American Playwrights Since 1945

American
Playwrights Since
1945

A GUIDE TO SCHOLARSHIP, CRITICISM, AND PERFORMANCE

Edited by PHILIP C. KOLIN

GREENWOOD PRESS
NEW YORK • WESTPORT, CONNECTICUT • LONDON

Library of Congress Cataloging-in-Publication Data

American playwrights since 1945 : a guide to scholarship, criticism,
   and performance / edited by Philip C. Kolin.
      p.   cm.
   Includes index.
   ISBN 0–313–25543–1 (lib. bdg. : alk. paper)
   1. American drama—20th century—Bibliography.   2. Dramatists,
American—20th century—Biography—Indexes.   3. Theater—United
States—History—20th century—Bibliography.   4. American
drama—20th century—History and criticism—Bibliography.
I. Kolin, Philip C.
Z1231.D7A53   1989
[PS350]
016.812′54′09—dc19   88–10245

British Library Cataloguing in Publication Data is available.

Library of Congress Catalog Card Number: 88–10245
ISBN: 0–313–25543–1

First published in 1989

Greenwood Press, Inc.
88 Post Road West, Westport, Connecticut   06881

Printed in the United States of America

The paper used in this book complies with the
Permanent Paper Standard issued by the National
Information Standards Organization (Z39.48–1984).

10   9   8   7   6   5   4   3   2

Contents

Preface

Many of the greatest triumphs on the American stage have occurred since 1945. In its diversity, inventiveness, social and dramatic power, and sheer quantity, American drama of this evolving period has achieved unprecedented national attention and, in many instances, international acclaim. With the exception of the plays of Eugene O'Neill (most of which were written before 1945), this period of American theatre history has witnessed the work of our greatest playwrights. At the pinnacle of such achievement are Tennessee Williams's passionate lyricism, Arthur Miller's social realism, Edward Albee's existential games, Sam Shepard's mythic narratives, David Mamet's energized street poetry, and David Rabe's failed rituals of war and drug-torn America. A variety of other voices have also been responsible for achievements in the American theatre. Many significant black playwrights have made lasting contributions to the theatre in post–World War II America. In the 1950s, for example, Lorraine Hansberry, in the 1960s and 1970s Amiri Baraka (LeRoi Jones), Ed Bullins, and Charles Gordone (the first black American playwright to receive the Pulitzer Prize), and in the 1980s August Wilson have created plays of immense power and terrifying beauty. Women playwrights such as Megan Terry, Beth Henley, Wendy Wasserstein, and Marsha Norman—some in the tradition of Lillian Hellman—have provided a feminist perspective and genius. Hansberry and Ntozake Shange have contributed to the American theatre as both women and blacks. Other ethnic groups are represented in American drama since 1945 through the works of Maria Irene Fornes, Israel Horovitz, Albert Innaurato, and Ronald Ribman. Social consciousness in this period reached new dramatic heights in the works of such playwrights as Arthur Kopit, Jean-Claude van Itallie, Jack Gelber, and Rabe. The comic muse has spoken eloquently and frequently during this forty-five-year period in the plays of, among others, John Guare, Christopher Durang, Terrence McNally, and Neil Simon. Playwrights have come from and written about nearly every section of the country—William Inge's Kansas and Oklahoma, Lanford Wilson's and Romulus Linney's North Carolina, Beth Henley's Mississippi, Preston Jones's Texas, Sam Shepard's West and California, and Neil Simon's Brooklyn. Some of the most distinguished playwrights are also the most successful screenwriters—Robert Anderson, Paddy Chayefsky, Michael Weller, Sam Shepard, and David Mamet, for example. New voices have also produced startling innovations. Richard Foreman has charted new dramatic terra incognitas with his transformational plays, and lyricist-composer-playwright Stephen Sondheim has been equally adventurous in his haunting musicals and satisfying plots. A final sign of the power of the American playwrights of the last forty-five years is that even writers better known for their work in other literary genres have produced some of the most impressive plays; James Baldwin, Robert Lowell, Carson McCullers, and Paul Zindel come to mind.

Documenting the variety of achievements on the American stage, *American Playwrights Since 1945* provides the first scholarly, in-depth study of the state of research on and history of performances of forty American playwrights whose work has won acclaim at home and (in many cases) abroad. Rather than a fast-paced critical overview of the works of these playwrights, this collection contains forty analytical bibliographic essays that assess the playwrights' reputations, offer a production history of their works, and classify, survey, and evaluate scholarly and critical opinion. The essays were written by experts on the American theatre whose credentials and academic affiliations represent the interdisciplinary talent it often requires to write knowledgeably about contemporary dramatists. Clearly there are other important dramatists who have written works for the American theatre since 1945 than can be contained in this book. But this collection does contain valuable bibliographic information on forty representative, influential playwrights whose works have unquestionably shaped the course of the American theatre since World War II. Some of the playwrights represented in this book are unchallenged superstars (such as Williams, Miller, Albee, and Shepard), and others have reputations in the making. A knowledge of the works of these forty, though, is essential for an understanding of contemporary American theatre.

The organization of each essay reveals how the aims of the collection are accomplished. Each contributor has followed a structured format that contains information on the six major areas of research described as follows:

1. *Achievements and Reputation*

This introductory section assesses the playwright's reputation and achievements in the theatre as perceived by reviewers and critics. It provides a brief analysis of the playwright's main contributions to American theatre in terms of significant awards, innovations, themes, language, characters, and dramatic techniques. Contributors often include a quotation (or more for a major writer with an extensive canon) from a critic or reviewer to pinpoint a unique or especially impressive achievement or characteristic.

2. *Primary Bibliography*

This section is divided into categories to show the extent and variety of a playwright's canon. Listed first are all of the playwright's plays, published and unpublished, arranged in chronological order. Following, where appropriate, are the playwright's other works, divided into categories (also arranged chronologically), such as screenplays, essays, novels/short stories/poetry, and interviews. I regard an interview as the playwright's oral work subsequently preserved in print.

3. *Production History*

Relying on theatre reviews, published stage histories, and even interviews, contributors in this section document where, how often, and how successfully the playwright's work has been performed. For major figures (such as Williams, Albee, and Miller), contributors have had to be highly selective. Not every review of a production of *Glass Menagerie* or *Zoo Story*, for example, could be cited and summarized within the limits of space. All contributors, however, have emphasized the premiere production of a playwright's work and/or the first time it appeared on Broadway. Each essay includes representative responses from the New York critics or those elsewhere, many times incorporating direct quotations from the reviews, with special emphasis on the overall critical reception of the play, its ideas and language, theatrical innovations, directorial approach and influence, and cast, staging, and set. Contributors have paid special attention to reviewers' comments linking one of the playwright's works to another.

4. *Survey of Secondary Sources*

Bibliographies

Contributors have identified major bibliographies on the playwright, often with an assessment of their scope, strengths, and weaknesses and whether they include primary as well as secondary material. They call attention to any useful bibliographic listings on the playwright and his or her work that have appeared in articles, standard reference works, or specialized serial bibliographies.

Biographies

This section contains commentary on book-length biographies, as well as on chapters of books and relevant articles that significantly focus on biographical details revealing important information. Standard biographical sources with relevant information on the playwright also are cited. Of invaluable assistance to anyone interested in the playwright's life will be the identification of and

commentary on key interviews that the contributor believes contain biographical facts or interpretations of the playwright's works.

Influences—Dramatic and Nondramatic—on the Playwright

Surveyed here are the critical works (articles, dissertations, books, and so on)
that identify, document, and discuss sources that influenced the playwright
and his or her works. "Sources" has been broadly interpreted to include
specific works and figures, as well as larger psychoanalytical and historical
forces. Also included, where appropriate, is a review of studies pointing out
how and where the playwright may have influenced other dramatists of the
period.

General Studies of the Playwright

Important titles—books, articles, and so on—that concentrate exclusively on the
playwright's themes and techniques are surveyed first. For a playwright of
the stature of Williams or Albee, emphasis rightfully falls on books. For
playwrights with smaller canons and still emerging reputations, articles on
American literary and dramatic topics or other broad topics—the Vietnam
War, for example—in which the playwright is prominently mentioned receive
consideration.

Analyses of Individual Plays

For major plays of major figures, critical studies are grouped according to various
relevant topics. As with reviews in the production history section, contributors
surveying critical works on major figures had to be more selective than those
assessing the criticism on other playwrights. In every instance, though, each
contributor has cited what he or she believes are the most valuable critical
studies of a particular play. Weaknesses of various critical approaches are
also frequently considered part of this review of criticism.

5. *Future Research Opportunities*

In this section, one of the most valuable parts of each essay, contributors alert
readers to particular scholarly and critical problems that need to be solved
or issues that need further investigation. For example, contributors indicate
whether a new biography, bibliography, or reassessment is necessary or
whether key influences on a playwright's work have been neglected. They
may also comment on whether a critical approach may be especially fruitful.
In short, this section plots the groundwork for future studies of the playwright
as it offers guideposts for researchers.

6. *Alphabetical Checklist of Secondary Sources*

This section contains a bibliography of all the sources contributors have cited
parenthetically throughout their essays.

Given the importance of these playwrights to the American theatre
over the last forty-five years, I believe that this reference work will be
as welcome as it is essential. No similar reference guide to reputations,
stage histories, and critical and scholarly studies exists, though one has
been needed for some time. Despite their usefulness for plot summaries

and capsule biographies, general reference works on contemporary drama offer limited bibliographical information and assessment; they provide little or no production histories, contain skimpy secondary bibliographies, and offer almost no evaluation of secondary sources. Unlike these reference works, *American Playwrights Since 1945* is a guide to research for readers who want to know what scholarly and critical resources are available for the forty playwrights covered here. I hope this book will be a useful, and frequently consulted, tool for anyone interested in theatre history and criticism; American literature and drama; American studies; for librarians concerned about developing or supplementing a collection; and for individuals charting the course and methods of critical opinion in contemporary America.

Philip C. Kolin

Acknowledgments

I am grateful to a number of individuals for their help. Marilyn Brownstein, humanities editor at Greenwood Press, gave generously of her encouragement and wise counsel; President Aubrey Lucas, Dean Glenn T. Harper, and Dr. David Wheeler, Chair of the English Department, at the University of Southern Mississippi have given generously of their friendship and support; Kathleen Rossman, my graduate assistant, wore out the pavement between my office and the library to answer the innumerable questions that arose in editing this volume; my wife Janeen, as always, assisted me at every stage of this book; and my son Eric and daughter Kristin joined with friends and family in praying for my work.

American
Playwrights Since
1945

Edward Albee

(28 MARCH 1928–   )

MATTHEW C. ROUDANÉ

ASSESSMENT OF ALBEE'S REPUTATION

The only detectable consistency in Albee scholarship is its lack of consistency. Any examination of three decades of books, articles, and reviews reveals the balkanization of Albee criticism, the Albeephobe's outrageous attack countered by the Albeephile's heated defense. Indeed ever since *The Zoo Story*, each new Albee play has produced nothing less than divided loyalties. Such varied audience responses come from the productions themselves, for Albee delights in challenging the orthodox aesthetics of Broadway and in refusing to repeat dramatic formulas that might raise his reputation in commercial and, perhaps, critical terms. Still, whether praising or attacking Albee as a nihilist, social protester, moralist, dramatic innovator, affirmative existentialist, or absurdist, critics acknowledge Albee's unmistakable influence on contemporary American drama. Albee reinvented the American stage in the 1960s by carrying on the moral seriousness of American drama established by O'Neill, Williams, and Miller.

Albee animates his theatre through language. In fact, language stands as the most conspicuous feature of his dramaturgy, as well as his major contribution to American drama. In both text and performance, Albee's technical virtuosity emanates from an ability to capture the values, personal politics, and perceptions of his characters through language. He "revolutionized the language of the American stage, extending verbal metaphor into the visual settings of his plays, working isolated ironic meanings into a complex network of interrelated ironic reverberations, and using epic topography to maintain allegorical simplicity," writes Paolucci in her influential *From Tension to Tonic: The Plays of Edward Albee* (15). "The accusative dialogue, and its cruelties" in *Who's Afraid of Virginia*

Woolf? contends Cohn, "are the wittiest ever heard on the American stage" (*Currents*, 72). Similarly, in *A Critical Introduction to Twentieth-Century American Drama*, Bigsby characterizes Albee's language thus: "By turns witty and abrasive, and with a control over language, its rhythms and nuances, unmatched in the American theater, he broke new ground with each play, refusing to repeat his early Broadway success" (II, 327). Although the language from *A Delicate Balance* onward becomes, as Adler argues, more stylized, elliptical, even "pretentious and obscure" ("Art or Craft," 45), Albee's repartee—when he is at his best—still generates compelling mimetic energy within each play.

Albee's theatrical strategy minimizes the actor-audience barrier. "What makes Albee stand out . . . is his insistence on giving us the Pirandellian sense of realism on stage, drawing us into the play and slowly pulling away the scaffolding that separates us from the core of the experience, casting us as participants in the drama" (Paolucci, "Albee and the Modern Stage," 11). As active participants in the play, the audience contributes to the ritualized forms of confrontation and expiation that characterize much of Albee's work.

Albee's theatre reflects the sweep and play of a nation thinking in front of itself. If Albee dominated the stage during the 1960s, however, his later works do not compare as favorably. His language, most critics report, has become more mannered, abstract, more difficult to apprehend in text or performance. The demonic energy of *Who's Afraid of Virginia Woolf?* dissipated in his plays of the 1970s and 1980s. Many of the later plays, which may seem more like daring, unfinished experiments than polished works, cannot always sustain the dramaturgic burdens Albee places on them. The later plays, many critics feel, simply repeat what have become outworn themes (see Copeland; Brustein, "Trashing"). Nevertheless, Albee remains one of the most influential and controversial American dramatists.

PRIMARY BIBLIOGRAPHY OF ALBEE'S WORKS

Tyce provides a relatively complete primary bibliography of Albee's works—plays, poems, short stories, articles.

Plays

"Schism." *Choate Literary Magazine* 32 (1946): 87–110.
The Zoo Story and The American Dream. New York: Signet, 1960.
The Zoo Story, The Death of Bessie Smith, The Sandbox. New York: Coward-McCann, 1960.
The Zoo Story and Other Plays. London: Jonathan Cape, 1962.
The American Dream. New York: Coward-McCann, 1961.

Fam and Yam. New York: Dramatists Play Service, 1961.

Who's Afraid of Virginia Woolf? New York: Atheneum, 1962; London: Jonathan Cape, 1964.

The Sandbox, The Death of Bessie Smith, with Fam and Yam. New York: New American Library, 1963.

Tiny Alice. New York: Atheneum, 1964; London: Jonathan Cape, 1966.

A Delicate Balance. New York: Atheneum, 1966; New York: Pocket, 1966; London: Jonathan Cape, 1968.

Box and Quotations from Chairman Mao Tse-tung. New York: Atheneum, 1969; London: Jonathan Cape, 1970.

All Over. New York: Atheneum, 1971; London: Jonathan Cape, 1972.

Seascape. New York: Atheneum, 1975; London: Jonathan Cape, 1976.

Two Plays: Counting the Ways and Listening. New York: Atheneum, 1977.

The Lady from Dubuque. New York: Atheneum, 1980.

The Plays. Vols. 1–4. New York: Coward, McCann, and Geoghegan, 1981, 1983, 1984.

Walking. 1984. Unpublished play.

Finding the Sun. 1983. Unpublished play.

Envy. Vignette; part of Nagel Jackson's *Faustus in Hell*. Produced in Princeton, New Jersey in January 1985.

The Man Who Had Three Arms. Forthcoming.

Second Marriage. Produced in Vienna, May 1987.

Adaptations

Bartleby. With James Hinton, music by William Flanagan. Unpublished libretto adaptation of Herman Melville's short story. Produced 1961.

The Ballad of the Sad Café. Boston: Houghton Mifflin, 1963. London: Jonathan Cape, 1965. Adaptation of Carson McCullers's novella of the same name.

Malcolm. New York: Atheneum, 1964; London: Jonathan Cape, 1967. Adaptation of James Purdy's novel of the same name.

Breakfast at Tiffany's. Music by Bob Merrill. Produced in Philadelphia, 1966. Musical adaptation of Truman Capote's novella of the same name.

Everything in the Garden. New York: Atheneum, 1967. Adaptation of Giles Cooper's play of the same name.

Lolita. New York: Dramatists Play Service, 1984. Adaptation of Vladimir Nabokov's novel *Lolita*.

Other Early Plays

These plays are unpublished and unperformed. The manuscripts, held at the New York Public Library at Lincoln Center, may be seen only after Albee grants special permission. They are not intended for performance. (See Bigsby's *Edward Albee: Bibliography, Biography, Playography*.)

"The City of People." 1949. 177-page manuscript.
"Untitled Play" (perhaps "In a Quiet Room"). 1949. 34-page manuscript.
"Ye Watchers and Ye Lonely Ones." 1951.
"The Invalid." 1952. 18-page manuscript.
"The Making of a Saint." 1953–1954. 76-page manuscript.
"The Ice Age." N.d. 35-page manuscript.
"An End to Summer." N.d. 40-page manuscript.
"Untitled Play" (perhaps "The Recruit"). N.d. 9-page manuscript.
"Untitled Opera" (perhaps "Hatchet, Hatchet"). N.d.

Short Stories

"*L'Apres-midi d'un faune.*" *Choate Literary Magazine* 21 (1944): 43–44.
"Empty Tea." *Choate Literary Magazine* 31 (1945): 53–59.
"A Place on the Water." *Choate Literary Magazine* 32 (1945): 15–18.
"Well, It's Like This." *Choate Literary Magazine* 32 (1945): 31–34.
"Lady With an Umbrella." *Choate Literary Magazine* 32 (1946): 5–10.
"A Novel Beginning." *Esquire* 60 (July 1963): 59–60.
"Peaceable Kingdom, France." *The New Yorker* 29 December 1975: 34.

Articles

"Richard Strauss." *Choate Literary Magazine* 31 (1945): 87–93.
"Chaucer: The Legend of Phyllis." *Choate Literary Magazine* 32 (1945): 59–63.
"What's It About?—A Playwright Tries to Tell." *New York Herald Tribune Magazine*
     The Lively Arts (22 January 1961): 5.
"Which Theatre Is the Absurd One?" *New York Times Magazine* (25 February
     1962): 30–31, 64, 66.
"Some Notes on Non-Conformity." *Harper's Bazaar* (August 1962): 104.
"Carson McCullers—The Case of the Curious Magician." *Harper's Bazaar* (Jan-
     uary 1963): 98.
Review of Lillian Ross's novel, *Vertical and Horizontal*. *Village Voice* (11 July 1963):
     1.
"Who's Afraid of the Truth?" *New York Times* (18 August 1963): 1.
"Albee on Censorship." [Letter] *Newsweek* 62 (30 September 1963): 4.
"Ad Libs on Theatre." *Playbill* May 1965.
Review of Sam Shepard's *Icarus' Mother*. *Village Voice* (25 November 1965): 19.
Three Plays by Noel Coward. Introduction by Edward Albee. New York: Dell, 1965.
"Who Is James Purdy?" *New York Times* (9 January 1966): 1, 3.
"Creativity and Commitment." *Saturday Review* (4 June 1966): 26.
"Judy Garland." In *Double Exposure*, pp. 198–99. Edited by Roddy McDowall.
     New York: Delacorte, 1966.
"Apartheid in the Theater." *New York Times* (30 July 1967): 1, 6.
"Albee Says 'No Thanks' to John Simon." *New York Times* (10 September 1967):
     1, 8.
"The Decade of Engagement." *Saturday Review* (24 January 1970): 19–20.
"The Future Belongs to Youth." *New York Times* (26 November 1971): 1.

"Albeit." In *The Off-Broadway Experience*, pp. 52–62. Edited by Howard Green-
    berger. Englewood Cliffs, N.J.: Prentice-Hall, 1971.
"On Making Authors Happy." *Cinebill* (American Film Theatre) (1 October 1973)
    (program accompanying the AFT production of *A Delicate Balance*).
"Edward Albee on Louise Nevelson: The World Is Beginning to Resemble Her
    Art." *Art News* (1980): 99–101.
Foreword to James Purdy, *Dream Palaces*, pp. vii–ix. New York: Viking, 1980.
"New York! New York!" Introduction to *New York in Photographs*, photography
    by Reinhart Wolf, text by Sabina Lietzmann. New York: Vendome, 1980.
The Wounding: An Essay on Education. Charleston, W.Va.: Mountain State Press,
    1981.
"The New Work of Mia Westerlund Roosen." *Arts Magazine* 56 (1982): 120–21.

Interviews

Kolin's *Conversations with Edward Albee* (Jackson: University Press of
Mississippi, 1988) gathers twenty-seven Albee interviews, including four
that were previously unpublished. In a lengthy introduction, Kolin identifies the major themes Albee has emphasized over the last twenty-five
years and the various roles that he has played with interviewers. In
addition to the interviews in Kolin, the following should be consulted:

Roudané, Matthew C. "An Interview with Edward Albee." *Southern Humanities
    Review* 16 (1982): 29–44.
———. "Albee on Albee." *RE: Artes Liberales* 10 (1984): 1–8.
———. "A Playwright Speaks: An Interview with Edward Albee." In *Critical
    Essays on Edward Albee*, pp. 193–99. Edited by Philip C. Kolin and J. Mad-
    ison Davis. Boston: G. K. Hall, 1986.

PRODUCTION HISTORY

Albee's early plays were first produced in Germany and later in the
fertile environs of off-Broadway. After *The Zoo Story* premiered on 28
September 1959 at the Schiller Theatre Werkstatt, West Berlin, Germany, Friedrich Luft reviewed the play, calling it "a shiningly sickly and,
at the same time, painfully interesting, one-acter," a play that embodies
a "study of fright in dialogue" (41). When he saw its 14 January 1960
American debut at the Provincetown Playhouse in New York City, Hewes
wrote that Albee "has written an extraordinary first play" ("Benchmanship," 32). Although the play garnered many favorable reviews, Driver
concluded, "It is more than a little melodramatic, and the only sense I
could draw from it is the conviction that one shouldn't talk to strangers
in Central Park" (194). Brustein labeled the play beat generation "claptrap" (1960, 22). Despite some detractors, *The Zoo Story* received largely
positive responses. Copeland, reflecting two decades after its debut, calls
it "probably the finest first play ever written by an American" (30).

Albee produced a brief sketch, *The Sandbox*, on 15 April 1960 at the Jazz Gallery in New York City, a work about the "shameless organized exploitation which encourages the survivors to buy peace of mind about the deceased they have abused or ignored while they were alive" (Debusscher, 32). He followed with *Fam and Yam* on 27 August 1960 at the White Barn in Westport, Connecticut, a comic playlet attacking "the unwillingness of the theatrical establishment to help the next generation of artists" (Rutenberg, 55). *The Death of Bessie Smith*, which premiered at the Schlosspark Theatre, West Berlin, Germany, on 21 April 1960, had its American debut at the York Playhouse in New York City on 1 March 1961. Luft reviewed the German premiere, writing that the play is "an evilly talented thing, a piece of shrill human deprecation.... [Albee] drives his evil theme right to the heart of the matter with talent and tension" ("The German Review," 45). After viewing the American production, Hatch registered a positive response, although he quarreled with Bessie Smith's absence: "Bessie Smith never appears in the play ... nor is her death its subject. The subject is mutilation as a substitution for love" (116–17).

The American Dream, which premiered on 24 January 1961 at the York Playhouse, offended some reviewers (Meyers felt the play was "shallow and negative" [72]), though most judged the work positively. "Mr. Albee," said Kerr, "has taken a good nasty look at most of our success images and found them marvelously empty" ("First Night,"12) and Watts wrote that the play "is packed with untamed imagination, wild humor, gleefully sardonic satirical implications, and overtones of strangely touching sadness, and I thought it was entirely delightful" ("Two on the Aisle," 51).

On 13 October 1962 Albee stormed Broadway with *Who's Afraid of Virginia Woolf?* at the Billy Rose Theatre, a play assuring his place in world drama. The original cast included Arthur Hill and Uta Hagen as George and Martha, and George Grizzard and Melinda Dillon as Nick and Honey, under the directorship of Alan Schneider. Schneider originally did not want to stage such an intense and (for 1962 audiences) potentially offensive play on Broadway, but Albee insisted. With a performing time of three and one-half hours, Schneider had to enlist four other actors for matinee shows: Sheppard Strudwick and Kate Reid as George and Martha, Bill Berger and Avril Petrides as Nick and Honey. William Ritman designed the claustrophobic set, which featured a portrait of George and Martha Washington hanging on the wall. Truth and illusion, the subversion of audience expectation, Strindbergian sexual dynamics, its charting of what Albee perceives as a decline of humanistic values in Western culture, its relevancy to Eric Berne's psychological theories popularized to a mass public in *Games People Play* (1964), its allegorical, archetypal, sociopolitical, and existentialist dimensions—

these qualities invited audiences to revel in its mysteries and anxieties. "The quarrel over *The American Dream* had scarcely died down," Debusscher observed, "when Albee exploded a veritable bomb. *Who's Afraid of Virginia Woolf?* immediately became the subject of the most impassioned controversies, the object of criticism and accusation which recall the storms over the first plays of Ibsen and, closer to our own time, Beckett and Pinter. If we are able to examine this play today with more serenity, we are nonetheless forced to acknowledge its content might well have outraged the orthodox public of Broadway" (47).

Many attacked the play for its destructive theme. Clurman acknowledged Albee's "superbly virile and pliant" dialogue but concluded that "the pessimism and rage of *Who's Afraid of Virginia Woolf?* are immature" (27 October 1962, 274). For Trilling, the play celebrated bleakness: "The 'message' of Mr. Albee's play couldn't be more terrible: life is nothing, and we must have the courage to face our emptiness without fear" (85). Schechner implied that the play celebrates decadent values, embracing "self-pity, drooling, womb-seeking weakness . . . the persistent escape into morbid fantasy" (8). Above all, this play inspired the reviewers to react. Wrote Taubman in the *New York Times*: "Only a fortnight after its opening . . . it has piled up an astonishing impact. You can tell from the steady stream of letters it has precipitated. Elated, argumentative and vitrolic, they have been pouring across my desk and, no doubt, into the offices of my colleagues. Whether they admire or detest the play, theatergoers cannot see it and shrug it off. . . . They hail the play's electricity and condemn it as obscene. . . . The public is aroused" ("Cure for Blues," 1). A reviewer for *Time* granted the play its power but found the son myth unconvincing: "Coming after two acts of cascading turbulence, this plot resolution is woefully inadequate and incongruous, rather like tracing the source of Niagara to a water pistol" (Anon., "Blood Sport," 84). Such differing responses characterized the reviews, and the Pulitzer Prize committee refused to bestow on it the award it so clearly earned. Members of the committee who supported Albee's nomination resigned in protest. In one of the more hysterical reviews, Coleman wrote: "[It is] a sick play about sick people. They are neurotic, cruel and nasty. They really belong in a sanitarium for the mentally ill rather than on a stage. This sordid and cynical dip into depravity is in three lengthy and repetitious acts. . . . We do not enjoy watching the wings being torn from human flies" (20). Trewin admitted the play was "cruel" but found it filled with "savage comedy" (288). Watts, on the other hand, claimed it was "the most shattering drama I have ever seen since O'Neill's 'Long Day's Journey Into Night' " ("Shattering Play," 14). Gassner, a member of the Pulitzer Prize jury who resigned in protest of the play's being denied the award, called the play "*the* negative play to end all negative plays, yet also a curiously compassionate . . . and exhilarating one"

("Broadway in Review," 1963, 80). Brustein found it "an ambitious play" but felt it "collapses" because of the son myth ("Medusa-Head," p. 29–30).

The 1966 Warner Brothers film version, starring Elizabeth Taylor and Richard Burton, was a critical and financial success, as articles in the *Motion Picture Daily* (24 June 1966) and the *Hollywood Reporter* (6 July 1966) indicate. Predictably the play courted controversy. It was censored, altered, labeled "for adults only," even banned in certain cities (see *Variety*, 17 August 1966; *London Times*, 19 July 1966; *Variety*, 1 June 1966; *Daily Variety*, 13 June 1966; and *Motion Picture Daily*, 21 July 1966).

After his adaptation of Carson McCullers's *The Ballad of the Sad Café* on 30 October 1963 at the Martin Beck Theatre, Albee staged *Tiny Alice*, which opened on 19 December 1964 at the Billy Rose Theatre and has since been regarded as one of his most baffling works. With Alan Schneider directing Irene Worth and Sir John Gielgud in the lead roles, the play drew eager crowds. William Ritman's set—an ornate library in a mansion, complete with a replica of the castle, 38-foot-high walls, giant 17-by-7-foot doors, a 6-foot candelabra, and a phrenological head placed on a huge reading table—was impressive. Most felt that the excellent cast and set covered for a less than satisfying play, however.

Not surprisingly, the reviews were as mixed as the play was mysterious. "In ten years that I have been reviewing, I have not encountered so completely baffling a play," wrote one reviewer for *Newsday* (Oppenheimer), while Clurman in the *Nation* said the play was "the sort of thing a highly endowed college student might write" (18 January 1965). The play, for Taubman, was "a large, modern allegory . . . about the passion of a Christ-like figure, if not Christ himself." But, Taubman conceded, Albee has not "cast fresh light on this theme." Finally, he said, "Mr. Albee is reduced to illustrating rather than illuminating his theme" ("*Tiny Alice* Opens," 14). Brustein thought that Albee presented "a huge joke on the American culture industry" ("Three Plays," 33). Roth called the play "a homosexual day-dream" and found *Tiny Alice* utterly "unconvincing," "remote," and a "sham" (4). Perhaps the best source presenting the contradictory reviews is Henry Hewes's "The *Tiny Alice* Caper": "Some have used such phrases as 'a masterpiece,' 'one of the capstones of the drama's long and adventurous history,' 'every minute a totally engrossing evening,' and 'establishes Albee as the most distinguished American playwright to date.' Others have deprecated it with such terms as 'prolix,' 'tedious,' 'pretentious' 'ostentatious.' 'ugly.' 'willfully obscure,' 'an intellectual shell game.' 'a set trap that has no bait' " (38–39). One reviewer called the play a "battle of three devils for a good man's soul" (Ulanov, 383), while another claimed that "*Tiny Alice* is a corrupt work" (Cavenaugh). Another reviewer suggested that "one leaves the theater with the feeling of having seen the most dynamic play of the season—

and one wonders why!" (Lewis, 337). The 1969 revival at the American Conservatory Theater drew more favorable reviews (see Gottfried, *"Tiny Alice,"* 40; Probst).

Albee produced an adaptation of James Purdy's novel by the same name, *Malcolm*, on 11 January 1966 at the Shubert Theatre in New York City. Even Albee admits it was a disaster, as the following advertisement he placed in the *New York Times* indicates: "To those who have come to *Malcolm*, my thanks. To those who were pleased, my gratitude. To those who were disappointed, my apologies. See you next play. Edward Albee" (quoted in Rutenberg, 165).

With the following play, however, Albee redeemed himself, garnering a Pulitzer Prize (his first) for *A Delicate Balance*. The play opened on 12 September 1966 at the Martin Beck Theatre in New York City. Of course, certain reviewers and critics disliked the production. Complaining of its lack of mimetic energy, Kerr said of the play that "breathlessness is its ultimate condition, immobility its sole activity" ("Only Time Really Happens," 1). Kemper, however, praised Albee's "gifts for language" but found the play morally "too small" (1447). Gassner attacked the play, arguing that "it is altogether vacuous, as a result of the fuzzy failure of Agnes and Tobias as either separate individuals or as a married couple" (1966, 451). Brustein in *The Third Theater* contended that "Albee seems to be stimulated by mere artifice, and the result is emptiness, emptiness, emptiness." Summed up Brustein, it was "a very bad play" (83).

After *Breakfast at Tiffany's* (1966), a musical based on Truman Capote's book, and an adaptation of Giles Cooper's play, *Everything in the Garden* (1968), Albee staged the inventive companion plays, *Box* and *Quotations from Chairman Mao Tse-tung*, which opened at the Studio Arena Theatre in Buffalo, New York, on 6 March 1968 and on Broadway 30 September 1968 at the Billy Rose Theatre. One reviewer said he had not witnessed "more garbage since John Lindsay last asked Nelson Rockefeller for a favor" (Gottfried, *"Box-Mao-Box,"* 24). "It is a good play to dress up for," deadpanned Kerr, "because the members of the audience are going to spend quite a bit of time looking at one another" (*"Mao,"* 1). Kroll produced the most perceptive review, alluding to the play's musicality, structure, and theme. He went to the heart of the plays, suggesting that "the 'box' may indeed be a coffin for the flesh and spirit of a self-annihilated species" ("Inside," 109; see also his "Busted *Box*").

All Over opened 27 March 1971 at the Martin Beck Theatre in New York City. Initial reviews were highly negative. Kalem, for instance, claimed that "so thin and sketchy are the characterizations that one or two stereotypical words serve to define and exhaust the nature of the people involved" (69). Kroll said that "Albee's idea in 'All Over' has its interest and possibilities, but they are annihilated by the deadness of every element of the play" ("Disconnections" 52).

Seascape opened on 26 January 1975 at the Sam S. Shubert Theatre in New York City and won Albee his second Pulitzer. Kauffmann found the dialogue "undistinguished," "artificial," and "in character, in texture, in theme *Seascape* is an echoingly hollow statement of bankruptcy" ("Kauffmann on Theater," 22); Kalem found the dialogue nothing but "aimless chatter" ("Primordial Slime," 57). In contrast, Kissel thought the play "delightful and amusing" (10), and Gill in the *New Yorker* enthused, "Of all Mr. Albee's plays, *Seascape* is the most exquisitely written" (75).

Albee presented two relatively minor plays after *Seascape: Listening*, commissioned as a radio play for BBC Radio Three and heard on 28 March 1976, and *Counting the Ways*, which had its American premiere (after its first performance at the National Theatre in London on 6 December 1976) at the Hartford Stage Company, Hartford, Connecticut, on 28 January 1977. Barnes called *Listening* "a chamber opera and a symbolic poem about communication as a present branch of catatonia" (3). Adler in his review said that *Counting the Ways* "can delight with its considerable charm and wit and occasional beauties of language" (408).

The Lady from Dubuque opened 31 January 1980 at the Morosco Theatre, New York City, and received a familiar critical response: a great deal of scathing hostility and somewhat lesser amounts of praise. Simon called the drama "one of the worst plays about anything, ever" (74), and Brustein seconded: It is "an awful piece" ("Self-Parody," 26). Schlueter argued that "the problem with *The Lady from Dubuque* is not that Albee has said what has already been said—Beckett, after all, keeps repeating himself—but simply that, in dramatic terms, he has not said it effectively" ("Is It 'All Over'?" 115). Rounding out the scores of negative reviews was Kroll, who lamented that "the air of the theatre seemed scorched by a negative charge, the electrocution of creative force" ("Going to Hell," p. 102). Although there were a few positive reviews, the most surprising was that from Gerald Clarke, whose shrill response seems nothing less than absurd: the play represents Albee's "best since *Who's Afraid of Virginia Woolf?*" (69).

Albee staged a controversial and unsuccessful adaptation of Vladimir Nabokov's *Lolita*, which closed after nineteen performances in March 1981 in New York City. Amazingly Brustein thought "*Lolita* contains some of his most vigorous writing since *Virginia Woolf*. With all its flaws, *Lolita* is engrossing, terse, and, above all, dangerous" ("Trashing of Albee," 27; see also Amacher, who discusses the reviewers' revulsion to the play, 115–18).

The Man Who Had Three Arms opened 4 October 1982 at the Goodman Theatre in Chicago. One reviewer called it "brutal, obscene, always intense, often eloquent" (Christiansen, 7, 9). Another thought that Albee composed a text "so restrictive, so flat, so full of evasions" that we experience merely a "prospectus" of a play (Feingold, 106). Reviewing the New York production, Kroll claimed that what Albee had "written is not a play at all but a nasty and embarrassing display of bad manners" ("Albee's Hymn," 54). Adler conceded, "Albee can still pen those wonderful arias . . . yet even for an Albee aficionado, this isn't much of a play" ("The Man," 124). Albee continues to display an acute sensitivity to European dramatic tradition, the courage to experiment with the essence of theatre, and to restructure the stage in the spirit of a dramatic innovator, as evident from his *Walking* (1984), *Finding the Sun* (1984) (see Ben-Zvi; Sullivan *"Walking"*), and *Envy* (see Gussow, "Stage," p. 55), highly experimental and seemingly unfinished pieces.

SURVEY OF SECONDARY SOURCES

Bibliographies

Giantvalley, Tyce, King, Green, and Amacher and Rule are the major bibliographies. King's and Giantvalley's are particularly useful for their wide-range coverage and annotations. Tyce's, although not annotated or comprehensive, contains primary and secondary listings, totaling over 2,700 entries. The bibliographies by Wilson, and by Evans and Reed are limited and dated. Useful are Kolin's classified checklists, Carpenter's bibliographic essay, Bigsby's *Edward Albee: Bibliography, Biography, Playography*, and Owen's bibliography of interviews and topical index. Undoubtedly the most comprehensive and impressive bibliographic essay to date is Kolin and Davis's Introduction to their *Critical Essays on Edward Albee*, which surveys the criticism and research tools through 1986. Kolin and Davis survey more than 200 items of Albee scholarship.

Biographies

There is no biography on Albee. Accordingly biographical details remain skimpy, somewhat superficial and often appear speculative. The following sources, however, contain limited but useful information: Gould (1966); Morgan (1967); La Fontaine (1968); Kolin (1975); Smilgis (1980); MacNicholas (1981); and Brenner (1983). Each provides a brief sketch on Albee's personal life. Hardy's feature in *Architectural Digest* (1982) also gives us an idea of Albee's tastes (in decorating at least). Making more scholarly and theoretical connections are Debusscher (7–9), Amacher (1–12), and Bigsby (1984, 249–56).

Influences

When asked what artists might have influenced his work, Albee replied: "I admire Chekhov, Sophocles, Beckett. . . . I think of the experience of seeing O'Neill's *The Iceman Cometh* . . . which *Who's Afraid of Virginia Woolf?* is a response to. Then there is Williams's *Suddenly Last Summer*. I think of my first experience with Beckett and Genet as being *authentic* experiences for me" (Roudané, "Albee on Albee," 5–6). Bradish offers a few interesting comments on the "Ironic Connection between O'Neill and Albee" (12). Pinpointing influences on Albee, though, are as varied as the plays and responses to the plays. "Critics have identified numerous and diverse influences, from Unamuno to Strindberg to *The Tatler* to Tennessee Williams to medieval moralities to vaudeville to piano pieces by Satie to humorous sketches by Thornton Wilder" (Kolin and Davis, 1). Esslin links Albee to the great European innovators, as does Debusscher. Harris connects Albee with Maeterlinck. Paolucci often refers to Dantean motifs in her *From Tension to Tonic*. In his *Understanding Edward Albee*, Roudané points to Artaud and Elizabeth Kübler-Ross as influences in certain plays. Most recently, Luere has argued that a possible source for Albee's imaginary child in *Who's Afraid of Virginia Woolf?* comes from a short story by British writer Elizabeth Taylor. In turn, Albee's impact within the off-Broadway theatre world in the 1960s probably influenced such aspiring writers as Shepard (Hart, 16, 84), Mamet (Rogoff, 1977), and Baraka (Debusscher, 57–58), all of whom were young writers struggling to forge craft into art. Albee, it seems, provided some kind of inspiration to these writers.

General Studies

Debusscher's *Edward Albee: Tradition and Renewal* (1967), the first book on the playwright, places Albee in a useful historical context, citing him as the American dramatist most worthy of carrying on the legacies of O'Neill, Miller, and Williams. According to Debusscher, Albee assimilated rather than copied the French avant-garde style in the early plays but produced a distinctly American cadence. Examining the plays through *Malcolm*, Debusscher claims that Albee is technically sound but often lapses into " 'theater for theater's sake' " (83). Debusscher concludes that Albee is a nihilist: "Albee's work contains no positive philosophical or social message. His theatre belongs in the pessimistic, defeatist or nihilistic current which characterizes the entire contemporary theatrical scene" (82). Subsequent studies challenge Debusscher's conclusions.

Four studies on Albee appeared in 1969, and Bigsby's remains the best. His *Albee* locates Albee's impulse to dramatize the human need "to break out of his self-imposed isolation" and establish "contact with his fellow man," to experience a "revival of love" (9). Despite his social protests, Albee's interest lies in a more "fundamental sense of alienation" (21). Bigsby concludes that Albee explores the "source of a limited but genuine hope" in human encounters (96), a point he established in his *Confrontation and Commitment* (1968).

Cohn's *Edward Albee* (1969) is a brief but substantive study. For Cohn, Albee is obsessed with stripping away illusions within human experience: "Whereas Sartre, Camus, Beckett, Genet, Ionesco, and Pinter represent that reality in all its alogical absurdity, Albee has been preoccupied with illusions that screen man from reality" (6).

Rutenberg's *Edward Albee: Playwright in Protest* (1969) investigates Albee's sociopolitical quarrels with American culture. An illuminating chapter on *Box* and *Quotations from Chairman Mao Tse-tung* and two interviews with Albee are a valuable resource, though unfortunately diminished by time. Such statements as Albee's "supreme ability to present plays of shocking social protest which reflect present-day thinking"(12–13) and Albee "is into what is happening" (16) make the book very much a product of the 1960s. Still it is a well-documented study that makes its point clearly.

Amacher's *Edward Albee* (1969) explicates the plays, making connections between Greek drama and Albee. In his revised version (1982), Amacher covers the plays through *Lolita*. Hayman's *Edward Albee* (1971) discusses the plays through *All Over*. With no introduction or conclusion, the book is less than satisfying; like Amacher's, it presents detailed plot summaries rather than rigorous analyses.

From Tension to Tonic: The Plays of Edward Albee, Paolucci's provocative 1972 book, rivals Bigsby's work in its analytical rigor and critical insights. For Paolucci, "Albee is the only playwright, after O'Neill, who shows real growth, the only one who has made serious effort to break away from the 'message' plays which have plagued our theater since O'Neill. Experimentation, for Albee, is a slow internal transformation of the dramatic medium. . . . His arrogance is not an empty gesture. He is the only one of our playwrights who seems to have accepted and committed himself to serious articulation of the existential questions of our time, recognizing the incongruity of insisting on pragmatic values in an age of relativity" (3). Paolucci covers the plays through *Box-Mao-Box* in what must be essential reading for Albee scholars.

The year 1975 saw the first collection of essays on Albee: *Edward Albee: A Collection of Critical Essays*, edited by Bigsby. Four others have since been published: *Edward Albee: Planned Wilderness*, edited by De La Fuente (1980); *Edward Albee: An Interview and Essays*, edited by Wasserman (1983); *Critical Essays on Edward Albee*, edited by Kolin and Davis (1986); and *Edward Albee: Modern Critical Views*, edited by Bloom (1987). Although all are helpful, Kolin and Davis's—with thirty-nine essays—stands out as the exemplary collection.

Hirsch's *Who's Afraid of Edward Albee?* (1978) argues largely from a pyschobiographical perspective, citing Albee's homosexuality as influencing his characterizations. The book covers the plays through *Counting the Ways* and *Listening*. As the themes, characters, and language become increasingly abstract and "rarefied" (3), the plays have become more distant, boring. Therefore, says Hirsch, the question to ask at "this diminished moment" in Albee's career is, "Who's afraid of Edward Albee?" The answer, for Hirsch, is Albee himself. Although Albee is not an absurdist, Hirsch seems intent on labeling him one, since for Albee reality serves only as an invitation to the surreal and the fantastic (1–16).

Stenz's *Edward Albee: The Poet of Loss* (1978), a solid psychological reading of characters, discusses the plays through *Seascape*. She concludes: "In all of Albee's plays the moral imperative is the obligation for everyone to live with awareness. The demands of institutions and the barriers people build around themselves prevent them from seeing the realities of their condition and foster the creation of self-destructive illusions" (132). And here Stenz makes the important distinction: "Albee does not damn an institution in itself but insists that its demands should not override the natural human need for self-development and constructive relationships with other people" (132).

Bigsby's authoritative *A Critical Introduction to Twentieth-Century American Drama* (1984) is essential reading. He relies extensively on Albee's unpublished materials. Bigsby's sense of social history and existentialism enhances his illuminating study. Albee has tackled, concludes Bigsby, "issues of genuine metaphysical seriousness in a way that few American dramatists before him have claimed to do, and done so, for the most part, with a command of wit and a controlled humour which has not always characterized the work of O'Neill, Miller and Williams. He has set himself the task of probing beneath the bland surface of contemporary reality and created a theatre which at its best is luminous with intelligence and power" (328). Bigsby's books on Albee are the best there are.

Roudané's *Understanding Edward Albee* (1987) argues that the plays embody an affirmative vision, one dispelling Albee's reputation as a nihilist. Roudané discusses nine original plays through *The Man Who Had Three Arms*. "When he is at his best," writes Roudané, "Albee produces in certain characters and, ideally, the audience 'a momentary stay against confusion,' a still point in the messy business of living that paves the way for the possibility of existing with a heightened sense of self-responsibility. Heated repartee, sexual tensions, death, a preoccupation with vital lies, a withdrawal from meaningful human encounters, indifference—these are the issues that Albee mines, but not from the position of a nihilist" (193–94). Roudané concludes that Albee's goal often centers on shocking the audience into self-reflection and "participating in living fully" (196).

McCarthy's *Edward Albee* (1987), a title in the Modern Drama Series edited by Bruce and Adele King, provides a somewhat hasty though valid overview of Albee's key themes and techniques. McCarthy is rewarding on matters of staging and performance but less than satisfying in his overall view of Albee's achievements and biography.

Analyses of Individual Plays

The Zoo Story, in Anderson's words, can be "explained as a sociopolitical tract, a pessimistic analysis of human alienation, a modern Christian allegory of salvation, and an example of absurdist and nihilist theater," but the play "has managed to absorb these perspectives without exhausting its many levels of meaning" ("Ritual," 93). For Anderson, the play stands "as a portrayal of a ritual confrontation with death and alienation in which Jerry acts the role of shaman-guide who directs the uninitiated Peter through the initiatory rite necessary for Peter to achieve his maturity and autonomy" (93). Zimbardo views the play as a religious allegory, arguing that Albee's images are "traditional Christian symbols which . . . retain their original significance" (10). Hayman states: "*The Zoo Story* is not a homosexual play, not an absurd play, and not a religious play, but it is a moral play"(17). Hirsch thinks that "Albee presents Jerry's agonizing loneliness as a universal condition, rather than a specifically gay one" (122), and Hassan writes that the play registers "a macabre success" (150). Gabbard explains the play through Jerry's immersion in fantasy and death as an escape from "the hostility and despair of rejection" ("Triptych," 14–15).

Most scholars find the ending of the play life affirming (Bennett, 65). In *The Onstage Christ*, Ditsky suggests that "*The Zoo Story* rests upon a foundation of Christ-references, and indeed derives its peculiar structure from Jesus's favourite teaching device, the parable" (147). Perhaps Force best captures the majority opinion of the play: "The diversity of judgement and analysis elicited by Edward Albee's *The Zoo Story* tempts one to wonder whether such varied critical response was induced by a viewing of the same play" (47).

The Death of Bessie Smith, although important insofar as revealing Albee's emerging unity of vision and skill as a master of dialogue, is not a major work. Kolin provides a fine reading of the play, concentrating on its structure. Kolin sees Albee's Bessie as the "heroine" but identifies analogues and links (as well as contrasts) between the black and white strands of the play ("Cars and Traveling"). Although many critics have focused on the play's overt subject matter, racism (Rutenberg, 77–88; Grande), Bigsby identifies what also engages Albee: "But over and above the level of social protest this is a play about individuals trapped in their own myths, condemned to act out their fictions to the point at which they are forced to deny their own humanity and desires" (*Critical Introduction*, 260–61).

The American Dream exerted a tremendous influence on American theatre. Esslin identifies the play as a "promising and brilliant first example of an American contribution to the Theatre of the Absurd" (268). Miller calls Albee's portrait of the "American family home" a "modern prefabricated chamber of horrors" (195), and Rutenberg sees the play as social protest theatre reflecting "the hypocrisy of much of American life" (74). The play parodies language and social conventions, as Paolucci observes: "A curious feature of Albee's work is his early experimentation (in *The American Dream* and *The Sandbox*, for instance) along the lines of Beckett and Ionesco—the defleshed abstract stage where language becomes an irritating puzzle and familiar conventions are struck down harshly, without any effort at salvaging some measure of our experience" ("Albee and the Modern Stage," 14–15). Although Hamilton argues that Albee falls victim to the very dream he is attacking in the play, most other critics feel that the play stands as one of Albee's major works.

Who's Afraid of Virginia Woolf? dominated the theatre world during the 1960s. The play ran for 664 consecutive performances. Many critics call it a "war between the sexes" (Amacher, 68), and in his *The Theater of Protest and Paradox* Wellwarth contends that "there is nothing more in this than a dissection of an extremely ambiguously conceived sick marriage. . . . *Who's Afraid of Virginia Woolf?* [makes] Albee looks like a man expending a tremendous amount of energy on furiously pedaling backwards" (284). Many critics acknowledge the ultimately affirmative nature of the play (Roudané, *Understanding Edward Albee*, 67), as does Albee. The play challenges, Albee points out, the sorts of illusions paralyzing the figures in O'Neill's *The Iceman Cometh*, one of the plays that motivated Albee to present George and Martha's condition. "It's about going against the 'pipe dreams.' After all, *Who's Afraid of Virginia Woolf?* just says have your pipe dreams if you want to but realize you are kidding yourself" (Roudané, "Interview with Edward Albee," 1982, p. 38). Harris writes that the play "contains much more assurance of the possibility of meaningful choice" (249), Adler locates in the play's closure an affirmative dimension ("Long Night's Journey," 1973), and Hankiss sees that play's febrile action as culminating in the characters' coming to consciousness. "Exposure of the [son] myth—it could concern God and America as well as the imaginary son of George and Martha—opens the way for harrowing reconciliations," explains Hassan (152). Leff tackles the 1966 film version of *Who's Afraid of Virginia Woolf?* (1981), while in his *Modern Tragicomedy and the British Tradition*, Dutton explains the play thus: "In its structure and thematic patterns, its mixture of game-play and quasi-religious ritual, its exploration of sterile symbiotic relationships—it is a copy-book modern tragicomedy" (113–14). "In *Who's Afraid of Virginia Woolf?*" writes Paolucci in *From Tension to Tonic*, "the existential dilemma is dramatized with full sympathy in its most painful human immediacy. The weak are redeemed in their helplessness, and the vicious are forgiven in their tortured self-awareness" (46). The critical and popular success of the play "consolidated Albee's reputation. The first of his generation successfully to accomplish the transition from Off-Broadway to Broadway, he did so without making any concessions... to that audience's supposed sensibility. Twenty years later the play still holds up and has deservedly come to be regarded as one of the classics of the American stage" (Bigsby, *Critical Introduction*, 264). Or as Debusscher puts it, with *Virginia Woolf* Albee gave "the American stage its first great work in years" (57).

Tiny Alice invited an incredible variety of critical interpretations. For Coe, the play is absurdist but fails to "communicate the absurdist themes to the bulk of its audience" (373). Witherington sees the play's "form and language" in the gothic tradition (151). Davison finds the play Albee's most "metaphysically provocative" (54), seeing it as an "aesthetically unified view of man's struggle in an equivocal and enigmatic universe" (56). The play, argues Morrison, exhibits a "profound hostility toward women" (261). Because the "play is non-realistic and is indeed essentially symbolic, allegorical, allusive," Campbell concentrates on the "naming of the five characters" as a key to understanding the play's mysteries (22–23), and Casper ("The Expense of Joy") and Grunes ("God and Albee") think much of the play's power emanates from the mysteriousness of its mysteries. Anderson provides a Jungian psychoanalytic reading ("Staging the Unconscious"), while Lucey explores the truth-illusion motif of the play. Although recognizing its moral seriousness, Mandanis concedes that "it is possible that Albee's vision is too dishonestly disguised and falsified by the baroque surface of neo-Platonism, homosexuality, masturbation, and prurience" (98). Stenz argues that Albee demonstrates the ways in which faith sometimes "can become a substitute for full participation in life" (61).

A Delicate Balance, which earned Albee his first Pulitzer Prize, marked a return to critical favor for the playwright, with most citing language as his major source of power. *A Delicate Balance* "represents one of the incredibly few major advances in the use of language in the contemporary theatre," writes von Szeliski (124), and Bachman adds that the play's "lyrical language, its dramatic movement, its beautifully appropriate naturalistic-expressionistic characterization, and its rich structure, overtones and insights make it a significant and rewarding drama of the modern theatre" (630). Von Szeliski believes Agnes's language "has been a handy substitute for an ability to love or to enforce a decision based on love—and it has also been a wonderful subconscious weapon for domination" (126). Perry points out that Agnes's language also correlates to the illusion of her well-being: "Verbal dexterity is Agnes's weapon against what she cannot understand, articulateness her mooring in the world" (59). Fumerton concludes that language in this play "forms an impenetrable blockage, a thick layer of skin within which each individual may rest secure: isolated and lonely and—tragically—invulnerable" (210). In what remains one of the best analyses of the play, Porter points out that the mimetic fallacy to which critics object actually "serves as the center of the plot" and, "becoming a fully developed existential noth-ingness, the emptiness at last is both significant and basic to the play's strength" (398). Some focus on the cat story (Sykes), and one critic argues that Albee constructed the play "as a comedy, with a lyrical ending in keeping with its comic structure" and that it is best produced as a "com-edy of contemporary manners" (Robinson, 26). In his *Mirror on the Stage*, Adler also finds the play a "metaphysical drawing room comedy" and correctly concludes, "The 'delicate balance' of the title refers to a con-dition of stasis and stagnation" (120–21).

Box and *Quotations from Chairman Mao Tse-tung* demonstrated Albee's eagerness to experiment with what Bigsby would later call "conventional notions of theatrical propriety" (*Collection*, 9). The two best essays on the play are by Cohn and Bigsby. Cohn writes convincingly of the play's musicality ("Albee's *Box* and Ours"), while Bigsby argues that the two interrelated plays "examine the role and function of imagination, in the form of ideological constructs no less than artistic creations" (153).

Despite largely negative reviews, *All Over* has stood up better in later studies. Vos notes that the play's subject matter concerns "the failure of love," which becomes a "form of dying" (81), a distinction Jones cites as well: "love" lies at the center of the play (87). Moses writes that "Albee in this play forcefully combats resignation to dehumanization and de-grading death" (68) and that "for Albee, death . . . is a metaphor for the quality of life. The irony in this play is that there is more life in the dead man than in the survivors" (76), a conclusion that Schvey repeats. James Neil Harris provides a comparative study linking one of Albee's sources for the play as Maeterlinck, and Bigsby observes that in the play, "Albee pursues this flight from reality to its source in personal betrayal, to a flaw in human character which must be faced if it is to be understood and remedied" (Bigsby, "Brink of the Grave," 169).

Seascape invited scholars to explore its mythical, existentialist, and archetypal patterns. Adler sees the play as a reverse mirror image of *A Delicate Balance*, identifying the regenerative possibilities within the two couples ("Humanity at the Second Threshold"); he confirms this point in *Mirror on the Stage*: "[Nancy] believes that man must create his own happiness by making a Kierkegaardian leap of faith and finding some positive value" (139). Agreeing with Adler is Roudané, who discusses the existentialist growth of the characters ("Animal Nature"). Exploring the archetypal patterns of the play is Gabbard ("An Adult Fairy Tale"). Concerning the language in *Seascape*, Bernstein writes that Albee's "ability to heighten and intensify naturalistic speech endows the conversation with a wonderful energy" (118). For Purdon, the play "functions in the tradition of the medieval morality play with its more clearly defined figures serving as emblems for the distinct parts of the human consciousness" (141). Kolin argues that the sound of the jets over the *Seascape* beach is an ominous reminder of death and suggests a parallel and contrast with the "Booms" in Williams's *The Milk Train Doesn't Stop Here Anymore* ("Of Jets").

Two instructive essays on *The Lady from Dubuque* are by Roudané and Adler. Roudané argues that the play revolves around the central theme of waste ("On Death, Dying"; see also his "Communication as Therapy"), and Adler discusses Albee's obsession with "knowing" and his Pirandellian techniques in the play ("The Pirandello in Albee").

Little has been published on *Lolita*, but two sensible essays are by Davis ("Albee's Struggle with Nabokov") and Adler ("Meta-Lolita"). Both discuss the problems of adapting the novel to the play.

Counting the Ways and *Listening* have not generated much critical discussion. Kolin provides the most detailed analysis on *Counting the Ways*, focusing affirmatively on language, character, and the way in which Albee's stage differs from Tennessee Williams's ("Ways of Losing Heart"). Condemning both plays, Hirsch writes: "The strict limitations that Albee sets himself—no stories, no fully developed characterizations, the monosyllabic language—are a denial of his virtuosity, his lush sense of language, his harsh satire, his joy in creating explosive, rampaging, exhibitionistic neurotics" (99).

In the first critical discussion of *The Man Who Had Three Arms*, Roudané suggests that Albee presents a hero savagely divided against himself and his world. Himself, the protagonist, lashes out at the theatregoer. Himself berates the audience in an attempt to come to terms with the incubi haunting his soul: his undeserved fame and subsequent fall from undeserved stardom. *The Man* quickly establishes itself as a play whose words, gestures, character changes, and repartee transform the action into a metatheatrical experience. The play blatantly calls attention to its artificiality, deliberately makes the spectators aware of the theatricality of the theatre, and calls attention to its own language while simultaneously exposing the meaninglessness of that language ("Monologue of Cruelty").

FUTURE RESEARCH OPPORTUNITIES

Despite nearly 200 theses and dissertations, at least sixteen book-length studies, and hundreds of essays and reviews, there is still room for Albee scholarship. There is a pressing need for a biography. A study of Albee on the world stage is also in order, given his international reputation. More studies on the musicality of Albee's theatre would shed light on such plays as *Box*. Paolucci is right when she calls for a new set of critical terms to deal adequately with the plays (*Modern Drama*, 1980). Schlueter and Simard are suggestive of the ways in which new critical methods and ideologies may help scholars better come to terms with Albee's aesthetic. No scholar has fully dealt with a deconstructionist approach, a critical angle—given Albee's distrust of language in the later plays—that could yield provocative results. Essays with a more detached interest, says Meserve, would help Albee scholarship (386). But unless Albee returns to producing plays of the quality of his early years, it remains debatable how much more can be said about him that has not already been said. Still, Albee remains one of the most influential and dynamic American dramatists, one who, most scholars feel, rescued the American theatre at a most propitious moment.

SECONDARY SOURCES

"$75,000 to Charity at *Woolf* New York Debut." *Motion Picture Daily* (24 June 1966): 1, 3.

"$1,300,000 for *Virginia Woolf* First Week ..." *Hollywood Reporter* (6 July 1966): 1.

Adler, Thomas P. "Albee's *Virginia Woolf:* A Long Night's Journey into Day." *Educational Theatre Journal* 25 (1973): 66–70.

———. Review of *Counting the Ways. Educational Theatre Journal* 29 (1977): 407–8.

———. "Albee's *Seascape:* Humanity at the Second Threshold." *Renascence* 31 (1979): 107–14.

———. "Art or Craft: Language in the Plays of Albee's Second Decade." In *Edward Albee: Planned Wilderness*, pp. 45–57. Edited by Patricia De La Fuente. Edinburg, Tex.: Pan American University, 1980.

———. " '*The Man Who Had Three Arms.*' " *Theatre Journal* 35 (1983): 124.

———. "The Pirandello in Albee: The Problem of Knowing in *The Lady from Dubuque*." In *Edward Albee: An Interview and Essays*, pp. 109–19. Edited by Julian N. Wasserman. Lee Lecture Series. University of St. Thomas, Houston. Syracuse: Syracuse University Press, 1983.

———. "Albee's Meta-Lolita: Love's Travail and the Artist's Travail." *Publications of the Mississippi Philological Association* (1986): 122–29.

———. *Mirror on the Stage: The Pulitzer Plays as an Approach to American Drama*. West Lafayette: Purdue University Press, 1987.

Amacher, Richard E. *Edward Albee*. Rev. ed. Boston: Twayne, 1982.

———, and Margaret Rule. *Edward Albee at Home and Abroad: A Bibliography 1958-June 1968*. New York: AMS Press, 1973.

Anderson, Mary C. "Staging the Unconscious: Edward Albee's *Tiny Alice*." *Renascence* 32 (1980): 178–92.

———. "Ritual and Initiation in *The Zoo Story*." In *Edward Albee: An Interview and Essays*, pp. 93–108. Lee Lecture Series. University of St. Thomas, Houston. Syracuse: Syracuse University Press, 1983.

Anon. "Blood Sport," *Time* (26 October 1962): 84.

"Aussie Pic Censors Unafraid of *Woolf*." *Variety* (17 August 1966): 15.

Bachman, Charles R. "Albee's *A Delicate Balance:* Parable as Nightmare." *Revue des langues vivantes* 38 (1972): 619–30.

"Ban on *Virginia Woolf* Film." *Times* (London) (19 July 1966): 19.

"The Banning of *Virginia Woolf*." *Stage and Television Today* (17 October 1963): 15.

Barnes, Clive. *"Listening:* A Review." *New York Times* (4 February 1977): C3.

Bennett, Robert B. "Tragic Vision in *The Zoo Story*." *Modern Drama* 20 (1977): 55–66.

Ben-Zvi, Linda. *"Finding the Sun."* *Theatre Journal* 36 (1984): 102–3.

Bernstein, Samuel. *The Strands Entwined: A New Direction in American Drama.* Boston: Northeastern University Press, 1980.

Bigsby, C. W. E. *Confrontation and Commitment: A Study of Contemporary American Drama 1959–1966.* Columbia: University of Missouri Press, 1968.

———. *Albee.* Edinburgh: Oliver and Boyd, 1969; New York: Chip's Bookshop, 1978.

———, ed. *Edward Albee: A Collection of Critical Essays.* Englewood Cliffs, N.J.: Prentice-Hall, 1975.

———. *Edward Albee: Bibliography, Biography, Playography.* Theatre Checklist No. 22. London: Theatre Quarterly Publications, 1980.

———. *A Critical Introduction to Twentieth-Century American Drama.* Vol. 2. Cambridge: Cambridge University Press, 1984.

Bloom, Harold, ed. *Edward Albee: Modern Critical Views.* New Haven: Chelsea House, 1987.

Bradish, Gaynor R. "Edward Albee." In *Contemporary Dramatists.* Fourth Edition, pp. 11–13. Ed. D. L. Kirkpatrick. Chicago: St. James Press, 1988.

Brenner, Marie. "Tiny Montauk: On and Off the Beach." *New York* (22 August 1983): 13–15.

Brustein, Robert. "Krapp and a Little Claptrap." *New Republic* (22 February 1960): 21–22.

———. "Albee and the Medusa-Head." *New Republic* (3 November 1962): 29–30.

———. *Seasons of Discontent.* New York: Simon and Schuster, 1965.

———. "Three Plays and a Protest." *New Republic* (23 January 1965): 32–34, 36.

———. *The Third Theater.* New York: Knopf, 1969.

———. "The Trashing of Edward Albee." *New Republic* 11 (April 1981): 27–28.

———. "Self-Parody and Self-Murder." *New Republic* 182 (8 March 1980): 26.

Campbell, Mary Elizabeth. "Tempters in Albee's *Tiny Alice*." *Modern Drama* 13 (1970): 22–33.

Carpenter, Charles A. "American Drama: A Bibliographic Essay." *American Studies International* (1983): 37–39.

Casper, Leonard. *"Tiny Alice:* The Expense of Joy in the Persistence of Mystery." In *Edward Albee: An Interview and Essays*, pp. 83–92. Edited by Julian N.

Wasserman. Lee Lecture Series. St. Thomas University, Houston. Syracuse: Syracuse University Press, 1983.

"Catholic Office's A-4 Rating to *Woolf:* Industry's Own Seal Still Not Bestowed." *Variety* (1 June 1966): 7.

Cavenaugh, Arthur. "Play Reviews: *Tiny Alice." Sign* 44 (March 1965): 27.

Christiansen, Richard. "Albee's 'Arms' Is an Eloquent Ordeal." *Chicago Tribune* (6 October 1983): 7, 9.

Clarke, Gerald. "Theater: Night Games." *Time* (11 February 1980): 69.

Clurman, Harold. "Theatre." *Nation* (27 October 1962): 273–74.

———. "Theater." *Nation* (18 January 1965): 65.

"Code Review Board Overrules Shurlock, Gives *Woolf* Seal." *Daily Variety* (13 June 1966): 1.

Coe, Richard M. "Beyond Absurdity: Albee's Awareness of Audience in *Tiny Alice." Modern Drama* 18 (1975): 371–83.

Cohn, Ruby. *Edward Albee.* Minneapolis: University of Minnesota Press, 1969.

———. "Albee's *Box* and Ours." *Modern Drama* 14 (1971): 137–43.

———. *Currents in Contemporary Drama.* Bloomington: Indiana University Press, 1969.

Coleman, Robert. "The Play You'll Love to Loathe." *New York Daily Mirror* (15 October 1962): 20.

Copeland, Roger. "Should Edward Albee Call It Quits?" *Saturday Review* (February 1981): 28–31.

"Court Permits *Woolf?* to Resume in Nashville." *Motion Picture Daily* (21 July 1966): 1, 8.

Davis, J. Madison. "Albee's Struggle with Nabokov." *Publications of the Mississippi Philological Association* (1986): 101–11.

Davison, Richard Allan. "Edward Albee's *Tiny Alice:* A Note of Re-examination." *Modern Drama* 11 (1968): 54–60.

Debusscher, Gilbert. *Edward Albee: Tradition and Renewal.* Translated by Anne D. Williams. Brussels: American Studies Center, 1967.

De La Fuente, Patricia, ed. *Edward Albee: Planned Wilderness: Interviews, Essays, and Bibliography.* Living Author Series No. 3. Edinburg, Tex.: Pan American University, 1980.

Ditsky, John. *The Onstage Christ: Studies in the Persistence of a Theme.* London: Vision Press, 1980.

Driver, Tom. "Drama: Bucketful of Dregs." *Christian Century* (17 February 1960): 193–94.

Dutton, Richard. *Modern Tragicomedy and the British Tradition.* Norman: University of Oklahoma Press, 1986.

Esslin, Martin. *The Theatre of the Absurd.* Rev. ed. Woodstock, N.Y.: Overlook Press, 1969.

Evans, James L., and Michael D. Reed. "Edward Albee: An Updated Checklist of Scholarship, 1977–1980." In *Edward Albee: Planned Wilderness,* pp. 121–29. Edited by Patricia De La Fuente. Edinburg, Tex.: Pan American University, 1980.

Feingold, Michael. "Small Craft Warnings." *Village Voice* (19 April 1983): 106.

Force, William M. "The *What* Story? or Who's Who at the Zoo?" *Studies in the Humanities* 1 (1969–1970): 47–53.

Fumerton, M. Patricia. "Verbal Prisons: The Language of Albee's *A Delicate Balance.*" *English Studies in Canada* 7 (1981): 201–11.

Gabbard, Lucina P. "Albee's *Seascape*: An Adult Fairy Tale." *Modern Drama* 21 (1978): 307–17.

———. "Edward Albee's Triptych on Abandonment." *Twentieth Century Literature* 28 (1982): 14–33.

———. "The Enigmatic *Tiny Alice.*" *Journal of Evolutionary Psychology* 6 (March 1985): 73–86.

Gassner, John. "Broadway in Review." *Educational Theatre Journal* 15 (1963): 77–80.

———. "Broadway in Review." *Educational Theatre Journal* 18 (1966): 450–52.

Giantvalley, Scott. *Edward Albee: A Reference Guide.* Boston: G. K. Hall, 1987.

Gill, Brendan. "The Theatre: Among the Dunes." *New Yorker* (3 February 1975): 75–77.

Gottfried, Martin. "Theatre: *Tiny Alice.*" *Women's Wear Daily* (30 December 1964): 40.

———. "Theatre: Albee's *Box-Mao-Box.*" *Women's Wear Daily* (11 March 1968): 24.

Gould, Jean. *Modern American Playwrights.* New York: Dodd, Mead, 1966.

Grande, Luke. "Existentialism and Modern Drama." *Critic* 21 (1963): 33–38.

Green, Charles Lee. *Edward Albee: An Annotated Bibliography 1968–1977.* New York: AMS Press, 1980.

Grunes, Dennis. "God and Albee: *Tiny Alice.*" *Studies in American Drama, 1945–Present* 1 (1986): 150–60.

Gussow, Mel. "Theatre: Albee's *Box-Mao-Box.*" *Women's Wear Daily* (11 March 1968): 24.

———. "Stage: A New Look at Seven Deadly Sins." *New York Times* (3 February 1985): A55.

Hamilton, Kenneth. "Mr. Albee's Dream." *Queen's Quarterly* 70 (1963): 393–99.

Hankiss, Elemér. "Who's Afraid of Edward Albee?" *New Hungarian Quarterly* 5 (1964): 168–74.

Hardy, Hathaway. "Edward Albee." *Architectural Digest* 39 (1982): 150–55.

Harris, James Neil. "Edward Albee and Maurice Maeterlinck: *All Over* as Symbolism." *Theatre Research International* 3 (1978): 200–8.

Harris, Wendell V. "Morality, Absurdity, and Albee." *Southwest Review* 49 (1964): 249–56.

Hart, Lynda. *Sam Shepard's Metaphorical Stages.* Westport, Conn.: Greenwood Press, 1986.

Hassan, Ihab. *Contemporary American Literature: 1945–1972.* New York: Ungar, 1973.

Hatch, Robert. "Theater: Arise, Ye Playgoers of the World." *Horizon* 3 (July 1961): 116–17.

Hayman, Ronald. *Edward Albee.* London: Heinemann, 1971; New York: Ungar, 1973.

Hewes, Henry. "Benchmanship." *Saturday Review* (6 February 1960): 32.

———. "Broadway Postscript: The *Tiny Alice* Caper." *Saturday Review* (30 January 1965): 38–39, 65.

Hirsch, Foster. *Who's Afraid of Edward Albee?* Berkeley, Calif.: Creative Arts, 1978.

Jones, David Richard. "Albee's *All Over*." In *Edward Albee: Planned Wilderness*, pp. 87–98. Edited by Patricia De La Fuente. Edinburg, Tex.: Pan American University Press, 1980.

Kalem, T. E. "Club Bore." *Time* (5 April 1971): 69.

——. "Primordial Slime." *Time* (10 February 1975): 57.

Kauffmann, Stanley. "Edward Albee: All Over?" *Saturday Review* (15 March 1980): 34–35.

——. "Stanley Kauffmann on Theater: *Seascape*." *New Republic* (22 February 1975): 22.

Kemper, Robert Graham. "Drama: A Weekend with the 'Can Do' Family." *Christian Century* 83 (23 November 1966): 1447.

Kerr, Walter. "First Night Report: *The American Dream*." *New York Herald Tribune* (25 January 1961): 12.

——. "Only Time Really Happens to People." *New York Times* (2 October 1966): 2: 1.

——. "*Mao*—But What Message?" *New York Times* (17 March 1968): 2:1, 3.

King, Kimball. *Ten Modern American Playwrights: An Annotated Bibliography*. New York: Garland, 1982.

Kissel, Howard. "*Seascape*." *Women's Wear Daily* (27 January 1975): 10.

Kolin, Philip C. "A Classified Edward Albee Checklist." *Serif* 6 (1969): 16–32.

——. "A Supplementary Edward Albee Checklist." *Serif* 10 (1973): 28–39.

——. "Two Early Poems by Edward Albee." *Resources for American Literary Study* 5 (Spring 1975): 95–97.

——. "Edward Albee's *Counting the Ways:* The Ways of Losing Heart." In *Edward Albee: An Interview and Essays*, pp. 121–40. Edited by Julian N. Wasserman. Lee Lecture Series. St. Thomas University, Houston. Syracuse: Syracuse University Press, 1983.

——. "Of Jets, Milk Trains, and Edward Albee's *Seascape*." *Notes on Modern American Literature* 9 (1986): item 9.

——. "Cars and Traveling in Edward Albee's *The Death of Bessie Smith*." *CLA Journal* 30 (June 1987): 39–46.

——, and J. Madison Davis, eds. *Critical Essays on Edward Albee*. Boston: G. K. Hall, 1986.

——. *Conversations with Edward Albee*. Jackson: University Press of Mississippi, 1988.

Kroll, Jack. "Busted *Box*." *Newsweek* (14 October 1968): 117.

——."Inside the Cube." *Newsweek* (18 March 1968): 109–10.

——. "The Disconnection." *Newsweek* (5 April 1971): 52.

——. "Going to Hell with Edward Albee." *Newsweek* (11 February 1980): 102–3.

——. "Edward Albee's Hymn of Self-Disgust." *Newsweek* (18 April 1983): 54.

La Fontaine, Barbara. "Triple Threat On, Off and Off-Off Broadway." *New York Times Magazine* (25 February 1968): 36–37, 39–40, 42, 44, 46.

Leff, Leonard. "Play into Film: Warner Brothers' *Who's Afraid of Virginia Woolf?*" *Theatre Journal* 33 (1981): 453–66.

Lewis, Theophilus. "*Tiny Alice*." *America* (6 March 1965): 336–37.

Lucey, William F. "Albee's *Tiny Alice:* Truth and Appearance." *Renascence* 21 (1969): 76–80, 110.

Luere, Jeane. "A British Parallel for Edward Albee's Imaginary Child: 'A Dedicated Man' and Who's Afraid of Virginia Woolf?" *Studies in American Drama, 1945–Present* 3 (1988).

Luft, Friedrich. [Review of *The Zoo Story*.] In *Critical Essays on Edward Albee*, p. 41. Edited by Philip C. Kolin and J. Madison Davis. Boston: G. K. Hall, 1986.

———. "[*The Death of Bessie Smith:* The German Review.]" In *Critical Essays on Edward Albee*, p. 45. Edited by Philip C. Kolin and J. Madison Davis. Boston: G. K. Hall, 1986.

McCarthy, Gerry. *Edward Albee*. New York: St. Martin's, 1987.

MacNicholas, John. "Edward Albee (1928–)." In *Twentieth-Century American Dramatists: Dictionary of Literary Biography*. 7:3–22. Edited by John MacNicholas. Detroit: Gale Research Co., 1981.

Mandanis, Alice. "Symbol and Substance in *Tiny Alice*." *Modern Drama* 12 (1969): 92–98.

Meserve, Walter J. "American Drama." In *American Literary Studies, 1985*, pp. 347–66. Edited by J. Albert Robbins. Durham: Duke University Press, 1987.

[Meyers, Harold.] "*The American Dream* and *The Death of Bessie Smith*." *Variety* (8 November 1961): 72.

Miller, Jordan Y. "Myth and the American Dream: O'Neill to Albee." *Modern Drama* 7 (1964): 190–98.

Morgan, Thomas B. "Angry Playwright in a Soft Spell." *Life* (26 May 1967): 90–90B, 93–94, 96–97, 99.

Morrison, Kristin. "Pinter, Albee, and 'The Maiden in the Shark Pond.' " *American Imago* 35 (1978): 259–74.

Moses, Robbie Odom. "Death as a Mirror of Life: Edward Albee's *All Over*." *Modern Drama* 19 (1976): 67–77.

Oppenheimer, George. "Gielgud Stars in Albee's *Tiny Alice*." *Newsday* (30 December 1964): C3.

Otten, Terry. *After Innocence: Visions of the Fall in Modern Literature*. Pittsburgh: Pittsburgh University Press, 1982.

Owen, Lea Carol. "An Annotated Bibliography of Albee Interviews, with an Index to Names, Concepts, and Places." In *Critical Essays on Edward Albee*, pp. 200–18. Edited by Philip C. Kolin and J. Madison Davis. Boston: G. K. Hall, 1986.

Paolucci, Anne. *From Tension to Tonic: The Plays of Edward Albee*. Carbondale: Southern Illinois University Press, 1972.

———. "Pirandello and the Waiting Stage of the Absurd (with Some Observations on a New 'Critical Language')." *Modern Drama* 23 (1980): 102–11.

———. "Albee and the Restructuring of the Modern Stage." *Studies in American Drama, 1945-Present* 1 (1986): 4–16.

Perry, Virginia I. "Disturbing Our Sense of Well-Being: The 'Uninvited' in *A Delicate Balance*." In *Edward Albee: An Interview and Essays*, pp. 55–64. Edited by Julian N. Wasserman. Lee Lecture Series. University of St. Thomas, Houston. Syracuse: Syracuse University Press, 1983.

Porter, M. Gilbert. "Toby's Last Stand: The Evanescence of Commitment in *A Delicate Balance*." *Educational Theatre Journal* 31 (1979): 398–408.

Probst, Leonard. Review of *Tiny Alice*. WNBC-TV. New York. 29 September 1969.

Purdon, Liam O. "The Limits of Reason: *Seascape* as Psychic Metaphor." In *Edward Albee: An Interview and Essays*, pp. 141–53. Edited by Julian N. Wasserman: Lee Lecture Series. University of St. Thomas, Houston. Syracuse: Syracuse University Press, 1983.

Robinson, Fred Miller. "Albee's Long Night's Journey into Day." *Modern Language Studies* 11 (1981): 25–32.

Rogoff, Gordon. "Theater: Albee and Mamet: The War of the Words." *Saturday Review* (2 April 1977): 36–37.

Roth, Philip. "The Play That Dare Not Speak Its Name." *New York Review of Books*, (25 February 1965): 4.

Roudané, Matthew C. "On Death, Dying, and the Manner of Living: Edward Albee's *The Lady from Dubuque*." In *Edward Albee: An Interview and Essays*, pp. 65–81. Edited by Julian N. Wasserman. Lee Lecture Series. University of St. Thomas, Houston. Syracuse: Syracuse University Press, 1983.

———. "Animal Nature, Human Nature, and the Existentialist Imperative: Edward Albee's *Seascape*." *Theatre Annual* 38 (1983): 31–47.

———. "Communication as Therapy in the Theater of Edward Albee." *Journal of Evolutionary Psychology* 6 (1985): 302–17.

———. "A Monologue of Cruelty: Edward Albee's *The Man Who Had Three Arms*." In *Critical Essays on Edward Albee*, pp. 187–92. Edited by Philip C. Kolin and J. Madison Davis. Boston: G. K. Hall, 1986.

———. *Understanding Edward Albee*. Columbia: University of South Carolina Press, 1987.

Rutenberg, Michael E. *Edward Albee: Playwright in Protest*. New York: Drama Book Specialists, 1969.

Schechner, Richard. "Who's Afraid of Edward Albee?" *Tulane Drama Review* 7 (1963): 7–10.

Schlueter, June. *Metafictional Characters in Modern Drama*. New York: Columbia University Press, 1979.

———. "Is It 'All Over' for Edward Albee?: *The Lady from Dubuque*." In *Edward Albee: Planned Wilderness*, pp. 112–19. Edited by Patricia De La Fuente. Edinburg, Tex.: Pan American University, 1980.

Schvey, Henry I. "At the Deathbed: Edward Albee's *All Over*." *Modern Drama* 30 (September 1987): 352–63.

Simard, Rodney. *Postmodern Drama: Contemporary Playwrights in America and Britain*. Lanham, Md.: University Press of America, 1984.

Simon, John. "From Hunger, Not Dubuque." *New York* 13 (11 February 1980): 74–75.

Smilgis, Martha. "Edward Albee Blames His Newest Broadway Flop on the Critics and Cast for *Lolita* on Subways." *People* (25 February 1980): 70, 73.

Stenz, Anita M. *Edward Albee: The Poet of Loss*. The Hague: Mouton, 1978.

Sullivan, Dan. "*Walking*." *Los Angeles Times* (26 May 1984): E2.

———. "*Finding the Sun*." *Los Angeles Times* (26 May 1984) E2.

Sykes, Carol. "Albee's Beast Fables: *The Zoo Story* and *A Delicate Balance*." *Educational Theatre Journal* 25 (1973): 448–55.

Taubman, Howard. "Cure for Blues." *New York Times* (28 October 1962): 1.

————. "Theater: Albee's *Tiny Alice* Opens." *New York Times* (30 December 1964): 14.

Trewin, J. C. "Nights with the Ripsaw." *Illustrated London News* (22 February 1964): 288.

Trilling, Diana. "The Riddle of Edward Albee's *Who's Afraid of Virginia Woolf?*" In *Edward Albee: A Collection of Critical Essays*, pp. 80–88. Edited by C. W. E. Bigsby. Englewood Cliffs, N.J.: Prentice-Hall, 1975.

Tyce, Richard. *Edward Albee: A Bibliography*. Metuchen, N.J.: Scarecrow Press, 1986.

Ulanov, Barry. "*Luv* and *Tiny Alice*." *Catholic World* 200 (March 1965): 383–84.

von Szeliski, John J. "Albee: A Rare Balance." *Twentieth Century Literature* 16 (1970): 123–30.

Vos, Nelvin. "The Process of Dying in the Plays of Edward Albee." *Educational Theatre Journal* 25 (1973): 80–85.

Wasserman, Julian N., ed. *Edward Albee: An Interview and Essays*. Lee Lecture Series. University of St. Thomas, Houston. Syracuse: Syracuse University Press, 1983.

Watts, Richard. "Two on the Aisle: Another Striking Play by Albee." *New York Post* (25 January 1961): 51.

————. "Two on the Aisle: Shattering Play by Edward Albee." *New York Post* (15 October 1962): 14.

Wellwarth, George. *The Theater of Protest and Paradox*. New York: New York University Press, 1964.

Wilson, Robert A. "Edward Albee: A Bibliographical Checklist." *American Book Collector* 5 (1983): 37–42.

Witherington, Paul. "Albee's Gothic: The Resonances of Cliche." *Comparative Drama* 4 (1970): 151–65.

Zimbardo, Rose A. "Symbolism and Naturalism in Edward Albee's *The Zoo Story*." *Twentieth Century Literature* 8 (1962): 10–17.

Robert Anderson

(28 APRIL 1917–   )

THOMAS P. ADLER

ASSESSMENT OF ANDERSON'S REPUTATION

Robert (Woodruff) Anderson once generalized that every time a writer sits down to work, he faces two challenges: one posed by the material, the other by the need to discover an adequate form. Anderson's recurrent subject is—as he indicated when linking his works with those of William Inge—married sexuality. His usual mode is the well-made play, though he manages to introduce some, even at times considerable, variety through nonrepresentational techniques. The title of Adler's 1975 article, which served as the genesis of his later monograph, suggests the parameters that define Anderson's particular achievement. He is the "playwright of middle-aged loneliness," exploring incessantly the aloneness that exists inside (as well as outside) marriage. This loneliness especially plagues Anderson's older male characters: disillusioned that their lives have not turned out as they planned and doubly aware that time's passage has seriously limited their future options; embarrassed by their feelings when those around them regard sensitivity as unmanly, yet sublimating their fears and even their cynicism in sexuality, though often leaving their wives emotionally starved in the process. Three of Anderson's dramas that have mined this area of experience have been named Best Plays, two of his filmscripts have garnered Academy Award nominations, and their author was inducted into the Theatre Hall of Fame in 1981.

PRIMARY BIBLIOGRAPHY OF ANDERSON'S WORKS

Plays

Come Marching Home. Unpublished. 1945.
The Eden Rose. Unpublished. 1948.

Love Revisited. Unpublished. 1951.
Tea and Sympathy. New York: Random House, 1953. Reprinted in *Theatre Arts*
    38, no. 9 (September 1954): 34–61.
All Summer Long. New York: Samuel French, 1955.
Silent Night, Lonely Night. New York: Random House, 1960.
The Days Between. New York: Random House, 1965. Rev. ed. New York: Samuel
    French, 1969.
You Know I Can't Hear You When the Water's Running. New York: Random House,
    1967.
I Never Sang for My Father. New York: Random House, 1968.
Solitaire/Double Solitaire. New York: Random House, 1972.
Free and Clear. Unpublished play, 1983.

Screenplays

Tea and Sympathy. Unpublished. 1956.
Until They Sail. Unpublished filmscript based on James Michener's *Return to
    Paradise.* 1957.
The Nun's Story. Unpublished filmscript based on Kathryn Hulme's novel. 1959.
The Sand Pebbles. Unpublished filmscript based on Richard McKenna's novel.
    1966.
I Never Sang for My Father. New York: New American Library, 1970.
The Patricia Neal Story. Unpublished television script. 1981.

Novels

After. New York: Random House, 1973. London: Barrie and Jenkins, 1973.
Getting Up and Going Home. New York: Simon and Schuster, 1978.

Essays and Interviews

"Walk a Ways with Me." *Theatre Arts* 38, no. 1 (January 1954): 30–31.
"Some Notes on *Tea and Sympathy*." *Exonian* (3 March 1954): 14–16.
"Draw Your Own Conclusions." *Theatre Arts* 38, no. 9 (September 1954): 32–33.
"A Playwright Talks to Us." *Cue* 30, no. 3 (Spring 1955): 2–3.
"The Playwright and His Craft." *Writer* 68, no. 5 (May 1955): 152–54.
"A Postscript . . . Not a Post-Mortem." *Theatre Arts* 39, no. 8 (August 1955): 32–
    33.
"The Playwright: Man and Mission." *Theatre Arts* 42, no. 3 (March 1958): 49.
"Introduction to *Silent Night, Lonely Night*." *Theatre Arts* 45, no. 12 (December
    1961): 26.
"Who's to Blame? The Albee Debate." *New York Times* (25 April 1965): J4.
"Notes to APT Producers." Mimeographed production script of *Days Between*
    (1965).
"The Theatre Is Such an Impossible Place, Maybe It's Only Meant for Miracles."
    Dramatists Guild Quarterly 2, no. 1 (Spring 1965): 3–5.

"APT: Here's a Chance for Playwrights to Work in a More Stable Theater."
    Dramatists Guild Quarterly 4, no. 2 (Spring 1967): 4–8. Reprinted as "Amer-
    ican Playwrights Theater: More than Fifty Productions Coast to Coast."
    In *The Best Plays of 1966–67*, pp. 49–53. Edited by Otis L. Guernsey, Jr.
    New York: Dodd, Mead, 1967.
Introduction to *I Never Sang for My Father*. In *The Best Plays of 1967–68*, pp. 278–
    80. Edited by Otis L. Guernsey, Jr. New York: Dodd, Mead, 1968.
"Thoughts on Playwriting." *Writer* 83, no. 9 (September 1970): 12–14.
"Recent Study of Broadway Theatre Is Welcome, But Too Optimistic." *Dramatists
    Guild Quarterly* 9, no. 1 (Spring 1972): 6, 10–11.
"Robert Anderson—An Interview" (with Patricia Bosworth). *Publishers Weekly* (9
    July 1973): 16–17. Reprinted in *The Author Speaks: Selected "Publishers
    Weekly" Interviews 1967–1976*, pp. 3–5. New York: Bowker, 1977.
Untitled comment. In *Contemporary Dramatists*, pp. 32–33. Edited by James Vin-
    son. London: St. James, 1973. (4th ed., 1988. Pp. 16–17).
Untitled Homage to Elia Kazan. In *Working with Kazan*. Edited by Jeanine Bas-
    inger et al. Middletown, Conn.: Wesleyan, 1973.
"Maxwell Anderson: An Appreciation." *American Film Theatre/Cinebill* 1, no. 8
    (January 1974).
"Writing for Performance." Marvin Borowsky Memorial Lecture, Academy of
    Motion Picture Arts and Sciences. 29 April 1974.
"Forum's Pair of One-Acters: Two Kinds of Loneliness." *Chicago Sun-Times* (21
    July 1974): C2.
"No Final Curtain on the Ghosts of Grief." *Prism* (August 1974): 50–53. Re-
    printed as "Notes of a Survivor." In *The Patient, Death, and the Family*,
    pp. 73–82. Edited by Stanley B. Troup and William A. Greene. New York:
    Charles Scribner's Sons, 1974.
" 'Every Play I've Ever Written Is Me. I Am Naked When I Finish': A Conver-
    sation" (with Janet Baker-Carr). *Harvard Magazine* 77, no. 8 (April 1975):
    40–45.
"Interview with Robert Anderson." In *Playwrights Talk about Writing*, pp. 257–
    84. Edited by Lewis Funke. Chicago: Dramatic Publishing Co., 1975.
"*Tea and Sympathy*" (with Terrence McNally and Elia Kazan). *Dramatists Guild
    Quarterly* 19, no. 4 (Winter 1983): 11–27. Reprinted in *Broadway Song and
    Story: Playwrights/Lyricists/Composers Discuss Their Hits*, pp. 24–39. Edited by
    Otis L. Guernsey, Jr. New York: Dodd, Mead, 1985.
"A Multi-Media Dramatist's Inner Space." In *Broadway Song and Story*, pp. 165–
    71. Edited by Otis L. Guernsey, Jr. New York: Dodd, Mead, 1985.
"The Value of Criticism" (with A. R. Gurney, Jr., James Kirkwood, Marsha
    Norman, and Peter Stone). In *Broadway Song and Story*, pp. 331–44. Edited
    by Otis L. Guernsey, Jr. New York: Dodd, Mead, 1985.
"An Interview with Robert Anderson" (with Jackson Bryer). *Studies in American
    Drama, 1945–Present* 3 (1988).

PRODUCTION HISTORY

Although Anderson's plays have been seen in regional theatres across
the United States and in over twenty other countries, he is known pri-

marily as a writer for Broadway, where six of his plays appeared between 1953 and 1972. Anderson received his first New York—though not yet Broadway—exposure with a limited run of *Come Marching Home* at the Blackfriars Guild in May 1946. Written while he was on duty in the Pacific during World War II and performed earlier at the Pasadena Playhouse and at Iowa (where it was directed by Hallie Flanagan and the playwright's wife, Phyllis), *Home* pits the quixotic idealism of an ex-serviceman turned political candidate against a complacent electorate. In giving Anderson his first substantial notice, Nathan, while agreeing with others about the play's "honest conviction," found it too much "a forum harangue" (25).

Anderson's first Broadway play is—and seems likely to remain—the work by which he will be most remembered. *Tea and Sympathy*, which opened on 30 September 1953 and ran for 712 performances, was universally applauded for the sensitivity of Elia Kazan's direction, the evocativeness of Jo Mielziner's multilocale setting, the stellar performances of Deborah Kerr and John Kerr (Ingrid Bergman later triumphed in it in Paris), and the indelible effect of its breathtaking curtain as the older married woman offers herself to the adolescent boy so that he will be reassured of his normality after unjust accusations of homosexuality, reflecting the McCarthy era's paranoid guilt-by-association mentality. Sievers, who felt the play held "greater psychoanalytic insight" than John Van Druten's *Young Woodley* (1925) to which it seems heavily indebted, termed *Tea* "the most mature and important play of the 1953–54 season" (411). Although sympathetic to Anderson's emphasis on how the pack mentality tries to "dull [the] sensitivities" of the young man and enforce a stereotypical equation of manliness with macho toughness, Hewes found that the "perfectly carpentered" structure exacted its toll: the antagonist who projects his own guilt over his latent homosexuality on to the boy is made too villainous and unsympathetic ("Pekoe," 35); Kerr (*How Not To*, 108–11) and Bentley (149–53) would concur. And Gibbs criticized Anderson's "vacant rhetoric when some distinction of thought is demanded" (71). Even Kronenberger, choosing *Tea* because of its "moral force" as one of the best plays of the season, let a note of reservation creep in when he alluded to William Archer's old categorization of " 'bad literature but a good play' " (8).

In retrospect, fifteen years after the event, Gottfried overreacted that what was once an "affecting play" with a "theme [that] seemed bold" had become "dreadful now and its attitude embarrassingly naive" (*Theatre Divided*, 247). But Tynan, in his review of the 1957 London production, had already objected that Anderson failed to investigate, or even admit, "the possibility that the hero might in fact be an invert" (172). When Anderson adapted *Tea* for Hollywood, the Code would not countenance any mention of homosexuality and demanded that the woman's giving of herself to the young man cause, rather than follow, the irrevocable breakup of her marriage (Schumach, 144). Along with Crowther (24), Alpert faulted the resultant "heavy-handed moralizing" inherent in the guilt and "remorse and retribution" syndrome that the woman suffers for failing her husband in order to fulfill the adolescent's cry for help (31).

Although *All Summer Long* was first performed at Washington's Arena Stage before Broadway had heard Anderson's name, it did not reach New York until a year after *Tea* established him as one of America's bright new dramatists. Opening on 23 September 1954, it managed, in its director Alan Schneider's words, only a "disappointingly brief run" (193) of sixty performances. Adapted from Donald Wetzel's novel, *A Wreath and a Curse*, this rites-of-passage play treats the redemptive interaction of two brothers—and therein lay part of the perceived difficulty. The reviewers felt more uneasy than they should have over what they saw as the work's diffused focus. Yet the play, boasting an ingenious Mielziner set that simulated a destructive river, found at least a guarded champion in Atkinson. Despite cautious reservations about the somewhat "vapory . . . symbolism," "desultory" plot, and lack of a "clarifying point of view" ("Coming of Age," 39), he still judged Anderson's dramatization a "poignant play" and a "tender and beautiful work of art" in the manner of a "Chekovian portrait" ("*Summer*," 1).

If not the briefest of Anderson's Broadway runs—it held for 124 performances after opening on 3 December 1959—*Silent Night, Lonely Night* prompted the most muted, if ordinarily respectful, reviews of the playwright's career. Essentially a two-character play (fetchingly performed by Henry Fonda and Barbara Bel Geddes), *Night* asserts that perhaps the only hope for assuaging the loneliness besetting two basically decent and well-intentioned people might lie in overthrowing absolute moral strictures in favor of a situation ethic permitting them to respond to one another sexually in time of need. The critics, for the most part, did not object to Anderson's anti-puritanical and open point of view. Allan Lewis, for one, found that "the Christmas background" helped to suggest "the religious approval of resurrection through adultery" (155). Almost alone, Gassner supported *Night* as "an exercise in restraint [and a] finely spun web of feeling and insight" (*Crossroads*, 293), while most others judged it a talky and undramatic affair—in Weales's words "a relentlessly dull play. . . . simply a long double narrative" (51). Hewes added that the very brief encounter seemed somewhat joyless, although he blamed that decisively "on a Broadway that now appears to demand that all sex be therapeutic" ("Wrecks," 24).

Reconciling himself to the increasing difficulty of finding financial backing for a Broadway venture but aware as well of a potentially vast theatre audience beyond the Great White Way, Anderson offered *The*

Days Between to the newly formed American Playwrights Theater (APT) for production in fifty community and college playhouses during the 1965–1966 season, in places as farflung as Dallas, Texas (where it premiered), and Berea, Ohio. In his article assessing the APT's inaugural venture, Ayers surveyed the reviewers' responses to the initial production of this work about the way in which an egotistical novelist's blocked creativity threatens to destroy his marriage and turn his wife into simply an appendage of himself. As Taubman noted, it "digs deeply . . . into the psychology of a woman" (quoted in Ayers, "Progress Report," 254). Here was a dramatist especially sympathetic to the feminist agenda beginning to be felt and heard. Hewes faulted the play's structure for "manufactur[ing] dramatic climaxes and explanations somewhat too unrelievedly" and found the final staying together of the couple ill prepared for ("Aptitude," 28), sentiments Stanton would later echo (93). Although Taubman believed it "unthinkable that *The Days Between* will not eventually reach Broadway" (251), it never has. It did, however, finally have a brief run in New York City in 1979 as the premiere production of the Playhouse Repertory Company. Corry, confirming the initial impression that Anderson had created a "stunning" role for an actress, regretted that the playwright's very strengths as "a civilized, literate . . . and . . . immensely theatrical" writer contribute to making the play much too "genteel. It makes you wish that one of its characters, all of whom are guilty about one thing or another, might use a dirty word" (C:5).

Anderson's second Best Play and greatest (755 performances) Broadway success—actually an evening of four one-acters—opened on 13 March 1967, with one of the longest titles ever to appear on a marquee, *You Know I Can't Hear You When the Water's Running*, featuring a masterfully comic Martin Balsam. It secured for director Alan Schneider his surest financial return, though he initially doubted its commercial viability and continued to find it "superficial and showy" next to the works of Beckett and Albee with which he will always be associated (387). Schneider did, however, give *Water* credit for being "the first Broadway play that concerned itself seriously and organically with the issue of nudity" (387)—for which Kerr would gently chide Anderson for knowing not what he did (*Gymnasium Floor*, 105). And indeed the central critical debate, if such can exist over what purports to be little more than entertainment, has centered on whether Anderson should be considered a pacesetter or is actually retrograde in his attitude toward sexuality. While Emory Lewis (98) and Guernsey (12) stressed the fun, Gottfried (*Opening Nights*, 37–38), Lahr (7–8), and Simon (109–10) castigated Anderson as an apologist for puritanism at heart. Clurman captured the ambiguity behind their uneasiness with *Water*: "Its sophistication veils a puerile fascination with sex, a determination to be free and frank in talk about it, together with an equal degree of embarrassment. There is some uncertainty as to whether sex is to be embraced on a biologic level or to be ridiculed as something less significant than what we romantically suppose it to be" (444). For the hugely amused audiences, perhaps this was much ado about little. Theatre practitioners might be interested in Kamlot's behind-the-scenes look at a hit from optioning to closing (24–25).

In naming *I Never Sang for My Father* one of the Best Plays of 1967–1968, Guernsey called it "a triumph of American playwriting combined with Broadway stagecraft" (20). And yet the work, which opened on 25 January 1968 and gave Anderson, for the second time in his career, two plays running simultaneously on Broadway, closed after only 124 performances. It partially fell victim to reviews that found its characters too stereotyped, its sentiment too sentimental, and its situations too predictable. Finally, the play's overall effect was evidently not helped by Mielziner's cavernous and dreary, if functional, setting. The London reviewers, aware especially of the "classics" America exports, understandably noticed *Father*'s derivative nature: its memory structure borrowed from that other and better guilt play, *The Glass Menagerie;* its father-son conflict was reminiscent of *Death of a Salesman*. Wardle, for example, stated bluntly, "We have met these people before" (16). Back home, Kerr felt "the play . . . over-insistent, asking more . . . emotional return than its figues . . . justify" ("Feel," 368), though Loney, focusing on the love between middle-aged children and aged parents, countered that "Anderson is writing on a higher level [than soap opera]" (235).

Cates, the play's—and later the film version's—producer, encapsulated its theme as "the battle for primacy of soul, for the right to live life one's own way" (19), with Hewes sensing the connection between this need and "the way we all manipulate each other by guilt" ("Best," 13). One of the more intriguing aspects of *Father* is, in fact, the way in which the son, unable to accuse the too-close mother of guilt, transfers her possessiveness to the father. Anderson originally conceived *Father* as a screenplay, and when finally released on film in 1970 (with haunting performances by Melvyn Douglas and Gene Hackman) it appeared richer and more at home, shorn of its narrative passages and filled out by probing the son's relationships with his deceased wife, mistress, and fiancée; now "direct and largely non-subjective" (Cates, 19), it becomes, paradoxically, more affecting. *Father* was given a major revival during the 1987–1988 theatrical season.

Before opening in New York City on 30 September 1971 for an undeservedly brief thirty-six performances, Anderson's second evening of one-act plays, *Solitaire/Double Solitaire*, premiered earlier that year at New Haven's Long Wharf Theatre and then traveled to the Edinburgh (Scotland) International Festival, where Birrell declared that only "rarely can the subject [marriage] have been treated with such startling insight and compassion" (19). Although the dystopian curtain raiser, *Solitaire*, was, except for its house-of-illusion Call Families who provide the sole warmth available in an antiseptic technocracy, found lacking in originality, the longer *Double Solitaire* about relationships on the rocks garnered a number of superlatives, Hewes terming it Anderson's "best writing to date" ("Undoing," 35). In a review singling out the superlative performance of Joyce Ebert, Gill delineated Anderson's "bleak theme: that the consolations of family life, uncertain and fugitive as they may be, are not only the best we have but *all* we have" (95). While respecting Anderson's "honest" and "uncompromising" examination of a marriage grown lonely because of diminished sexual intensity (on one side) and opposing needs, Hughes still declared the evening "tiresome, tedious" and somewhat "bland" (322). Leone would agree with this assessment yet acclaimed *Solitaire/Double Solitaire* notable if for no other reason than its being "the first contemporary pro-woman plays to have been written, produced and directed by men" (134). Reviewing a 1974 revival in Chicago, Adler criticized the director's decision to downplay Anderson's emphasis on how a husband's adolescent idealization of physical sexuality as the sine qua non has "victimized" and "atrophied" the wife and threatened their continued marriage ("*Solitaire*," 530).

Free and Clear, Anderson's most recent work to be given a major production, had a limited run (22 March–1 May) in 1983, again under Arvin Brown's direction at the Long Wharf Theatre. It generated not just mixed but contradictory notices. What was gripping or powerful or provocative to some was old-fashioned or overly explicit or predictable to others. Dialogue that was tense and meticulous in its perfect pitch to one ear was whiney, stilted, and repetitive to another. As Viagas noted in his largely negative review, Anderson derived not only his title from *Death of a Salesman* but much of his "subject matter and mood" from that drama and *Long Day's Journey* as well (C5). Two grown sons, one unhappy in his marriage and career and the other a clearly autobiographical fledgling writer on the verge of marrying an older woman, come home to cut belatedly the cords tying them to their castrating parents: a socially charming but autocratic father who sees them as "dividends" who will pay back his investment by fulfilling his expectations and an artistic but now arthritic mother who depends emotionally on her "jewels" to "make her life for her." Love, to be worth anything, must be given freely, and not out of duty, Anderson says. In one of the most laudatory reviews, Pronechen predicted that this "touching...thought-provoking" work ought to "take its place alongside other lasting family-relationship dramas of the American theatre" (6). The lack of further productions—and the absence as yet of a printed text—would seem to lend considerable weight, however, to Klein's verdict that the "seemingly interminable barrage of torturous family bickering" makes *Free and Clear* "an irredeemable play" (2:4).

SURVEY OF SECONDARY SOURCES

Bibliographies

No full-scale bibliography for Anderson is yet available. A selected one can be found at the end of Ayers's 1969 dissertation, and still briefer lists of references appear in Adler's 1978 book (with annotations, 179–80) and at the conclusion of both Pedersen's (40) and Witkoski's (45) articles.

Biographies

In the absence of any full-length biography of Anderson, the most extensive "brief life" available in print appears in Adler's *Robert Anderson* (15–23). The dramatist himself provided a short autobiographical narrative stressing his early development (Wakeman, 54–56). Ayers's dissertation, a "professional biography" of the playwright's lengthy "apprenticeship," contains much useful information. Lawrence sketched a brief portrait of his fellow writer of "civilized" plays (35–38); Wood has recounted her long friendship with Anderson as his theatrical agent (262–77); and Wharton has detailed Anderson's association with the Playwrights Producing Company.

Influences

At a 1983 thirtieth anniversary symposium on *Tea and Sympathy* sponsored by the Dramatists Guild, Anderson admitted being drawn to poetic drama as an undergraduate and to the plays of Clifford Odets, S. N. Behrman, and Philip Barry—and the last two do appear to have influenced his early unpublished comedies. Although he claimed not to have warmed up to O'Neill until late in life, Anderson certainly felt the presence of *Long Day's Journey* when he penned *Free and Clear* and of Miller's *Death of a Salesman* in both that work and *I Never Sang for My Father*. The influence of Chekhov on the mood of *All Summer Long* has already been noted, as has that of the plot of *Young Woodley* on *Tea and Sympathy* (for a full discussion, see Adler's book, 69–70). Anderson alludes purposively to Shaw's *Candida* both early (*Tea*) and late (*Free and Clear*) in his career.

General Studies

A decade after its publication, Adler's *Robert Anderson* remains the only monograph devoted solely to the playwright. Analyzing each of the dramatist's plays (and screenplays and novels) in sequence, Adler focuses on autobiographical elements in the works and their technical variety, particularly on thematic motifs: the need to set aside traditional value systems when they conflict with a higher affective response to the emotional wounds of others; the diminishing possibilities for choice and change with the passage of time; an adolescent idealization of physical sexuality that, while it might counter fear of mortality and a metaphysical terror of the void, breaks down communion between couples; the fathers' tendency to confuse strength and aggression with manliness and thus their failure to foster the teaching emotions of sensitivity and compassion in their sons. Cognizant of, though perhaps too sanguine about, Anderson's evident shortcomings—his forced happy endings, his tendency to tell rather than to dramatize—Adler finally prizes Anderson's "humanity and compassion in portraying his distraught and lonely creatures" as second only to Williams's (166).

There exist two other, albeit very brief, overviews of Anderson's canon. In his grudgingly appreciative treatment, Witkoski (adopting Adler's lead) considers Anderson a writer of "carefully crafted, deeply felt" dramas of "loneliness"; he criticizes the plays, however, for their overdependence on dialogue, since their conflicts do not lend themselves well to "overtly dramatic representation" and for too often resorting to endings that are "too tidy and obvious to be convincing" (35–45). Pedersen balances Anderson's admittedly limited themes and motifs against his attempt to make the stage "more frank and open in its treatment of sex." Arguing for *I Never Sang for My Father* as the most successful in exploring relationships, she concludes that the autobiographical impulse makes aesthetic distance difficult for Anderson (30–40). The most satisfying short commentary comes from C. W. E. Bigsby, who finds in Anderson, despite his drawbacks, "power" and "subtlety," especially in seeing "growth away from innocence into experience as the first stage in the extinction of genuine feeling and human compassion" (34–35). Gassner, though critical of particulars, praises Anderson's "feeling and insight" in his brief discussion (*Crossroads*, 288–94), while Herron finds much to admire in Anderson's early efforts at "dramatizing lonely townspeople" (457–65). Three other critics take a decidedly negative posture on Anderson for quite similar reasons. Brustein chides him for presenting "object lessons" on adultery as self-sacrifice more appropriate from a "psychological counselor" (254) and Meserve for penning sentimental comedies and melodramas that espouse "illicit sex as a solution to man's problems" (351–52) and Weales for much the same (49–56).

Analyses of Individual Plays

For detailed analyses of Anderson's individual works, one must ordinarily consult Adler's *Robert Anderson*. The only other discussions of any length concern *Double Solitaire:* Leone expresses delight over Anderson's espousal of a feminist point of view (134–36), and Bernstein surveys the critical response to the play, praises its "trenchant criticism" of marriage, discusses its handling of time and space and its use of the motif of photography, inexplicably declaims against its being considered a well-made play—which no one would argue anyway—and unconvincingly links it with the absurdist movement because of its sense of "frustration" and "contingency" and its use of a "bare setting" (87–109). Gunton and Stine offer a representative sampling of critical responses to the various plays by many of the better-known commentators on modern drama (28–34).

FUTURE RESEARCH OPPORTUNITIES

Because of Anderson's extensive theatrical activity and wide associations over a period of three decades or more, as well as because of the deeply autobiographical nature of much of his writing, there would seem to be a need—or at least a fruitful opportunity—for a critical biography. A thorough examination of Anderson's language, his rhetoric that tends to abstract and enunciate ideas explicitly, has yet to be done, though it would more likely reveal perhaps his major deficiency rather than his strengths. An extended look at Anderson's plays from a feminist perspective, given the hints in this direction in Adler's monograph and Leone's essay, might be one approach that would most keep him in the critical eye, since what Gassner once viewed as Anderson's mark of distinction—his being "a gentleman in the age of literary assassins" (*Best*, 314)—now appears a liability that links Anderson inescapably with the insular domestic (melo)drama of the 1950s.

SECONDARY SOURCES

Adler, Thomas P. *Robert Anderson*. Boston: Twayne, 1978.
———."Robert Anderson: Playwright of Middle-Aged Loneliness." *Ball State University Forum* 16, no. 2 (Spring 1975): 58–64.
———. *"Solitaire/Double Solitaire."* *Educational Theatre Journal* 26, no. 4 (December 1974): 529–30.
Alpert, Hollis. "What Hangs Over." *Saturday Review* (29 September 1956): 31.
Atkinson, Brooks. *"All Summer Long."* *New York Times* (3 October 1954): B1.
———. "Coming of Age." *New York Times* (24 September 1954): 39.
Ayers, David H. "American Playwrights Theatre—A Progress Report." *Educational Theatre Journal* 17, no. 3 (October 1965): 251–56.

————. "The Apprenticeship of Robert Anderson." Ph.D. dissertation, Ohio State University, 1969.

Bentley, Eric. *The Dramatic Event: An American Chronicle*. London: Dennis Dobson, 1956.

Bernstein, Samuel J. *The Strands Entwined: A New Direction in American Drama*. Boston: Northeastern University Press, 1980.

Bigsby, C. W. E. "Robert Anderson." In *Contemporary Dramatists*, 4th ed., pp. 16–18. Ed. D.L. Kirkpatrick. Chicago: St. James Press, 1988.

Birrell, George. *"Solitaire/Double Solitaire." Edinburgh Evening News* (7 September 1971): 19.

Brustein, Robert. *Seasons of Discontent: Dramatic Opinions 1959–65*. New York: Simon and Schuster, 1965.

Cates, Gilbert. "Notes on Making the Film." In *I Never Sang for My Father*, pp. 15–19. New York: New American Library, 1970.

Clurman, Harold. "Theatre." *Nation* (3 April 1967): 444.

Corry, John. "New Group Gives *The Days Between*." *New York Times* (8 June 1979): C5.

Crowther, Bosley. *"Tea and Sympathy." New York Times* (28 September 1956): 24.

Gassner, John. *Best American Plays: Fifth Series—1957–63*. New York: Crown, 1963.

————. *Theatre at the Crossroads: Plays and Playwrights of the Mid-Century American Stage*. New York: Holt, Rinehart and Winston, 1960.

Gibbs, Wolcott. "Minority Opinion." *New Yorker* (10 October 1953): 71–72.

Gill, Brendan. "No Place Like Home." *New Yorker* (9 October 1971): 95–96.

Gottfried, Martin. *Opening Nights: Theatre Criticism of the Sixties*. New York: G. P. Putnam's Sons, 1969.

————. *A Theatre Divided: The Postwar American Stage*. Boston: Little, Brown, 1967.

Guernsey, Otis L., Jr., ed. *The Best Plays of 1967–68*. New York: Dodd, Mead, 1968.

Gunton, Sharon R., and Jean C. Stine, eds. *Contemporary Literary Criticism*, Vol. 23. Detroit: Gale Research, 1983.

Herron, Ima Honaker. *The Small Town in American Drama*. Dallas: Southern Methodist University Press, 1969.

Hewes, Henry. "Aptitude Test." *Saturday Review* (19 June 1965): 28.

————. "A Husband's Undoing." *Saturday Review* (16 October 1971): 35.

————. "Oedipus Wrecks." *Saturday Review* (19 December 1959): 24.

————. "Orange Pekoe." *Saturday Review* (17 October 1953): 35–36.

————. "The Best of the 1967–68 Theatre Season." *Saturday Review* (1 June 1968): 13.

Hughes, Catharine. *"Solitaire/Double Solitaire." America* (23 October 1971): 322.

Kamlot, Robert. "What Does a General Manager Do?" *New York Theatre Review* 1, no. 1 (March 1976): 24–25.

Kerr, Walter. *God on the Gymnasium Floor and Other Theatrical Adventures*. New York: Delta, 1973.

————. *How Not to Write a Play*. New York: Simon and Schuster, 1955.

————. "Why Can't I Feel Anything?" *New York Times* (4 February 1968). Reprinted in *New York Theatre Critics' Reviews* (5 February 1968): 367–68.

Klein, Alvin. "*Free and Clear* Is Ponderous Stuff." *New York Times* (17 April 1983): B4.

Kronenberger, Louis, ed. *The Best Plays of 1953–54*. New York: Dodd, Mead, 1954.

Lahr, John. *Up Against the Fourth Wall: Essays on Modern Theatre*. New York: Grove Press, 1970.

Lawrence, Jerome. "Living Playwrights in the Living Theatre." *Dramatics* 52, no. 3 (January 1981): 35–38.

Leone, Vivien. "Notes from an Accidentally Passionate Playgoer." *Drama and Theatre* 10, no. 3 (Spring 1972): 134–36.

Lewis, Allan. *American Plays and Playwrights of the Contemporary Theatre*. Rev. ed. New York: Crown, 1970.

Lewis, Emory. *Stages: The Fifty-Year Childhood of the American Theatre*. Englewood Cliffs, N.J.: Prentice-Hall, 1969.

Loney, Glenn. "Broadway in Review." *Educational Theatre Journal* 20, no. 2 (May 1968): 229–36.

Meserve, Walter J. *An Outline History of American Drama*. Totowa, N.J.: Littlefield, Adams, 1965.

Nathan, George Jean. *The Theatre Book of the Year 1946–47: A Record and an Interpretation*. Rutherford, N.J.: Fairleigh Dickinson University Press, 1947.

Pedersen, Lise. "Robert Anderson." In *Critical Survey of Drama: English Language Series*, 1: 30–40. Edited by Frank H. Magill. Englewood Cliffs, N.J.: Salem Press, 1985.

Pronechen, Joseph. "Anderson Scores; Simon Bores." *Trumbull Times* (7 April 1983): 6.

Schneider, Alan. *Entrances: An American Director's Journey*. New York: Viking, 1986.

Sievers, W. David. *Freud on Broadway: A History of Psychoanalysis and the American Drama*. New York: Hermitage House, 1955.

Schumach, Murray. *The Face on the Cutting Room Floor: The Story of Movie and Television Censorship*. New York: Da Capo Press, 1974.

Simon, John. *Uneasy Stages: A Chronicle of the New York Theatre, 1963–1973*. New York: Random House, 1975.

Stanton, Stephen S. Review of *Robert Anderson*. *Comparative Drama* 14, no. 1 (Spring 1980): 90–93.

Tynan, Kenneth. *Curtains*. New York: Atheneum, 1961.

Viagas, Robert. "*Death* Haunts *Free and Clear*." *Fairpress* (Fairfield, Conn., 6 April 1983): C5.

Wakeman, John, ed. *World Authors 1950–1970*. New York: H. W. Wilson, 1975.

Wardle, Irving. "*I Never Sang for My Father*." *The Times* (London, 28 May 1970): 16.

Weales, Gerald. *American Drama Since World War II*. New York: Harcourt, Brace, 1962.

Wharton, John H. *Life among the Playwrights: Being Mostly the Story of the Playwrights Producing Company*. New York: Quadrangle/Times, 1974.

Witkoski, Michael. "Robert Anderson." In *Dictionary of Literary Biography/Twen-*

tieth Century American Dramatists, 7, pt. 1: 35–45. Edited by John MacNicholas. Detroit: Gale Research, 1981.

Wood, Audrey, with Max Wilk. *Represented by Audrey Wood*. Garden City, N.Y.:
Doubleday, 1981.

James Baldwin
(2 AUGUST 1924–1 DECEMBER 1987)

DAVID H. ROBERTS

ASSESSMENT OF BALDWIN'S REPUTATION

Noted more for his fiction than his drama, James Baldwin nonetheless is an important voice in the American theatre. Of Baldwin's eight plays and scripts, two—*The Amen Corner* (1955) and *Blues for Mister Charlie* (1964)—are regarded as major achievements. They expand the major themes of his fiction and essays: racism and religion. As Darwin T. Turner rightly states, "In drama, as in his other writing, Baldwin repeatedly preaches that people must love and understand other people if they wish to save the world from destruction" (30). It is no wonder that *Newsweek* called him "our black Jeremiah" (Prescott, 86). The *Washington Post* proclaimed him the "voice of the witness" (Williams, B6). The *New York Times* called him an "eloquent essayist" (Daniels, D1).

Baldwin received many awards and fellowships. He was given the Eugene Saxton Memorial Trust Award in 1945, a Rosenwald Foundation Fellowship in 1948, a Guggenheim Fellowship in 1954, a National Institutes of Arts and Letters Award in 1956, and a Partisan Review Fellowship in 1956. Baldwin won a Ford Foundation Fellowship in 1958. The University of British Columbia conferred an honorary doctorate on him in 1963. In 1962 the National Conference of Christians and Jews gave him their organization's Brotherhood Award. He won a George Polk Award in 1963 and the Foreign Drama Critics Award in 1964, the year his sensational *Blues for Mister Charlie* rocked the New York stage. Also in 1964, he was named a member of the National Institute of Arts and Letters. Morehouse College bestowed an honorary doctorate on him in 1976, and in 1978 he won the Martin Luther King, Jr., Award from the City College of the State University of New York.

Baldwin lived in France for more than forty years and was the second black to be awarded the Legion of Honor by France ("Author James Baldwin Gets France's Top Honor," 4). After his death of cancer on 1 December 1987, he was eulogized in the *Washington Post* by Williams as "a great American writer [whose] writings became a standard of literary realism" (B1).

PRIMARY BIBLIOGRAPHY OF BALDWIN'S WORKS

Books

Go Tell It on the Mountain. New York: Alfred A. Knopf, 1953.
Notes of a Native Son. Boston: Beacon Press, 1955.
Nobody Knows My Name. New York: Dial Press, 1961.
Another Country. New York: Dial Press, 1962.
Giovanni's Room. New York: Dial Press, 1962.
The Fire Next Time. New York: Dial Press, 1963.
Nothing Personal. New York: Atheneum Publishers, 1964.
Going to Meet the Man. New York: Dial Press, 1965.
Tell Me How Long the Train's Been Gone. New York: Dial Press, 1968.
A Rap on Race: Margaret Mead and James Baldwin. Philadelphia: J. B. Lippincott, 1971.
No Name in the Street. New York: Dial Press, 1972.
A Dialogue: James Baldwin and Nikki Giovanni. Philadelphia: J. B. Lippincott, 1973.
If Beale Street Could Talk. New York: Dial Press, 1974.
Little Man, Little Man. A Story of Childhood. New York: Dial Press, 1976.
The Devil Finds Work. An Essay. New York: Dial Press, 1976.
Just Above My Head. New York: Dial Press, 1979.

Plays and Productions

The Amen Corner. (Produced Washington, D.C.: Howard University, 1955; New York: Barrymore Theatre, 1965; Philadelphia: Zellerbach Theatre, 1986; London: Tricycle Theatre, 1987.) New York: Dial, 1968.
Giovanni's Room. Actor's Studio Workshop, 1957.
Blues for Mister Charlie. (Produced New York: ANTA Theatre, 1964; Atlanta: Performance Gallery, 1987.) New York: Dial Press, 1964; London: Joseph, 1965.
A Deed from the King of Spain. (Produced New York: American Center for Stanislavsky Theatre Art, 1974.)
Amen Corner. Musical (Produced Washington, D.C.: Ford's Theatre, 1983; New York: Nederlander Theatre, 1983.) New York: Dial Press, 1964; London: Joseph, 1965.
"*Go Tell It on the Mountain*." Television production. *PBS American Playhouse*, January 14, 1985.
One Day, When I Was Lost: A Scenario Based on Alex Haley's "The Autobiography of Malcolm X." London: Michael Joseph, 1972. New York: Dial Press, 1973.

The Welcome Table. Mentioned in O'Reilly (91:F14).
The Woman at the Well. Listed in *Who's Who 1987*, p. 79.

Screenplay

The Inheritance. 1973.

PRODUCTION HISTORY

The Amen Corner was first performed at Howard University in 1955 and then at the Robertson Playhouse in Los Angeles in 1964 (Standley, 45). The play opened in New York City on 15 April 1965, ten years after its initial performance at Howard University, at the Ethel Barrymore Theatre, for eighty-four performances (Woll, 7). Taubman found the script sketchy and the action slow but added that "a number of notable performances" overcame those weaknesses ("Frank Silvera," 35). Nevertheless, Taubman also credited the play with shedding "some light on the barrenness of the lives of impoverished Negroes who seek surcease from their woes in religion." Other critics insisted that Bea Richards's performance gave the play a "moment of inflated glory" (Drake, 51:D4).

The European premiere in Vienna at the Theatre An Der Wein in June 1965 was part of the celebration of Austria's tenth anniversary of freedom from occupation by military forces. The Vienna performance received a standing ovation despite the difficulty the Austrians had in understanding Harlem vernacular ("Play by Baldwin," 82). Fifty other European performances were scheduled during the summer of 1965.

The play was well received in Tel Aviv, where Baldwin showed up, unannounced, just before the play began. In Jerusalem as part of the 1965 Israel Festival, the play was "warmly received," and Bea Richards, who played Sister Margaret on Broadway, was rewarded with shouts of "Bravo!" for "her performance in the closing scene [which] was the highlight of the play" ("Baldwin Play," 19). The London *Times* critic who did not like an earlier production of *Blues for Mister Charlie* also cared little for *The Amen Corner*, accusing Baldwin of having a "fatally simple-minded way" of writing about important issues ("Uneven Play," 11). The critic said that the London production of *The Amen Corner* was only "marginally better" than *Blues*. The Edinburgh production pace was "limping," although Claudia McNeil portrayed a "powerful, authoritative and moving Sister Margaret" ("A Victory," 13).

The Amen Corner was revived in 1978 by the Afro/American Total Theatre at the New York Arts Consortium. Lask assessed the production as "at once full of pathos and caustic humor, irritating superstition and shrewd folk wisdom," though Baldwin's script was too long "and sometimes soft" (Lask, 54). The Chicago-based Kuumba Workshop Theatre's 1979 revival of the play was called "a small classic" (Webster, 40), and the Kuumba group's performances were praised around the country ("Kuumba Theatre Group," 64).

Revived again in 1983 as a musical and described before the Broadway opening as "ebullient" ("What's New on Broadway," 122), the play was termed "modest" (Gill, 208); "trite, obvious, graceless, and boring" (Simon, 68); and "an attempt at a retread of *Purlie*" (" 'Amen Corner' Full of True Believers," D2). Watt said the New York production was in need of a miracle to improve it (Watt 50:D3); however, it was heralded as "a musical of power and joy" in Baltimore (Gardner, 34:C1).

A 1985 run of *The Amen Corner* for two performances by the Cambridge Players in Los Angeles was anticipated eagerly because the Broadway version had originated there in 1964. Because of the play's modest success on Broadway, "it was something one wanted to see again" (Drake, 51:D4). But the production was terrible. Lighting was poor, the ceiling was too high, the stage was too shallow, the set was dull, and the action was slow (Drake, 51:D4).

Radin called a 1987 London production of the musical version by the Carib Theatre Company a "finely-imagined production" (24), and Algeo believed the production captured "both the spirit and for the most part the sound of Harlem" (126). Smith characterized a Memphis production of the play as "a bold, moving drama that's almost relentlessly charged with emotion" (9:A7). By contrast, the Annenberg Center's Zellerbach Theatre production in late 1985 was passionless (Collins, 106:G14).

The New York debut of *Blues for Mister Charlie* was 23 April 1964 at the ANTA Theatre, under the direction of Burgess Meredith. It closed a month later. Based on the murder of Emmett Till, a Mississippi black man killed in 1955, the play was dedicated to the memory of Medgar Evers, with whom Baldwin had investigated Till's murder. *Blues*, a play that "throbs with fierce energy and passion" (Taubman, "James Baldwin's Play," 24), was disliked in London (Feron, 52). The 1964 New York production was seen as "an angry sermon and a pain-wracked lament" (Taubman, "Common Burden," 11). A 1987 revival of the play in Atlanta was "compelling" (Crouch, 127:F5).

Baldwin's other plays—*Giovanni's Room, A Deed from the King of Spain,* "*Go Tell It on the Mountain*" (a television production of the book), *The Welcome Table* (mentioned in O'Reilly, 91:F13), *One Day, When I Was Lost* (based on Alex Haley's *Autobiography of Malcolm X* [Pratt, 98]), *The Woman at the Well* (listed in *Who's Who, 1987*)—have been performed infrequently.

SURVEY OF SECONDARY SOURCES

Bibliographies

Standley and Standley, the most important Baldwin bibliography to date, supply an excellent, detailed, and nearly complete bibliography covering the years 1946 through 1978. Bobia analyzes the French critics' reception of Baldwin and presents an annotated bibliography of French criticism on Baldwin up to 1986.

Biography

The most significant biographical treatment of Baldwin is by Pratt, who probes the constant conflicts of Baldwin's life and the themes of his writings. Briefer biographies are offered by Standley in volumes 2 and 7 of *Dictionary of Literary Biography* and by Roberts in volume 33. Turner's concise biography also provides some insights to Baldwin's life and work. The Winter 1987 issue of *The Massachusetts Review* contains an impassioned four-part dedication to Baldwin, the first part ending with a paraphrase of an old slave song, "James Baldwin got a home in the rock of immortality. Ain't that good news?" (Terry, et al.).

Influences

Auchincloss and Lynch outline the motives of Baldwin's social activism. In an interview with the *Black Scholar* that ranges from Malcolm X to civil rights to Stokley Carmichael to Stevie Wonder, Baldwin himself discussed the effects of racism and oppression on his development as a writer. Gates explores various influences on Baldwin's life, while Pratt discusses the common experiences that Baldwin shared with other Americans, black and white. Weixlmann identifies the influences of O'Neill's *All God's Chillun* (which Baldwin uses with "little of the finesse of his predecessor") on *Blues for Mister Charlie*.

General Studies

Several recent general studies of Baldwin and his works merit mention. Sylvander offers a useful survey of the canon. Baylor examines the theme of the Fall of Man in Baldwin's novels, and Montgomery reads *Go Tell It on the Mountain* in the light of the "impending doom and destruction" found in several other black writers.

Other studies of Baldwin are included in works that focus on the black community or on Baldwin's activism as an integrationist, as in Davis's essay, "James Baldwin," one of a collection in *From the Dark Tower: Afro-American Writers, 1900 to 1960*. Hayes explores *The Amen Corner* and two other plays from what he terms "the Theatre of Negro Participation-Protest Aspect." In a carefully argued, historically informed article, Bigsby discussed *Blues For Mister Charlie* as protest literature. Bigsby provides a valuable background study for Baldwin's play. Taking another point of view, Simon suggests that the play, like Baraka's *Dutchman*, is closer to a piece of propaganda.

Two works provide insight on the effect of black culture on Baldwin. Dobson asserts that a "tension between orality and literacy underlies that between the two main characters of 'Sonny's Blues.'" And Hubbard studies the linguistic structure of sermons by black preachers and compares them with the structure of sermons by black preachers in the novels. Harris investigates the women of Baldwin's works in depth, with some reference to female characters in his plays.

Analyses of Individual Plays

The Amen Corner is "concerned with the way religion is used as an escape by impoverished and emotionally troubled Negroes" (Taubman, "Jones and Baldwin," 11). The scene is a storefront church in Harlem with Sister Margaret the central character. She is "a minister of enormous verbal power and magnetic leadership abilities" (Roberts, 8) who turns to religion for consolation following a miscarriage and the resulting rejection of Luke, her husband. In the final act, Sister Margaret, rejected by her congregation, discovers that religious legalism perpetuates suffering and love promotes forgiveness: "To love the Lord is to love all his children—all of them, everyone!" (in Standley, 48). Among other things, the play demonstrated to the critics that religion, properly applied, demands that the members of one race love and accept the members of all other races.

From the personal conflict of *The Amen Corner* to the public and racial conflict of *Blues for Mister Charlie*, Baldwin had difficulty externalizing conflict but no difficulty creating a setting that exemplifies the conflict. The stage of *The Amen Corner* contains the church and its pulpit, plus Sister Margaret's apartment, symbolizing her personal conflict between family life and church life. The *Blues* set shows a black church and a courthouse separated by a street in a Southern town, a moving contrast (Meserve, 178).

FUTURE RESEARCH OPPORTUNITIES

A number of major research opportunities await students of Baldwin's plays. The women in Baldwin's dramas deserve special attention. Pryse and Spillers's collection of essays serve as models for such an investigation. Research on Baldwin's lesser-known plays is equally necessary, especially in revealing how Baldwin explores the themes of perdition, destruction, and chaos through his characters. Significantly enough, Baldwin's earlier works do not exhibit the militancy of his later prose and drama. I would like to see a detailed, book-length analysis of the plays in light of the novels and other prose works. His development as a militant and whether he sees militancy or social degeneration as the agent of destruction and chaos needs to be studied and chronicled. Baldwin's religious experiences and his theology also need to be analyzed through the language, setting, and characters in his plays to determine to what extent Baldwin's theology reflects what is commonly known as liberation theology, and especially the theology of Sister Margaret. Finally, a complete bibliography of Baldwin's works from 1978 until his death in 1987 is needed.

SECONDARY SOURCES

Algeo, John. " 'The Amen Corner.' " *Studies in American Drama, 1945–Present* 2 (1987): 123–26.

" 'Amen Corner' Full of True Believers." *New York Post* (11 November 1983). Newsbank, Performing Arts, 50:D2.

Auchincloss, Eve, and Nancy Lynch. "Disturber of the Peace: James Baldwin." In *The Black American Writer.* Vol. 1: *Fiction*, pp. 199–215. Edited by C. W. E. Bigsby. Deland, Fla.: Everett/Edwards, 1969.

"Author James Baldwin Gets France's Top Honor." *Jet* (7 July 1986): 4.

"Baldwin Play Wins Acclaim in Tel Aviv." *New York Times Theatre Reviews* (9 August 1965): 19.

Baylor, Cherry Revona. "James Baldwin and the Fall of Man." *DAI* 47 (May 1987): 4005A-6A.

Bigsby, C. W. E. "The Committed Writer: James Baldwin as Dramatist." *Twentieth Century Literature* 13 (April 1967): 39–48.

"The Black Scholar Interviews James Baldwin." *Black Scholar: Journal of Black Studies and Research* 5 (December 1973–January 1974): 33–42.

Bobia, Rosa Mae Williamson. "James Baldwin and His Francophone Critics: An Analysis and Annotated Bibliography (1952–1981)." *DAI* 46 (February 1986): 2287A.

Collins, William. " 'Amen Corner' Opens at Annenberg Center." *Philadelphia Inquirer* (4 December 1985). Newsbank, Performing Arts, 106:G14.

Crouch, Paula. "Performance Gallery's 'Blues for Mister Charlie' Timely and Compelling." *Atlanta Journal* (10 February 1987). Newsbank, Performing Arts, 127:F5.

Daniels, Lee. "James Baldwin, Eloquent Essayist in Behalf of Civil Rights, Is Dead." *New York Times* (2 December 1987): D1.

Davis, Arthur P. "James Baldwin." In *From the Dark Tower: Afro-American Writers, 1900 to 1960*, pp. 216–26. Washington, D.C.: Howard University Press, 1982.

Dobson, Frank Edward. "The Use of Oral Tradition and Ritual in Afro-American Fiction." *DAI* 47 (July 1986): 177A.

Drake, Sylvie. "Cambridge Players Bring Back 'The Amen Corner.' " *Los Angeles Times* (21 October 1985). Newsbank, Performing Arts, 51:D.

Feron, James. " 'Charlie' Scored by London Critics." *New York Times Theatre Reviews* (5 May 1965): 52.

Gardner, R. H. "Amen! to 'Amen Corner.' " *Baltimore Sun* (16 September 1983). Newsbank, Performing Arts, 34:C1.

Gates, Henry Louis. "An Interview with Josephine Baker and James Baldwin." *Southern Review* 21 (July 1985): 594–602.

Gill, Brendan. "Waifs." *New Yorker* (21 November 1983): 208–9.

Harris, Trudier. *Black Women in the Fiction of James Baldwin.* Knoxville: University of Tennessee Press, 1985.

Hayes, Donald. "An Analysis of Dramatic Themes Used by Selected Black-American Playwrights from 1950–1976 with a Backgrounder: The State of the Art of the Contemporary Black Theater and Black Playwriting. Volumes I and II." *DAI* 45 (June 1985): 3483A.

Hubbard, Dolan. "Preaching the Lord's Word in a Strange Land: The Influence of the Black Preaching Style on Black American Prose Fiction." *DAI* 47 (January 1987): 2585A.

"Kuumba Theatre Group Praised for 'Amen Corner.' " *Jet Magazine* 15 (January 1981): 64.

Lask, Thomas. " 'Amen Corner' by Baldwin Staged by Arts Consortium." *New York Times Theatre Reviews* (23 April 1978): 54.

Meserve, Walter. "James Baldwin's 'Agony Way.' " In *The Black American Writer.* Vol. 2: *Poetry and Drama*, pp. 171–86. Edited by C. W. E. Bigsby. Deland, Fla.: Everett/Edwards, 1969.

Montgomery, Maxine Lavon. "The Modern Black Novelist and the Apocalyptic Tradition." *DAI* 47 (March 1987): 3428A.

O'Reilly, David. "A Play This Time." *Philadelphia Inquirer* (2 December 1986). Newsbank, Performing Arts, 91:F12–F14.

"Play by Baldwin Opens in Vienna." *New York Times Theatre Reviews* (13 June 1965): 82.

Pratt, Louis. *James Baldwin.* Boston: Twayne, 1978.

Prescott, Peter. "The Dilemma of a Native Son." *Newsweek* (14 December 1987): 86.

Pryse, Marjorie, and Hortense Spillers. *Conjuring: Black Women, Fiction, and Literary Tradition.* Bloomington: Indiana University Press, 1985.

Radin, Victoria. "Rituals." *New Statesman* (20 March 1987): 23–24.

Roberts, John W. "James Baldwin." In *Afro-American Writers after 1955. Dictionary of Literary Biography*, 33: 3–16. Edited by Thadious Davis and Trudier Harris. Detroit: Gale Research Company, 1984.

Simon, John. "Brotherhood Weak." *New York* (21 November 1983): 65, 68.

———. "Theatre Chronicle." *Hudson Review* 17 (1964): 421–430.

Smith, Whitney. "Hallelujah for 'Amen Corner.' " *Commercial Appeal* (21 June 1985). Newsbank, Performing Arts, 9:A7.

Standley, Fred L. "James Baldwin." In *American Novelists since World War II. Dictionary of Literary Biography.* Vol. 2, pp. 15–22. Detroit: Gale Research Company, 1978.

———. "James Baldwin." In *Twentieth-Century American Dramatists. Dictionary of Literary Biography.* Vol. 7, pp. 45–49. Detroit: Gale Research Company, 1981.

Standley, Fred L., and Nancy V. Standley. *James Baldwin: A Reference Guide.* Boston: G. K. Hall, 1980.

Sylvander, Carolyn W. *James Baldwin*. New York: Ungar, 1980.

Taubman, Howard. "Common Burden." *New York Times Theatre Reviews* (3 May 1964): 11.

——. "Frank Silvera and Bea Richards Head Cast." *New York Times Theatre Reviews* (16 April 1965): 35.

——. "James Baldwin's Play Opens at the ANTA." *New York Times Theatre Reviews* (24 April 1964): 24.

——. "Jones and Baldwin." *New York Times Theatre Reviews* (25 April 1965): 11.

Terry, Esther, Chinua Achebe, Michael Thelwell, and John Wideman. "James Baldwin, 1924–1987: A Dedication." *The Massachusetts Review*, 38 (Winter 1987): 552–560.

Turner, Darwin T. "James Baldwin." In *Contemporary Dramatists*, 4th ed., pp. 29–31. Edited by D. L. Kirkpatrick. Chicago: St. James Press, 1988.

"Uneven Play by James Baldwin." London *Times* (24 August 1965): 11.

"A Victory for Miss McNeil." London *Times* (13 October 1965): 13.

Watt, Douglas. " 'Amen Corner': Pray for a Miracle." *New York Daily News* (11 November 1983). Newsbank, Performing Arts, 50:D3.

Weales, Gerald. "Drama." In *Harvard Guide to Contemporary American Writing*, pp. 396–438. Edited by Daniel Hoffman. Cambridge: Harvard University Press, 1979.

Webster, Ivan. "This Amen Corner Is a Bit Cramped." *Encore American and Worldwide News* (18 June 1979): 40–41.

Weixlmann, Joe. "Staged Segregation: Baldwin's *Blues for Mister Charlie* and O'Neill's *All God's Chillun Got Wings*." *Black American Literature Forum* 11, no. 1 (1976): 35–36.

"What's New on Broadway." *Business Week* (10 October 1983): 122.

Williams, Juan. "Baldwin: The Voice of the Witness." *Washington Post* (2 December 1987): Bl.

Woll, Allen. *Dictionary of the Black Theatre: Broadway, Off-Broadway, and Selected Harlem Theatre*. Westport, Conn.: Greenwood Press, 1983.

Amiri Baraka (LeRoi Jones)
(7 OCTOBER 1934–   )

THOMAS BONNER, JR.

ASSESSMENT OF BARAKA'S REPUTATION

Baraka has contributed substantially to the continued rise of drama in the tradition of American letters. His plays move from the exploration of self in the American milieu toward the enigma of race in the national order, and to the exploration of economic systems directly affecting society. Although Baraka has had broad aesthetic, political, and philosophical interests articulated in several literary genres, his major form of art is drama.

Baraka's achievement lies in his subject: blacks in a white world—their postures, fears, and hopes for fulfillment. The programmatic nature of the plays has drawn criticism for didacticism, but it is this very aesthetic, with its inherent heightened rhetorical form, that came to be a hallmark of literature by black Americans during the 1960s. Baraka, like many others, defends this juncture of politics and art as a distinction between black art and other American art.

Although more than twenty-five of Baraka's plays have been performed, the most influential come from early in his career, when inspiration, energy, and the times collided in a nearly unique explosion of dramatic activity. *Dante* (later *The Eighth Ditch*), *Dutchman* (1964 Obie Award), *The Slave* (Second Prize, Dakar International Arts Festival, 1966), and *A Black Mass* show Baraka turning his attention to a black audience from one of mixed races, establishing a black aesthetic and moving toward cultural nationalism. Later works from the 1970s such as *S-1* and *The Motion of History*, reveal broadened themes and less dramatic intensity. The 1980s finds Baraka extending his use of ritual as devices into the adoption of technology. With his reputation as the great catalyst of the black aesthetic movement secure, he has devoted himself to poetry and non-fiction prose. A declining number of critical essays on his plays balances a rising number devoted to his other arts.

PRIMARY BIBLIOGRAPHY OF BARAKA'S WORKS

Plays

Dutchman and The Slave: Two Plays. New York: Morrow, 1964; London: Faber & Faber, 1965.

A Black Mass. In *Liberator* 6 (June 1966): 14–16.

The Baptism and The Toilet. New York: Grove, 1967.

Arm Yrself or Harm Yourself. Newark, N.J.: Jihad, 1967.

Police. In *Drama Review* 12 (Summer 1968): 112–15.

Home on the Range. In *Drama Review* 12 (Summer 1968): 106–11.

Slave Ship. Newark, N.J.: Jihad, 1969.

Rockgroup. In *Cricket*, no. 4 (December 1969): 41–43.

The Death of Malcolm X. In *New Plays from the Black Theatre*, pp. 1–20. Edited by Ed Bullins. New York: Bantam, 1969.

Four Black Revolutionary Plays. Indianapolis: Bobbs-Merrill, 1969. Contains *Experimental Death Unit #1, A Black Mass, Great Goodness of Life: A Coon Show,* and *Madheart.*

J-E-L-L-O. Newark, N.J.: Jihad, n.d.; Chicago: Third World, 1970.

Bloodrites. In *Black Drama Anthology*, pp. 25–31. Edited by Woodie King and Ron Milner. New York: Columbia University Press, 1971.

Junkies Are Full of S-H-H-H. In *Black Drama Anthology*, pp. 11–23.

Ba-Ra-Ka. In *Spontaeneous Combustion: Eight New American Plays*, pp. 175–81. Ed. Rochelle Owens. New York: Winter House, 1972.

The Motion of History and Other Plays. New York: Morrow, 1978. Includes *Slave Ship* and *S-1.*

Selected Plays and Prose of Amiri Baraka/LeRoi Jones. New York: Morrow, 1979. Includes *Dutchman, The Slave, Great Goodness of Life,* and *What Was the Relationship of the Lone Ranger to the Means of Production?*

The Sidney Poet Heroical in 29 Scenes. Berkeley: Reed & Cannon, 1979.

Screenplays

Dutchman. Gene Person Enterprises, 1967.

Black Spring. Jihad Productions, 1967.

A Fable (from *The Slave*). MFR Productions, 1971.

Phonographic Recording

A Black Mass. Jihad Productions, n.d.

Interviews

Ossman, David. "LeRoi Jones." In *The Sullen Art: Interviews with Modern American Poets*, pp. 77–81. New York: Corinth Books, 1963.
"Black Revolution and White Backlash." *National Guardian* 4 (July 1964): 5–9.
"The Roots of Violence: Harlem Reconsidered." *Negro Digest* 13 (August 1964): 16–26.
Gottlieb, Saul. "They Think You're an Airplane and You're Really a Bird! An Interview with LeRoi Jones." *Evergreen Review* 12 (December 1967): 51–53, 96–97.
Coleman, Michael. "What Is Black Theatre? Michael Coleman Questions Imamu Amiri Baraka." *Black World* 20 (April 1971): 32–36.
"Waitin' for the 70's." *Black Theatre*, no. 5 (1971).
"Interview: Imamu Amiri Baraka." *Black Collegian* 3 (March-April 1973): 30–33.
Benston, Kimberly W. "Amiri Baraka: An Interview." *Boundary* 26 (Winter 1978): 303–16.

Critical Essays

"The Myth of a Negro Literature." *Saturday Review* 44 (20 April 1963): 19–21, 40.
"In the Ring." *Nation* (29 June 1964): 661–62.
"The Revolutionary Theatre." *Liberator* 5 (July 1965): 4.
"In Search of the Revolutionary Theatre." *Negro Digest* 16 (April 1966): 20–24.
"Communication Project." *Drama Review* 12 (Summer 1968): 53–57.
"The Black Aesthetic." *Negro Digest* 18 (November 1969): 5–6.
"Black Power Chant." *Black Theatre* 5 (April 1970): 35.
"For Maulano and Pharaoh Saunders." *Black Theatre* 5 (April 1970): 4.
"Negro Theatre Pimps Get Off Nationalism." In *J-E-L-L-O*, pp. 5–8. See "Plays."
"A Symposium on 'We Righteous Bombers.' " *Black Theatre* 5 (April 1970): 15–25.
"Black (Art) Drama Is the Same as Black Life." *Ebony* 26 (February 1971): 74–76.
Spirit Reach. Newark, N.J.: Jihad, 1972.
"Black Revolutionary Poets Should Also Be Playwrights." *Black World* 21 (April 1972): 4–7.
"Comments on a Recent Killing." *New York Times* (13 March 1973): 30.
"Afro-American Literature and the Class Struggle." *Black American Literature Forum* 14 (1980): 5–14.
"The Descent of Charlie Fuller into Pulitzerland and the Need for Afro-American Institutions." *Black American Literature Forum* 17 (1983): 73–78.
Daggers and Javelins: Essays. New York: Morrow, 1984.

Introductions

Moderns: An Anthology of New Writing in America. Edited by LeRoi Jones. New York: Corinth Books, 1963.

Black Fire: An Anthology of Afro-American Writing. Edited by LeRoi Jones and
    Larry Neal. New York: Morrow, 1968.
Neal, Larry. *Black Boogaloo (Notes on Black Liberation).* San Francisco: Journal of
    Black Poetry Press, 1969.

Autobiography

The Autobiography of LeRoi Jones/Amiri Baraka. New York: Freundlich Books, 1984.

PRODUCTION HISTORY

Baraka's plays have been produced largely off-Broadway and off-off-
Broadway in New York and in Newark, New Jersey, with one production
premiering in Washington, D.C. The most intense period of production
coincides with the height of the civil rights movement and the flashing
emergence of the black power movement from 1964 to 1975.

A Good Girl Is Hard to Find opened at Sterington House in Montclair,
New Jersey, in August 1958 to little response. In October 1961 *Dante*
was produced at the Off-Bowery Theatre in New York City; it was
revived as *The Eighth Ditch* at the New Bowery in March 1964. Tallmer
acknowledged the play's rhythm and force.

After a January 1964 run at Village South Theatre in New York City,
Dutchman reopened at the Cherry Lane Theatre, New York City, in
March. This play caught the attention of the critics. Gruen expressed
overwhelming approval of this new talent as did Clurman. Even *Newsweek*
responded with laudatory hyperbole (Review of *Dutchman*). Taubman
essentially saw it as "the shock of the new." The play has received the
most positive responses of all Baraka's works.

In May 1964 *The Baptism* opened at Writers' Stage Theatre in New
York City. Tallmer in the context of an earlier performance recognized
the play's humor but failed to be impressed with its characterization. In
December *The Slave* and *The Toilet* made a twin bill at St. Mark's Playhouse
in New York City. Taubman observed that *"The Slave* is not so well
designed a play as *The Toilet"* (51), pointing out the dichotomy between
Baraka's talent and rage. Clurman showed some disappointment but
emphasized the importance of its racial subject. Most of the reviews were
negative and emotional; *Time*'s is representative (Review of *The Slave*).

In 1965 the Black Arts Repertory Theatre of New York featured
J-E-L-L-O, and in March *Experimental Death Unit #1* came to the St. Mark's
Playhouse there. The year 1966 brought *A Black Mass* to Proctor's Theatre
in Newark, New Jersey.

In a year similar to the intensity of 1964, *Slave Ship: A Historical Pageant*
was performed at Spirit House in Newark, New Jersey in March. Later
productions brought generally acceptable reviews. Riley commented that

"the design [was] a curriculum in grief" and observed that through it "we discover some portion of ourselves" (3). Barnes and Kerr indicated disappointment with its structure. Writing later, Bentley recognized the power of its protest theme and recalled it as a strong play. *Madheart* opened at San Francisco State College in May. A review by Gussow of a later production saw both *Madheart* and *A Black Mass* (Afro-American Studio Productions) as less than successful. Spirit House in Newark, New Jersey, brought out *Arm Yrself, or Harm Yourself!* (date not available). In November *Great Goodness of Life (A Coon Show)* closed the year at Spirit House. In 1969 it was revived as part of *The Black Quartet* at the Chelsea Theatre Center. Gilroy commented on its "dreamlike murkiness" (92) and questioned the premise of the plot. Kerr observed that the "stage effectively becomes a rattled state of mind" (11). Shepard saw the play as "above the average in the message category" (28). Barnes recognized *Great Goodness* as a play for blacks and a new turn in drama. And Riley noted the play's criticism of the black middle class.

In March 1968, near the time LeRoi Jones changed his name to Baraka, Spirit House in Newark, New Jersey, presented *Home on the Range*. Sullivan in a mixed review commented on Baraka's power to use "words as weapons" and observed that the repetition of words in the play is boring. The frequently leveled charge of "propagandist" surfaced again here. Limited attention accompanied productions through 1969. *Resurrection in Life* was on the stage in Harlem during August. *Junkies Are full of S-H-H-H* and *Bloodrites* were at New York's New Federal Theatre earlier in January. Howard University's Spirit House Movers presented *Columbia the Gem of the Ocean* in Washington, D.C., four years later.

A Recent Killing, written nearly a decade before its production, was Baraka's first play of conventional length, the others being quite brief. It opened at Spirit House in Newark, New Jersey, on January 26, 1973, but it did not represent the aggressive and militant plays Baraka was writing and producing then. Gussow recognized its power of language and dramatic effect, but he criticized it for its length and loose structure. Novick similarly had difficulties with its plot, but he also saw it as different from Baraka's current work. L. Dace's discussion of reviews in *Black American Writers* should be consulted (149–50).

Baraka's plays continued to reach the stage, but the responses from critics waned. In February 1974, *The New Ark's a Moverin* was staged at Spirit House in Newark, New Jersey. *Sidnee Poet Heroical or If in Danger of Sun, the Kid Poet Heroical* opened in New York at the New Federal Theatre in May 1975. Afro-American Studios produced *S-1* in New York in July 1976. *The Motion of History* was performed by the New York City Theatre Ensemble in May 1977. The decade ended with *What Was the Relationship of the Lone Ranger to the Means of Production?* at Ladies Fort in New York City during May 1979.

The 1980s began with Columbia University's production *At the Dim' Crackr Party Convention* in July 1980. *Boy & Tarzan Appear in a Clearing* was staged during October 1981 in New York at the New Federal Theatre. In January 1982 La Mama Experimental Theatre in New York produced *Money*. Baraka's *Primitive World* played in New York during 1984.

SURVEY OF SECONDARY SOURCES

Bibliographies

The basic, although now outmoded, accounting of works by and about Baraka is Dace's *LeRoi Jones* (1971), which is especially strong on first printings of primary sources. Her evaluative essay in *Black American Writers* (1978), required reading for any student of Baraka, covers bibliography, editions, manuscripts, biography, letters, plays, criticism, nonfiction, fiction, and poetry. Arata and Rotoli provide a list of published plays, commentary by Baraka, and criticism through the early 1970s. The listing of reviews, though understandably incomplete, is helpful. *The Glenn Carrington Collection* lists a major repository of works by and about Baraka. Hatch provides locations of published plays. Carpenter offers a nearly up-to-date listing of secondary sources, especially foreign publications. The bibliography in Hudson's *From LeRoi Jones to Amiri Baraka* is still useful, as is the one in Sollors's study. Peavy has a bibliography of primary and secondary sources with annotations in *Afro-American Literature and Culture*. Gaffney's 1985 list of primary and selected secondary sources in *Afro-American Writers After 1955* is indicative of the growing quality of this type of information in general and specific reference works.

Biography

There is no biographical study. One of the most coherent and precise accounts of Baraka's life and works is Gaffney's essay in *Afro-American Writers after 1955*, which supersedes and complements Hurst's essay (1981). *Contemporary Authors* (1977) has a stronger and more accurate image of Baraka than the 1969 edition; in the newer volume, Irving Howe is quoted describing Baraka as "a pop-art guerilla warrior" (459). Hudson's *From LeRoi Jones*, while not primarily a biographical study, shows a real and coherent grasp of the dramatist's life. T. Dace's 1979 essay calls attention to the revolutionary and contradictory elements from his life and work. Hill emphasizes the "fierceness" (66) that exerts itself through his work.

Dace's bibliographical essay gives close attention to the myriad of newspaper and periodical articles describing Baraka and incidents in which he was involved. She discusses his new black consciousness, his arrests, his trials, his political shifts, and his personal life. Also important is her analysis of incidental sources, like Birenbaum's *Something for Everybody Is Not Enough*, in which there is a story of Baraka's being hired at the New School for Social Research.

Most book-length studies of Baraka's works include varying amounts of biography. Brown's 1980 study is a useful example, especially with its chronology. Despite problems with specificity and accuracy, Baraka's autobiography (1984) provides some necessary connections and introductions to incidents and people. Ossman's interview in 1960 of Baraka as Jones before his much vaunted changes reveals reservations about "Negro literature" and sources of influence.

Influences

The book-length studies of Baraka (Benston, Brown, Hudson, Lacey, and Sollors) discuss a range of influences affecting Baraka's writing and responses to the political climate. Nelson, addressing *Dutchman*, links Baraka to the Wagnerian tradition and the modern theatre of Strindberg. Peavy delineates the psychosocial influences on *Dutchman, The Slave, Home on the Range*, and *Police*. Adams in " 'My Christ' " comments on Christian and biblical influences in *Dutchman*. Fabre shows the presence of Marxist politics on Baraka's artistry, as does Andrews in his examination of *The Motion of History* and *S-1*. The effect of cultural nationalism is central to Ricard's study. In *Great Writers* Dace relates Antonin Artaud's ideas on nonverbal communication with Baraka's works. In her bibliographic essay, she points to the artists and art in several fields touching Baraka, especially the Black Mountain group. Writing in *Obsidian*, Brown connects Baraka's fiction, notably *The System of Dante's Hell*, to the image of Ulysses in works by Homer, Dante, Tennyson, and Joyce.

As an influence himself, Baraka has marked an entire generation of playwrights, especially black ones, including Ed Bullins, Charles H. Fuller, Jr., N. R. Davidson, Jr., Ben Caldwell, Salimu, Sonia Sanchez, Herbert Stokes, Martin X Loyalty, and Kingsley B. Bass, Jr. In this context, Jeffers connects Baraka with Bullins and Elder as a "new black humanity" (32); Canaday forges another link to Bullins. Kaufman discusses the revolutionary nature of Jimmie Farrett's *And We Own the Night* and *The Slave*. Both Williams and Sanders place Baraka at the center of the new movement in black theatre and aesthetics. Hill (Fourth edition) offers a concise and incisive summary of Baraka's achievements and declares his role to be one of "summoning black playwrights to a new and urgent mission" (34).

General Studies

Sollor's *Amiri Baraka* provides the most reliable, clear, and comprehensive study, charting the playwright's changes through the years with particular attention to the texts. In *Baraka, the Renegade*, Benston devotes the second part of his sound study to drama and traces Baraka's movement from concern for the individual to the community. Hudson's pioneering study not only treats the texts carefully but also focuses on Baraka's changes by skillful use of biographical material gleaned from interviews with the writer. In *To Raise* Lacey focuses on the 1960s as the decade crucial to Baraka and the black revolution with reliable and clear discussions. Brown's 1980 Twayne study devotes one chapter to drama; in a cautious assessment, he introduces the plays and places them in a coherent pattern. Ricard's *Théâtre et nationalism*, focusing on the pre-1969 plays, gives perceptive attention to ritual. Benston's collection of essays has a solid selection on drama covering *Dutchman, The Slave, The Toilet, Great Goodness of Life, Madheart*, and *Slave Ship*.

Among the shorter studies, Fischer is typical in giving a controlled overview without breaking new ground as he follows Baraka's pattern of change. In *Native Sons*, Margolies shows concern that Baraka's rage overwhelms his artistic control. Costello also addresses the problem of art and propaganda. Despite these concerns, Lahr cites Baraka as critical to performance theatre and theatre imagination. In *Black Drama* (1967), Mitchell offers an early view of the plays as a drama of change. A careful survey of the plays can be found in Ferruggia's essay.

Baraka's role in the black theatre movement has several perspectives. Reed sees his position in starting the movement as the basis of his reputation in the years to come. Dodson cites Baraka in the context of black and white playwrights addressing the black experience. The need for whites and the incompleteness of black self-determination in his plays is the subject of Freydberg's essay. Johnson and Neal comment on Baraka's leadership in the growth of plays by blacks for blacks. Jeyifous writes of Baraka's role in the rejection of commercial theatre as part of the movement. Redding observes the limitations affecting black writers, including Baraka, but Pearson places Baraka outside Western formalism and in the context of the black movement. Similarly Turner in the *Iowa Review* argues that he should be approached outside the formalistic but within the questions he raises on human nature.

Several other approaches raise important questions. Cohen examines the efficacy of the violent language; Richards addresses the negative images of women; and Turner in the volatile year of 1968 comments on Baraka's being one of the few playwrights to explore black life in northern cities.

T. Dace's bibliographic essay in the section on general discussions

(150–56) offers a chronological survey through 1976. The section on general criticism (173–78) is also helpful in building a complete image of Baraka's work. Burford traces his development and calls him the most important black dramatist on the American scene.

Analyses of Plays

Most attention has gone to *Dutchman* and *The Slave*, with little and sometimes no attention to others. Lattin observes that the early plays—*The Toilet, Dutchman,* and *The Slave*—point up the emptiness of people's lives regardless of race and the empty rituals they follow. Rice offers one of the best examinations of *Dutchman*'s text and language, focusing on the play's mythic, social, and folkloric elements. Political and social expression in the play define Riach's perspective, and the play as social alarm (to the establishment) is the subject of Adams's essay on the black militant drama. The element of race relations persists over the years in considering the play, as Ralph's note attests. Bermel discusses black identity and its use in characterization, especially Lula's. Hagopian also centers on her possibilities of interpretation. Martin focuses on the one and the many using the subway as a melting pot. Werner centers on Clay's change in his study of dramatic rhetoric in *Dutchman* and *Slave Ship*. Lula's questions addressed to Clay contribute to Ceynowa's study of dramatic structure. Levesque uses metaphoric foreshadowing and implied action in his approach to myth and allegory in *Dutchman*.

Brady claims that *The Slave* is a revolutionary response to Clay *(Dutchman)*. While he continues to see *Dutchman* as Baraka's major contribution, Lindberg cites *The Slave* as the critical moment when revolution begins to take priority over art in Baraka's work. He also links the plays through the themes of search and sanity. In discussing contemporary black playwrights, Turpin comments on the play's role in creating a new dignity for black characters. Taylor, as several other writers have, uses *The Slave* as evidence that among the new writers, black blood is a positive element rather than the conventional negative one. Emphasizing violence as the key to the play's effectiveness, Lederer points to language and characterization as contributing factors. The tendency toward seeing a new theatre continues as Kgositsile in *Black Expression* suggests that its inspiration comes from the myth and ritual of *A Black Mass;* limited attention to that play can be found in contextual articles by Neal, Miller, and Burford.

Mootry notes the direction toward violence and racial self-esteem in *The Baptism* and *The Toilet*. Brady in an essay in *Educational Theatre Journal* extends this idea in the latter play as he points up problems of duality and identity of the black individual in a white society. Witherington sees the violence in *The Toilet* as symbol and ritual of change, an aspect in the process of group maturation, the subject of a study by Tener.

About *Home on the Range*, Velde voices concern that the art be appreciated no matter how intense the propaganda. In an essay on *Slave Ship*, Brecht cuts through to the theme of black survivability through intense opposition to whites. Despite his sympathy with the play's idea, he criticizes the use of spectacle as a means of its expression. He also notes the play's being aimed at a solely black audience. Elam in a "Theatre of Color" issue of *Theatre Journal* offers an insight in ritual and politics through a comparative study.

In an essay on contemporary black drama, Peavy comments on *Police, Home on the Range*, and *Madheart* as satire directed against whites and less militant blacks. In a separate article on *Madheart*, he writes one of the two best analyses of a Baraka play as he studies the protagonist's growth to manhood through mythic and psychological processes.

Marxist and political themes are the interest in the later plays. Andrews observes that Marxist theory is not very effective in *The Motion of History* and *S-1*. In a brief commentary, San Juan pursues the characters in the context of political themes in *What Was the Relationship of the Lone Ranger to the Means of Production*. Dace's bibliographic essay (138–50) includes a section on individual plays generally in the order of production; it is most helpful.

FUTURE RESEARCH OPPORTUNITIES

Work on Baraka is still in its infancy; the need for more disinterested and pluralistic approaches is evident. A comprehensive bibliography is needed; the last one appeared in 1971. Specific bibliographic studies are needed in the areas of little magazines, small presses, and community organization publications. A biography focused on Baraka's life through 1970 would clarify many of the discrepancies that Dace notes in her evaluative essay. The field for influence studies is wide open; the list in the section "Influences" would be a good start. Revised editions of the earlier general studies would be helpful, and there is a need for a new one whose author is quite apart from the political and racial turmoil of the 1960s. No play has been explicated definitively, although Peavy's and Rice's efforts on *Madheart* and *Dutchman*, respectively, offer excellent models. Essays on technique should be especially welcome. As there is a growing list of foreign-authored studies, an examination of Baraka's influence abroad should open up some new approaches.

SECONDARY SOURCES

Adams, George R. "Black Militant Drama." *American Imago* 28 (Summer 1971): 107–28.

————." ' My Christ' in *Dutchman*." *College Language Association Journal* 15 (September 1971): 54–58.

Andrews, W. D. E. "The Marxist Theatre of Amiri Baraka." *Comparative Drama* 18 (1984): 137–61.

Arata, Esther Spring, and Nicholas John Rotoli. *Black American Playwrights 1800 to the Present: A Bibliography*. Metuchen, N.J.: Scarecrow Press, 1976.

Barnes, Clive. Review of *Great Goodness of Life*. *New York Times* (22 September 1969): 36.

————. Review of *Slave Ship*. *New York Times* (13 September 1970): 11, 1.

Benston, Kimberly W. *Baraka, the Renegade and the Mask*. New Haven: Yale University Press, 1976.

————, ed. *Imamu Baraka: A Collection of Critical Essays*. Englewood Cliffs, N.J.: Prentice-Hall, 1978.

Bentley, Eric. Review of *Slave Ship*. *New York Times* (23 January 1972): 2, 1.

Bermel, Albert. "Dutchman or the Black Stranger in America." *Arts in Society* 9 (1972): 423–34.

Birenbaum, William. *Something for Everybody Is Not Enough*. New York: Random House, 1972.

Brady, Owen E. "Cultural Conflict and Cult Ritual in LeRoi Jones's *The Toilet*." *Educational Theatre Journal* 28 (1976): 69–77.

————."LeRoi Jones's The Slave: A Ritual of Purgation." *Obsidian* 4 (1978): 5–18.

Brecht, Stefan. "LeRoi Jones' *Slave Ship*." *Drama Review* 14 (1970): 212–19.

Brown, Lloyd W. *Amiri Baraka*. Boston: Twayne, 1980.

————. "Jones (Baraka) and His Literary Heritage in *The System of Dante's Hell*." *Obsidian* 1, no. 1 (Spring 1975): 5–17.

Burford, Walter W. "LeRoi Jones: From Existentialism to Apostle of Black Nationalism." *Players* 47, no. 2 (1971): 60–64.

Canaday, Nicholas. "Ellison, Baraka, and Bullins: A Setting and Two Characters." *Contemporary Literature* 15, no. 2 (May 1985): 2.

Carpenter, Charles A. *Modern Drama Scholarship and Criticism, 1966–1980*. Toronto: University of Toronto Press, 1986.

Ceynowa, Andrej. "The Dramatic Structure of *Dutchman*." *Black American Literature Forum* 17 (1983): 15–18.

Clurman, Harold. Review of *Dutchman*. *Nation* 198 (1964): 383–84.

————. Review of *The Slave*. *Nation* (4 January 1965): 16–17.

Cohen, Ruby. *Dialogue in American Drama*. Bloomington: Indiana University Press, 1971.

Contemporary Authors, 21–24R. Edited by Christine Nasso. Detroit, Michigan: Gale, 1977.

Costello, Donald P. "LeRoi Jones Black Man as Victim." *Commonweal* 88 (1968): 4436–40.

Dace, Letitia. "Amiri Baraka (LeRoi Jones)." In *Black American Writers*, 2:121–78. Edited by M. Thomas Inge, Maurice Duke, and Jackson R. Bryer. New York: St. Martin's, 1978.

————. *LeRoi Jones (Imamu Amiri Baraka): A Checklist of Works by and about Him*. London: Nether Press, 1971.

————. "LeRoi Jones: Black Revolutionary Playwright." In Letitia Dace and

Wallace Dace. *The Theatre Student: Modern Theatre and Drama.* New York: Richard Rosens Press, 1973.

Dace, Tish. "LeRoi Jones." In *Great Writers of the English Language: Dramatists.* New York: St. Martin's, 1979.

Dodson, Owen. "Who Has Seen the Wind? Playwrights and Black Experience." *Black American Literature Forum* 11 (1977): 108–16.

Elam, Harry J. "Ritual Theory and Political Theatre: *Quinta Temporada* and *Slave Ship.*" *Theatre Journal* 38 (December 1986): 463–72.

Fabre, Michel. "Les Avatars d'Amiri Baraka, Citoyen—dramaturge: un montage documentaire." *Revue français d'études américaines* 5 (1980): 285–301.

Ferruggia, Gabriella. "Il Teatro di LeRoi Jones." *Studi Americani* 19–20 (1976): 339–60.

Fischer, William C. "Amiri Baraka." In *American Writers: A Collection of Literary Biographies*, suppl. 2, pt. 1: 29–63. New York: Scribners, 1981.

Freydberg, Elizabeth Hadley. "The Concealed Dependence upon White Culture in Baraka's 1969 Aesthetic." *Black American Literature Forum* 17 (1983): 27–29.

Gaffney, Floyd. "Amiri Baraka." In *Dictionary of Literary Biography.* Vol. 38: *Afro-American Writers after 1955: Dramatists and Prose Writers*, pp. 22–42. Edited by Thadious Davis and Trudier Harris. Detroit: Bruccoli Clark, 1985.

Gilroy, Harry. Review of *Great Goodness of Life.* *New York Times* (27 April 1969): 92.

The Glenn Carrington Collection: A Guide to the Books, Manuscripts, Music, and Recordings. Washington, D.C.: Moreland-Springarn Research Center, Howard University, 1977.

Gruen, John. Review of *Dutchman.* *New York Herald Tribune* (25 March 1964): n.a.

Gussow, Mel. Review of *Madheart* and *A Black Mass.* *New York Times* (20 September 1972): 18.

———. Review of *A Recent Killing.* *New York Times* (30 January 1973): 25.

Hagopian, John V. "Another Ride on Jones's Subway." *College Language Association Journal* 20 (1977): 269–74.

Hatch, James V. *Black Image on the American Stage: A Bibliography of Plays and Musicals, 1770–1970.* New York: Drama Book Specialists, 1970.

Hill, Errol. "Baraka, Amiri." In *Contemporary Dramatists.* Fourth Edition, pp. 33–36. Edited by D. L. Kirkpatrick. Chicago and London: St. James Press, 1988.

———. "Baraka, Amiri." In *Contemporary Dramatists.* Third Edition, pp. 60–66. Edited by James Vinson. New York: St. Martin's, 1982.

Hudson, Theodore. *From LeRoi Jones to Amiri Baraka: The Literary Works.* Durham, N.C.: Duke University Press, 1973.

Hurst, Catherine Daniels. "Amiri Baraka (LeRoi Jones)." In *Dictionary of Literary Biography Vol. 7: Twentieth Century American Dramatists*, pp. 49–66. Edited by John MacNicholas. Detroit: Bruccoli Clark, 1981.

Jeffers, Lance. "Bullins, Baraka, and Elder: The Dawn of Grandeur in Black Drama." *College Language Association Journal* 16 (1972): 32–48.

Jeyifous, Abiodun. "Black Critics on Black Theatre in America." *Drama Review* 18 (1974): 34–45.

Johnson, Helen Armstead. "Playwrights, Audiences, and Critics." *Negro Digest* 19 (April 1970): 17–24.

Kaufman, Michael W. "The Delicate World of Reprobation: A Note on the Black Revolutionary Theatre." *Educational Theatre Journal* 23 (December 1971): 446–51.

Kerr, Walter. Review of *Great Goodness of Life*. *New York Times* (4 May 1969): 11,1.

———. Review of *Slave Ship*. *New York Times* (22 November 1969): 46.

Kgositsile, K. William. "Towards Our Theater: A Definitive Act." In *Black Expression*, pp. 146–48. Edited by Addison Gayle, Jr. New York: Weybright and Talley, 1969.

Lacey, Henry C. *To Raise, Destroy, and Create: The Poetry, Drama, and Fiction of Amamu Amiri Baraka*. Troy, N.Y.: Whitston, 1981.

Lahr, John. "America: The Collapsing Underground." *Gambit* 17 (1971): 64–69.

Lattin, Linda G. "Paying His Dues: Ritual in LeRoi Jones' Early Dramas." *Obsidian* 2, no. 1 (1976): 21–31.

Lederer, Richard. "The Language of LeRoi Jones' *The Slave*." *Studies in Black Literature* 4 (Spring 1973): 14–16.

Levesque, George A. "LeRoi Jones' *Dutchman*: Myth and Allegory." *Obsidian* 5, no. 3 (1979): 33–40.

Lindberg, John. " 'Dutchman' and 'the Slave': Companions in Revolution." *Black Academy Review* 2, nos. 1–2 (1971): 101–7.

Margolies, Edward. *Native Sons: A Critical Study of Twentieth Century Negro American Authors*. Philadelphia: Lippincott, 1968.

Martin, Thaddeus. "*Dutchman* Reconsidered." *Black American Literature Forum* 11 (1977): 62.

Miller, Jean-Marie A. "The Plays of LeRoi Jones." *College Language Association Journal* 14 (March 1971): 331–39.

Mitchell, Loften. *Black Drama*. New York: Hawthorn Books, 1967.

Mootry, Maria K. "Themes and Symbols in Two Plays by LeRoi Jones." *Negro Digest* 18 (April 1969): 42–47.

Neal, Larry. "The Black Arts Movement." *Drama Review* 12 (Summer 1968): 31–37.

Nelson, Hugh. "LeRoi Jones' *Dutchman*: A Brief Ride on a Doomed Ship." *Educational Theatre Journal* 20 (1968): 53–59.

Novick, Julius. Review of *A Recent Killing*. *New York Times* (4 February 1973): 3.

Ossman, David. "LeRoi Jones: An Interview on Yugen." *TriQuarterly* 43 (1978): 317–23.

Pearson, Lou Anne. "LeRoi Jones and a Black Aesthetic." *Paunch* 35 (1972): 33–66.

Peavy, Charles D. "Myth, Magic, and Manhood in LeRoi Jones' *Madheart*." *Studies in Black Literature* 1 (1970): 12–20.

———. *Afro-American Literature and Culture Since World War II*. Detroit: Gale, 1979.

———. "The Revolutionary Theater and the Black Power Movement." In *Some Reflections Upon Modern America*. College Station: Texas A&M, 1969.

————. "Satire and Contemporary Black Drama." *Satire Newsletter* 7 (Fall 1969): 40–49.

Ralph, George. "Jones's *Dutchman.*" *Explicator* 43, no. 2 (1985): 58–59.

Redding, Saunders. "The Problems of the Negro Writer." *Massachusetts Review* 6 (1964): 57–70.

Reed, Daphne S. "LeRoi Jones: High Priest of the Black Arts Movement." *Educational Theatre Journal* 22 (1970): 53–59.

Review of *Dutchman.* *Newsweek* (13 April 1964): 60.

Review of *The Slave.* *Time* (25 December 1964): 62–63.

Riach, W. A. D. "Telling It Like It Is: An Experiment of Black Theatre as Rhetoric." *Quarterly Journal of Speech* 56 (1970): 179–86.

Ricard, Alain. *Théâtre et nationalism: Wole Soyinka et LeRoi Jones.* Paris: Présence africaine, 1972.

Rice, Julian. "LeRoi Jones' *Dutchman:* A Reading." *Contemporary Literature* 12 (Winter 1971): 42–59.

Richards, Sandra. "Negative Forces and Positive Non-Entities: Images of Women in the Dramas of Amiri Baraka." *Theatre Journal* 34 (1982): 233–40.

Riley, Clayton. Review of *Great Goodness of Life.* *New York Times* (3 August 1969): 11, 1.

————. Review of *Slave Ship.* *New York Times* (23 November 1969): 11, 3.

Sanders, Leslie Catherine. *The Development of Black Theater in America: From Shadows to Selves.* Baton Rouge: Louisiana State University Press, 1988.

San Juan, E., Jr. "Amiri Baraka, Revolutionary Playwright." *Stepping Stones* (1985): 151–56.

Shepard, Richard. Review of *Great Goodness of Life.* *New York Times* (31 July 1969): 28.

Sollors, Werner. *Amiri Baraka/LeRoi Jones: The Quest for a "Populist Modernism."* New York: Columbia University Press, 1978.

Sullivan, Dan. Review of *Home on the Range.* *New York Times* (21 May 1968): 42.

Tallmer, Jerry. Review of *The Baptism.* *New York Post* (24 March 1964): 20.

————. Review of *The Eighth Ditch.* *New York Post* (16 March 1964): 16.

Taubman, Howard. Review of *Dutchman.* *New York Times* (25 March 1964): 46.

————. Review of *The Slave* and *The Toilet.* *New York Times* (17 December 1964): 51.

Taylor, Willene P. "The Reversal of the Tainted Blood Theme in the Works of Writers of the Black Revolutionary Theater." *Negro American Literature Forum* 10 (1976): 88–91.

Tener, Robert L. "The Corrupted Warrior Heroes: Baraka's *The Toilet.*" *Modern Drama* 17 (1974): 207–15.

Turner, Darwin. "Negro Playwrights and the Urban Negro." *College Language Association Journal* 12 (1968): 19–25.

————. "Visions of Love and Manliness in a Blackening World: Dramas of Black Life from 1953–1970." *Iowa Review* 6 (1975): 82–99.

Turpin, Waters E. "The Contemporary American Negro Playwright." *College Language Association Journal* 9 (1965): 12–24.

Velde, Paul. "LeRoi Jones: Pursued by the Furies." *Commonweal* 88 (1968): 440–41.

Werner, Craig. "Brer Rabbit Meets the Underground Man: Simplification of

Consciousness in Baraka's *Dutchman* and *Slave Ship.*" *Obsidian* 5, nos. 1–2 (1979): 35–40.

Williams, Mance. *Black Theatre in the 1960s and 1970s: A Historical-Critical Analysis of the Movement.* Westport, Connecticut: Greenwood, 1985.

Witherington, Paul. "Exorcism and Baptism in LeRoi Jones' *The Toilet.*" *Modern Drama* 15 (1972): 159–63.

Ed Bullins

(2 JULY 1935–)

LESLIE SANDERS

ASSESSMENT OF BULLINS'S REPUTATION

Two playwrights presided over the black theatre in the 1960s: Amiri Baraka (LeRoi Jones) and Ed Bullins. Baraka was crucial to that theater's flowering, but Bullins provided the more enduring and substantial model for what it was to become. No matter how critics quarreled with particular plays or productions, they all acknowledged Bullins, in the words of Gussow, as "one of the most interesting of American playwrights, and [perhaps] one of the most significant" (27 January 1971, 28), a playwright with "his hand on the jugular vein of the people" (Barnes, 10 March 1972, 46).

Building on the artistic freedom that Baraka's forthright and controversial attacks on white America had declared for black writers, Bullins established a range of possibilities for the theatrical depiction of black experience. In his most notable plays—*Goin'a Buffalo, Clara's Ole Man, In the Wine Time, In New England Winter* and *The Duplex*—plays he described as theater of black experience, Bullins depicts the lives of ghetto residents and, through their sense of life, articulates not only an implicit social critique but also the contours of human dreams and desires. *The Fabulous Miss Marie*, which received an Obie in 1971, depicts the black middle class with equal eloquence; *The Taking of Miss Janie*, which won the New York Drama Critics Award for 1975, dissects American race relations. *In New England Winter* was awarded a Black Arts Alliance Award (1971). Institutional support has been forthcoming as well: American Place Theatre (1967), two Guggenheim fellowships (1971, 1976), three Rockefeller grants (1968, 1970, 1972), a Creative Artists' Public Service Program Award (1973), and an honorary doctorate from Columbia College in Chicago (1976). Moreover, as editor, in particular of two highly influential anthologies—*Drama Review*, Black Theatre Issue, (1968) and *New Plays from The Black Theatre* (1969)—Bullins helped to dictate the terms and define the shape of black theatre of the period.

PRIMARY BIBLIOGRAPHY OF BULLINS'S WORKS

Plays

How Do You Do? (first produced San Francisco, 1965). Mill Valley, Cal.: Illuminations Press, 1967.

Dialect Determinism (or The Rally) (first produced San Francisco, 1965). Included in *The Theme is Blackness*, 1973.

Clara's Ole Man (first produced San Francisco, 1965). Included in *Five Plays*, 1969.

It Has No Choice and *A Minor Scene* (first produced San Francisco, 1966). Included in *The Theme is Blackness*, 1973.

The Game of Adam and Eve, by Bullins and Shirley Tarbell (first produced Los Angeles, 1966).

The Theme Is Blackness (first produced San Francisco, 1966). Included in *The Theme is Blackness*, 1973.

The Electronic Nigger and Others (including *Clara's Ole Man* and *A Son, Come Home*, first produced New York, 1968). Included in *Five Plays*, 1969.

Goin'a Buffalo (first produced New York, 1968). Included in *Five Plays*, 1969.

In the Wine Time (first produced New York, 1968). Included in *Five Plays*, 1969.

The Corner (first produced Boston, 1968). Included in *The Theme is Blackness*, 1973.

We Righteous Bombers, as Kingsley B. Bass, Jr. (attributed to Bullins), adapted from Albert Camus's *The Just Assassins*, (first produced New York, 1969). Included in *New Plays from the Black Theatre*, 1969.

The Gentleman Caller (first produced New York, 1969). Included in *A Black Quartet: Four New Black Plays*, (with Ben Caldwell's *Prayer Meeting*, Amiri Baraka's *Great Goodness of Life*, Ron Milner's *The Warning—A Theme for Linda*) introduction by Clayton Riley (New York: New American Library, 1970).

A Ritual to Raise the Dead and Foretell the Future (first produced New York, 1970). New York: New Lafayette Publications, 1971.

The Pig Pen (first produced New York, 1970). Included in *Four Dynamite Plays*, 1971.

The Duplex: A Black Love Fable in Four Movements (first produced New York, 1970). New York: Morrow, 1971.

The Helper (first produced New York, 1970). Included in *The Theme is Blackness*, 1973.

The Man Who Dug Fish (first produced Boston, 1970). Included in *The Theme is Blackness*, 1973.

It Bees Dat Way (first produced London, 1970). Included in *Four Dynamite Plays*, 1971.

Death List (first produced New York, 1970). Included in *Four Dynamite Plays*, 1971.

Street Sounds (first produced New York, 1970). Included in *The Theme is Blackness*, 1973.

The Devil Catchers (first produced New York, 1970).

In New England Winter (first produced New York, 1971). Included in *New Plays from the Black Theatre*, 1969.

The Fabulous Miss Marie (first produced New York, 1971). In *The New Lafayette Theatre Presents*, 1974.

Next Time (first produced New York, 1972). In *City Stops*.

You Gonna Let Me Take You Out Tonight, Baby? (first produced New York, 1972). In *Black Arts*. Edited by Ahmad Alhamisi and Harun Wangala. Detroit: Black Arts Publishing, 1969.

The Psychic Pretenders (A Black Magic Show) (first produced New York, 1972).

House Party, a Soul Happening (music by Pat Patrick, lyrics by Ed Bullins; first produced New York, 1973).

The Taking of Miss Janie (first produced New York, 1975). In *Famous American Plays of the 1970s*. Edited by Ted Hoffman. New York: Dell, 1981.

The Mystery of Phyllis Wheatley (first produced New York, 1976).

Home Boy, music by Aaron Bel, lyrics by Bullins (first produced New York, 1976).

Jo Anne! (first produced New York, 1976).

Storyville (book by Bullins, music and lyrics by Mildred Kayden; first produced La Jolla, 1977).

DADDY! (first produced New York, 1977).

Sepia Star (book by Bullins, music and lyrics by Mildred Kayden; first produced New York, 1977).

Michael (first produced New York, 1978).

C'mon Back to Heavenly House (first produced Amherst, Massachusetts, 1978).

Leavings (first produced New York, 1980).

Steve and Velma (first produced Boston, 1980).

Collections

Five Plays: Goin'a Buffalo. In the Wine Time. The Electronic Nigger. A Son, Come Home. Clara's Ole Man. Indianapolis: Bobbs-Merrill, 1969: revised as *The Electronic Nigger and Other Plays.* London: Faber & Faber, 1970.

Four Dynamite Plays: It Bees Dat Way. Death List. The Pig Pen. Night of the Beast. New York: Morrow, 1972.

The Theme Is Blackness: The Corner and Other Plays: Dialect Determinism, or The Rally. It Has No Choice. The Helper. A Minor Scene. The Theme Is Blackness. The Man Who Dug Fish. Street Sounds. Black Commercial No. 2. The American Flag Ritual. State Office Bldg. Curse. One-Minute Commercial. A Street Play. A Short Play for a Small Theatre. The Play of the Play. New York: Morrow, 1973.

Other

"Malcolm: '71, or Publishing Blackness," *Black Scholar* 6 (June 1975): 84–86.

Fiction

The Hungered One: Early Writings. New York: Morrow, 1971.
The Reluctant Rapist. New York: Harper & Row, 1973.

Anthologies

Drama Review. Black Theatre Issue. Edited by Ed Bullins. 12 (Summer 1968).
Black Theatre. Edited by Bullins. (6 issues, 1969–1972).
New Plays from The Black Theatre. Edited with contributions by Ed Bullins. New
    York: Bantam, 1969.
*The New Lafayette Theatre Presents the Complete Plays and Aesthetic Comments by Six
    Black Playwrights*. Edited by Ed Bullins. Garden City, N.Y.: Doubleday,
    1974.

Nonfiction

"The Polished Protest: Aesthetics and the Black Writer." *Contact* 4 (July 1963):
    67–68.
"Ed Bullins." In "The Task of the Negro Writer as Artist: A Symposium," *Negro
    Digest* 14 (April 1965): 54–83.
"Theatre of Reality." *Negro Digest* 15 (April 1966): 60–66.
"The So-Called Western Avant-Garde Drama." *Liberator* 7 (December 1967): 16–
    17.
"Black Theatre Groups: A Directory." *Drama Review* 12 (Summer 1968): 172–
    75.
"Black Theatre Notes." *Black Theatre*, no. 1 (1968): 4–7.
"Short Statements on Street Theatre." *Drama Review* 12 (Summer 1968): 93.
"What Lies Ahead for Black Americans." *Negro Digest* 19 (November 1968): 8.
"Next Time." *The Magazine of Black Culture* 1 (Spring 1975).

Interviews

Marvin X. "Interview with Ed Bullins." In *New Plays from the Black Theatre*, pp. vi-
    xv. Edited by Ed Bullins. New York: Bantam Books, 1969.
Ed Bullins. "Talking of Black Art, Theatre, Revolution and Nationhood." *Black
    Theatre* 5 (1971): 23–24.
Riley, Clayton. "Bullins: 'It's Not the Play I Wrote.' " *New York Times* (19 March
    1972): D1,D7.
Erika Munk. "Up From Politics—An Interview with Ed Bullins." *Performance* 2
    (July/August 1972): 52–60.
Jervis Anderson. "Profiles—Dramatist." *New Yorker* 49 (16 June 1973): 40–59.
O'Brien, John. "Interview with Ed Bullins." *Negro American Literature Forum* 7
    (Fall 1973): 108–12.
Wesley, Richard. "An Interview with Playwright Ed Bullins." *Black Creation* 4
    (Winter 1973): 8–10.

PRODUCTION HISTORY

Between 1968 and 1973, the period of his greatest influence, Bullins was frequently produced at an array of off and off-off-Broadway theatres. The most important of those many productions were those done at or by Harlem's New Lafayette Theater and directed by Robert Macbeth: in 1968, at the American Place Theatre because the New Lafayette had burned down, *Three Plays by Ed Bullins (Clara's Ole Man, A Son, Come Home,* and *The Electronic Nigger),* which earned Bullins the Vernon Rice Drama Desk Award for 1968; and in their newly renovated theater in Harlem, *In the Wine Time, The Duplex* (1970), and *The Fabulous Miss Marie* (1971). The New Lafayette also performed *The Devil Catchers* (1970), a satiric political piece, and his rituals, *A Ritual to Raise the Dead and Foretell the Future* (1970) and *The Psychic Pretenders (A Black Magic Show)* (1972), according to Larry Neal and Tom Dent with less success.

The New Lafayette productions are significant because the theatre's aims, ambience, artistic intention, and typical audience formed and were informed by Bullins's plays of this period. Particularly the often-noted quality of intimacy in his plays of the black experience demands an audience sympathetic to the people depicted, an audience capable of judging them on their own terms rather than moralizing about the lives they lead. The New Lafayette provided the context Bullins sought for his plays and modes of direction that honored the quality of intimacy that marks his best work. The fact that so many of Bullins's plays found their way to various New York theatres is also important because prior to 1968, the New York theatre saw relatively few plays by black writers.

On the whole, New York theatre critics served Bullins well, from the start providing sensitive readings of his plays. Black critics Riley and Patterson immediately identified the veracity of his ear and eye; white critics Gussow, Barnes, Oliver, and Clurman were especially enthusiastic; only Kerr remained stridently unappreciative, although he too acknowledged Bullins's talent. Some white critics condemned what they did not understand, but others, in particular Oliver, noted when black audiences responded to aspects of the plays that left them baffled. Reviewers consistently praised Bullins's characters and his language, his ability to turn street argot to poetry; most also valued the illusion in his plays of life overheard, particularly when apparently insignificant snippets of conversation shed light on an era. Others censured this quality as the cause of his tendency to write plays that these critics regarded as formless and lacking in point of view.

Reviewers found more troubling Bullins's plays that deal explicitly with black revolution. For example, *The Gentleman Caller,* presented with three other plays (by Ron Milner, Ben Caldwell, and Amiri Baraka) as a *Black Quartet*, elicited wildly diverse responses. Bullins supporters Barnes (1969), Riley, and Clurman (1969) found it weak, but Kerr (1969) and Shepard were quite enthusiastic. The more discerning critics, an anonymous reviewer of *Death List* and Barnes, in a review of *How Do You Do? A Minor Scene, Dialect Determinism* and *It Has No Choice*, understood Bullins's satire, as well as his serious meaning and purpose ("Short Bullins," 59).

It is through his plays of the black experience that Bullins acquired his stature. His New York debut, the evening of three plays originally entitled *The Electronic Nigger and Others*, met with immediate critical success. "[Bullins] is promising because he performs. The mark of his promise is the diversity of his attack, subject matter and style," wrote Clurman (420). Oliver, who was to become Bullins's most consistently enthusiastic and perceptive reviewer, called *A Son, Come Home*, "sad and haunting" ("Three Cheers," 133). Barnes saluted the "authentic presence of a dramatist" ("American Place Stages," 23).

In the same year, the New Lafayette offered Bullins's first full-length play and the first in his projected twenty-play cycle, *In the Wine Time*. Patterson found it "deeply moving," full of revelation, rare in its truthful presentation of ghetto dwellers, and occasionally hilarious, although melodramatic in its ending, and, in his view, not entirely well served by Macbeth's production (2:7). Not much noted at its first production, *In the Wine Time* is now regarded as one of Bullins's most important plays. Macbeth revived it eight years later to acclaim.

Kerr's judgment of *The Pig Pen*, Bullins's next major New York production, as "causal, rambling, silent as to its intentions, unwritten, arrogant," was shared by no one else (2:1). Oliver noted that upon reflection, the play's apparently random events assumed a tighter and tighter underlying design (72). Barnes admired it as a "strangely authentic tape recording of history," observing that Bullins maintains "a real feeling for time and place," although the play's formlessness troubled him ("Night of Malcolm X," 47). Clurman found it disturbing and gratifying, heartening in its "candor and intensity" (1 June 1970, 668). These reviews established how critics would measure Bullins's work from then on. Later the same year, when Gussow described *Street Sounds* approvingly as "black and very Bullins," he was also proclaiming that Bullins had made his mark on American theatre ("Street Sounds," 32).

Kerr remained the dissenting voice. He charged *In New England Winter*, the second play in the cycle, with being formless, difficult to follow, and bound together by theatrical tricks ("Good Black Plays," II:3). Conversely Gussow, representing the majority, speculated, on the basis of the same play, that Bullins would become one of America's most significant playwrights ("Bullins Drama Opens," 28).

The New Lafayette Theatre production of *The Fabulous Miss Marie* occasioned acknowledgment of the special relation between the playwright and his preferred audience for his plays of the black experience. "[The New Lafayette] is home ground for Mr. Bullins and it feels right for this play," Gussow observed. He found it more shaped than its predecessors and delightfully allusive to other plays in the cycle ("The Fabulous Miss Marie" 28). In her admiring review, Oliver also remarked on the extraordinary rapport that the actors established with their audience ("An Evening," 94).

Regarding *Goin'a Buffalo*, Gussow noted the playwright's customary "power and . . . insight into human behavior" (" WPA Stages," 28). Oliver particularly praised his ability to turn the "obscene and profane argot his characters talk into a kind of poetry that is all its own" (*"Goin'a Buffalo,"* 83). In the same vein, concerning the Public Theatre's revival of *The Corner*, she observed, "The rough argot of the streets [is] transformed into a special kind of beauty" (*"The Corner,"* 53).

When the Forum Theatre of the Lincoln Center Theatre mounted *The Duplex*, a play earlier done at the New Lafayette Theatre, Bullins disowned the production, accusing Lincoln Center director Jules Irving of turning it into a "minstrel show" and thus turning it into the most notorious, if not the most noteworthy, production of a Bullins play. Kerr ("Mr. Bullins," 1) and Anderson ("Profiles," 41) suggested that Bullins sought to "cause a play in the real world"; Sanders ("Ed Bullins," 49) proposed that Bullins's reaction may have been honest, if not legitimate. Critical response to the production was almost univocally enthusiastic. "[A] playwright with his hand on the jugular vein of people, [he] writes with conviction and sensitivity," Barnes began his review of the production (*"The Duplex,"* 46).

This production of *The Duplex* brought into focus the debate about Bullins's form. Most critics commented on the play's lack of conventional form; Barnes (*"The Duplex,"* 46), Hughes (*"The Duplex,"* 50–51), and Oliver (*"The Duplex,"* 85) defended its apparent shapelessness, while Simon and Kerr ("Mr. Bullins," 1) were sharply critical, each raising an issue that academic critics also took up. Kerr accused Bullins of including anything he observes and overhears without providing his material with a meaningful structure. Simon argued that Bullins failed to "take [his black audience] beyond mere self-recognition" (*"The Duplex,"* 85). Bullins's next production, *House Party*, essentially a series of dramatic monologues, exacerbated the disagreement. Oliver delighted in its free form, saying, "Mr. Bullins's writing has never been stronger; his irony, his understanding, his ability to catch a whole life in a sing speech or song lyric, and his mocking, parodic humor have never been more apparent" ("Marvellous Party," 91). Kerr acknowledged Bullins's range and the occasionally brilliant line but termed the play "cavalier collage" ("We've Heard," 7).

The same debate, with more participants, occurred over Bullins's best-known work, *The Taking of Miss Janie.* "Mr. Bullins has rarely been wittier or, for that matter, more understanding and vigorous," wrote Oliver ("Fugue," 62). "Approaching allegory, Mr. Bullins is trading in stereotypes but he never loses sight of the truth that informs the cliché," said Gussow of the New Federal Theatre production (*"The Taking of Miss Janie,"* 29). Barnes similarly admired the play's "intellectual and emotional density." He faulted the playwright with the play's slight lack of focus but added that Bullins "writes like an angel" ("Bullins Race," 40). By and large, other critics concurred, finding the play "dramatically compelling" (Gottfried, "A Radical Idea," 244). They particularly admired the play's ring of truth told with energy and wit. But some dissented. Kerr ("A Blurred Picture," 5), Kauffmann, and Simon (*"The Taking of Miss Janie,"* 36) found the play formless and slight. Mackay, particularly disturbed by the play's use of rape, judged it politically retrograde.

After *The Taking of Miss Janie*, Bullins produced three new major works: *Home Boy, Jo Anne!* and *DADDY! Home Boy*, a return to his twentieth-century cycle, was, according to Gussow, "a fragmented play with music," its episodic structure its main weakness ("Fifth Work," 42). In contrast, *Jo Anne!* directed by Carl Weber, a veteran of the Berliner Ensemble, was, according to Gussow ("Jo Anne!" 53) and Oliver ("Jo Anne!" 62) a strong and remarkable examination of the Joan Little case, the story of a black woman who killed the prison guard who raped her. Most reviewers found *DADDY!* disappointing. While acknowledging the pungency of Bullins's language, Lask saw the playwright as torn between "making a play and making a point" ("DADDY," C12). *Michael,* a one-act version of *"DADDY!"* appeared in 1978. An evening of short plays— *You Gonna Let Me Take You Out Tonight, Baby?, How Do You Do?* and *Clara's Ole Man* at La Mama and directed by Robert Macbeth in 1980— was warmly welcomed by Gussow, who hoped for revivals of Bullins's longer works ("Three One-Act Plays," C9). His hope has not to date been fulfilled.

SURVEY OF SECONDARY SOURCES

Bibliographies

The only extensive scholarly bibliography on Bullins, in King's *Ten Modern American Playwrights: An Annotated Bibliography*, is quite thorough. Hatch and Abdullah's compendium, aimed at theatre groups rather than scholars, lists all Bullins's known plays, cast requirements, and sources for scripts and permissions.

Biographies

Biographical information is available in *Contemporary Authors*, and there are two interpretive essays in the *Dictionary of Literary Biography*. Scharine sees Bullins's plays of the black experience as formally reliant on black rituals and forms and as concerned thematically with exorcising whiteness in their main characters. Sanders concentrates in more detail on Bullins's dramatic methods and on his concern with how people refuse the responsibility of choosing their own freedom.

Influences

Bullins acknowledges having learned from the work of Edward Albee, Samuel Beckett, Jean Genet, and Arthur Miller and mentions many other writers, black and white, as influencing his thought (Bullins, *Negro Digest* 1966; Anderson, 73). Of LeRoi Jones, he insists, he "created me" (Marvin X, xv). Canaday, Williams, and Sanders (*Black Theater*) address the relation between Bullins and Baraka. No one has analyzed the other influences Bullins mentioned or speculated on others.

General Studies

Three chapter-length discussions of Bullins's plays occur in studies of Afro-American theatre, one in a study of trends in contemporary American drama, and one in a study of five major contemporary American dramatists. In all, the fact of Bullins's inclusion is in itself a measure of his importance, although each critic values him for somewhat different reasons. Fabre claims that "no playwright better demonstrates how drama can alternate between political commitment and ethnic expression free from the constraints of ideology," the two poles that constitute the foci of her excellent study (168). Williams argues that "Bullins more than Baraka clarified techniques of Black dramaturgy"; thus Bullins is central to his discussion of the history of the black theatre movement (21). Sanders devotes an entire chapter to Bullins, focusing on his *Five Plays* as evidence of the new black theatre's artistic freedom and assurance. Bernstein cites Bullins's use of realistic and absurdist forms in *The Taking of Miss Janie* as an example of a more general trend in American theatre. And Herman's chapter on Bullins praises him as "the great black dramatist of sexual relations," the great artist of "the dreams and drives of the black culture" (169).

Several briefer but still sustained discussions in books and articles provide useful assessments of his work. Bigsby in *The Second Black Renaissance* describes Bullins's technique in *Street Sounds* as "literary pointillism gradually building up a picture of the black community," a comment one might usefully extend to all his plays of the black experience (247). He sees Bullins as having "declared a hegemony over black experience and a commitment to the real world of private passions locked within a public world characterized by economic and social constrictions" (247) and as absurdist and romantic, as well as naturalist, in both form and thought (*A Critical Introduction to Twentieth Century American Drama*).

Also in the context of a discussion of black theatre, Cohn judges that "Bullins has produced no single play as powerful as Baraka's *Dutchman*, but he is a more consistent dramatic craftsman" (107). She praises his command of black colloquial speech and his memorable portraits of "Black vigour and courage, against overwhelming odds," but she is disturbed by what she sees as uncertain politics and lamentable portraits of women (107).

Early general essays on Bullins by Evans, Smitherman, and Hay still are useful. Evans and Smitherman in particular seek to explain how Bullins captures his ghetto characters with power and accuracy. Evans attributes his effect largely to the "unerring honesty of his realistic style" (16). Smitherman attributes the power of his plays to their blues roots and to their melding of the oral and literary traditions. Hay argues, in what essentially was a response to Kerr's attack on the play, that the appropriate analogue for the structure of Bullins's *The Duplex* is that attributed to Chekhov's major work, an argument True extends convincingly. Tener provides an early overview of Bullins's fictive universe, finding it "filled with the hunger and absurdity trapped in the Black life style" (533). Andrews defines Bullins's mode as blues, basing his judgments on protracted and rich readings of *Clara's Ole Man* and *In New England Winter*. More recently, Sanders attended to Bullins's black revolutionary plays, analyzing how they test and criticize the rhetoric of the black power movement while still affirming the movement's political thrust and aims ("Rhetoric"). Canaday finds some of Bullins's early work derivative of Baraka and gleans from the alienation of the characters in early plays a similar alienation in the playwright. Scharine attempts to read a Bullins biography in the various fictional and dramatic manifestations of Bullins's character Steve Benson, a claim the playwright refutes in a reply published along with the article (Scharine, "Who Is He Now"; Bullins, "Replies"). Bruck interprets Bullins as trying to create a populist, utopian theatre in the Baraka tradition and failing because he lacks "ethnic" vision in his work. Moore makes a convincing case for the originality in Bullins's rewrite of Camus's *Les Justes*.

Several essays in the two-volume Hill anthology of essays on black theatre, most of which have been published elsewhere, touch on Bullins's work. Notably, Hatch suggests the "African continuum" as a formal principle that accounts for the frequent "meandering" plot structure in Afro-American plays. He cites approvingly the frequent attribution of a "jazz structure" to Bullins plays but points out that it has never been demonstrated (Hatch, et al, 28). Steele discusses ritual and expressionist elements in the work of Bullins and others. Cook concludes regarding *In the Wine Time* that "given the destruction that waits outside the door, [and] Cliff's ineffectiveness, Ray is lost to the world beyond Derby Street" (179). Thus he confirms, at least in tone, the conclusions reached by Turner, who described Bullins's vision of black life as the "absence of vision" (93), a conclusion with which more recent work takes issue. Reilly succinctly surveys Bullins's major plays, identifying Bullins as "the most prolific" figure in "black American theater" (72).

FUTURE RESEARCH OPPORTUNITIES

Work on Bullins has barely begun. His various dramatic forms, particularly his characteristic blend of naturalistic and expressionist presentation, and his preference for the episodic, need examination. The matter of his influences is complex. How traditional Afro-American and African forms influence his work presents one area for study; another is whether and how American and European writers have influenced him. Reviewers and critics mention other writers as touchstones, for example, Anton Chekhov, Eugene O'Neill, Edward Albee, Tennessee Williams, and Amiri Baraka, but few have studied either the influences on Bullins or his on other playwrights. Finally, while critics and scholars alike univocally praise his language, none has yet provided an analysis of its veracity or its lyricism.

SECONDARY SOURCES

Anderson, Jervis. "Profiles—Dramatist." *New Yorker* (16 June 1973): 40–79.

Andrews, W. D. E. "Theatre of Black Reality: The Blues Drama of Ed Bullins." *Southwest Review* 65 (Spring 1980): 178–90.

Barnes, Clive. "American Place Stages 'Electronic Nigger.' " *New York Times* (9 March 1968): 23.

———. Review of *The Gentleman Caller. New York Times* (22 September 1969): 36.

———. "Night of Malcolm X's Death Is Examined." *New York Times* (21 May 1970): 47.

———. Review of "Short Bullins." *New York Times* (5 March 1972): 59.

———. Review of *The Duplex. New York Times* (10 March 1972): 46.

———. "Bullins Race Play Is at Mitzi Newhouse." *New York Times* (5 May 1975): 40.

Bernstein, Samuel J. *The Strands Entwined: A New Direction in American Drama.* Boston: Northeastern University Press, 1980.

Bigsby, C. W. E. *A Critical Introduction to Twentieth-Century American Drama.* Vol. 3. Cambridge: Cambridge University Press, 1985.

———. *The Second Black Renaissance: Essays in Black Literature.* Westport, Conn.: Greenwood Press, 1980.

Bruck, Peter. "Ed Bullins: The Quest and Failure of an Ethnic Community Theatre." *Essays on Contemporary Drama*, pp. 123–40. Hedwig Bock and Albert Wertheim, eds. Munich: Hueber, 1981.

Canaday, Nicholas. "Toward Creation of a Collective Form." *Studies in American Drama, 1945–Present* 1 (1986): 33–47.

Clurman, Harold. Review of *The Electronic Nigger and Others*. *Nation* (25 March 1968): 420–21.

———. Review of *The Gentleman Caller*. *Nation* (12 May 1969): 612.

———. Review of *The Pig Pen*. *Nation* (1 June 1970): 668.

Cohn, Ruby. *New American Dramatists: 1960–1980*. London: Macmillan, 1982.

Cook, William. "Mom, Dad and God: Values in Black Theater." In *The Theater of Black Americans*. Vol. 1: *A Collection of Critical Essays*, pp. 168–84. Edited by Errol Hill. Englewood Cliffs, N.J.: Prentice-Hall, 1980.

Death List. Review. *Show Business* (17 October 1970). Reprinted in *Contemporary Literary Criticism*, 1:47. Carolyn Riley, ed. Detroit: Gale Research Company, 1973.

Dent, Tom. "Black Theater in the South: Report and Reflections." In *The Theater of Black Americans*. Vol. 2. *A Collection of Critical Essays*, pp. 63–71. Edited by Errol Hill. Englewood Cliffs, N.J.: Prentice-Hall, 1980.

Evans, Don. "The Theatre of Confrontation: Ed Bullins, Up against the Wall." *Black World* 23 (April 1974): 20–29.

Fabre, Genevieve. *Drumbeats, Masks and Metaphor: Contemporary Afro-American Theatre*. Translated by Melvin Dixon. Cambridge and London: Harvard University Press, 1983.

Gottfried, Martin. "A Radical Idea." *New York Post* (5 May 1975). Reprinted in *New York Theatre Critics' Reviews* (1975): 244–45.

Gussow, Mel. Review of *Street Sounds*. *New York Times* (23 October 1970): 32.

———. "Bullins Drama Opens on Henry Street." *New York Times* (27 January 1971): 28.

———. Review of *The Fabulous Miss Marie*. *New York Times* (12 March 1971): 28.

———. "W. P. A. Stages Bullins Play on Young Adults." *New York Times* (16 February 1972): 28.

———. Review of *The Taking of Miss Janie*. *New York Times* (18 March 1975): 29.

———. "Fifth Work in Bullins Cycle Focuses on Country Life." *New York Times* (27 September 1976): 42.

———. Review of *"Jo Anne!" New York Times* (19 October 1976): 53.

———. Review of Three One-Act Plays by Ed Bullins. *New York Times* (31 December 1980): C9.

Hatch, James V. "Some African Influences on the Afro-American Theatre." In *The Theater of Black Americans*. Vol. 1: *A Collection of Critical Essays*, pp. 13–29. Edited by Errol Hill. Englewood Cliffs, N.J.: Prentice-Hall, 1980.

Hatch, James V. and OMANii Abdullah, eds. *Black Playwrights, 1823–1977: An Annotated Bibliography of Plays*. New York: Bowker, 1977.

Hay, Samuel A. "Structural Elements in Ed Bullins' Plays." In *The Theater of Black Americans*. Vol. 1: *A Collection of Critical Essays*, pp. 185–91. Edited by Errol Hill. Englewood Cliffs, N.J.: Prentice-Hall, 1980.

Herman, William. " 'The People in This Play Are Black': Ed Bullins." In his *Understanding Contemporary American Drama*. Columbia, S.C.: University of South Carolina Press, 1987.

Hill, Errol, ed. *The Theater of Black Americans*. 2 vols. Englewood Cliffs, NJ: Prentice-Hall, 1980.

Hughes, Catharine. Review of *The Duplex*. *Plays and Players* 19 (May 1972): 50–51.

Kauffmann, Stanley. *"The Taking of Miss Janie." New Republic* (June 1975). Reprinted in *Contemporary Literary Criticism*, 7:36. Phyllis Carmel Mendelson and Dedria Bryfonski, eds. Detroit: Gale Research Company, 1977.

Kerr, Walter. Review of *The Gentleman Caller*. *New York Times* (4 May 1969): 2: 1,5.

————. Review of *The Pig Pen*. *New York Times* (31 May 1970): II:1:6.

————. "Good Black Plays—But Those Strobe Lights." *New York Times* (7 February 1971): II:3:1.

————. "Mr. Bullins Is Himself at Fault." *New York Times* (19 March 1972): II 1:1.

————. "We've Heard It All Before." *New York Times* (4 November 1973): II:7:1.

————. "A Blurred Picture of a Decade." *New York Times* (11 May 1975): II:5:1.

King, Kimball. *Ten Modern American Playwrights: An Annotated Bibliography*. New York: Garland, 1982.

Lask, Thomas. Review of "DADDY!" *New York Times* (17 June 1977): C12.

Mackay, Barbara. "Studies in Black and White." *Saturday Review* (12 July 1975): 52.

Marvin X. "Interview with Ed Bullins." In *New Plays from the Black Theatre*, pp. vi–xv. Edited by Ed Bullins. New York: Bantam Books, 1969.

Moore, Jack B. "The (In)humanity of Assassination: Plays by Albert Camus and Kingsley B. Bass, Jr." *MELUS* 8 (Fall 1981): 45–56.

Neal, Larry. "Into Nationalism, Out of Parochialism." In *The Theater of Black Americans*. Vol. 2: *A Collection of Critical Essays*, pp. 95–102. Edited by Errol Hill. Englewood Cliffs, N.J.: Prentice-Hall, 1980.

Oliver, Edith. "Three Cheers." *New Yorker* (9 March 1968): 133–34.

————. Review of *The Pig Pen*. *New Yorker* (30 May 1970): 72–73.

————. "An Evening with Bullins & Co." *New Yorker* (20 March 1971): 94–95.

————. Review of *Goin' a Buffalo*. *New Yorker* (4 March 1972): 83.

————. Review of *The Duplex*. *New Yorker* (18 March 1972): 85.

————. Review of *The Corner*. *New Yorker* (1 July 1972): 53.

————. "A Marvellous Party." *New Yorker* (5 November 1973): 89–91.

————. "Fugue for Three Roommates." *New Yorker* (24 March 1975): 61–63.

————. Review of *"Jo Anne!" New Yorker* (25 October 1976): 62.

Patterson, Lindsay. "Theater in Harlem." *New York Times* (22 December 1968): 2:7.

Reilly, John M. "Ed Bullins." In *Contemporary Dramatists*. Fourth Edition. pp. 72–74. Edited by D. L. Kirkpatrick. Chicago: St. James Press, 1988.

Riley, Clayton. Review of *The Gentlemen Caller*. *New York Times* (3 August 1969): 2:1.

Sanders, Leslie. "Ed Bullins." In *Dictionary of Literary Biography*, Vol. 38. Detroit: Gale Research Company, 1985.

————. " 'Dialect Determinism': Ed Bullins' Critique of a Rhetoric of the Black Power Movement." In *Studies in Black American Literature*. Vol. 2: *Belief vs. Theory in Black American Literary Criticism*, pp. 161–76. Edited by Joe Weixlmann and Chester J. Fontenot. Greenwood, Fla.: Penkevill Publishing Company, 1986.

————. *The Development of the Black Theater in America*. Baton Rouge: Louisiana State University Press, 1988.

Scharine, Richard G. "Ed Bullins." In *Dictionary of Literary Biography*, Vol. 7. Detroit: Gale Research Company, 1985.

————. "Ed Bullins Was Steve Benson But Who Is He Now?" *Black American Literature Forum* 13 (Fall 1979): 103–9.

Shepard, Richard. "One-Act Plays Arrive at Gate Theater." *New York Times* (31 July 1969): 2:3.

Simon, John. Review of *The Duplex*. Reprinted in *Contemporary Literary Criticism*, 5:85. Carolyn Riley and Phyllis Carmel Mendelson, eds. Detroit: Gale Research Company, 1976.

————. Review of *The Taking of Miss Janie*. *New York Magazine* (19 May 1975). Reprinted in *Contemporary Literary Criticism*, 7:36. Phyllis Carmel Mendelson and Dedria Bryfonski, eds. Detroit: Gale Research Company, 1977.

Smitherman, Geneva. "Ed Bullins/Stage One: Everybody Wants to Know Why I Sing the Blues." *Black World* 23 (April 1974): 4–13.

Steele, Shelby. "Notes on Ritual in the New Black Theater." In *The Theater of Black Americans*. Vol. 1: *A Collection of Critical Essays*, pp. 30–44. Edited by Errol Hill. Englewood Cliffs, N.J.: Prentice-Hall, 1980.

Tener, Robert L. "Pandora's Box—A Study of Ed Bullins's Dramas." *College Language Association Journal* 19 (June 1976): 533–44.

True, Warren Roberts. "Bullins, Chekhov, and the Drama of Mood," *CLA Journal* 20 (June 1987): 531–32.

Turner, Darwin. "Visions of Love and Manliness in a Blackening World: Dramas of Black Life from 1953–1970." *Iowa Review* 6 (Spring 1975): 82–99.

Williams, Mance. *Black Theatre in the 1960s and 1970s: A Historical-Critical Analysis of the Movement*. Westport, Conn.: Greenwood Press, 1985.

Woll, Allen. *Dictionary of the Black Theatre: Broadway, Off-Broadway, and Selected Harlem Theatre*. Westport, Conn.: Greenwood Press, 1983.

Paddy Chayefsky

(29 JANUARY 1923–1 AUGUST 1981)

DAVID H. GOFF

ASSESSMENT OF CHAYEFSKY'S REPUTATION

Paddy (Sidney) Chayefsky is important for his critical and commercial successes in three dramatic formats: live television, motion pictures, and theatre. His earlier works offer vivid characterizations of ordinary people and settings, revealing, in Shub's opinion, "alert topicality, keen humor, and a rare ear for the common speech" (523). As Chayefsky's biographer, Clum notes that Chayefsky's "favorite topic" is "man's sense of meaninglessness in a senseless world" (131), describing his "primary theme" as "the depersonalization of modern American society" (127). According to Clum, Chayefsky's style evolves from " 'slice-of-life' Realism" to a "more eclectic mixture of dramatic techniques" (131), from "sentimental, Realistic comedy to satire" (134). His most famous work, *Marty*, moved audiences with its story of love found by two ordinary people. The single most celebrated program of the Golden Age of Television, *Marty* was named the best television drama of 1953–1954 and received the Donaldson and Sylvania Television awards (Brown, 113). The 1955 film version received the Best Picture and Best Screenplay Academy Awards. Chayefsky also earned Oscars for his screenplays *The Hospital* (1971) and *Network* (1976). *The Goddess*, (1958) won the Critic's Prize at the Brussels Film Festival (Brown, 116).

PRIMARY BIBLIOGRAPHY OF CHAYEFSKY'S WORKS

Plays

Middle of the Night. New York: Random, 1957.
The Tenth Man. New York: Random, 1960.
Gideon. New York: Random, 1962.

The Passion of Josef D. New York: Random, 1964.
The Latent Heterosexual. New York: Random, 1967.

Motion Picture Screenplays

The Bachelor Party. New York: NAL, 1957.
The Goddess. New York: Simon, 1958.

Books

Television Plays. New York: Simon, 1955. This collection includes the television plays *Holiday Song, Marty, Printer's Measure, The Big Deal, The Bachelor Party,* and *The Mother.*
Altered States. London: Hutchinson, 1978; New York: Harper, 1978.

Chapters in Books

"Good Theatre in Television." In *How to Write for Television*, pp. 44–48. Edited by William I. Kaufman. New York: Hastings, 1955.

Interviews

"An Interview with Paddy Chayefsky." With Nora Sayre and Robert B. Silvers. *Horizon* (3 September 1960): 50–56.
"We Were Writing for Criers, Not for Laughers." With John Brady. *American Film* (December 1981): 60–63.

Articles

"Not So Little." *New York Times* (15 July 1956): 2:1.
"Art Films—Dedicated Insanity." *Saturday Review* (21 December 1957): 16–17.
"The Giant Fan." *Harper's Bazaar* (February 1959): 122–23, 182–85.
"Has Broadway Had It?" *New York Times* (23 November 1969): 2:7.
"An Ad Lib for Four Playwrights." By Chayefsky, Israel Horowitz, Arthur Laurents, and Leonard Melfi, *Dramatists Guild Quarterly* 5 (Winter 1969): 4–19.

Unpublished Works

Plays

No T.O. for Love. 1945.

Motion Picture Screenplays

True Glory. With Garson Kanin. 1945.
Marty. 1955.
Middle of the Night. 1959.

The Americanization of Emily. 1964.
Paint Your Wagon. 1969.
The Hospital. 1971.
Network. 1976.
Altered States. 1980.

   Television Screenplays

The Reluctant Citizen. 1952.
The Sixth Year. 1953.
Catch My Boy on Sunday. 1953.
Middle of the Night. 1953.
The Catered Affair. 1955.
The Great American Hoax. 1957.

PRODUCTION HISTORY

Chayefsky's television plays were tremendously important for his future as a writer and for the young medium of television. Written about lower-middle-class people and settings familiar to the Bronx-raised Chayefsky, *Printer's Measure*, for example, is considered semiautobiographical. Frank describes his characters as "mundane people whose problems were universal and who, therefore, touched a deep nerve with the viewing public" (84). According to Brown, Chayefsky's "universal themes" were "independence, uncertainty, and loneliness," which "underscore Chayefsky's ability to focus on the commonplace" (112). The first of Chayefsky's six 1953 television plays, *Marty* (24 March 1953) became the symbol of the Golden Age of Television and his most famous work. *Marty* is the story of a lonely, unattractive butcher who against his mother's wishes falls in love with an unattractive woman. The two share what Brown calls "their need for a sense of worth in a world where looks are too highly rated" (112). Ironically Chayefsky, who thought *Marty* was a satire of lower-middle-class social values, was startled to learn that viewers had cried at the end of the show. "And then I realized that in television we were writing for criers, not for laughers" (quoted in Brady, 62).

   Chayefsky's first Broadway play, *Middle of the Night*, opened 8 February 1956 at the ANTA Theatre. A commercial success, the play was noted almost as much for bringing Edward G. Robinson back to the stage as for Chayefsky's writing. Robinson starred as a lonely fifty-three-year-old widower who falls in love with a younger married woman. Atkinson (9 February 1959) noted that "Chayefsky has written it in a minor key, deliberately holding down the emotion and laying emphasis on the homeliness of the material" (39). Critics, however, were quick to compare the work with television plays. Atkinson commented that "everyone is . . . average" and the "dialogue is composed of average talk," adding that "this technique was successful in *Marty*," but is "less successful in the theatre where size is important" (39). Hayes (663) described *Middle of the Night* as "a play of harsh and angular surfaces, all of which are stained with the synthetic dyes of television," contrasting it with the "urban lyricism" of *Marty*. Bentley accused Chayefsky of writing "with his audience, not his characters in mind," condemning such writing as "all calculation and contrivance" (21). This particular criticism would dog Chayefsky throughout his theatre experience.

Middle of the Night enjoyed a brief revival by the Equity Library Theater in New York City in 1971. Expressing wonder at the revival, Thompson commented that it "is much better than many of us, perhaps, remember it" (22).

Chayefsky's first original stage play, *The Tenth Man*, opened at the Booth Theatre on 5 November 1959 and proved to be his most successful play commercially (623 performances) and critically. Atkinson ("Decanting a Dybbuk") hailed it as the "first new play of the season that brings both distinction and enjoyment to the theatre" (2, 1). Critics praised the play's setting and its "comic juxtaposition of Old World simplicity and New World complexity" (Brustein, 94). Atkinson ("Story of Exorcism") called Tyrone Guthrie's direction "inspired" (24). Questioning the depiction of Jews in the play, Tynan complained of Chayefsky's use of stereotypes, calling its image of Jews "as limited in its way as the image of Uncle Tom" (326). Hewes ("Inside Job") also voiced dissatisfaction because *Tenth Man* lacked "that degree of emotional revelation that would make us more interested in the people and less in the events" (31) and that it "settles for less than its full potential" (34). Even more stridently, Brustein observed that while this was Chayefsky's "most entertaining dramatic work, it openly betrays that omnipresent molasses which seeps under the flinty exterior of all his writings." Sounding a critique he would repeat, Brustein feared that Chayefsky "melts down all doctrines into the gluey ooze of Love" (97).

When *The Tenth Man* was produced in London in April 1961, reviews were mixed, with the *Daily Telegraph* and *Times* critics praising the play but the mass circulation papers panning it ("London Critics," 23). Craig asserted that the work was "cheapened by its patter of Jewish jokes" (639). The play was also produced as an American contribution to Berlin's Twelfth Annual Cultural Festival in 1962, taking on added overtones due to its Jewish characters and story (" 'The Tenth Man' Opens").

Gideon, also directed by Guthrie, opened at the Plymouth Theatre in New York City on 9 November 1961, and ran for 236 performances. Gassner (March 1962) described it as the "most ambitious American play of the season" but noted that Chayefsky's "widening talent and intentions came up against the difficulty of his subject" (70). Taubman ("Chayefsky's 'Gideon' ") and McCarten praised the dialogue between Gideon and the Angel, but Lewis labeled the script "a television writer's approach to God" (126).

Brustein again criticized Chayefsky for writing for the audience. "If Paddy Chayefsky had never existed, Broadway would surely have invented him" (122). "Chayefsky knows exactly who is in the theatre party out front, and writes for them as if he were privy to their inmost desires" (123). In Brustein's view, Chayefsky "squeezes" a work "dry of all significance, power, and depth, and adapts it to the more conventional expectations of his audience" committing again the sin of "dropping the whole mess into the yawning cavern of Love" (123).

The Passion of Josef D., which Chayefsky also directed, was, in the words of Gilman, "a dreadful play" (178). The play about Stalin and other figures of the Russian Revolution opened at the Ethel Barrymore Theater in New York City on 11 February 1964, and closed after only fifteen performances. Chayefsky depicted Stalin as "a deflected religious fanatic whose unrequited passion for the Lord came to settle upon Lenin" (Gilman, 177). Taubman found Stalin's character and Peter Falk's portrayal "entirely credible" but called the treatment of Lenin "as the voice of anti-Communism" "another and graver failure" ("Passion"). And he accused Chayefsky of having an "intoxication with the thunder of the English language," calling the play "vastly oversimplified" ("Author Directs," 29). Lewis used *Passion* to illustrate his criticism of "the television writer now dedicated to the theatre" (181). For him, the play's most successful scenes were "those played in the manner of a nightclub review," which "attempted a political burlesque" in the style of Brecht (181). Lewis felt that in this play, unlike in *Marty*, "The language has no unity of style" (183).

Chayefsky's final play, *The Latent Heterosexual*, opened at the Kalita Humphreys Theatre in Dallas on 15 March 1968 (Brown, 116). Directed by Burgess Meredith and starring Zero Mostel, *The Latent Heterosexual* is the story of a homosexual writer's efforts to protect his income from taxation and was generously received by critics. Barnes called it "Mr. Chayefsky's most serious work," noting that "he seems at last to have lost the soft core of sentimentality" (52). Brown saw the theme as one of self-preservation "through the worship of a capitalist god" and Morley's suicide as "Chayefsky's portent not only of man's fate but also of man without identity" (116). Hewes ("Lone Starshine") found the suicide scene "less moving than it should be" because Morley has been a willing participant in his own dehumanization, but he considered this a "slight flaw" (20). *The Latent Heterosexual* was produced later the same year by London's Royal Shakespeare Company. French noted that the play represented a stylistic departure, with more in common with the film *The Americanization of Emily* than with earlier Chayefsky plays.

Screenplays

The 1955 film version of *Marty* was directed by the original television director, Delbert Mann. Ernest Borgnine was cast as Marty despite having been typically cast as a "heavy" (Einstein, 1080). Frank considered Borgnine "too gregarious" and Betsy Blair "too attractive" as Clara (86). Nonetheless, the film received eight Academy Award nominations, winning Best Screenplay and Best Picture.

Chayefsky's next two films, *The Catered Affair* (1956) and *The Bachelor Party* (1957), were also based on television plays. The screenplay for *The Catered Affair* was written by Gore Vidal. Expanding *The Bachelor Party* for the film screen allowed Chayefsky to overcome the limitations of the television anthology format. The film version was directed by Mann. Crowther ("The Bachelor Party") described it as "excellent 'slice of life' portraiture" (37). Frank, however, described the story as "tolerable to the public on television, but downright uncomfortable on screen" (87). The film was shown at the annual Cannes Film Festival.

With *The Goddess* (1958), Chayefsky departed from his television screenplays and New York settings. This original work was filmed in three acts, each depicting a phase in the unhappy life of a Hollywood sex symbol. Crowther ("*The Goddess*") noted that while the film explored Chayefsky's familiar theme of loneliness, *The Goddess* avoided the humor of *Marty* and "is scored for ironic tragedy" (24). Frank noted that "*The Goddess* was neither a critical nor popular success" (87). Crowther, however, called it a "shattering but truly potent film," praising John Cromwell's "beautiful" direction, Chayefsky's "finely written scenes and dialogue," and Kim Stanley's performance in the lead role (24).

The film version of *Middle of the Night*, the final television script adapted for film by Chayefsky, was released in 1959. This was also Mann's final collaboration with the writer. The film starred Frederic March in the role Robinson had defined on Broadway. Although March was lauded in the role, Crowther ("*Middle of the Night*") found him "a little too old and doddering" (36). *Middle of the Night* also played at the Cannes Festival (Brown, 116).

The Americanization of Emily (1964), an adaptation of a William Bradford Huie novel, began a trend toward black comedy that marked Chayefsky's later film work. Crowther ("*Americanization of Emily*") praised Chayefsky's "slashing irreverence," calling the film "a deadly satiric thrust at the whole myth of war being noble" (51). Hanson noted that the film was considered controversial in 1964 but became a "cult film enjoying wide popularity with new audiences" (67).

As a musical comedy, *Paint Your Wagon* represents an oddity in Chayefsky's career. The 1969 film was a box office failure for a number of reasons. Chayefsky's adaptation of the Lerner and Loewe play was largely rewritten (Frank, 89).

Chayefsky's next two films were critical triumphs. Like *The Americanization of Emily*, *The Hospital* and *Network* satirized American institutions. In Frank's opinion, *The Hospital* succeeded "because the public was ready for a sacred cow to be attacked" (89). *Network* makes a similar, although more vicious and possibly self-indulgent, attack on the television industry. Thompson described it as "thunderously written and as contentious as . . . *The Hospital*" (122).

Chayefsky's final screenplay was based on his only novel, *Altered States*. He saw his satire of scientific research transformed by the producer-director into "a symbol-heavy, special-effects laden film" and "withdrew his name from the credits in protest" (Frank, 90). Moss claimed that in *Altered States*, Chayefsky "has become one of his own characters. He has battled another institution—Hollywood" (25).

SURVEY OF SECONDARY SOURCES

Bibliographies

Although no comprehensive bibliography on Chayefsky exists, Salem and Eddleman list major reviews. By comparison, Adelman and Dworkin and Breed and Sniderman cover the writer's work superficially. Samples lists sources of Chayefsky's television plays, as well as plays for the theatre.

Biographies

Clum's is the only comprehensive biography. It is valuable, but it dates back to 1976, thereby missing the significant *Network*. Brown's excellent short biography covers all three areas of Chayefsky's career, with major attention to the theatre. Covering the television and film years, Frank's work is the necessary companion piece.

Influences

Many writers (especially Field and Chayefsky himself) have commented on the impact of Chayefsky's Jewish and Bronx roots on his writing. Lewis compares and contrasts *Gideon* and *J.B.* by Archibald MacLeish but reports that Chayefsky did not welcome such comparisons (128). The literary figure most often cited as a source or parallel is Clifford Odets. Shub pointed out, "Like Odets, Chayefsky writes mostly about immigrants . . . , draws upon Jewish folk humor, and is more inventive at comedy than at serious drama" (523). Shub (and Clum) also identify differences between the two.

General Studies

To date, Clum, Brown, and Frank stand as the major general studies of Chayefsky's work. Also worth notice are Lewis's two chapters concerning Chayefsky. Lewis examines Chayefsky's notions of God and religion as revealed in *The Tenth Man* and *Gideon* and critiques the writer as one of "The Refugees from Television." Field develops the thesis that in Chayefsky's television and stage works, he is foremost a Jewish playwright. EmanuEl's dissertation on *The Passion of Josef D.* also supplies a useful general study of the writer.

Analyses of Individual Works

Given Chayefsky's success, especially in film, it is ironic that the major study of an individual work is EmanuEl's examination of Chayefsky's biggest failure. Though brief, the critiques of five of Chayefsky's films in *Magill's Survey of Cinema* offer a fresh perspective (1981), discussing each film in its relationship to other work by Chayefsky.

FUTURE RESEARCH OPPORTUNITIES

Much scholarly and critical work needs to be done on Chayefsky. Most necessary is a comprehensive biography, including reviews of his plays and films done abroad. Although Clum's study is admirable in many ways, it needs to be updated to include Chayefsky's final two works. A full-length critical study on Chayefsky also has priority status. Such a study needs to explore in detail Chayefsky's major themes, techniques, and sources. Studies of his relationship to other Jewish writers—Saul Bellow, Norman Mailer, Philip Roth; his contributions to screen writing; and his contribution to the social impact of film are high on the agenda as well. Finally, I would ask for a study of the relationship between Chayefsky and David Mamet, another playwright, screenwriter, and historian of loneliness.

SECONDARY SOURCES

Adelman, Irving, and Dworkin, Rita. *Modern Drama: A Checklist of Critical Literature on 20th Century Plays*. Metuchen, N.J.: Scarecrow Press, 1967.

Atkinson, Brooks. "Decanting a Dybbuk." *New York Times* (15 November 1959): 2: 1.

———. Review of *Middle of the Night. New York Times* (9 February 1956): 39; (19 February 1956): 11:1.

———. "Story of Exorcism of Dybbuk at Booth." *New York Times* (6 November 1959): 24.

Barnes, Clive. "Zero Mostel Triumphs in Chayefsky Play." *New York Times* (22 March 1968): 52.

Bentley, Eric. "Theatre." *New Republic* (27 February 1956): 21.

Bodeen, Dewitt. Review of *The Goddess*. *Magill's Survey of Cinema*. Edited by Frank N. Magill. Vol. 2. New Jersey: Salem Press, 1981. 896–99.

Brady, John. " 'We Were Writing for Criers, Not for Laughers': An Interview With Paddy Chayefsky." *American Film* (December 1981): 60–63.

Breed, Paul F., and Sniderman, Florence M. *Dramatic Criticism Index: A Bibliography of Commentaries on Playwrights from Ibsen to the Avant-Garde*. Detroit: Gale Research, 1972.

Brown, Francie C. "Paddy Chayefsky." In *Dictionary of Literary Biography*. Vol. 7: *Twentieth-Century American Dramatists*, pp. 111–17. Edited by John MacNicholas. Detroit: Gale Research, 1981.

Brustein, Robert. *Seasons of Discontent: Dramatic Opinions 1959–1965*. New York: Simon, 1965.

Clum, John. *Paddy Chayefsky*. Boston: Twayne, 1976.

Clurman, Harold. "Theatre." *Nation* (25 November 1961): 437–38.

Craig, H. A. L. "Mad Due-West." *New Statesman* (21 April 1961): 639.

Crowther, Bosley. Review of *As Young As You Feel*. *New York Times* (3 August 1951): 10.

———. Review of *The Bachelor Party*. *New York Times* (10 April 1957): 37.

———. Review of *The Catered Affair*. *New York Times* (15 June 1956): 32.

———. Review of *The Goddess*. *New York Times* (25 June 1958): 24.

———. Review of *Marty*. *New York Times* (12 April 1955): 25.

———. Review of *Middle of the Night*. *New York Times* (18 June 1959): 36.

———. Review of *The Americanization of Emily*. *New York Times* (28 October 1964): 51.

Desmaris, James J. Review of *Network*. *Magill's Survey of Cinema*. Edited by Frank N. Magill. Vol. 3. New Jersey: Salem Press, 1981. 1190–92.

Eddleman, Floyd Eugene, ed. *American Drama Criticism: Interpretations 1890–1977*. Hamden, Conn.: Shoe String Press, 1979.

Einstein, Daniel. Review of *Marty*. *Magill's Survey of Cinema*. Edited by Frank N. Magill. Vol. 3. New Jersey: Salem Press, 1981. 1079–82.

Emanuel, Edward Frank. "A Study of the Playwright Paddy Chayefsky with a Special Emphasis on the Play, *The Passion of Josef D*." Ph.D. dissertation, University of Minnesota, 1983.

Feeney, F. X. Review of *The Hospital*. *Magill's Survey of Cinema*. Edited by Frank N. Magill. Vol. 2. New Jersey: Salem Press, 1981. 766–69.

Fidell, Estelle A., ed. *Play Index, 1961–1967*. New York: H. W. Wilson, 1968.

———. *Play Index, 1968–1972*. New York: H. W. Wilson, 1973.

Fidell, Estelle A., and Peake, Dorothy Margaret. *Play Index, 1953–1960*. New York: H. W. Wilson, 1963.

Field, Leslie. "Paddy Chayefsky's Jews and Jewish Dialogues." In *From Hester Street to Hollywood*, pp. 137–51. Edited by Sarah B. Cohen. Bloomington: Indiana University Press, 1983.

Frank, Sam. "Paddy Chayefsky." In *Dictionary of Literary Biography*. Vol. 44: *Amer-*

ican Screenwriters, 2d ed., pp. 83–91. Edited by Randall Clark. Detroit: Gale Research, 1986.

French, Philip. "Queer Pegs in Square Circles. *Latent Heterosexual.*" *New Statesman* (20 September 1968): 371.

Gassner, John. "Broadway in Review." *Educational Theatre Review* 12 (March 1960): 37–38.

———. "Broadway in Review." *Educational Theatre Review* 14 (March 1962): 69–70.

Gilman, Richard. *Common and Uncommon Masks: Writings on Theatre 1961–1970.* New York: Random, 1971.

Gunton, Sharon R., and Stine, Jean C., eds. *Contemporary Literary Criticism: Excerpts from Criticism of the Works of Today's Novelists, Poets, Playwrights, Short Story Writers, Filmmakers, Scriptwriters, and Other Creative Writers.* Detroit: Gale Research, 1983.

Hanson, Stephen L. Review of *The Americanization of Emily. Magill's Survey of Cinema.* Edited by Frank N. Magill. Vol. 2. New Jersey: Salem Press, 1981. 65–67.

Hayes, Richard. "Democratic Vistas." *Commonweal* (30 March 1956): 663.

Hewes, Henry. "An Inside Job." *Saturday Review* (21 November 1959): 31, 34.

———. "Lone Starshine." *Saturday Review* (6 April 1968): 20.

Houston, Penelope. "Marty." *Sight and Sound* 25 (Summer 1975): 31–32.

Lewis, Allan. *American Plays and Playwrights of the Contemporary Theatre.* New York: Crown, 1970.

"London Critics Split on 'The Tenth Man.'" *New York Times* (14 April 1961): 23.

Magill, Frank N., ed. *Magill's Survey of Cinema.* Englewood Cliffs, N.J.: Salem Press, 1981.

McCarten, John. "God's Sometime Chum." *New Yorker* (18 November 1961): 96.

Moss, Robert F. "The Agonies of a Screenwriter." *Saturday Review* (April 1981): 20–24.

Novick, Julius. Review of *The Latent Heterosexual. New York Times* (31 March 1968): 2: 3.

Rosenberg, Howard. "Fifties TV: Gold or Dross?" *American Film* (December 1981): 58–61, 72.

Salem, James M. *A Guide to Critical Reviews.* Part I: *American Drama, 1909–1969.* 2d ed. Metuchen, N.J: Scarecrow Press, 1973.

Samples, Gordon. *The Drama Scholars' Index to Plays and Filmscripts: A Guide to Plays and Filmscripts in Selected Anthologies, Series, and Periodicals.* Metuchen, N.J.: Shoe String Press, 1974, 1980.

Shub, Anatole. "Paddy Chayefsky's Minyan: 'The Tenth Man' on Broadway." *Commentary* (December 1959): 523–27.

"'The Tenth Man' Opens in Berlin." *New York Times* (3 October 1962): 46.

Taubman, Howard. "Author Directs Drama at the Barrymore—Stalin Is Portrayed by Peter Falk." *New York Times* (12 February 1964): 29.

———. "Chayefsky's 'Gideon' Opens at Plymouth." *New York Times* (10 November 1961): 38.

————. "Humanist Spirit." *New York Times* (19 November 1961): 2: 1.

————. " 'Middle of the Night' Gets Fine Equity Revival." *New York Times* (11 December 1971): 22.

————. "Passion of Josef D." *New York Times* (23 February 1964): 2:1.

Thompson, David. "Network." *Sight and Sound* 46 (Spring 1977): 122–23.

Tynan, Kenneth. *Curtains.* New York: Atheneum, 1961.

Christopher Durang

(2 JANUARY 1949–   )

WILLIAM W. DEMASTES

ASSESSMENT OF DURANG'S REPUTATION

Christopher Durang is part of a breed of playwrights that critics such as Gussow and Rich have called America's new angry young playwrights. Theirs is an "anger of despair" (Rich, "New Angry Young Playwrights," 1), which, for Durang, has led to a style that Gussow notes "has the wiggishness of four Marxes and the malice of a Jonathan Swift" ("History of American Film," 22). Durang's main satirical focus has been the Catholic church, but the subjects of his satires and parodies extend well beyond Catholicism to the roots of modern American culture itself, including the myth-making of cinema, the "solutions" found in psychoanalysis, and the sense of identity developed by family.

Although he has received a Tony nomination, Broadway critics have questioned Durang's art and durability. Beyond Broadway, Durang has met with general approval. He has won two Obies, and his plays are regularly revived in regional and university theatres throughout the country. He has also been awarded fellowships from CBS and the Rockefeller and Guggenheim foundations.

PRIMARY BIBLIOGRAPHY OF DURANG'S WORKS

Plays

The Greatest Musical Ever Sung. Unpublished. 1969.
I Don't Generally Like Poetry But Have You Read "Trees"? With Albert Innaurato. Unpublished. 1972.
Better Dead Than Sorry. Unpublished. 1973. Music by Jack Feldman; lyrics by Durang.
The Life Story of Mitzi Gaynor; or Gyp. With Albert Innaurato. Unpublished. 1973.

Titanic. 1974. New York: Dramatists Play Service, 1983. Reprinted in *Christopher Durang Explains It All for You.* New York: Avon, 1983.

The Idiots Karamazov. With Albert Innaurato. 1974. New York: Dramatists Play Service, 1981.

Death Comes to Us All, Mary Agnes. 1975. In *Three Short Plays.* New York: Dramatists Play Service, 1979.

Das Lusitania Songspeil. With Sigourney Weaver. Unpublished. 1976. Revised 1979.

The Vietnamization of New Jersey. 1976. New York: Dramatists Play Service, 1978.

A History of the American Film. 1977. New York: Avon, 1978.

When Dinah Shore Ruled the Earth. With Wendy Wasserstein. Unpublished. 1978.

'dentity Crisis. 1978. In *Three Short Plays.* New York: Dramatists Play Service, 1979. Reprinted in *Christopher Durang Explains It All for You,* pp. 39–59. New York: Avon, 1983.

The Nature and Purpose of the Universe. 1975 (radio version); 1979. In *Three Short Plays.* New York: Dramatists Play Service, 1979. Reprinted in *Christopher Durang Explains It All For You,* pp. 1–36. New York: Avon, 1983.

Sister Mary Ignatius Explains It All for You. 1979. In *Two Plays,* pp. 25–52. New York: Dramatists Play Service, 1982. Book club edition, Garden City, N.Y.: Nelson Doubleday, 1981. Reprinted in *Christopher Durang Explains It All for You,* pp. 121–51. New York: Avon, 1983.

Beyond Therapy. 1981. New York: Samuel French, 1983. Book club edition, Garden City, N.Y.: Nelson Doubleday, 1981. Reprinted in *Christopher Durang Explains It All for You,* pp. 159–214. New York: Avon, 1983.

The Actor's Nightmare. 1981. In *Two Plays,* pp. 5–21. New York: Dramatists Play Service, 1982. Book club edition, Garden City, N.Y.: Nelson Doubleday, 1981. Reprinted in *Christopher Durang Explains It All for You,* pp. 99–119. New York: Avon, 1983.

Baby with the Bathwater. 1983. New York: Dramatists Play Service, 1984. Also by Garden City, N.Y.: Nelson Doubleday, 1983.

The Marriage of Bette and Boo. 1973; revised 1985. New York: Dramatists Play Service, 1985. Book club edition, Garden City, N.Y.: Nelson Doubleday, 1985.

Sloth. In *Faustus in Hell* (produced 1985, Princeton).

Laughing Wild. New York: Dramatists Play Service, 1988.

Screenplay

Beyond Therapy. With Robert Altman. 1987.

Articles and Essays

"Addenda" (to *The Nature and Purpose of the Universe*). In *Three Short Plays,* pp. 35–36. New York: Dramatists Play Service, 1979. Excerpt reprinted as "Addendum" in *Christopher Durang Explains It All for You,* pp. 37–38. New York: Avon, 1983.

"Co-Author's Notes" (with Albert Innaurato). In *The Idiots Karamazov,* pp. 66–68. New York: Dramatists Play Service, 1981.

"Christopher Durang's Guilty Pleasures." *Film Comment* (January–February 1982): 62–65.

"Addendum (Author's Notes)" (to *Sister Mary Ignatius Explains It All for You*). In *Two Plays*, pp. 53–61. New York: Dramatists Play Service, 1982. Reprinted as "Addendum" in *Christopher Durang Explains It All for You*, pp. 152–57. New York: Avon, 1983.

"Introduction." In *Christopher Durang Explains It All for You*, pp. ix–xix. New York: Avon, 1983.

"Author's Notes." In *Beyond Therapy*, pp. 82–95. New York: Samuel French, 1983.

"Author's Notes." In *Titanic*, pp. 3–8. New York: Dramatists Play Service, 1983.

"Author's Notes." In *Baby with the Bathwater*, pp. 55–62. New York: Dramatists Play Service, 1984.

"Naked Lunch: A Feast of Caviar and Innuendo with Sigourney Weaver and Christopher Durang" (with Sigourney Weaver). *Esquire* (July 1984): 73–76.

"Shadings: Dianne Wiest." *Film Comment* (March–April 1985): 46–47.

"Wrestling with Wrath." *Esquire* (July 1986): 62–63.

"Out of Sorts in Africa" (with Sigourney Weaver). *Esquire* (November 1986): 130–35.

Interview

David Savran. "Christopher Durang." *In Their Own Words: Contemporary American Playwrights*. pp. 18–34. New York: Theatre Communications Group, 1988.

PRODUCTION HISTORY

Durang developed his dramatic skills at the Yale Repertory Theatre while studying drama under Robert Brustein. The first play to reach New York was one he cowrote with fellow student and playwright Albert Innaurato, entitled *I Don't Generally Like Poetry But Have You Read "Trees"?* performed at the Manhattan Theater Club in December 1972 and sponsored by the Yale Cabaret. During this period (1972–1975), however, Durang received his greatest exposure in New Haven with productions of *The Nature and Purpose of the Universe* (the play that won him admission to the Yale School of Drama in 1972), *'dentity Crisis* (stemming from an interest in case studies on schizophrenia by R. D. Laing), and *Titanic* (an assignment in a class led by Howard Stein). In 1974, Yale's University Theatre produced *Death Comes to Us All, Mary Agnes*. Durang also cowrote (with Innaurato) *The Idiots Karamazov* (a spoof of Dostoyevsky), performing in its 1974 Yale Repertory premiere.

A radio play version of *The Nature and Purpose of the Universe* was briefly produced in 1975 by the Direct Theatre as part of its After-Theater Series. In March 1976 *Titanic* also opened as part of the Direct's After-Theater Series and later briefly moved off-Broadway to the Van

Dam Theater (eight performances) with *Das Lusitania Songspeil*, a cabaret companion piece spoofing Brecht/Weill collaborations cowritten with fellow Yale classmate Sigourney Weaver.

Much of Durang's work through this period were pieces that brought him little genuine critical attention. In 1976, however, *A History of the American Film* was given a reading at the O'Neill National Playwrights Conference, and in 1977 the play's rights were jointly secured by Hartford's Stage Company, Los Angeles's Mark Taper Forum, and Washington's Arena Stage for simultaneous world premieres. The piece is an "elaborate spoof of more than a half-century of everything worth spoofing on the screen" (Chemasi, "Inner Circles," 66). These regional productions were well received, the play being labeled "a significant act of film criticism as well as wise social commentary" (Gussow, "History of American Film," 22) and "a comic memorial to our movie mania" (Clarke, 108) that shows a "satiric bite and a certain rueful affection for a fantasy-fed nation" (Kroll, 63). Several critics (Clarke; Gussow, "History of American Film"; Kerr, "An Ambitious, Ambiguous Satire"; Chemasi, "A History of American Film") have noted with approval Durang's efforts to capture America's hunger for Hollywood's manufacture of American mythology. But Chemasi noted, "While the critics were generally delighted, there was a good deal of uncertainty about exactly what Durang's intentions were" ("Inner Circles," 66). When the Arena Stage production was transferred to Broadway (the ANTA) on 30 March 1978, reviews played down the pleasure of the production and attacked Durang's indirection. Of the Broadway production, Kerr observed that "our playwright hasn't the stamina or the wit to see his off-with-their-heads attitude through" ("An Ambitious, Ambiguous Satire," 3), while Gill noted, "Durang's skill at parody is on an undergraduate level" (91). Working to understand the failure, Simon suggested it involved the shift from intimate theatres to the large ANTA Theater ("Film Flam," 100), and Gottfried has studied the failure by comparing Durang to a typical Broadway show running simultaneously, Bob Fosse's *Dancing* (42). Nevertheless, Durang was nominated for a Tony for Best Book of a Musical Play. Despite the short run and poor reviews on Broadway, the play quickly became a favorite of regional theatre in the 1979–1980 season in Cleveland, San Francisco, Seattle, and Ottawa, Canada.

During the same 1976–1978 period, the Yale Repertory produced *The Vietnamization of New Jersey*, a play parodying David Rabe's *Sticks and Bones* in particular and "socially significant drama" (Chemasi, "A History of American Film," 27) in general. The character Hazel, played by Ben Halley, Jr., received the greatest acclaim, being called "a supreme caricature" of the black servant stereotypes presented "in countless Hollywood movies" (Gussow, "Less May Be More," 3). In October 1978 the

Yale Rep produced *'dentity Crisis* as part of a double bill entitled "Mistaken Identities," a play that anticipates much of Durang's later work.

In February 1979, a revised version of *The Nature and Purpose of the Universe* opened at the Direct Theatre and ran for twenty-six performances. It is a play that "seems to be parodying the life of a conventional American family with problems" (Eder, 15). Durang's intentions were again at issue. The play focuses on a Catholic-American family comically gone berserk, and events result in the kidnapping and assassination of the pope. Eder's assessment of the play, finally, was, " 'Nature' is not only toothless but gumless as well" (15).

Sister Mary Ignatius Explains It All for You opened November 1979 at the Ensemble Studio Theatre as part of a bill including works by David Mamet, Marsha Norman, and Tennessee Williams entitled "Invitational." It won an Obie in 1980, and in October 1981 it opened at the Playwrights Horizons with a companion piece, *The Actor's Nightmare*, running for 947 performances (closing January 1984), his greatest commercial success to date. Kalem and others identify *The Actor's Nightmare* as an "in joke" (119) involving an actor thrust onto stage in a play he has not prepared for. It is a curtain raiser for the much more controversial feature play. Opening as a simple catechism given to the audience and a seven-year-old on-stage student, *Sister Mary Ignatius Explains It All for You* turns into a murderous confrontation between Sister Mary Ignatius and former students.

Most critics acknowledge the comically satiric bite of the play, which for Rich "rid[es] waves of demonic laughter" ("One-Acters," 21) and for Weales "retreats from direct didacticism into black farce" ("Fr. Tim, Sister Sade," 51). But two fundamental concerns about Durang's art surfaced in this work. One involves his craft. Weales noted, "The play goes to pieces with the arrival of the accusatory former students" ("Fr. Tim, Sister Sade," 51), and Kerr similarly noted that at the end of the play, "A struggle ensues, for the gun and for the shape and tone of the play" ("Durang's 'Sister,' " 3). The play shifts from playfully uncovering incongruities in Sister Ignatius's literalist perspective to what some consider a brutal and vicious indictment of Catholicism in the second half. Oliver noted that the "comedy dissolves entirely into rage" ("Sister Mary Ignatius," 66). The confusing tone in turn led to confusion about theme. Although Brustein saw the play "directed less toward social and political targets than toward the nightmares of his [Durang's] own personal history" ("Sister Mary Ignatius," 24), others claimed that the play is "a vision of Catholicism that is as trite as it is myopic" (Lauder, 418). Gilman, in fact, claimed that Durang presented a Catholic version of anti-Semitism; it is a "viciousness . . . that grinds up wit, social observation, and moral criticism" (650). On the other hand, Weales claimed to "suspect something less serious" ("Fr. Tim, Sister Sade," 51). And though Rich felt Durang's bite, he was less damning, noting that Durang "may well have shocked the likes of... Lenny Bruce, and yet he never lets his bitter emotions run away with his keen theatrical sense" ("One-Acters," 21). Though the play became a popular regional selection, Schaeffer and Pollitt note that the outrage over the play's seemingly anti-Catholic focus reached a fever pitch when a group in St. Louis tried to stage the play in 1983 (and eventually succeeded), prompting widespread debate on such issues as freedom of religious expression and the public's right to censor offensive art.

Beyond Therapy was a commissioned work that opened January 1981 at the Phoenix (thirty performances), starring Sigourney Weaver and Stephen Collins as two people hungry for meaningful relationships but thwarted in their efforts by the counseling of their respective therapists. The play was reworked and opened May 1982 on Broadway (Brooks Atkinson Theatre), featuring Dianne Wiest and John Lithgow, but once again Broadway reviews condemned Durang's work and succeeded at cutting the run short (eleven performances). Gussow (" 'Beyond Therapy' ") and Rich ("Durang's 'Beyond Therapy' ") noted that Durang's concentration on the two patients rather than on the more comical two psychiatrists moves away from the play's true source of humor into the less rich love affair. Where such criticism was less damaging off-Broadway (Gussow's review), it was a much more central concern on Broadway (Rich's review). Though Simon enjoyed the off-Broadway production ("Beyond Therapy"), he later observed that Durang's humor "is a kind of joke that does not bear repetition" ("Beyond Therapy... and Then There Were Nuns," 62), deserving one viewing at most, and preferably off-Broadway. However, Durang's work again won regional support, being produced as early as 1983, for example, at the Berkeley Repertory Theatre.

Baby with the Bathwater premiered April 1983 at the American Repertory Theatre's Hasty Pudding Theatre, then opened at the Playwrights Horizons in New York in November 1983 (closing January 1985 after eighty-four performances). Oliver noted that the play "is not nearly as acrid" as Durang's other works, having an ending that is "hopeful" (213). Denby observed that "psychoanalysis, which took a beating in *Beyond Therapy*, actually looks good in *Baby*" (423). Structurally Henry noted that Durang does work toward a narrative but concluded that problems still exist in the piece: "If Durang could bring a touch of the play's final forgiveness to its early scenes, *Baby with the Bathwater* would mark a major advance in an already noteworthy career" (96).

Marriage of Bette and Boo, a 1973 play produced by the St. Nicholas Theater in 1976, was rewritten in 1985. It opened 16 May 1985 at the Public Theatre (thirty-nine performances). It earned Durang his second

Obie and was named one of the year's ten best plays by Guernsey. The production also won Obies for direction (Jerry Zaks) and for Best Ensemble Performance. Durang himself played Matt, the son of Bette and Boo, working as narrator of and participant in the play's thirty-three scenes. Most critics noted the autobiographical elements of the play. Rich in fact called it "Mr. Durang's version of "The Glass Menagerie" ("Bette and Boo," 3), and Brustein ("Combating Amnesia") and Klein identified the work as Durang's *A Long Day's Journey Into Night*. Cohen saw "a remarkable new dimension" in this play in which Durang uses his brand of black humor while "touch[ing] our feelings at the same time" (24). Not all reviewers were captivated, however. Simon, for example, identified the work as interesting absurdist theatre but noted that it left him "lukewarm" ("The Public Goes Private," 83). The play has been revived in several regional productions, the most recent being by the Boston Post Road Stage Company in February 1987 (see Klein).

SURVEY OF SECONDARY SOURCES

Bibliographies

There is no extensive bibliography on Durang, though Salem includes a bibliography of New York reviews through to 1982, and both Marowski and Stine and Locher provide limited bibliographical data.

Biographies

Although no extended biography of Durang exists, Durang's various addenda and author's notes to the performance scripts provide valuable autobiographical insights, and his Introduction to *Christopher Durang Explains It All for You* is a brief but informative autobiography of his professional career. Flippo, Gussow ("Less May Be More"), and Chemasi ("A History of the American Film") also include biographical details. Herbert, Baxter, and Finley; Marowski; Stine; and Locher have entries on Durang as well. See also Savran's interview.

Influences

Clarke calls Durang "a grandchild of the movie age" (108) and suggests that cinema has influenced more than just *A History of the American Film*. Gussow ("History of American Film") notes in particular the influence of Marx Brothers' films. In "Christopher Durang's Guilty Pleasures," Durang acknowledges his obsession with cinema, listing his favorite classic films and providing some insight into their influences on him. Several critics (Cohen; Brustein, "Combatting Amnesia"; Simon, "Beyond Therapy") have noted an absurdist influence on Durang's works, with Denby noting in particular that "perhaps only Ionesco has combined farce and philosophical despair in quite so disturbing a way" (358). Given Durang's college and Catholic background, Brustein ("The Naked and the Dressed") suggests a literary influence—James Joyce—that Durang himself confirms, noting that *Portrait of the Artist as a Young Man* was influential in his personal development (Flippo, 41). Others (see Gussow "History of American Film"; Oliver, "Sister Mary Ignatius") see Jonathan Swift as a critical influence on Durang's satire.

General Studies

No major scholarly assessment of Christopher Durang's work exists, though several brief articles suggest directions in which to pursue Durang. Brustein's "The Crack in the Chimney" is perhaps the most fruitful. It identifies Durang as an important modern dramatic innovator. Brustein discusses America's seeming obsession with rationally motivated, essentially naturalist drama, citing O'Neill and Miller as standard representatives of American tastes and then arguing that Durang's work breaks from that past and "has deep roots in a controlled anger, which can only be expressed through a comedy of the absurd" (25). Moe also offers a short general essay on Durang's comedy.

That Durang is part of a new breed of American playwrights is addressed by Gussow, who discusses Durang, David Mamet, Albert Innaurato, and William Cristofer, calling them part of a "broad spectrum of the post-Albee American theater" that has its "roots in regional theater" ("The Daring Visions," 1) as opposed to the more restrictive Broadway theatre world. Rich similarly sees Durang as part of a new breed, grouping him with writers like Charles Fuller and calling them modern-day angry young men who have turned to "an anger of despair that tends to minimize the existence of villains or heroes" ("New Angry Young Playwrights," 1). Neither Gussow nor Rich, however, fully develops his points. In regard to this new breed, Samuel Freedman posits the question that since most great art has been centered around national controversy, can good art be produced in tranquil times? He uses Durang as a central example and concludes that "the suburban generation has a tale to tell that does not depend on having endured gunfire or breadlines" (1).

Analyses of Individual Plays

Although Durang's works are generally short pieces, four plays have received particular critical attention. Brustein's "The Crack in the Chimney" concentrates on *The Vietnamization of New Jersey* as its example of Durang's movement away from rationalism and toward other forms of unity. Chemasi ("A History of American Film") in particular looks at *A History of the American Film* and notes how Durang uses cinematic icons to reveal both the building up and recent steady decay of American myth (see also Gussow, "History of American Film"; Kerr, "An Ambitious, Ambiguous Satire"; Clarke), though a close study has yet to be attempted.

The central issue surrounding *Sister Mary Ignatius Explains It All for You* is censorship. Gilman and Lauder charge that the play is an intellectual version of anti-Semitism in which Catholicism is attacked instead of Judaism. Pollitt, however, defends the play, noting that "anticlericalism has a long and honorable history in literature" (23). Schaeffer wonders at the "brouhaha," noting that "this deeply flawed little play did not deserve all that uproar" (220).

Brustein sees *The Marriage of Bette and Boo* as an answer to Nightingale's charge that American drama has recently produced only "diaper plays" ("Combating Amnesia," 28), arguing, "If this is a 'diaper play,' then so is *A Long Day's Journey into Night*" (28). The play, he argues, is a mature product that addresses a growing realization that "the past is the present" (28), and it marks yet another breakthrough (*The Vietnamization of New Jersey* is the first) in Durang's career in particular and in modern American drama in general. Others have also noted the significance of this play: Klein observes that the play is "Durang's own 'Long Day's Journey into Night' " (24), and Rich calls it "Durang's version of 'The Glass Menagerie' " ("Bette and Boo," 3). Neither critic, however, pursues his comparison. *The Marriage of Bette and Boo* has even drawn the attention of avant-garde critics. Elinor Fuchs, for example, points out that Durang's theatre often addresses avant-garde, experimentalist issues. Using *The Marriage of Bette and Boo* as her example, Fuchs notes that the question of authority, presence, and writing itself are concerns that Durang has effectively introduced to mainstream theatre.

FUTURE RESEARCH POSSIBILITIES

Brustein sees American theatre growing up in the works of Christopher Durang. Others see Durang more generally as part of a group of young playwrights working to change the way American drama sees the world. Although he is still young and currently active in theatre, Durang has already produced a large body of material, warranting studies on a variety of subjects, including his unique satiric form, the influence of popular culture on his drama, and the autobiographical nature of his works. Alone or as part of a group, Durang is a writer who deserves more attention than scholars have recently given him.

SECONDARY SOURCES

Brustein, Robert. "Combating Amnesia." *New Republic* (1 July 1985): 28.
————. "The Crack in the Chimney: Reflections on Contemporary American

Playwrighting." *Theatre* 9, no. 2 (Spring 1978): 21–29. Reprinted in *Images and Ideas in American Culture*, pp. 141–57. Edited by Arthur Edelstein. Hanover, N.H.: University Press of New England, 1979.

———. "The Naked and The Dressed." *New Republic* (9 Dec. 1981): 21, 24–25.

———. "Sister Mary Ignatius." *New Republic* (9 December 1981): 21, 24–25.

Chemasi, Antonio. "A History of the American Film: In Which Playwright Christopher Durang Spoofs a Half Century of Movie Myths—and Takes a Fresh Look at Our Past." *Horizon* (March 1978): 26–31.

———. "Inner Circles." *American Film* 2, no. 10 (September 1977): 66–67.

Clarke, Gerald. "The Reel Truth, As Time Goes By." *Time* (23 May 1977): 108.

Clurman, Harold. "A History of the American Film." *Nation* (15 April 1978): 443.

Cohen, Ron. "The Marriage of Bette and Boo." *Women's Wear Daily* (20 May 1985): 24.

Denby, David. "Chris Durang—Funny Baby: Off-Broadway Theater's Malevolent Choirboy Finds Hope and Mental Health Beyond Therapy." *Vogue* (February, 1984): 358, 423.

Eder, Richard. "Durang's 'Nature and Purpose' at the Direct." *New York Times* (24 February 1979): 15.

Flippo, Chet. "Is Broadway Ready for Christopher Durang?" *New York* (15 March 1982): 40–43.

Freedman, Samuel. "Can Tranquil Times Yield Great Works?" *New York Times* (25 August 1985): 2: 1, 18.

Fuchs, Elinor. "Presence and the Writing of Revenge: Re-thinking Theatre After Derrida." *Performing Arts Journal* 26/27 (1985): 163–173.

Gill, Brendan. "A History of the American Film." *New Yorker* (10 April 1978): 91.

Gilman, Richard. "Sister Mary Ignatius Explains It All for You, The Actor's Nightmare." *Nation* (12 December, 1981): 649–50.

Gottfried, Martin. "The Razzle-Dazzle of Bob Fosse." *Saturday Review* (27 May 1978): 42.

Guernsey, Otis L., Jr., ed. *The Best Plays of 1984–1985*. New York: Dodd, Mead, 1985.

Gussow, Mel. " 'Beyond Therapy' by Durang at Phoenix." *New York Times* (6 January, 1981): C11.

———. "The Daring Visions of Four New Young Playwrights." *New York Times* (13 February, 1977): 2: 1.

———. " 'History of American Film,' a Play, Is Glorious Montage of U.S. Myth." *New York Times* (23 May 1977): 22.

———. "Less May Be More for Christopher Durang." *New York Times* (26 May 1986): B 3–4.

Henry, William A., III. "Mad House: 'Baby with the Bathwater' by Christopher Durang." *Time* (18 April 1983): 96.

Herbert, Ian, Christine Baxter, and Robert E. Finley. "Christopher Durang." In *Who's Who in the Theatre*, 17th ed. 1:192. Detroit: Gale Research Co., 1981.

Kalem, T. E. "Avaunt, God." *Time* (9 November 1981): 119.

Kerr, Walter. "An Ambitious, Ambiguous Satire." *New York Times* (5 June 1977): II: 3, 33.

―――. "Durang's 'Sister' Is Malicious Fun." *New York Times* (8 November 1981): II: 3, 12.

Klein, Alvin. "Durang's 'Marriage of Bette and Boo' Staged in Fairfield." *New York Times* (22 February 1987): 13: 24.

Kroll, Jack. "Sprocket Yocks." *Newsweek* (10 April 1978): 63.

Lauder, Robert E. "Theatrical Catholics." *America* (26 December 1981): 417–18.

Locher, Frances C., ed. "Christopher Durang." In *Contemporary Authors*, 105:151–53. Detroit: Gale Research, 1982.

Marowski, Daniel G., ed. "Christopher (Ferdinand) Durang." In *Contemporary Literary Criticism*, 38: 170–75. Detroit: Gale Research, 1986.

Moe, Christian H. "Christopher Durang." *Contemporary Dramatists*. Fourth Edition. Ed. D. L. Kirkpatrick. Chicago: St. James, 1988. 130–32.

Oliver, Edith. "Baby with the Bathwater." *New Yorker* (21 November 1983): 210, 213.

―――. "Sister Mary Ignatius." *New Yorker* (2 November 1981): 66.

Pollitt, Katha. "Bookends: 'Sister Mary Ignatius Explains It All for You.' " *Nation* (2 July 1983): 23–24.

Rich, Frank. " 'Bette and Boo' by Durang at the Public." *New York Times* (17 May 1985): III: 3.

―――. "Durang's 'Beyond Therapy.' " *New York Times* (27 May 1982): III: 19.

―――. "New Angry Playwrights Are Taking Center Stage." *New York Times* (3 January 1982): II: 1, 24.

―――. "One-Acters by Durang." *New York Times* (22 October 1981): III: 21.

Salem, James M. "Christopher Durang." In *A Guide to Critical Reviews: Part I: American Drama, 1909–1982*, 3d ed., pp. 143–45. Metuchen, N.J.: Scarecrow Press, 1984.

Schaeffer, Pamela. "St. Louis Brouhaha over 'Sister Mary.' " *Christian Century* (2 March 1983): 219–20.

Simon, John. "Beyond Therapy...and Then There Were Nuns." *New York* (7 June 1982): 62.

―――. "Film Flam." *New York* (17 April 1978): 100–101.

―――. "The Public Goes Private." *New York* (3 June 1985): 83–84.

Stine, Jean C., ed. "Christopher (Ferdinand) Durang." In *Contemporary Literary Criticism*, 107: 87–93. Detroit: Gale Research, 1984.

Weales, Gerald. "American Theater Watch, 1981–1982." *Georgia Review* 36 (Fall 1982): 517–26.

―――. "Fr. Tim, Sister Sade: Anguish and Anger." *Commonweal* (29 January 1982): 50–51.

Richard Foreman

(10 JUNE 1937–   )

DAVID SAVRAN

ASSESSMENT OF FOREMAN'S REPUTATION

Among modern American playwrights, Richard Foreman is the foremost explorer and poet of consciousness. His plays, composed in a richly allusive and utterly concrete language and free of the constraints of linear plot and traditional character development, abound in absurdities and discontinuities. These deeply poetic and challenging works scramble narrative, action, and image to explore, through performance, the workings of consciousness itself. As a result, they are less about the peculiarities of an objectively real world than about the process of perception, feeling, and understanding. They perform consciousness—consciousness understood as being itself a performance, a play of intuition and expression, external stimuli, and endless reflection. His scripts, hostage not to real but to written time, document Foreman's attempts, as he has explained, "to notate at every moment, with great exactness, what was going on as the 'writing was written' " (qtd. in Davy, 24). They read less like mimetic jottings than "like notations of my own process of imagining a theatre piece."

PRIMARY BIBLIOGRAPHY OF FOREMAN'S WORKS

Performed Plays

Angelface. 1968. In Richard Foreman. *Plays and Manifestos*. Edited by Kate Davy. New York: New York University Press, 1976.
Elephant Steps. Music by Stanley Silverman. Unpublished. 1968.
Ida-Eyed. Unpublished. 1969.
Real Magic in New York. Music by Stephen Dickman. Unpublished. 1969.
Sophia = (Wisdom): Part I. Unpublished. 1969.

Total Recall (Sophia = Wisdom: Part 2). 1970. In Richard Foreman. *Plays and Manifestos*. Edited by Kate Davy. New York: New York University Press, 1976.

HcOhTiEnLa (or) Hotel China. 1971. In *Plays and Manifestos*. Edited by Kate Davy. New York: New York University Press, 1976.

Evidence. Unpublished. 1971.

Dream Tantras for Western Massachusetts. Music by Stanley Silverman. Unpublished. 1971.

Sophia = (Wisdom) Part 3: The Cliffs. 1971. In *Plays and Manifestos*. Edited by Kate Davy. New York: New York University Press, 1976.

Daily Life. Unpublished. 1972.

Hotel for Criminals. Music by Stanley Silverman. Unpublished. 1972.

Dr. Selavy's Magic Theatre. Music by Stanley Silverman. Lyrics by Tom Hendry. Unpublished. 1972.

Classical Therapy or A Week under the Influence . . . 1972. In *Plays and Manifestos*. Edited by Kate Davy. New York: New York University Press, 1976.

Particle Theory. Unpublished. 1972.

Vertical Mobility (Sophia = (Wisdom): Part 4). 1973. In *Plays and Manifestos*. Edited by Kate Davy. New York: New York University Press, 1976.

Pandering to the Masses: A Misrepresentation. 1974. In Bonnie Marranca. *The Theatre of Images*. New York: Drama Book Specialists, 1977.

Pain(t). In *Plays and Manifestos*. Edited by Kate Davy. New York: New York University Press, 1976.

Rhoda in Potatoland (Her Fall-Starts). 1974. In *Plays and Manifestos*. Edited by Kate Davy. New York: New York University Press, 1976.

Thinking (One Kind). Unpublished. 1974.

Out of the Body Travel. Unpublished. 1975.

Livre des Splendeurs. 1975. In *Reverberation Machines: The Later Plays and Essays*. Barrytown, N.Y.: Station Hill Press, 1985.

Book of Splendors: Part Two (Book Of Levers): Action at a Distance. 1976. In *Reverberation Machines: The Later Plays and Essays*. Barrytown, N.Y.: Station Hill Press, 1985.

Blvd. de Paris. 1977. In *Reverberation Machines: The Later Plays and Essays*. Barrytown, N.Y.: Station Hill Press, 1985.

Slight. Unpublished. 1977.

Place + Target. 1978. In *Reverberation Machines: The Later Plays and Essays*. Barrytown, N.Y.: Station Hill Press, 1985.

American Imagination. Music by Stanley Silverman. Unpublished. 1978.

Madness and Tranquility. Unpublished. 1979.

Madame Adare. Music by Stanley Silverman. In *Theater* 12, no. 3 (Summer 1981).

Penguin Touquet. 1981. In *Reverberation Machines: The Later Plays and Essays*. Barrytown, N.Y.: Station Hill Press, 1985.

Cafe Amerique. 1981. In *Reverberation Machines: The Later Plays and Essays*. Barrytown, N.Y.: Station Hill Press, 1985.

Faust ou la Fête Électrique. Unpublished. 1982.

Egyptology (My Head Was a Sledgehammer). 1983. In *Reverberation Machines: The Later Plays and Essays*. Barrytown, N.Y.: Station Hill Press, 1985.

La Robe de chambre de Georges Bataille. Unpublished. 1983.

Miss Universal Happiness. Unpublished. 1985.
Africanis Instructus. Music by Stanley Silverman. Unpublished. 1986.
The Cure. Unpublished. 1986.
Film Is Evil: Radio Is Good. Unpublished. 1987.
Love and Science. Unpublished. 1987.
Symphony of Rats. Unpublished. 1988.

Screenplays

Out of the Body Travel. 1975.
City Archives. 1977.
Strong Medicine. 1978.

Essays

"Critique: Glass and Snow." *Arts Magazine* (February 1970): 20–22.
"Ontological-Hysteric Manifesto I." "Ontological-Hysteric Manifesto II." "On-
    tological-Hysteric Manifesto III." In Richard Foreman. *Plays and Mani-
    festos*. Edited by Kate Davy. New York: New York University Press, 1976.
"Notes on the Process of Making It." "How Truth...Leaps (Stumbles) Across
    the Stage." "14 Things I Tell Myself." "The Carrot and the Stick." "How
    to Write a Play." "How I Write My (Plays: Self)." In Richard Foreman.
    Reverberation Machines: The Later Plays and Essays. Barrytown, N.Y.: Station
    Hill Press, 1985.
"Putting the DEMAND into the work." *Two and Two*. Amsterdam, 1985.

Interviews

Feingold, Michael. "An Interview with Richard Foreman." *Yale/Theatre* 7, no. 1
    (Fall 1975): 6–29.
Shyer, Laurence. "A Night at the Opera: Richard Foreman Talks about *Madame
    Adare*." *Theater* 12, No. 3 (Summer 1981): 16–21.
Savran, David. "Richard Foreman." In *In Their Own Words: Contemporary American
    Playwrights*. New York: Theatre Communications Group, 1988. 35–50.
Bartow, Arthur. "Interview with Richard Foreman." In *The Director's Voice*. New
    York: Theatre Communications Group, 1988.

PRODUCTION HISTORY

Since 1968 Richard Foreman has presented his plays under the aegis of
his own producing organization, the Ontological-Hysteric Theatre. He
has directed almost all of his own work and has established a reputation
as a major director of classical and contemporary plays and operas in
the United States and Europe. When working in New York, Foreman
has produced his plays in non-traditional theatre spaces. During the
theatre's first years, from 1968 until 1972, he presented his work at the

tiny Cinematheque Theatre on Wooster Street in Soho. In 1973 he moved his performance space to a loft farther north on Wooster Street and in 1975 took over a theatre on Lower Broadway, which remained the theatre's home until 1979. Thereafter he began to work in somewhat more conventional theatre spaces, ranging from New York's Public Theatre to the Performing Garage. Although Foreman's work has been produced principally off-off-Broadway, he has written many plays for European theatres and since 1973 has worked widely abroad, especially in France, where his writing and directing are widely admired. At the same time that he has composed his series of spoken dramas, he has written and directed five music theatre works with the composer Stanley Silverman, most of which have been produced in New York by the Music Theater Laboratory/Lenox Art Center.

Foreman's critics, and Foreman himself, acknowledge that his work falls into two major periods, each with its own internal development. The first, from 1968 until 1975, under the primary influence of Brecht and Stein, was marked by Foreman's interest, as Bigsby has pointed out, "in a process of recuperating the real through a systematic defamiliarisation" (191). By repeating and slowing down action and constantly reworking and varying material, Foreman tried to lead his audience to reconceive the world in radically subjective terms. For both Shank (160) and Marranca (4), this work was in essence phenomenological—theatre that disrupted cause and effect, restricted empathy, and atomized experience in an attempt to dramatize the substratum out of which everything arises. Putting most of his dialogue on tape and using untrained performers not allowed, as Shank explains, "to be expressive in the traditional theatrical way," Foreman worked to defy "the logic of our expectations" and luxuriate "in the prolongation of the moment" (160).

In these early works, Foreman worked from an outline, a story that used elements of boulevard drama, especially the erotic triangle, to force a reexamination of traditional dramatic forms and devices. The main characters reappeared in one play after another: Ben, the figure originally representing Foreman himself; Max, at first, in Foreman's words, the "father figure" (Rockwell, 5) but later "the pivotal figure," in Marranca's words, the writer who "embodies Foreman, the creative artist" (4); Rhoda (usually played by Kate Manheim, Foreman's long-term associate and partner) whom Marranca describes as the "thematic representative of sexuality" (4); and Sophia, the goddess of wisdom or, in Foreman's phrase, the "demon/muse" (Rockwell, 5).

Beginning around 1975, Foreman began, as Bigsby describes it, to detail "his own shifting obsessions, presenting a series of fragments, each displacing one another at speed" (191–92). Shank notes that "increasingly he became interested in a form of theatre which, as a direct reflection of his notebooks, was a collection of fragments" (160–61). No longer working from an outline, Foreman juxtaposed discrete passages from his notebooks, using much more music and allowing the action to move faster and faster—to capture the buzz of consciousness. Instead of attempting the phenomenological drenching of the self in the bracketed object, Foreman began working toward undercutting the solidity and stability of the object. He strove to dramatize the web of relations that gives rise to objects, or in Bigsby's words, the "process whereby the human mind in a sense summons them into being by observing them and then generates meaning by relating them to other objects or events" (192).

Beginning in the 1980s, Foreman started to look more intently to the real world for objects and concerns to insert into the buzz of consciousness. Both *Egyptology* and *Miss Universal Happiness* abound in historical and political references in an attempt to examine cultural imperialism and the workings of various authoritarianisms. Both call into question what Bigsby considers Foreman's basic "apoliticism" (194). During this same period, Foreman's work has become less severe and fatalistic. Rather than dramatizing the tragedy of consciousness doomed to incessant self-representation, *The Cure*, for example, embodies a dream of positive values. *Film Is Evil: Radio Is Good* delights in the play of presence and absence that produces the manifold systems of representation and celebrates the free play of the mind and of the world.

The reaction of the popular press to Foreman's work has varied widely, from adulation to disgust. In recognition, however, of the importance and singularity of his theatrical vision, the *Village Voice* has regularly reviewed his work since 1971 and the *New York Times* since 1974. For both newspapers' reviewers, the articulation of a response to the work and the explanation of Foreman's strategies to an uninitiated public have proved extremely difficult. Gussow, for example, has noted that "it is almost more difficult to talk about the acting in Mr. Foreman's plays than it is to talk about the plays (they should be seen, not described)" ("Stage: Two," 37). Nevertheless, most reviewers have resorted to description (rather than analysis) of the action combined with documentation of their subjective response to the experience. Few critics writing for the popular press have attempted a carefully worked out exegesis.

In the early years, the critics tended to be torn between fascination and boredom. In 1971, Sainer, while describing *Total Recall* as "cunning, forceful and brilliant work," also observed that it was "austere, overly long . . . and at times impossibly clumsy" (55). Gussow, reviewing *Pain(t)*, noted that "the evening lacks drama in the traditional sense, but it is charged with cause and effect." While observing that Foreman's images "linger in the consciousness," he also reported that "some members of the audience seem infected with sleeping sickness, nodding and dozing until they gather enough energy to walk out" ("Stage: Two," 37). In

perhaps the most thoughtful equivocation of the period, Smith and
Sainer described the "powerful negative magnetism" of Foreman's work,
explaining that he likes the "sheer idiosyncrasy," the "twinkle," the "care
and consistency . . . I can enjoy expressions of sheer fuck-you hostility,
healthy and politically apt or not, just for vitality and exuberance. But
the style . . . doesn't so often release the spirit as crush it" (68–69).

During the late 1970s, most critics found that the newly found fre-
neticism made Foreman's work more accessible. Reviewing *Book of Splendors*, Gussow noted that "Mr. Foreman is even more fun now that his
plays have become shorter" ("Stage: Two," C3). Munk recognized in the
piece a significant "leap in tone," reporting that "this play is shorter,
faster, denser, noisier, funnier, more sensual, more 'acted,' less tied to
'character,' " than Foreman's earlier pieces (81). Writing on *Blvd. de Paris*,
Feingold characterized Foreman as the "arch sensualist of the avant-
garde" (73), while Rabkin, more finely attuned to the methods of experimental theatre, noted "the whirl of visual transformation and inventiveness, the volition of objects, the 'alienation' of performance, the
crescendo and diminuendo of sound, the sepulchral authority of the
playwright/director's voice—above all, the now still, now frenzied presence of Kate Manheim's Rhoda, increasingly the physical center around
which all revolves" (47).

By the 1980s, Foreman had become a recognized master of the avant-
garde. Rich called *Penguin Touquet*, the first Foreman piece to be performed in a conventional auditorium, "one of the season's most audacious displays of fantastic stagecraft" (C14). Feingold hailed *Egyptology*
as a "masterwork," noting the explicit concern "with the state of the
world and with [Foreman's] own position in our culture." He judged the
piece "political art of the highest order" and observed that "in the crumbling of our Egypt, Richard Foreman has made a hieroglyph everyone
can read" (91). But the critics were not unanimous. Brustein found the
piece "entirely random" and deemed it "a personal and quite impenetrable series of disjointed images" (23–24).

SURVEY OF SECONDARY SOURCES

Bibliographies

No full-scale, up-to-date bibliography for Foreman is available. A comprehensive one is included in Davy's book (242–48), but it ends at 1976.
An extensive bibliography, particularly useful for its inclusion of European material, is contained in Quadri (135–40). Bode also contains a
list of Foreman publications.

Biographies

No full-length biography of Foreman has been written, although Davy includes considerable information in her Introduction and chapter 10, and *Current Biography* is helpful. Interviews and articles containing the useful biographical information are Bartow, Rockwell, Savran, and Shewey.

Influences

The most comprehensive analysis of the sources that have influenced Foreman, especially Brecht and Stein, is found in Davy. In a much shorter essay, Marranca also focuses on the impact of Brecht and Stein (6–11), while Kirby discusses the relation of Foreman's work to European experimental film (20–22) and surrealism (27). Falk sees Jarry and Artaud as Foreman's precursors ("Physics," 396), while Leverett studies the influence of Stein and cinema (10–14).

General Studies

Davy's full-length study remains the only monograph. Having worked closely with Foreman for several years during the 1970s, she assembled a wealth of material detailing both the creation and construction of a Foreman play and the aesthetic laws of his theatre. Although her book tends to be more descriptive than speculative, her chapters on Foreman's work as playwright, scenographer, and director are an invaluable source for scholars intent on studying the different phases of his creative process.

Among the more speculative critics, Pasquier provides both an excellent overview of Foreman's work as a whole and an analysis of what is perhaps the most elusive quality of his work—its playfulness. Describing him as "a great comic writer" (534) in the tradition of "Harold Lloyd, Buster Keaton, the Marx Brothers, Charlie Chaplin" (544), she identifies his obsession with wonderfully grotesque and erotic play, with "topsy-turviness" and "sexually incongruous behavior" (538). Among other general studies, Bigsby's is particularly important for the historical context he provides, for his close reading of Foreman's *Manifestos*, and for his focus on stage-audience interaction: "The dynamism of his work is to derive not from a struggle between discrete persons or forces, or between being and the threat of non-being (existential or absurd drama), but from the activity of the mind coerced into activity by the theatre artist" (194). Schechner provides a more "autobiographical" key, focusing on Foreman's existential "soap opera": the "sexual struggle" in which men attempt to deny "personhood to women" (124).

In contrast to the structural and thematic approaches, Scarpetta and

Falk examine Foreman's art from the perspective of his scenography. In his semiotic study, Scarpetta concentrates on Foreman's "scenic 'writing' " that, he believes, "cuts across all theatrical codes" (23) in an attempt to "ruin representation," to allow "the spectacle's infernal rhythm and tempo" to consume space and "the objects that rise into view there" (30–31). Falk pursues a more phenomenological line of inquiry, maintaining that "Foreman's theatre is designed to reorient the spectator's perception toward nonlinear forms of consciousness" ("Setting," 51). She catalogs Foreman's scenographic technique to support her contention that he uses "setting as a metaphor for consciousness" ("Setting" 59).

Analyses of Individual Plays

There are very few studies that restrict themselves to single works because, as Cohn has explained, "the corpus of Foreman's Ontological/ Hysteric Theatre is so full of repetitions that it is hard to see any piece as a whole" (161) or self-contained entity. The two extensive analyses of a single work, Falk (1977) and Kirby, use the pieces under scrutiny, *Particle Theory* and *Sophia = (Wisdom) Part 3: The Cliffs*, respectively, as a way of approaching Foreman's theatre as a whole.

FUTURE RESEARCH OPPORTUNITIES

Foreman's work has elicited a considerable body of criticism; however, the beauty and flamboyance of his work as director and scenographer has inhibited critics from approaching his plays as complex literary texts. A closer reading of his plays as poetry would be extremely useful, as would an up-to-date and complete international bibliography. Because Foreman's way of working has been extensively documented and his plays described in great detail, a less formalist and more speculative criticism is called for. Foreman's theatre tends to undermine the self-containment of the work of art and valorize the radical subjectivity of all interpretation. If Foreman is correct and his art is indeed "a *contest* between object (or process) and viewer," then the viewer-critic should feel free to play his or her part more aggressively, subjecting Foreman's work to greater historical and political scrutiny or, alternatively, using it as the basis for psychoanalytical and autobiographical conjecture.

SECONDARY SOURCES

Bigsby, C. W. E. *A Critical Introduction to Twentieth-Century American Drama*, 3: 190–203. Cambridge: Cambridge University Press, 1985.
Bode, Walter. "Richard Foreman." In *Contemporary Dramatists*. Fourth Edition. pp. 156–58. Edited by D. L. Kirkpatrick. Chicago: St. James Press, 1988.

Brustein, Robert. "Theater with a Public Dimension." *New Republic* (1 August 1983): 23, 24.

Cohn, Ruby. *New American Dramatists, 1960–1980.* New York: Grove Press, 1982.

Davy, Kate. *Richard Foreman and the Ontological-Hysteric Theatre.* Ann Arbor: UMI Research Press, 1981.

Falk, Florence. "Physics and the Theatre: Richard Foreman's *Particle Theory.*" *Educational Theatre Journal* 29 (October 1977): 395–404.

———. "Setting as Consciousness." *Performing Arts Journal* 1, no. 1 (Spring 1976): 51–61.

Feingold, Michael. "Dis-Orient Express." *Village Voice* (2 January 1978): 73.

———. "Tut, Tut, Hurray!" *Village Voice* (31 May 1983): 91.

Gussow, Mel. "Stage: New Shocks, 'Splendors,' " *New York Times* (4 March 1977): C3.

———. "Stage: Two by Foreman." *New York Times* (3 April 1974): 37.

Kirby, Michael. "Richard Foreman's Ontological-Hysteric Theatre." *Drama Review* 17 (June 1973): 5–32.

Leverett, James. "Richard Foreman and Some Uses of Cinema." *Theater* 9, no. 2 (Spring 1978): 10–14.

Marranca, Bonnie. *The Theatre of Images.* New York: Drama Book Specialists, 1977.

Munk, Erika. "Foreman Pushes, Theatre Shifts." *Village Voice* (21 March 1977): 81.

Pasquier, Marie-Claire. "Richard Foreman: Comedy Inside Out." *Modern Drama* 25 (December 1982): 534–44.

Quadri, Franco. *Invenzione di un teatro diverso.* Turin: Giulio Einaudi editore, 1984.

Rabkin, Gerald. "Rhoda and Richard: The Shocking Truth." *Soho Weekly News* (29 December 1977): 47, 49.

Rich, Frank. "Stage: 'Penguin Touquet,' Richard Foreman's Dream." *New York Times* (2 February 1981): C14.

"Richard Foreman." *Current Biography* 49, no. 7 (July 1988): 6–9.

Rockwell, John. "The Magic Theater of Richard Foreman." *New York Times* (8 February 1976): B1, B5.

Sainer, Arthur. "A Hot Tip for a Bitter Winter." *Village Voice* (21 January 1971): 55.

Scarpetta, Guy. "Richard Foreman's Scenography: Examples from His Work in France." *Drama Review* 28 (Summer 1984): 23–31.

Schechner, Richard. "If Heidegger Wrote Soaps, He'd Be Richard Foreman." *Village Voice* (23 February 1976): 124.

Shank, Theodore. *American Alternative Theater.* New York: Grove Press, 1982.

Shewey, Don. "Richard Foreman Remains Provocative." *New York Times* (15 May 1983): B14, B26.

Smith, Michael, and Arthur Sainer. "Theatre Dialogue: Bubbles of Joy in a Sober Field." *Village Voice* (11 April 1974): 68–69.

Maria Irene Fornes

(14 MAY 1930–   )

SCOTT T. CUMMINGS

ASSESSMENT OF FORNES'S REPUTATION

Maria Irene Fornes has been called "one of the last of the real bohemians
among the writers who came to prominence in the sixties" (Marranca,
34) and "arguably our most inventive experimental playwright" (Munk,
"Cross Left," 93). She embodies the off-off-Broadway ethic, one dedicated to a direct, intimate, and sometimes visceral meeting of audience
and theatrical event. Her twenty-five-year career represents a unique
maturation of that ethic beyond its early communal preoccupations into
a highly personal artistic vision.

The crossroads of character, thought, and language has always been
the locus of Fornes's dramatic concerns. Some critics speak of the "invisible trajectory" of her career, one that has led from antic abstraction
to three-dimensional realism (Wetzsteon, 42). Her '60s plays are honestly
absurdist, full of language and logic games, zany transformations, and
fanciful incongruities. Her '70s plays suggest a discomfiting period of
growth, a search for a more personal voice, the fruition of which is
signaled by the turning point of *Fefu and Her Friends* (1977). Her '80s
plays, undoubtedly her most lasting work, achieve a crystalline balance
of lyricism, emotionalism, and formalism that makes them stunning objects of art that ask to be contemplated as much as experienced.

Since 1968, Fornes has directed the original production of each new
play, giving script and staging a seamless integrity. Her plays have been
seen off-Broadway and across the country, in regional theaters and on
college campuses, in vestpocket theatres and legitimate houses, and in
unconventional spaces such as an open field or a dusty loft or an empty
warehouse. Over the years, she has received seven Obies (only Samuel
Beckett and Sam Shepard have more), including one for Sustained

Achievement (1982), and many grants, including a prestigious grant from the National Endowment for the Arts in 1974. Although far from obscure today, the evanescent nature of Fornes's work mitigates against the widespread popularity that often passes for artistic achievement in the United States.

PRIMARY BIBLIOGRAPHY OF FORNES'S WORKS

Plays

Date listed for an unpublished play is the year of the first performance.

La viuda (The Widow). In *Teatro cubano: Cuatro obras recomendadas en el II Concurso Literario Hispanoamericano de la Casa de Las Américas,* pp. 7–54. Havana: Casa de las Américas, 1961.

Tango Palace and *The Successful Life of 3.* In *Playwrights for Tomorrow: A Collection of Plays,* 2: 7–74. Ed. Arthur H. Ballet. Minneapolis: University of Minnesota Press, 1966.

Promenade. In *The Bold New Women.* Greenwich, Conn.: Fawcett, 1966.

The Successful Life of 3. In *Eight Plays from Off Off Broadway,* pp. 205–52. Edited by Nick Orzel and Michael Smith. New York: Bobbs Merrill, 1966.

The Office. Unpublished. 1966.

The Annunciation. Adaptation of Rainer Maria Rilke's "The Life of Mary," the Gospel of St. John, and the Gospel of St. Luke. Unpublished. 1967.

Promenade. In *The New Underground Theatre,* pp. 1–32. Edited by Robert J. Schroeder. New York: Bantam, 1968.

Dr. Kheal. Yale/Theatre 1 (Winter 1968): 32–40.

Tango Palace. In *Concepts of Literature,* pp. 434–45. James William Johnson. Englewood Cliffs, N.J.: Prentice-Hall, 1971.

Promenade and Other Plays. Includes *Tango Palace, The Successful Life of 3, Promenade, A Vietnamese Wedding, Molly's Dream, The Red Burning Light,* and *Dr. Kheal.* Edited by Michael Feingold. New York: Winter House, 1971. (Rev. ed.: Performing Arts Journal Publications, 1987.

Molly's Dream. In *The Off Off Broadway Book.* pp. 304–16. Edited by Albert Poland and Bruce Mailman. New York: Bobbs Merrill, 1972.

The Curse of Langston House. Unpublished. 1972.

Aurora. Unpublished. 1974.

Cap-a-Pie. Unpublished. 1975.

Lines of Vision (lyrics). Book by Richard Foreman, music by George Quincy. 1976.

Lolita in the Garden. Unpublished. 1977.

Fefu and Her Friends. Performing Arts Journal 2 (Winter 1978): 112–40.

In Service. Unpublished. 1978.

Dr. Kheal. In *A Century of Plays by American Women,* pp. 179–84. Edited by Rachel France. New York: Richards Rosen Press, 1979.

Promenade. In *Great Rock Musicals,* pp. 507–60. Edited by Stanley Richards. New York: Stein and Day, 1979.

Eyes on the Harem. Unpublished. 1979.

Fefu and Her Friends. In *Word Plays*, pp. 5–41. Edited by Bonnie Marranca and Gautam Dasgupta. New York: PAJ Publications, 1980.

Blood Wedding. Translation and adaptation of Lorca. Unpublished. 1980.

Evelyn Brown (A Diary). Adaptation of 1909 diary of New Hampshire domestic worker. Unpublished. 1980.

A Visit. Unpublished. 1981.

Life Is a Dream. Translation and adaptation of Calderon. Unpublished. 1981.

The Danube. In *Plays from Padua Hills*. pp. 1–23. Edited by Murray Mednick. Pomona: Pomona College, 1984.

Maria Irene Fornes: Plays. Includes *The Danube, Mud, Sarita*, and *The Conduct of Life*. New York: PAJ Publications, 1986.

Drowning. In *Orchards: Seven Stories by Anton Chekhov and Seven Plays They Have Inspired*, pp. 55–62. New York: Alfred A. Knopf, 1986.

Cold Air. Translation and adaptation of a play by Virgilio Piñera. In *New Plays USA 3*, pp. 211–63. Edited by James Leverett and M. Elizabeth Osborn. New York: Theatre Communications Group, 1986.

The Trial of Joan of Arc in a Matter of Faith. Adaptation of W. P. Barrett's translation of fifteenth-century transcripts of Joan of Arc's interrogation by the Bishop of Beauvais. Unpublished. 1986.

Lovers and Keepers. Plays in Process Series. New York: Theater Communications Group, 1986.

The Mothers. Unpublished. 1986.

Box. Unpublished. 1986.

The Conduct of Life. In *On New Ground, Contemporary Hispanic-American Plays*, pp. 45–72. Edited by M. Elizabeth Osborn. New York: Theatre Communications Group, 1987.

Abingdon Square. *American Theatre* (February 1988): 1–10.

Hunger. Unpublished. 1988.

Interviews and Essays

Creese, Robb. " 'I Write These Messages That Come.' " *Drama Review* 21 (December 1977): 25–40.

Marranca, Bonnie. *Performing Arts Journal* 2 (Winter 1978): 106–11.

"Women in the Theatre." Roundtable discussion with Doris Abramson, Carolee Schneemann, Florence Falk, Bonnie Marranca, and Rosette C. Lamont. *Centerpoint: A Journal of Interdisciplinary Studies* 3 (11 [3–4]): 31–37.

Statement included in "The 'Woman' Playwright Issue." *Performing Arts Journal* 7, no. 3 (Fall 1983): 87–102.

Austin, Gayle. "Entering A Cold Ocean: The Playwrighting Process." *Theatre Times* (March 1984): 3–4.

"Creative Danger." *American Theatre* 2, no. 5 (September 1985): 10–15.

Cummings, Scott T. "Seeing with Clarity: The Visions of Maria Irene Fornes." *Theater* 17 (Winter 1985): 51–56.

Morrow, Lee Alan and Frank Pike. *Creating Theater: The Professionals' Approach to New Plays*. New York: Vintage, 1986.

Interviews with Contemporary Women Playwrights. Edited by Kathleen Betsko and Rachel Koening. New York: Beech Tree Books, 1987.

Savran, David. "Maria Irene Fornes." *In Their Own Words: Contemporary American Playwrights*. New York: Theatre Communications Group, 1988. 51–69.
"The Playwright in the Regional Theater." (Discussion with A. R. Gurney, Jr., Austin Gray, Eric Overmyer.) *Dramatists Guild Quarterly* (Spring 1988): 9–16.

PRODUCTION HISTORY

Although Fornes served her theatrical apprenticeship off-off-Broadway, her first production was at the Actors Workshop in San Francisco where Herbert Blau directed *There! You Died* (later retitled *Tango Palace.*) Local reviewers immediately pigeonholed this "lunatic farce" between the androgynous Isidore and the youthful Leopold as theatre of the absurd, "inflated with murky symbolism and gaudy poetics," yet "oddly hypnotic" (MacKenzie, D27). The play was performed the following year at the Actors Studio in New York City where Fornes was a member of the playwrights' unit. It was done again in 1965 at the Firehouse Theatre in Minneapolis in a production underwritten by Arthur Ballet's Office for Advanced Drama Research at the University of Minnesota.

On the same bill, marking Fornes's directing debut, was *The Successful Life of 3*, with music by Joseph Chaikin who directed the play at the Sheridan Square Playhouse a few months later with the Open Theatre. Soon after Richard Gilman redirected this "skit for vaudeville," which Pasolli described as a brightly colored, brisk tour de force: "a deeply pessimistic observation of the way we live our lives [that] refuses not to be gay" (65). In 1968, the Open Theatre performed *The Red Burning Light* as part of its European tour.

The other Greenwich Village group that nurtured Fornes's fledgling work was the Judson Poets Theatre on Washington Square. Fornes (book and lyrics) teamed up with its artistic directors, Al Carmines (music) and Lawrence Kornfeld (director), to create *Promenade*, a zany musical for which she received an Obie for distinguished playwriting in 1965. Fornes's beguiling mixture of comedy and pathos challenged the reviewers' synoptic powers. Tallmer of the *New York Post* called it "a Jeanette MacDonald movie co-scripted by Bertolt Brecht and Jean Genet, directed by Groucho Marx" (59), while Smith of the *Village Voice* wrote, "The dominant emotion is romantic melancholia but the tone is vapid frivolity and the delicate tension this creates gives the event its distinction" (21). Judson also provided a showcase for *The Annunciation* (1967, an adaptation of religious texts), and for one of Fornes's most frequently performed pieces, *Dr. Kheal* (1968), a monodrama in the manner of Nikolai Evreinov.

In 1969, *Promenade* became Fornes's first and only true commerical hit when it ran for 259 performances as the inaugural production of the new Promenade Theatre, a production marked by a rare combination of Broadway professionalism and off-off-Broadway exuberance. Producers Edgar Lansbury and Joseph Beruh hired designers Rouben Ter-Arutunian, Willa Kim, and Jules Fisher to join the original trio of Fornes, Carmines, and Kornfeld, creating what Kroll called "the apotheosis of Judson" (107). Critics quibbled or carped about the book's being "cryptic" (Watts, 78) and "incomprehensible" (Gottfried, 214) but forgave it this flaw in the face of Fornes's free-spirited lyrics, Carmines's nearly nonstop eclectic score and a first-rate cast that included Madeline Kahn. A 1983 revival by Theatre Off Park suggested that *Promenade*'s "joyful irreverence hasn't tarnished over the years" (Massa, 98). Both Massa of the *Village Voice* (98) and Holden of the *New York Times* (C8) praised the "perfect" collaboration of lyricist and composer, a quality that would seem to guarantee *Promenade*'s status as an offbeat musical of lasting interest.

The 1969 off-Broadway production of *Promenade* was not Fornes's first uptown showing. In 1966, *The Office*, directed by Jerome Robbins and starring Elaine May, Jack Weston, Tony Lo Bianco, and Ruth White, previewed at the Henry Miller Theatre, making Fornes perhaps the first "off-off" playwright on Broadway. The producers withdrew the play before it opened. In 1971, Fornes co-founded with Julie Bovasso, the New York Theater Strategy, a theatre cooperative devoted to the continued promotion of new plays and playwrights. For much of the 1970s, administrative duties cut into her playwriting work; still, several of her own plays premiered there (*Molly's Dream*, 1973; *Aurora*, 1974).

The most important play to be introduced at New York Theater Strategy was *Fefu and Her Friends*. The play, set in the 1930s yet oddly contemporary, presents a meeting of eight women in a New England country home to plan a fund-raising event designed to promote "art as a tool for learning." This gathering becomes the occasion for a series of encounters around the theme of women being with women. The most remarked-upon aspect of this and all subsequent productions is its environmental and processional second act. The first and third act take place in a conventional proscenium arrangement that represents Fefu's living room, but for the second act, the audience is divided into four groups, each of which visits four "rooms" elsewhere in the house.

The positive response to the short run at the Relativity Media Lab in May 1977 led to another production of the play the following January at Wynn Handman's American Place Theatre, one that attracted widespread attention. Reviewers, both positive and negative, found the play enigmatic, challenging, plotless, and abstract. Kerr and Watt were outwardly hostile. Kauffmann (38) found it "too ill-developed to be rewarding." But Clurman wrote, "The mixture of elements—symbolism, abstracted or semi-surrealistic discourse, stream-of-consciousness rumination and hysteria along with quirks of humor—keep one, by turn, alert and dazed" (154).

Despite the misgivings of the Broadway press, *Fefu* has achieved a life of its own. Notable productions have taken place at Padua Hills Festival (1979), Eureka Theatre in San Francisco (1981), the Empty Space in Seattle (1981), and At the Foot of the Mountain in Minneapolis (1986, 1987), a feminist theatre collective that had rejected the play ten years earlier for political reasons.

If *Promenade* brought Fornes a momentary commercial esteem in the late 1960s, *Fefu* brought critical recognition in the late 1970s. Since then, Fornes has returned to American Place Theatre twice. In 1982, she directed *The Danube*, a play set in Budapest in which human love and innocence are besieged by a decay of language and an unfolding natural disaster of seemingly nuclear origin. Again, the critics were split over the value of a play built around a gnawing, unexplained mystery. Rich dismissed it as trivially apocalyptic and the work of an impoverished imagination (C3), but Feingold found it "one of the most startlingly original and devastating things I can ever remember seeing on a stage" (20 March 1984, 83).

The most recent play that Fornes directed at American Place Theatre, *Abingdon Square* (1987), was produced by Julia Miles's Women's Project. It presents an epic in miniature about a child bride whose growth into sexual maturity and desire is in conflict with her loving marriage to a much older man. Munk credited Fornes with presenting this melodramatic story "with the uniqueness and emotional weight it would have if it happened to our own relatives" (27 October 1987, 112). Gussow found the play impressionistic, languid, and vague, much more a reflection of his attention than the play itself (17 October 1987, 16).

The uptown and downtown reviewers are almost perfectly split in their respective dismissal and praise of Fornes's work. The key issue seems to be the challenge that a Fornes play presents to the audience's understanding. The uptowners do not mind riddles as long as they get the answers by the end. The downtowners value the puzzle itself in its ineffable splendor. This is partly a matter of taste, but it is also a matter of Fornes's aesthetic strategy. Her plays do not provide tidy messages in either domestic homilies or zealous politics; they provoke thought in an open-ended, often haunting way. If the plays are hollow, it is because they carve out a cavernous space in which those thoughts can resonate after the final curtain. They are the audience's thoughts, though, not Fornes's; she has only instigated them, allowed them to bubble up to the surface and pop as they hit the hostile air of consciousness.

The period since *Fefu* has been a prolific one for Fornes. She has written and directed at the rate of more than one new play a year. *Eyes on the Harem* (INTAR, 1979) and *A Visit* (1981) suggest a return to the polymorphous perversity and satirical thrust of the earlier off-off-Broadway plays. *Eyes on the Harem* is a loosely structured revue on sexual politics in the Ottoman Empire. *A Visit* presents a Victorian weekend-in-the-country situation, which quickly turns into the springboard for a licentious romp. Feingold called it "a whole new genre—human pornography" (30 December-5 January 1982, 69). Both plays reflect Fornes's interest in sexual politics, this time using historical settings and source materials.

Evelyn Brown (A Diary) (Theatre for the New City, 1980) presented Fornes's staging of passages drawn from the diary of a New Hampshire domestic worker. It exemplifies Fornes's fondness for found texts—Sontag describes this as a preliterary attraction to "the authority of documents" (8)—and her interest in finding evocative public images for private thoughts and feelings. This method was manifest again in *The Trial of Joan of Arc on a Matter of Faith* (Theater for the New City, 1986), in which Fornes staged selected passages from the transcripts of Saint Joan's interrogation by the Bishop of Beauvais on the charge of heresy. Fornes has been credited with making these characters her own by virtue of handling them with a "tenderness completely without sentimentality, without deception, and not for interpretation" (Munk, 21 April 1980, 83).

These two adaptations also reflect Fornes's interest since *Fefu*, a play about women as a group, as an entity, in individual female heroines, a development fully borne out in *Sarita*, *Mud*, and *The Conduct of Life*. Syna called *Sarita* (INTAR, 1984) a female *Woyzeck:* "not so much in the story line"—although it is a tale of desperate and destructive passion—"but in Fornes's use of short, episodic scenes and terse, often symbolic and enigmatic dialogue" (7B). This method has marked much of Fornes's recent work. *Mud* (Theater for the New City, 1983) presents the story of a lower-depths love triangle in seventeen scenes, each of which is followed by a freeze that gives the effect of a still photograph. In his review, Feingold extended the analogy: "The reality seems to have had its details airbrushed out; the actions happen with the hypnotic slowness of a dream, unnerving you, making you restless, and finally eating into the mind like etchers' acid" (20 November 1988, 130). A subsequent production of *Mud* produced by the Omaha Magic Theatre and also directed by Fornes caused a minor stir when it visited the 1986 Boston Women in Theatre Festival. In a panel discussion after the play, audience members questioned the "necessity" of Mae's death and the presentation of a female heroine as, ultimately, a trapped, powerless victim. Similar feminist criticisms have been made about *Sarita* and, oddly, *Fefu and Her Friends*, but Fornes steadfastly insists on the truthfulness of her vision, however disturbing her audience may find it.

Sexual oppression takes its most violent form in *The Conduct of Life* (Theater for the New City, 1985), which presents "the home life of a Latin American army captain who is a professional torturer and a domestic sadist" (Munk, 26 March 1985, 69). His wife and his captive mistress both suffer variously under his shadow until the final act of violence that rings down the curtain. Berman found both the play and the production "uneven" but "incomparably more serious than any of the new plays on Broadway" (413) and called for a quick revival.

Despite the harsh living conditions in which Fornes places her characters, her fondness and respect for them as creatures of her imagination has been commented upon often. Only Orlando in *The Conduct of Life* seems purely evil. Otherwise Fornes's characters are imbued with what Marranca calls the "loveliness of presence," a quality she defines as "a humanism that guilelessly breathes great dignity into the human beings [she] imagines into life and, and so proposes to reality" (33). Occasionally this tenderness toward her characters borders on sentimentality, as in *Lovers and Keepers* (INTAR, 1986; Pittsburgh's New City Theatre, 1986), a trio of short musical plays that lightheartedly celebrate the partnership of love. Contrasted to her other work, critics found it pleasant but undemanding (Gussow, "Lovers," C25; Smith D3). Feingold sensed an ambivalent return to the capricious romps of her early plays: "It may be that her grapples with the tragic have disenchanted her with the side of her sensibility that is all ease and affectionate fun, sentimental in the clean, open way of a good melodrama or romance" ("Fornes's Incompatibles," 92). Comments like this attest to one of the few constants in Fornes's ever-changing experiments: an engaging mixture of tones, moods, and emotions (exuberant despair, pathetic comedy) that at first seem contradictory or mutually exclusive but gradually take on the truthfulness of life's unrelenting paradoxes.

Since the demise of the New York Theater Strategy in the late 1970s, Fornes has been associated with George Bartenieff and Crystal Field's Theater for the New City and Max Ferra's INTAR, as well as the annual Padua Hills Festival in southern California. Fornes works frequently with a trio of designers: Donald Eastman (scenery), Gabriel Berry (costume), and Anne Militello (lighting). The only performers closely associated with Fornes's work are Sheila Dabney, who appeared in *Sarita, The Conduct of Life, The Trial of Joan of Arc on a Matter of Faith,* and *Lovers and Keepers,* and Margaret Harrington, who appeared in *Fefu and Her Friends, Evelyn Brown, Life Is a Dream* and *Danube.* In recent years, Fornes's interest in directing has begun to extend beyond her own work to include classic and Latin American plays. For productions at INTAR, she translated, adapted, and directed Calderon's *Life is a Dream* and Virgilio Piñera's *Cold Air.* In 1987 she directed *Hedda Gabler* at the Milwaukee Rep and *Unce Vanya* at the CSC Repertory in New York, as well as the premiere of her *Abingdon Square* and a workshop of a play in development at the Guthrie called *Oscar and Bertha*. Both Gussow ("Abingdon Square," A16) and Munk ("Conduct," 112) heaped special praise on the directing of *Abingdon Square*, and Fornes has admitted a particular satisfaction with the recognition of her directing efforts. This may suggest a slight shift in priorities for her future work. She continues to teach playwriting at INTAR and in workshops around the country, and a book on the subject, *The Anatomy of Inspiration*, is forthcoming.

SURVEY OF SECONDARY SOURCES

Bibliographies

There is no significant bibliography of secondary sources on Fornes.

Biographies

There is no extensive biography of Fornes, although sketchy thumbnail biographies can be found in reference volumes such as MacNicholas, Hall, and Riley and in newspaper features such as Winks.

Influences

Sontag (8) characterizes Fornes as an autodidact influenced more by certain styles of painting and film than literature and theater. Marranca in *American Playwrights* (53) mentions the influence of the Open Theatre and the Judson Poets' Theatre on specific works. In the Cummings interview (52), Fornes acknowledges two 1950's productions that had an impact on her dramatic imagination: Roger Blin's original production of *Waiting for Godot* and Burgess Meredith's production of *Ulysses in Nighttown* with Zero Mostel. Comparisons have been made to a variety of absurdist playwrights as well as to Gertrude Stein, but there has been no systematic study of verifiable influences on Fornes's work.

Fornes's influence on other dramatists has been chiefly felt through the playwriting workshops she teaches in New York and around the rest of the country, but no study of this has been undertaken.

General Studies

There have been no book-length treatments of Fornes's work to date, although I am preparing one.

The most comprehensive and brilliant introduction is Sontag, although it is synoptic almost to a fault. For example, Sontag states that Fornes's "work is both a theatre about utterance (i.e. a meta-theatre) and a theatre about the disfavored—both Handke *and* Kroetz, as it were"

(9). This statement is provocative in its insight but is left to be fleshed out by a lesser critic. Of equal merit is Wetzsteon's excellent profile of Fornes's playwriting and directing. At once anecdotal and analytical, it captures a sense of her creative process and its varyingly startling results.

More workmanlike introductions have been provided by Cohn, Keyssar, and Marranca within chapters of longer books. For Cohn, Fornes shares a chapter ("Actor Activated") with Jack Gelber, Israel Horovitz, Jean-Claude van Itallie, and Megan Terry because of their '60s affiliation with actor-centered ensembles such as the Open Theatre and the alleged influence on them of experimental acting techniques such as transformation (73). Keyssar discusses Fornes together with Adrienne Kennedy, Rochelle Owens, Julie Bovasso, and Rosalyn Drexler and credits Fornes, largely on the basis of *Fefu and Her Friends*, with being the woman playwright to articulate most systematically the problem of recognition of women by women (121). Still, like most other quick and comprehensive surveys of contemporary playwrights, these passages are virtually outdated by the time they are published and distributed.

Delicacy of tone, lightness of spirit, economy of style, and keen intelligence are the Fornes trademarks that Marranca delineates in her more thorough and insightful chapter on Fornes (53). Marranca is among the first to observe (and to celebrate) the "new move into realism" (62) suggested by *Fefu and Her Friends*. She extends the argument in a major essay, "The Real Life of Maria Irene Fornes," in which the new realism is variously described as emotive, aggressive, quotational, iconic, miniaturist, distilled, and gestural. Marranca credits Fornes (along with '70s European neorealists such as Edward Bond, Franz Xaver Kroetz, and Michel Vinaver) with lifting "the burden of psychology, declamation, morality, and sentimentality from the concept of character" (30). This frees Fornes characters for the emotional process of thought or of coming to thought, an action often paralleled or exemplified by the acquisition of language (32–33).

Also worthy of mention is Austin's essay.

Analyses of Individual Plays

Extensive analysis of individual Fornes plays has centered on *Fefu and Her Friends*. Cummings has seized on Marranca's ideas about the relationship of language, thought, and action in his reading of *Fefu and Her Friends*. Pevitts provides a balanced feminist account of the play in her essay in *Women in American Theatre*. No other Fornes play has received detailed scholarly attention, but Gilman, Wetzsteon, and Marranca are all useful in their brief discussions of a number of other individual works.

FUTURE RESEARCH OPPORTUNITIES

Scholars have only begun to recognize Fornes's importance. This neglect is due in part to Fornes's commitment to directing the initial productions of each new play. Often, she begins rehearsals for a new play with an unfinished script and uses the rehearsal process, her work with the actors, and formal directoral elements to integrate text and performance more fully than in conventionally logocentric plays. The finished play stands on its own as dramatic text, but the built-in symbiosis of word and image suggests that Fornes scholarship will have to be based as much on performance criticism as textual analysis.

Two well-established critical issues warrant further debate. Both stem from *Fefu and Her Friends*. The first concerns Fornes's emotional and ontological realism and the nature of character in her recent work. What is the relationship of character to thought and action in her plays? How does Fornes's style as a director operate as an aesthetic control on her realism? The second, and much thornier, issue is that of Fornes and feminism. Does a feminist approach limit or open up her work? How does the feminist label affect her work and the attention of the broader, male-dominated scholarly community?

A host of unexplored questions awaits investigation. How does Fornes's bicultural background and early training as a painter affect her work, particularly in reference to the role of language in her work and its visual composition? To what extent does her mature work amalgamate the lessons learned during her brief period of study at the Actors Studio and her off-off-Broadway apprenticeship in the 1960s? As scholars turn to these issues, they will join the ranks of downtown critics and editors, foundation people, regional theatre artistic directors, playwriting students, feminists, and academics whose continuing support of Fornes's work attests to her stature as one of this nation's foremost playwrights.

SECONDARY SOURCES

Aaron, Jules. "Padua Hills Playwriting Workshop." *Performing Arts Journal* 3 (Winter 1979): 121–26.

Austin, Gayle. "Madwoman in the Spotlight: Plays of Maria Irene Fornes." In *Feminist Perspectives on Contemporary Women Playwrights*. Edited by Lynda Hart. Ann Arbor: University of Michigan Press, forthcoming.

Berman, Paul. "The Conduct of Life." *Nation* (6 April 1985): 412–13.

Clurman, Harold. "Theatre." *Nation* (11 February 1978): 154.

Cohn, Ruby. *New American Dramatists, 1960–1980*. Grove Press Modern Dramatists. New York: Grove Press, 1982.

Cummings, Scott T. "Notes on Fefu, Fornes, and the Play of Thought." *Ideas and Production*, Issue 8 (Winter 1988): 91–103.

Feingold, Michael. "Found in Translation." *Village Voice* (20 March 1984): 83.

————. "Fornescations." *Village Voice* (30 December–5 January 1982): 69.

————. "Clearer Than Anything." *Village Voice* (20 November 1983): 130, 32.

————. "Fornes's Incompatibles." *Village Voice* (29 April 1986): 92.

"Fornes, Maria Irene, Writer and Director." *Contemporary Theatre, Film and Television* 1 (1984): 181. Monica M. O'Donnell, ed. Detroit: Gale Research Co., 1984.

Gilman, Richard. Introduction to *Promenade and Other Plays*, by Maria Irene Fornes. Winter Repertory 2. Edited by Michael Feingold. New York: Winter House, 1971.

Gottfried, Martin. "Promenade." *Women's Wear Daily* (5 June 1969).

Gussow, Mel. "Stage: Fornes's 'Abingdon Square.' " *New York Times* (17 October 1987): A16.

————. "Stage: 'Lovers' at Intar." *New York Times* (17 April 1986): C25.

Hall, Sharon K., ed. "Maria Irene Fornes: The Conduct of Life." In *Contemporary Literary Criticism Yearbook 1985*, pp. 135–38. Detroit: Gale Research, 1986.

Holden, Stephen. " 'Promenade,' Carmines-Fornes Work." *New York Times* (25 October 1983): C8.

Kauffmann, Stanley. "Away from Broadway." *New Republic* (25 February 1978): 38.

Kerr, Walter. "Two Plays Swamped by Metaphors." *New York Times* (22 January 1978): B3.

Keyssar, Helene. *Feminist Theatre*. Grove Press Modern Dramatists. New York: Grove Press, 1985.

Kroll, Jack. "Apotheosis." *Newsweek* (16 June 1969): 107.

MacKenzie, Bob. "Workshop Offers a Puzzling Pair." *Oakland Tribune* (2 December 1963): D27.

Mael, Phyllis. "Maria Irene Fornes." In *Twentieth Century American Dramatists*. Pt. 1: *Dictionary of Literary Bibliography*, 7: 188–91. Edited by John MacNicholas. Detroit: Gale Research, 1981.

Marranca, Bonnie. "The Real Life of Maria Irene Fornes." *Performing Arts Journal* 8, no. 1 (1984): 29–34.

Marranca, Bonnie, and Gautam Dasgupta. *American Playwrights: A Critical Survey*. New York: Drama Book Specialists, 1981.

Massa, Robert. "Pomp and Circumstance." *Village Voice* (25 October 1983): 98.

Munk, Erika. "Cross Left." *Village Voice* (2 April 1985): 93.

————. "The Conduct of Love." *Village Voice* (27 October 1987): 112.

————. "Let Us Now Praise Famous Women." *Village Voice* (21 April 1980): 83.

————. *Village Voice* (26 March 1985): 69.

Pasolli, Robert. *A Book on the Open Theater*. New York: Avon, 1970.

Pevitts, Beverly. " 'Fefu and Her Friends.' " In *Women in American Theatre*, pp. 316–20. Edited by Helen Krich Chinoy and Linda Walsh Jenkins. New York: Crown, 1981.

Rich, Frank. "Theatre: 'The Danube' at the American Place." *New York Times* (13 March 1984): C13.

Riley, Carolyn, ed. "Fornes, Maria Irene." In *Contemporary Authors*, 25–28: 261–62. Detroit: Gale Research, 1971.

Smith, Michael. "Theatre: Devices and The Promenade." *Village Voice* (15 April 1965): xxx.

Sontag, Susan. Preface. In *Plays*, by Maria Irene Fornes, pp. 7–10. New York: Performing Arts Journal, 1986.

Syna, Sy. "Maria Fornes's Vision and Dabney's Talent Work Well in 'Sarita.' " *New York Tribune* (1 February 1984): 7B.

Tallmer, Jerry. "Here Comes Irene Fornes." *New York Post* (11 April 1965): 59.

Watt, Douglass. "What's Doing Here, Fefu?" *New York Daily News* (14 January 1978): 12.

Watts, Jr., Richard. "A Cascade of Musical Numbers." *New York Post* (5 June 1969): 78.

Wetzsteon, Ross. "Irene Fornes: The Elements of Style." *Village Voice* (29 April 1986): 42–45.

Winks, Michael. "Encore." *Pittsburgh Press* (28 September 1986): 26–28, 31.

Jack Gelber

(12 APRIL 1932–   )

VINCENT F. PETRONELLA

ASSESSMENT OF GELBER'S REPUTATION

Jack Gelber's work defies easy categorization within the sweep of contemporary American drama. His first play, *The Connection*, has its origins not only in the literary achievements of Pirandello and Brecht but also in the musical achievement of American jazz. Just as the improvisational mode of jazz requires spatial or harmonic flexibility and a close relationship of performer and audience, so do Gelber's plays open up new spaces on and off the stage and ask the audience to play along with the dramatic material. We also see this in *The Apple*. What is more, *Square in the Eye*, achronologically shows us how the artist needs to play with time in order to dramatize how time plays ironic tricks on all of us. It is as if Gelber does a variation on Hamlet's "The time is out of joint" in order to make it swing to a different rhythm section. *The Cuban Thing* also exemplifies this need to drive home rhythmically a dramatic point. It is a festive celebration of the Castro revolution, requiring not so much Afro-American music as Cuban/Afro-Cuban culture to energize it. The effect, like that of *Rehearsal* and the earlier work, is free-wheeling spontaneity, apparently improvised choruses on the fundamental changes of "All the world's a stage." Drama as jam session is one way of characterizing Gelber's plays.

PRIMARY BIBLIOGRAPHY OF GELBER'S WORKS

Plays

The Connection. 15 July 1959, Living Theatre, New York. New York: Grove, 1960. London: Faber, 1961.

The Apple. 7 December 1961, Living Theatre, New York. New York: Grove, 1961.

Square in the Eye. 19 May 1965, Theatre de Lys, New York. New York: Grove, 1966.

The Cuban Thing. 24 September 1968, Henry Miller's Theatre, New York. Summer 1968 at Berkshire Festival Theatre, Stockbridge, Massachusetts. New York: Grove, 1969.

Sleep. 10 February 1972, American Place Theatre, New York. New York: Hill and Wang, 1972.

Barbary Shore. Adapted from Norman Mailer's novel. 18 December 1973, Public/Ansapcher Theater, New York.

Farmyard. Translation by Gelber and Michael Roloff from Franz Xaver Kroetz's play. 22 January 1975, Yale Theatre, New Haven.

Rehearsal. 8 October 1976, American Place Theatre, New York.

Starters. 1980. Yale Theatre, New Haven.

Screenplay

The Connection. 1962.

Novel

On Ice. New York: Macmillan, 1964; London: Deutsch, 1965.

Essays

"Julian Beck (1925–1985)." *Drama Review* 30 (Spring 1986): 11.
"Julian Beck, Businessman." *Drama Review* 30 (Summer 1986): 6–29.

PRODUCTION HISTORY

Almost all of Gelber's plays have been produced in off-Broadway and way-off-Broadway theaters. In his review of the first production of *The Connection* at the Living Theatre, Calta said the play is about "jazz and junk...an attempt to depict the sordid world of the narcotics addict.... But [the play] proves to be nothing more than a farrago of dirt, small-time philosophy, empty talk and extended runs of 'cool' music" (30). The impact upon the audience, said Calta, is that of the excessive use of heroin, which causes listlessness and stupor (30). Atkinson also commented on the same production by describing the effect on audiences who leave the theatre in "various frames of mind—horror, terror or ironic amusement—finding it difficult to pull themselves together after the performance" (11). Atkinson pointed out that the play was being performed in repertory with Pirandello's *Tonight We Improvise* to suggest that improvisatory elements link the two playwrights. These elements create another kind of link or "connection": the one with the audience, who are not permitted to remain overly detached from the onstage events. The lukewarm reception from Calta and the warmer reaction of Atkinson was followed by a rowdy response from the London audience when the play opened there: "Some members of the audience jeered, some applauded ironically, and others walked out. There was booing at the final curtain" (*New York Times*, 23 February 1961, 30). Similarly the Paris critics accorded *The Connection* a cold reception. Falb records that of the three plays in repertory at the Odéon (William Carlos Williams's *Many Loves* and Brecht's *In the Jungle of Cities* were the other two), Gelber's *The Connection* "got the most attention and the loudest denunciation" (84). For most of the Parisian critics, says Falb, the play "represented . . . the naturalistic theatre 'dans tout son orgueil, dans toute son absurdité, dans toute sa folie' " (85). By contrast, Italian critics were quite positive in their evaluations of *The Connection* in Rome. The afternoon newspaper *Giornale d'Italia* offered the following: "In Mr. Gelber the effort to discover the link between truth and fantasy, memories and aspirations, and between dreams of an impossible world and the waiting for an impossible salvation reaches a rare clarity" (*New York Times*, 16 June 1961, 29).

Gelber's next play, *The Apple*, was also produced at New York's Living Theatre and like *The Connection* baffled some reviewers. Taubman commented on the way the audience was distracted deliberately by irrelevancies as that audience attempted to catch what Gelber was trying to say (8 December 1961). "Before the play begins," wrote Taubman, "the audience is drawn into the core of the make-believe. And even the make-believe shades over into reality. In the intermission the actors serve you real coffee, potable cider, and edible fortune cookies" (44). In this production, James Earl Jones played the Black Man as other members of the cast played the Jew, the homosexual, the Oriental, the spastic, the prostitute, and the con man. Ritual, phantasmagoria, and improvisation combined to present the drama of the death and resurrection of a silent screen actor. As the actor is restored to life, his acquaintances become more and more insect- or animal-like. Taubman concluded that *The Apple* (the Edenic apple?) added up to "an unconscionable amount of nonsense" (44). The French audience at a Paris performance of the same play by the Living Theatre was caught up in the experimental features, especially the actor-audience intimacy before the opening curtain and during the intermission (*New York Times*, 20 April 1962, 22), but the French critics were not as receptive, finding it "sordid, depressing . . . devoid of any meaningful message" (*New York Times*, 23 April 1962, 33).

Square in the Eye, Gelber's next effort, was presented by the Establishment Theatre Company at the Theatre de Lys and again found Taubman unmoved. This play is about the lack of communication between Ed and Sandy Stone, whose married life is characterized by one quarrel after another. Taubman described *Square in the Eye* as "capricious, circuitous and boring" (20 May 1965, 54) and had little use for Gelber's approach to dramatic freedom, which he said created ambiguity and tedium. A chameleon-like character called Doc (played in the original production by later television star Conrad Bain who played a comic physician in the the situation comedy series "Maude") changes roles within the play (from physician to funeral director to preacher) and makes a sardonic, presumably interesting, impact. But all in all, Taubman was not pleased with the play. Gelber, Taubman wrote, "diffuses his fire over too many targets and his characters shift uneasily between realism and caricature" (6 June 1965, 11).

Gelber continued to look dramatic history and dramatic critics square in the eye and without flinching or blinking conceived *The Cuban Thing*, which opened and very quickly closed, a day later, on Broadway at Henry Miller's Theatre. Barnes spoke of the way Gelber was intending to dramatize the effect of the Cuban revolution on a middle-class, liberal-thinking Havana head of household (Roberto played by Rip Torn) who supports Castro and who instructs his family in the ways of the revolutionary thought. But the intention was not artistically realized, according to Barnes. The play, he wrote, "was flat, stale and unprofitable stuff" (8 October 1976, 36), but he did respond favorably to the acting of Rip Torn and of Maria Tucci as Roberto's daughter, Alicia. But between the shakiness of the dramatic material onstage and the noisy anti-Castro demonstrators outside the theatre, *The Cuban Thing* was not bound to last long. "The characters," said Barnes, "all lacked the life-blood of likelihood" (36). Apparently much more vibrancy came from the anti-Castro demonstrators.

Theatrical experimentation continued with *Sleep*, which appeared at New York's American Place Theatre. This play deals with scientists in a sleep laboratory. Here scientific experimentation and analysis is a metaphor for dramatic exploration. The scientists study a sleeper-dreamer whose dreams produce still other characters in the play. As the scientists look into the psyche of the patient, the fictional dramatic world undergoes psychoanalysis. Barnes found "the concept of the play...a great deal better than the play itself" (25 September 1968, 36), but Stasio explained that the "central device is dramatically sound" and that the "writing is excellent and thematic concerns intriguing" (244). In a helpful article, Gale tells us that the concepts found in Gelber's novel *On Ice* (1964) are, in part, found in *Sleep* (1984, 737).

Two other plays, *Barbary Shore*, an adaptation of Norman Mailer's novel by that name (1974 at the Public/Anspacher Theater in New York), and *Farmyard*, a translation by Gelber and Michael Roloff of the Franz Xaver Kroetz play (1975 at the Yale Theatre in New Haven), have not received critical attention. But *Jack Gelber's New Play: Rehearsal* prompted Barnes to pose the questions that he believes Gelber is asking in this piece: What is a play? How does it happen? What makes it work? (8 October 1976). Gelber's play, which is set in prison and shows the influence of the Attica prison uprisings of the 1970s, is called a rehearsal, but it is not in fact a rehearsal. It is a Pirandellian exploration of the fine line between reality and fiction. According to Sainer, "The play hardly gives us a sense of the forces that go to make up prison society. ... [Nevertheless] Gelber's script and his direction of it evoke a keen sense of humanity under the system's ax of theatre people tearing at each other, often without knowing it, to keep themselves going in this economic jungle" (95).

SURVEY OF SECONDARY SOURCES

Bibliographies

The most recent and complete bibliography is by Gale (1986), who includes about 150 entries, at least two of which are dated as recently as 1986 (in particular, two articles Gelber wrote on Julian Beck). Gale offers astute annotations throughout his bibliography. In addition, a handy checklist for earlier Gelber is in Coleman and Tyler's. *Checklist of Interpretation since 1940 of English and American Plays. Contemporary Literary Criticism* (Gale series) itemizes excerpts from reviews, articles, and book chapters. Also see *Contemporary Authors* and *Twentieth-Century American Dramatists*. Several references to shorter articles on *The Connection* appear in Bonin.

Biographies

Detailed biographical accounts of Jack Gelber can be found in Wilcox and Brandish. Together the result is a full discussion of the life and career of Gelber. Brandish says that Gelber's "dramatic world describes a society that seems to have begun with a mythic expulsion [cf. the title of *The Apple* and *The Fall in the Garden*], a communal and pragmatic place without heroes where man has become his ordinary self and disappointment and death are inevitable" (290). Wilcox concludes that Gelber "still hews to the ideals of his early work: to express the elusive qualities of consciousness, to expand the function and reach of theatrical conventions, and to experiment with nontraditional subject matter" (199). Gelber, according to Bradish, is a "chronicler of the American drama" that makes connections between contemporary theatre and the world it reflects (290). Other biographical statements are in *Critical Survey of Drama, Contemporary Authors*, and the *National Playwrights Directory*. Also see Bermel; "Talk with the Author" (*Newsweek*); and "Young Playwright" (*New Yorker*). Two recollections by Gelber himself on the Living Theatre's

Julian Beck (1925–1985) are important for biographers. Gelber writes (Spring 1986): "Those of us who have some idea of what it takes to keep theatre alive stand in awe of Julian's accomplishments" (11). The second, lengthier recollection (Summer 1986) gives insightful details regarding Beck's role as principal administrator of the Living Theatre, a moving account of the economics of theatre life, and Beck's struggle against enormous odds to keep the Living Theatre alive. He also discusses his own play, *The Connection*, making brief references to *The Apple* (15–17).

Influences

Wilcox points out that Brecht and Pirandello "were Gelber's immediate precursors in their exploration of the relationship between audience and actor, while Gelber's dramatic construction, with its naturalistic surface overlaying poetic drama, owes much to the works of O'Neill, Chekhov, and Strindberg" (196). Gilman adds to this list Beckett and the theme of waiting, which links *Waiting for Godot* and *The Connection*. Gilman admires *The Connection* for its universal impact, but he calls Gelber a "junior Genet" who hardly matches the French playwright in *The Apple*, a play that goes counter to Pirandello's view that to dramatize a chaos does not mean to present it chaotically. *The Apple*, says Gilman, is "almost nothing but chaotic...there is nothing organic, no image, of chaos or anything else" (173). So Pirandello is and is not an influence in Gelber, according to Gilman. More negatively, Lewis speaks of *The Connection* as a "play of dubious merit" (199), *The Apple* as a play that "could not be sustained even by friendly critics" (202), and *The Cuban Thing* as "lost in sterile engagement with new techniques" (202). At the same time, Lewis invokes the names of Pirandello, Beckett, and O'Neill (*The Iceman Cometh* in particular) to specify influences upon Gelber. Jeffrey is somewhat more positive about the Gelber-Genet link, which is considered in detail by Eskin. Itzin, without explicitly indicating a line of influence, says that Gelber in *The Connection* determines the direction of American theater in much the way that Osborne's *Look Back in Anger* (1956) did for British drama. Admitting the heavy influence of Pirandello and Beckett on *The Connection*, Herman points out that "it was nevertheless an original theatrical fomulation that opened new horizons for others" (232). Gelber's own influence might be found in many of the alternate theatre achievements of the 1960s and 1970s. At least three nonliterary influences on Gelber's work need to be noted: that deriving from American jazz, with its pulsating, inventive, controlled freedom, and that from scientific sleep experimentation; and what Herman sees as Gelber's "important use of the film makers" in *The Connection* (232).

General Studies

Gould discusses *The Connection* as a play that prompted audiences into action against drug peddling but says nothing of the value of the play as dramatic art (289). And about *The Apple*, Gould writes that Gelber "failed to live up to the promise of his earlier work" (289). In Bigsby's chapter on the Living Theatre, he offers astute commentary on *The Connection*, a static play with static characters offering "less realistic detail than metaphysical observation" (76). But Bigsby sees a dynamic in the jazz music, "itself a powerful image of the way in which spontaneous individual freedoms can be merged into a form which is generated rather than imposed" (77). If we are seeking affirmation in *The Connection*, we have to explore the music that is part of the drama.

Spiller gives only a few paragraphs on the place of Gelber in American literature since 1945. Reference is made not only to the *Godot*-like theme of waiting in *The Connection* but also to the "zany violence and theatrical horseplay" of *The Apple*, which blasts "every kind of bigotry that stifles human awareness" (1441). Gelber's avant garde theatre, according to Spiller "tells the story of postwar literature even while advancing its frontiers" (1441). This is quite different from the assessment of Köhler, who summarizes Gelber's dramaturgy as follows: "The works of Gelber, their content and form taken together, disintegrate, commit suicide, so to speak, in the opening scene" (185; my translation). Tennessee Williams, Arthur Miller, Eugene O'Neill, and Edward Albee fare much better in this volume. Abel calls Gelber a "talented young playwright" (123) but takes serious issue with *The Connection* and *The Apple*. Abel sees them as confused in their dramatic purpose. The drug addicts of *The Connection*, for example, "are not people who have paid a great price for a great joy; if they were, they would be on a higher level than the audience; they would have a right to be on the stage. They don't have that right, in fact, except that Jack Gelber was cunning enough to put them there. . . . They dominate mainly by being so similar to the people watching them, which means also to you" (124). Abel's book is given over largely to the European tradition from Shakespeare to Beckett; interestingly, the only American dramatist considered is Gelber. Gale (*Critical Survey of Drama*) analyzes in detail *The Connection* (2:739–42), offering also succinct commentaries on *The Apple* (742–43) and *Square in the Eye* (743–45).

Analyses of Individual Plays

One study that focuses attention on a single play of Gelber is Kostelanetz's analysis that is useful in itself and particularly in tandem with Bigsby's comments (3:77–78). For Eskin, Gelber shares the critical stage with Genet, but *The Connection* again receives individual attention. The primary focus here is the self-conscious theatricality that finds characters engaged in significant role playing (219).

FUTURE RESEARCH OPPORTUNITIES

The dearth of studies concentrating on Gelber reveals a need to assess his position in contemporary American drama. For the most part, response to Gelber has been negative, but he does have his defenders, and even his harshest critics speak of his talent for dramatic writing. Where does Gelber fit in among the Rabes and Mamets and Albees? His place in American dramatic history is assured on the basis of one play, *The Connection*, but an evaluation has to be done of all of his work of the 1960s and 1970s. Critical reassessment should include his dramatic work as the subject matter for new theoretical approaches. Cultural poetics would address instructively Gelber's dramatic interest in and use of American jazz. Even a technical semiotic study of his plays may prove quite useful, as would feminist or deconstructionist readings. Indeed Jack Gelber, the playwright who has said much about the fault lines of society and human relationships, may be viewed and studied as one of America's dramatic deconstructionists.

SECONDARY SOURCES

Abel, Lionel. *Metatheatre: A New View of Dramatic Form*. New York: Hill & Wang, 1963.

Alden, Robert. "*Apple* Disliked by Paris Critics." *New York Times* (23 April 1962): 33.

Atkinson, Brooks. "Theatre Review." *New York Times* (7 February 1960): 11.

Barnes, Clive. "*The Cuban Thing:* A Play by Jack Gelber." *New York Times* (25 September 1968): 36.

———. "Gelber's *Rehearsal*, A Play within a Play." *New York Times* (8 October 1976): C4.

Bermel, Albert. "Jack Gelber Talks about Survival in the Theatre." *Theatre* 9 (1978): 46–58.

Bigsby, C. W. E. *Critical Introduction to Twentieth-Century American Drama*. 3 vols. Cambridge: Cambridge University Press, 1985.

Bonin, Jane F. *Prize-Winning American Drama*. Metuchen, N.J.: Scarecrow, 1973.

Brandish, Gaynor F. "Jack Gelber." In *Contemporary Dramatists*, 4th ed., pp. 188–89. Edited by D. L. Kirkpatrick. Chicago: St. James Press, 1988.

Calta, Louis. "*Connection* Offered in Premiere Here." *New York Times* (16 July 1959): 30.

Coleman, Arthur and Gary R. Tyler, eds. *Drama Criticism*. Vol. 1: *A Checklist of Interpretation since 1940 of English and American Plays*. Denver: Swallow, 1966.

"*Connection* Booed at London Opening." *New York Times* (23 February 1961): 30.

Contemporary Authors. Edited by Ann Evory. Detroit: Gale, 1981.

Eskin, Stanley G. "Theatricality in the *Avant-Garde* Drama: A Reconsideration of a Theme in the Light of *The Balcony* and *The Connection*." *Modern Drama* 7 (1964): 213–22.

Falb, Lewis. *American Drama in Paris, 1945–1970*. Chapel Hill: University of North Carolina Press, 1973.

Gale, Steven H. "Jack Gelber: An Annotated Bibliography." *Bulletin of Bibliography* 44 (1987): 102–10.

———. "Jack Gelber." In *Critical Survey of Drama*. British and American Authors. Ed. Walton Beacham. 6 vols. Pasadena, Calif.: Salem, 1984. 2: 737–46.

"Gelber's *Apple* Hailed by Paris." *New York Times* (20 April 1962): 22.

Gilman, Richard. *Common and Uncommon Masks: Writings on Theatre, 1961–1970*. New York: Random House, 1971.

Gould, Jean. *Modern American Playwrights*. New York: Dodd, Mead, 1966.

Herman, William. *Understanding Contemporary American Drama*. Columbia: University of South Carolina Press, 1987.

Itzin, Catherine. *Plays and Players* (October 1974): 41.

Jeffrey, David K. "Genet and Gelber: Studies in Addiction." *Modern Drama* 7 (1964): 213–22.

Köhler, Klaus. "Das 'Underground Theatre.'" In *Studien zum Amerikanischen Drama nach dem Zweiten Weltkrieg*. Edited by Eberhard Bruning, Köhler, and Bernhard Scheller. Berlin: Rutten & Loening, 1977.

Kostelanetz, Richard C. "*The Connection:* Heroin as Existential Choice." *Texas Quarterly* 5 (1962): 159–62.

Lewis, Allan. *American Plays and Playwrights of the Contemporary Theatre*. New York: Crown, 1970.

National Playwrights Directory. Edited by Phyllis Johnson Kaye. 2d ed. Detroit: Gale, 1981.

"Rome Is Receptive to Living Theatre." *New York Times* (16 June 1961): 29.

Sainer, Arthur. "Gelber Revisits the Survival Junkies." *Village Voice* (25 October 1976): 95.

Spiller, Robert E. et al., eds. *Literary History of the United States*. New York: Macmillan, 1974.

Stasio, Marilyn. "Jack Gelber." In *Contemporary Authors*, 2: 244. Edited by Ann Evory. Detroit: Gale, 1981.

"Talk with the Author." *Newsweek* 58 (18 December 1961): 72.

Taubman, Howard. "Judith Malina Directs Experimental Work." *New York Times* (8 December 1961): 4.

———. "*Square in the Eye* Is Offered at the de Lys." *New York Times* (20 May 1965): 54.

———. "Theatre Reviews." *New York Times* (6 June 1965): 11.

Twentieth-Century American Dramatists. Vol. 7. Edited by John MacNicholas. Detroit: Gale, 1981.

Wilcox, Agnes. "Jack Gelber." In *Twentieth-Century American Dramatists*, pt. 1. Edited by John MacNicholas. Detroit: Gale, 1981.

"Young Playwright." *New Yorker* 36 (9 July 1960): 24–25.

Charles Gordone

(12 OCTOBER 1925–   )

SUSAN HARRIS SMITH

ASSESSMENT OF GORDONE'S REPUTATION

The first black playwright to win a Pulitzer Prize, Charles Gordone, an actor and director, rose to brief prominence because of *No Place to Be Somebody*, which not only was awarded the Pulitzer in 1970 but was also the first off-Broadway play to be so honored. Repeatedly eschewing the label of "black" playwright, Gordone became controversial by holding firmly to his belief that his work is universal. "I write out of an American experience," he explained in an interview in *Contemporary Authors*; "I don't write out of a black or white experience; it's American" (85). Not only did Gordone confound many of the critics by refusing to be merely black, he also annoyed them by challenging a basic assumption about categories of drama: "I do believe there has never been such a thing as 'black theater' " ("Yes, I Am a Black Playwright, But . . . " 1).

PRIMARY BIBLIOGRAPHY OF GORDONE'S WORKS

Plays

A Little More Light Around the Place. Unpublished. 1964. Produced in 1964 at the Sheridan Square Playhouse, New York. Adaptation of Stanley Easton's novel.

No Place to Be Somebody: A Black-Black Comedy. 1967. Produced 4 May 1969, Shakespeare Festival Public Theatre. Indianapolis: Bobbs-Merrill, 1969.

Worl's Champeen Lip Dansuh an' Wahtah Mellon Jooglah. Unpublished. 1969.

Gordone Is a Muthah. 1970. Produced 8 May 1970, Carnegie Recital Hall, New York. In *Best Short Plays of 1973*. Edited by Stanley Richards. Philadelphia: Chilton Press, 1973.

Baba Chops. Unpublished. 1974. Produced 26 July 1974, Wilshire Ebell Theatre, Los Angeles.

The Last Chord. Unpublished. 1976. Produced May 1976, Billie Holiday Theatre.
A Qualification for Anabiosis. Unpublished. 1978. Produced at the Ensemble Studio's Theatre Marathon '78. Revised as *Anabiosis.* Unpublished. 1979. Produced 9 March 1979, City Players, St. Louis, Missouri.
Mamzel Jolie. Unpublished. 1982. Produced in 1982 by the American Stage, Berkeley, California. Adaptation of Strindberg's *Miss Julie.*
Roan Brown and Cherry. Unpublished. 1985. Produced 2 March 1985, Live Oak Theatre, Berkeley, California.

Screenplays

No Place to Be Somebody. 1972.
From These Ashes. 1965.
The W.A.S.P. Adaptation of Julius Horowitz's novel.
Liliom. Adaptation.
Under The Boardwalk. 1976. Stage version produced 1979 by City Players, St. Louis, Missouri.

Interviews

"A Quiet Talk with Myself." *Esquire* 73 (January 1970): 78–81, 174.
"Yes, I Am a Black Playwright, But..." *New York Times* (25 January 1970): B1, B11.
Kroll, Jack. "From the Muthah Lode." *Newsweek* 75 (25 May 1970): 95.
"Beyond the Pulitzer: An Interview with Charles Gordone." *Sepia* (February 1971): 14–17.
Ross, Jean W. *Contemporary Authors,* 93–96: 184–87. Edited by Frances C. Lochar. Detroit: Gale, 1980.
Glackin, William. "Gordone's Search for Self Filled Time between Plays." *Sacramento Bee* (10 March 1985): 2:1, 5.
Arkatov, Janice. "Gordone's Win, 'Place,' and Shows." *Los Angeles Times* (17 July 1987): Calendar: 1, 21.
Smith, Susan Harris. "An Interview with Charles Gordone." *Studies in American Drama, 1945-Present* 3 (1988): 123–24.

PRODUCTION HISTORY

Not surprisingly, *No Place to Be Somebody* is Gordone's most produced and most reviewed work; translated into Spanish, Russian, French, and German, it continues to be produced throughout the world. Originally it opened at the Sheridan Square Playhouse in 1967, was picked up for Joseph Papp's workshop, The Other Stage, in May 1969, moved to the larger New York Shakespeare Festival's Public Theatre, and then to the ANTA Theater in December 1969 and, finally to the Promenade Theater early in 1970. In all, there were 903 off-Broadway performances. The play made regional tours with three companies and then was revised and revived in 1971 in a production directed by Gordone at the Morosco Theatre on Broadway. The most recent revival (July 1987) at Actors for

Themselves in Los Angeles opened to good reviews that attest to the relevant timelessness of *No Place to Be Somebody*.

The reviewers' reception of the first version of *No Place to Be Somebody* ranged from Kerr's paean to Gordone as "the most astonishing new American playwright to come along since Edward Albee" (1) to Wetzsteon's condemnation of the work as a "huge, sprawling, shapeless mess of a play slopped all over the stage with appalling carelessness" (41). Riley blamed producer Papp for an unedited, shabby presentation and director Ted Cornell for a confused and slothful production. *Playboy* found it "ill-kempt and in need of editing" (35), and Simon characterized it as a "typical protest play" which would have gone unnoticed had it been written by a white dramatist (203). That *No Place to Be Somebody*, a play "of small worth," should have been given the Pulitzer was, for Kauffmann, proof of the bankruptcy of the prize and an example of "reverse Uncle-Tomming" (12).

Those who liked the play were more cautious than the effusive Kerr. Gill found the "eloquent" and "rough" work to be the most interesting play of the year (64). Lewis hailed it as a play of social as well as dramatic significance. Atkinson praised the "lyricism and fury" and the fact that it was not just a black play but a play about life (287). Like so many of the other critics, Watts cited the affinities with O'Neill's and Saroyan's barroom plays.

For those with mixed responses, the major problem was the lengthy and melodramatic form, which hampered a promising playwright. O'Connor credited Gordone for struggling beyond the clichés of racial relations but, like several other reviewers, did not like the "30's-movies surface." The reviewer for *Time*, Edith Oliver, and "Humm" at *Variety* found the play to be too long but praised the tough humor. For Hewes, the acting elevated the essential despair of the piece above its "melodramatic crudities" (31 May 1969, 18). Rudin hedged a bit by calling *No Place to Be Somebody* "the most notable Negro play of the season" and found it to be disarmingly powerful despite its rambling longwindedness (587).

Of the revisions Gordone made to *No Place to Be Somebody* for the ANTA and Morosco productions, Kraus complained that the play was "literally ruined by the 'improvements' " (132), but most reviewers such as Barnes and Gussow preferred the less self-indulgent version, which they agreed had grown in raw energy. Hewes felt that the rewritten role of a dream character, in particular, brought the play closer to its symbolic objective (28).

SURVEY OF SECONDARY SOURCES

Bibliographies

No definitive or comprehensive bibliography exists for Gordone. Furthermore, all material should be approached with this caveat: reference material compiled by both Ross and by Arata and Rotoli seem to have conflated some works of Charles Gordone (b. 1925) with Charles Gordon ([Oyamo] b. 1943), and the results are confusing and misleading. Sketchy primary bibliographical material can be found in standard reference works such as the *National Playwrights Directory* and *Black Playwrights 1823–1977*. The most complete guide to secondary material can be had by combining the information in Arata and Rotoli's *Black American Playwrights, 1800 to the Present* and *More Black American Playwrights*. Keyssar-Franke's Afro-American checklist is useful, if less complete than Arata and Rotoli's. Washington's dissertation contains the most extensive bibliography of theatrical reviews.

Biographies

The scant biographical information on Gordone can be found primarily in two articles, one in *Crisis* that discusses his youth and religious background, and the other in his own piece for *Esquire*, which provides his political views on racial tension. The citation in *Twentieth-Century Dramatists* provides general information about his career as an actor and director. Basic biographical details are supplied in *Black American Writers: Past and Present*, *Who's Who in the Theatre*, and *Contemporary Dramatists*.

Influences

There is no formal study of influences on Gordone who himself is adamant about resisting any influences. The only thing Gordone will say is that he was writing *No Place* in the early 1960s while he was acting in Jean Genet's *The Blacks* and that he was influenced by Genet. Otherwise he is trying to find his own style (personal conversation, 10 May 1988). Yet despite Gordone's protestations, Keyssar succinctly lists a number of likely sources for *No Place*, including O'Neill (*The Iceman Cometh*), Gorky, Williams, Bullins, Baraka, and even Hawthorne ("Charles Gordone," 200–201).

General Studies

No general study of Gordone exists, and all critical appraisals concern *No Place to Be Somebody*. The absence of even a mention of Gordone in dozens of basic critical and scholarly surveys of modern black drama suggests an antipathy toward him perhaps caused by his own disinclination to be narrowly labeled as "black." As a consequence, Gordone is absent not only from many works on American drama in general but from many works on black drama as well.

This problem is central to Williams's placement of Gordone as "one voice opposed to the basic tenet of the Black Theatre Movement—that the Black experience is a singular and unique phenomenon" (124). In many instances, Gordone receives only passing notice, such as the one in Bigsby's history of American drama in which *No Place to Be Somebody* is merely cited as "unconventional" (26). Some critics, such as Bonin and Archer, do little more than note themes or summarize the plot. Others, such as Scott and Johnson, simply refer to the play as one of many in the late 1960s forcefully expressing a yearning for social equality.

Studies of *No Place to Be Somebody*

The critical opinions of *No Place to Be Somebody* are as divided as the reviewers' assessments. Although Washington's analysis of the critics' evaluations of the play implies a white, racist bias against it, this is not the case. In fact, several black critics are upset by the ideological implications of Gordone's characterization of blacks. More often than not, however, the critical judgments have more to do with the melodramatic and uneven structure of the play and its disillusioned message than with specific racial implications.

The most important study of *No Place to Be Somebody*, Taeni's ambitious article (in German), analyzes the disgruntled critical responses to Gordone and boldly attempts to reconcile him with the black arts movement. Invoking Marcuse, Brecht, and Larry Neal, Taeni presses to make sense of the Gordonian paradox that a black playwright writing a play about the black experience has written a mainstream, Saroyanesque melodrama lacking a revolutionary, agitative spirit. First, Taeni, somewhat apologetically, sets up Gordone as a psychological realist concerned with the disfiguring disease of capitalism as it affects both races. Second (and here he is on shakier ground), Taeni argues that Gordone really is in the forefront of the black liberation movement because of the style, not the substance, of the play. Arguing that there is a surreal, epic, and moralistic structure that frames wholly symbolic action, Taeni suggests that ultimately the play is a liberating ritual in which the suicide heralds new life for blacks.

None of the other critics who deal with Gordone even begins to address the major dramaturgical, historical, or critical issues that Taeni tackles so provocatively. Oliver praises *No Place to Be Somebody* as an exemplary melodrama in an extended analysis that also stresses the metaphorical structure of the play. Carter-Harrison, on the other hand, finds the melodrama "unpardonable" and faults Gordone's dramaturgy as shifting "from realism to surrealism" and as suffering from a lack of clear focus (172). He blames Gordone for abandoning his "African sensibility" in lieu of "a confused network of sociological imperatives" (229–30). Fabre judges the play a failure, criticizing it for the mixed modes that result in a "diminished plausibility" (116). The nonillusionistic, fragmented structure, however, is, for Adler, an effective dramatic pattern that repeats the action of Albee's *The Zoo Story*.

The theme draws as much mixed response as the structure. Largely a plot summary, Hughes's assessment of Gordone's play as powerful and lacerating echoes Kerr's in that she faults the eulogistic epilogue for a false tone that fails to jibe with the vital, ironic humor that precedes it. Lee places *No Place to Be Somebody* in "one of a long line of Black works which speak to the problems of relationship and identity through analogous metaphors of inaudibility, invisibility, and anonymity" (402). In a similar vein, Curb, in her examination of the American dream, aligns Gordone with other black American playwrights such as Lorraine Hansberry, Lonne Elder, and Amiri Baraka (LeRoi Jones) who dramatize the tragic consequences of racial discrimination.

Several other critics also see *No Place to Be Somebody* as a generic complaint play characteristic of the period. Record hails Gordone's play as an example of the new freedom black writers were feeling in the late 1960s to express the seamy side of black life. Allan Lewis echoes this opinion, suggesting that *No Place to Be Somebody* is most representative of the work of the new black playwrights who replaced revolutionary zeal with an exposé of social illness. Less content with this new perspective, Turner, in a study of traditional black drama, finds much of *No Place to Be Somebody* to be "a mockery of the Black people and Black dreams" and controversial and unsatisfactory because it does not offer any social solution except escape (96).

Two critics have examined Gordone's language. Walcott reads *No Place to Be Somebody* through the prologue to Ralph Ellison's *The Invisible Man*; in his thorough analysis, he sees Gabe, the protagonist, as a conscious stylist who examines his life through an ahistorical dialectic, through the word and the blues, an exercise doomed to failure. Hatch makes only passing references to Gordone's use of rap and dialect in both his articles.

The most controversial reading of *No Place to Be Somebody* is Clayborne's insistence that Gordone has an implicit homosexual theme that portrays "gays as emasculated dupes" (383). Williams is the only critic to consider the black humor of *No Place to Be Somebody*; he argues that it is based on a "metaphysical incongruity between station and aspiration" (126).

FUTURE RESEARCH OPPORTUNITIES

Clearly Gordone is a neglected playwright ripe for study; he needs everything from a reliable and comprehensive bibliography to a thoughtful analysis of all his writing. Although a number of critics refer to the resemblances between Gordone and Miller, Saroyan, O'Neill, and Albee, influences Gordone readily admits to in "Yes, I Am a Black Playwright, But..." no thorough comparison has been done placing Gordone in the tradition of American plays about spiritual isolation. Furthermore no one has followed up on Genet's profound impact on Gordone, who repeatedly claims that his life was changed by acting in the original off-Broadway and subsequent touring company productions of *The Blacks*. With the exception of such short reviews as those by Gussow on *Gordone Is a Muthah* and *The Last Chord* (Theater), virtually nothing has been written about Gordone's other work.

SECONDARY SOURCES

Adler, Thomas P. *Mirror on the Stage*. West Lafayette, Ind.: Purdue University Press, 1987.

Arata, Esther S., and Nicholas J. Rotoli. *Black American Playwrights, 1800 to the Present: A Bibliography*. Metuchen, N.J.: Scarecrow Press, 1976.

———. *More Black American Playwrights: A Bibliography*. Metuchen, N.J.: Scarecrow Press, 1978.

Archer, Leonard C. *Black Images in the American Theatre*. Brooklyn, N.Y.: Poseidon, 1973.

Atkinson, Brooks. "Charles Gordone: *No Place to Be Somebody*." In *The Lively Years*, pp. 286–89. New York: Association Press, 1973.

Barnes, Clive. Review of *No Place to Be Somebody*. *New York Times* (10 September 1971): 1: 43.

Bigsby, C. W. E. *A Critical Introduction to Twentieth-Century American Drama*, 3: 26. Cambridge: Cambridge University Press, 1985.

"Black Pulitzer Prize Awardees." *Crisis* 77 (May 1970): 186–88.

Bonin, Jane F. *Major Themes in Prize-Winning American Drama*. Metuchen, N.J.: Scarecrow Press, 1975.

———. *Prize-Winning American Drama*. Metuchen, N.J.: Scarecrow Press, 1973.

Carter-Harrison, Paul. *The Drama of Nommo*. New York: Grove Press, 1972.

Clayborne, Jon L. "Modern Black Drama and the Gay Image." *College English* 36 (November 1974): 381–84.

Curb, Rosemary Keefe. "The Idea of the American Dream in Afro-American Plays of the Nineteen-Sixties." Ph.D. dissertation, University of Alabama, 1977.

Fabre, Geneviève, *Drumbeats, Masks, and Metaphor*. Translated by Melvin Dixon Cambridge: Harvard University Press, 1983.

Garland, Phyl. "Prize Winners." *Ebony* 25 (July 1970): 29–32, 36–37.

Gill, Brendan. "Last of the Red Hot Theories." *New Yorker* 45 (10 January 1970): 64–65.

Gussow, Mel. "The Last Chord." *New York Times* (18 May 1976): A39.

———. Review of *No Place to Be Somebody*. *New York Times* (31 December 1969): 1: 17.

———. "Theater: An Evening with Gordone." *New York Times* (10 May 1970): 72.

Hatch, James V. "Speak to Me in Those Old Words, You Know, Those La-La

Words, Those Tong-Tong Sounds (Some African Influences on the Afro-American Theatre)." *Yale/Theatre* 8 (Fall 1976): 31, 33.

———. "A White Folks Guide to 200 Years of Black and White Drama." *Drama Review* 16 (December 1976): 8, 11.

———, and Omanii Abdullah, eds. *Black Playwrights, 1823–1977: An Annotated Bibliography of Plays*. New York: R. R. Bowker Company, 1977.

Herbert, Ian, ed. *Who's Who in the Theatre*, 1:267–68. 17th ed. Detroit: Gale Research Company, 1981.

Hewes, Henry. "The Theater." *Saturday Review* 52 (31 May 1969): 18.

———. "The Theater." *Saturday Review* 53 (14 February 1970): 30.

———. "The Theater." *Saturday Review* 53 (17 January 1970): 28.

Hughes, Catharine. *Plays, Politics, and Polemics*. New York: Drama Book Specialists, 1973.

"Humm." Review of *No Place to Be Somebody. Variety* (28 May 1969): 72.

Johnson, Helen Armstead. "Black Influences in the American Theatre: Part II, 1960 and After." In *The Black American Reference Book*, p. 708. Edited by M. Smythe. Englewood Cliffs, N.J.: Prentice-Hall, 1976.

Kauffmann, Stanley. *Persons of the Drama*. New York: Harper & Row, 1976.

Kaye, Phyllis Johnson, ed. *National Playwrights Directory*. 2d ed. Waterford, Conn.: Eugene O'Neill Theatre Centre, 1981.

Kerr, Walter. Review of *No Place to be Somebody. New York Times* (18 May 1969): B1. Reprinted in *God on the Gymnasium Floor*, pp. 210–13. New York: Simon and Schuster, 1970.

Keyssar, Helene. "Charles Gordone." *Contemporary Dramatists*. Fourth Edition, pp. 200–201. Edited by D. L. Kirkpatrick. Chicago: St. James Press, 1988.

Keyssar-Franke, Helene. "Afro-American Drama and Its Criticism, 1960–1972: An Annotated Check List with Appendices." *Bulletin of the New York Public Library* 78 (Spring 1975): 276–346.

Kraus, Ted M. "Theatre East." *Players* 47 (February-March 1972): 132.

Lee, Dorothy. "Three Black Plays: Alienation and Paths to Recovery." *Modern Drama* 19 (December 1976): 397–409.

Lewis, Allan. *The Contemporary Theatre: The Significant Playwrights of Our Time*. New York: Crown, 1971.

Lewis, Theophilus. Review of *No Place to be Somebody. Time* (6 September 1969): 144–45.

"New Plays: Bar Stool in a Black Hell." *America* (6 September 1969): 145–46.

O'Connor, John J. "The Theater: On the 'Charley Fever.'" *Wall Street Journal* (6 May 1969). Reprinted in *New York Theatre Critics' Reviews* (1969): 266–67.

Oliver, C. F. "Charles Gordone." In *Contemporary Black Drama*, pp. 383–93. Edited by C. F. Oliver and Stephanie Sills. New York: Charles Scribner's Sons, 1971.

Oliver, Edith. "A Good Place to Be." *New Yorker* 44 (17 May 1969): 112, 114.

"Playboy after Hours: Theater." *Playboy* 16 (August 1969): 34–35.

Record, Wilson. "The Negro Writer and the Communist Party." In *The Black American Writer*, 1:227. Edited by C. W. E. Bigsby. Deland, Fl.: Everett Edwards, 1969.

Riley, Clayton. Review of *No Place to Be Somebody. New York Times* (18 May 1969): B22.

Ross, Jean W. *Twentieth Century American Dramatists*, 1:227-31. Edited by John MacNichols. Detroit: Gale Research Company, 1981.

Rudin, Seymour. "Theatre Chronicle: Winter-Spring 1969." *Massachusetts Review* 10 (Summer 1969): 583–93.

Rush, Theressa Gunnels, Carol Fairbanks Meyers, and Esther Spring Arata, eds. *Black American Writers: Past and Present*. Metuchen, N.J.: Scarecrow Press, 1975.

Scott, John. "Teaching Black Drama." *Players* 47 (February-March 1972): 131.

Simon, John. "Underwriting, Overreaching." *New York* (9 June 1969): 56. Reprinted in *Uneasy Stages: A Chronicle of the New York Theater 1963–1973*. New York: Random House, 1976.

Taeni, Rainer. "Gordone: *No Place to Be Somebody*." In *Das amerikanische Drama*, pp. 319–38. Edited by Paul Goetsch. Dusseldorf: August Bagel Verlag, 1974.

Turner, Darwin. "Visions of Love and Manliness in a Blackening World: Dramas of Black Life from 1953–1960." *Iowa Review* 6, no. 2 (1975): 82–99.

Vinson, James, ed. *Contemporary Dramatists*. 3d ed. New York: St. Martin's, 1982.

Walcott, Ronald. "Some Notes on the Blues Style and Space." *Black World* 22 (December 1972): 4–29.

Washington, Rhonnie Lynn. "The Relationship between the White Critic and the Black Theatre from 1959–1969." Ph.D. dissertation, University of Michigan, 1983.

Watts, Richard Jr. "Second Best New American Play." *New York Post* (7 June 1969). Reprinted in *New York Theatre Critics' Reviews* (1969): 265.

Wetzsteon, Ross. "Theatre Journal." *Village Voice* (22 May 1969): 41.

Williams, Mance. *Black Theatre in the 1960's and 1970's: A Historical-Critical Analysis of the Movement*. Westport, Conn.: Greenwood, 1985.

John Guare
(5 FEBRUARY 1938–   )

DON B. WILMETH

ASSESSMENT OF GUARE'S REPUTATION

With the release in 1981 of the critically acclaimed film *Atlantic City*, for which Guare wrote the screenplay, the productions in 1982 of his *Lydie Breeze* and *Gardenia*, the first two plays in a projected tetralogy, and the highly successful revival in 1986 of *The House of Blue Leaves*, John Guare is no longer simply one of America's most promising young playwrights, a phrase identified with him for over a decade. In 1982 Markus called Guare "one of the most successful American playwrights to forge to the front of the public's attention since Edward Albee," tagging him a "witty, exuberant, and perceptive playwright" (331). Miller has pointed out that Guare has established himself as an "adventurous, critically acclaimed playwright" despite frequent commercial failures (427).

Guare, who has been termed a "high-risk playwright" by critic Walter Kerr (quoted in Wakeman, 325), has produced about twenty plays, most of which have been classified as savage farce (an alliance of Feydeau and Strindberg), a kind of melodrama pulled into farcical structures by the energy of his wit, although recent work suggests a new direction toward a more tragic outlook. On the other hand, one critic suggests that in *Lydie Breeze*, Guare, "the Jackson Pollock of playwrights" (Wetzsteon, *New York*, 35), has reached the culmination of his career with "an artful assimilation of all his influences, the long-searched-for resolution of all his themes" (37). Critical comment has centered on his grotesque wit and his rich language (Guare believes the theatre is the last refuge for poetry), though some critics find him "diffuse and self-indulgent" (Cohn, *New American Dramatist*, 39) and believe his plays are "overwritten and dialogue pivots on the banal" (Marranca and Dasgupta, 52). All recognize his satiric vivacity, vital theatricality, and bizarre characters (often at the expense of credibility), frequently of the middle class showing their vacant inner lives and expressing "their anguish through senseless violence or festering hate" (Marranca and Dasgupta, 41). Frankly autobiographical, Guare's plays, most often based on the realities of contemporary life, are built around colliding ideas, plots concerned with family relationships, and the individual's consuming desire for success.

Guare's work has been honored in many ways, beginning with an Obie for *Muzeeka* in 1968. In 1968–1969, he was named the most promising playwright in *Variety*'s poll of New York drama critics for *Cop-Out*. *The House of Blue Leaves* won both an Obie and the New York Drama Critics Circle Award for the Best American Play, 1970–1971. The following year *Two Gentlemen of Verona* was awarded the Tony and the New York Drama Critics Circle awards for best muscial, the Tony for best book of a musical, and the Drama Desk Award for best lyrics and book, and the Variety poll for best lyricist. In 1977 he was the recipient of a Joseph Jefferson Award for playwrighting and in 1981 received an Award of Merit from the American Academy and Institute of Arts and Letters. *Atlantic City*, though not winning an Academy Award for Guare's screenplay, did receive a number of honors for Guare's effort, including best screenplay by the National Society of Film Critics, the Los Angeles Film Critics Society, and the New York Film Critics Circle. Guare received Rockefeller Grants in 1968 and 1977.

PRIMARY BIBLIOGRAPHY OF GUARE'S WORKS

Theatre Girl (produced 1959).
The Toadstool Boy (produced 1960).
Did You Write My Name in the Snow (produced 1963).
To Wally Pantoni, We Leave a Credenza (produced 1965).
The Loveliest Afternoon of the Year and *Something I'll Tell You Tuesday*. New York: Dramatists Play Service, 1968.
Muzeeka. New York: Dramatists Play Service, 1968.
Cop-Out and *Home Fires*. New York: Samuel French, 1968.
Muzeeka and Other Plays (*Cop-Out* and *Home Fires*). New York: Grove Press, 1970.
Muzeeka. In *Showcase 1: Plays from the Eugene O'Neill Foundation*. Edited by John Lahr. New York: Grove Press, 1970.
Muzeeka and *Cop-Out*. In *Off-Broadway Plays*. Vol. 1. London: Penguin, 1970.
A Day for Surprises. In *Best Short Plays of 1970*. Edited by Stanley Richards. Philadelphia: Chilton, 1970.
Kissing Sweet and *A Day for Surprises*. New York: Dramatists Play Service, 1971.
Taking Off (with Milos Foreman) New York: New American Library, 1971.
The Loveliest Afternoon of the Year and *Something I'll Tell You Tuesday*. In *The Off Off Broadway Book*. Edited by Albert Poland and Bruce Mailman. Indianapolis: Bobbs-Merrill, 1972.
The House of Blue Leaves. New York: Samuel French, 1971.
The House of Blue Leaves (excerpts). In *Best Plays of 1970–1971*. Edited by Otis L. Guernsey, Jr. New York: Dodd, Mead, 1971.

Two Gentlemen of Verona. Music by Galt MacDermot and lyrics by Guare. New
    York: Tams Witmark, 1971.
The House of Blue Leaves. New York: Viking Press, 1972.
"Playwrights on Playwriting." *Dramatists Guild Quarterly* 9 (Summer 1972): 6–10.
    Reprinted as "From Atlantic Beach to Broadway: A Playwright Grows in
    New York." In *Playwrights, Lyricists, Composers on Theatre*. Edited by Otis
    L. Guernsey, Jr. New York: Dodd, Mead, 1974.
Two Gentlemen of Verona (with Mel Shapiro). New York: Holt, Rinehart & Winston,
    1973.
Rich and Famous. New York: Dramatists Play Service, 1977.
Marco Polo Sings a Solo. New York: Dramatists Play Service, 1977.
Landscape of the Body. New York: Dramatists Play Service, 1978.
Introduction to *Ibsen's Notebooks*. New York: Da Capo Press, 1979.
Bosoms and Neglect. New York: Dramatists Play Service, 1980.
In Fireworks Lie Secret Codes. New York: Dramatists Play Service, 1981.
Gardenia. New York: Dramatists Play Service, 1982.
Lydie Breeze. New York: Dramatists Play Service, 1982.
Three Exposures: House of Blue Leaves, Landscape of the Body, and Bosoms and Neglect.
    Foreword by Louis Malle. San Diego: Harcourt Brace Jovanovich, 1982.
The Talking Dog. In *Orchards: Seven Stories by Anton Chekhov and Seven Plays They
    Have Inspired*. New York: Alfred Knopf, 1986.
*The House of Blue Leaves and Two Other Plays: Landscape of the Body, Bosoms and
    Neglect*. New York: NAL Penguin, 1987.
" 'Living in that Dark Room': The Playwright and His Audience" (Guare inter-
    viewed by John Harrop). *New Theatre Quarterly* 10 (May 1987): 155–59.
In Their Own Words. Contemporary American Playwrights. Interviews by David Sa-
    vran. New York: Theatre Communications Group, 1987, pp. 84–99.

PRODUCTION HISTORY

Guare is undeniably a product of the off-Broadway of the 1960s. With
the exception of four productions, two transferred to Broadway from
off-Broadway and two having had runs under eight performances, he
has not been a mainstream playwright. His first play of note, *Did You
Write My Name in the Snow?* was staged at Yale while he was a student at
the Drama School. In 1964, back in his native New York, his one-act *To
Wally Pantoni, We Leave a Credenza* was presented by the New Dramatists
Workshop, followed in October 1966 by a double bill of *The Loveliest
Afternoon of the Year* and *Something I'll Tell You Tuesday* at the Caffe Cino
in New York. *Muzeeka*, Guare's premiere success, was first seen at the
Mark Taper Forum in 1967 and in 1968 at New York's Provincetown
Playhouse. This was also his first play seen in London, at the Open Space
in February 1969. His one-acts *Cop-Out* and *Home Fires* were seen briefly
on Broadway at the Cort Theatre in 1969, closing after seven performances. Other than noting good performances by Linda Lavin and Ron

Leibman, the critics, including Barnes, Gill, Chapman, Gottfried, and Kerr, soundly attacked the plays.

The year 1971 was a banner one for Guare, for twin successes finally established his reputation. The musical version of *Two Gentlemen of Verona*, adapted by Guare and Mel Shapiro with music by Galt MacDermot, was produced by the New York Shakespeare Festival (Delacorte Theatre, 22 July, transferred to the St. James, 1 December 1971), and *The House of Blue Leaves* opened 10 February at the Truck and Warehouse Theatre in the East Village.

Blue Leaves, termed by the *New York Time*'s Kerr "the most striking new American play of the season" (B3), received mostly positive reviews, although Novick some weeks after its opening concluded that "the farce and the agony seem to violate instead of reinforcing each other" (B9). Barnes, however, although he found faults ("a straggling but lovely play"), commented on the "chillingly and accurately depressing setting" by Karl Eigsti and the "fliply crisp staging" by Mel Shapiro, Guare's favorite director over the years (11 February 1971, 54). Hewes was well aware of one of Guare's repeating themes when he noted that, in Artie, Guare had personified "the American dream of success and the destructive forces unleashed by the frustration of never achieving it" ("Under the Rainbow," 10). Performances by Harold Gould, Anne Meara, and Katherine Helmond received strong notices, clearly affecting the impressions summarized by the critics, most notably Davis, Watts, and Gottfried, although Clurman found Gould as Artie and Helmond as Bananas miscast, creating the effect of a "psychological" drama. He was also distressed by the literal replica of a grubby apartment, whereas the "background for such a play demands some manner of humorous stylization" (286). Gottfried represents the typical critical conclusion when he wrote: "Guare remains a playwright with a powerful personal vision and a vivid sense of theatre. If he could only get it all together" (355).

The 1986 revival of *The House of Blue Leaves* gave Guare renewed recognition. The play was no longer seen as a formless, unfinished work but a play that "becomes even better with time," as Gussow noted, adding that Jerry Zaks's production with John Mahoney, Stockard Channing, and Swoosie Kurtz at Lincoln Center "remains a joyful affirmation of life—and of Mr. Guare's artistry" (6 April 1986, 3). Rich found that the tone of the play had shifted and that Guare's "characters and themes have gained the weight and gravity so lacking in his more pretentious recent plays" (20 March 1986), and Oliver agreed that the play now seemed "deeper, sadder, more passionate, and even funnier" (31 March 1986, 66). Outstanding in this revival was the wonderful performance by Kurtz as Bananas, called "a metaphor for the state of all the characters" in Henry's review. Also notable in this revival were the physical trappings. Wilson commented on Tony Walton's set, "in which a glowing, nightmarish neon jungle surrounds Artie's seedy apartment; Ann Roth's garish costumes, and Paul Gallo's sensitive lighting" (31). The success of this revival stimulated a number of retrospective essays, most notably by Freedman, Bennetts, and Gussow in the *New York Times*.

Two Gentleman of Verona, a critical and popular success, was praised for its interracial casting, its updating of Elizabethan values and assumptions, and its lively rock music. Having first been seen in Central Park, the production was restaged for Broadway, losing some of its spirit, according to Kroll of *Newsweek*, in the process. The scaffold setting by Ming Cho Lee was adapted successfully for the St. James Theater, noted Watt (2 December 1971), and for the first time Guare's lyrics were recognized. Gottfried wrote that the lyrics were "a marvelous combination of technical devil-may carelessness and inspired inanity" (355). A dissenting voice was Kalem in *Time* who condemned the production totally and concluded: "The excuse for ventures of this sort is that they render the classics accessible. Actually, such shows are merely masked in the accessories of modernity—rock music, randy deshabille, silly props and lofty panfraternal sentimentality" (172). Nonetheless, the majority opinion was positive, with special notice given to performances by Raul Julia, Clifton Davis, Jonelle Allen, and Diana Davila.

The next notable Guare production was of a play set on a Norwegian iceflow and described by Kerr as "a vaudeville tour of the human condition in the year 1999," presenting "a series of images and acts, more than a coherent play; and some are underbaked and some drag on," though at its best, said Kerr, it was "a brilliantly absurdist comedy of ideas" (Kerr quoted in Wakeman, 325). *Marco Polo Sings a Solo*, after its premiere at the Nantucket Stage Company's tiny Cyrus Pierce Theater in Massachusetts in 1973, presented as a work-in-progress for six weeks, received a brief run at Joseph Papp's Public Theatre in 1977. The critical response was generally negative. Wetzsteon in *Plays and Players* believed that the results demonstrated "both the most luxuriant imagination of any American playwright and the least capacity for structuring a play" (37). Barnes found the play totally obscure (7 February 1977), while Gottfried considered it "a glib and strident comedy" (7 February 1977, 344) and *Time*'s Clarke in a typical response concluded that "ideas meet, collide and cancel one another out, like so many errant atoms, and his play explodes in a dozen directions" (346).

Rich and Famous, staged first at the Academy Theatre in Lake Forest, Illinois, in 1974, and then at the New York Shakespeare Festival's Newman Theatre in 1976, received equally harsh reviews, typified by Kauffmann's conclusion in the *New Republic*: "The script has no dramatic conclusion or thematic issue. Guare is the writing equivalent of a talented actor who needs a good director and flounders without one" (29). The only unique production device noted in reviews was the use of two actors for many roles. *Landscape of the Body*, combining the brutal and the bizarre in its telling of a young woman blamed with the savage murder of her son, with the ultimate blame placed on chance or, as some thought, on society in general, also presented at the Public Theatre (in 1977), was generally rejected by the critics. Oliver, however, did admit that the "play was filled with surprises and theatrical resourcefulness" (24 October 1977, 144). When the play was revived at the Second Stage in 1984, Oliver found that the "puzzling, grisly comedy" had been given a drab, tame production and that the evening, despite good performances, was "pretty depressing" (21 May 1987, 98).

Bosoms and Neglect, which dramatizes the neglect and guilt of a parent-child relationship, opened 3 May 1979 at the Longacre Theatre but was considered too abstract and disorganized and closed after four performances. Subsequent productions in October 1979 at Providence's Trinity Repertory (seen also in Boston) and at the Yale Repertory Theater and a brief 1986 revival by the New York Theatre Workshop at the Perry Street Theatre were more successful, though the last was deemed by Oliver as simply "more acceptable and definitely funnier" but nonvintage Guare nonetheless (21 April 1986, 109), and Gussow concluded that the production had "kept its assets and its flaws intact" (13 April 1986, 66). Of the original production, the strongest support came from Gottfried and Fox, who declared that "Guare is a fine writer of farces; he has the moralist's outrage at the imperfection of the world and the good satirist's delight in the foibles of his own kind" and decried the lack of acceptance of this intelligent, deeply felt, painful comedy ("Premature Burial," 96).

Guare's most recent work is his Lydie Breeze tetralogy, "a fusion of Civil War history, the search for an American Utopia, and the fabulous" (Stuart, 17). The first two plays of the cycle, *Lydie Breeze* and *Gardenia*, opened in quick succession in 1982 at New York's American Place Theatre and Manhattan Theatre Club. The third, *Women and Water*, was produced in July 1985 at the Goodman Theatre after its premiere at Los Angeles Actors' Theatre; in December 1985 it received a large production at Washington's Arena Stage, demonstrating to Gussow that "Guare continues to be a playwright as architect, with a view of life as interlocking 'similitude' " (8 December 1985, 102). The fourth play, *Bullfinch's Mythology*, is still in process. In general, critics have not been kind to these recent efforts, although they clearly mark a departure in Guare's writing. Brustein found in the first two that the intent was more impressive than the execution. Rich, who was not fond of *Lydie Breeze*, considered *Gardenia* even weaker and bemoaned the evasive and disembodied qualities of both works. Similar conclusions were forthcoming from most other critics. Watt, who found *Lydie* bogged down with too much imagery and atmosphere, concluded that *Gardenia*, given a marvelous production, was a bold work of the imagination and striking theatre.

In addition to working on *Bullfinch's Mythology*, Guare is reportedly collaborating with Leonard Bernstein, Jerome Robbins, and Stephen Sondheim on an adaptation with music of Bertolt Brecht's *Exception and the Rule*, a project that Guare had initiated a number of years ago but had put aside. After *Atlantic City*, written for the director Louis Malle, Guare completed another screenplay for Malle, *Moon over Miami* (now being adapted into play form), which was put aside upon the death of the star, John Belushi. Guare is also involved with a project with the Steppenwolf Company in Chicago and another for Malle, a screenplay tentatively called *Eye Contact*. Important in Guare's activities is his position on the Council of the Dramatists Guild, the vice-presidency of Theatre Communications Group, and involvement as a Fellow at the New York Institute for the Humanities.

SURVEY OF SECONDARY SOURCES

Bibliographies

Other than a brief listing of sources or checklist of Guare plays, only one significant bibliography has been done on Guare. The most useful basic checklists are to be found in MacNicholas's *Twentieth Century American Dramatists*, Giantvalley's entry on Guare in *Critical Survey of Drama*, and Markus's entry in *Contemporary Dramatists*. The fullest bibliography on Guare, though indiscriminate in its selection of entries, is included in "NTQ Checklist No. 3" compiled by Harrop. Harrop includes not only primary material but secondary literature and a good smattering of selected reviews.

Biographies

Although no book-length biography of Guare has been written, the autobiographical nature of his plays has resulted in numerous essays and feature articles focusing on his life, as well as most standard biographical reference sources. Of the latter, the most complete are the works by Giantvalley and MacNicholas, Moritz, Locher, and Blackwell. Of the more succinct biographical entry, the following are recommended: Kaye, Kopper, Esslin, McGill, *Who's Who in America*, and Hartnoll. The most in-depth interview would appear to be in Savran's *In*

Their Own Words, although Harrop's recent interview is quite extensive. In part of a three-section feature on Guare, Harrop also includes a useful chronology of major events in Guare's career. Other helpful interviews, often insightful in terms of autobiographical influences on specific plays, include Bosworth (especially good on *Blue Leaves*); Winer's "Nice Guys Can Finish First" (*Blue Leaves* and *Atlantic City*); Richards (general comments on state of the theatre and influences); Brandt (general observations and specifics on *Marco Polo Sings a Solo*); Tallmer (*Blue Leaves*); and finally, an imaginative interview between a critic and Ibsen ("Exclusive Interview") drawing interesting parallels between Ibsen and Guare.

Influences

Since most of Guare's major influences are autobiographical or social, the sources in the preceding sections are relevant in this section as well. Most recent plays have moved away from personal history to broader topics, almost epic in scope (the Lydie cycle). Two recent essays shed a good deal of light on the influences on these plays: Stuart's "Stars and Strife Forever" and Rose's "A New American Master." Both also contain general comments on the plays and his style, the latter commenting on other plays as well. Guare is especially helpful in his introduction to the published text of *Blue Leaves*. His entry in *Current Biography* is surprisingly helpful in terms of explicating influences and providing general criticism of specific plays.

General Studies

There have been no book-length studies of Guare to date, although three critics have included major chapters on Guare. Bernstein's chapter is the most detailed, offering a review of Guare criticism, a detailed analysis of *Blue Leaves*, and a comparison of this play with David Rabe's *Sticks and Bones*. Cohn, in *New American Dramatists*, provides an overview of all his major plays through *Bosoms and Neglect* (1980). In *Comic Relief* she discusses, even more succinctly, *Muzeeka, Blue Leaves*, and *Rich and Famous*. Dasgupta (in Marranca and Dasgupta) is the most critical of Guare's work, providing an overview of all of his work up to *Bosoms and Neglect* and exploring all aspects of the playwright's work, including style, influences, and themes. Leiter includes mention of Guare's New York–produced plays in the 1970s in *Ten Seasons*, providing a useful context for much of Guare's work. Briefer, recommended general assessments are Goetz, Markus, Giantvalley, Hewe's "The Playwright as Voyager," Miller, and the entries in *World Authors* (Wakeman) and *Twentieth Century American Dramatists* (MacNicholas). Excerpts from various reviews of his work are reprinted in Bryfonski and Harris. A useful overview of Guare's work appears in Harrop's " 'Ibsen Translated by Lewis Carroll' " and in the "NTQ Checklist No. 3." Harrop lists all of Guare's plays with production and publication data and provides succinct criticism and synopses. The most recent overview of Guare's work is Steven H. Gale's essay in the fourth edition of *Contemporary Dramatists*, edited by D. L. Kirkpatrick.

Analyses of Individual Plays

Other than sources indicated above, few specific essays have been written on individual Guare plays. Of these, the following are recommended: on *Blue Leaves*, Bennetts's "The Duality in 'House of Blue Leaves,' " Freedman's " 'Blue Leaves' is Back and Guare's in the Pink," and Gussow's "Revisiting a Realm of Broken Dreams"; on *Bosoms and Neglect*, Kroll's brief comments (with general remarks as well on other works) in "Laugh When It Hurts"; on *Landscape*, Fox's "At Long Last, 'Landscape' " (also providing a retrospective survey); and on *Lydie Breeze*, Wetzsteon's "The Coming of Age of John Guare" and Berkvist's "John Guare Stirs Up a 'Breeze.' " Two features on Guare's filmscript, *Atlantic City*, include comments on the plays as well: Winer's " 'Atlantic City' Pays Off for John Guare" and Chase's "Good Days in the Life of a Screenwriter." Lahr provides a brief analysis of *Muzeeka*.

FUTURE RESEARCH OPPORTUNITIES

Despite Guare's reputation as one of our most important active playwrights, a full-length study of his work has yet to appear. Such a detailed, critical overview is now warranted, correcting a somewhat distorted critical picture that has evolved over the past twenty years. Thematic studies of his plays are certainly needed, especially given the various threads that run through clusters of his texts, as is a more analytic application of the autobiographical touches found in much of his work.

The comparative study undertaken by Bernstein suggests a useful strategy for more criticism as well. Given the shift in the assessment of *Blue Leaves* from its premiere in 1971 to its revival in 1986, a reexamination of earlier Guare plays criticized for their lack of form and clear structure might be justified, especially given the perspective of time. Certainly a structural study of his plays would be useful. With the completion of the *Lydie* cycle, a number of examinations of this late work will be possible. Guare, articulate and outgoing, will always prove a fruitful subject for personal interview, and, despite a number of previously published dialogues, none is as deep or as detailed as might be possible. Finally, given the innovative nature of much of Guare's work, especially in terms of production requirements, an in-depth performance study could be quite revealing, as would be analyses of individual plays from directorial points of view.

SECONDARY SOURCES

Barnes, Clive. "Theater: Guare's Humorous 'Cop-Out.' " *New York Times* (8 April 1969): 42. Reprinted in *New York Theatre Critics' Reviews* (1969): 310.

———. "Theater: John Guare's 'House of Blue Leaves' Opens." *New York Times* (11 February 1971): 54.

———. " 'Marco Polo Sings a Solo,' a Play by John Guare, Opens at the Public." *New York Times* (7 February 1977): 30. Reprinted in *New York Theatre Critics' Reviews* (1977): 344.

Bennetts, Leslie. "The Duality in 'House of Blue Leaves.' " *New York Times* (9 April 1986): C19.

Berkvist, Robert. "John Guare Stirs Up a 'Breeze.' " *New York Times* (21 February 1982): B4.

Bernstein, Samuel J. *The Strands Entwined: A New Direction in American Drama.* Boston: Northeastern University Press, 1980.

Blackwell, Earl, ed. in chief. *Celebrity Register.* New York: Simon and Schuster, 1973.

Bosworth, Patricia. "Yes for a Young Man's Fantasies." *New York Times* (7 March 1971): 2: 1, 12.

Brandt, Claudia. "Dear John." *Soho Weekly News* (17 February 1977): 14.

Brustein, Robert. "Unsound Breeze from the Sound." *New Republic* (24 March 1982): 26–27.

———. "Back at the Starting Post." *New Republic* (19 May 1982): 24–25.

Bryfonski, Dedria, and Laurie Lanzen Harris, eds. *Contemporary Literary Criticism.* Vol. 14. Detroit: Gale Research Co., 1980.

Bryfonski, Dedria, and Phyllis Carmel Mendelson, eds. *Contemporary Literary Criticism.* Vol. 8. Detroit: Gale Research Co., 1978.

Chapman, John. "Play Critic Cops Out." *New York Daily News* (8 April 1969). Reprinted in *New York Theatre Critics' Reviews* (1969): p. 310.

Chase, Chris. "Good Days in the Life of a Screenwriter." *New York Times* (29 May 1981): C8.

Clarke, Gerald. "Fissionable Confusion." *Time* (21 February 1977). Reprinted in *New York Theatre Critics' Reviews* (1977): 346.

Clurman, Harold. "Theatre." *Nation* (1 March 1971): 285–86.

Cohn, Ruby. "Camp, Cruelty, Colloquialism." In *Comic Relief: Humour in Contemporary American Literature*, pp. 288–89. Edited by Sarah Blacher Cohen. Urbana: University of Illinois Press, 1978.

———. *New American Dramatists, 1960–1980.* New York: Grove Press, 1982.

Davis, James. " 'House of Blue Leaves' a Brilliant New Play." *New York Daily News* (11 February 1971). Reprinted in *New York Theatre Critics' Reviews* (1971): 354.

Esslin, Martin, ed. *The Encyclopedia of World Theater.* New York: Charles Scribner's Sons, 1977.

"Exclusive Interview with Henrik Ibsen: 'We're Just Friends.' " *Village Voice* (14 February 1977): 43.

Fox, Terry Curtis. "John Guare: At Long Last, 'Landscape.' " *Village Voice* (15 August 1977): 34–35.

———. "Premature Burial." *Village Voice* (14 May 1979): 95–97.

Freedman, Samuel G. " 'Blue Leaves' Is Back and Guare's in the Pink." *New York Times* (16 March 1986): B1, B16.

Gale, Steven H. "Guare, John (Edward)." In *Contemporary Dramatists.* 4th ed. Edited by D. L. Kirkpatrick. Chicago and London: St. James Press, 1988.

Giantvalley, Scott. "John Guare." In *Critical Survey of Drama. English Language Series. Authors Cow-Gua.* Edited by Frank N. Magill. Englewood Cliffs, N. J.: Salem Press, 1985.

Gill, Brendan. "Pranks." *New Yorker* (19 April 1969): 98.

Goetz, Ruth. "John Guare." *Dramatics* (May 1983): 5–6, 28–30.

Gottfried, Martin. "Theatre." *Women's Wear Daily* (8 April 1969). Reprinted in *New York Theatre Critics' Reviews* (1969): 311.

———. "Theatre: 'Two Gentlemen of Verona.' " *Women's Wear Daily* (3 December 1971). Reprinted in *New York Theatre Critics' Reviews* (1971): 172.

———. "Theatre: 'The House of Blue Leaves' . . . 'Exasperating.' " *"Women's Wear Daily* (11 February 1971). Reprinted in *New York Theatre Critics' Reviews* (1971): 355.

———. "Marco Polo's Sinking Solo." *New York Post* (7 February 1977). Reprinted in *New York Theatre Critics' Reviews* (1977): 344.

———. "An Unmerry Month of May." *Saturday Review* (7 July 1979): 40.

"Guare, John (Edward)." In *World Authors 1970–1975*, pp. 323–26. Edited by John Wakeman. New York: H. W. Wilson Co., 1980.

Gussow, Mel. "Revisiting a Realm of Broken Dreams." *New York Times* (6 April 1986): B3, B16.

———. "Stage: John Guare's 'Bosoms and Neglect.' " *New York Times* (13 April 1986): A66.

———. "The Stage: Guare Chronicle, 'Women and Water.' " *New York Times* (8 December 1985): 102.

Harrop, John. " 'Ibsen Translated by Lewis Carroll': The Theatre of John Guare." *New Theatre Quarterly* 3 (May 1987): 150–54.

———. " 'Living in that Dark Room': The Playwright and His Audience" (interview). *New Theatre Quarterly* 3 (May 1987): 155–59.

———. "NTQ Checklist No. 3: John Guare." *New Theatre Quarterly* 3 (May 1987): 160–77.

Hartnoll, Phyllis, ed. *The Oxford Companion to the Theatre.* 4th ed. Oxford and New York: Oxford University Press, 1983.

Henry, William A., III. "Irreverence: 'The House of Blue Leaves.' " *Time* (31 March 1986): 77.

Herbert, Ian. *Who's Who in the Theatre.* Vol. 1: *Biographies.* Detroit: Gale Research Co., 1981.

Hewes, Henry. "Under the Rainbow." *Saturday Review* (20 March 1971): 10.

———. "The Playwright as Voyager." *Saturday Review/World* (20 November 1973): 48.

Kalem, T. E. "Cultural Vandalism." *Time* (13 December 1971). Reprinted in *New York Theatre Critics' Reviews* (1971): 172.

Kauffmann, Stanley. "Off-Broadway Offerings." *New Republic* (13 March 1976): 28–29. Reprinted in Bryfonski and Harris, pp. 219–20.

Kaye, Phyllis Johnson, ed. *National Playwrights Directory.* Waterford, Conn.: O'Neill Theater Center, 1977.

Kerr, Walter. "The Silliest Question of the Year." *New York Times* (20 April 1969). Reprinted in *New York Theatre Critics' Reviews* (1969): 312–13.

———. "The Most Striking New American Play." *New York Times* (4 April 1971): 2:3.

Kopper, Philip. "Guare, John." In *1983 Britannica Book of the Year.* Chicago: Encyclopedia Britannica, 1983.

Kroll, Jack. "Avon Rock." *Newsweek* (13 December 1971). Reprinted in *New York Theatre Critics' Reviews* (1971): 173.

———. "Laugh When It Hurts." *Newsweek* (14 May 1979): 85–86.

Lahr, John. *Up against the Fourth Wall.* New York: Grove Press, 1970.

Leiter, Samuel L. *Ten Seasons: New York Theatre in the Seventies.* Westport, Conn.: Greenwood Press, 1986.

Locher, Frances Carol, ed. *Contemporary Authors.* Vols. 73–76. Detroit: Gale Research Company, 1978.

McGill, Raymond D., ed. *Notable Names in the American Theatre.* Clifton, N.J.: James T. White and Co., 1976.

MacNicholas, John, ed. *Dictionary of Literary Biography.* Vol. 7: *Twentieth Century American Dramatists. Part 1: A-J.* Detroit: Gale Research Co., 1981.

Markus, Thomas B. "Guare, John." In *Contemporary Dramatists.* 3d ed. Edited by James Vinson. New York: St. Martin's Press, 1982.

Marranca, Bonnie, and Gautam Dasgupta. *American Playwrights: A Critical Survey.* Vol. 1. New York: Drama Books Specialists, 1981.

Miller, Terry. "Guare, John [Edward]." In *McGraw-Hill Encyclopedia of World Drama,* Vol. 2. Edited by Stanley Hochman. New York: McGraw-Hill, 1984.

Moritz, Charles, ed. *Current Biography Yearbook 1982.* New York: H. W. Wilson Co., 1983.

Novick, Julius. "Very Funny—or a Long Sick Joke." *New York Times* (21 February 1971): sec. B9.

Oliver, Edith. "Old and Improved." *New Yorker* (31 March 1986): 66, 68.

———. "Betty and Bert in New York." *New Yorker* (24 October 1977): 144–46.

———. "Off Broadway." *New Yorker* (21 May 1984): 98.

———. "Off Broadway." *New Yorker* (21 April 1986): 109.

Rich, Frank. "Theater: John Guare's 'House of Blue Leaves.' " *New York Times* (20 March 1986): C21.

———. "Stage: Guare's 'Gardenia' Antedates His 'Lydie.' " *New York Times* (29 April 1982): C20.

Richards, David. "Critics, Happiness and Sex: 2 Playwrights' Views." *Washington Sunday Star* (16 January 1972): C5.

Rose, Lloyd. "A New American Master." *Atlantic Monthly* (March 1984): 120–22, 124.

Savran, David. *In Their Own Words. Contemporary American Playwrights.* New York: Theatre Communications Group, 1987.

Stuart, Jan. "Stars and Strife Forever." *American Theatre* (April 1985): 12–18.

Tallmer, Jerry. "Huck Finn Strikes Back." *New York Post* (26 February 1971).

Wakeman, John, ed. *World Authors, 1970–1975.* New York: H. W. Wilson Co., 1980.

Watt, Douglas. "The Park Comes to Broadway with 'Two Gents,' Joy and Love." *New York Daily News* (2 December 1971). Reprinted in *New York Theatre Critics' Reviews* (1971): 174.

———. " 'Lydie Breeze.' " New York *Daily News* (25 February 1982). Reprinted in *New York Theatre Critics' Reviews* (1982): 345.

———. "Pre-'Lydie,' a Vital Drama." *New York Daily News* (29 April 1982). Reprinted in *New York Theatre Critics' Reviews* (1982): 271.

Watts, Richard. "The Day the Pope Was Here." *New York Post* (11 February 1971). Reprinted in *New York Theatre Critics' Reviews* (1971): 354.

Wetzsteon, Ross. "The Coming of Age of John Guare." *New York* (22 February 1982): 35–39.

———. "New York." *Plays and Players* (June 1977): 37–38.

Who's Who in America. 43d ed. Chicago: Marquis Who's Who, 1984.

Wilson, Edwin. "Theater: A Smash Revival." *Wall Street Journal* (19 April 1986): 31.

Winer, Laurie. "Playwright John Guare: Nice Guys Can Finish First." *Wall Street Journal* (15 May 1986): 26.

Winer, Linda. " 'Atlantic City' Pays Off for John Guare." *New York Daily News* (15 May 1981): "Manhattan" magazine: 1–2.

Lorraine Hansberry

(19 MAY 1930–12 JANUARY 1965)

FRANCIS DEDMOND

ASSESSMENT OF HANSBERRY'S REPUTATION

Lorraine Hansberry was the first black woman to have a play produced on Broadway and the first black and youngest American ever to receive the New York Drama Critics Circle Award. She was, as Carter has observed, a trailblazer whose phenomenal success with *A Raisin in the Sun* (1959) enabled other black playwrights to get their plays produced. Her success also made her one of the most important voices in black theatre. She argued that art could be and should be social and that Negro writers must participate in intellectual affairs everywhere. Her purpose was, through her plays and her other works, to tell America about the world and her people. As Gerald Weales pointed out, "her strengths as a playwright lie in her ability to create an almost intangible milieu—particularly out of Chicago and the Greenwich Village settings that she knew so well—and in her understanding of and affection for human complexity" ("Hansberry," 654).

PRIMARY BIBLIOGRAPHY OF HANSBERRY'S WORKS

With Stan Steiner (coauthor). "Cry for Colonial Freedom Jostles Phony Youth
 Meet." *Freedom* (September 1951): 6.
"Noted Lawyer Goes to Jail: Says Negroes' Fight for Rights Menaced." *Freedom*
 (May 1952): 3.
"Harlem Children Face Mass Ignorance in Old, Overcrowded, Understaffed
 Schools." *Freedom* (November 1952): 3.
"Child Labor Is Society's Crime against Youth." *Freedom* (February 1955): 2.
"No More Hiroshimas." *Freedom* (May-June 1955): 7.
"Willy Loman, Walter Younger, and He Who Must Live." *Village Voice* (12 August
 1959): 7–8. Reprinted as "An Author's Reflections: Willy Loman, Walter

Younger, and He Who Must Live." *Village Voice Reader*, pp. 194–99. Edited by Daniel Wolf and Edwin Fancher. New York: Doubleday, 1962.

A Raisin in the Sun. New York: Random House, 1959; London: Methuen, 1960.

"A Challenge to Artists." *Freedomways* 31 (1st quarter 1963): 33–35.

"Black Revolution and the White Backlash." Transcript of Town Hall Forum. *National Guardian* (4 July 1964): 5–9. Reprinted in *Black Protest: History, Documents and Analysis, 1619 to the Present*, pp. 442–48. Edited by Joanne Grant. New York: Fawcett World Library, 1968.

The Movement: Documentary of a Struggle for Equality. New York: Simon and Schuster, 1964. Reprinted as *A Matter of Colour: Documentary of a Struggle for Equality*. London: Penguin Books, 1965.

"The Scars of the Ghetto." *Monthly Review* 16 (February 1965): 588–91.

The Sign in Sidney Brustein's Window. New York: Random House, 1965; included in *Three Negro Plays*. London: Penguin, 1969.

A Raisin in the Sun and The Sign in Sidney Brustein's Window. New York: New American Library, 1966.

To Be Young, Gifted and Black: A Portrait of Lorraine Hansberry in Her Own Words. Adapted with a foreword and postscript by Robert Nemiroff. Introduction by James Baldwin. Englewood Cliffs, N.J.: Prentice-Hall, 1969.

"The Negro in American Culture." *The Black American Writer*. Vol. 1: *Fiction*, pp. 78–108. Edited by C. W. E. Bigsby. Baltimore: Penguin Books, 1971.

To Be Young, Gifted and Black. Caedmon TRS 342, 1971.

To Be Young, Gifted and Black. Adapted by Robert Nemiroff. Acting edition. New York: Samuel French, 1971.

Les Blancs. The Collected Last Plays of Lorraine Hansberry. Edited by Robert Nemiroff. Introduction by Julius Lester. New York: Random House, 1972; Vintage Books, 1973; New American Library, 1983.

Lorraine Hansberry Speaks Out: Art and the Black Revolution. Selected and edited by Robert Nemiroff. Caedmon TC 1352, 1972.

A Raisin in the Sun. Caedmon TRS 355, 1972.

To Be Young, Gifted and Black. Film. NET, Educational Broadcasting Corp., 1972.

Lorraine Hansberry: The Black Experience in the Creation of Drama. Princeton: Films for the Humanities (FFH 128), 1976.

"The Negro Writer and His Roots: Toward a New Romanticism." *Black Scholar* (March-April 1981): 2–12.

Lorraine Hansberry's A Raisin in the Sun. Twenty-fifth anniversary edition, Revised by Robert Nemiroff. New York: Samuel French, 1984.

PRODUCTION HISTORY

A Raisin in the Sun—with Ruby Dee as Ruth Younger, Sidney Poitier as Walter Lee Younger, Diana Sands as Beneatha, and Claudia McNeil as Momma Younger—opened on Broadway at the Ethel Barrymore Theatre on 11 March 1959 and ran for 530 performances. On 7 April, four weeks after its opening, Hansberry was awarded the New York Drama Critics Circle Award for the best American play of the season. From opening night on, the newspaper critics were unanimous in their praise of the production. Coleman said that Hansberry had brought a moving story to the stage and had told it with dramatic impact. Aston and Atkinson were impressed with the honesty of the play, and Watts was particularly taken with the real-life characters the playwright had brought to the stage, especially Momma Younger, the family matriarch.

The magazine reviewers were also lavish in their praise. Richard Tynan found the opening night performance by the cast to be flawless. "The supreme virtue of 'A Raisin in the Sun,' " he wrote, "is its proud, joyous proximity to its source, which is life as the dramatist lived it" (100). Harold Clurman in his review in *Nation* agreed with Tynan about the acting and authenticity of the play. "The play is organic theatre," he wrote (302). The reviewer for *Theatre Arts* called attention to the unanimously favorable verdict of the newspaper critics and noted that "the Negro has come a long way in the American theatre, both as performer and as subject matter, yet it is rare to find him as free from stereotypes as he is in the play at hand" (" 'A Raisin in the Sun,' " 22–23).

Between 1959 and 1979, according to Kaiser and Nemiroff, *A Raisin in the Sun* was produced on stage and radio in more than thirty languages. In the 1980s, there were a number of significant revivals of the play in the United States and in England, most of them part of the celebration of the twenty-fifth anniversary of the original production. Normant (" 'Raisin' Celebrates Its 25th Anniversary") noted that "the first major celebration was held at Chicago's Goodman Theatre, followed by a major production by the Yale Repertory Theatre, whose artistic director, Lloyd Richards, directed the original Broadway *Raisin*" (58). The revival opened in Chicago on 3 October 1983. The next day Christiansen said that the play, "wearing the true mantle of a classic" yet "rooted in its own time," speaks "through the years to our own" (B8). The play was staged at Yale in November 1983.

Normant's article was published before other significant twenty-fifth anniversary productions were staged. For instance, the review by Pollack of the production by the Repertory Theatre of St. Louis in September 1984 was captioned "A Magnificent Revival of 'Raisin in the Sun.' " The *London Theatre Record* for 10–23 April 1985 reprinted portions of eight reviews that had appeared in British newspapers of the Black Theatre Co-operative production of the play at the Tricycle Theatre. After its Richmond run in March 1985, the Virginia Museum Theatre brought the play to the McCarter Theatre at Princeton, New Jersey, in April to rave notices. At the same time that the play was running at Princeton, the *Daily Utah Chronicle* reported that the play was "mesmerizing" audiences in Salt Lake City. And in early December, the *Philadelphia Inquirer* said that local incidents of recent racial troubles in southwest Philadelphia made the revival of *Raisin* by the Philadelphia Drama Guild timely indeed; and the *Philadelphia Daily News* declared the play to be "still as fresh as dawn 26 years after its maiden splash on Broadway" (79). Amiri Baraka wrote on 16 November 1986, the morning after the opening of *A Raisin in the Sun* at the Kennedy Center, that "no doubt part of the renewed impact of the play comes with the fresh interpretation by both directors and actors. But we cannot stop there. The social materials Hansberry so brilliantly shaped into drama are not lightweight" (F2).

Hansberry's *The Sign in Sidney Brustein's Window* opened on Broadway on 15 October 1964. Reviews by the newspaper critics were mixed, ranging from Gottfried's blast at "the stinking triviality of it all" (21) to Reed's statement that "I shall never, as long as I live, hope to see such perfection in the theatre again" (10). But the play was doomed from the beginning and survived on stage for 101 performances only because of the sacrificial devotion of numerous actors and actresses, such as Shelley Winters and Ruby Dee. Robert Nemiroff, Hansberry's husband, described the struggle for survival in his essay, "The 101 'Final' Performances of *Sidney Brustein.*" The play closed on 12 January 1965. Playgoers were turned off by the story of a disenchanted egghead and his actress wife in their unorthodox quest for meaningful lives in an age of corruption, alienation, and cynicism. They found meaning for their lives only when they came to recognize the necessity for individual commitment and activism.

The magazine critics echoed Gottfried in their attacks on the play. Sheed wrote that " 'Sidney Brustein' is a compendium of Village legends—homosexual playwright, junkie-prostitute, miscegenation blues— all jostling for equal time. There is more than a hint of parody, particularly in solemn quotes from Thoreau and Kafka. . . . The individual segments have been sharpened to a squeaky point, but the Grand Design has been lost" (197). Hewes agreed with Sheed about the design, finding in the script material for at least a half-dozen plays. However, Hansberry's accuracy of observation, honesty, and superior dialogue, he said, compensated to a considerable extent for her failure in design.

In late January 1972, *The Sign in Sidney Brustein's Window* returned to Broadway and the Longacre Theatre in a new production, but this time it lasted only five performances. In Gill's words ("All Thumbs"), *The Sign*—"poor enough as a play eight years ago"—was not improved by the adaptation it received at the hands of Robert Nemiroff and Charlotte Zaltzberg, who, it seemed to Gill, had given it "a patting over of cosmetic scatological invective in the vain hope of making it sound more timely" (69). The incidental songs that had been added to the production, Gill said, were mindless and "reedily sung by four Woodstockian wraiths, who came on at intervals to stop the play dead in its tracks" (69).

To Be Young, Gifted and Black is a dramatic testament of black life assembled by Robert Nemiroff from Hansberry's published work and from the unpublished work she left at her death. The play opened at the Cherry Lane Theatre in 1969 and enjoyed enormous off-Broadway success. In 1970–1972, the play was taken on a two-year national tour, with the several casts having in them such performers as Cicely Tyson, Claudia McNeil, Barbara Baxley, and Tina Sattin. In 1973, a television production of the play featured Roy Scheider, Claudia McNeil, Ruby Dee, and Blythe Danner. During its New York run, though, it received relatively little critical attention. However, Clurman did note in his "Theatre" column (for 28 April 1969) that he had seen the play, which was "comprised of excerpts from letters, public addresses, diaries, and several scenes from her two produced plays, *A Raisin in the Sun* and *The Sign in Sidney Brustein's Window* . . . together with a brief passage from *Les Blancs*, a play to be given next season" (548). He found the play touching and the playwright perceptive and dignified, thus giving, in his view, her obvious propaganda a special forcefulness.

Hansberry started writing *Les Blancs* in 1960 but had not, by her death, polished it to her full satisfaction. It was left to Nemiroff to produce the final text and to bring the play to the Longacre Theatre in 1970. The play opened on 15 November to mixed reviews, an interesting account of which may be found in Nemiroff's comments in *Les Blancs: The Collected Last Plays of Lorraine Hansberry* (1972). Gill in his review ("Things Going Wrong") pointed out that the play was out of date. So much, he said, had happened in Africa since 1961 that a play "laid in a Schweitzer-like medical mission in some vast equatorial country, plagued by white colonial rule and black terrorism, has an air of being far less current than it claims to be" (104). Late in the play, the plot erupts into melodrama with people being gunned down all over the stage, Gill said. But this made little difference since the characters had degenerated into symbols of set beliefs and were not individuals capable of being murdered in cold blood. Gill did find one redeeming feature in the evening: the splendid performance of James Earl Jones. Clurman (30 November 1970) could have been replying to the views expressed by Gill in the *New Yorker* for 21 November. He liked the play; it was not propaganda; it transcended banalities; it was "a fanciful and intelligent statement of the tragic impasse of white and black relations all over the world" (573). It was an honest, thought-provoking play, he said. Nonetheless, it closed in late December after only forty-seven performances.

In October 1973, Nemiroff was back on Broadway at the Forty-sixth Street Theatre, this time with *Raisin*, a musical based on *A Raisin in the Sun*. He and Charlotte Zaltzberg had done the book, Judd Waldin the music, and Robert Brittan the lyrics. The action and conflict in the musical were essentially the same as in the play, except that the musical moved beyond the Youngers' apartment into the streets, bars, churches, and workaday world of the people of Chicago's South Side. The score incorporated idioms of gospel, jazz, blues, and soul, along with dances based on Afro-American and African tradition. According to Bailey,

Raisin "rode into the 'Great White Way' . . . on a tidal wave of rave reviews it amassed as a traveling road show" (74). Gill ("A Black Rose") admitted that Hansberry's plot was faithfully reproduced, even if the musical did come across as little more than a stock Jewish-American melodrama in black terms with stereotyped characters on a level scarcely above that of "Abie's Irish Rose." Kalem complained that the musical *Raisin* did not update *A Raisin in the Sun* but shoved it into the realm of soap operetta. Bailey told the readers of *Ebony* that what Hansberry was after in *A Raisin in the Sun* did not lend itself to treatment in the Broadway musical theatre. Nevertheless, *Raisin* won the Tony Award as the best Broadway musical of 1973. Most recently, Washington focuses on the social and political elements of *Raisin* while emphasizing that the characters of Walter Lee and Lena Younger each deserve "a proportionate share of the spotlight" (111).

SURVEY OF SECONDARY SOURCES

Bibliographies

Anyone interested in the life, works, and criticism of Lorraine Hansberry is blessed with a number of useful bibliographies. By far the most comprehensive is Kaiser and Nemiroff's, which lists her works by categories (books, parts of books, magazine and newspaper articles, and recordings and films); and it lists writings about her and her works in books, dissertations, scholarly journals, magazines, and newspapers. Cheney has an excellent selected bibliography of primary sources and an annotated bibliography of some of the best secondary sources. The Hansberry bibliography in Arata and Rotoli is especially helpful in its listing of anthology publications of Hansberry's plays. Also useful are "Lorraine Hansberry" in Ora Williams (1973) and a similar bibliography in Rush, Myers, and Arata. Hatch and Abdullah's *Black Playwrights, 1823–1977* provides excellent plot summaries of Hansberry's plays. Eddleman and Salem list selected reviews of Hansberry's plays together with a list of selected articles about the plays.

Biographies

A full-length study of Hansberry's life and works is in Cheney. Although it traces her life and career, it suffers from the restrictions imposed by the Twayne United States Authors Series format and is not an in-depth study of her life. Scheader's short biography, written for children, is generously illustrated with photographs and Hansberry's drawings of herself and, according to Kirkwood, provides the young with a picture of an attractive and complex personality. The book *To Be Young,*

Gifted and Black is, in essence, an informal autobiography that offers interesting personal comments on the highlights of Hansberry's life. In addition, a number of useful and trustworthy biographical sketches of Hansberry are available, the best being Abramson's (1980).

Influences

Critics such as Hays and Cheney have pointed to Sean O'Casey's influence on Hansberry, especially the influence on her of his *Juno and the Paycock* as reflected in *A Raisin in the Sun*. Cheney also treats at some length the influence on Hansberry of Frederick Douglass, W. E. B. Du Bois, Paul Robeson, and Langston Hughes. What Hansberry learned from Douglass, she put to use in *The Drinking Gourd*. From Du Bois she acquired an admiration for the black intellectual and black leadership. Robeson inspired her to be an activist, and Hughes explained to her her own race.

General Studies

Freedomways devoted its fourth quarter 1979 issue to Hansberry. According to Bond, the special issue—consisting of nineteen articles—was designed to make the journal's readers aware of the range of Hansberry's work and to encourage the study and understanding of her activity. Many of the articles are simply appreciative or personal reminiscences. However, Gresham's is an interesting study of Hansberry's prose style. Wilkerson's "Lorraine Hansberry: The Complete Feminist" makes the point that if Hansberry had been writing in 1979, she would have been labeled a feminist, yet her works "bring an invaluable perspective to the confused, heated dialogue between contemporary men and women, for her feminism is predicated on a deep love and empathy for all mankind" (244). Haley argues that Hansberry was not the first black writer to play up the relationship between the American black and Africa, but "she was the first to *popularize* the notion" (279). Killens found Hansberry to be "a one-woman literary warrior for change—qualitative and fundamental change" (273), and Giovanni discovered in Hansberry a visionary who enables all of us to look deeper. Ward says that *A Raisin in the Sun* is history but not just history; it is art through which we can discover new aspects of ourselves.

Beyond doubt the two best general studies of Hansberry are by Wilkerson and Carter. Carter's essay is by far the best available introduction to Hansberry; it is scholarly yet readable and comprehensive. Generally both essays cover the same material. They touch on the salient points of Hansberry's life, emphasizing her role as an activist artist as that role is portrayed in her plays. Wilkerson concluded that Hansberry's finely crafted themes "forced the American stage to a new level of excellence and human relevance" (13), and Carter concluded that her artistry, intelligence, and deeply committed life will ensure that she will be remembered "as one of the most important Afro-American writers" (133).

Lorraine Hansberry has figured, along with other black novelists and playwrights, in several doctoral dissertations. Zietlow found that, unlike Richard Wright in *Native Son* and Ralph Ellison in *Invisible Man* who used the absurdity of the social scene as a backdrop, James Baldwin and Lorraine Hansberry dealt with the problems of individual human beings rather than with representative figures in an absurd social situation. Friedman studied the feminist concerns of Susan Glaspell, Rachel Crothers, Lillian Hellman, and Lorraine Hansberry and found, in Hansberry's case, that her female characters were not simply nurturing and supportive but revolutionary as well. The most significant dissertation to date is Grant's, the best piece of extended scholarly work that has been done on Hansberry.

Analyses of Individual Plays

A Raisin in the Sun has received an unusual amount of critical attention. According to Mance Williams, *A Raisin in the Sun* was one of the plays in the 1950s that "expressed a new form of protest, one that not only exhorted Black people to stand up for their rights but warned Whites that Blacks would settle for nothing less than their full share of the American Dream" (112). The best single study of the play is the chapter devoted to the play in Keyssar. It is an excellent, balanced critical analysis—free from adulation—of the dramaturgy, dramatic tricks, and flaws of the play. *A Raisin in the Sun*, the critics found, was not a perfect play. Yet despite its flaws, the play, according to Gassner, "earned critical approbation and popular success with its simple and concentrated realism. The young author was completely in rapport with her material, yet intellectually detached in her judgments" (308). Miller agrees that Hansberry kept the play "within the bounds of the conventional realistic well-made play, something almost anachronistic amidst the styles of the 1960s" (161). He found something almost Ibsenesque about the scene, incidents, convincing characters, and dialogue. Lewis said *A Raisin in the Sun* is "an Odets' drama with Negro replacements" (112). Weales (*American Drama Since World War II*) agrees, and later noted that *Raisin* is a "black play, in its characters and its concerns" but that it was "also a combination of two pervasive American subjects, a maturation play containing a critique of the American dream" ("Hansberry," 654). But Keyssar argues that *A Raisin in the Sun* was successful because Hansberry's strategy proved successful; she attempted to make the white audience desire the fulfillment of the personal dreams of the characters in the play—and succeeded—succeeded, as Cheney put it, because the playwright was successful in universalizing a family and its hopes. From New Haven during the out-of-town tryouts of *A Raisin in the Sun*, Hansberry wrote to her mother that "it is a play that tells the truth about people, Negroes and life and I think it will help a lot of people to understand how we are just as complicated as they are—and just as mixed up—but above all, that we have among our miserable and downtrodden ranks—people who are the very essence of human dignity. That is what, after all the laughter and tears, the play is supposed to say. I hope it will make you very proud" (*To Be Young, Gifted and Black*, 109).

In the view of most critics, Hansberry succeeded in her purpose—but not in the view of all. Notable among the dissenters is Cruse, who argues that Hansberry was born into an affluent family and knew nothing at first-hand about the plight of the Negro working class. *A Raisin in the Sun* was successful because it provided the American theatre, which had not been kind to black playwrights, a chance to assuage the commercial theatre's guilt with "a good old-fashioned, home-spun saga of some good working-class folk in pursuit of the American dream . . . in their fashion" (277). In fact, many whites did not even look upon it as a "Negro play." Hansberry made theatre history, Cruse said, "with the most cleverly written piece of glorified soap opera I, personally, have ever seen on stage" (278). Weales earlier had also declared the play to be "as clumsy as it is old-fashioned," but, unlike Cruse, he found that "it had virtues that commend it" (*American Drama*, 233).

Some of the source and "similarity" hunters have come up with some interesting findings. For instance, Hays has pointed to the similarity in theme and situation between *A Raisin in the Sun* and O'Casey's *Juno and the Paycock*, and Abramson has found striking similarities between Hansberry's play and Richard Wright's *Native Son*, but what she calls "a more revealing comparison can be made between Theodore Ward's *Big White Fog* and *A Raisin in the Sun*" (*Negro Playwrights*, 242).

Wilkerson has noted that following its Broadway success, *A Raisin in the Sun* was subsequently translated into over thirty languages on all continents, including the language of East Germany's Sorbische minority ("The Sighted Eyes," 8). The translations and productions in most of the foreign countries did not inspire critical studies. But in Germany, the situation was different. The essays of Breitinger, Guttman, Hajek, and Brüning indicate the German interest in the black liberation movement, racial integration, and black nationalism as set forth in the works of Hansberry and other Afro-American dramatists. And even one of the few critical studies of *The Sign in Sidney Brustein's Window*—Habicht's essay—appeared in a German publication.

With the production of *The Sign in Sidney Brustein's Window* (1964), many of Hansberry's fellow black artists felt that with her Jewish play, she was abandoning the black cause. Nonetheless, Mitchell wrote that on many levels, the play was far more mature than *A Raisin in the Sun*. Cheney finds—in Hansberry's still-life study of modern man and woman caught up in the conflict between not caring and caring too much—the playwright pleading for maturity and commitment in such closely linked things as sexuality and creativity. And although it leaves unresolved many problems eternally old and eternally new, Miller says that Hansberry's comedy of sensibility is a "charming, delightful, and touching play, and, furthermore, it is a very moral play" that thus places her "completely outside the world of racial dogma and protest" (168).

The play *To Be Young, Gifted and Black* (1969) does not lend itself to scholarly concern. In 1972, Nemiroff edited and published *Les Blancs: The Collected Last Plays of Lorraine Hansberry*. The most available general studies of these plays—*Les Blancs, The Drinking Gourd*, and *What Use Are Flowers?*—are found in chapter 6 of Cheney and in Farrison, both of which contain some analysis but are largely given over to plot summaries. Ness attempts to get at the theme of *Les Blancs*, which seems to be, Ness says, that the hero Tshembe comes to realize that as an African at heart, he cannot separate himself from the African struggle, regardless of how much he would like to. Powell, who compares the black experience in Margaret Walker's *Jubilee* to the plantation experience of both blacks and whites in Hansberry's *The Drinking Gourd*, says that Hansberry reveals that both groups, by virtue of their being born at a certain place and at a certain time, became victims of a viciously destructive system over which they had no control, but a system, nonetheless, that they refused to allow to destroy their humanity.

FUTURE RESEARCH OPPORTUNITIES

Much critical attention has been devoted to Lorraine Hansberry. Needed now is a definitive, full-length, critical biography that will consider her unpublished works along with her published works and that will go beyond the present scholarship in an effort to present a realistically coherent, unbiased picture of the life and works of this many-faceted, complex artist. She was, more than most other writers, a product of her time and place, and her time and place and the plight of her people infuse her art. She developed a theory of art that has not yet received proper attention in studies of her life and work. A critical biography should carefully assess her creative works against her theory of art and should judge her work, especially her plays, in the context of her stated social purpose.

SECONDARY SOURCES

Abramson, Doris E. "Lorraine Hansberry." In *Notable American Women, The Modern Period: A Bibliographical Dictionary*, pp. 310–12. Edited by Barbara Sicherman and Carol H. Green. Cambridge: Harvard University Press, 1980.
———. *Negro Playwrights in the American Theatre, 1925–1959*. New York: Columbia University Press, 1969.
Arata, Esther, and Nicholas J. Rotoli. "Hansberry, Lorraine." In *Black American Playwrights, 1800 to the Present: A Bibliography*, pp. 93–101. Metuchen, N.J.: Scarecrow Press, 1976.
Aston, Frank. " 'Raisin in Sun' Is Moving Tale." *New York World Telegram* (12 March 1959). Reprinted in *New York Theatre Critics' Reviews* (1959): 346.
Atkinson, Brooks. "The Theatre: 'A Raisin in the Sun.' " *New York Times* (12 March 1959). Reprinted in *New York Theatre Critics' Reviews* (1959): 345.
Bailey, Peter. " 'Raisin': Lorraine Hansberry's Award Winning Play Becomes Musical Hit on Broadway." *Ebony* (May 1974): 74–80.
Baraka, Amiri. " 'Raisin in the Sun's' Enduring Passion." *Washington Post* (16 November 1986): F1–3.
Bond, Jean. "Lorraine Hansberry: To Reclaim Her Legacy." *Freedomways* 19 (4th quarter 1979): 183–85.
Breitinger, Eckhard. "Lorraine Hansberry: *A Raisin in the Sun*." In *Das Amerikanische Drama der Gegenwart*, pp. 153–68. Edited by Herbert Grabes. Kronberg: Athenaum, 1976.
Brüning, Eberhard. " 'Schwarze Befreiungsbewegung' und Afroamerikanische." In Eberhard Brüning, Klaus Kohler, and Bernhard Scheller, eds. *Studien zum Amerikanischen Drama nach dem Zeiten Weltkrieg*, pp. 214–18, Berlin: Rütter und Loening, 1977.
Carter, Steven R. "Lorraine Hansberry (19 May 1930—12 January 1965)." In *Dictionary of Literary Biography*. Vol. 38: *Afro-American Writers after 1955: Dramatists and Prose Writers*, pp. 120–34. Edited by Thadious M. Davis and Trudier Harris. Detroit: Gale Research Co., 1985.
Cheney, Anne. *Lorraine Hansberry*. Boston: Twayne Publishers, 1984.
Christiansen, Richard. "Goodman Taps Fine Wine with 'Raisin.' " *Chicago Tribune* (4 October 1983): B8.
Clurman, Harold. "Theatre." Review of *Les Blancs*. *Nation* (30 November 1970): 573.
———. "Theatre." Review of *A Raisin in the Sun*. *Nation* (4 April 1959): 301–2.
———. "Theatre." Review of play *To Be Young, Gifted and Black*. *Nation* (28 April 1969): 548.
Coleman, Robert. " 'Raisin in Sun' Superior Play." *New York Daily Mirror* (12 March 1959). Reprinted in *New York Theatre Critics' Reviews* (1959): 347.
Collins, William B. "Drama Guild Revives 'A Raisin in the Sun.' " *Philadelphia Inquirer* (5 December 1985): C1, C9.
Cook, Louis. " 'A Raisin in the Sun' a Hit at McCarter." *Trentonian* (8 April 1985): 18.
Cruse, Harold. *The Crisis of the Negro Intellectual*. New York: William Morrow and Co., 1967.

Eddleman, Floyd Eugene. *American Drama Criticism: Interpretations, 1890–1977.* 2nd. Edition. Hamden, CT: Shoestring, 1979.

Farrison, W. Edward. "Lorraine Hansberry's Last Dramas." *CLA Journal* 16 (December 1972): 188–97.

Friedman, Sharon P. "Six Female Black Playwrights: Images of Blacks in Plays." *DAI* 41 (1980): 3104.

Gassner, John. *Theatre at the Crossroads: Plays and Playwrights of the Mid-Century American Stage.* New York: Holt, Rinehart and Winston, 1960.

Gill, Brendan. "All Thumbs." Review of *The Sign in Sidney Brustein's Window. New Yorker* (5 February 1972): 69.

———. "A Black Rose." Review of *Raisin. New Yorker* (29 October 1973):107.

———. "Things Going Wrong." Review of *Les Blancs. New Yorker* (21 November 1970): 104.

Giovanni, Nikki. "An Emotional View of Lorraine Hansberry." *Freedomways* 19 (4th quarter 1979): 281–82.

Gottfried, Martin. Review of *The Sign in Sidney Brustein's Window. Women's Wear Daily* (16 October 1964): 21.

Grant, Robert H. "Lorraine Hansberry: The Playwright as Warrior-Intellect." *DAI* 82–22 (1982): 634.

Gresham, Jewell H. "Lorraine Hansberry as Prose Stylist." *Freedomways* 19 (4th quarter 1979): 192–204.

Gussow, Mel. "Stage: 'A Raisin in the Sun' at Yale." *New York Times* (9 November 1983): C23.

Guttman, Allen. "Integration and Black Nationalism in the Plays of Lorraine Hansberry." In *Amerikanisches Drama und Theater in 20. Jahrhundert,* pp. 248–60. Edited by Alfred Weber and Siegfried Neuweiler. Göttingen: Vandenhoech, 1975.

Habicht, Werner. "Lorraine Hansberry: *The Sign in Sidney Brustein's Window.*" In *Theatre und Drama en Amerika: Aspekte und Interpretation,* pp. 364–74. Edited by Edward Lohner and Rudolf Haas. Berlin: Schmidt, 1978.

Hajek, Friederike. "Lorraine Hansberry und Ihre Kinder: zur Rezeption von Lorraine Hansberry Stuck *A Raisin in the Sun,*" *Wissenschaftliche Zeitschrift der Pedagogischen Hochschule* [Potsdam] 21 (1977): 257–94.

Haley, Alex. "The Once and Future Vision of Lorraine Hansberry." *Freedomways* 19 (4th quarter 1979): 277–80.

Hatch, James V., and Omanii Abdullah, eds. *Black Playwrights, 1823–1977: An Annotated Bibliography of Plays.* New York: R. R. Bowker, 1977.

Hays, Peter L. "*Raisin in the Sun* and *Juno and the Paycock.*" *Phylon* 33 (2d quarter 1972): 175–76.

Hewes, Henry. "Broadway Postscript: He Who Laughs First." Review of *The Sign in Sidney Brustein's Window. Saturday Review* (31 October 1964): 31.

Kaiser, Ernest, and Robert Nemiroff. "A Lorraine Hansberry Bibliography." *Freedomways* 19 (4th quarter 1979): 285–304.

Kalem, T. E. "The Faith That Fades." Review of *Raisin. Time* (29 October 1973): 99.

Keyssar, Helene. *The Curtain and the Veil: Strategies in Black Drama.* New York: Burt Franklin and Co., 1981.

Killens, John O. "Lorraine Hansberry: On Time!" *Freedomways* 19 (4th quarter 1979): 273–76.

Kirkwood, Porter Jr. "Two Portraits of Lorraine Hansberry." *Freedomways* 18 (4th quarter 1978): 222–25.

Lewis, Allan. *American Plays and Playwrights of the Contemporary Theatre.* New York: Crown Publishers, 1965.

"Lorraine Hansberry." In *American Drama Criticism: Interpretations—1890–1977,* 2d ed, pp. 138–40. Compiled by Floyd E. Eddleman. Hamden, Conn.: Shoe String Press, 1979.

"Lorraine Hansberry." In Ora Williams. *American Black Women in the Arts and Social Sciences: A Bibliographic Survey.* Metuchen, N.J.: Scarecrow Press, 1973.

Miller, Jordan Y. "Lorraine Hansberry." In *The Black American Writer.* Vol. 2: *Poetry and Drama,* pp. 157–70. Edited by C. W. E. Bigsby. Deland, Fla.: Everett/Edwards, 1969.

Mitchell, Loftin. *Black Drama: The Story of the American Negro in the Theatre.* New York: Hawthorne Books, 1967.

Nemiroff, Robert. "The 101 'Final' Performances of *Sidney Brustein:* Portrait of a Play and Its Author." In Lorraine Hansberry. *A Raisin in the Sun and The Sign in Sidney Brustein's Window,* pp. 138–83.

Ness, David. "Lorraine Hansberry's *Les Blancs:* The Victory of the Man Who Must." *Freedomways* 13 (4th quarter 1973): 294–306.

Normant, Lynn. " 'Raisin' Celebrates Its 25th Anniversary." *Ebony* (March 1984): 57–60.

Pollack, Joe. "A Magnificent Revival of 'Raisin in the Sun.' " *St. Louis Post-Dispatch* (10 September 1984), 4B: 1–2.

Powell, Bertie. "The Black Experience in Margaret Walker's *Jubilee* and Lorraine Hansberry's *The Drinking Gourd.*" *CLA Journal* 21 (December 1977): 304–11.

" 'A Raisin in the Sun.' " *London Theatre Record* (10–23 April 1985): 338–40.

" 'A Raisin in the Sun.' " *Theatre Arts* (May 1959): 22–23.

Reed, Rex. "The Curtain Opens," Review of *The Sign in Sidney Brustein's Window.* *New York Express* (29 October 1964): 10.

Robertson, Nan. "Dramatist against Odds." *New York Times* (8 March 1959): 2:3.

Rush, Theressa, Carol F. Myers, and Esther Arata. *Black American Writers Past and Present: A Biographical and Bibliographical Dictionary.* 2 vols. Metuchen, N.J.: Scarecrow Press, 1975.

Salem, James M. *A Guide to Critical Reviews: Part I: American Drama, 1909–1982.* 3d ed. Metuchen, N.J.: Scarecrow Press, 1984.

Scheader, Catherine. *They Found a Way: Lorraine Hansberry.* Chicago: Children's Press, 1978.

Sheed, Wilfred. "The Stage: The Three Minute Laugh." Review of *The Sign in Sidney Brustein's Window.* Commonweal (6 November 1964): 197–98.

Tunks, Larry. " 'Raisin in Sun' Is Mesmerizing." *Daily Utah Chronicle* (5 April 1955): 5.

Turkel, Studs. "An Interview with Lorraine Hansberry." *WFMT Chicago Fine Arts Guide* 10, no. 2 (April 1961): 8–14.

Tynan, Richard. " 'A Raisin in the Sun.' " *New Yorker* (21 March 1959): 100–102.

Ward, Douglas Turner. "Lorraine Hansberry and the Passion of Walter Lee." *Freedomways* 19 (4th quarter 1979): 223–25.

Washington, J. Charles. "*A Raisin in the Sun* Revisited." *Black American Literature Forum* 22 (Spring 1988): 109–24.

Watts, Richard. "Honest Drama of a Negro Family." Review of *A Raisin in the Sun. New York Post* (12 March 1959). Reprinted in *New York Theatre Critics' Reviews* (1959): 344.

Weales, Gerald. *American Drama Since World War II*. New York: Harcourt, Brace and World, 1962.

———. "Lorraine Hansberry." *Contemporary Dramatists*. Fourth Edition, pp. 653–54. Edited by D. L. Kirkpatrick. Chicago: St. James Press, 1988.

Wilkerson, Margaret. "Lorraine Hansberry: The Complete Feminist." *Freedomways* 19 (4th quarter 1979): 235–45.

———. "The Sighted Eyes and Feeling Heart of Lorraine Hansberry." *Black American Literature Forum* 17, no. 1 (Spring 1983): 8–13. Reprinted from *Essays on Contemporary American Drama*, pp. 91–104. Edited by Hedwig Bock and Albert Wertheim. Munich: Max Hueber, 1981.

Williams, Mance. *Black Theatre in the 1960s and 1970s: A Historical-Critical Analysis of the Movement*. Westport, Conn.: Greenwood Press, 1985.

Zietlow, Edward R. "Wright to Hansberry: The Evolution of Outlook in Four Negro Writers." *DA* 28 (1967): 701A.

Beth Henley

(8 MAY 1952–   )

COLBY H. KULLMAN AND MIRIAM NEURINGER

ASSESSMENT OF HENLEY'S REPUTATION

The dramatic world of Beth Henley is a mixture of bizarre tragedy and pathetic comedy. Rich asserts, "When Beth Henley is really flying, her comic voice has the crazed yet liberating sound of a Rebel yell.... Who but Miss Henley can describe one tragedy after another and send us home smiling" (C11). Henley's dramas are deeply rooted in the southern oral tradition. A strong sense of family, the ability to make the improbable real, a grotesque mixture of humor and horror, the laying on of Gothic overtones, the appreciation of eccentricity no matter how bizarre, the use of southern vernacular in a particular southern setting—these are the hallmarks of Henley's scripts for stage and screen.

Critics celebrate her best work by praising the complexity of her characters, the preciseness of her dialogue, the weird humor of her southern grotesques, the subtlety of her exposition, the liveliness of her action, and the richness of small details. Rafferty explains that her characters are "troupers streaming bravely ahead with their lives, though what they're performing is a shambles of what they've rehearsed" (66). The critics have found fault with her weaker scripts for their worn situations, stereotyped characters, flimsy structure, stale comic dialogue, and lack of wit and humor. At the beginning of what promises to be a productive career in the theatre, Henley has won the Pulitzer Prize for *Crimes of the Heart*, which also was chosen co-winner of the Actors' Theatre of Louisville's Great American Play Contest and received the New York Drama Critics Circle Award for Best New American Play as well as the George Oppenheimer/*Newsday* Playwriting Award. Meserve aptly observes, "Maintaining that level of creativity has been her constant challenge" (245).

PRIMARY BIBLIOGRAPHY OF HENLEY'S WORKS

Plays

Drafts, notebooks, typescripts, xerographies, and holographs of many of these items are on deposit with the Department of Archives and Special Collections, University of Mississippi.

Am I Blue. 1972. New York: Dramatists Play Service, 1982.
Parade. Unpublished. 1975.
The Miss Firecracker Contest. Garden City, N.Y.: Nelson Doubleday, 1979, 1985; New York: Dramatists Play Service, 1985.
Crimes of the Heart. New York: Viking, 1982; New York: Dramatists Play Service, 1982.
The Wake of Jamey Foster. New York: Dramatists Play Service, 1982.
The Debutante Ball. Unpublished. 1985.
The Lucky Spot. Unpublished. 1986.

Screenplays

Moonwatcher. Unpublished filmscript. 1976. Multiple revisions between 1982 and 1985.
Crimes of the Heart. Unpublished filmscript. 1985.
Nobody's Fool. Unpublished filmscript. 1986.
True Stories. Co-authored with David Byrne and Stephen Tobolowsky. New York: Viking Penguin, 1986.
A Family Tree. Unpublished television script co-authored with Budge Threlkeld, 1986.
Strawberries. Unpublished filmscript. 1987.
The Miss Firecracker Contest. Unpublished filmscript. 1987.

Miscellaneous

Sisters of the Winter Madrigal. Unpublished manuscript. N.d.
Hymn in the Attic. Unpublished manuscript. N.d.
Rosamond. Unpublished notes. N.d.

Interviews

Berkvist, Robert. "Act 1: The Pulitzer, Act 11: Broadway." *New York Times* (25 Octctober 1981): D4, D22.
Haller, Scot. "Her First Play, Her First Pulitzer Prize." *Saturday Review* (November 1981): 40–44.
Raidy, William A. "Mississippi Playwright Tells Home-State Tales on and off Stage." *Memphis Commercial Appeal* (15 November 1981): 3

Bent, Ted. "Playwright Beth Henley's Only Crime Is Stealing the Hearts of Broadway Critics." *People Weekly* 16 (21 December 1981): 124–25.

Corliss, Richard. "I Go with What I'm Feeling." *Time* (8 February 1982): 80.

Lawson, Carol. "Henley's 'Wake of Jamey Foster' Taking Shape." *Jackson Clarion-Ledger* (22 September 1982): D6.

Buckley, Peter. "Beating the Odds." *Horizon* (December 1982): 49–55.

Jones, John Griffin. "Beth Henley." In *Mississippi Writers Talking*, pp. 169–90. Jackson: University Press of Mississippi, 1982.

Drake, Sylvie. "Henley's Heart Is in the Theatre." *Los Angeles Times* (16 April 1983):V1, V8.

Sherbert, Linda. "Life after the Pulitzer: 'Crimes' Playwright Aims for Acting Career." *Atlanta Constitution* (8 June 1984): H1, H10.

Myers, Leslie R. "Mississippi Playwright Downplays Her Success." *Jackson Clarion-Ledger* (21 July 1985): E1-2.

Morrow, Mark. "Beth Henley." In *Images of the Southern Writer*, pp. 42-43. Georgia: University of Georgia Press, 1985.

Walker, Beverly. "Beth Henley." *American Film* 12, 3 (December 1986): 30–31.

Rafferty, Terrence. "Nobody's Fool: Mississippi-born Playwright Beth Henley May Want to be Invisible, But These Days She's Just about Inescapable." *Savvy* (8 January 1987): 66–68.

Rochlin, Margy. "The Eccentric Genius of 'Crimes of the Heart.' " *Ms* (February 1987): 12–14.

Betsko, Kathleen, and Rachel Koenig. "Beth Henley." In *Interviews with Contemporary Women Playwrights*, pp. 211–22. New York: Beech Tree Books, 1987.

PRODUCTION HISTORY

Am I Blue, Beth Henley's first play, was written in 1972 while she was a sophomore (she used the pseudonym Amy Peach) at Southern Methodist University and produced there her senior year. This one-act play was not presented again until 1981 when Connecticut's Hartford Stage Company revived it. The following year, New York's Circle Repertory Theatre Company presented it, and it received favorable reviews. It is the story of a sixteen-year-old, dreamy urchin, Ashbe Williams, who meets eighteen-year-old fraternity boy John Polk Richards in a squalid section of New Orleans where they confess their insecurities and loneliness to each other, forming a tentative bond of affection. Humm praised her "off-the-wall humor" ("The Good Parts," 88), and Simon saw in the play "both the promise of the lovely *Crimes of the Heart* and the besetting peril of this young playwright: a leaning toward bizarre cuteness derived from any number of Southern writers" ("Slow Flow," 56).

In 1975, her first year away from SMU, she wrote the book for a 1940s musical, *Parade*, which was performed just before she left Texas for a year of graduate work at the University of Illinois. Her father was one of her worst critics this time; she explains that "he hated it because he'd been in World War II" and thought the play "completely and historically inaccurate" (Betsko and Koenig, 214).

When Henley finished *Crimes of the Heart* in 1978, she submitted it to several regional theatres, without success. Unknown to her, Frederick Bailey, a friend and fellow playwright, entered it in the Great American Play Contest sponsored by the Actors' Theatre of Louisville. Chosen as cowinner for 1977–1978, it was performed in February 1979 as part of the company's annual Festival of New American Plays. It was so well received that the Loretto-Hilton Repertory Theatre in Saint Louis, the Center Stage in Baltimore, the California's Actor's Theatre in Los Gatos, and the Immediate Theatre Company in Chicago added it to their 1979–1981 seasons. When it played off-Broadway at the Manhattan Theatre Club from 9 December 1980 to 11 January 1981, this limited engagement of thirty-two performances was sold out. By the time it transferred to Broadway and opened on 4 November 1981, it had already won the Pulitzer Prize for Drama, the first play to win the prestigious award before opening on Broadway. Shortly after, *Crimes* received the New York Drama Critics Circle Award for Best New American Play, as well as the George Oppenheimer/*Newsday* Playwriting Award, a Guggenheim Award, and a Tony nomination. A smash hit at Broadway's John Golden Theatre, it enjoyed a run of 535 performances. Among the many successful regional productions that followed were those staged by the Bush Theatre in London; the Blackstone Theatre, Chicago; the Olney Theatre, Washington, D.C.; the Alliance Theatre, Atlanta; the Center Theatre Group, Los Angeles; the Plaza Theatre, Dallas; the Alaska Repertory Theatre, Anchorage/Fairbanks; and the Alley Theatre, Houston.

Celebrating Henley's "charm, warmth, style, unpretentiousness, and authentically individual vision," Simon summed up the prevailing praise for *Crimes:* "Henley is marvelous at exposition, cogently interspersing it with action, and making it just as lively and suspenseful as the actual happenings." Equally fine, her dialogue is "always in character . . . , always furthering our understanding while sharpening our curiosity, always doing something to make us laugh, get lumps in our throats, care" ("Sisterhood Is Beautiful," 42). Adler explained, "Babe's 'crime' is by no means the worst of those uncovered during the play—the things people do to one another, and to themselves, in a desperate search for love" (44). Considering this compelling combination of the tragic and the comic, Kroll observed: "Her strength, a rare one, is a sunny subtlety: she finds the theatrical flash point that fuses humor and pathos" (123). Marching along at a "pace that keeps us from ever questioning the degree of clever manipulation that we are made subject to," Gill thought *Crimes* had "a daffy complexity of plot that old pros like Kaufman and Hart would have envied" ("The Theatre: Backstage," 182). Kauffmann explained that underneath the play's insanity, its "molasses meandering, there is madness, stark madness; and that the only factor that keeps these characters out of asylums (insofar as they *are* kept out) is their mad humor which translates almost chillingly into our looking at them as comic" ("Two Cheers for Two Plays," 54). Alluding to the fact that there are seldom strong resolutions or startling conclusions to the action in Henley's scripts, Kauffmann maintained that the play "presents a condition that, in miniscule, implies much about the state of the world, as well as the state of Mississippi, and about human chaos; it says, 'Resolution is not my business. Ludicrously horrifying honesty is' " ("Two Cheers for Two Plays," 55).

Not all the critics were so positive. Registering the first major dissenting view, Kerr found that the play left him "too often and in spite of everything, disbelieving—simply and flatly disbelieving" because Henley presses the offbeat too far with her "beginner's habit of never letting well enough alone, of taking a perfectly genuine bit of observation and doubling and tripling until it's compounded itself into a parody" (D3). Weales regarded the play as "both overwritten and overacted, a refugee from Eudora Welty country punching for show-biz success in the big town" (526). For Heilpern, it suffered from "a serious culture gap" when he saw the Broadway production, which left him mostly cold and bewildered. "I could only see Southern types, like a cartoon," he explained (11).

In December 1986, Henley's screenplay for the film *Crimes of the Heart* was directed by Bruce Beresford and starred Diane Keaton as Lenny, Jessica Lange as Meg, and Sissy Spacek as Babe. The reviews were mixed. Most agreed that something went wrong with this Hollywood production, which did not hold up as well as the play did. Kauffmann thought that the screenplay kept "the braided deception and truth of the original" ("The Three Sisters," 26); Cunliffe saw it as "a comedy of manners rather than an hysterically amusing film" (23); and Corliss attacked the movie for turning what was once a comedy into "a sad-sack elegy" ("Once a Comedy," 70).

The Miss Firecracker Contest, Henley's next play, was performed in 1981 and 1982 at the University of Illinois' Krannert Center, Buffalo's Studio Arena Theatre, Chicago's Steppenwolf Theatre Company, and Britain's Bush Theatre to generally appreciative reviews. The Manhattan Theatre Club production followed with 131 performances from 1 May to 25 August 1984. Nightingale applauded this production as "a thoroughly beguiling addition to the Henley archives," finding "an element of caricature in her work," which he differentiated from "the thin monochrome sort one associates with the parodist or theatre puppeteer." Her people are "grotesque yet sentient, outrageous yet vulnerable, sometimes even pathetic" (H3). Also considering Henley's strength her characters, Oliver praised "the strangeness and depth and validity of their emotions, in the lines she has written for them to speak, and in her own astonishing humorous vision" ("The Theatre: Off Broadway," 112). Celebrating this comic power, Rich reported that "the evening's torrential downpour of humor—alternately Southern Gothic absurdist, melancholy, and broad—almost never subsides" (11). But Simon disagreed: "The agglomeration of studied bizarreness is at first coy, then cloying, and finally intolerable" ("Repeaters," 80). The Manhattan Theatre Club production was so successful that it moved to larger off-Broadway quarters that fall, playing for another 113 performances and thirteen previews at the Westside Arts Theatre.

Henley's *The Wake of Jamey Foster* was produced by the Hartford (Connecticut) Stage Company in January 1982 and transferred to Broadway's Eugene O'Neill Theatre later in the year. Opening 14 October, it closed on 23 October after only twelve performances. Jamey Foster, a failed poet and would-be historian (who left his wife for a twice-divorced, yellow-haired, sweet shop baker), has died, and his family and friends have gathered for his wake. Most of the reviewers agreed that the play struggled too hard to be funny. Considering its caprices "more obvious and ersatz" than those in *Crimes of the Heart*, Brustein claimed *The Wake* was "watered-down porridge for the stage" and that Henley "should be encouraged to do more with her talents than hang crepe on regional family pictures" (26). Humm noted that "eccentric characters and regional flavor don't compensate for an absence of action and structure" ("*The Wake of Jamey Foster*", 331). Finding "authentic laughs" and "good, or good enough, performances" in *The Wake*, Simon concluded that "the characters have been totally consumed by eccentricity" ("All's Well That Ends Good," 78–79).

Opening 9 April 1987 at South Coast Repertory in Costa Mesa, California, Henley's *The Debutante Ball* was fairly well received. Once again, she gathers southern eccentrics at a family celebration—this time a debutante ball for Teddy Parker held in Hattiesburg, Mississippi, at her stepfather's nouveau riche mansion. Bask enjoyed this "funny play" (one scene ranked among the funniest the reviewer had ever seen) "leavened with sadness" but lamented that this sadness "is not as affecting as one feels it's meant to be" and that one does not care enough for the futures of the characters (228).

Henley first presented her two-act comedy *The Lucky Spot* in Williamstown, Massachusetts, during the summer of 1986. It opened the following spring on 28 April at the Manhattan Theatre Club, playing until 17 May. Set in Pigeon, Louisiana, in 1934 during the depth of the Great Depression, the play tells of Reed Hooker, a former bootlegger who is trying to create a new life for himself by making a big success of his rural dance hall. Oliver enjoyed Henley's "erratic, eruptive and always surprising" material, praising the action and the humor for being entertaining ("The Theatre," 80–81). Humm, however, found Henley's "latest effusion of Dixie whimsy-and-water" disappointing. Considering the play "deficient in character and fresh in comic dialogue," he saw it as "a synthetic self-parody, in which the plight of the characters becomes tedious rather than sympathetic" (*"The Lucky Spot,"* 615).

While some critics like Gussow celebrate Henley's optimism about her characters' abilities to pursue paths of self-determination (25), others like Austin point out that feminists criticize playwrights Henley and Marsha Norman, among others, for failing to challenge custom and for accepting the safer tradition of the male realists (189). Henley considers herself a feminist, explaining, "Women's problems are people's problems. . . . There are certain subjects I mightn't get into, simply because I don't have the necessary knowledge, but I don't think my being a woman limits my concerns" (Berkvist, D22).

SURVEY OF SECONDARY SOURCES

Bibliographies

No full-scale bibliography for Henley is available. Selected listings appear in Durham (192, 197), Harbin (94), Hargrove (69–70), and McDonnell (104).

Biographies

In the absence of any full-length biography for Henley, the most helpful essays appear in Durham (192–94) and Tarbox (302–305). The best sources for biographical information are the Berkvist, Haller, Jones, and Walker interviews.

Influences

Henley's storytelling ability is deeply rooted in the southern oral tradition, perhaps her most significant influence. Simon praises the MaGrath sisters in *Crimes of the Heart* as "wonderful creations": "Lenny out of Chekhov, Babe out of Flannery O'Connor, and Meg out of Tennessee Williams in one of his benign moods" ("Sisterhood Is Beautiful," 42). There is irony in this evaluation, for Henley admits that she had not read O'Connor until she saw in the reviews that she was like her (Haller, 44). She does admit to being influenced by Chekhov, Beckett, Shaw, and Shakespeare whose works she discovered as "alive theatre" when she was an acting major at SMU (Corliss, "I Go with What I'm Feeling," 80). In 1986 Claudia Reilly published *Crimes of the Heart*, a novel based on Henley's play.

General Studies

Although no book or monograph is devoted to Henley, a few articles provide excellent overviews. Hargrove reveals Henley's vision of humanity and human experience as "essentially a tragicomic one, revealing both the despicable and the admirable elements of human nature as well as the duality of the universe which inflicts pain and suffering on man but occasionally allows a moment of joy or grace" (69). Studying familial bonds in her plays, Harbin notes that in all of them Henley "takes up themes related to the disintegration of traditional ideals, such as the breakup of families, the quest for emotional and spiritual fulfillment, and the repressive social forces within a small Southern community." Unnurtured by family or peers, he concludes, "they reach adulthood hungering for bonds of affection, longing to connect with family, home, and siblings" (93). In a general analysis of Henley's works, Durham observes, "Whereas Henley's dramatic material is confined to small Southern towns and the misfits who inhabit them, her humorous but sympathetic treatment of human foibles has a universality and originality that make her one of the most imaginative dramatists writing for the American theatre" (197). "Throughout her plays," Meserve asserts, "Henley is at her best in scenes with women who long for freedom, love to remember the past, and tend to be sentimental and gossipy" (246). McDonnell's consideration of "diverse similitude" in the plays of Henley and Norman, concludes that Henley (an actress by training) approaches playwriting from the standpoint of "theatre" while Norman (a teacher before becoming a playwright) shows more attention to "literary" forms and devices (103). Morrow argues that both Marsha Norman's *'night, Mother* and Henley's *Crimes of the Heart* present women whose identities are defined largely through orality, through their attitudes towards eating, drinking, smoking, and speech. The protagonists in both plays, she argues, have been influenced by mothers who were literally or figuratively abandoned by their husbands, and who responded to their isolation by substituting self-destructive oral habits for genuine human interaction.

Analyses of Individual Plays

Laughlin tests *Crimes* against the insights of several contemporary feminist theorist and asserts that the play rejects "patriarchal forces" for "a vision of female bonding and community" (49). Harris delves beneath the stereotypes in *The Miss Firecracker Contest* to show how the characters try to escape "the rigid, shallow, stereotypical roles that define and confine them, roles imposed by a society that threatens to suppress all traces of nonconformity" (4).

FUTURE RESEARCH OPPORTUNITIES

Most necessary, perhaps, is a critical biography. More needs to be known about influences on Henley, as well as about those whom she has now influenced. Sometimes attacked by feminists for accepting the safer tradition of the male realists, a more detailed study of this issue would be clarifying. Differences between writing for theatre and for film are frequently noted, yet no one has compared and contrasted her playwriting and screenwriting abilities. Her use of significant, unusual details is often mentioned but has yet to be the focus of a full-length study itself. A study of her revision strategies might prove a worthy research project. On deposit at the Department of Archives and Special Collections of the University of Mississippi, her manuscripts (sometimes revised many times over long periods of time) need to be thoroughly investigated, resulting in a necessary bibliography.

SECONDARY SOURCES

Adler, Thomas P. *Mirror on the Stage: The Pulitzer Plays as an Approach to American Drama.* West Lafayette, Ind.: Purdue University Press, 1987.

Austin, Gayle. "Women/Text/Theatre." *Performing Arts Journal* 9 (1985): 185–90.

Bask. "The Debutante Ball." *Variety* (17 April 1985): 228.

Bent, Ted. "Playwright Beth Henley's Only Crime Is Stealing the Hearts of Broadway's Critics." *People Weekly* 16 (21 December 1981): 124–25.

Berkvist, Robert. "Act I: The Pulitzer, Act II: Broadway." *New York Times* (25 October 1981): D4, D22.

Betsko, Kathleen, and Rachel Koenig. *Interviews with Contemporary Women Playwrights.* New York: Beach Tree Books, 1987.

Brustein, Robert. "Robert Brustein on Theatre." *New Republic* (29 November 1982): 24–26.

Chinoy, Helen Krich, and Linda Walsh Jenkins, eds. *Women in the American Theatre*, pp. 344, 347–350, and 374. Rev. ed. New York: Theatre Communications Group, 1988.

Corliss, Richard. "I Go with What I'm Feeling." *Time* (8 February 1982): 80.

———. "Once a Comedy, Now an Elegy." *Time* (22 December 1986): 70.

Cunliffe, Simon. "A Confederacy of Dunces." *New Statesman* 113 (24 April 1987): 23.

Durham, Ayne C. "Beth Henley." In *Critical Survey of Drama: Supplement*, pp. 192–97. Edited by Frank N. Magill. Pasadena, Calif.: Salem Press, 1987.

Gill, Brendan. "The Theatre: Backstage." *New Yorker* (16 November 1981): 182–83.

———. "The Theatre: Off Broadway." *New Yorker* (12 January 1981): 81.

Gussow, Mel. "Women Playwrights: New Voices in the Theatre." *New York Times Sunday Magazine* (1 May 1983): 22–35.

Haller, Scot. "Her First Play, Her First Pulitzer Prize." *Saturday Review*, Nov. 1981: 40–44.

Harbin, Billy J. "Familial Bonds in the Plays of Beth Henley." *Southern Quarterly* 25, no. 3 (Spring 1987): 80–94.

Hargrove, Nancy D. "The Tragicomic Vision of Beth Henley's Drama." *Southern Quarterly* 22, no. 4 (Summer 1984): 50–70.

Harris, Laurilyn J. "Delving beneath the Stereotypes: Beth Henley's *The Miss Firecracker Contest.*" *Theatre Southwest* 14 (May 1987): 4–7.

Heilpern, John. "Great Acting, Pity about the Play." *London Times* (5 December 1981): 11.

Humm. "The Good Parts." *Variety* (27 January 1982): 88.

———. "The Lucky Spot." *Variety* (6 May 1987): 615.

———. "The Wake of Jamey Foster." *Variety* (20 October 1982): 331.

Kauffmann, Stanley. "The Three Sisters." *New Republic* (2 February 1987): 26–27.

———. "Two Cheers for Two Plays." *Saturday Review* (January 1982): 54–55.

Kerr, Walter. "Offbeat—But a Beat Too Far." *New York Times* (15 November 1981): D3, D31.

Kroll, Jack. "Birthday in Manhattan." *Newsweek* (16 November 1981): 123.

Laughlin, Karen L. "Criminality, Desire, and Community: A Feminist Approach to Beth Henley's *Crimes of the Heart.*" *Women & Performance* 3, no. 1 (1986): 35–51.

McDonnell, Lisa J. "Diverse Similitude: Beth Henley and Marsha Norman." *Southern Quarterly* 25, no. 3 (Spring 1987): 95–104.

Meserve, Walter J. "Henley, Beth." *Contemporary Dramatists*. 4th ed. Chicago: St. James Press, 1988.

Morrow, Laura. "Orality and Identity in *'night, Mother* and *Crimes of the Heart.*" *Studies in American Drama, 1945–Present* 3 (1988).

Myers, Leslie R. " 'Firecracker' Cast Arrives in Yazoo City," *The Clarion-Ledger/ Jackson Daily News* 22 May 1988: E3.

Nightingale, Benedict. "A Landscape That Is Unmistakably Henley." *New York Times* (3 June 1984): H3, H7.

Oliver, Edith. "The Theatre." *New Yorker* (11 May 1987): 80–81.

———. "The Theatre: Off Broadway." *New Yorker* (11 June 1984): 112.

Rafferty, Terrence. "Nobody's Fool: Mississippi-born Playwright Beth Henley May Want to Be Invisible, But These Days She's Just about Inescapable." *Savvy* 8 (January 1987): 66–68.

Reilly, Claudia. *Crimes of the Heart*. New York: NAL/Signet, 1986.

Rich, Frank. "Theatre: *Firecracker*, A Beth Henley Comedy." *New York Times* (28 May 1984): C11.

Simon, John. "All's Well That Ends Good." *New York* 15 (25 October 1982): 78–79.

———. "Repeaters." *New York* 17 (4 June 1984): 79–80.

———. "Sisterhood Is Beautiful." *New York* 14 (12 January 1981): 42–44.

———. "Slow Flow." *New York* 15 (25 January 1982): 56–57.

Tarbox, Lucia. "Beth Henley." In *Dictionary of Literary Biography Yearbook: 1986*, pp. 302–305. Edited by J. M. Brook. Detroit, Michigan: Gale Research Company, 1986.

Weales, Gerald. "American Theatre Watch, 1981–1982." *Georgia Review* 36 (Fall 1982): 517–26.

Israel Horovitz

(31 MARCH 1939–)

MARTIN J. JACOBI

ASSESSMENT OF HOROVITZ'S REPUTATION

Israel Horovitz has written over four dozen plays and been translated into over twenty languages, yet he has not become the important dramatic voice some predicted of him when *The Indian Wants the Bronx* appeared. When this play opened at the Astor Place Theatre in 1968, Kerr and Oliver praised his dialogue; Gottfried concurred and also included "dramatic flair" among Horovitz's attributes, while Watts thought that in the future "we may be hearing fine news of him." Kerr, Barnes, and others saw potential in *Indian* and other early plays, but as early as 1971 he was being told to "get on with a full-length play" (Kerr, 1971).

Horovitz has grown and developed. The short, early works, which "staked out his claim to a share in the Beckett-Ionesco tradition of modern absurdity" (Giantvalley, 958), focused often on senseless urban violence and the inability of people to communicate; the later plays, lengthier and somewhat more realistic, have expanded his range into familial and small town social problems while maintaining felicity and wit in language. Bigsby notes, "The early, arcane plays—*Indian* and *Plum*—gave way to rather more accessible works such as *The Arthur Trilogy* and *The Quannapowitt Quartet*, which partly celebrated and partly dissected an American rural world" (27). It is difficult to determine whether these later works will gain for Horovitz the status so long promised him. So far they have received little critical commentary.

Horovitz has received numerous honors and awards that suggest he yet may rise to importance. He has received a Fulbright Grant and a Guggenheim Fellowship, and he was a Rockefeller Foundation fellow, as well as a fellow of the Royal Academy of Dramatic Art. He has received two Obies (for *Indian* and *Schnozzola*) and numerous other awards for his drama, an Emmy Award shared with Jules Feiffer for "VD Blues," and a Cannes Film Festival Prix de Jury for *The Strawberry Statement*. He was the Fanny Hurst Visiting Playwright at Brandeis University, the first American playwright in residence at the Royal Shakespeare Company, and a playwright in residence at the City University of New York and at New York University.

PRIMARY BIBLIOGRAPHY OF HOROVITZ'S WORKS

Published Plays

First Season: The Indian Wants the Bronx, Line, It's Called the Sugar Plum, Rats. New York: Random House, 1968.

Morning, Noon, and Night. With Terrence McNally and Leonard Melfi. New York: Random House, 1969.

Leader and *Play for Trees*. New York: Dramatists Play Service, 1971.

Acrobats and *Line*. New York: Dramatists Play Service, 1971.

The Honest-to-God Schnozzola. New York: Breakthrough Press, 1971.

Shooting Gallery and *Play for Germs*. New York: Dramatists Play Service, 1973.

Dr. Hero. New York: Dramatists Play Service, 1973.

The Primary English Class. New York: Dramatists Play Service, 1976.

The Qwannapowitt Quartet (produced New Haven, Connecticut, 1976; including *Hopscotch, The 75th, Stage Directions*, and *Spared*).

Uncle Snake: An Independence Day Pageant. New York: Dramatists Play Service, 1976.

Man with Bags. Adapted from Eugene Ionesco, *L'Homme aux valises*. New York: Grove, 1977.

The Wakefield Plays (including *Alfred the Great, Our Father's Failing, Alfred Dies, Hopscotch, The 75th, Stage Directions*, and *Spared*). New York: Avon, 1979.

Mackerel. Vancouver, Canada: Talonbooks, 1979.

A Christmas Carol: Scrooge and Marley. Adapted from Charles Dickens, *A Christmas Carol*. New York: Dramatists Play Service, 1979.

The Widow's Blind Date. New York: Theatre Communications Group, 1981.

The Former One-on-One Basketball Champion and *The Great Labor Day Classic*. New York: Dramatists Play Service, 1982.

The Good Parts. New York: Dramatists Play Service, 1983.

An Israel Horovitz Trilogy (including *Today, I Am a Fountain Pen, A Rosen by Any Other Name, The Chopin Playoffs*). Garden City, N.Y.: Fireside Theatre, 1987.

Other Plays

The Comeback. 1958.

The Death of Bernard the Believer. 1960.

This Play Is about Me. 1961.

The Hanging of Emmanuel. 1961.

Hop, Skip, and Jump. 1963.

The Killer Dove. 1963.

The Simon Street Harvest. 1964.
Le Premiere. 1972.
Turnstile. 1974.
The First, the Last, the Middle: A Comedy Triptych. 1974.
The Reason We Eat. 1976.
The Lounge Player. 1977.
Cappella (with David Boorstin), 1978.
Sunday Runners in the Rain. 1980.
Park Your Car in the Harvard Yard. 1980.
Henry Lumper, 1985.
The Year of the Duck, 1986.
North Shore Fish. 1987.

Novels

Cappella. New York: Harper & Row, 1973.
Nobody Loves Me. Paris: Editions de Minuit, 1975; New York: Braziller, 1976.

Poetry

Spider Poems and Other Writing. New York: Harper & Row, 1973.

Screenplays and Television Scripts

Play For Trees (television), 1969.
Machine Gun McCain (screenplay, English adaptation), 1970.
The Strawberry Statement. Adapted from a novel by James Somon Kunen. MGM, 1970.
Believe in Me (Speed Is of the Essence). MGM, 1970.
Alfredo (screenplay), 1970.
The Sad-Eyed Girls in the Park (screenplay), 1971.
Camerian Climbing (screenplay), 1971.
Acrobats (screenplay), 1972.
"VD Blues." New York, WNET-TV, 1972.
Start to Finish (television), 1975.
The Making and Breaking of Splinters Braun (television), 1976.
"Bartleby the Scrivener." Adapted from Herman Melville's short story. Baltimore: Maryland Public TV, 1977.
A Day with Conrad Green (from a story by Ring Lardner, television), 1978.
"Growing Up Jewish in Sault Ste. Marie." Adapted from a novel by Morley Torgov. Canadian Broadcasting, 1978.
"The Deer Park." Adapted from a novel by Norman Mailer. Lorimar Productions, 1979–80.
Fast Eddie (screenplay), 1980.
Fell (screenplay), 1982.
Berta (screenplay), 1982.

Author! Author! MGM, 1982.
Light Years (screenplay), 1985.

PRODUCTION HISTORY

Horovitz's plays have been produced all over the world, and he consistently ranks as one of the most frequently produced playwrights in American colleges and universities (Kovac, 303). His premieres have been predominantly on off-Broadway, but his work also has appeared in regional theatres.

His first play staged in New York City, *Line*, opened at the La Mama Experimental Theatre Club (also the starting place for Sam Shepard and Lanford Wilson, among others). When the lead actor left for Hollywood after the dress rehearsal, Horovitz also performed his role. Both author and actor were praised in the reviews, and when the play was revised and staged in 1971, the reviews remained generally positive. Kerr called it "a brilliantly imagined conceit executed with wit and an almost inexhaustible inventiveness" (1971, 2:3), and Oliver noted the playwright's "extraordinary ability to create a group of people and to conjure up, by the words they speak and by the rhythms of those words, the atmosphere of the special segment of society that they represent" (1971, 83).

The reviews were not all positive, however. Barnes complimented Horovitz on his "true and dazzling dialogues," his "sense of heightened realistic speech," and his "very fine technique" but complained that "the meaning beneath the words, the internal story, is far too obvious" (1971, 26). Watts thought the play more concerned with befudding the audience than with telling a recognizable story, although he still included Horovitz among the "promising playwrights" (1971). At the negative extreme are Kalem's description of Horovitz as one of "the new playwrights who . . . are seventh-rate Schopenhauers posing as third-rate Neil Simons" (350), and Harris's description of the play as "a travesty of the Theatre of the Absurd" (350).

Perhaps the negative reviews of *Line* were conditioned in part by the force of an earlier work, *The Indian Wants the Bronx*. This 1968 play, with John Cazale as the Indian and Al Pacino as one of the young toughs, is considered by many to be Horovitz's best and helped establish him as a forceful and effective commentator on urban violence. The play won Obies for Pacino and Cazale, an Obie for Best American Play of 1968, and numerous other awards. Watts (1968) recognized affinities with Albee's *The Zoo Story* and Oliver (January 1968) compared it to Pinter's *The Caretaker*. Kerr praised the language highly, saying that "each line of dialogue is a pebble skipped skillfully across the water's surface, its particular curve attended to; that a last, well-aimed stone might kill is perfectly reasonable" (*Thirty Plays* 1968, 73), and Clurman emphasized the play's social statement: characters "produce shivers because their menace and violence are part of the greater beastliness inherent in our society, which, because it does not inspire creative action based on human thought and energy, turns to wanton and senseless destructiveness" (221). Clurman's comments on the play's power and Kerr's on its language were echoed in most other reviews, and the elements of social statement and verbal felicity have continued as hallmarks of Horovitz's critical reception.

A number of critics, however, while praising the play and the potential they saw in the young playwright, thought the work flawed. Sullivan asked rhetorically if Horovitz had done more than to drag a street fight into the theatre, although he also found the "abstract beauty" of the violence and the "accuracy of the dialogue" to be undeniable (270). And while Gottfried saw Horovitz as a "playwright of unmistakable talent," he also thought he lacked "the ability to create characters and situations" (1968, 268), a complaint Watts echoed.

Appearing on the same bill with *Indian* was *It's Called the Sugar Plum*. *Plum* was considered the inferior work by almost all the critics, although its reviews were generally positive. Oliver, however, thought it "the more original of the two plays—funny while it is going on but ultimately no less chilling than *The Indian*" (January 1968, 87).

While *Indian* was in rehearsal, Horovitz was working on *Rats*, a short play billed with eleven other works under the title *Collision Course*. Included were works by Leonard Melfi, Terrence McNally, Jean-Claude van Itallie, Lanford Wilson, Sam Shepard, and Jules Feiffer. Barnes called *Rats* the best of the bill, "rough, tough, funny and moving, and both Mr. Horovitz's considerable skill and dramatic originality are again outstanding" (9 May 1968, 55). Oliver said it was "original and dramatic," calling it and Feiffer's play the only good ones on the bill (18 May 1968, 74).

Yet another play by Horovitz, *Morning*, was performed in 1968. On a bill called *Morning, Noon, and Night* (McNally and Melfi, respectively, wrote the other two plays), it was Horovitz's first appearance on Broadway. Barnes called Horovitz "disturbingly funny" and a "superb comic writer" (29 November 1968, 52), and Kerr called it "the only good one" of the three; however, Kerr also noted that the play was far inferior to *Indian*, "being psychologically slighter and structurally sloppier" (8 December 1968, 2:7), while Gill gave it a poor review, calling it a play that "would suit the fancy of the most brazen Southern racist" (1968, 140).

In 1969, *The Honest-to-God Schnozzola* premiered and won for Horovitz his second Obie. Billed with *Leader*, *Schnozzola* received positive reviews from Oliver (1969) and Barnes, who said of both plays that their endings have the "predictable unexpectedness of the pay-off to an O. Henry story. Yet when the trick has been turned, even though we have an idea of how it has been done, it remains pretty effective" (1969, 40). Kroll, however, declared that *Schnozzola* "is a sophomore's anthology of moist dreams from *Steppenwolf*, old German flicks and frat-house bull sessions about Brecht. . . . *Leader* is even worse as Horovitz has his incoherent raucous say about the particular bankruptcy of the American political system" (118).

In 1971 Horovitz began work on his Wakefield plays, seven works that premiered intermittently from 1972 through 1977. They have received little attention from the New York reviewers, since for the most part they have opened in regional and college theatres. During this period, Horovitz also wrote, among other works, *The Primary English Class*, which included Diane Keaton among its cast members. It was received less favorably than were some of the earlier works. Barnes repeated an oft-stated observation that "Mr. Horovitz is better at setting a situation than plotting a play" and called it "a slight play but an amusing one" (1976, 335); Schickel saw it as a one-joke disappointment kept alive by the "delightful comic force" of Keaton (337), and Gottfried called it "dumb and irritating, a combination definitely to be missed" (1976, 336). A 1982 production in Washington, D.C., was "as entertaining as a fingernail on a blackboard . . . a poorly conceived play" (Rosenfeld, 46). On a more positive note, Kovac noted that the play was much better received in Poland, Germany, and Japan and is Canada's longest-running play (305), and Sogliuzzo claimed it as Horovitz's "outstanding success" (267).

The Good Parts, which premiered in 1982, continued the poor reviews. Beaufort claimed that Horovitz's "characters seem more like vehicles to be maneuvered than vessels to be filled" (18); Rich asserted that it had "too many cheap jokes . . . and the plot hasn't even been worked out to fruition" (C3); and Simon called it a "ripe, maybe overripe, specimen of ["Jewish Absurdism"]. . . . It is all parts, though with not even absurdist paralogic to hold them together; as for *the good*, the other half of the title, I can see very little of it here" (1982, 70).

The most recent plays, however, suggest that Horovitz might finally be tackling the kind of material in the kind of structure that will fulfill his early promise. Of *North Shore Fish*, Gussow said that the playwright "is artful in his delineation of a dying economy and in his small but sensitive group portrait of people allied by geography, their Roman Catholic upbringing, and their limited aspirations. [The play] resonates with local color" (12 January 1987, C20). In a later review, Gussow noted that Horovitz "performs the double obligation of humanizing his characters and of making a statement about the troubles of the American economy [and in the process] amasses color, character, and sensitivity" (25 January 1987, H4). Gold wrote that Horovitz "makes no pretense of having any interest in other threatened professions. He sticks to his fish so his play [is] small but true" (16).

The observations of smallness and control are repeated in reviews of his "Growing Up Jewish" plays, which are based on Morley Torgov's book, *A Good Place to Come From*. Gussow claimed of *Today, I Am a Fountain Pen* that it "is small in scope but wide in its appreciation of family values and the yearnings of youth.... Horovitz communicates a genuine fondness for his characters and their environment ... [and] his play is quietly disarming" (3 January 1986). The second play of the trilogy, *A Rosen by any Other Name*, also received a strongly positive review from Gussow, who closed by saying, "Move over, *Star Wars*. This is a trilogy with dimension" (5 March 1986). Like *Fountain Pen* and unlike the science fiction trilogy, the "action is made up of little scenes.... The story is serviceable enough, but it is the details that count—the vignettes that the author blends with some skill" (Oliver, 24 March 1986). The last play, *The Chopin Playoffs*, was less successful in its comic execution. "Sad to say, though the pen is willing, the inspiration has dwindled ... [and] one wonders where the Horovitz humor has gone and concludes that it remains lodged in the first two plays" (Gussow, 16 May 1986). Taken together, though, this trilogy shows Horovitz heeding the earlier advice of critics to write longer plays, and indicates a control over character and plot development missing in his earlier efforts.

SURVEY OF SECONDARY SOURCES

Bibliographies

No bibliography devoted to Horovitz exists.

Biographies

Biographical material is contained in two long magazine articles—Wetzsteon's "Author! Author!—It's Israel Horovitz" and Sagal's "The Mellowing of Israel Horovitz"—and in a recent piece by Forsberg in the *New York Times*. Perhaps the most important piece of biographical information to surface in these reports is Horovitz's statement that until the "Growing Up Jewish" plays, he never used events from his own childhood in his works. It seems reasonable to suppose that a connection exists between this fact and the greater control over character and plot development shown in these plays. It might also seem reasonable to wonder whether Horovitz has elsewhere used aspects, if not events, from his life; the playwright was born in Wakefield, and Sogliuzzo suggests that "Horovitz probes into the roots of his own psyche by dramatizing the adventures of Alfred, a celebrated citizen of Wakefield," in the collected Wakefield plays (266).

Influences

Horovitz is listed in *Critical Survey of Drama, Contemporary Authors, Dictionary of Literary Biography*, and *Contemporary Dramatists*. Opinion among these researchers is that Horovitz has been influenced primarily by Samuel Beckett and Eugene Ionesco—particularly in his early works. In *The Arthur Trilogy*, however, "there are echoes, stylistic and thematic, of Kafka, Albee, Pinter . . . [and] classical forms" (Kovac, 306). Researchers have also noted the trilogy's affinities with *The Oresteia* (Kovac, 306; Wetzsteon, 30; Williams, 230).

General Studies

As yet little scholarly attention has been given to Horovitz's plays. One exception is the article by Williams, which in part analyzes the three Arthur plays. Williams notes the relationships among these plays and *The Oresteia:* incest as the precipitating event in both cycles; the homecomings in *Alfred the Great* and *Agamemnon;* and the trial in *Alfred Dies* and *The Eumenides*. He points out, however, that the plays are not about Greece but modern America, and, focusing on *Alfred Dies*, he notes the symbolic America contained in the play's setting: "a green park with a white gazebo built over a swamp." The vision of modern society presented in this play is bleak and unredeemable yet honest, an "attempt to assess [recent events] so that we can understand where we have been and what we have learned" (232). Another general study can be found in Sogliuzzo.

Analyses of Individual Plays

Aside from individual reviews of his plays, there is no critical assessment of a single Horowitz play.

FUTURE RESEARCH OPPORTUNITIES

The Horovitz canon, since it is relatively unexamined by scholars, stands open to manifold approaches. Three lines of thought seem most worthy of development.

The first would analyze dramatic influences. Here one should consider not only the Greek influence—Williams asserts that parallels to the Orestes legend exist throughout the works (230)—but also the influence of Beckett, Ionesco, and Albee. In what ways has Horovitz used these and other playwrights' absurdist visions and in what ways has he developed his own variation?

Second, critics, especially those interested in psychological and sociological readings, might consider the themes of alienation and lack of communication, which are woven throughout the body of plays. This analysis should also consider the contribution Horovitz has made to the depiction of violence in modern America. He has dealt continually with variations on the theme of violence—with physical violence, in such works as *Indian* and *Rats;* with psychic violence, in, for example *Sugar Plum, Acrobats,* and *The Primary English Class;* and with economic violence, in *Rats, Mackerel,* and *North Shore Fish.* Often violence results from the alienation of people who cannot communicate with each other. Other works that develop this line of analysis include the plays about foolish Americans abroad—*The Honest-to-God Schnozzola* and *The Good Parts*— and, especially worthy, the Wakefield cycle.

Finally, stylistic and rhetorical critics also have a great deal of material with which to work. Throughout Horovitz's career, critics have noted the humor, the felicity of expression, and the intensity of image in the plays, and so far no one has examined this aspect of the plays critically. He can combine, sometimes within a single sentence, elements of terror and slapstick humor, and his playful uses and misuses of words are not only delightful in themselves but also often effective in developing plot and character. While Horovitz has significant points to make about violence, alienation, and lack of communication, the verbal ability he exhibits in making these points sets him apart from other playwrights of his generation. If Horovitz is to gain a place among the important American dramatists, a good deal of the credit will go to the ways in which he uses language.

SECONDARY SOURCES

Barnes, Clive. "Theater: 11 Short Plays." *New York Times* (9 May 1968): 55.
———. "Theater: *Honest-to-God Schnozzola.*" *New York Times* (22 April 1969): 40.
———. "Theater: Horovitz Double Bill Opens at the De Lys." *New York Times* (16 February 1971): 26.
———. "Theater: *Morning, Noon,* and *Night.*" *New York Times* (29 November 1968): 52.
———. "Theater: *The Primary English Class* Is Staged." *New York Times* (17 February 1976). Reprinted in *New York Times Theatre Critics' Reviews* (1976): 335.
Beaufort, John. "The American Tourist Is Still Good for Laughs." *Christian Science Monitor* (21 January 1982): 18.
Bigsby, C. W. E. *A Critical Introduction to Twentieth Century American Drama: Beyond Broadway.* Vol. 3. New York: Cambridge University Press, 1985.
Clurman, Harold. "Theatre." *Nation* (12 February 1968): 221.

Davis, James. "Two Horovitz Plays Are Lightweight Fare." *New York Daily News* (16 February 1971). Reprinted in *New York Theater Critics' Reviews* (1972): 349.

Evory, Ann, ed. *Contemporary Authors: A Bio-Bibliographical Guide to Current Authors and Their Works*, 33–36: 416–18. Detroit: Gale Research Co., 1978.

Forsberg, Myra. "A Playwright Seeks the Truths of His Childhood." *New York Times* (2 March 1986): H4, H26.

Giantvalley, Scott. "Israel Horovitz." In *Critical Survey of Drama: English Language Series*, 3: 957–64. Edited by Frank Magill. Englewood Cliffs, N.J.: Salem Press, 1985.

Gill, Brendan. "Triumph and Disaster." *New Yorker* (7 December 1968): 139–40.

Gold, Sylviane. "Life at the Fish Factory." *Wall Street Journal* (19 January 1987): 16.

Gottfried, Martin. "A Tower of Babel." *New York Post* (17 February 1976). Reprinted in *New York Theatre Critics' Reviews* (1976): 336.

———. *Opening Nights: Theater Criticism of the Sixties*. New York: G. P. Putnam's Sons, 1969.

———. "Theatre: *Acrobats* and *Line*." *Women's Wear Daily*. (17 February 1971). Reprinted in *New York Theater Critics' Reviews* (1972): 350.

———. "The Indian Wants the Bronx." *Women's Wear Daily* (18 January 1968). Reprinted in *New York Theatre Critics' Reviews* (1968): 268.

Gussow, Mel. "Stage: *Chopin Playoffs* Third of H's Tales." *New York Times* (16 May 1986): C3.

———. "Stage: *Fish*, by Horovitz." *New York Times* (12 January 1987): C20.

———. "Stage: *Fountain Pen*." *New York Times* (3 January 1986): C3.

———. "The Theater: *Rosen*, New Play by Horovitz." *New York Times* (5 March 1986): C19.

———. "When the Group Becomes the Star." *New York Times* (25 January 1987): H4.

Harris, Leonard. "*Line* and *Acrobats*." WCBS-TV. 15 February 1971. Reprinted in *New York Theater Critics' Reviews* (1972): 350.

Kalem, T. E. "The Theater: Cosmic Jokers." *Time* (1 March 1971). Reprinted in *New York Theater Critics' Reviews* (1972): 350.

Kerr, Walter. "A Brilliantly Drawn *Line*." *New York Times* (7 March 1971): 2: 3.

———. "*Futz*:—and Eugene O'Neill." *New York Times* (30 June 1968): B1. Reprinted in Kerr, *Thirty Plays Hath November: Pain and Pleasure in the Contemporary Theater*. New York: Simon and Schuster, 1968.

———. "It's No One Going Nowhere." *New York Times* (8 December 1968): 2: 1, 5.

Kovac, Kim Peter. "Israel Horovitz." In *Dictionary of Literary Biography: Twentieth Century American Dramatists*, 7, pt. 1: 301–8. Detroit: Gale Research Co., 1981.

Kroll, Jack. "Theater of Crisis." *Newsweek* (5 May 1969): 118.

Little, Stuart W. and Arthur Cantor. *The Playmakers*. New York: Dutton, 1970.

Oliver, Edith. "Off Broadway: Hayf Dy Doretob!" *New Yorker* (18 May 1968): 73–76.

———. "Off Broadway: More of the Same." *New Yorker* (24 March 1986): 108–11.

———. "Off Broadway: Queue." *New Yorker* (27 February 1971): 82–84.

———. "Off Broadway: *The Indian* and *Sugar Plum.*" *New Yorker* (27 January 1968): 86–87.

———. "Off Broadway: The Soft-Edged Pirandello." *New Yorker* (3 May 1969): 107–9.

Rich, Frank. "Farce: Tony Roberts in Horovitz's *Good Parts.*" *New York Times* (7 January 1982): C3.

Rosenfeld, Megan. "Too Many Languages, Not Enough Class." *Washington Post* (9 October 1982): 46.

Sagal, Peter. "The Mellowing of Israel Horovitz." *Boston Magazine* (October 1986): 172, 239–48.

Schickel, Richard. "Filling the Vacuum." *Time* (1 March 1976). Reprinted in *New York Theatre Critics' Reviews* (1976): 337.

Shepard, Richard. "Three Young Playwrights Talk Shop." *New York Times* (10 December 1968): 54.

Simon, John. "Half-Truths." *New York Magazine* (18 January 1982): 70.

———. *Uneasy Stages: A Chronicle of New York Theater, 1963–1973.* New York: Random House, 1975.

Sogliuzzo, A. Richard. "Israel Horovitz." *Contemporary Dramatists* (4th Ed.). Ed. D. L. Kirkpatrick. Chicago: St. James Press, 1988: 264–7.

Sullivan, Dan. "Theater: Two One-Acters." *New York Times* (18 January 1968). Reprinted in *New York Times Theatre Critics' Reviews* (1968): 269–70.

Watts, Richard, Jr. "The Indian and the Sugar Plum." *New York Post* (18 January 1968). Reprinted in *New York Theatre Critics' Reviews* (1968): 268.

———. "Five People on Line." *New York Post* (16 February 1971). Reprinted in *New York Theater Critics' Reviews* (1972): 349.

Wetzsteon, Ross. "Author! Author!—It's Horovitz." *New York Magazine* (2 August 1982): 28–35.

Williams, Barry B. "Images of America." *Theatre Journal* 34 (May 1982): 223–32.

William Inge

(3 MAY 1913–10 JUNE 1973)

MAARTEN REILINGH

ASSESSMENT OF INGE'S REPUTATION

William Motter Inge was one of America's most popular playwrights in
the 1950s. *Come Back, Little Sheba*, Inge's first Broadway play, was quickly
recognized with the George Jean Nathan and Theatre Time awards.
Sheba was followed in 1953 by *Picnic*, which won the Pulitzer Prize and
New York Drama Critics Circle Award. *Bus Stop* in 1955 and *The Dark
at the Top of the Stairs* in 1957 were also popular successes. Although later
plays were not as well received, these four dramas, which were rapidly
developed into successful motion pictures, established Inge's position in
American theatre and letters. In 1961, he wrote the Academy award–
winning *Splendor in the Grass*.

Working within the long-established tradition of naturalism, Inge was
regarded as a pioneer among American playwrights in his use of the
Midwest and of Freudian psychology as motivational elements in his
plays. By placing characters in intimate contact with careful plotting,
authentic-sounding dialogue, and sympathy, Inge typically depicted ordinary people in their struggles with hidden neuroses in the face of
middle-class repression and prejudice. Inge shows these people coming
to terms with each other and with their ordinary lives. As Bigsby notes,
Inge's "subject is compromise" (13). According to Shuman, his early
biographer, Inge "presented with astounding veracity the oppressive
banality of the lives of his characters" and "may justifiably be called the
first playwright to examine the Midwest . . . to have concern for the sociological uniqueness of the area and for the psychological manifestations
of this uniqueness as it is revealed in the reactions of its people" (17–
18).

By the 1960s, however, social revolution was in the air, and neither
theatre audiences nor scholars were interested in social or personal com-

promise. The poignant, gentle plays of the Midwestern gentleman did not attract audiences or critics during these years. The ferment of the 1960s, however, also planted the seeds in the 1970s and 1980s of a renewed interest in popular culture and rural America and with it a renewed interest in the study and production of his drama. Inge's birthplace, Independence, Kansas, is the home of an annual festival of performance and scholarship convened in his honor. As McIlrath so eloquently expresses, Inge is still the "Great Voice of the Heart of America" (45).

PRIMARY BIBLIOGRAPHY OF INGE'S WORKS

Unless they constitute the only edition, anthologized or paperback editions or acting editions of plays are not listed below. Listings for anthologized and paperback plays, acting editions, and additional essays by Inge may be found in the Shuman, McClure and William Inge Collection bibliographies.

Full-Length Plays

Come Back, Little Sheba. New York: Random House, 1950.
Picnic. New York: Random House, 1953.
Bus Stop. New York: Random House, 1955.
The Dark at the Top of the Stairs. New York: Random House, 1958.
Four Plays by William Inge. New York: Random House, 1958. Contains *Come Back, Little Sheba, Picnic, Bus Stop,* and *The Dark at the Top of the Stairs.*
A Loss of Roses. New York: Random House, 1960.
"Summer Brave." In *Summer Brave and Eleven Short Plays,* pp. 1–113. New York: Random House, 1962.
Natural Affection. New York: Random House, 1963.
Where's Daddy? New York: Random House, 1966.

One-Act Plays

"Glory in the Flower." In *Twenty-four Favorite One-Act Plays,* pp. 133–50. Edited by Bennett Cerf and Van H. Cartmell. New York: Doubleday, 1958.
"The Sounds of Triumph." In *Plays as Experience: One-Act Plays for the Secondary School.* Rev. ed. Edited by Irwin J. Zachar. New York: Odyssey Press, 1962.
Summer Brave and Eleven Short Plays. New York: Random House, 1962. Contains *Summer Brave, To Bobolink, for Her Spirit, People in the Wind, A Social Event, The Boy in the Basement, The Tiny Closet, Memory of Summer, Bus Riley's Back in Town, The Rainy Afternoon, The Mall, An Incident at the Standish Arms,* and *The Strains of Triumph.*
"The Disposal." In *The Best Short Plays of the World Theatre, 1958–1967.* Edited by Stanley Richards. New York: Crown Publishers, 1968.
Two Short Plays: The Call, and A Murder. New York: Dramatists Play Service, 1968.

"Midwestern Manic." In *Best Short Plays, 1969*, pp. 37–77. Edited by Stanley
    Richards. Philadelphia: Chilton, 1969.
"Margaret's Bed." In *Best Short Plays of the World Theatre 1968–1973*, pp. 254–
    63. Edited by Stanley Richards. New York, Crown, 1973.

Screenplay

Splendor in the Grass. New York: Bantam Books, 1961.

Novels

Good Luck, Miss Wyckoff. Boston: Little, Brown, 1970.
My Son is a Splendid Driver. Boston: Little, Brown, 1971.

Essays

"The Schizophrenic Wonder." *Theatre Arts* 34, no. 5 (May 1950): 22–23. Also in
    American Playwrights on Drama, pp. 89–93. Edited by Horst Frenz. New
    York: Hill and Wang, 1965.
"Concerning Labels; 'Most Promising Playwright' Discusses Handicaps Imposed
    by Designation." *New York Times* (23 July 1950): 2: 1.
" 'Picnic': Of Women." *New York Times* (15 February 1953): 2: 3.
"From 'Front Porch' to Broadway." *Theatre Arts* 38, no. 4 (April 1954): 32–33.
"How Do You Like Your Chopin?" *New York Times* (27 February 1955): 2: 1, 3.
"Culled from the Author's Past." *New York Times* (1 December 1957): 2: 1, 3.
Foreword to *Four Plays by William Inge*. New York: Random House, 1958. Also
    as "The Taste of Success." In *American Playwrights on Drama*, pp. 127–33.
    Edited by Horst Frenz. New York: Hill and Wang, 1965.
"Forgotten Anger." *Theatre Arts* 42, no. 2 (February 1958): 68–69, 94.
"More on the Playwright's Mission." *Theatre Arts* 42, no. 8 (August 1958): 19.

Interviews

Interview. In *Counterpoint*, pp. 356–63. New York: Edited by Roy Newquist.
    Simon and Schuster, 1964.
Interview. In *The Playwrights Speak: Interviews with 11 Playwrights*, pp. 110–39.
    Edited by Walter Wager. New York: Delacorte Press, 1967.

PRODUCTION HISTORY

In 1947, Margot Jones produced Inge's *Farther Off from Heaven* which
ran for fourteen performances at her Theatre 47 in Dallas. Her account
of this production of Inge's yet unpublished script is valuable. *Farther
Off from Heaven* was eventually rewritten and produced on Broadway as
The Dark at the Top of the Stairs.

Inge's most well-known play, *Come Back, Little Sheba*, opened at the

Booth Theatre on 15 February 1950 and was directed for the Theatre Guild by Daniel Mann. Taking royalty and salary cuts, Inge and his loyal cast kept *Sheba* on Broadway for 190 performances. Many critics were troubled by Inge's first-act portrait of domestic routine, distinguished primarily by Shirley Booth's incessantly cheerful Lola. These critics characterize *Sheba* as an excellent first effort for a new playwright, its weaknesses hidden by the guild's first-class production and the bravura performances of Booth and Sidney Blackmer. The unidentified *Newsweek* critic complained that the "author risks monotony in reporting the boredom and defeat of Doc's existence with Lola (*"Come Back Little Sheba,"* 74), and Beyer noted that it was Booth who "manages to make [Lola] humanly sympathetic, and so the reconciliation is deeply moving" (345). Clurman, however, reserved credit for Inge and declared that "the drab spiritual desert that forms the atmosphere for these people would justify our calling 'Come Back, Little Sheba' a form of suicide literature were it not for an element of tenderness that sweetens it" ("A Good Play," 22). Clurman also suggested that *Sheba* was "true Americana of a kind that has become rather rare" in a theatre accustomed to serving more "hyped-up" realism to its audiences (22). Inge did make a bow to hyped-up realism with his heavily dramatic second act, which culminates with Doc's hatchet-wielding attack on Lola. This scene was played vividly, the reviewer for *Life* noting that Blackmer broke two ribs during the run of the show. Mann (interview by M. Wood), Anderson, and Audrey Wood discuss details concerning the production, acting, and staging of *Sheba* and of Inge's frame of mind at this time.

For the Paramount film of *Come Back, Little Sheba* in 1952, Daniel Mann and Shirley Booth were joined by Burt Lancaster (who replaced Blackmer as Doc) successfully playing a role very much different from his usual muscular types. A playwright herself, Ketti Frings who wrote the screenplay remained faithful to the original. The ability of the camera to focus on small details helped to make the quieter proceedings of the first act more significant in a production that Brog claimed still delivered "well-directed wallops of emotions" (*"Come Back, Little Sheba"*). Mann discussed the process of filming *Sheba* and the differences between the two versions (interview by M. Wood).

Picnic opened on 19 February 1953 at the Music Box Theatre, produced by the Theatre Guild and Joshua Logan. Spanning two seasons for 477 performances, this production featured Ralph Meeker as the virile Hal Carter and included noteworthy performances by Kim Stanley (Millie), dancer Janice Rule (Madge), Peggy Conklin (Flo), Ruth McDevitt (Helen Potts), Eileen Heckart (Rosemary), Arthur O'Connell (Howard), and Paul Newman (Alan). With this sensational production, Inge established himself as a master of theatrical technique. Hayes noted that *Picnic* is "orchestrated . . . with a subtlety of detail and breadth of reference dazzling in their sensibility" (603), and Gibbs pointed to "accurately ob-served detail, sensitively recorded speech, and . . . rare . . . humor" (65). The heavy sensuality of this production was vividly photographed for *Life* (1953). *Catholic World* critic Rensselaer Wyatt observed that "William Inge . . . has sensed with graphic perception the effect of six feet of un-inhibited manhood in sudden proximity to four women" (69). While Bentley accused Inge of pandering to prurient public taste (1953), the responsibility of this particular effect was not only to be laid at the playwright's door alone. Clurman noted that director Joshua Logan had transformed "a laconic delineation of a milieu seen with humor and intelligent sympathy" into "a rather coarse boy-and-girl story with a leeringly sentimental emphasis on naked limbs and 'well-stacked' fe-males" ("*Picnic,*" 176). Nathan confirmed these remarks (1953) ("*Come Back, Little Sheba,*" 232) as did the reviewer in *Saturday Review* who also provided many specific details of Logan's treatment. That Inge and Logan did not agree on many key issues is well known. Inge subsequently acknowledged the efficacy of Logan's manipulations (1954; foreword, 1958). However, *Summer Brave,* a reworked *Picnic,* was staged in 1973. Details of these differences are recounted in Logan's memoirs and those of Audrey Wood.

The Columbia Pictures 1956 film of *Picnic* was highly successful; it garnered four Academy Award nominations, including for Best Picture and Best Director. Joshua Logan directed a cast that included William Holden as Hal, with Kim Novak (Madge), Rosalind Russell (Rosemary), and Susan Strasburg (Millie). While they faithfully retold Inge's story, Logan and screenwriter Daniel Taradash also opened up the action to include the festivities, which are only mentioned in the play. Weiler points out, "While the titular picnic of this sprawling dramatization is inventive, eye-catching and eye-filling, it is not particularly germane to the dramas [of the various characters] at hand" (13). *Picnic*—in both versions—established Inge as a fine delineator of the midwestern milieu and of characters who were at the same time ordinary and interesting. The enduring popularity of Inge's love story was exemplified by the 1987 television version of *Picnic* which starred Michael Learned.

Bus Stop, Inge's next success, also premiered at the Music Box Theatre where it opened on 2 March 1955 and ran for 478 performances. Pro-duced by Robert Whitehead and Roger Stevens and directed by Harold Clurman, the cast featured Kim Stanley as Cherie opposite Albert Salmi's Bo Decker and included Phyllis Love (Elma), Elaine Stritch (Grace), Lou Polan (Will), Anthony Ross (Lyman), Patrick McVey (Carl), and Crahan Denton (Virgil). Gibbs noted that "Stanley . . . is nasal, brassy, incredibly vulgar, and altogether a delight" (64). Ensuring its success by unequi-vocally labeling it a comedy, reviewers were also aware that this play was directed with more subtlety than its more dramatic predecessors. "It is delicate work," noted Hatch, "the night-club girl who is vulgar but not cheap; the cowboy who is absurd but not ridiculous; the professor who is pitiable but not maudlin; the restaurant owner who is tough but not callous. This is partly technique, of course, but even more it is the way Inge and Clurman see people" (246). Kronenberger praised *Bus Stop* for its "largely Chekhovian mood" ("*The Best Plays of 1954–1955*," 54). While Hewes credited him for writing "banal characters with most of their sentimental fat off," he "wishes that Mr. Inge might more completely free himself from the demands of the commonplace" (1955, 24). Bentley found fault with Inge's "curiously morbid insistence on healthy instinct" ("*Bus Stop*," 22).

Unlike the Broadway version, which featured ensemble playing, the 1956 Twentieth Century Fox *Bus Stop* was a one-woman show. That woman was Marilyn Monroe as Cherie. She was supported by Don Murray (Bo), Betty Field (Grace), Arthur O'Connell (Virgil), Eileen Heckart (Vera), Hope Lange (Elma), and others. Scripted by George Axelrod "without too much literal attachment to the play of Mr. Inge," according to Crowther ("*Bus Stop*," 19), and directed by Joshua Logan, the film emphasized Cherie and her relationship to Bo.

Produced by Arnold Saint Subber and Elia Kazan, *The Dark at the Top of the Stairs* opened at the Music Box Theatre on 5 December 1957. Inge's last Broadway hit, *Dark* ran for 469 performances. Kazan directed a talented cast that featured Pat Hingle as Rubin Flood, Teresa Wright as Cora, and Eileen Heckart as Lottie Lacey. Other performers included Charles Saari (Sonny), Judith Robinson (Reenie), Evans Evans (Flirt), Frank Overton (Morris), and Timmy Everett (Sammy Goldenbaum). Kerr called this reworking of the autobiographical *Farther Off from Heaven* "a touching example" of a "memory play" (238). *Dark* was generally well received by the daily critics as an honest, gentle portrait of conventionally pathetic individuals. Once again, however, the question of Inge's treatment by a director was raised, this time by Brustein, who noted that where "Inge proposes calm and lassitudes, Kazan imposes theatrical high-jinks...and in a play almost devoid of climaxes we are served a climax every five minutes" (53). Brustein, Driver, and Kronenberger ("*Dark*" reviews) offered similar reservations concerning Inge's use of a prescriptive, underlying psychology.

Warner Brothers released the film version of *The Dark at the Top of the Stairs* in 1960 with Robert Preston as Rubin, Dorothy McGuire as Cora, and Eve Arden as Lottie. Delbert Mann directed, and Harriet Frank, Jr., and Irving Ravetch produced the script. And once more Inge was recognized for his memorable characters and compassionate realism. The *Variety* reviewer Ron noted that Preston's Rubin shared a "manner" with his Harold Hill (the role he created in *The Music Man*), more serious but still the hustler with "strength and independence" ("*Dark*").

Arnold Saint Subber teamed up with Lester Osterman to produce Inge's ill-fated *A Loss of Roses* at the Eugene O'Neill Theatre on 28 November 1959. The production, directed by Daniel Mann, featured Betty Field (replacing Shirley Booth during the out-of-town tryout) as Helen Baird, Warren Beatty as Kenny, Carol Haney as Lila, and Michael J. Pollard as Jelly Beamis. The play closed after only twenty-five performances. Watts, whose comments are typical, noted that its "weakness lies in its curiously plodding dullness and the lack of emotional vitality, in the absence of the author's usual deep and sympathetic insight into character and motive. The play seems at the same time shallow, pallid and undramatic" (211). Daniel Mann (interview by M. Wood) and Audrey Wood offered some useful assessments of working with Inge and the actors.

A frequent criticism leveled at *A Loss of Roses* was that its mother-son theme was inconsistently developed by the more theatrical and titillating character of Lila and her relationship to Kenny. These reviews, however, were apparently ignored by the producers of the film version, which was retitled *The Stripper* and released by Twentieth Century Fox in 1963. Directed by Franklin Schaffner and scripted by Meade Roberts, the cast included Joanne Woodward as Lila, Richard Beymer as Kenny, and Claire Trevor as Helen. Crowther indicated only disgust for the entire project, noting that its plot was inconsequential and dull ("*The Stripper*").

Two years earlier, Crowther had passed an entirely different judgment on Inge's first screenplay, *Splendor in the Grass*, released in 1961 by Warner Brothers. Directed by Elia Kazan, this drama of young lovers and their parents expertly played by Natalie Wood, Warren Beatty, Pat Hingle, and Audrey Christie provided the twin values of sensitivity and sensation that had come to characterize Inge's stage plays. Crowther stated that "Mr. Inge has written and Mr. Kazan has hurled upon the screen a frank and ferocious social drama that makes the eyes pop and the modest cheek burn" ("*Splendor*," 53).

Natural Affection, which lasted for only thirty-six performances, opened at the Booth Theatre on 31 January 1963. Produced by Oliver Smith, directed by Tony Richardson, with Kim Stanley as Sue Barker, Harry Guardino as Bernie Slovenk, Tom Bosley and Monica May as Vince and Claire Brinkman, respectively, and Gregory Rozakis as Donnie Barker, the sexual and violent nature of the play's theme and its staging generated quick condemnation from most critics. Writing at season's end, Hewes noted that "while the play's shape was interesting and theatrical, it too often seemed gratuitously preoccupied with presenting the earthy details instead of rising to a poetic and incisive savagery. And here and there we are aware of psychological theory guiding the playwright's hand" (*The Best Plays of 1962–1963*, 6).

Produced by Michael Wager at the Billy Rose Theatre, *Where's Daddy?* opened on 2 March 1966, but closed later that month after only twenty-two performances. Harold Clurman directed a cast that included Barbara Dana as Teena, Beau Bridges as Tom, Betty Field as Mrs. Bigelow, Hiram Sherman as Pinky, Barbara Ann Teer as Helen, and Robert Hooks as Razz. While praised by a few reviewers as a minor sentimental comedy, most of them condemned the play for its overly broad humor and moralizing.

Inge's last New York premieres occurred off-Broadway. *The Last Pad* opened at the Thirteenth Street Theatre on 27 November 1970 and ran for six performances. Gussow, one of the few critics to review it, noted that "it is another slice of the Inge landscape—full of strong women and suffocating men—but without the emotional intimacy, the small insights into human nature, and those little twists of humor that make the mundane seem self-satirizing" (61). *Summer Brave* received an Equity Library Theatre production on 5 April 1973 running for twelve performances.

Several unpublished Inge plays were produced while he was teaching on an occasional basis in the late 1960s in California.

SURVEY OF SECONDARY SOURCES

Bibliographies

McClure's *William Inge: A Bibliography* is the most complete listing of works by or about Inge. Briefly annotated, McClure's bibliography is classified to guide the user to appropriate material. Using McClure's guide, one must still fend for oneself when seeking material published after 1980.

The bibliography of the William Inge Collection at the Independence Community College (ICC) library, though not widely available, is available from the library. Intended as a guide to the collection, it functions as a comprehensive, annotated bibliography to Inge material published before 1980. The collection itself, and two other smaller Inge collections, are described in Young's helpful guide to theatre manuscripts and collections in the United States and Canada. The ICC library supplies copies of the programs of the William Inge Festival and Conference.

Shuman offers an annotated, selective bibliography in addition to extensive notes. Although his coverage stops in 1965, his notes make his study a fine starting point for any Inge project and a good source for play reviews of the Broadway productions. Further reviews are cited in Palmer and Dyson's bibliography of dramatic criticism and the McClure and Inge Collection bibliographies.

Biographies

Voss (1986) analyzes Inge's personal battles with alcoholism, homosexuality, and loneliness in a thoughtful essay that relies on many of the
unpublished resources of the William Inge Collection. This is the most
comprehensive biographical treatment in print. Voss's contribution to
Twentieth-Century American Dramatists also provides information that has
eluded the many Inge biographers forced until recently to rely solely
on the playwright's public remarks.

Tennessee Williams notes in his *Memoirs* that Inge was a private individual. A typical example of the biographical material he commonly
supplied, limited almost completely to the years before he arrived in
New York, can be found in Bracker. This material remains largely unchanged and unsupplemented in Newquist's collection of interviews of
American authors. Similar material is supplied by Frenz in his collection
of documents by American playwrights.

The settings of Inge's plays, his typically Midwestern upbringing, and
his early life have received much coverage. Shuman reviews these years,
always careful to note similarities between incidents in the playwright's
life and in his plays. Gould also treats these early years in detail. Inge's
life in St. Louis receives careful treatment in Burgess's well-documented
essay. Focusing on *Front Porch* (*Picnic*) and *Come Back, Little Sheba*, which
were drafted during these years, Burgess convincingly demonstrates the
impact of Inge's St. Louis experience on his plays.

Influences

Although he was reluctant to give others credit for influencing his
work, it is clear that Inge was deeply moved when he saw Tennessee
Williams's *The Glass Menagerie* starring Laurette Taylor in Chicago. Yet
contrary to many critical assumptions, Inge does not seem to have con-
sciously emulated Williams. In an interview with Wager, Inge expressed
his appreciation for Williams and also for Sean O'Casey and Anton
Chekhov—an appreciation he recorded in his first essay for *Theatre Arts*,
seventeen years earlier. He confessed as well to an intellectual attraction
to the ideas associated with existentialism (122–23).

Inge was unquestionably influenced by his own Midwestern background and the particular ideas and ideals that characterized many
Americans who lived through the war years into the 1950s. While Adler
clearly demonstrates the presence of characteristics in the plays of Inge,
Robert Anderson, and Arthur Laurents that spring from these general
sources, he states emphatically that "there can be no question . . . of literary influence" (113). Discussions of his childhood, the Midwest, Freud-

ian psychology, or popular culture as influences on his work are integral to many general assessments of Inge.

General Studies

In terms of volume, Inge has not attracted the attention of scholars that might be expected for one of America's most successful playwrights of the 1950s. Although several well-warranted dissertations exist, to date there has been published no full-length retrospective analysis of Inge or his complete works. He received only one book-length treatment during his lifetime—R. Baird Shuman's 1965 study. An issue of *Kansas Quarterly* (Fall 1986) may prompt more work on Inge; it contains twelve articles on Inge's plays, novels, and films of his works.

Shuman's *William Inge* contains an introductory chapter focusing on the details of Inge's life prior to his career in the theatre and then discusses the Broadway successes of the 1950s and Inge's work of the early 1960s, the failed Broadway plays and *Splendor in the Grass*. Shuman examines Inge's plays with particular attention to theme as revealed through characterization and to dramaturgical technique, ideas, characters, and techniques that are shared by more than one play. Shuman caps his book with a cautious but sympathetic assessment of the playwright's achievement that shows an implicit awareness of the mixed critical reception of Inge's work. Although Inge was to write *Where's Daddy?* and his two novels after Shuman's study was published, it remains a solid introductory survey of the thematic and dramaturgical nature of Inge's principal work.

In the 1950s, critics seemed about evenly divided between those who thought Inge an important, sensitive playwright in the realistic mode who captured an essential American experience and those who looked disparagingly upon his Broadway successes as a result of his reliance on stock characters, prosaic themes, and simple technique. Bentley used his *New Republic* venue to suggest that Inge's appeal lay in easily recognized character stereotypes that did not challenge his audiences ("*Bus Stop*" and "Pity the Dumb Ox"). According to Bentley, the adventures of the "stud" characters in *Come Back, Little Sheba* and *Picnic* appealed to prurient interests while maintaining a veneer of politeness that protected both the author and his audiences. Wolfson notes that the "strength and truth of [*Come Back, Little Sheba*] are in its picture of how essentially unheroic people can wrest some dignity from a crushing nexus of ignorant upbringing and untoward circumstance" (225). "If the particular problems of Inge's characters are not specifically those of the audience," claims Wolfson, "the basic insecurities they feel, and the particular values for which they strive have near-universal import" (227). Yet *Picnic*, observed Wolfson, "is shot through with tawdry pandering to popular taste, and as *Bus Stop* was to do in even worse fashion, it presents a gallery of characters who, despite Inge's intention, do not interrelate in a finally meaningful way" (225).

In a frequently quoted and much anthologized essay, Brustein suggests that Inge's drama had the effect of relieving the audience of their insecurities. Inge's drama was, to Brustein, "ameliorative." Despite Inge's apparent frankness, his work was ultimately reducible to a theme of love and compromise in an ordered world "not far different from the Midwest of Rodgers and Hammerstein, a land where the gift of milky happiness is obtained when some obstacle ('pore Jud' or resistance to love) is removed" (57). Brustein astutely generalizes that "each of Inge's plays reads a little like *The Taming of the Shrew* in reverse"; Brustein points out that each of the major plays is resolved when a male character sacrifices his manhood—often a false vision to begin with—in order to achieve some level of domestic or conjugal happiness (56).

Recapping his reviews in *Theatre at the Crossroads*, Gassner expressed disappointment over the facile endings of *The Dark at the Top of the Stairs* and *A Loss of Roses* in the light of Inge's apparent gifts for realistic dialogue and characterization. According to Gassner, these endings were renunciations, last-minute diversions from true tragic conclusions. Gassner's view, though sympathetically expressed, remains essentially unchanged in subsequent essays—in 1963, 1968. In *American Drama Since World War II*, Weales places Inge among a group of playwrights "so involved in the prejudices and the preoccupations of their society that their work reflects the values of its audience. Inevitably, in their attempts to be serious, they get sidetracked into sentiment, romance, theatrical and ideational cliché, but, for a time at least, their new dressing of old bromides wins them commercial and critical success" (40). Like Brustein, Weales charges that Inge's drama too often came to an ameliorative conclusion: "that love is the solution to all problems" (73).

Although the late 1960s saw the publication of Shuman's full-length study, no new or interesting observations on Inge or his work emerged at this time. Acknowledging Inge's naturalistic technique, Lewis echoes the criticism of Weales and Driver when he notes that Inge's utilization of these techniques did not protect him from dramatic and thematic cliché. Gottfried analyzes the plays through *Where's Daddy?* showing how Inge developed themes or techniques introduced in earlier works. While claiming in his brief treatment that Inge had been "unfairly dismissed by critics," Lumley draws attention to Inge's own statements regarding dramatic composition and values (1967, 329).

Scholarly interest in Inge increased in the 1970s. In a thoughtful, substantial essay Miller builds on Wolfson's thesis that Inge's strength lies in his treatment of ordinary characters and mundane ideas ("William

Inge: Last of the Realists"). Placing Inge squarely in the tradition of dramatic naturalism, Miller convincingly demonstrates a fundamental universality in each of his plays. Concentrating on the plays of the 1950s, Jain believes that each of Inge's major characters is forced out of a state of innocence or dreams and made to confront life on more realistic and healthy terms. Mitchell notes that Inge repeatedly presented school-teachers as ineffectual observers rather than as participants in life ("Teacher as Outsider").

In the 1980s, Inge's plays continue to generate discussion. Bigsby notes that at his best Inge "offers . . . a kind of soft-centered naturalism in which his characters are products of their own inner compulsions and of the small-town environment in which they live" (14). While we can identify with these characters who verge on mythic stereotypes, Inge presents them in a "world deprived of transcendence, with no spiritual dimension, no purpose to serve beyond a sexual impulse which is only momentarily liberating" (15). From her feminist perspective, Juhnke successfully attacks the notion that Inge's plays lack any sort of transcendent vision in her excellent critique of Brustein's influential response to Inge. Thoughtful appreciations by McIlrath and Bailey appear in a special issue of *Kansas Quarterly* (Fall 1986) dedicated to Inge. Knudsen analyzes Inge's two novels and explains how they recapitulate themes first expressed in his dramas.

Inge's use of the Midwestern or small town environment has been a recurring issue in Inge criticism. Shuman, who claims that Inge was the first playwright to "write seriously" of the Midwest and "to have concern for the sociological uniqueness of the area and for the psychological manifestations of this uniqueness as it is revealed in the reactions of its people" (17–8), supports his claim with detailed analysis of individual plays. Herron effectively characterizes the small town settings of the Inge plays within the context of a skillful exposition of Inge's plots and themes. In contrast to those who would call Inge a provincial playwright, Miller demonstrates that Inge's Midwestern settings contributed a universal appeal ("William Inge: Playwright of the Popular") and declares that Inge "so successfully focused not on the surroundings and what they do to his characters, but what his characters do to themselves and each other as a function of these surroundings . . . [and] without those surroundings themselves having the ghost of a reason to take any meaningful part in the action" (1–3). Noting that they constitute "a major element . . . that establishes, expresses, and reinforces his themes" (90), Gale thoroughly analyzes small town images in Inge's plays. Any examination of Inge's Midwest inevitably leads to an examination of Inge himself as he experienced and remembered it throughout his life. Mitchell demonstrates convincingly that Inge closely identified with his characters. Most telling is the line Mitchell cites from *My Son Is a Splendid Driver* (155): "Maybe the poems grew out of my feeling of hopelessness . . . for if we can mold our grief into some shapeful form, we have objectified it and put it into a shape that we can hold" (310).

Inge's use of the Midwest was tied both to his general understanding of human psychology and behavior and to his more specific experience with feelings relating to psychoanalysis and homosexuality. These issues are also common themes in Inge criticism. Sievers points out the very palpable Freudian characteristics of *Come Back, Little Sheba* and *Picnic* and claims that Inge was able to incorporate psychoanalytical "insights without following outworn literary patterns" (353). Driver directly challenged Sievers's thesis that American drama had matured as a result of new understanding in psychology by claiming that the playwright's strict adherence to certain conceptions of character amounted to little more than a mundane and prosaic preoccupation, which pervaded and limited his work. Goldstein describes a tendency of American playwrights to turn from social issues in the 1930s to more introspective, psychological issues in the 1950s and notes that, after *Bus Stop*, Inge seemed to place less significance on the economic circumstances of his characters. Though ideologically based, Goldstein's contention about the social consequences of this orientation is stimulating. In an essay on "homosexual spite" in Inge's plays Sarotte views *The Boy in the Basement* as an archetype of which each of the full-length plays is a version diluted or disguised for Broadway audiences.

Analyses of Individual Plays

Of the works previously cited, the essays or relevant chapters of Wolfson, Brustein, Bentley, Weales, Miller, Burgess, Sarotte, Voss, Gale, and Adler deserve attention for their extended discussions of individual plays. Shuman's study is also important because of its detail and as the sole source of an extended discussion of the one-act plays, with the exception of Sarotte's analysis of *The Boy in the Basement*.

Dusenbury presents *Come Back, Little Sheba* along with Arthur Miller's *Death of a Salesman* and Eugene O'Neill's *The Iceman Cometh* as exemplars of the theme of personal failure and attendant feelings of loneliness and isolation. She notes that *Sheba* "describes the journey of a couple from loneliness to complete isolation . . . and back to a feeling of sense of belonging to each other because of the suffering each has undergone" (14), adding that this resolution is not a simple happy ending, since the characters are once again returned to routine patterns of communication and living. Dusenbury's analysis of *Sheba*'s plot, though geared to her theme, is detailed and lucid. Centola discusses the effects of sexual denial and repression in *Come Back, Little Sheba* and Arthur Miller's *A View from the Bridge*. He also describes in Freudian terms the resolution of *Sheba* as an unhealthy one for its protagonists. Among the critical reactions that emerged with the first appearance of *Come Back, Little Sheba*, those of Nathan and Beyer provided a measured, perceptive analysis of the play's method, theme, and impact. Inge explained his own feelings and intentions in writing *Sheba* in his 1950 *Theatre Arts* essay.

Its primal nature has led several critics to find archetypes in *Picnic*. In a thoughtful analysis, Armato sees a modern scapegoat ritual comparable to those in ancient times in which an individual was driven from the tribe into the wilderness carrying with him the sins of the community. In one way or another, each of the townspeople in *Picnic* transfers to Hal their own shortcomings and sins before he is driven off. According to Armato, Madge's decision to follow Hal is no simple romanticized ending; it is the playing out of a kind of "messianic neurosis" that drives her to sacrifice the comforts and virtues of home. Donovan, who draws striking parallels between *Picnic* and *The Bacchae* of Euripides, delves into another ritual, that of the dance—the intoxicating ritual where social conventions and traditional behavior patterns are thrown aside—as the centerpiece of his argument on the play's Dionysian theme. Hal is Dionysus entering the town in disguise in order to visit a "kinsman," in this case, a fraternity brother. The women characters are the maeneds, irresistibly drawn toward the god. In tying *Picnic* to myths and fairy tales, Wentworth recapitulates and broadens the conclusions reached by Armato and Donovan.

Taking a sociological approach, Lange effectively studies *Picnic* against the background of a post–World War II America caught in the throes of materialism, changing sexual values and roles, malaise over the hydrogen bomb, and political hysteria. Emphasizing its Chekhovian features, Hamblet analyzes *Picnic* for the purpose of comparing it to a play by the French-Canadian playwright Marcel Dubé. Inge's own ideas concerning *Picnic* can be found in two brief *New York Times* essays—1953, 1954.

Although it received no major theatre awards, *Bus Stop* was almost universally commended by critics. Although praised by Miller as "one of the finest examples of the comedy of sensibility" ("William Inge: The Last of the Realists," 23), it has yet to receive an extended treatment. Perhaps its simplicity discourages detailed analysis. The assessments of Driver and Brustein written on the occasion of *The Dark at the Top of the Stairs* have greatly influenced subsequent scholarship. Driver identifies the basic tenets of "Freudianity" that are epitomized in *Dark*. Inge also published his thoughts on *Dark* in the *New York Times* (1957). The later plays have received little, if any, extensive treatment. Studying its principal character, Scheick examines the autobiographical *My Son Is a Splendid Driver* to reveal Inge's attitude toward a relationship between life and art.

FUTURE RESEARCH OPPORTUNITIES

The annual William Inge Festival and Conference at Independence Community College has stimulated scholarship and doubtless will continue to be a forum for Inge scholars and performers. The William Inge Collection at Independence, housing his manuscripts and notes, has yet to be fully exploited. A second book-length study of the entire Inge canon is an important book that needs to be written. Of the plays, only *Picnic* has received extensive treatment.

Although at least two book-length treatments are reported to be in progress, a comprehensive biography of Inge—one that penetrates beyond the barrier of shyness he maintained throughout his life—is needed. Several aspects of Inge's life might be carefully explored to shed direct light on his plays. These include details concerning Inge's feelings of isolation, his social, professional, and familial relationships, his experiences with alcoholism, and his sexuality. The nature of Tennessee Williams's influence on Inge's work and career has not been fully documented, though its existence is treated as received wisdom. The creative processes behind Inge's writing and rewriting his plays in production and as screenplays also have not been thoroughly treated. Such a study merits special attention in view of the controversy in Inge's own lifetime regarding the direction of his plays by Logan and Kazan.

While Inge's classics—*Come Back, Little Sheba* and *Picnic*—will certainly continue to attract diverse critical attention, detailed studies of his other plays, including the Broadway failures, are long overdue. The instructive essays on *Picnic* by Armato, Donovan, and Wentworth demonstrate a fruitful approach that might be transferred to Inge's neglected texts. Although the Oedipus experience that Inge dramatizes in *The Dark at the Top of the Stairs*, *A Loss of Roses*, and *Natural Affection* is universal, one wonders if the later plays contain the same kinds of transcendent archetypes as *Picnic*. However, Dusenbury's essay on the theme of loneliness in *Come Back, Little Sheba* might well point the way to an existentialist reading of the entire Inge canon. Inge acknowledged his appreciation for existentialism, though he denied its direct influence. In a sense, the Inge plays may be popular philosophical archetypes that reflect a malaise typical of postwar America. Miller and Lange epitomize another approach that will pay dividends to those willing to follow a sociological bent. Inge does present visions—of the Midwest, of homosexuality, of interpersonal relationships, of the family—that need explanation in their social or cultural context. The public and critical response to Inge can also be explored as a sociotheatrical phenomenon. Finally, no one appears to have explored in detail the similarities between Inge's plays and those of O'Casey, Chekhov, or Williams, all of whom he admired.

SECONDARY SOURCES

Adler, Thomas P. "The School of Bill: An Inquiry into Literary Kinship (William Inge, Robert Anderson, and Arthur Laurents)." *Kansas Quarterly* 18, no. 4 (Fall 1986): 113–19.

Anderson, Phyllis. "Diary of a Production." *Theatre Arts* 36 (November 1959): 58–59.

Armato, Philip M. "The Bum as Scapegoat in William Inge's Picnic." *Western American Literature* 10 (Winter 1976): 273–82.

Bailey, Jeffrey. "William Inge: An Appreciation in Retrospect." *Kansas Quarterly* 18 (Fall 1986): 139–147.

Bentley, Eric. *Bus Stop* review. *New Republic* (2 May 1955): 22.

———. "Pity the Dumb Ox." *New Republic* (16 March 1953): 22–23.

Beyer, W. H. "The State of the Theatre." *School and Society* 71 (3 June 1950): 342–46.

Bigsby, C. W. E. *A Critical Introduction to Twentieth-century American Drama*. Vol. 3: *Beyond Broadway*. Cambridge and New York: Cambridge University Press, 1985.

Bracker, Milton. "Boy Actor to Broadway Author." *New York Times* (22 March 1953): 2:1, 3.

Brog. *Come Back, Little Sheba* review. *Variety* (3 December 1952). Reprinted in *Variety Film Reviews 1949–1953*.

Brustein, Robert. "The Men-Taming Women of William Inge." *Harper's Magazine* (November 1958): 52–57.

Burgess, Charles E. "An American Experience: William Inge in St. Louis 1943–49." *Pennsylvania Language and Literature* 12 (Fall 1976): 438–68.

Centola, Steven R. "Compromise as Bad Faith: Arthur Miller's 'A View from the Bridge' and William Inge's 'Come Back, Little Sheba.'" *Midwest Quarterly* 28 (Autumn 1986): 100–113.

Clurman, Harold. "A Good Play." *New Republic* (13 March 1950): 22–23.

———. *Picnic* review. *Nation* (7 March 1953): 176.

Come Back, Little Sheba unattributed review. *Life* (17 April 1950): 93–96.

Come Back, Little Sheba unattributed review. *Newsweek* (27 February 1950): 74.

Crowther, Bosley. *Bus Stop* review. *New York Times* (1 September 1956): 19. Reprinted in *New York Times Film Reviews*. Vol. 4: *1949–1958*, p. 2942.

———. *Splendor in the Grass* review. *New York Times* (11 October 1961): 53. Reprinted in *New York Times Film Reviews*. Vol. 5: *1959–1968*, p. 3281.

———. *The Stripper* review. *New York Times* (20 June 1963): 29. Reprinted in *New York Times Film Reviews*. Vol. 5: *1959–1968*, pp. 3394–95.

Donovan, Robert Kent. "The Dionysiac Dance in William Inge's 'Picnic.'" *Dance Chronicle* 7, no. 4 (1984–1985): 413–34.

Driver, Tom F. "Psychologism: Roadblock to Religious Drama." *Religion in Life* 29 (Winter 1959–1960): 107–9.

Dusenbury, Winifred L. *The Theme of Loneliness in Modern American Drama*. Gainesville: University of Florida Press, 1960.

Frenz, Horst, ed. *American Playwrights on Drama*. New York: Hill and Wang, 1965.

Gale, Steven H. "Small Town Images in Four Plays by William Inge." *Kansas Quarterly* 18, no. 4 (Fall 1986): 89–100.

Gassner, John. *Natural Affection* criticism. *Educational Theatre Journal* 15 (May 1963): 185–86.

———. *Theatre at the Crossroads.* New York: Holt, Rinehart and Winston, 1960.

———. *The Theatre in Our Times.* New York: Crown Publishers, 1966.

Gibbs, Wolcott. *Bus Stop* review. *New Yorker* (12 March 1955): 62–64.

———. *Picnic* review. *New Yorker* (28 February 1953): 62–64.

Goldstein, Malcolm. "Body and Soul on Broadway." *Modern Drama* 7 (February 1965): 411–21.

Gottfried, Martin. *A Theater Divided.* Boston: Little, Brown, 1967.

Gould, Jean. *Modern American Playwrights.* New York: Dodd, Mead, 1966.

Gussow, Mel. "William Inge's Latest Opens in 'Village.'" *New York Times* (8 December 1970): 61.

Hamblet, Edwin J. "The North American Outlook of Marcel Dubé and William Inge." *Queen's Quarterly* 77 (1970): 374–87.

Hatch, Robert. *Bus Stop* review. *Nation* (19 March 1955): 245–46.

Hayes, Richard. *Picnic* review. *Commonweal* (20 March 1953): 603.

Herron, Ima Honaker. "Our Vanishing Towns: Modern Broadway Versions." *Southwest Review* 51 (1966): 209–20. Also in *The Small Town in American Drama*, pp. 419–27. Dallas: Southern Methodist University Press, 1969.

Hewes, Henry. *The Best Plays of 1962–1963.* New York: Dodd, Mead, 1963.

———. "Mr. Inge's Meringueless Pie." *Saturday Review* (19 March 1955): 24.

Jain, Jasibir. "William Inge: Confrontation with Reality." *Indian Journal of American Studies* 4, nos. i-ii (1974): 72–77.

Jones, Margo. *Theatre-in-the-Round.* New York: Rinehart and Company, 1951.

Juhnke, Janet. "Inge's Women: Robert Brustein and the Feminine Mystique." *Kansas Quarterly* 18, no. 4 (Fall 1986): 103–11.

Kerr, Walter. *The Theatre In Spite of Itself.* New York: Simon and Schuster, 1963.

Kronenberger, Louis. *The Best Plays of 1957–1958.* New York: Dodd, Mead, 1958.

———. *The Best Plays of 1954–1955.* New York: Dodd, Mead, 1955.

Knudsen, James. "Last Words: The Novels of William Inge." *Kansas Quarterly* 18, no. 4 (Fall 1986): 121–129.

Lange, Jane W. "'Forces Get Loose': Social Prophecy in William Inge's *Picnic.*" *Kansas Quarterly* 18, no. 4 (Fall 1986): 57–70.

Lewis, Allan. "The Emergent Deans: Kingsley, Inge, and Company." In *American Plays and Playwrights of the Contemporary Theatre.* New York: Crown Publishers, 1965.

Logan, Joshua. *Josh: My Up and Down, In and Out Life.* New York: Delacorte Press, 1976.

McClure, Arthur F. *William Inge: A Bibliography.* New York: Garland Publishing, 1982.

McIlrath, Patricia. "William Inge, Great Voice of the Heart of America." *Kansas Quarterly* 18, no. 4 (Fall 1986): 45–53.

Miller, Jordan Y. "William Inge: Last of the Realists?" *Kansas Quarterly* 2, no. 2 (1970): 17–26.

———. "William Inge: Playwright of the Popular." In *Proceedings of the Fifth*

National Convention of the Popular Culture Association, St. Louis, Missouri,
March 20–22, 1975. Compiled by Michael T. Marsden. Bowling Green,
Ohio: Popular Culture Association, 1975. (Available from the Center for
Archival Collections, Jerome Library, Bowling Green State University of
Ohio, 43403.)

Mitchell, Marilyn. "Teacher as Outsider in the Works of William Inge." *Midwest
Quarterly* 17 (July 1976): 385–93.

———. "William Inge." *American Imago* 35 (1978): 297–310.

Nathan, George Jean. *"Come Back, Little Sheba."* In *Theatre Book of the Year, 1949–
1950,* pp. 232–36. New York: Alfred A. Knopf, 1950.

———. "Director's Picnic." *Theatre Arts* 37 (May 1953): 14–15.

———. "William Inge." In *The Theatre in the Fifties,* pp. 71–76. New York: Alfred
A. Knopf, 1953.

Newquist, Roy. *Counterpoint.* New York: Simon and Schuster, 1964.

Palmer, Helen H., and Jane Ann Dyson. *American Drama Criticism.* Hamden,
Conn.: Shoe String Press, 1967.

" 'Picnic' Tells Conquest of a Kansas Casanova." *Life* (16 March 1953): 136–37.

"Picnic and More Fun." *Saturday Review* (7 March 1953): 33–34.

Rensselaer Wyatt, Euphemia Van. "Picnic." *Catholic World* 177 (April 1953): 69–
70.

Ron. *The Dark at the Top of the Stairs.* Review. *Variety* (14 September 1960). Reprinted in *Variety Film Reviews, 1959–1960.*

Sarotte, Georges-Michel. "William Inge: 'Homosexual Spite' in Action." In *Like
a Brother, Like a Lover,* pp. 121–33. Translated by Richard Miller. Garden
City, N.Y.: Anchor Press/Doubleday, 1978.

Scheick, William J. "Self and the Art of Memory in Inge's *My Son Is a Splendid
Driver.*" *Kansas Quarterly* 18, no. 4 (Fall 1986): 131–37.

Shuman, R. Baird. *William Inge.* New York: Twayne, 1965.

Sievers, W. David. *Freud on Broadway.* New York: Hermitage House, 1955. Reprint ed., New York: Cooper Square Pub., 1970.

Voss, Ralph. "William Inge." *Dictionary of Literary Biography; Twentieth Century
American Dramatists,* vol. 7. Detroit: Gale Research, 1981.

———. "William Inge and the Savior/Specter of Celebrity." *Kansas Quarterly* 18,
no. 4 (Fall 1986): 25–40.

Wager, Walter. *The Playwrights Speak: Interviews with 11 Playwrights.* New York:
Delacorte Press, 1967.

Watts, Richard, Jr. "Everything Didn't Come Up Roses." *New York Post* (30 November 1959). Reprinted in *New York Theatre Critics' Reviews* (1959): 211.

Weales, Gerald C. *American Drama since World War II.* New York: Harcourt, Brace
and World, 1962.

Weiler, A. H. *Picnic* review. *New York Times* (17 February 1956): 13. Reprinted
in *New York Times Film Reviews.* Vol. 4, *1949–1958,* p. 2909.

Wentworth, Michael. "The Convergence of Fairy Tale and Myth in William
Inge's *Picnic.*" *Kansas Quarterly* 18, no. 4 (Fall 1986): 57–63.

William Inge Collection of Independence Community College Library. *Annotated
Bibliography.* Independence, Kans.: Independence Community College,
1986. Available from the library.

Williams, Tennessee. "The Writing Is Honest." In *The Dark at the Top of the Stairs.*

New York: Random House, 1958. Also in *The Passionate Playgoer*, pp. 246–49. Edited by George Oppenheimer. New York: Random House, 1958.

Wolfson, Lester M. "Inge, O'Neill, and the Human Condition." *Southern Speech Journal* 22 (Summer 1957): 221–32.

Wood, Audrey, with Max Wilk. "Come Back, Sweet William." In *Represented by Audrey Wood: A Memoir*. Garden City, N.Y.: Doubleday, 1981.

Wood, Michael. "An Interview with Daniel Mann (The Director of Inge's First Success and His First Failure)." *Kansas Quarterly* 18, no. 4 (Fall 1986): 7–22.

Young, William C. *American Theatrical Arts: A Guide to Manuscripts and Special Collections in the United States and Canada*. Chicago: American Library Association, 1971.

ACKNOWLEDGMENT

My thanks to David Radavitch of Eastern Illinois University, who graciously supplied me with bibliographic assistance.

Albert Innaurato

(2 JUNE 1948–   )

LINDA E. McDANIEL

ASSESSMENT OF INNAURATO'S REPUTATION

Productions of Innaurato's best-known dramas—*Gemini* and *The Trans-figuration of Benno Blimpie*—contributed in large part to the excitement of the 1976–1977 New York season. Both plays opened off-Broadway within the same week and earned Obies for playwriting and acting. *Gemini*, with its Italian-American family and raucous spaghetti dinner, appealed with its new realism and subsequently became one of the longest-running nonmusicals on Broadway. For *Benno*, Innaurato was honored as "a leader in the new emphasis on language in the theater" (Gunton, 190). Reviewers repeatedly noted the humor and compassion that mark Innaurato's treatments of fat people, sexual nonconformists, deformed rejects, aging losers, and lonely outcasts. Mingling realistic, absurdist, and surrealistic techniques for humorous and profound effect, Innaurato deals with "sexual crises" and with survivors' creative, flamboyant ways of "coping" in a loveless world (Introduction, x, xiii).

PRIMARY BIBLIOGRAPHY OF INNAURATO'S WORKS

Plays

Urlicht. First produced, 1971. Included in *Bizarre Behavior*.
I Don't Generally Like Poetry, But Have You Read "Trees"? With Christopher Durang. First produced, 1972.
The Life Story of Mitzi Gaynor, or Gyp. With Christopher Durang. First produced, 1973.
The Transfiguration of Benno Blimpie. First produced, 1973. Included in *The Best Short Plays, 1978*, pp. 261–98. Edited by Stanley Richards. Radnor, Pa.: Chilton Book Company, 1978. Also in *Bizarre Behavior*.

The Idiots Karamazov. With Christopher Durang. First produced, 1974. New York: Dramatists Play Service, 1981.

Earth Worms. First produced, 1974. Included in *Bizarre Behavior*.

Gemini. First produced, 1976. New York: Dramatists Play Service, 1977. Included in *Bizarre Behavior*.

Gemini [and] *The Transfiguration of Benno Blimpie: Two Plays*. Clifton, N.J.: J. T. White, 1978.

Ulysses in Traction. First produced, 1977. New York: Dramatists Play Service, 1978. Included in *Bizarre Behavior*.

Bizarre Behavior: Six Plays. New York: Avon, 1980, 1985. Contains *Gemini, The Transfiguration of Benno Blimpie, Ulysses in Traction, Earth Worms, Urlicht*, and *Wisdom Amok*.

Passione. First produced, 1980. New York: Dramatists Play Service, 1981.

Coming of Age in Soho. First version produced, 1984. Rewritten play produced, 1985. New York: Dramatists Play Service, 1985.

Television Scripts

Verna: U.S.O. Girl. PBS, 1978.

Just Plain Folks. Unproduced.

Articles

"Author's Notes for Production" of *The Transfiguration of Benno Blimpie*. In *The Best Short Plays, 1978*, pp. 293–98. Edited by Stanley Richards. Radnor, Pa.: Chilton Book Company, 1978.

Introduction to *Bizarre Behavior*. New York: Avon, 1980, 1985.

"A Playwright Decries an Era of 'Hit Flops.' " *New York Times* (20 July 1986): B1, B50.

Interviews

Berkvist, Robert. "Innaurato's Characters Even Surprise Himself." *New York Times* (22 September 1980): C16. Reprinted in *New York Times Biographical Service* 11 (September 1980): 1271–72.

Span, Paula. "Making Plays the Hard Way." *Philadelphia Inquirer* (19 May 1985). Located in Newsbank Microform, Performing Arts, 1985, 122:G3–5, fiche.

DiGaetani, John. "An Interview with Albert Innaurato." *Studies in American Drama, 1945–Present* 2 (1987): 87–95.

PRODUCTION HISTORY

The outstanding successes of *Gemini* and *Benno* followed earlier productions of Innaurato's plays in New Haven and in theatres off-off-Broadway. *Gemini* ran the gamut of off-off-Broadway, regional theatre, off-Broadway, and Broadway productions. As it continued successfully, *Earth Worms* and *Ulysses in Traction* played to less receptive audiences. Before *Gemini* closed in 1981, Innaurato saw *Passione* move from Playwrights Horizon to Broadway. Then followed a four-year hiatus until Joseph Papp produced *Coming of Age in Soho*.

While working toward his M.F.A. at the Yale School of Drama, Innaurato saw on stage his one-act *Urlicht* (1971), *Benno* (1973), and three works coauthored with Christopher Durang (the controversial satirist): *I Don't Generally Like Poetry But Have You Read "Trees"?* (1972); *The Life Story of Mitzi Gaynor; or, Gyp* (1973); and, in 1974, *The Idiots Karamazov*, with Meryl Streep as the old crone translator, Constance Garnett.

The off-Broadway productions of *The Transfiguration of Benno Blimpie* and *Gemini* brought Innaurato fame and the *Village Voice* Off-Broadway Awards for Distinguished Playwriting and Performances. *Benno* appeared with William Dews's *Side Show* on a program entitled *Monsters*, which opened at the Astor Place Theater on 10 March and ran through 1 May 1977. James Coco's highly lauded performance as Benno won him the Obie for Distinguished Performance, and Rosemary De Angelis drew accolades in the role of Benno's mother. Wilson found the production "riveting throughout," and he described the "interesting" staging: a hugely obese young man remained sitting on a platform eating while other characters performed brief scenes. If Benno had a part in a scene from the past, the family talked to "empty space," and Benno answered from his "sidelines" position (24). Gottfried admired the dramatist's "great skill" in "maneuvering neatly between brief scenes and Benno's monologues" and commended Coco's "heartbreaking performance" and Robert Drivas's "steady" direction (305). Barnes praised Innaurato's "complex, intricately textured play," which despite its "chilling" and "modern-Gothic horrors" showed a "compassion and an understanding of what it is like to be a freak in an unfeeling society" ("Monsters," C3). *Benno* was produced in London in 1978 and revived at Playwrights Horizons in 1983.

On 13 March 1977, the same week that the *Monsters* program began, the Circle Repertory Company presented *Gemini* off-Broadway. Peter Mark Schifter, who had first directed the drama at Playwrights Horizons and then at the regional Performing Arts Foundation Playhouse in Huntington, Long Island, continued to direct a changing cast and revised script. After sixty-three performances off-Broadway, the Circle Repertory Company transferred *Gemini* to the Little Theater on Broadway on 21 May 1977, where it ran over four years, closing on 5 September 1981. Critics generally praised the writing and acting in the dramatization of Francis Geminiani's confusion about his sexual orientation after a WASP brother and sister arrive for an unexpected visit. While an occasional critic sidetracked into argument about "gayism" (Wetzsteon), other reviewers praised the comedy and lauded the cast, giving special kudos to Danny Aiello and Anne DeSalvo, who later received Obies for their performances. Gussow favorably reviewed the writing and the production ("Gemini"), and Barnes called it a "well-crafted, popularly styled play" (" 'Gemini' Continues," A31). Although Watt expressed reservations about the "design" and the "happy ending," he observed the "decency and compassion" in the characters' relationships (306). Productions mounted in Chicago, Cleveland, Washington D.C., and Philadelphia attested to the appeal of *Gemini*, which was adapted for the movie *Happy Birthday, Gemini* in 1980 (Gunton, 217).

As *Gemini* met with enthusiastic audiences on its way to Broadway, Innaurato's *Earth Worms* played at the Long Wharf Theatre, New Haven, Connecticut, in March 1977 and at Playwrights Horizons in May. Reviewing the second production, Gussow commended the characterizations of the couple in the "Pygmalion-Galatea relationship"—the seventy-year-old transvestite and the young hillbilly wife neglected by her sexually ambivalent husband. But the "wavering focus" and "cluttered background," declared Gussow, indicated "flaws of the script" ("Earth Worms," C3). The Circle Repertory Company's performances of *Ulysses in Traction* from 8 December 1977 to 22 January 1978 fared even worse, despite the performances of Trish Hawkins and William Hurt. While Valentine lambasted *Ulysses*, Eder found the drama about the rehearsal of a play during a race riot "interesting" and "amusing"; but, he opined, "the play is a mess" (C3).

Innaurato's television play, *Verna: U.S.O. Girl*, aired on PBS and won an Emmy nomination in 1978. Although Dunning drubbed the production, Mordden considered the adaptation of Paul Gallico's short story an "excellent" example of television drama (307). Innaurato's other scripts include *Coming Out, Matter Between Friends*, and *Just Plain Folks*, coauthored with Mort Lauchman (DiGaetani, 87).

In 1980, Innaurato returned to Broadway with *Passione*, which presents a WASP mother's return to the South Philadelphia apartment, the Italian-American ex-husband, and the son she deserted ten years earlier. Berkvist's interview-article includes an account of its history. Frank Langella saw the 17 May production directed by Innaurato at the Playwrights Horizons off-off-Broadway, made notes and suggestions that impressed the dramatist, and subsequently directed the play, which transferred to the Morosco on Broadway on 23 September 1980. Yet *Passione* flopped. The Italian meal, the fat woman, and the South Philadelphia setting led reviewers to compare it to *Gemini*. Kerr, for example, considered *Passione* a "recyling" of old material, and he found the direction and acting too strained ("Stage View," 18). Cohen, however, declared the writing "more mature, more complex"; the cast—featuring Jerry Stiller and Laurel Cronin—"accomplished"; and the directing "admirable" (160). Rich admired Innaurato's creation of a "new and often hilarious place of his own startling design" while paying "lip service to kitchen-sink realism" (C23).

Four years passed before Innaurato presented a new stage play, *Coming of Age in Soho*. Freedman provides one account of its unique production history. Joseph Papp produced the play with Innaurato directing it at the Public Theatre; but at previews of the original version, the audience hissed the leading character, a woman composer harshly rejecting her son. After Papp suggested changes in the script and closed *Coming of Age* for three weeks, Innaurato rewrote the play to make Gioconda's neighbor the central character, a divorced bisexual male novelist whose long-lost son shows up. The rewritten drama opened on 3 February 1985, with John Procaccio as a changed Beatrice Dante. Gussow described a production "bustling with the frenzy of imaginative life"; but the play, he concluded, was not "well-made" ("Innaurato Survives," 3). Oliver, on the other hand, praised the "action" as "bountiful, brimming over with comic and dramatic ingenuity—wonderful surprises" (110). Despite a much more positive reception to the rewritten version, the show closed on 31 March 1985.

SURVEY OF SECONDARY SOURCES

Bibliographies

O'Donnell and Bradish provide bibliographies of Innaurato's works; O'Donnell also includes references to some productions. Gunton's listings, however, offer the most extensive gathering of secondary sources.

Biographies

The *Current Biography* essay on "Innaurato" contains a valuable, comprehensive account of the life and work. O'Donnell, Miller, and Bradish provide brief, sketchy basics. In 1985 Span garnered informative details about the playwright's childhood, schooling, and family. Focusing on the problematic history of the production of *Coming of Age in Soho*, Span and Freedman recorded accounts of the Innaurato and Papp partnership. Lester and Berkvist elicited comments from the dramatist about his schooling, his love of opera, and his own problems with gaining weight. The dramatist expanded on his recurring lament about the difficulties and frustrations of contemporary playwriting in "A Playwright Decries an Era of 'Hit Flops.' "

Interviews and essays also include instructive authorial commentary on methods and themes. The Introduction to *Bizarre Behavior* and the "Author's Notes for Production" of *The Transfiguration of Benno Blimpie* provide autobiographical and interpretative background for individual plays. In his most recent interview, Innaurato discusses his interest in those who fit neither "a gay identity" nor a "straight identity," his views of a "cosmetic" society, and his emphasis on character rather than action (DiGaetani, 89–94).

Influences

While no specific study deals with influences, critics have identified possible parallels to the work of Eugene Ionesco and Franz Kafka (Gussow, "Perplexed Men") and to Leoncavallo and Verdi (Simon). Innaurato specifically names or alludes to others in his Introduction (*Bizarre*) and throughout the plays.

General Studies

No extended general study of Innaurato has appeared. Bradish includes useful generalizations and short summaries in a brief discussion of Innaurato as a dramatist who has "a unique, powerfully held vision of the human condition." After commenting on Innaurato's "skillful manipulation of vividly contrasting dramatic elements," Bradish discusses "the multiple dualities" of *Gemini;* compares ideas in the "more interesting" *Soho* to themes of Edward Albee and Peter Shaffer; describes *Earth Worms* as "one of the most wildly imaginative plays by any recent dramatist"; and praises the "brilliant, darkly beautiful" *Benno* (277).

Analyses of Individual Plays

Treatments of single plays are short and few. Ventimiglia discusses *Gemini* as "new realism" and as "comedy" presenting Francis Gemaniani's "rite of passage" and "search for identity" on his twenty-first birthday. Innaurato's "greatest strength," according to Ventimiglia, "is his gift for creating characters who transcend stereotype" (202). Hoffman remarks the contrasts between seeing *Gemini* on stage and reading the script closely; funny and attractive actors obscure "the troubled heartache of aging elders and hopelessly confused youngsters burning out their life energies" which the printed page reveals (24). For his book, Kerr revised a review in which he contrasted attitudes toward sex in *Romeo and Juliet* and *Benno Blimpie* to postulate theories about the modern view of sex as "poison" and "killer" (*Journey*, 164–67); and in his reviews, Gussow presents useful interpretive commentary on *Benno* ("Perplexed Men") and on *Earth Worms* ("Earth Worms").

Since these relatively short treatments often generalize rather than examine these unique, complex dramas in detail, Innaurato's own remarks about individual plays suggest other useful starting points for extended analysis. In his Introduction, Innaurato discusses each play in the collection, explaining, for instance, what *Ulysses in Traction* "is about" and providing indispensable annotations for *Urlicht* (xiv). The "Author's Notes for Production" of *Benno* could serve as external starting point for interpretation of that play.

FUTURE RESEARCH OPPORTUNITIES

Analyses of individual plays, interpretation of recurring themes and motifs, and examinations of methods and structures would establish points of departure for more comprehensive studies. Since Innaurato's wide-ranging and erudite allusions figure prominently in his work, the plays invite investigations of sources and influences. Most obvious topics include the influence of the opera on the structure, characterizations, and staging of the plays. Other allusions and echoes—ranging from Sophocles to pop culture, from Henry James to the Theater of the Ridiculous—call for commentary on the way they develop thematic contrasts between art and life, past and present, traditional ideals and contemporary obscenities. Finally, a biography and a bibliography could facilitate research and interpretation.

SECONDARY SOURCES

Barnes, Clive. " 'Gemini' Continues New-Realism Trend." *New York Times* (24 May 1977): A31.
———. "Stage: Harrowed by 'Monsters.' " *New York Times* (11 March 1977): C3. Reprinted in *New York Theatre Critics' Reviews* (1977): 309.
Bradish, Gaynor F. "Albert Innaurato." In *Contemporary Dramatists*, 4th ed., pp. 276–77. Chicago: St. James Press, 1988.
Cohen, Ron. " 'Passione.' " *Women's Wear Daily* (24 September 1980). Reprinted in *New York Theatre Critics' Reviews* (1980): 160.
Dunning, Jennifer. "TV: 'Verna,' Trouper for U.S.O." *New York Times* (25 January 1978): C18.
Eder, Richard. "Drama: Innaurato Falters." *New York Times* (9 December 1977): C3. Reprinted in *New York Times Theater Reviews* (1977–1978): 77–78.
Freedman, Samuel G. "Reshaping a Play to Reveal Its True Nature." *New York Times* (24 February 1985): B1, B38.
Gottfried, Martin. "Coco Tops Career in 'Monsters.' " *New York Post* (11 March 1977). Reprinted in *New York Theatre Critics' Reviews* (1977): 305.
Gunton, Sharon R., ed. "Innaurato, Albert." In *Contemporary Literary Criticism*, 21:190–99. Detroit: Gale Research, 1982.
Gussow, Mel. " 'Gemini' Is Exceptional." *New York Times* (14 March 1977): A36. Reprinted in *New York Theatre Critics' Reviews* (1977): 305–6.
———. "Innaurato Survives a Period of Adjustment." *New York Times* (10 February 1985): B3, B14.

————. "Stage: 'Earth Worms,' Innaurato's Grand Opera." *New York Times* (27 May 1977): C3. Reprinted in *New York Times Theater Reviews* (1977–1978): 105.

————. "Stage: 2 Perplexed Men." *New York Times* (8 May 1976): 15. Excerpted in Gunton, 21: 190.

Hoffman, Ted. Introduction to *Famous American Plays of the 1970s*. New York: Laurel Drama Series. 1981.

"Innaurato, Albert." *Current Biography* 49.3 (March 1988): 19–22.

Kerr, Walter. *Journey to the Center of the Theater*. New York: Alfred A. Knopf, 1979.

————. "Stage View: 'Passione' Is Familiar Innaurato." *New York Times* (28 September 1980): B5, B18.

Lester, Elenore. "Innaurato—His Passion for the Outcast Is Finding a Place on Stage." *New York Times* (29 May 1977): B1, B5.

Miller, Terry. "Innaurato, Albert." *McGraw-Hill Encyclopedia of World Drama*. 2d ed. New York: McGraw-Hill, 1984. 3:48.

Mordden, Ethan. *The American Theatre*. New York: Oxford University Press, 1981.

O'Donnell, Monica, ed. "Innaurato, Albert." In *Contemporary Theatre, Film, and Television*, 4:233–34. Detroit: Gale Research, 1987.

Oliver, Edith. "The Theatre: Off Broadway." *New Yorker* (18 February 1985): 110.

Rich, Frank. "Theater: 'Passione,' Innaurato Comedy." *New York Times* (24 September 1980): C23. Reprinted in *New York Theatre Critics' Reviews* (1980): 162.

Simon, John. *"Aria da capo." New York Magazine* (9 June 1980): 58–59. Excerpted in Gunton 21:197–98.

Valentine, Dean. "Theater of the Inane." *New Leader* (2 January 1978): 28–29. Excerpted in Gunton, 21:195.

Ventimiglia, Peter J. "Recent Trends in American Drama: Michael Christopher, David Mamet, and Albert Innaurato." *Journal of American Culture* 1 (Spring 1978): 195–204. Excerpted in Gunton, 21:196–97.

Watt, Douglas. "Boisterous But Uneven 'Gemini.' " *New York Daily News* (14 March 1977). Reprinted in *New York Theatre Critics' Reviews* (1977): 306.

Wetzsteon, Ross. "Gay Theatre after Camp: From Ridicule to Revenge." *Village Voice* (18 April 1977): 87. Excerpted in Gunton, 21:192–93.

Wilson, Edwin. "Innaurato: A Promising Talent." *Wall Street Journal* (16 March 1977): 24. Reprinted in *New York Theatre Critics' Reviews* (1977): 310.

Preston Jones
(7 APRIL 1936–19 SEPTEMBER 1979)

CHARLOTTE S. McCLURE

ASSESSMENT OF JONES'S REPUTATION

Between 1962 and 1979, Texas playwright Preston Jones not only achieved a regional and national reputation but also, Busby observes, became "one of the first post–World War II dramatists to break New York's hold on American Theater" (*Preston Jones*, 48–49). Jones's career of acting, directing, and playwriting at the Dallas Theater Center occurred during the years when regional theatres concentrated on developing new playwrights and original work to counteract New York's commercial theatre. Jones's most well-known work, *A Texas Trilogy* (1976), received acclaim from critics and audiences in Dallas and Washington, D.C., before going to Broadway. Jones earned national recognition in several other ways. In 1975 he gained time to concentrate on writing with the Rockefeller Foundation Playwright-in-Residence Fellowship, and he received the Golden Apple Award from *Cue* in 1976 and both the Outer Critics Circle Award and the Drama Desk Award in 1977 (Sewell, 54). *The Last Meeting of the Knights of the White Magnolia*, offered in 1975 to American Playwrights Theatre, a group formed to promote regional playwrights' work, was produced 500 times in towns and on college campuses across the country and was enthusiastically received by London audiences in 1977 (*London Times*, 3 March 1977). Weales proclaimed Jones's national reputation. In April 1980, seven months after Jones's death at forty-three, NBC paid tribute to him by broadcasting from Dallas a special performance of *The Oldest Living Graduate*, starring Henry Fonda and Cloris Leachman.

PRIMARY BIBLIOGRAPHY OF JONES'S WORKS

Published Plays

"Red Grover, On Thanksgiving: A Short Play." *New York Times* (25 November 1976): L29.
A Texas Trilogy. With "Author's Note." New York: Hill and Wang, Mermaid Dramabook, 1976.
Santa Fe Sunshine. New York: Dramatists Play Service, 1977.
The Oldest Living Graduate and *The Last Meeting of the Knights of the White Magnolia.* In *The Best Plays of 1976–77*, pp. 168–82, 183–97. New York: Dodd, Mead, 1977.
A Place on the Magdalena Flats. New York: Dramatists Play Service, 1984.

Unpublished Plays

"The Night of the Hunter: A Play in Three Acts." Unpublished thesis. Trinity University, 1966.
Juneteenth. 1978.
Remember. 1979.

Interviews

Interview. With Bruce Cook. *National Observer* (5 June 1974).
"Preston Jones: Alive and Well and Writing in the Southwest." With J. Peter Coulson. *Theater Southwest* 4 (October 1978): 15–19.
Preston Jones: An Interview. With Annemarie Marek. Dallas: New London Press, 1978.
"Preston Jones: In the Jaws of Time." In *Talking with Texas Writers: Twelve Interviews*, pp. 157–78. With Patrick Bennett. College Station: Texas A&M University Press, 1980.

Articles

"A Little Town in West Texas." *Washington Post* (25 April 1976): G1.
"Reflections on a 'Trilogy.' " *New York Times* (17 October 1976): O3.
"Smith and Whatstheirname." *Dallas Morning News* (15 April 1979).
"Tales of a Pilgrim's Progress: From Bradleyville to Broadway." *Dramatists Guild Quarterly* (Winter 1977): 7–18.
"West Texas Talk." *Visions* 1 (1978): 17–19.

PRODUCTION HISTORY

All but one of Jones's plays (*Juneteenth*) had premieres at Dallas Theater Center. His three best-known plays, combined as *A Bradleyville Trilogy* after opening in Dallas, had favorable reviews by Neville in Dallas and

Coe in Washington (1976) before opening as *A Texas Trilogy* in repertory on Broadway in September 1976. Because of the mixed reviews of critics Barnes and Kerr of the *New York Times* and of others, *Trilogy* closed after sixty-three performances. During the same year, however, Neville reported that *Trilogy* was booked into theatres in Houston, Seattle, Chicago, Cleveland, and Louisville (10 January 1976), and Marek recorded that Jones praised the theatre-in-the-round productions of *Trilogy* by Roy Bowman at the Ohio State University. *The Last Meeting*, the most often produced of the three plays, was warmly received by London audiences; Curtis praised its "beautifully" workable copy-book shape. The *Trilogy*, revived at Dallas Theater Center in November 1978, earned enthusiastic reviews as Neville observed, "Age has not dimmed the show" (10 December 1978). Mitchell estimated that the NBC live broadcast of *The Oldest Living Graduate* from the stage of the Bob Hope Theatre of Southern Methodist University on 7 April 1980 brought Jones's play to 10 million to 12 million viewers (2 March 1980, H1; 6 April 1980, 1, 3), although O'Connor complained about its predictable plot.

Jones's three post-*Trilogy* plays, focusing on his theme of time, opened at Dallas Theater Center and played in other theatres in Texas and New Mexico. *A Place on the Magdalena Flats* (1976) and *Santa Fe Sunshine* (1977) did not attract much critical enthusiasm or interest outside Dallas according to Dallas critic Mitchell ("Preston Jones Rings Down," 4E). When Jones's last play, *Remember*, opened in August 1979, Werts (10 August 1979) and Coe (21 September 1979) claimed the play showed several improvements in Jones's playwriting. Taitte described *Remember* as Jones's "most ambitious, most carefully crafted, and richest drama" (1979, 166), emphasizing the play's classic concentration on one day's experience of an aging actor rather than the twenty-year expansiveness of *Trilogy*. Sewell observed that Jones's one-act play, *Juneteenth*, an invited contribution to a series of American celebratory dramas by Actors' Theatre in Louisville and performed there in 1978, satirizes small town racism, a purpose that Busby evaluates as not allowing Jones to advance his dramatic talent (41).

Jones's presentation of *Trilogy* in repertory on Broadway was the most significant performance of all of his work. Its production gave evidence, as a *Time* reviewer claimed, that regional theatre had gained nationwide attention and in a "Texas Triple Play" had invaded Broadway ("Texas Triple Play"). Yet reviewers also wrote that the enthusiastic reception of *Trilogy* in Washington, D.C., and elsewhere in the months prior to its opening in New York raised expectations too high. A cover story on *Trilogy* by Cook in *Saturday Review* and Prideaux in *Smithsonian* made claims for it that supported what Coe had declared: "Not since the late 1940's when Miller and Williams were breaking in on us, has one heard so assured, so American a dramatic voice" (9 May 1976, K1). Although

Clurman generally praised the plays, noting the "ripe and racy" language, their originality that "makes us laugh," and the remarkably good cast (348–50), the mediocre reviews of Barnes, Kerr, and Gill, among others, predicted its early closing. Both Barnes and Kerr referred to the high expectations for *Trilogy*, and both mentioned echoes of early Williams and Inge in it but not necessarily to praise Jones's work. Reviewing *Trilogy* after seeing all three plays, Kerr declared they lacked idea, conflict, and originality, being "ghosts of plays" in which the characters "never quite inhabit domains of their own." In addition, Kerr revealed that Broadway was concerned about regional theatre in his ambiguous remark, "What the present venture suggests is that 'regional theater,' for all its slight variations of background and tongue, is still taking too many of its cues from Broadway outlines of the past." Reviewing each play after its opening performance as if to see what *Trilogy* would reveal, Barnes acknowledged that Jones "can write, can create atmosphere" (22 September 1976, 30) with a great gift for language, but he complained that if Jones were to be a new voice in American theatre he must provide more than slices of life (24 September 1976) and not use art or texture for substance (23 September 1976). In general, the major critics praised the direction of Alan Schneider, the staging, and the cast, especially the characterization of Lu Ann and Colonel Kinkaid, noting that the plays interpreted a region far away from New York.

SURVEY OF SECONDARY SOURCES

Bibliographies

To date, the most complete bibliographies are found in Busby's monograph and, among other entries, in Sewell's dissertation. Data on production and reviews of *A Texas Trilogy, Santa Fe Sunshine*, and *A Place on the Magdalena Flats* can be found in Salem.

Biographies

No biography of Jones exists, but brief capsule statements are found in Busby's and Sewell's studies. Biographical facts appear in Bruegge and in *Contemporary Authors* ("Preston Jones"). Bennett's interview with Jones teases the playwright into discussion of his writing habits and attitudes, which are interspersed with anecdotes from various periods of his life.

Influences

Dramatic or nondramatic influences on Jones's work or of his influence on other writers are mentioned in Busby (*Literary History*), who links

Jones with other playwrights prominent since the 1960s such as Sam Shepard, Lanford Wilson, and Mark Medoff (1232). While reviewers early on compare Jones with O'Neill, Inge, or Williams, Jones told Bennett that he admired Thornton Wilder's *Our Town* and Arthur Miller's *The Price*. Both Bennett and Busby observe that Jones was influenced by the humor of Robert Flynn's novel, *North to Yesterday*, and the work of other Texas writers such as Larry McMurtry and D. L. Coburn, whose Pulitzer Prize play, *The Gin Game*, Jones influenced. Porterfield also notes these Texas influences on Jones's work.

General Studies

General studies of Jones are found in Busby's monograph and Sewell's dissertation. Sewell's study draws on two interviews with Jones in November and December 1978, as well as on specific historical and cultural information concerning the region where Jones lived and worked and that inspired his themes, settings, and characterizations. This knowledge and her direct contact with the playwright enabled her to evaluate specifically the effect of Jones's long association with the Dallas Theater Center on his artistic development, his self-conflicts and dependence on tradition, especially in religious belief, and his childlike qualities that permitted him to observe people and places with a sort of wonder. Busby's monograph provides the background for his assessment of Jones's contribution to American theatre: "acute sensibility about the human condition presented in humorous, lively, audience-centered plays" (48). Latimer combines biography, analysis, and assessment and concludes that Jones "lived and worked entirely outside New York" and "helped to establish a new acceptance of the work of regional theaters and writers around the country" (1013).

Analyses of Individual Plays

Jones's *Trilogy* has attracted the most critical attention. Because the three plays have a single setting, Bradleyville in West Texas, shared characters, and common themes of confrontation with time's effect on people and places, the plays become a tightly constructed unit that breathes Jones's dramatic storytelling talent. Analyses by Busby, Latimer, and Sewell emphasize this theme of time and several associated elements: passing southwestern frontier values, the playwright's humorous ambivalence toward his characters, group relationships, especially in the family, the realistic yet sometimes poetic speech of Bradleyville inhabitants, and sharp characterization of people caught between diminishing expectations and escape from small town stagnation. Busby remarks that *Trilogy* plays well, "reaching beyond regionalism through theme and character while remaining deeply rooted in the Southwest" (*Preston Jones*, 48), and Latimer adds that Bradleyville acquires a dense reality akin to that of Faulkner's fictional county (1011), yet Jones told Bennett that initially he did not write the plays with such a region in mind. Sewell's knowledge of West Texas complements Busby's assertion that the three plays examine the different values of the southwestern frontier (16): the loss of the natural world in *The Oldest Living Graduate*, the hard times of women on this frontier in *Lu Ann Hampton Haverty Oberlander*, and the racism of southwesterners in *The Last Meeting of the Knights of the White Magnolia*. A failure by most standards, Lu Ann, in Latimer's view, is Jones's survivor, "worthy of sympathy and praise" (1010).

Jones reveals his own analysis of *Trilogy* and its destiny in two articles, "Reflections on a Trilogy" and "Tales of a Pilgrim's Progress from Bradleyville to Broadway." "I write to tell stories about people," he reflected (D3). Small things triggered his imagination to create incidents and characters in *Trilogy:* a certain waitress inspired his characterization of Lu Ann and a television news story about a school's reunion and its oldest living graduate gave birth to Colonel Kinkaid. Only after director Paul Baker prepared *Lu Ann* for possible performance at Dallas Theater Center did Jones think about Bradleyville as a locale for other stories and interweaving the lives of the characters in a trilogy, "plays tied together by time, place and related characters" that were subsequently performed under the title *A Bradleyville Trilogy* ("Tales," 9–10). The fate of *A Texas Trilogy* on Broadway Jones attributed to the difficulty of selling a trilogy to theatregoers, to traditional characteristics of New York audiences, to a lack of "western" environment in the Broadhurst Theatre to acclimate the audience to the sounds and sights of a small West Texas town and its characters, and to the nature of the critical response to theatrical performances in New York (18).

Concerning the three New Mexico plays, Busby, Latimer, and Sewell agree that *Remember* represents a new direction in Jones's writing: better educated and more self-aware characters (Latimer, 1012); concern with ideas, especially the decline of religous values (Busby, *Jones*, 43), which Anthony explains as Jones's philosophical questioning of death; and imagery and music to engage the audience in consideration of their own mortality (Sewell, 519).

FUTURE RESEARCH OPPORTUNITIES

Scholars will find opportunities for future research in three sources: Jones's manuscripts held by his widow, Mary Sue Jones, of Santa Fe; unclassified historical materials related to the operation of Dallas Theater Center to 1982, owned by Dallas Public Library; and data on the production of *The Last Meeting* through the auspices of American Playwrights

Theatre at Ohio State University. An expanded biography can integrate these materials through further discussions, like those of Nikki Greenberg and Pam Johnson, with Mary Sue Jones, with Paul Baker, director of the Dallas Theater Center up to 1982, with directors of Jones's plays, and with actors who worked with him. Sewell's observation on aspects of Jones's life suggests that a psychoanalytic approach might uncover influences on his work that his remarks on influences do not reveal. A deeper study of Jones's humor, his universalization of familial relationships and of his southwestern region's small town people (Madden calls them "stunted people"), and his theatrical technique of characterization would help to illuminate how these elements might account for his nationwide appeal and to identify the voice of his own that told stories of ordinary people that New York critics failed to hear.

SECONDARY SOURCES

Anders, John. "Mr. Jones Goes to Broadway." *Dallas Morning News* (26 September 1976): G1, G6.

Anthony, Ole. "The Long Nights of Preston Jones." *Texas Monthly* (December 1979): 180–89.

Ayers, David. American Playwrights Theatre. Telephone conversation. 22 April 1987.

Barnes, Clive. "Preston Jones's 'Texas Trilogy' Opens with Portrait of a Loser." *New York Times* (22 September 1976): 30.

———. "A Sentimental Texas Journey." *New York Times* (23 September 1976): 51.

———. "Stage: The Last of 'Texas Trilogy.'" *New York Times* (24 September 1976): C3.

Bennett, Patrick. *Talking with Texas Writers: Twelve Interviews.* College Station: Texas A&M University Press, 1980.

Bruegge, Andrew Vorder. "Preston Jones." In *Dictionary of Literary Biography*, 7:337–44. Edited by John MacNicholas. Detroit: Gale, 1981.

Busby, Mark. "Contemporary Western Drama." In *Literary History of the American West*, pp. 1232–35. Forth Worth: Texas Christian University Press, 1987.

———. *Preston Jones*. Western Writers Series. Boise: Boise State University, 1983.

Clurman, Harold. *Nation* (9 October 1976): 348–50.

Coe, Richard L. "Playwright Preston Jones, 43, Dies." *Washington Post* (21 September 1979): 86.

———. "'A Texas Trilogy': In Affirmation of Wonder." *Washington Post* (9 May 1976): K1, K3.

Cook, Bruce. "Preston Jones: Playwright on the Range." *Saturday Review* (15 May 1976): 40–42.

Curtis, Anthony. "Plays in Performance." *Drama* 124 (Spring 1977): 49.

Dunn, Si. "Q. What Have You Been Doing since 'Texas Trilogy'? A: Been Working, Pal." *New York Times* (22 May 1977): D5, D32.

Durham, Weldon. "The Last Meeting of the Knights of the White Magnolia." *Educational Theater Journal* 28 (March 1976): 109–10.

Eason, Robert. Theatre librarian, Dallas Public Library. Letter, 10 February 1987.

Gill, Brendan. "Open for Business." *New Yorker* (4 October 1976): 75–76.

Greenberg, Nikki Finke. "High Profile: Mary Sue Jones." *Dallas Morning News* (2 May 1982): E1, E4.

Johnson, Pam. "At Home with Preston Jones." *Dallas Morning News* (15 January 1979).

Jones, Mary Sue. Telephone interview. 16 March 1987.

Kerr, Walter. "The Buildup (and Letdown) of 'Texas Trilogy.' " *New York Times* (3 October 1976), D3, D6.

Kroll, Jack. "Branch Water." *Newsweek* (4 October 1976): 97.

Latimer, Kathleen. "Preston Jones." In *Critical Survey of Drama*, 3:1007–13. Edited by Frank N. Magill. Englewood Cliffs, N.J.: Salem Press, 1985.

London *Times* (3 March 1977): E13.

Madden, David. "A Texas Trilogy." In *Magill's Literary Annual*, 812–16. Edited by Frank N. Magill. Englewood Cliffs, N.J.: Salem Press, 1977.

Marek, Annemarie. *Preston Jones: An Interview*. Dallas: New London Press, 1978.

Mitchell, Sean. "The Champion Playwright Texas Loved." *Dallas Times Herald* (6 April 1980): Q1, Q3.

———. "NBC's 'Graduate' from Dallas: A Bitter Pill for Some." *Dallas Times Herald* (2 March 1980): H1.

———. "Preston Jones Rings Down a Final Curtain." *Dallas Times Herald* (20 September 1979): E1, E4, E9.

Neville, John. "And Then Along Came Jones." *Dallas Morning News* (10 January 1976): F1, F4.

———. "Bradleyville Is Revisited with Return of 'Trilogy.' " *Dallas Morning News* (10 December 1978): C7.

———. "Down Center Debut for Jones' 'Lu Ann.' " *Dallas Morning News* (7 February 1974): A43.

———. "Magnolia Blooms at DTC." *Dallas Morning News* (6 December 1973): A14.

O'Connor, John. "TV: 'Live Theatre.' 'Nurse,' 'Henry IV.' " *New York Times* (9 April 1980): C27.

Porterfield, Bill. "Preston Jones: An Unsentimental Genius." *Dallas Times Herald* (20 September 1979): A19.

———. "The Texas of Jones, Greene and Graves." *Dallas Times Herald* (6 April 1980): M3.

"Preston Jones." In *Contemporary Authors*, 73–76:3210. Detroit: Gale, 1987.

Prideaux, Tom. "The Classic Family Drama Is Revived in 'A Texas Trilogy.' " *Smithsonian* 7 (October 1976): 49–54.

Salem, James M. *A Guide to Critical Reviews*. Pt. I: *American Drama, 1909–1982*, 3d ed., pp. 264–65. Metuchen, N.J.: Scarecrow Press, 1984.

Sewell, Betty Brady. "The Plays of Preston Jones: Background and Analysis". Ph.D. dissertation. University of California at Los Angeles, 1984.

Taitte, W. L. "Keeping up with Jones." *Texas Monthly* 3 (December 1975): 50–52.

————. "This Little Play Goes to Market." *Texas Monthly* 7 (May 1979): 166–67.

"Texas Triple Play." *Time* (27 September 1976): 67–68.

Weales, Gerald C. "Drama." In *Harvard Guide to Contemporary American Writing*, p. 422. Edited by Daniel Hoffman. Cambridge: Harvard University Press, 1979.

Werts, Diane. "Playwright Preston Jones Dies." *Dallas Morning News* (20 September 1979): F2.

————."Preston Jones' 'Remember' Gives Wistful Look into Past." *Dallas Morning News* (10 August 1979): C1.

————. "Preston Jones Remembered." *Dallas Morning News* (23 September 1979): E3.

Arthur Kopit

(10 MAY 1937–   )

LAURA H. WEAVER

ASSESSMENT OF KOPIT'S REPUTATION

The major plays of Arthur Lee Kopit, who became immediately successful as a young playwright at Harvard University in the late 1950s, are *Indians* (1968) and *Wings* (1978). He has been the recipient of awards for specific plays: for *Oh Dad, Poor Dad, Mamma's Hung You in the Closet and I'm Feelin' So Sad* in 1962, the Vernon Rice Award and the Outer Circle Award; for *Wings* in 1979, the Italia Prize for the radio version and the Pulitzer Prize for the stage version. He was elected to the American Academy of Arts and Letters in 1971, has been a member of the council of the Dramatists Guild since 1982, and has received the following awards and grants: Guggenheim Fellowship (1967), Rockefeller Grant (1968), National Institute of Arts and Letters Award (1971), and National Endowment for the Arts Grant (1974). Dasgupta provides a useful assessment of Kopit's achievement: "Working within the then fashionable dramatic mode of European absurdism, he had in the sixties integrated social and existential questions in a way that addressed the American way of life. In all instances, Kopit's social commentary is grounded in a cohesive dramatic and theatrical premise, a reason why his plays succeed as well as they do on stage" (24–25). Kopit is also significant for the diversity of modes he uses: realism (*The Questioning of Nick*), absurdism (*Oh Dad, Poor Dad*), Brechtian epic theatre and Pirandellian drama *(Indians* and *End of the World)*, and poetic stream of consciousness (*Wings*). His versatility is demonstrated especially in his two very different major plays. The political theatre of *Indians*, a play on the process of mythmaking, places the Vietnam War in the context of American history; and *Wings*, a brilliant interior monologue incorporating Joycean stream of consciousness, treating language not only in one clinical case but also in universal terms, reaches the level of "high poetry" and "true tragedy" (Esslin, 24).

PRIMARY BIBLIOGRAPHY Of KOPIT'S WORKS

Plays

The Questioning of Nick. 1957. Televised WNHC, New Haven, Conn., June 1959. Published in *The Day the Whores Came Out to Play Tennis and Other Plays.* New York: Hill & Wang, 1965.

Gemini. Unpublished. 1957.

Don Juan in Texas, with Wally Lawrence. Unpublished. 1957.

On the Runway of Life, You Never Know What's Coming Off Next. Unpublished. 1957.

Across the River and into the Jungle. Unpublished. 1958.

Aubade. Unpublished. 1959.

Sing to Me Through Open Windows. 1959. In *The Day the Whores Came Out to Play Tennis and Other Plays.* New York: Hill & Wang, 1965.

To Dwell in a Place of Strangers. 1959. Act I published in *Harvard Advocate* (May 1959).

Oh Dad, Poor Dad, Mamma's Hung You in the Closet and I'm Feelin' So Sad: A Pseudoclassical Tragifarce in a Bastard French Tradition. New York: Hill & Wang, 1960; New York: Samuel French, 1960; London: Methuen, 1962; New York: Pocket Books, 1966.

Mhil'daim. Unpublished. 1963.

Asylum: or, What the Gentlemen Are Up To, And as for the Ladies. (Kopit also considered the title, *Asylum: or What the Gentlemen Are Up To, Not to Mention the Ladies).* 1963. Published as *Chamber Music* in *The Day the Whores Came Out to Play Tennis and Other Plays.* New York: Hill & Wang, 1965; and as *Chamber Music and Other Plays.* London: Methuen, 1969.

The Conquest of Everest. 1964. Published in *The Day the Whores Came Out to Play Tennis and Other Plays.* New York: Hill & Wang, 1965.

The Hero. 1964. Published in *The Day the Whores Came Out to Play Tennis and Other Plays.* New York: Hill & Wang, 1965.

The Day the Whores Came Out to Play Tennis and Other Plays (Chamber Music, The Questioning of Nick, Sing to Me Through Open Windows, The Hero, The Conquest of Everest). New York: Hill & Wang, 1965. Published as *Chamber Music and Other Plays.* London: Methuen, 1969.

An Incident in the Park. In *Pardon Me, Sir, But Is My Eye Hurting Your Elbow?* Edited by Bob Booker and George Foster. New York: Geis, 1968.

Indians. New York: Hill & Wang, 1969; London: Methuen, 1970; New York: Bantam, 1971.

What Happened to the Thorne's House? Unpublished. 1972.

Louisiana Territory; or, Lewis and Clark—Lost and Found. Unpublished. 1975.

Secrets of the Rich. Unpublished. 1976. (Although several bibliographies list this as published by Hill and Wang, it has never been published.)

Wings. New York: Hill & Wang, 1978; New York: Samuel French, 1978; London: Eyre Methuen, 1979; Paris: Gallimard, 1979.

Good Help Is Hard to Find. New York: Samuel French, 1982.
Nine. A musical. Book by Arthur Kopit, music and lyrics by Maury Yeston (adaptation from the Italian by Mario Fratti). New York: Samuel French, 1983; Garden City, N.Y.: Nelson Doubleday, 1983.
End of the World. New York: Hill & Wang, 1984; New York: Samuel French, 1984.
Ghosts: A Drama by Henrik Ibsen. New translation by Arthur Kopit. New York: Samuel French, 1984.

Radio Play

Wings. 1977.

Television Plays

The Conquest of Television. NETV. 1966.
Promontory Point Revisited. WNET (PBS). 1969.

Essays and Interviews

Barnett, Jane, Susan Merrill, and Mopsy Strange. "Looking for Answers: Guest Editors Interview Six Creative People." *Mademoiselle* 55 (August 1962): 248, 360.
Berkvist, Robert. "Playwright Arthur Kopit Tells How 'Wings' Took Flight." *New York Times* (25 June 1978): 2:1.
Funke, Lewis. "Origins of *Indians* as Recalled by Kopit." *New York Times* (15 October 1969): 37.
Hennessy, Brendan. "Arthur Kopit." *Transatlantic Review* 30 (Autumn 1968): 68–73. Reprinted in *Behind the Scenes: Theater and Film Interviews from the Transatlantic Review*, pp. 70–76. Edited by Joseph F. McCrindle. New York: Holt, 1971.
Kopit, Arthur. Introduction to *The Day the Whores Came Out to Play Tennis and Other Plays.* New York: Hill & Wang, 1965.
———. Preface to *Wings.* New York: Hill & Wang, 1978.
———. "The Vital Matter of Environment." *Theatre Arts* 45, no. 4 (April 1961): 12–13.
Lahr, John. "*Indians*: A Dialogue between Arthur Kopit and John Lahr." Edited by Anthea Lahr. Unpaginated insert in Bantam edition of *Indians.* New York: Bantam, 1971.
Parker, Judith. "A Play Has to Breathe." *Harvard Magazine* (March/April 1979): 90–91.
Shewey, Don. "Arthur Kopit: A Life on Broadway." *New York Times Biographical Service* 15 (29 April 1984): 505–7.
Wilson, Harry R. " 'Indians' Playwright Clarifying History." In *Authors in the News*, Vol. 1. Detroit: Gale, 1976. 288.

PRODUCTION HISTORY

Kopit's first plays, written while he was a student at Harvard University, were produced there before his graduation in 1959: *The Questioning of Nick; Gemini; Don Juan in Texas; On the Runway of Life, You Never Know What's Coming Off Next; Across the River and Into the Jungle; Aubade; Sing to Me Through Open Windows;* and *To Dwell in a Place of Strangers.* Also written during Kopit's undergraduate days was his first major play, *Oh Dad, Poor Dad, Mamma's Hung You in the Closet, and I'm Feelin' So Sad,* which was initially produced in the Adams House competition at Harvard and then at the Agassiz Theatre in Cambridge, Massachusetts, in 1960. In 1961, it opened at the Lyric Opera House in London, in 1962 at the Phoenix Theatre (off-Broadway) (with 454 performances), and in 1963 at the Morosco (with 47 performances). Its London performance, viewed as "a hilarious skit on the Ionesco School of Playwrights" ("A Skit," 19a), was considered both "baffling" ("Oh Dad," 19) and "superb"—"a sick and bitter joke . . . of considerable beauty and not a little truth" (Gellert, 64). As Gellert observed, this play contained a "wildly funny blend of Firbank, Tennessee Williams and Charles Addams" (64).

The Phoenix production was, for Taubman, clever ("One Work," 1), but for Simon not "self-sustaining" ("Theater," 268). Although Gassner had some reservations about *Oh Dad* ("entertaining yet gruesome; playful yet labored; and varied . . . yet monotonous"), he labeled Jerome Robbins's direction excellent and praised Jo Van Fleet's performance as Mrs. Rosepettle (170). When the play opened at the Morosco, it was characterized by "bizarre energy" (Nadel, 294), "bright, brash theatricality," and "a gift for grotesquerie" (Altshuler, 296). Music, setting, and lighting were also considered effective.

Between the production of *Oh Dad* and his next major play, *Indians,* Kopit wrote *Asylum: Or, What the Gentlemen Are Up To, And As for the Ladies,* which was scheduled to open at the off-Broadway Theatre de Lys in 1963, but after only five preview performances, Kopit cancelled it, though the play was later produced as *Chamber Music* at the Society Hill Playhouse in Philadelphia in 1965 and in London in 1971. *The Conquest of Everest* was produced in New York in 1964 and then again at the Assembly Theatre in New York in 1970 and off-Broadway at Playwrights Cooperative in 1973. *The Hero* was produced in New York in 1964, at Playwrights Cooperative in 1973, at Playbox in New York in 1970, and in London in 1972. In 1965 two plays, *The Day the Whores Came Out to Play Tennis* (originally scheduled, with *Mhil'daim,* to be produced at the Tyrone Guthrie Theatre but withdrawn by Kopit after a disagreement with the University of Minnesota in 1964) and *Sing to Me Through Open Windows* (cancelled as a curtain raiser to *Oh Dad* in New York in 1962), were performed at the Players Theatre in Greenwich

Village, with twenty-four performances. Taubman found the "grotesque and sardonic" *The Day* only "sporadically amusing" and lamented the unclear motivation; the second play, *Sing to Me*, was, he thought, "pretentious and arty" ("Short," 45).

The world premiere of *Indians* was at the Aldwych Theatre in London on 4 July 1968 because of, according to Kopit, "its strong political underpinnings" (a parallel to the Vietnam War): "In New York it wouldn't have been judged on its own merits. Not in 1968" (Parker, 91). Another reason was the expensive production costs in New York. Directed by Jack Gelber, the play elicited uneven reviews. Although "fired with moral passion and grow[ing]...out of a splendid and hitherto unused theatrical form," this play, by presenting Buffalo Bill's life "from a vantage point of ultimate failure," denied him "a positive role." While at the end Buffalo Bill "achieves a pathos that embraces the whole situation,...by then it is rather too late" (Wardle, 7a). Finding this production only partially successful, Barnes claimed it needed "more seriousness" (9 July 1968, 30). However, despite a few misgivings, Taylor declared the contrasting scenes from Cody's memory "a daring notion" and "remarkably successful" and the play as a whole "a brilliant piece of stage machinery" (17, 19). For Esslin the Vietnam application was "under-explicit and over-discreet," though Kopit's idea was "brilliant" and Gelber's direction effective (21 July 1968, 12).

The American premiere of *Indians* at the Arena Stage on 6 May 1969 presented a revised version emphasizing the Wild West Show and the 1886 Indian Commission hearing. Novick praised this "neo-Brechtian chronicle" for its contrasts, the Arena Stage's rectangular stage surrounded on four sides by the audience, and Stacy Keach's acting as Buffalo Bill (3). Barnes found that, in general, the acting was "not as polished" as in the London production but that this production had "a better director," Gene Frankel, and that Keach was "more convincing" as Buffalo Bill (27 May 1969, 43). On 13 October 1969 *Indians* moved to the Brooks Atkinson Theater on Broadway, running for ninety-six performances. Although designated "almost entirely exposition" and a "penitential exercise" by Kerr (11), the production was "a spectacular leap forward," according to O'Connor (233). Particular strengths were its revelation that plays do not need to be "linear" but can be "a group of images" (Barnes, "Stacy," 51) and for its avoidance of "strident polemics" even though it confronted the audience "with the specter of genocide" (O'Connor, 233). Technically the play was successful in its staging (a proscenium-style version of a thrust stage), lighting, costumes, music, and choreography.

Between the success of *Indians* and his later *Wings*, Kopit's *Secrets of the Rich* was produced at the National Playwrights Conference at the

Eugene O'Neill Theater Center, Waterford, Connecticut, in 1976. Also during this time, an Arthur Kopit Festival was held at the Impossible Ragtime Theatre in New York (1977): *Chamber Music, The Conquest of Everest, The Day the Whores Came Out to Play Tennis, The Hero, The Questioning of Nick, and Sing to Me Through Open Windows.*

Wings, Kopit's next major play, commissioned by Earplay for National Public Radio, was aired in 1977; it subsequently opened at the Yale Repertory Theatre on 3 March 1978 and ran for twenty-eight performances. It later had a limited run (sixteen performances) at the New York Shakespeare Festival's Public Theatre in June 1978 and then opened at the Lyceum Theatre on Broadway in January 1979 (113 performances). Almost uniformly, critics praised this play for its poetry, staging, setting, lighting, John Madden's direction, and Constance Cummings's acting. Although the play was based on research, many critics thought that it transcended a medical case history; a representative critical accolade was Eder's praise for the "chaotic landscape of the mind" portrayal achieved by Madden's direction and Andrew Jackness's set (385).

In the 1980s Kopit continued to have plays on both off-Broadway and on Broadway. In 1981 his *Good Help Is Hard to Find* was presented off-off-Broadway in Marathon 1981, a month-long session of one-act plays at the Ensemble Studio Theatre. The domestic crisis in this "bitter black comedy about the servant problem" was, according to Gussow, handled by Kopit with "humor and finesse" ("Theater: 3," 66). Kopit's *End of the World* was produced at the Kennedy Center, Washington, D.C., in March 1984 and on Broadway at the Music Box Theatre in May 1984. While Kopit was applauded for treating nuclear destruction, reviewers like Simon thought that the private investigator conceit did not work ("Bangs," 104), and Rich believed that "little is done with the Pirandellian device of having a playwright writing a play that may be the play we're watching" ("Stage," 274). Weales, however, found that since a "direct approach" would have been "undramatizable," the use of a "human story" and the playwright-detective analogy constituted a successful solution to the problem (598–99). Another strength of the play was its "mixture of comedy and documentary [which] prevent[ed] . . . [it] from being a simplistic antinuke diatribe" (Shewey, 506).

Kopit also has done the book for the musical *Nine* (1982) (a version of Federico Fellini's movie *8½*). The style of Kopit's book, based on a previous adaptation from the Italian by Mario Fratti, was "sometimes stylish" (Rich, "Theatre," 288–89), polished and witty (Kroll, 293) but also "flat" (Watt, 289). Kroll also found that Kopit's book "waffles fatally with Guido himself"; the audience does not care about the hero (293). In August 1982, when Kopit's adaptation of Ibsen's *Ghosts* appeared at the Brooks Atkinson Theatre, Gussow observed that the translation was "colloquial and faithful to its source" and that the production did "not illuminate Ibsen" ("Theater: Liv," 238).

Two film versions of Kopit's plays also deserve comment. In 1967 *Oh Dad, Poor Dad, Mamma's Hung You in the Closet and I'm Feelin' So Sad* was produced by Paramount Pictures, with Rosalind Russell playing Madame Rosepettle and Jonathan Winters the ghost of the father as observer and commentator, a part not included in the play. This film, considered not as successful as the play, struggled "too hard to be outlandish" (Crowther, 32). In 1976 Robert Altman produced and directed *Buffalo Bill and the Indians, or Sitting Bull's History Lesson*, based on Kopit's *Indians*. Despite some "attempts at conscious intellectualizing," Altman's film was praised for its portrayal of mythmaking (Stabiner, 54–55).

SURVEY OF SECONDARY SOURCES

Bibliographies

The only bibliography (primary and secondary) on Kopit is the section on Kopit in King. Although generally useful for its coverage of criticism and reviews, King includes items only up to 1979 and contains a number of errors (for example, listing the unpublished *Secrets of the Rich* as published). Two other bibliographies are in Eddleman (1979 and 1984) and Salem (1973 and 1984). Neither of those bibliographies is complete, however. Another current bibliography of criticism appears in Carpenter (1986) (containing fourteen entries and eight cross-reference items on Kopit).

Biographies

In the absence of a full-scale biography of Arthur Kopit, consult the entries in Bradish, Gale, Harley, and Popovich. Helpful biographical details can be gleaned in interviews by Hennessy and Shewey. Finally, information about Kopit's composition of specific plays and about his personal experiences is contained in interviews done by Funke, Wilson, and Berkvist. Kopit's preface to *Wings* also sheds light on the playwright and his writing.

Influences

The only study of influence on Kopit is Rinear's article, which argues that Kopit's play *The Day the Whores Came Out to Play Tennis* is "a parody of *The Cherry Orchard*" and similar to Chekhov's play in setting, tone, characters, and theme. Rinear concludes that Kopit's play, "in spite of its self-conscious absurdist elements, dramatically develops the same central idea used in *The Cherry Orchard*" (22–23). Scattered throughout Kopit criticism are references to writers with whom Kopit appears to have affinities: Ionesco, Beckett, Pirandello, Pinter, Brecht, and (as revealed in *Wings*) James Joyce. Kopit himself, however, has denied the influence of these specific writers. Called Ionesco's "young American cousin" by Parker in her interview, Kopit replied, "I've never once thought of Ionesco in connection with my work. . . . I'm not conscious of the influence of other playwrights at all. Except indirectly, I suppose" (90).

General Studies

No book-length studies on Kopit exist. Auerbach's book, however, devotes five of thirteen chapters to Kopit, supplying an introductory and separate chapters on *Oh Dad, Indians, Chamber Music,* and *Wings.* Her useful overview provides information on production history and analysis. Helpful brief overviews of Kopit's works can be found in Cohn, Harley, and Weales (*Contemporary Dramatists*). More detailed analysis appears in Dasgupta, whose thesis is that "the nightmarish dimensions" of the world are "the projections of the inner world of his characters. . . . Forever in search of his identity, the quintessential Kopit character rearranges his universe in a desperate attempt to make it conform to a sense of order and to establish his own identity. But the world eludes him at every point" (15). Demonstrated throughout Kopit's works, this controlling idea seems to work especially well in the early plays.

Several articles, discussing one theme or motif, treat all or most of Kopit's plays. Dieckman and Brayshaw argue that "windows or theatres, as prisons, are constructed by various social forces in Kopit's plays: the family, social or sexual class, or the national myth-making process" (196). Kopit's works show a development from a portrayal of characters' "succumbing to their limitations" to, in *Wings* and in *Nine*, their "transcending these limitations" (Dieckman and Brayshaw, 210). An equally convincing analysis of Kopit's works, also including early plays like *The Questioning of Nick* and *Sing to Me Through Open Windows*, is Wolter's essay, which argues that Kopit's works "show a strong coherence in their subject matter: . . . Kopit is concerned with an individual's interior landscape and the question of his identity; the protagonist's visionary self-portrait is tested and exposed as a fallacious dream which, revealing his true soul, turns into an apocalyptic nightmare" (55).

Analyses of Individual Plays

Studies of individual plays have appeared in articles and in chapters in books. Not surprisingly, the plays that have received the most attention are *Wings* and *Indians*. (*Oh Dad* was treated more often, however sketchily, in earlier surveys of the American theatre.) *Wings* is the subject of several articles and a section in a book on American drama. A few critics found weaknesses in this play. For example, Geraths, in comparing *Wings* with Beckett's *Not I*, concludes that *Wings* is not suited for the stage. Rosen observes that "the clinical nature," the "literalness," limits this play; lacking is "the poetic transformation of a social system into a microcosm" (79–80). However, the play has been praised by Cohn, Harley, and others. Edgerton concludes that despite differences between radio and stage (for example, the subjective mode of perception in radio and the combined subjective and objective modes on the stage), "*Wings* in the two media has demonstrated that the same kind of material, once modified to suit the presentation, can work in both" (158).

Discussions of *Indians* have focused on both form and theme. Weales contends that "the comedy is thematic" ("Kopit," 302). Wilz contrasts the text of the first version (as produced in London) with the revised one (produced in the United States). Jones's excellent article claims that the theme, the United States's fabrication of myths "about her more unpleasant behavior," is communicated "through the formal characteristics or 'shape' of *Indians*," in which the theatre is used "as a metaphor for the process of myth-making" (443). To establish his thesis, Jones includes a breakdown of scenes. Jiji discusses Kopit's use of a "mosaic," a term Kopit himself used (Lahr, "*Indians*" n.p., and Funke, 37), to show "how Kopit counterposed four disparate kinds of theatrical conventions" and why the play is ultimately not successful. While she admires the play, Jiji thinks it fails because of too heavy reliance on the Brechtian method; the audience does not sympathize enough with Buffalo Bill. Consequently "the split personality of Cody [does not] coalese . . . into one struggling human being" (230, 236).

Most of the other articles on *Indians* focus on the play's relationship to history and its depiction of mythmaking. Kleinen does a scene-by-scene comparison of the historical material with the dramatic form, and Grant explores, in the context of past "*commemorative* tradition" plays about American history, the "revisionist history" dramatized in *Indians* (328, 330). Agreeing with Lahr's designation of *Indians* as "not a protest play, but a process play" ("Arthur," 67), Weiher observes that "the process of history-making" is manifested in the form of this play: "a montage of scenes" (406, 409). O'Neill's discussion of history in *Indians* concentrates on Kopit's use of musical strategies in an untraditional way: "collage . . . depending upon counterpoint" (496). Kopit has attempted, O'Neill argues, "to redefine history poetically as an eternal present"; but the play also "looks to triumph over time, to move its audience away from the post-Hegelian, linear view of history" (503–4).

Other Kopit plays have received less attention. In raising the question of parodies (Williams, Ionesco, Ibsen, Beckett, O'Neill, and Dürrenmatt) and satire of Freudianism in *Oh Dad*, Szilassy concludes that "the significance of this play,... apart from any parodistic effects, lies... in offering a grand metaphysical farce, giving the clown-sized interpretation of human life as it is mirrored by theatrical convention and innovations" (147). Weales briefly discusses a "fusion of genres" in *End of the World*" (302). Kopit's *Chamber Music* for Murch focuses not on social or political concerns but on "a ritual killing." The killing leads not to reintegration of the characters into society but to further imprisonment. The ritual helps the participants "to act out the rejection of the existing social order" and to try to reach "some new plane of individual consciousness where, the 'enemy' having been ostensibly disposed of, the individual may experience at least temporary fulfillment and harmony" (371, 375–76).

FUTURE RESEARCH POSSIBILITIES

Possibilities for research on Kopit are many. Both primary (especially on Kopit's unpublished works) and secondary bibliographies need to be updated and corrected. Critically, a book-length study of Kopit's plays is in order. Ironically no critical book exclusively on Kopit has been published. A critical biography and a stage history are also necessary. Specific areas most in need of investigation are Kopit's comedy, his language, a reevaluation of his Harvard plays, and Kopit's unpublished plays and the ways in which they foreshadow later themes and techniques.

SECONDARY SOURCES

Altshuler, Jerry. " 'Oh Dad' Hilarious Novelty." *New York Mirror* (28 August 1963). Reprinted in *New York Theatre Critics' Reviews* (1963): 296.

Auerbach, Doris. *Sam Shepard, Arthur Kopit, and the Off Broadway Theater.* Boston: Twayne, 1982.

Barnes, Clive. Review of *Indians. New York Times* (9 July 1968): 30.

———. Review of *Indians. New York Times* (27 May 1969): 43.

———. "Stacy Keach Is Starred in Study on Genocide." Review of *Indians.* New York Times (14 October 1969): 51. Reprinted in *New York Theatre Critics' Reviews* (1969): 234–35.

Berkvist, Robert. "Playwright Arthur Kopit Tells How 'Wings' Took Flight." *New York Times* (25 June 1978): 2:1.

Bradish, Gaynor F. "Kopit, Arthur (Lee)." In *Contemporary Dramatists*, Third Edition, pp. 455–58. Edited by James Vinson. New York: St. Martin's Press, 1982.

Carpenter, Charles A. *Modern Drama: Scholarship and Criticism 1966–1980: An International Bibliography.* Toronto: University of Toronto Press, 1986.

Cohn, Ruby. *New American Dramatists, 1960–1980.* 1st Evergreen ed. New York: Grove, 1982.

Crowther, Bosley. Review of *Oh, Dad, Poor Dad, Mamma's Hung You in the Closet, and I'm Feelin' So Sad* [film]. *New York Times* (16 February 1967): 32. Reprinted in *New York Times Film Reviews (1959–1968)* 5:3662–63.

Dasgupta, Gautam. "Arthur Kopit." In *American Playwrights: A Critical Survey*, pp. 15–25. Edited by Bonnie Marranca and Gautam Dasgupta. New York: Drama Book Specialists, 1981.

Dieckman, Suzanne Burgoyne, and Richard Brayshaw. "Wings, Watchers, and Windows: Imprisonment in the Plays of Arthur Kopit." *Theatre Journal* 35, no. 2 (May 1983): 195–212.

Eddleman, Floyd E. "Arthur Kopit." In *American Drama Criticism: Interpretations 1890–1977*, 2d ed., pp. 199–201. Hamden, Conn.: Shoe String Press, 1979. *Supplement to the Second Edition*, pp. 93–94. 1984.

Eder, Richard. "Theater: 'Wings' Comes to Broadway." *New York Times* (29 January 1979). Reprinted in *New York Theatre Critics' Reviews* (1979): 385.

Edgerton, Gary. "*Wings*: Radio Play Adapted to Experimental Stage." *Journal of Popular Culture* 16, no. 4 (1983): 152–58.

Esslin, Martin. "*Osborne's* Author and Kopit's *Indians*." Review of *Indians*. *New York Times* (21 July 1968): 11:12.

———. Review of *Wings*. *Plays and Players* 27 (October 1979): 23–24.

Funke, Lewis. "Origins of *Indians* as Recalled by Kopit." *New York Times* (15 October 1969): 37.

Gale, Steven H. "Arthur Kopit." In *Critical Survey of Drama*, pp. 1064–76. English Language Series. Edited by Frank N. Magill. Englewood Cliffs, N.J.: Salem Press, 1985.

Gassner, John. "Broadway in Review." Review of *Oh Dad*. *Educational Theatre Journal* 14 (May 1962): 169–71.

Gellert, Roger. "Black Widow." Review of *Oh Dad*. *New Statesman* 62 (14 July 1961): 64.

Geraths, Armin. " 'Verarmung' and 'Bereicherung' Literarischer Texte durch Bühne Funk, Film und Fernsehen: P. Shaffers *Equus*, Becketts *Not I* und Kopits *Wings*." In *Literatur in Film und Fernsehen: von Shakespeare bis Beckett*, pp. 150–87. Edited by Herbert Grabes. Königstein: Scriptor, 1980.

Grant, Thomas M. "American History in Drama: The Commemorative Tradition and Some Recent Revisions." *Modern Drama* 19 (December 1976): 327–39.

Gussow, Mel. "Theater: Liv Ullmann Is the Star of '*Ghosts*.' " *New York Times* (31 August 1982). Reprinted in *New York Theatre Critics' Reviews* (1982): 238.

———. "Theater: 3 New Works Displaying Originality." Review of *Good Help Is Hard to Find*. *New York Times* (14 June 1981): 66.

Harley, Carol. "Arthur Kopit." In *Dictionary of Literary Biography/Twentieth-Century American Dramatists*, vol. 7, pt. 2: 41–49. Edited by John MacNicholas. Detroit: Gale, 1981.

Jiji, Vera M. "*Indians*: A Mosaic of Memories and Methodologies." *Players* 47 (Summer 1972): 230–36.

Jones, John B. "Impersonation and Authenticity: The Theatre as Metaphor in Kopit's *Indians*." *Quarterly Journal of Speech* 59 (December 1973): 443–51.

Kerr, Walter. "But If the Play Is Sick at Heart . . ." Review of *Indians. New York*

Times (19 October 1969): 11:1. Reprinted in *New York Theatre Critics' Reviews* (1969): 235–36.

King, Kimball. "Arthur Kopit." In *Ten American Playwrights: An Annotated Bibliography*, pp. 167–78. New York: Garland, 1982.

Kleinen, Edgar. "Arthur Kopit: *Indians* (1968)." In *Amerikanische Geschichte im amerikanischen historischen Drama seit Maxwell Anderson: Forschungsbericht, Werkinterpretation, gattungsgeschichtlicher Wertungsversuch*, pp. 239–80. Frankfurt: Lang, 1982.

"Kopit, Arthur (Lee)." In *Contemporary Authors*, 81–84: 303–5. Detroit: Gale, 1979.

"Kopit, Arthur L(ee)." In *Current Biography*, pp. 263–66. New York: H. W. Wilson, 1972.

Kroll, Jack. "Fellini on Broadway." Review of *Nine*. *Newsweek* (24 May 1982). Reprinted in *New York Theatre Critics' Reviews* (1982): 293–94.

Lahr, John. "Arthur Kopit's *Indians*: Dramatizing National Amnesia." *Evergreen Review* 13 (October 1969): 19–21, 63, 67. Reprinted in John Lahr. *Up against the Wall: Essays on Modern Theater*, pp. 136–288. New York, 1970.

———. "*Indians*: A Dialogue between Arthur Kopit and John Lahr." Edited by Anthea Lahr. Unpaginated insert in Bantam ed. of *Indians*. New York: Bantam, 1971.

Murch, Anne C. "Genet-Triana-Kopit: Ritual as 'Danse Macabre.' " *Modern Drama* 15 (March 1973): 369–81.

Nadel, Norman. " 'Poor Dad' Back in Closet, This Time on Broadway." *New York World-Telegram and the Sun* (28 August 1963). Reprinted in *New York Theatre Critics' Reviews* (1963): 294.

Novick, Julius. " 'Liberty and Justice' for Indians?" Review of *Indians*. *New York Times* (18 May 1969): 11:3.

O'Connor, John J. "Kopit and the Indians." *Wall Street Journal* (15 October 1969). Reprinted in *New York Theatre Critics' Reviews* (1969): 233.

" 'Oh Dad, Poor Dad,' by Arthur Kopit, Opens." *New York Times* (6 July 1961): 19.

O'Neill, Michael C. "History as Dramatic Present: Arthur L. Kopit's *Indians*." *Theatre Journal* 34 (December 1982): 493–504.

Parker, Judith. "A Play Has to Breathe." *Harvard Magazine* (March-April 1979): 90–91.

Popovich, Helen Houser. "Kopit, Arthur (Lee)." In *20th-Century American Literature*, pp. 318–20. New York: St. Martin's Press, 1981.

Rich, Frank. "Stage: New Kopit Play." Review of *End of the World*. *New York Times* (7 May 1984). Reprinted in *New York Theatre Critics' Reviews* (1984): 273–74.

———. "Theater: 'Nine,' a Musical Based on Fellini's '8 1/2.' " *New York Times* (10 May 1982). Reprinted in *New York Theatre Critics' Reviews* (1982): 288–89.

Rinear, D. L. "*The Day the Whores Came Out to Play Tennis*: Kopit's Debt to Chekhov." *Today's Speech* 22 (Spring 1974): 19–23.

Rosen, Carol. *Plays of Impasse: Contemporary Drama Set in Confining Institutions*. Princeton: Princeton University Press, 1983.

Salem, James M. "Kopit, Arthur." In *A Guide to Critical Reviews*. Pt. 1: *American*

Drama, 1908–1969, 2d ed., pp. 269–70. Metuchen, N.J.: Scarecrow Press, 1973. Pt. 1: *American Drama, 1909–1982,* 3d ed. 1984., pp. 297–99.

Shewey, Don. "Arthur Kopit: A Life on Broadway." *New York Times Biographical Service* 15 (29 April 1984): 505–7.

Simon, John. "Bangs and Whimpers." Review of *End of the World. New York* (21 May 1984): 104–5.

———. "Theatre Chronicle." Review of *Oh Dad. Hudson Review* 15 (Summer 1962): 267–68.

"A Skit on the Ionesco Playwrights' School." Review of *Oh Dad. London Times* (6 July 1961): 19a.

Stabiner, Karen. *"Buffalo Bill and the Indians."* Review of film by Robert Altman and Alan Rudolph. *Film Quarterly* 30, no. 1 (Fall 1976): 54–56.

Szilassy, Zoltán. "Yankee Burlesque or Metaphysical Farce? (Kopit's *Oh Dad, Poor Dad . . . Reconsidered)." Hungarian Studies in English* 11 (1977): 143–47.

Taubman, Howard. "One Work at a Time." Review of *Oh Dad. New York Times* (11 March 1962): 11:1.

———. "Short Plays Presented Off Broadway." Review of *The Day the Whores Came Out to Play Tennis* and *Sing to Me Through Open Windows. New York Times* (16 March 1965): 45.

Taylor, John Russell. "Kopit Goes West." Review of *Indians. Plays and Players* 15 (September 1968): 16–19.

Wardle, Irving. "Moral Pageantry from the West." Review of *Indians. London Times* (5 July 1968): 7a.

Watt, Douglas. " 'Nine' a Pretentious Tiresome Musical." *New York Daily News* (10 May 1982). Reprinted in *New York Theatre Critics' Reviews* (1982): 289.

Weales, Gerald. Review of *End of the World. Georgia Review* 38 (Fall 1984): 597–99.

———. "Arthur Kopit." *Contemporary Dramatists.* Fourth Edition, pp. 301–3. Edited by D. L. Kirkpatrick. Chicago: St. James Press, 1988.

Weiher, Carol. "American History on Stage in the 1960s: Something Old, Something New." *Quarterly Journal of Speech* 63 (December 1977): 405–12.

Wilson, Harry R. " 'Indians' Playwright Clarifying History." In *Authors in the News,* 1:288. Detroit: Gale, 1976.

Wilz, Hans-Werner. "Arthur Kopit: *Indians."* In *Das amerikanische Drama der Gegenwart,* pp. 44–64. Edited by Herbert Grabes. Kronberg: Athenaüm, 1976.

Wolter, Jürgen. "Arthur Kopit: Dreams and Nightmares." In *Essays on Contemporary American Drama,* pp. 55–74. Edited by Hedwig Bock and Albert Wertheim. Munich: Max Heuber, 1981.

Romulus Linney

(21 SEPTEMBER 1930–)

DON B. WILMETH

ASSESSMENT OF LINNEY'S REPUTATION

Since the first production of one of his plays, *The Sorrows of Frederick*, in 1967, actor, director, novelist, and playwright Romulus Zachariah Linney V's reputation has never reached the status of other important playwrights of his generation. Despite critical recognition, including a National Endowment for the Arts Fellowship in playwriting in 1974, an Obie for *Tennessee* and a Guggenheim Fellowship, both in 1980, the Award in Literature from the American Academy and Institute of Arts and Letters in 1984, and a Rockefeller Foundation Fellowship in 1986, Linney, born in Philadelphia and raised in North Carolina, remains a largely unknown major American playwright. Martin Gottfried of the *New York Post* has called him "one of the best kept secrets of the American theatre, a playwright of true literacy, a writer in the grand tradition," and Schickel described him in 1984 as "one of the American theatre's most mysteriously buried treasures" (p. 74).

With over a dozen critically acclaimed plays to his credit, Linney's topics and themes are amazingly diverse. As Weales has noted, he is a "writer who deals in complexity whether he is working a literary vein—*The Sorrows of Frederick, Childe Byron*—or dealing in the apparent simplicities of the rural South, as in *Holy Ghosts*" (598). Linney is equally at home with folk plays, such as *Sand Mountain*, and contemporary commentaries on the human condition, such as the three short plays grouped under the title *Laughing Stock*.

PRIMARY BIBLIOGRAPHY OF LINNEY'S WORKS

Plays

Ten Plays for Radio. Edited with Norman A. Bailey and Domenick Cascio. Minneapolis: Burgess Publishing Co., 1954.

Radio Classics. Edited with Bailey and Cascio. Minneapolis: Burgess Publishing Co., 1956.

The Sorrows of Frederick. New York: Harcourt, Brace & World, 1968; New York: Dramatists Play Service, 1976; New York: Harcourt Brace Jovanovich, Harvest Edition, 1976 (with *Holy Ghosts*).

Armer Alter Fritz. Vienna: Universal Edition, 1970.

The Love Suicide at Schofield Barracks. A Play in Two Acts. New York: Dramatists Play Service, 1972; New York: Harcourt Brace Jovanovich, 1973 (with *Democracy* and *Esther*).

Democracy (with *The Love Suicide at Schofield Barracks* and *Esther*). New York: Harcourt Brace Jovanvich, 1973; New York: Dramatists Play Service, 1976.

Esther (with *The Love Suicide at Schofield Barracks* and *Democracy*). New York: Harcourt Brace Jovanovich, 1973.

Autopsie. Vienna: Universal Edition, 1973.

Holy Ghosts (with *The Sorrows of Frederick*). New York: Harcourt Brace Jovanovich, Harvest Edition, 1976.

Old Man Joseph and His Family. New York: Dramatists Play Service, 1978.

Tennessee. In *Best Short Plays, 1980.* Edited by Stanley Richards. Radnor, Pa.: Chilton Press, 1980; In *Dramatics* (January 1981): 19–25; New York: Dramatists Play Service, 1981.

El Hermano. New York: Dramatists Play Service, 1981.

The Captivity of Pixie Shedman. New York: Dramatists Play Service, 1981.

Childe Byron. New York: Dramatists Play Service, 1981.

The Death of King Philip. New York: Dramatists Play Service, 1984.

Why the Lord Come to Sand Mountain. New York: Theatre Communications Group (Plays in Process series), 1984.

F.M. in *Best Short Plays, 1984.* Edited by Ramon Delgado. Radnor, Pa.: Chilton Press, 1984.

Laughing Stock. (Includes *Goodbye, Howard, F.M.* and *Tennessee*). New York: Dramatists Play Service, 1985.

The Love Suicide at Schofield Barracks. A Play in One Act. New York: Dramatists Play Service, 1985; New York: Applause Theatre Books Publishers, 1986 (In *Best Short Plays 1986.* Edited by Ramon Delgado).

Sand Mountain. New York: Dramatists Play Service, 1986.

A Woman Without a Name. New York: Dramatists Play Service, 1986.

Pops. New York: Dramatists Play Service, 1987.

Novels

Heathen Valley. New York: Atheneum, 1962. London: Cassell, 1963.

Slowly, By Thy Hand Unfurled. New York: Harcourt, Brace & World, 1965; London: Cassell, 1966.

Jesus Tales. Berkeley: North Point Press, 1980.

Interviews

"An Interview with Romulus Linney." Edited by Michael Bigelow Dixon. *Houston on Stage* 2 (November 1984): 26–28.

"An Interview with Romulus Linney." Edited by Don B. Wilmeth. *Studies in American Drama, 1945–Present* 2 (1987): 71–84.

PRODUCTION HISTORY

Linney's plays have been produced primarily off and off off-Broadway, in repertory theatres of Great Britain, Canada, Germany, and Austria and in resident theatres throughout the United States. Of the many organizations producing Linney's work, the following are representative: Actors Theatre of Louisville, South Coast Repertory (Costa Mesa, Cal.), The Alley Theatre (Houston), the Philadelphia Festival for New Plays, Circle Repertory, Phoenix Theatre, Chelsea Theatre, Theatre for the New City, St. Clement's, Cubiculo, ANTA Theatre (New York City), Birmingham Alabama Festival Theatre, Virginia Museum Theatre, Barter Theatre (Virginia), Milwaukee Repertory Theatre, the Mark Taper Forum (Los Angeles), Roundabout Theatre (New York), the Denver Theatre Center, the Whole Theatre (Montclair, New Jersey), and the San Diego Repertory Theatre. Outside the United States, his plays have been produced by the Young Vic in London, the Vancouver Playhouse, the Vienna Burgtheatre, Linz and Innsbruck Landestheatres, Dusseldorf Theatre, and the Birmingham England Repertory Theatre.

His first produced play, *The Sorrows of Frederick*, was presented for six weeks during the opening season of the Mark Taper Forum, premiering 23 June 1967; subsequently it was proposed on numerous occasions for Broadway, but its large cast and the sweeping panorama of its subject, Frederick II of Prussia, has, to date, prevented such a production. Prior to its first New York production, in addition to Los Angeles, it was seen in Canada, West Germany, Austria, and Great Britain. In the last instance John Wood appeared as Frederick in a 1970 production directed by Finlay James. Most notable was Wood's performance, in which he, according to Young, played "the king in every aspect from nervous young philosopher to regal old dotard, maundering tearfully over the body of one of his too-well-beloved greyhounds." After its initial European production at the Schauspielhaus in Dusseldorf, a critically acclaimed performance was seen in January 1970 at Vienna's Burgtheater, a house often criticized for its lack of enterprise and the rigidity of its declamatory style. Under the management of Paul Hofmann and the direction of Leopold Lindberg and with Heinz Heincke as Frederick, this production apparently made full and intelligent use of the house's considerable resources (King). Rudolf Klein felt that, although the production was magnificently directed, too much was explained on the basis of frustration.

Frederick's New York premiere did not occur until February 1976, presented by St. Clement's Church and the Next Stage with Austin Pendleton as Frederick. This production received its most intelligent critical response principally from the *New York Times*'s Gussow, a champion of Linney's work. Gussow commented in some detail on the play's cinematic structure, utilizing frequent flashbacks but noted that the play is "not primarily an epic about wars and power plays, but an interior psychodrama about what goes on in the crumbling mind of a philosopher-king." Although Gussow was bothered by the other "faceless" characters and the enormous time span of the piece, he concluded that "the play is a rare example of a historical drama by a contemporary dramatist that commands our attention through its intelligence and theatricality. This is no wooden lumbering through history" (1976, 30). Alan Rich agreed that this is a major American play and also "a brilliant, haunting study of a tortured person who is both master and slave of his own intellect." Rich, who felt that Linney managed to deal "with majesty and frailty in a manner that neither glorifies nor condescends" (75), was especially smitten by the brilliance of the writing, a comment echoed by most other critics of this play. Pendleton, who gave, according to Rich, "an incandescent, wonderfully supple performance" at the Next Stage, repeated the role at the Whole Theatre in Montclair, New Jersey, from January through March 1985 in a production, though flawed, termed by Alvin Klein as "an evening of high theater, a powerful play of panoramic sweep, political intrigue, historical interest and contemporary resonance—a work of psychological insight and universal pertinence" (7).

Holy Ghosts, set in a snake-worshipping religious cult in the South, premiered in 1971 at New York's Garrick Theatre for a three-week run and was revived in spring 1976 at the Cubiculo in New York for a comparable period under the direction of John Olon-Scrymgeour.

Alan Rich, commenting on the revival, noted that "the flow of language and the rhythm of the play's construction are the work of a superior intellect," and although he found the irony of the ending too pat, he concluded that "as a portrait of a folkway the work is without flaw" (75). The Southwest premiere of the play, in April 1983 at Houston's Alley Theatre, directed by Linney, was termed by the *Houston Post* critic William Albright "an adroitly written play full of striking and memorable characters, and riveting theatricality." The play's most recent regional revival, at the San Diego Repertory Theater (8 June–19 July 1986), was part of a four-play American Theatre Exchange at New York's Joyce Theatre during the summer of 1987. Hagen, praising the direction of Douglas Jacobs, believed that it was the honesty with which Linney treats his characters and their bizarre beliefs that made the California production so effective: "Laugh with them, or even at them, he says, but their faith is no laughing matter." Other area critics were equally positive. Schneider, who found the play "raucous and mysterious, outspokenly hilarious and filled with unexpected compassion," agreed that Linney portrays his characters with great sympathy, "desiring something more than mere meliorist discourse." This theme dominated the reviews of this production. Jones stated: "Nothing is more amazing than the deftness with which the playwright handles his subject, neither catering to nor condescending to the sensibilities involved but instead simply tale-telling in a non-judgmental manner that lends dignity while stopping short of confirmation or approval."

Linney's one major New York production was also his greatest disappointment. *The Love Suicide at Schofield Barracks*, in a two-act version, was premiered at the ANTA Theatre in New York City on 9 February 1972 under the direction of John Berry and produced by Cheryl Crawford, Konrad Matthei, Hale Matthews, and Robert Weinstein, in association with the American National Theatre and Academy. An earlier version had been produced by Herbert Berghof at the H. B. Playwrights Foundation in 1971. The ANTA production, generally thought of as tedious and pretentious courtroom drama, lacking suspense, and relentlessly antiwar, closed after twelve performances. A number of critics praised the acting of Mercedes McCambridge in the featured role of Lucy Lake, but even the most supportive ultimately concluded, as did Watt, that despite some strong moments "its heart may be in the right place, I don't think its mind is" (1972, 376), or as did Watts and Gottfried that it was attempting to say too much about too many important matters.

A revised, one-act version of the play was performed in Louisville, Kentucky, as part of the 1984 Shorts Festival of the Actors Theatre of Louisville, directed by Frazier March. This version, also set on the dance floor of the Officers' Club ballroom, Schofield Barracks, Hawaii, in 1970, cut the cast size from over twenty to nine and condensed the inquiry into the ritualistic double suicide so as to create a more dramatic and credible whole, retaining much of the excitement originally found by the critics in the first half of the original version.

Childe Byron, possibly Linney's most literate and controversial play, based on the life of Byron and his daughter Ada, the countess of Lovelace, was originally commissioned by the Virginia Museum Theatre in Richmond where it premiered on 4 March 1977. *Variety* thought the ending was weak but found it to be a "brilliant, witty, searing work, that seeks and finds the man behind the romantic legend" (90). In November 1979 the Actors Theatre of Louisville gave the play a highly successful production. Once again, Linney was hailed as "an awesomely gifted American playwright" whose play, according to Mootz, "is a fantasy born from a striking theatrical imagination, and it is illumined with a richness of language thoroughly uncommon among contemporary playwrights." When the play finally made it to New York on 26 February 1981 for a six-week run, directed by Marshall W. Mason at the Circle Repertory Theater and boasting two major actors as Byron and Ada (William Hurt and Lindsay Crouse), Linney experienced his usual mixed response from the New York critics. Kalem dismissed the play as displaying "the industry of an ant and no discernible intelligence" (74). Kissel found it banal, while Watt and Frank Rich felt that Linney had only presented the ghost of Byron, although Watt felt that even as a ghost, Byron makes for lively company. Rich, recalling the calamitous production of *The Captivity of Pixie Shedman*, featuring the spirit of another character, the previous month at the Phoenix Theatre, warned Linney that the writing of ghost plays would wreck his work. Barnes, on the other hand, although unsure of the reasons for his response, found the play engrossing, as did most of the other critics, even those with the most negative remarks.

As with most other Linney productions, revivals of *Byron* outside New York were critically more successful. Critics recognized it as a piece that is "about" more than the scandalous life of Byron, though perhaps flawed in its exuberance to rehabilitate the title character. When staged at the South Coast Repertory Theatre in April 1981, Sullivan reported that it was a "witty and quietly satisfying play about a boy who insisted on not growing up." A production in August 1981 at the Young Vic in London, directed by Frank Dunlop, was considered by Hobson as mesmeric with an intricate text that required total attention from the audience, aided immeasurably by the "oratorical exactitude" of David Essex as Byron and Sara Kestelman as Ada. When revived at Philadelphia's Wilma Theatre in February 1986, the play was considered more timely than ever with the current movement of adopted children seeking their natural parents, though Collins concluded that "exculpation occasionally replaces dramatic momentum" (26 February 1986).

Of the numerous productions of other Linney plays, the following are most significant. *Tennessee*, the Obie winner of 1980, was produced first in November 1979 at the Ensemble Studio Theatre in New York City in a production that provoked a comment by Fox that echoes throughout much Linney criticism. Although the play is based on the simple notion of a backwoods woman who declares that she will marry only a man willing to sell off good North Carolina bottom land and take her to the wild, untamed mountains of Tennessee, Fox found the telling of the story extraordinary and concluded: "Each bit of narration is textured with rich detail so that an entire world emerges in which land is important not only as property but a ground for sustenance, independence, and family continuity" (106).

In April 1984 Linney revealed at the Manhattan Punch Line the most comedic side of his nature in *Laughing Stock*, three short plays deemed among the top ten of the year by *Time*. Gussow was taken by Linney's rich, Faulknerian sense of humor, demonstrating Linney "a homesteader, staking his claim to a bountiful side of Americana" through his ability to show how rustic lives are inextricably bound up with land, family and ancestral roots while combining "lyrical, homespun language" with a comic vision built around the themes of death and departure (1984). Schickel agreed with the superior nature of these plays and their production, especially *F.M.*, the centerpiece of the evening, and added: "They are marked by Linney's singular talent for stating wild ideas with high, simplifying intelligence and for drawing deft portraits of the half mad in which not a line is misplaced or wasted" (1984, 72).

Sand Mountain, two related one-act plays originally presented as part of the Philadelphia Festival for New Plays in June 1984, was successfully revived at the Whole Theatre in February 1986, with Gussow once more noting Linney's ability, in his "patented mountain Gothic style," never to patronize his earthy personages but to show "his people in their natural plummage, living full lives in the shadow of desperation and poverty" (28 February 1986, C3).

In two of his most recent productions, both staged by the author, Linney's proclivity toward simplicity in staging and economy in setting and movement has been evident. *Pops*, a series of six brief plays dealing with the subject of romantic love and structured around six familiar classical melodies (performed by the Boston Pops Orchestra), played 30 September–19 October 1986 at the Whole Theater. Gussow likened the plays to appetizers and concluded that together they substitute for the main course (14 October 1986). *Heathen Valley*, adapted from Linney's first novel, was part of the Philadelphia Festival for New Plays in May 1987. Gussow again offered the most insightful criticism, providing a useful summary of Linney's staging style and its appropriateness to most of his plays: "The play is presented on a raised platform on a bare stage. ... with six actors subtly evoking the landscape, both human and territorial. In the background, fiddle-harps and dulcimers are occasionally heard—and there is the additional music of Mr. Linney's local language" (12 May 1987, 14).

SURVEY OF SECONDARY SOURCES

Considering the literateness and thought-provoking nature of Linney's plays and the large number of them, it is surprising that so little of a critical or analytical nature has been written about his work other than reviews of specific productions and an occasional newspaper feature or interview.

Bibliographies

There are no bibliographies on Linney.

Biographies

There are no major biographies. The principal biographical sources are the standard ones: McGill, Herbert, Gaster, Ethridge and Kopala, and Kaye.

Influences

Most sources that deal with influences do so from the standpoint of autobiography. Dixon's interview with Linney, for instance, provides insight into his early life as it relates to *Frederick*. Papier's discussion of *Holy Ghosts* provides background on his southern years, as do Harris's piece and a detailed piece by Rothstein, the latter recommended as well for its insights into *Holy Ghosts*. Collins's and Seavor's features on *Byron* suggest autobiographical parallels in that play. The most detailed source for biographical insights, as well as literary influences, is my interview, which touches on his early life in the South, his army experiences and the influences of Japanese culture, the impact of religion on his work, and his training as an actor-director. The role of the playwright-director is discussed, along with an overview of his career and specific comments on *Pops*, in Wynne's feature.

General Studies

To date, there have been no general studies of Linney. The Wilmeth interview attempts to investigate major works with the author although without critical commentary. The only other overview is Christian H. Moe's succinct essay in the fourth edition of *Contemporary Dramatists*.

Analyses of Individual Plays

Other than Moe's summary analysis of the Linney canon and reviews of specific plays, the most insightful of which have already been mentioned, there is no body of critical work on Linney's plays. Taken as a whole, however, the criticism of Mel Gussow is highly recommended, offering sensitive analyses of the majority of Linney's most important work.

FUTURE RESEARCH OPPORTUNITIES

Since little meaningful criticism has yet been written on Linney, especially of a scholarly nature, opportunities are plentiful. A general study or overview is long overdue, as are studies of specific plays, themes, or techniques. For example, Linney's use of history, the adaptation of fiction to drama (he has adapted two of his novels), techniques in writing the short play, influences on his work such as O'Neill, Southern fiction writers, Japanese aesthetics, and the autobiographical nature of much of his work are topics for exploration. Certainly Linney's use of language, a constant subject of critical commentary, and his role as director of his own plays are worth analysis.

SECONDARY SOURCES

Albright, William. "Theater: 'Holy Ghosts.' " *Houston Post* (30 April 1983).

Barnes, Clive. " 'Childe Byron' Charms." *New York Post* (27 February 1981). Reprinted in *New York Theatre Critics' Reviews* (1981): 276.

Carr, Jay. " 'Pixie Shedman' Brings Charm of Dixie to Repertory Theatre." *Detroit News* (15 January 1982).

"Childe Byron." *Variety* (23 March 1977): 90.

Collins, William B. "A Playwright Turns to Byron's Story." *Philadelphia Inquirer* (23 February 1986).

———. " 'Childe Byron' Offers Fantasia of Poet's Life." *Philadelphia Inquirer* (26 February 1986).

Dixon, Michael Bigelow. "An Interview with Romulus Linney." *Houston on Stage* 2 (November 1984): 26–28.

Ethridge, James M., and Barbara Kopala, eds. *Contemporary Authors.* 4 vols. Detroit: Gale Research Co., 1967.

Fox, Terry Curtis. On *Tennessee. Village Voice* (26 November 1979): 106.

Gaster, Adrian, ed. *The International Authors and Writers Who's Who.* 9th ed. Cambridge, Eng.: Melrose Press, 1982.

Gottfried, Martin. " 'The Love Suicide at Schofield Barracks.' " *Women's Wear Daily* (10 February 1972). Reprinted in *New York Theatre Critics' Reviews* (1972): 377.

Gussow, Mel. "Stage: 'Frederick' at Last." *New York Times* (25 February 1976): 30.

———. "Stage: 3 Plays by Romulus Linney." *New York Times* (14 April 1984): A18.

———. "Theater: Linney's 'Sand Mountain.' " *New York Times* (28 February 1986): C3.

———. "Theatre: 'Pops,' by Romulus Linney." *New York Times* (14 October 1986): C14.

———. "Stage: Linney's 'Heathen Valley' in Philadelphia." *New York Times* (12 May 1987): C14.

————. "The Short Stories of the Stage." *New York Times* (14 June 1987): H5, H37.

Hagen, Bill. "Rep Opens Lyceum Space with Dazzling 'Holy Ghosts.' " *San Diego Tribune* (9 June 1986).

Harris, William. "Just Romulus Zachariah Linney V." *Soho Weekly News* (19 January 1978).

Herbert, Ian. *Who's Who in the Theatre*. 17th ed. 2 vols. Detroit: Gale Research Co., 1981.

Hobson, Harold. "Hearing Hallucinations." *The Times Literary Supplement* (London) (7 August 1981): 919.

Jones, Welton. " 'Ghosts' great, for heaven's snakes." *San Diego Union* (11 June 1986).

Kalem, T. E. "Bombette." *Time* (9 March 1981): 74.

Kaye, Phyllis Johnson, ed. *The National Playwrights Directory*. 2d ed., pp. 252–53. Waterford, Conn.: Eugene O'Neill Center.

King, Renee. "Memorable Production at the Burgtheater." *Stage and Television Today* (12 March 1970).

Kissel, Howard. " 'Childe Byron.' " *Women's Wear Daily* (2 March 1981). Reprinted in *New York Theatre Critics' Reviews* (1981): 277.

Klein, Alvin. " 'Frederick' Reigns." *New York Times* (3 March 1985): K7.

Klein, Rudolf. "American Play in Vienna Revives Burgtheater Style." *Christian Science Monitor* (12 January 1970): 6.

Linney, Romulus. "About O'Neill." *Eugene O'Neill Newsletter* (Winter 1982): 3–5.

McGill, Raymond D., ed. *Notable Names in the American Theatre*. Clifton, N.J.: James T. White and Co., 1976.

Moe, Christian. "Linney, Romulus." In *Contemporary Dramatists*. 4th ed., pp 324–26. Edited by D. L. Kirkpatrick. Chicago and London: St. James Press, 1988.

Mootz, William. "ATL Brings Fascinating New 'Childe Byron' to Blazing Life." *Louisville Courier-Journal* (10 November 1979).

Papier, Deborah. "A Dramatist's 'Pitch of Ecstasy.' " *Washington Star* (5 October 1980).

Rich, Alan. "Of Men and Other Beasts." *New York Magazine* (5 March 1976): 75.

Rich, Frank. "William Hurt in 'Childe Byron.' " *New York Times* (14 January 1981). Reprinted in *New York Theatre Critics' Reviews* (1981): 274.

Rothstein, Mervyn. "Romulus Linney Conjures Up His 'Holy Ghosts.' " *New York Times* (9 August 1987): C5, C11.

Schickel, Richard. "Laughing Stock." *Time* (30 April 1984): 72.

————. "Best of 84." *Time* (7 January 1985): 90.

Schneider, Christopher. "Rep Delivers with a Stunning, Compassionate 'Holy Ghosts.' " *La Jolla Light* (19 June 1986).

Seavor, Jim. "At Brown, Life Imitates Art." *Providence Journal-Bulletin* (22 April 1986): C11.

Sullivan, Dan. " 'Childe Byron': He Refused to Grow Up." *Los Angeles Times* (20 April 1981).

Watt, Douglas. " 'Love Suicide' Needs Suspense." *New York Daily News* (10 February 1972). Reprinted in *New York Theatre Critics' Reviews* (1972): 376.

————. "Casting a Clean Light on a Shadowy Byron." *New York Daily News* (27 February 1981). Reprinted in *New York Theatre Critics' Reviews* (1981): 275.

Watts, Richard. "Mystery of a Double Suicide." *New York Post* (10 February 1972). Reprinted in *New York Theatre Critics' Reviews* (1972): 376–77.

Weales, Gerald. "American Theater Watch, 1980–1981." *Georgia Review* 35 (Fall 1981): 598–99.

Wilmeth, Don B. "An Interview with Romulus Linney." *Studies in American Drama, 1945–Present* 2 (1986): 71–84.

The Writers Directory, 1986–1988. Chicago and London: St. James Press, 1986.

Wynne, Peter. "An Evening of Variations on Love Themes." *Bergen Record* (New Jersey) (26 September 1986).

Young, B. A. "The Sorrows of Frederick." *Financial Times*, London, (February 1970).

Robert Lowell

(1 MARCH 1917–12 SEPTEMBER 1977)

MICHAEL STUPRICH

ASSESSMENT OF LOWELL'S REPUTATION

Robert Lowell's reputation in the American theatre rests exclusively on *The Old Glory*, his trilogy of one-act verse dramas adapted from solid American materials: Hawthorne's short stories "Endicott and the Red Cross" and "My Kinsman, Major Molineaux" and Melville's novella *Benito Cereno*. Welcomed by one critic at the time of its 1964 off-Broadway premiere as perhaps signaling "a dramatic renaissance in America" (Brustein, 217), *The Old Glory* received mixed but generally affirmative reviews and at season's end was awarded five Obies, including one for Best Play. The response to the trilogy's 1976 bicentennial revival was also mixed. Barnes, for example, while admitting that *The Old Glory* had become "part of the younger glories of the American intellectual establishment," ultimately found Lowell's work "poetaster stuff—dull and gray, trying, with a certain intellectual arrogance, to say more than it means" ("The Old Glory," 268). The reaction from scholarly quarters (where the tendency has been to focus more on the play's literary and poetic qualities) has been more generously inclined, especially toward *Benito Cereno*, from the beginning considered the centerpiece of the trilogy.

Lowell's only other excursions into the theatre have been by way of two imitations—loose translations of Racine's *Phèdre* and Aeschylus's *Prometheus Bound*, each "distorted," in the words of Mazarro, "to accommodate events from Lowell's life and his various preoccupations" ("*Prometheus Bound*," 278). Both works escaped much notice at the time of their performances and are probably most usefully discussed in terms of Lowell's achievements as poet rather than dramatist.

PRIMARY BIBLIOGRAPHY OF LOWELL'S WORKS

The Lowell canon is extensive, running to almost twenty volumes of poetry and including numerous articles and interviews. The following list is restricted to works that bear directly on Lowell's contribution to the theatre. Much fuller bibliographies can be found in Procopiow, Mazarro, Fein, and Crick.

Plays

Phaedra. In *Phaedra and Figaro*, New York: Farrar, Straus and Cudahy, 1961; London: Faber, 1963, 1971. Also in *The Classic Theatre*, vol. 4. Edited by Eric Bentley. New York: Doubleday, Anchor Books, 1961.

The Old Glory. New York: Farrar, Straus and Giroux, 1965, with an Introduction by Robert Brustein; reprint, New York: Noonday Press (paperback), 1966, with Introduction by Brustein and a Director's Note by Jonathan Miller; rev. ed. 1968; London: Faber, 1966.

Prometheus Bound. Farrar, Straus and Giroux (hardback and paperback editions published simultaneously), 1969; London: Faber, 1970. First published in *New York Review of Books*, 13 July 1963.

Interviews

Kunitz, Stanley. "Talk with Robert Lowell." *New York Times Book Review* (4 October 1964): 34–38.

Alvarez, Alfred. "A Talk with Robert Lowell." *Encounter* (24 February 1965): 39–43.

Gilman, Richard. "Life Offers No Neat Conclusions." *New York Times* (5 May 1968): 2: 1, 5.

Carne-Ross, D. S. "Conversation with Robert Lowell." *Delos* 1 (1968): 165–75.

Alvarez, Alfred. "A Poet Talks about Making History into Theater." *New York Times* (4 April 1976): B1, B5.

PRODUCTION HISTORY

The Old Glory, which officially opened off-Broadway on 1 November 1964 and ran for thirty-six performances, was the premiere offering of the newly established American Place Theatre, a former Episcopal church on West Forty-sixth Street. This production was directed by Jonathan Miller, who dropped *Endecott and the Red Cross* shortly before opening night because of difficulties he discovered in capturing its "complex spiritual irony" (Miller, 221). *My Kinsman, Major Molineaux*, introduced that first evening by Lowell as a "political cartoon," was staged with an eye to the surreal and a sense of the *danse macabre*. In this grim, nightmarish story of the Boston Massacre of 1770, the actors were dressed as Hogarthian caricatures—with chalked faces and stiff cotton costumes so that they resembled "pieces of paper cut out of a coffee-house broadsheet" (Miller, 221). Critical response to *Molineaux* was not favorable. Oliver found it difficult "to sift anything worth bothering about from the elaborate, mannered, larky production" (1964, 144), and Taubman was even less kind, dismissing *Molineaux* as a "pretentious, arty trifle" (2 November 1964, 62). Miller's presentation of *Benito Cereno*, however, highlighted by the fine performance of Roscoe Lee Browne as Babu, elicited more enthusiastic response and seems indeed to have been the basis for the trilogy's subsequent rise to reputation. For Taubman, the play worked through a weak beginning to achieve "tragic size"; and in a letter to the editor of the *New York Times*, poet Randall Jarrell was moved to state flatly that he had "never seen a better American play than *Benito Cereno*" (2:3). Underlying much of this praise seems to have been the hope, echoed in a *Newsweek* review, that Lowell's debut as a playwright had given the "American theater an improbable impetus toward maturity" ("Triumph Off Broadway," 92). Quibblings about the play's dramatic weaknesses aside, the majority opinion was that an important new voice—speaking in "strong, supple, insinuating" verse (Finn, 323)—had been heard off-Broadway and that this newest "infusion of blood and talent" was a promising sign (Taubman, "Basic Ideal," 2:1). Speaking most sharply for the minority was Simon, who concluded his 1966 review of the published text of *The Old Glory* with this bleakly prophetic judgment: "The poet, as writer, may still have a place in the theater; poetry, barring a miracle, does not" ("Strange Devices," 83).

Following the earlier suggestion of Jonathan Miller that the play someday be "expanded" and "presented as a full length piece on its own" (221), *Endecott and the Red Cross* was staged at the American Place Theatre for fifteen performances, beginning 7 May 1968. Already the ghost of the original *Glory* could be sensed nostalgically by reviewers, one of whom called the John Hancock–directed production "oddly earthbound" and "discursive" and regretted that it failed "to achieve the impact of the earlier production" (Kroll, 13 May 1968, 110). Reviewing *Endecott* in the *New Yorker*, Oliver applauded Kenneth Haigh's performance in the title role but finally found the play "a disappointment, lacking fire and dramatic urgency, and even clarity" ("Mr. Lowell and Mr. Haigh," 86). "Disappointment" was also the key note sounded in the *Times* by Clive Barnes, whose sense that the "language" of *Endecott* was more important than its "ideas" may well touch the core of Lowell's problem in all three plays ("Endecott," 50).

The 1976 revival of *The Old Glory* opened on 18 April on the familiar stage of the American Place Theatre. On the first night, all three plays were presented together on a program lasting almost five hours; of the subsequent forty performances, however, some were devoted to *Benito*

Cereno alone and others to *Endecott* and *Molineaux* alone. As in the 1964 production, critical attention focused squarely on *Benito Cereno*, which in the dozen ensuing years had so risen in reputation that a reviewer in the *New York Post* could speak of it confidently as "a gorgeously written and powerful classic" (Gottfried, 269). Not all response was so laudatory, but even Barnes, in a strongly negative review, felt compelled to register his opinion as a "minority viewpoint" (" 'The Old Glory,' " 268). Though only time and critical evaluation will tell, what may prove to be the correct verdict on Lowell's trilogy was provided by Kroll, who judged *The Old Glory* to be "a magnificent accident, an isolated masterwork that bred no progeny" ("New Glory," 83).

The Yale School of Drama's 1967 production of *Prometheus Bound* (staged in May and June) brought together the considerable talents of Lowell, director Jonathan Miller, and actors Kenneth Haigh and Irene Worth. Reviewers were impressed with the various components, which included seventeenth-century costumes, a huge set made to resemble a ruined Roman fortress, and outstanding performances by all the principal actors, but generally disappointed with the whole. Novick, for example, found the production "lavish" and the acting "admirable" but could go no further than to label the work a "stimulating failure" (829–30). For Hewes, the insights of *Prometheus* were keen but the drama scant. "Still Bound," the title of Gilman's review in *Newsweek*, seems to have captured the critical consensus with sardonic accuracy and economy. The story of the play's production—perhaps more interesting than the play itself—was recounted by Jonathan Price in "The Making of Lowell's *Prometheus*."

During the same weeks that Yale was staging *Prometheus Bound*, the Theater of the Living Arts in Philadelphia was presenting Diana Sands in the title role of Lowell's *Phaedra*. Kerr called Lowell's adaptation "sturdy" but found the acting—with the exception of Sands—to be weak and often amateurish (50).

SURVEY OF SECONDARY SOURCES

Bibliographies

No comprehensive bibliographies of Lowell's work are available, though his solid reputation and the inevitable continuing study of him should guarantee the appearance of one soon. A recently published survey of the existing criticism, Norma Procopiow devotes some thirty pages to *The Old Glory* and is an invaluable guide to the researcher (though it makes no claims to comprehension). Readers may supplement Procopiow's work by consulting Mazarro's "Checklist: 1939–1968," as well as the more current—but shorter—bibliographies contained in the introductory studies of Fein and Crick.

Biographies

Anyone interested in the life of this most celebrated confessional poet would probably do best to begin with Lowell's poetry, and probably there with *Life Studies*, a tremendously influential work and arguably Lowell's masterpiece. Lowell's interviews, almost always entertaining, can also be revealing; Mazarro has collected a number of these in his *Profile of Robert Lowell*. There is as well a new, and copious, biography in the "life and works" tradition: Hamilton's *Robert Lowell: A Biography*. An approach more critically oriented can be found in Axelrod's *Robert Lowell: Life and Art*.

Influences

The question of influence in Lowell's dramatic work is a thorny one. Because each of his plays is, in one sense or another, an adaptation (Lowell's own slippery term is *imitation*), potentially multiple lines of influence insist on presenting themselves. An additional problem is defined by the contours of Lowell's career. He was a poet first, by temperament and design, and a dramatist second—a distant second, it seems safe to say (though one might argue that a confessional poet perpetually dramatizes himself). For these reasons perhaps, there are no studies that directly and exclusively confront the problem of influence in his dramatic work, although Simon's "Abuse of Privilege: Lowell as Translator," in considering Lowell's translations of *Phèdre* and *Prometheus Bound*, touches on analogous issues. Anyone interested in Lowell as translator, however, should begin with Lowell's own comments in his brief Preface to *Prometheus Bound* (where the reader may be delighted to ponder the questions implied by a translation that is only "derived" from the original). Lowell's vision of American history and his corresponding sense of his own New England heritage—important background concerns in *The Old Glory*—are examined by Holder.

General Studies

The best general introduction to Lowell may well be Fein's, whose intensely personal engagement with Lowell works well on this level. He devotes chapters to both *The Old Glory* and *Prometheus Bound*, and his reading of *Benito Cereno* is rewarding. Crick's brief study of Lowell offers a limited but intelligent introduction. Two more ambitious critical studies can also be helpful in establishing contexts: Williamson's *Pity the Monsters:*

The Political Vision of Robert Lowell (though Williamson has little to say about the plays as plays) and Axelrod's *Robert Lowell: Life and Work.* Ehrenpreis's "The Age of Lowell," though first published in 1965, remains an excellent brief appraisal of Lowell's artistic strengths. A number of essential articles (including "The Age of Lowell" and Mazarro's "Checklist") have been collected by London and Boyers.

Analyses of Individual Plays

While there have been no apparent recessions in the Lowell critical industry, examinations of the individual plays do not abound and since the mid-1970s have been particularly sparse. Of the works under discussion here, *The Old Glory* has naturally received most of the critical attention and *Benito Cereno* the lion's share of that. Of the very few available studies of *Prometheus Bound*, two can be recommended: Raizis's and, especially, Mazarro's scholarly "*Prometheus Bound:* Robert Lowell and Aeschylus." In *Pity the Monsters*, Williamson treats *Prometheus* briefly, within the context of Lowell's "political" concern with tyranny and rebellion. (Lowell himself nominated, as a modern embodiment of the archetypal tyrant Zeus, then-president Lyndon B. Johnson.) On *Phaedra*, Mazarro's "The Classicism of Robert Lowell's *Phaedra*" is an admirably thorough study—and defense—of Lowell's translation, while Solomon's "Racine and Lowell" finds little merit in the work, either as play or translation.

Of the studies that treat *The Old Glory* as a whole, three stand out: Mazarro's solid "Robert Lowell's *The Old Glory*: Cycle and Epicycle," Bigsby's interesting quasi-Marxist reading in "The Paradox of Revolution: Robert Lowell's *The Old Glory*," and especially Hochman's "Robert Lowell's *The Old Glory*," an overwritten but rewarding study that sees *The Old Glory* not so much as a play about American history as an intense, multiangled examination "of the dangers to moral and political life arising from the individual psyche and embodying themselves in the processes of history" (127).

Although there seem to be no studies that focus solely on *My Kinsman, Major Molineaux*, several find *Endicott and the Red Cross* worthy of detailed examination. Mazarro's "National and Individual Psycho-history" sees the Puritans' repression of Thomas Morton and the "jolly Merrymounters" as outlining "the key historical repression of the id by the superego," which *Molineaux* reverses (96). Sterne recounts the historical background to the "Maypole at Merrymount" incident and considers the differences in treatment between Lowell and Hawthorne.

Of the studies that treat *Benito Cereno* individually, most center on the question of the relationship between Melville's novella and Lowell's play. Ilson finds that Lowell's version sacrifices the "great complexity and indirection" (135) of Melville's original largely by insisting on moral judgments that Melville leaves suspended; while Estrin sees Lowell's "change in thematic emphasis" (424) as resulting in a powerful dramatic statement about American life. Knauf's essay on Lowell's "theatricalization" of the Melville novella provides a welcome focus on the more practical problems of adapting a work of fiction to the stage. Two earlier, largely supportive responses to *Benito Cereno* are also worth considering: Weales's "Lowell as Dramatist" and Yankowitz's "Lowell's *Benito Cereno*: An Investigation of American Innocence." George suggests that the play is most properly understood within the context of "prophetic theater and dramatic ritual" (155). What may remain the fullest treatment of the play was provided by Stone.

FUTURE RESEARCH OPPORTUNITIES

Some seventy years ago, T. S. Eliot began his speculations on "The Possibility of a Poetic Drama" by asking if there "is some legitimate craving, not restricted to a few persons, which only the verse play can satisfy" (60) and ended with a reply that was affirmative but in no palpable way optimistic of future "possibilities." Ironically Eliot's own later "successes" in the form, *Murder in the Cathedral* and *The Cocktail Party*, only beg the question that the student of Lowell's dramatic work must inevitably confront: whether the rich and measured cadences of poetic drama still provide a potential means of aesthetic communication in a society in which minimalism has become as much a mentality of response as expression. Such a question—not entirely separable from the question of ultimate value in Lowell's work—still needs to be confronted in a serious and sustained fashion, before too many more passing years make of *The Old Glory* the same quaint, antiquated curio as *The Cocktail Party*. Much has been done on *The Old Glory* as poetic-political-historical statement; future research would do best to consider whether its dramatic potentialities make it worthy of performance in the living theatre.

SECONDARY SOURCES

Axelrod, Steven Gould. *Robert Lowell: Life and Art*. Princeton, N.J.: Princeton University Press, 1978.

Barnes, Clive. "The Stage: Lowell's 'The Old Glory.' " *New York Times* (19 April 1976). Reprinted in *New York Theatre Critics' Reviews* (1976): 268.

———."Theatre: 'Endecott and the Red Cross.' " *New York Times* (7 May 1968): 50.

Bigsby, C. W. E. "The Paradox of Revolution: Robert Lowell's *The Old Glory*." *Recherches anglaises et américaines* 5 (1972): 63–79.

Brustein, Robert. Introduction to *The Old Glory*. Rev. ed. New York: Farrar, Straus and Giroux, 1968.

Crick, John. *Robert Lowell*. Edinburgh: Oliver and Boyd, 1974.

Ehrenpreis, Irvin. "The Age of Lowell." In *Robert Lowell: A Portrait of the Artist in His Time*, pp. 155–86. Edited by Michael London and Robert Boyers. New York: David Lewis, 1970.

Eliot, T. S. "The Possibility of a Poetic Drama." In *The Sacred Wood*, pp. 60–70. University Paperback ed. New York: Barnes and Noble, 1960.

Estrin, Mark W. "Robert Lowell's *Benito Cereno*." *Modern Drama* 15 (1973): 411–26.

Fein, Richard J. *Robert Lowell*. 2d ed. Boston: Twayne, 1979.

Finn, James. "The Old Glory." *Catholic World* 200 (1965): 323–24.

George, Ralph. "History and Prophecy in *Benito Cereno*." *Educational Theatre Journal* 22 (1970): 155–60.

Gilman, Richard. "Still Bound." *Newsweek* (22 May 1967): 109.

Gottfried, Marvin. "A Classic in 'The Old Glory.' " *New York Post* (19 April 1976). Reprinted in *New York Theatre Critics' Reviews* (1976): 269.

Hamilton, Ian. *Robert Lowell: A Biography*. New York: Random House, 1982.

Hewes, Henry. "Idol Conversation." *Saturday Review* (27 May 1967): 49.

Hochman, Baruch. "Robert Lowell's *The Old Glory*." *Tulane Drama Review* 11 (Summer 1967): 127–38.

Holder, Alan. "Flintlocks of the Fathers: Robert Lowell's Treatment of the American Past." *New England Quarterly* 44 (1971): 40–65.

Ilson, Robert. "*Benito Cereno* from Melville to Lowell." In *Robert Lowell: A Collection of Critical Essays*, pp. 135–42. Edited by Thomas Parkinson. Englewood Cliffs, N.J.: Prentice-Hall, 1969.

Jarrell, Randall. "A Masterpiece." *New York Times* (29 November 1964), 2:3.

Kerr, Walter. "Theatre: Robert Lowell's 'Phaedra' in Philadelphia." *New York Times* (22 May 1967): 50.

Knauf, David. "Notes on Mystery, Suspense, and Complicity: Lowell's Theatricalizational of Melville's *Benito Cereno*." *Educational Theatre Journal* 27 (1975): 40–55.

Kroll, Jack. "New Glory." *Newsweek* (3 May 1976): 82–83.

———. "Militant Movement." *Newsweek* (13 May 1968): 109–10.

London, Michael, and Robert Boyers, eds. *Robert Lowell: A Portrait of the Artist in His Time*. New York: David Lewis, 1970.

Mazarro, Jerome. "Checklist: 1939–1968." In *Robert Lowell: A Portrait of the Artist in His Times*, pp. 293–328. Edited by Michael London and Robert Boyers. New York: David Lewis, 1970.

———. "The Classicism of Robert Lowell's *Phaedra*." *Comparative Drama* 7 (1973): 87–106.

———. "Robert Lowell's *The Old Glory:* Cycle and Epicycle." *Western Humanities Review* 24, no. 4 (Autumn 1970): 347–58.

———. "National and Individual Psycho-history in Robert Lowell's 'Endecott and the Red Cross.' " *University of Windsor Review* 8, no. 1 (1972): 99–113.

———. *Profile of Robert Lowell*. Columbus: Charles E. Merrill, 1971.

———. "*Prometheus Bound:* Robert Lowell and Aeschylus." *Comparative Drama* 7 (1973): 278–90.

Miller, Jonathan. Director's Note to *The Old Glory*. Rev. ed. New York: Farrar, Straus and Giroux, 1968.

Novick, Julius. Review of *Prometheus Bound*. *Nation* (26 June 1967): 829–30.

Oliver, Edith. "Mr. Lowell and Mr. Haigh." *New Yorker* (11 May 1968): 85–87.

———. Review of *The Old Glory*. *New Yorker* (14 November 1964): 143–44.

Price, Jonathan. "The Making of Lowell's *Prometheus*." *Yale Alumni Magazine* 30 (June 1967): 30–37.

Procopiow, Norma. *Robert Lowell: The Poet and His Critics*. Chicago: American Library Association, 1984.

Raizis, M. B. "Robert Lowell's *Prometheus Bound*." *Papers on Language and Literature* 5 (Summer Supplement 1969): 154–68.

Simon, John. "Abuse of Privilege: Lowell as Translator." In *Robert Lowell: A Portrait of the Artist in His Time*, pp. 130–51. Edited by Michael London and Robert Boyers. New York: David Lewis, 1970.

———. "Strange Devices on the Banner." In *Robert Lowell: A Portrait of the Artist in His Time*, pp. 80–83. Edited by Michael London and Robert Boyers. New York: David Lewis, 1970.

Solomon, Samuel. "Racine and Lowell." *London Magazine* (6 November 1966): 29–42.

Sterne, R. C. "Puritans at Merry Mount: Variations on a Theme." *American Quarterly* 22 (1970): 846–48, 858.

Stone, Albert E. "A New Version of American Innocence: Robert Lowell's *Benito Cereno*." *New England Quarterly* 45 (1972): 467–83.

Taubman, Howard. "In Quest of Basic Ideal." *New York Times* (15 November 1964): 2:1.

———. "Theatre: Lowell, Poet as Playwright." *New York Times* (2 November 1964): 62.

"Triumph Off Broadway." *Newsweek* (16 November 1964): 92.

Weales, Gerald. "Robert Lowell as Dramatist." *Shenandoah* 20 (Autumn 1968): 3–28.

Williamson, Alan. *Pity the Monsters: The Political Vision of Robert Lowell*. New Haven: Yale University Press, 1974.

Yankowitz, Susan. "Robert Lowell's *Benito Cereno*: An Investigation of American Innocence." *Yale/Theatre* 2 (Summer 1968): 81–90.

David Mamet

(30 NOVEMBER 1947–)

JOYCELYN TRIGG

ASSESSMENT OF MAMET'S REPUTATION

A relatively young playwright, Mamet has already established himself as "a mainstay of the American theatre" (Bigsby, 13). In the last decade and a half, Mamet has written twenty plays, plus a number of short plays and several screenplays and adaptations; written a collection of essays, *Writing in Restaurants*; won numerous awards, including three Chicago Jefferson Awards for best new play of the season, two *Village Voice* Obies, two New York Drama Critics Circle Awards, the English Society of West End Theatres Award, the John Gassner Award, the Outer Critics' Circle Award for services to the American theatre, and the Pulitzer Prize for *Glengarry Glen Ross* (1984); and clearly established his rank among the top two or three playwrights of post-1975 American drama. *Speed-the-Plow*, which opened on Broadway in May 1988, was nominated for three Tony Awards—Best Play, Ron Silver as Best Actor in a Play, and Gregory Mosher as Best Director—and four Drama Desk Awards—Best Play, Joe Mantegna as Best Actor, Ron Silver as Best Actor, and Gregory Mosher as Best Director. Carroll recognizes Mamet as "the only playwright of several who emerged as 'promising' in the late 1970s ... who has so far managed to establish a significant international reputation" (2). In addition to playwriting, Mamet has distinguished himself as a screenwriter, winning an Oscar nomination in the Best Adaptation category for *The Verdict* in 1983.

Mamet "announced his arrival as a significant playwright in the American theatre in 1974," Christiansen recalls, with the opening of *Sexual Perversity in Chicago*, "his first professionally produced full-length play, ... filled with a jazzy, explosive use of coarse street language that immediately stamped the then-26-year-old writer as a fresh, invigorating force in drama" ("Mamet," *Contemporary Dramatists*, 339).

Mamet first achieved national importance as a major playwright with *American Buffalo* (1975), which Bigsby has called "a classic of the American theatre" (*Mamet*, 85). According to Ditsky, this powerful play "by itself establishes David Mamet's unique abilities and merits" (31). As in other Mamet plays, it is his concern with language that elicits reactions. While the critics may or may not like the language Mamet's characters speak, language—its role, its content, its lack of sincerity, its significance—is the Mamet hallmark. Kroll calls Mamet rare, "an American playwright who's a language playwright" ("Muzak Man," 79). Cohn writes, "David Mamet creates the most concentrated American stage speech since Edward Albee" (46). Viewers of performances and readers of the plays alike tune to the words, and the silences, of Mamet's salesmen, inventors, actors, petty thieves, who, like Mamet can create a fiction because someone wants to believe in it: for every sale, there is a buyer; for every performance, an audience.

Gussow claims that Mamet is one of four chief playwrights who "represent the broad spectrum of the post-Albee American theater" ("Daring Visions," 9). In 1977, as *American Buffalo* was about to open on Broadway, Gussow observed that these writers, "especially Mr. Mamet, can be dazzling in their use of contemporary language," recreating "everyday speech, finding the slips and elisions that give language its character" (9). Ditsky writes, "People *really speak* as Mamet's characters do; the sound of his plays has the fascination of an overheard phone conversation" (26). Nightingale adds that Mamet has "an eavesdropper's ear for striking idiom and a tape-recorder's precision in recording it" for his streetwise characters. He complains, however, that we do not hear "the voice of Mr. Mamet behind or within ("Shaping," 21).

Bigsby comments insightfully that Mamet "continues to bemuse those who resist his concern for metaphor and his fascination with character as a product of language and social myth. . . . Few playwrights have paid more attention to language, to the force of dramatic metaphor, to structure or to character as expression of psychological or social dislocation. None has given storytelling quite such a central role as method and subject" (*Mamet*, 13).

Similarly, Carroll points out that in "Mamet's world, the attempt to make contact is crucial" (22) as it is played out in three thematic areas: business, sex, and communion. "Mamet's importance, apart from the dialogue, lies in his unsentimental sense of personal and social morality, his wry but sharp sense of dialectic, and the vigour of his characters' intent. . . . His achievements already stamp him as a major American playwright of his generation, whose work has both the vividness and the power to cross national boundaries" (155).

Mamet has crossed genres as well and been highly acclaimed as a writer and director for the screen. According to Kroll, "Mamet has made the transition from Pulitzer Prize–winning playwright...to box-office screenwriter to personal-style film director with remarkable ease.... Mamet may be the first major American playwright to become a significant film director" ("Profane Poetry," 85).

PRIMARY BIBLIOGRAPHY OF MAMET'S WORKS

Plays

Mackinac. Unpublished. 1972 (?).
Marranos. Unpublished. 1972–73 (?).
American Buffalo. New York: Grove, 1976.
Sexual Perversity in Chicago and *The Duck Variations*. New York: French, 1977.
A Life in the Theatre. New York: French, 1977; New York: Grove, 1978.
Revenge of the Space Pandas; or Binky Rudich and the Two-Speed Clock. Chicago: Dramatic Publishing, 1978; New York: Grove, 1978.
The Water Engine: An American Fable and *Mr. Happiness*. New York: Grove, 1978.
Lone Canoe or The Explorer. Unpublished. 1979.
Reunion and *Dark Pony*. New York: Grove, 1979.
The Woods. New York: French, 1979.
Short Plays and Monologues. New York: Dramatists Play Service, 1981.
Lakeboat. New York: Grove, 1981.
The Poet and the Rent. New York: French, 1981.
Disappearance of the Jews. Unpublished. 1982.
Squirrels. New York: French, 1982.
Edmond. New York: Grove, 1983.
Red River. Adaptation of a play by Pierre Laville. Unpublished. 1983.
The Frog Prince. New York: Vincent and Fitzgerald, 1984.
Glengarry Glen Ross. New York: Grove, 1984; London: Methuen, 1984.
Joseph Dintenfass. Unpublished. 1984.
Dramatic Sketches and Monologues. New York: French, 1985. Includes *Five Unrelated Pieces, The Power Outrage, The Dog, Film Crew, 4 A.M., Food, Pint's a Pound the World Around, Deer Dogs, Columbus Avenue, Conversations with the Spirit World, Maple Sugaring, Morris and Joe, Steve McQueen, Yes, Dowsing, In the Mall, Cross Patch, Goldberg Street*.
Goldberg Street: Short Plays and Monologues. New York: Grove, 1985. Contains *Goldberg Street* (1985), *Cross Patch* (1984), *Two Conversations* (1982), *Two Scenes* (1982), *Yes But So What* (1982), *Conversations with the Spirit World* (1982), *Pints's a Pound the World Around* (1983), *Dowsing* (1983), *Deer Dogs* (1982), *In the Mall* (1983), *Maple Sugaring* (1981), *Morris and Joe* (1981), *The Dog, Film Crew* (1979), *Four A.M.* (1983), *The Power Outage* (1977), *Food* (1982), *Columbus Avenue* (1980), *Steve McQueen* (1983), *Yes* (1983), *The Blue Hour, City Sketches* (1981), *A Sermon* (1981), *Shoeshine* (1979), *Litko: A Dramatic Monologue* (1981), *In Old Vermont* (1981), *All Men Are Whores: An Inquiry* (1981).

The Shawl and *Prairie du Chien*. New York: Grove, 1985.
Three Children's Plays. New York: Grove, 1986.
Vint. Adaptation of a story by Chekhov. New York: Knopf, 1986.
The Cherry Orchard. Adaptation of a play by Chekhov. New York: Grove, 1987.
Speed-the-Plow, Unpublished. 1987.

Screenplays

The Postman Always Rings Twice. Directed by Bob Rafelson. With Jack Nicholson
     and Jessica Lange. Paramount, 1981.
The Verdict. Directed by Sidney Lumet. With Paul Newman. Columbia Pictures,
     1982.
The Untouchables. Directed by Brian De Palma. Paramount, 1985.
Malcolm X. Warner Brothers. Not released.
House of Games. Directed by David Mamet. With Linday Crouse and Joseph
     Mantegna. Grove, 1987. Orion, 1987.
Things Change. Directed by David Mamet. Written with Shel Silverstein. 1987.

For Children

The Owl. With Lindsay Crouse.
Warm and Cold. With drawings by Donald Sultan.

Nonfiction

"A Sad Comedy about Actors." *New York Times* (16 October 1977): B7.
"Essay: A National Dream-Life." *Dramatists Guild Quarterly* 15 (Fall 1978): 30–
     32.
"Learn to Love the Theater." *Horizon* (October 1978): 96.
"Playwrights on Resident Theaters: What Is to Be Done?" *Theater* 10 (Summer
     1979): 82.
"A Playwright Learns from Film." *New York Times* (20 July 1980): B6.
"Mamet in Hollywood." *Horizon* (February 1981): 54–55.
"First Principles." *Theater* 12 (Summer-Fall 1981): 50–52.
"My Kind of Town." *Horizon* (November 1981): 56–57.
"Air Plays." *Horizon* (May-June 1982): 20–23.
"Conventional Warfare." *Esquire* (March 1985): 110–14.
Writing in Restaurants. New York: Viking, 1986.
"I Lost It at the Movies." *American Film* (June 1987): 19–23.

Interviews

Fraser, C. Gerald. "Mamet Plays Shed Masculinity Myth." *New York Times* (5 July
     1976): A7.
Wetzsteon, Ross. "David Mamet: Remember That Name." *Village Voice* (5 July
     1976): 101.

Winer, Linda. "David Stages a Victory over a Village Goliath." *Chicago Tribune* (15 August 1976): F2.

Leogrande, Ernest. "A Man of Few Words Moves on to Sentences." *New York Sunday News* (13 February 1977): C3.

Raidy, William A. "Playwright with Paid-Up Dues." *Los Angeles Times* (27 November 1977): "Calendar" 72.

Gottlieb, Richard. "The Engine That Drives Playwright David Mamet." *New York Times* (15 January 1978): B1, B4–5.

Drake, Sylvie. "The Lunching of a Playwright." *Los Angeles Times* (5 February 1978): "Calender": 1, 54.

Vallely, Jean. "David Mamet Makes a Play for Hollywood." *Rolling Stone* (3 April 1980): 44–45.

Christiansen, Richard. " 'Postman' Script: David Mamet's Special Delivery." *Chicago Tribune* (15 March 1981): F5, F10.

———. "David Mamet." *Performing Arts Journal* 15, no. 3 (1981): 36–40.

Chase, Chris. "At the Movies." *New York Times* (20 March 1981): C6.

Taylor, Clarke. "Mamet and the Hollywood Wringer." *Los Angeles Times* (28 March 1981): B10.

Yakir, D. "Postman's Words." *Film Comment* (March-April 1981): 21–24.

Duka, John. "Hollywood's Long-Running Romance with James M. Cain." *New York Times* (5 April 1981): B15.

Lefko, Elliott. "Playwright's Talent Tapped." *Toronto Star* (14 April 1981): D1.

O'Toole, Lawrence. "Broadway to Hollywood." *Film Comment* (November-December 1981): 22–25.

Shewey, Don. "David Mamet Puts a Dark Urban Drama on Stage." *New York Times* (24 October 1982): B1, B4.

DeVries, Hilary. "In David Mamet's Hands a Pen Becomes a Whip." *Christian Science Monitor* (21 March 1984): 21.

Taylor, Clarke. "Mamet Is 'Thrilled' by His Pulitzer." *Los Angeles Times* (19 April 1984): F7.

Nuwer, Hank. "Two Gentlemen of Chicago: David Mamet and Stuart Gordon." *South Carolina Review* 17 (Spring 1985): 9–20.

———. "A Life in the Theatre: David Mamet." *Rendezvous* 21 (Fall 1985): 1–7.

Roudané, Matthew C. "An Interview with David Mamet." *Studies in American Drama, 1945–Present* 1 (1986): 73–81.

Savran, David. "Trading in the American Dream." *American Theatre* (September 1987): 12–18. Reprinted in *In Their Own Words: Contemporary American Playwrights*. New York: Theatre Communications Group, 1988. 132–44.

PRODUCTION HISTORY

As Carroll has noted, "Mamet's acclaim was not sudden or unanimous—it came in fits and starts" (1), beginning with his first production in Chicago in 1972, *Duck Variations*. Since then, most of Mamet's plays have "had their premieres in Chicago either at the St. Nicholas Theatre . . . or at the Goodman Theatre" (Christiansen, "Pulitzer," 2).

Three years after its Chicago debut, in October 1975, *Duck Variations* premiered in New York with *Sexual Perversity in Chicago* at the St. Clements, directed by Albert Takazauckas, and was well received. On 16 June 1976, the two plays moved to the Cherry Lane Theatre Off-Broadway, where they ran for 273 performances. *Sexual Perversity in Chicago*, which had premiered in the summer of 1974 at Chicago's Organic Theatre Company, was praised by Eder and others as "vastly successful" and the production as "flawless" (" 'Perversity,' " 29). Gussow hailed the "auspicious New York debut" of Mamet's "fresh and pungent comedies . . . a welcome gust of laughter from Chicago" ("Two Comedies," 15). The production on 1 December 1977 of *Sexual Perversity* and *Duck Variations* in London's West End at the Regent Theatre was Mamet's first production abroad. Receiving a lukewarm reception, the production did not last past 14 January (see Chaillet; Stothard); critics were not impressed (Carroll, 12), and some were downright hostile, especially over the posters of a woman spreading her legs across the Hancock Building. Sullivan reviewed the West Coast premiere in San Francisco's Magic Theatre of these two plays and honored Mamet as "A Young Playwright Who Listens." *About Last Night*, a film loosely based on *Sexual Perversity*, was produced in 1985. Although it was popular, the film lacked the irony and punch of Mamet's play.

In 1974, Chicago's St. Nicholas Players presented Mamet's *Squirrels* as their first production. Mamet himself directed the play, which is about two writers, one the employee and protégé of the other. Christiansen characterized the work as "so deeply and intimately connected with language, *Squirrels* needs unusually intense attention from its audience" (quoted in Carroll, 78).

One of Mamet's best-known plays, *American Buffalo* premiered on 23 October 1975 at Chicago's Goodman Theatre Stage Two. Christiansen auspiciously commented, "If you're looking for significant dates in the history of Chicago—and American—theater, there's one to remember" ("Young Lion," 12). When the play opened on Broadway in 1977, it had only a modest run and "was not unanimously praised" (Bigsby, *Mamet*, 72). Gussow complimented Mamet for tuning into the "subtext of everyday speech" and for having "intelligence, wit, an inventive mind, a restless imagination and a way with words" ("Daring Visions," 9, 13). Slightly critical of the play's "scatalogy and blasphemy," Porterfield nonetheless acknowledged Mamet's "infallible ear" and applauded the direction of Grosbard and performances of Kenneth McMillan (Donny), John Savage (Bob), and Robert Duval, (Teach) (54). The Broadway production at the Ethel Barrymore Theatre, however, was panned by Rogoff, who called the characters a "trio of charmless deadbeats," as well as by Duberman and Kerr. Mistakenly, Kerr criticized, "Nothing at all happens . . . which is what finally but firmly kills it as a possible event in the theater" ("Language Alone," 3).

A revival "played first at the Long Wharf Theatre in New Haven in 1980, then at the Circle in the Square Off-Broadway in 1981 and 1982, and finally...Broadway in 1983," proving "that the play could work in quite different interpretations" (Carroll 32). The Long Wharf Theatre production starred Al Pacino, J. J. Johnston, and Bruce MacVittie. Reviewing it, Bertin described *Buffalo* as "a complex, poetic work that stretches the imagination" (402). Exemplifying the diversity of critical responses to the play's original opening and its revival, Gill first called *Buffalo*, directed by Ulu Grosbard, a "curiously offensive piece of writing" composed of "tiresome small talk" and "monotony" ("No News," 54). Six years later he admitted that he had been "plainly unready for it and so mistook its nature" ("Valorous Failures," 149); the success of the later production was partly attributed to the change of directors (to Arvin Brown) and accompanying different readings. The 1983 production held Gill "spellbound" and was "an occasion worthy of vehement salute" ("Valorous Failures," 150). Another revival of *American Buffalo* opened 24 August 1983 at Kennedy Center's Terrace Theater in Washington, D.C.

Following its premiere at St. Nicholas Theatre Company in Chicago on 11 May 1977, Mamet's *Water Engine* opened in New York at the Off-Broadway Public Theatre Cabaret on 5 January 1978 to a wide variety of critical responses. Lape called it "a marvelously clever and nostalgic entertainment" with a "wonderfully well-rounded cast." Others applauded it as "totally fascinating" (Beaufort, "New Mamet Plays," 336), full of "emotional impact" (Kissel, "Water Engine," 336), the work of a writer with "true theatrical imagination" (Kroll, "Golden Age," 337). Sharp strongly criticized the play, setting, and performances. The production, very little changed, moved to the Plymouth Theater on Broadway, 6 March 1978. In response, Eder wrote enthusiastically about Mamet's "complex and quite beautiful work...one of Mr. Mamet's most interesting and subtle plays" ("'Water Engine' Uptown," 42). For Gottfried, the play was "a brilliant idea executed to perfection...mesmerizing, even enthralling" ("Cult," 41). Mordden praised *Engine* as "Mamet's most fully conceived piece" (317), and Watt found it "brilliantly unsettling...a vivid theatrical experience" ("'Engine' Works," 333). Others dismissed the play as a "trickle...simply not important enough to be taken seriously" (Kalem, "Trickle," 335), a "disappointing comedy ...a synthetic that doesn't work" (Oliver, "Watered," 69), plagued with "both superficial and substantive inconsistencies" (Wilson, "'Engine' Rolls," 334). Weales liked *Engine* but feared a short run at the Theatre Cabaret at the Public Theatre, a prediction that proved accurate ("Stronger than Water," 244).

Mamet's eighth play to be produced, *Dark Pony*, opened 14 October 1977 at the Yale Repertory Theatre, New Haven, and 18 October 1979 at the Circle Repertory Theatre, New York. One of three one-acters at the Circle Repertory, it was staged along with *Reunion* and *The Sanctity of Marriage*. These plays were Mamet's New York debut as a director, highly praised by Oliver, who described *Dark Pony* as "a charmer," *Reunion* as the best of the three—"Mamet's ear for the small rhythms and patterns of the speech of working people and his sense of the subtle inflections of emotion in his characters is unerring. . . . *Reunion*, like *Duck Variations*, is a poem for two voices"—and *Sanctity of Marriage* as unsuccessful ("Off Broadway," 81). While Gussow thought *Dark Pony* and *Sanctity of Marriage* weak, he did approve of the "small, quiet pleasures" of *Reunion* and Mamet's sensitive writing, "everyday language distilled into homely poetry" ("Stage: 'Reunion,' " 4). Clurman found *Reunion*, which had premiered on 6 January 1976 at the St. Nicholas Theatre, to be "more touching" than Mamet's other plays: "His writing here is marked by an honest sensibility and a humanity of perception" ("Theater," 572).

Following its premiere in the winter of 1976 at the Goodman Theatre in Chicago, *A Life in the Theatre* opened on 20 October 1977 at the Theatre de Lys, New York, where it ran for 244 performances. Slightly expanded and with a new set by John Lee Beatty, the New York production, directed by Gerald Gutierrez and starring Ellis Rabb (Robert) and Peter Evans (John), was widely praised as "A Comic Masterpiece" that "places its author in the very front rank of young American playwrights" (Watt, "Comic Masterpiece," 141), "a glorious new comedy . . . about the artifice of acting . . . [and] of living" (Gussow, "Illusion," 3). Gussow continued, "Mamet proves in this play . . . that he is an eloquent master of two-part harmony." Gottfried criticized the play for not having a plot yet recognized that "it creates satisfaction" and confirms Mamet's "profound abilities" (" 'Life' Surges," 143). Beaufort described *Life* as "beguiling entertainment superbly acted and beautifully staged" (" 'Life' Tops List," 143). Kissel also singled out the production, from directing to acting to lighting, as a "beautiful, wonderfully theatrical play" that "reconfirms Mamet's immense theatrical imagination and intelligence" ("Life," 144). *Life*'s two characters "shuttling between illusion and reality" (Kalem, "Curtain Call," 144) portray Mamet's fascination with the theatre—the illusions, the code of behavior, the mystery. Like *Water Engine*, the play moves through several levels of reality, offering a play within a play, performance as life, and arousing mystifying questions about the differences between them.

"A remarkable year for Mamet" (Carroll, 11), 1977 also saw the premiere of *The Revenge of the Space Pandas; or Binky Rudich and the Two-Speed Clock*, a children's play, in November at the St. Nicholas Theatre Company. Mordden called Mamet's play that satirizes television space shows as the "oddest of all" of Mamet's plays (316).

The Woods, directed by Mamet, opened on 11 November 1977 at the St. Nicholas Theatre Company, and on 25 April 1979 in New York, where Ulu Grosbard's production for Joseph Papp closed after only thirty-three performances. In Chicago the play received glowing notices, but the New York reception was generally unfavorable. Eder believed that the play in Chicago, under Mamet's direction, "showed beauty and strength," but the New York production had "gone very flat indeed," although it had not changed the critic's opinion that *Woods* is a "remarkably beautiful play" (" 'Woods' Redone," 251). Similarly, Kissel described the play as "an intriguing one to read" but complained that the New York production "realized very little of the play's potential" ("The Woods," 251). In contrast, Barnes praised the staging and performances as "perfect" and faulted the play itself (" 'Woods' Lumbers," 252). In a totally negative review, Beaufort insisted that the play "represents a step backward" for Mamet ("Woods," 251).

Mr. Happiness, a play in the tradition of Nathanael West's satire (*Miss Lonely Hearts*), opened on 6 March 1978 at the Plymouth Theatre in New York as a curtain raiser for *The Water Engine*. While some critics found the play "amusing" (Kissel, "Mr. Happiness," 336), Eder (" 'Engine' Is Uptown," 42), Watt (" 'Engine' Works Uptown," 333), and others criticized it for being filler that even detracted from *Water Engine*. Conversely, Kalem, who called *Engine* a failure, found *Happiness* "radio at its finest" and Charles Kimbrough's performance "absolutely superb. . . . This new sketch almost upstages the original play" ("Trickle," 335).

Lone Canoe, a play including music, opened on 24 May 1979 at Chicago's Goodman Theatre before an audience that included sixty critics at the American Theatre Critics' Association Convention. It was judged such an unmitigated failure (see Wilson, "Chicago"; Ellis) that, according to Carroll, Mamet did not publish the play and has said that he intends to work on it further (106). Also in 1979, the short *Shoeshine* opened 14 December at New York's Ensemble Studio Theatre (Lewis and Browne, 63).

Edmond opened in Chicago on 4 June 1982 at the Goodman Studio Theater. Gussow found it "not an easy play to like, but . . . a difficult one to forget," a play whose "writing is terse, the scenes staccato" in keeping with "the starkness of Mr. Mamet's vision" ("Stage: Mamet Explores," 17). As Carroll has noted, the play's reception in Chicago was mostly enthusiastic (Christiansen, for example, described the Chicago opening as "a brilliant premiere production" ["Mamet's 'Edmond' Savage," 14]), but it opened in New York to mixed notices. Rich was highly critical— "the author's ear has gone tone-deaf and his social observations have devolved into cliches"—and compared *Edmond* to Buchner's *Woyzeck*, to the screenplays *Taxi Driver* and *Hard Core*, the character's speech— "clipped, vague"—to *Beckett*, without the "substance and spice" (" 'Edmond' at Provincetown," 161). Also negatively, Solomon discussed the Provincetown Playhouse (Massachusetts) production, which opened on 27 October 1982 (and four other on and Off-Broadway plays of the same season). Solomon contrasted Mamet with Brecht and *Edmond* with Buchner's *Woyzeck*. Watt applauded the Provincetown opening, concluding that *Edmond* is "an example of masterly control over a dizzying experience and it will knock you for a loop" ("Round the Bend," 160). Weales summarized a great deal of critical reactions: "Newly cast and staged for New York, *Edmond* managed to get two Obie Awards (for writing and direction), but its general reception was unenthusiastic, the play being seen as anomalous Mamet" ("1982–1983," 604). Especially critical of the play's conclusion, Beaufort objected to "the notion that Edmond finds redemption and release" as being "simplistically contrived and incredible" ("On Stage: 'Edmond,' " 163).

The Pulitzer Prize–winning *Glengarry Glen Ross* premiered in London in November 1983. Mamet's friend and fellow playwright Harold Pinter, to whom Mamet had sent a copy of the play, had given the script to Peter Hall, director of the National Theatre of Great Britain. Mamet dedicated the play to Pinter. Lahr reviewed the world premiere in *New Society*, praising *Glengarry* as a major work, "a superb tale" told with "brilliant precision" (477). The play premiered in the United States in February 1984 at the Goodman Theatre and then moved to New York City's Golden Theatre on Broadway in March. In London, Chicago, and New York City, critics acclaimed the work as "Mamet's most mature and controlled" (Christiansen, "Chicago Playwright," 1). Billington described the London National Theatre production as "a complex, non-judgmental comedy" (6). Christiansen reviewed the New York production and reported that the immediate critical reaction to "this important work of American drama has ranged from coolly favorable to wildly enthusiastic" ("Rave, Coolly Favorable," 2). In *Glengarry*, Kauffmann wrote, "Mamet has found his voice most forcefully." He called the work "electric" and the "finest new American play since Pomerance's *The Elephant Man*" ("American Past," 59). Rich judged the play "one of his best. . . . As Mamet's command of dialogue has now reached its most dazzling pitch, so has his mastery of theatrical form" ("Theatre: 'Glengarry,' " 334). Nightingale extolled the play with this rave review: "Rarely have I been more confident of a play's built-in power to last. . . . People will be reviving and discussing it in 10, 20, 30 years time" ("Bard of Immorality," 23). Barnes declared Mamet's "bitterly humorous play" his "most considerable play to date," one to "see, remember and cherish" ("Glengarry," 336), and Siegel called it "one of the season's best new plays by one of our best playwrights" (*Glengarry* review, 339).

Mamet's most recent play, *Speed-the-Plow* (1987), opened mid-May, 1988, on Broadway. The play, with Madonna in the part of a temporary worker in the office of two Hollywood producers, attracted so much publicity that the Lincoln Center Theater premiered the play in its Royale Theatre "on Broadway instead of pursuing its plan for a five-week preliminary run at its uptown house" (Kroll, "Terrors," 82). Directed by Gregory Mosher (his twelfth Mamet play), *Speed-the-Plow* starred Joe Mantegna (Mike in *House of Games*) as Bobby Gould, who has just been promoted to head of production at one of the Hollywood studios, and Ron Silver as Charlie Fox, Bobby's old colleague and a would-be producer. Kroll describes the play, which involves a deal between Bobby and Charlie to produce a no-risk conventional movie being displaced by Karen's (Madonna) persuading Bobby to do one based on a novel about radiation and the end of the world, as "a brilliant black comedy...another tone poem by our foremost master of the language of moral epilepsy" ("Terrors," 82). He praised Mantegna and Silver as "gloriously Mametic; in their hair-trigger, interrupting, overlapping, undercutting exchanges" as well as Mosher's direction. "As for Madonna," Kroll continued, "she has a lot to learn, but she's a serious actress.... She doesn't yet have the vocal horsepower, the sparks and cylinders to drive Mamet's syncopated dialogue. But she has the seductive ambiguity that makes Karen the play's catalytic force" ("Terrors," 83). Oliver also lauded the play as "vintage Mamet, passionate and witty and terribly funny" and the "perfectly matched acting" of Mantegna as Bobby and Silver as Charlie as "a marvel to behold; not a word or gesture goes to waste. As for Madonna...her performance seemed to me just right" ("Mamet," 95). Gussow described *Speed-the-Plow* as "the wittiest and most fiendish comedy about American business since Mr. Mamet's own *Glengarry*" ("Hollywood," 51). Mamet "pinions the characters for their egocentricity and their complete lack of taste," he observes, recalling Mamet's earlier works and his ability to "sniff out a fishmonger no matter what his profession, be it real estate...or the movies" ("Hollywood," 5). Gussow cautiously commended Madonna's "playing the character as conceived by the author," somewhat in the shadow of Mantegna and Silver, who are "experts at playing Mamet" ("Hollywood," 51).

In contrast to these positive reviews, Henry criticized *Plow* for embodying Mamet's "moral ambiguity that verges on cynicism, coupled with a high-minded tone that verges on sanctimony." He expressed frustration with Mamet's idea that "by being oblique, even obscure, he forces spectators to think" and criticized the play for "two huge holes in the narrative," namely, the ambiguity regarding the quality of the book Madonna's character persuades Bobby to believe in and "Madonna's awkward, indecisive characterization" (99). Henry cites the varying opinions of Madonna's performance: *New York Times* critic Frank Rich complimented her "intelligent, scrupulously disciplined comic acting"; Clive Barnes of the *New York Post* acknowledged "a genuine, reticent charm here, but it is not ready to light the lamps on Broadway"; the lead review in the *New York Daily News* was headlined "NO, SHE CAN'T ACT"; WCBS-TV reviewer Dennis Cunningham "not only lambasted Madonna on the air but also later attacked Rich for praising her" (qtd. in Henry, 98). In a highly critical review, Simon complained of the "thinness (though not unwordiness) of the text"; the minimal plot and a script "which depends almost indecently on the skill of its interpreters"; the casting of Madonna, who is "unable to hold her own" and must have been cast "for the hype and fans she attracts" (106); and the limitations of Mamet's power theme, "how power translates itself into language and how language, in turn, translates into power. . . . Pinter did it all before; moreover, the concept may not provide quite as much mileage as Mamet supposes" (106).

Production histories and critical responses to Mamet's work to date are summarized in Carroll's informative opening chapter on Mamet (1–17). Also valuable is Lewis and Browne's list of selected productions of Mamet's plays through 1979 and plays published as books, which also provides biographical information along with discussion of each of the plays, including Mamet's techniques and various productions, surveying critical commentary. The authors generally applaud Mamet's work, especially his use of language (69), but they also find his work "fragile" and "uneven." The piece includes a page of revised typescript from *Sanctity of Marriage*.

On 27 June 1979, the WNET (New York) production of *A Life in the Theatre* was telecast nationwide by the Public Broadcasting System, and the drama became the first of Mamet's plays to be filmed. That was the beginning of Mamet's connection with film, foreshadowing his career ventures into writing both screenplay adaptations—*The Postman Always Rings Twice, The Verdict, The Untouchables*—and original screenplays—*House of Games*, Mamet's first, written and directed by him, and *Things Change*, written with Shel Silverstein and directed by Mamet.

In fall 1979 Mamet was hired by Hollywood director Bob Rafelson to write an adaptation for screen of *The Postman Always Rings Twice*, a novel by James M. Cain. Jack Nicholson and Jessica Lange starred as the obsessed lovers in the film, shot in spring 1980 (Carroll, 13). While Mamet had written adaptations of a couple of his own plays for film, none had been produced, and *Postman* was the first to be. In December 1982 *The Verdict*, adapted for director Sidney Lumet from a novel by Barry Reed, opened featuring Paul Newman as the lawyer hero. Unlike *Postman*, Mamet's adaptation of *Verdict*, which was very well received (see Sterritt; Maslin), differed greatly from its source to become "a parable of a man's oral regeneration and renewal of faith" (Carroll, 92). More recently, Mamet wrote the screenplay for *Malcolm X* (Warner Brothers, not released; Kroll, "Profane Poetry"), the box office hit *The Untouchables* (directed by Brian De Palma, Paramount, 1985), and *House of Games* (Orion, 1987), his first directorial effort. *House of Games* was the closing night selection at the New York Film Festival in October 1987. Lindsay Crouse stars in the role of a psychiatrist who tries to help a young compulsive gambler (played by Joe Mantegna) and gets caught up in an underworld of con men.

In late 1987, production began on *Things Change*, written with Shel Silverstein, produced by Michael Hausman (who also produced *House of Games*), and directed by Mamet. Mamet has said that the movie is about "an Italian immigrant, played by Don Ameche.... The mob asks him to take a jail rap for one of their guys who's a dead ringer for him. The old guy agrees, and they take him to Tahoe for his last weekend, where he's treated like a Mafia don" (Kroll, "Profane Poetry").

SURVEY OF SECONDARY SOURCES

Bibliographies

The most exhaustive bibliography to date is the Davis and Coleman listing of over 400 items. A record of publications by and about Mamet through late 1985, the bibliography is valuable as a starting point for research on Mamet. For a shorter bibliographic listing, see King. Also see Storey for an early bibliography of Mamet's works and Carroll for a bibliography of primary and secondary sources on Mamet, including archival collections and a listing of videocassettes in the TOFT (Theatre on Film and Tape) Collection. One of the most current bibliographies of Mamet's work accompanies Christiansen's recent essay in *Contemporary Dramatists*.

Biographies

Mamet and his career are both still relatively young. While a full-scale biography of Mamet has not been written, a few general works of criticism sketch in Mamet's life and background in the theatre (Cohn; Herman, 125–31; Witt; Kastor). In addition, Bigsby's opening chapter (*Mamet*, 11–21) offers a useful overview of biography, as does Carroll's (1–17). Also valuable for biographical information is Lewis and Browne's essay.

Standard biographic sources such as the *Playwrights Directory* and *Oxford Companion to American Literature* offer basic biographical material, including Mamet's education, awards, publications, and other theatrical activities.

In a particularly valuable biographical piece, Christiansen characterized Mamet as "The Young Lion of Chicago." Writing in 1982 for *Chicago*

Tribune Magazine, he reflected on Chicago-born Mamet's career and his personal and professional development through the 1982 production of *Edmond*. A friendly critic who has watched Mamet from the beginning— "yet to be praised as the bright new hope of American drama" (9)— Christiansen includes numerous enlightening comments by Mamet and others who have worked with him and gives an overview of Mamet's career.

Freedman traces the development of Mamet's career, discussing the plays, including the shorter ones. He has relied heavily on interviews with Mamet, Mamet's sister, and others who have worked with Mamet and in his plays. The article is valuable for its interweaving of Mamet's life and his plays and career and includes questions of where Mamet will go to follow up on *Glengarry*, "his most accomplished and rewarded work" (64).

Influences

Mamet has repeatedly and consistently acknowledged his indebtedness to Thorstein Veblen's *Theory of the Leisure Class* in numerous interviews, including the one with Roudané and a video interview ("Profile of a Writer"). Carroll discusses Veblen and others—Aristotle, the Stoics, Freud, Marx, Bruno Bettelheim, Joseph Campbell, Tolstoy, Stanislavsky—as sources for Mamet's moral vision (19). Writing on *Glengarry Glen Ross*, Roudané discusses the influence of Tocqueville on Mamet's aesthetic. Mamet's *Writing in Restaurants* is a source of much information on influences the playwright acknowledges. As Gerald Weales rightly points out in his review of Mamet's collection, "*Writing in Restaurants* is worth an effort for anyone who cares about Mamet's art. His view of the world, of America, of theatre, provides the intellectual content in which his plays take shape" ("Decay Is Our Destiny," 33).

The influences most often noted in Mamet are those of Pinter and Chekhov. Mamet wrote an adaptation of *The Cherry Orchard*, also the subject of an essay in *Writing in Restaurants* (118–25). Ditsky regards Mamet as "one of the more notable instances of genuine Pinter influence. . . . If there is one true follower of the Pinter fruition of Chekhov's observations of human speech, would his name not be David Mamet?" (26). Gale has also acknowledged similarities of Pinter's and Mamet's work, characterizing Mamet's as "less intellectual, philosophical, or theoretical . . . , and his writing is far more easily accessible" (207).

Critics have pointed out other influences. Almansi perceives Mamet as the "prince of contemporary blasphemers" and calls Louis Ferdinand Celine his "predecessor" (199). Jacobs discusses similarities between Mamet and other Chicago writers.

Schlueter and Forsyth note influences in their demonstration how, in *American Buffalo*, Mamet has used—and modified—the symbolism of the junkshop inherited from American literature and its relation to the American dream. Barbera has discussed the influence of Veblen, as well as that of Chicago history in general.

In the recent Savran interview, Mamet acknowledged the influences of several playwrights, including Lanford Wilson, Beckett, Pinter, Ionesco, and Brecht, as well as the significance of his training under acting teacher Sanford Meisner, which included methods based on what Mamet described as "Aristotle filtered through Stanislavsky and Boleslavsky" (15).

In an interview with Christiansen ("David Mamet"), Mamet discussed influences on his screenwriting, particularly the role of Bob Rafelson, the Hollywood director who first hired Mamet to write a screenplay, the adaptation of *The Postman Always Rings Twice*.

General Studies

Bigsby's *David Mamet*, the first book-length study of the playwright, expands his assessment of Mamet as a "poet of loss" in his *A Critical Introduction to Twentieth-Century American Drama: Beyond Broadway* (1985). Through eight chapters, Bigsby studies Mamet's works from his beginnings through *Glengarry Glen Ross*. An essential resource for the student of Mamet's work, the book recognizes Mamet's works as those of a major postwar writer and seeks "to illuminate not only those works but also in some degree the artistic, social and moral assumptions on which they rest" (6). Bigsby summarizes the essence of Mamet's art: "Beyond his central concern with the craft of theatre and its power to shape experience, language and thought, his plays stand as a consistent critique of a country whose public myths he regards as destructive, and whose deep lack of communality he finds disturbing" (14). Viewing Mamet as "a moralist...[whose] target is, in effect, less American realities than the myths that have deformed American possibility" (15), Bigsby examines Mamet in the context of theatrical traditions, and sensitively identifies Mamet's distinctive voice and considerable technical accomplishments throughout discussions of each of the plays. In addition, Bigsby offers information gained in interviews Mamet granted him, unpublished elsewhere.

In *David Mamet*, Carroll examines the playwright's career with emphasis on his themes: business, sex, learning, and communion. He offers rich discussions of the major plays and devotes the eighth and final chapter of his book to a consideration of "Mamet in Context," commenting on Mamet's "many-sided artistic talent" evident in essays and articles, adaptations of plays by playwrights other than himself, children's plays, work in progress, and short plays and sketches. Besides discussing selected works from these areas, Carroll considers "Mamet's place in the larger context of drama and theatre" (140). He discusses Mamet's career in the light of the creative work of playwrights slightly preceding him and of his peers such as Lanford Wilson, John Guare, Christopher Durang, Albert Innaurato, Michael Cristofer, Beth Henley, Marsha Norman, Wallace Shawn, and especially Sam Shepard and David Rabe (149–52). Carroll concludes that "Mamet's importance, apart from the dialogue, lies in his unsentimental sense of personal and social morality, his wry but sharp sense of dialectic, and the vigour of his characters' intent" (155).

Besides these two full-scale assessments, a number of useful general discussions of Mamet have been published. The most interesting and fruitful readings are in Almansi, Gale, Bigsby, Storey, and Herman. Almansi has found that a "comprehensive reading [of Mamet's plays] . . . reveals a strong line of plays in which characters are exclusively men who display all the male prejudices about women." He reads the best plays as "necessarily comic." When a Mamet character speaks, "His words have an ulterior meaning. Besides the meaning . . . , the act of speech itself *signifies*" (193–94). Gale sees Mamet's plays as "about relationships." His overview, "The Plays, 1972–1980," offers plot summaries and uncritical, superficial readings that might nevertheless be useful for an initial look at Mamet. In a significant though early short study, Storey explored Mamet's dramatic strategies, especially the function of language, focusing attention on plays through *The Woods*. Storey points out that in Mamet's work "language does not conceal but rather fabricates emotion" (3), and, indeed, the one character who gains "freedom from rhetoric"—John, in *A Life in the Theatre*—pays for it with an acute "sense of loss." Storey's essay offers succinct summaries and discussions of the plays, as well as biography and an early bibliography. Herman provides a biography of Mamet and a discussion of its relation to his approaches to his work. Mamet's "pervasive use of obscene language" is the "most famous element of his dramatic technique" (130), according to Herman, and his "obsessive themes are broken relations, the failure to form relations, the impossibility of forming relations, and yet the endless pursuit of these relations" (130). Herman gives individual attention to the major works (*Sexual Perversity, Duck Variations, American Buffalo, Life in the Theatre, Glengarry*) and what he calls "the most significant and interesting of his other works" (157)—*Water Engine, Reunion, Dark Pony*, and *The Woods*.

In her recent study, Jacobs discusses the "working world" as the setting for several of Mamet's plays, "essential to the dramas. . . . The men of *American Buffalo, Glengarry Glen Ross, Lakeboat*, and *A Life in the Theatre* are vitally engaged in their work" (47). She discusses Mamet's use of the work environment in relation to the dramas of Brecht, Odets, Miller, O'Neill, Hecht, and MacArthur and to the works of Hamlin Garland

and several novelists. Savran's recent interview with Mamet is introduced with general criticism of Mamet's works and contains important information about influences, techniques, Mamet's ideas about the American theatre and society, and the relationship between his work for stage and screen.

Christiansen's recent essay in *Contemporary Dramatists* is one of the best brief discussions available of Mamet's work in general. The Chicago critic begins with *Sexual Perversity* and follows Mamet's career through *House of Games*, providing important items of biography and influence, reporting critical reactions to each of the plays, and describing the focus of Mamet's work: "There are political repercussions.... But the most telling, most important battles and victories in Mamet's plays occur on the basic, personal levels of individual relationships. The bonds of friendship, family, and love are crucial in Mamet's world, and when they are broken, the world collapses for his characters." Christiansen predicts that Mamet's "best work in theater may lie ahead" (340).

In his collection of thirty essays on a variety of topics in the theatre and popular culture, Mamet offers some of the most insightful to be found of his work in general and of several specific plays. The book, extremely useful for students of his work, discloses Mamet's thoughts on radio drama, acting, Chicago history, writing screenplays, and other topics, illustrating Mamet's characteristic style filled with jabs and punches. The essays reveal Mamet as a student of the Stanislavsky school and his fundamental ideas that drama needs to present the soul of its age and that on stage, as much as everywhere else in life, "human beings must concern themselves with the truth of the individual moment" (28). Nichols praised Mamet's essays as "dead practical"; Lumet found them full of "passion, clarity, commitment, intelligence"; Albee has called it "serious, funny, intense, provocative and often outrageous; it reminds us once again that playwrights have minds as well as talents" (Jacket notes). Carroll comments, "Many of the essays reveal an overt didacticism that is stimulating, but fortunately absent from the plays themselves" (141).

Mamet himself is the best available source for information about his film career. "I am a playwright," Mamet wrote in *Writing in Restaurants*, "...hired to write a screenplay, and what had been—for better and worse—the most private of occupations became a collaborative endeavor" (75). In his essay on his work in Hollywood, Mamet describes the complementary effects of writing for both film and stage. He has also discussed his film activities in interviews with Christiansen ("David Mamet"), Savran ("Trading in"), Yakir ("Postman's Words"), and others, and in his essay "I Lost it at the Movies," which concerns both *The Untouchables* and *House of Games*.

Analyses of Individual Plays

American Buffalo is Mamet's most frequently discussed play. Characterizing *American Buffalo* as "new realism" (199), Ventimiglia claims that Mamet provides a new perspective of the subject matter—isolation, death, alienation—by suffusing it "with an optimism which is indeed new. . . . If Mamet's play is about acquisitiveness and greed, it is also about the human bond of friendship and its triumph over these influences" (203). Describing the play as "Chekhovian," he argues that it is "constructed with an extraordinary sense of the economics of dramatic representation" (199).

Writing on the "Ethical Perversity in America" portrayed in *American Buffalo*, Barbera answers criticism that assesses the play as lacking content and defends it as being of "intellectual interest" (272). Barbera reads the play as satirizing corrupt notions of American business and suggests reading the title: "for 'buffalo' read the slang verb 'to intimidate' " (274), as businessmen commonly buffalo the public. Barbera discusses *American Buffalo* in the light of the Chicago Exposition. He examines the urban nature of the play's language and explores the play's content that resides "in the relationships, tensions and contradictions in the patter of Don and Teach" (273). He credits Mamet's idea of "ethical perversity" to Veblen and considers the relations of *American Buffalo* to Veblen's thought.

Mamet's concern with the American business ethic in *Buffalo* and elsewhere has naturally received considerable attention. In an important interview with Gottlieb, he discusses his intent to expose that ethic in *American Buffalo*. Schlueter and Forsyth also emphasize the business ethic in the play, beginning with the central image, the buffalo nickel—money—which propels the business world: "Indeed, money is the object of all business deals and competition for that money the mainstay of the American business world" (493). The characters' speech reflects the language of "modern business-oriented America" (496), and the junkshop itself is "a powerful image for an America in which the business ethic has so infiltrated the national consciousness and language that traditional human values have become buried under current values of power and greed" (499).

Mamet's concern with language has also been a major topic of interviews (Wetzsteon), criticism, and reviews. Reviewing *American Buffalo*, Porterfield discusses Mamet, his background, and the development of his consciousness of language: "Mamet has an infallible ear for the cadences of loneliness and fear behind the bluntness [of the language], and he also knows how to make the bluntness very funny." Storey remarks on the "verbal busyness, glib, deft, quick" that is the foundation of Mamet's America, "the parenthetical asides that lace his dialogue (destined, undoubtedly, to become as celebrated as Pinter's pauses) suggest minds that abhor verbal vacuums, that operate, at all levels, on the energy of language itself" (2). Beaufort calls *American Buffalo* "a lower-depths tragicomedy," its strengths being "its word patterns, cadences, and rhythms, its verbal flights, odd turns, and sudden stops" (23).

Rogoff and Hughes have voiced representative dissatisfaction with Mamet. While others see Mamet's characters' street language as his forte, Rogoff criticizes: "With friends like [Mamet] ... words don't need enemies" (37). Reviewing the play in *America*, Hughes believed that the play's action "too often seems much ado about very little" (364).

Clurman briefly reviews *America Buffalo* in his introduction to *Nine Plays of the Modern Theater*. The play "breaks away from the tradition in our native drama which runs through O'Neill, Odets, Williams, to a play reminiscent of, though unlike, Pinter" (xiii). He continues, "A good part of [the play's] meaning is in its speech.... If the play finally achieves eloquence it is through the inarticulate" (xiii–xiv). Clurman perceives the characters as having friendship, albeit of "physical connection, a spastic reaching out for solace" (xiv).

Mamet's Pulitzer Prize–winning *Glengarry Glen Ross* has earned considerable critical attention as "Mamet's best play since *American Buffalo*" (Weales, "1983–84," 594). Almansi credits the play with "forcing the experts to reconsider the development of American theater in the last ten years" (191). He considers it "written to my opinion in the best American idiom to be found in the contemporary scene." In *Glengarry*, Mamet explores "the poetics, as well as the rhetoric, of salesmanship" (203). Criminals, yes, but first the characters of *Glengarry* are "just plain salesmen ... a model of normalcy" (205), not the exception but "the norm" for the millions in contemporary America who devote their lives to sales, "their whole emotional capital [vested] in their work." The play has earned Mamet the title of "Bard of Modern Immorality" (Nightingale, 5).

In a review of the play's world premiere in *New Society* (1983), Lahr comments that "Mamet is again dramatising The Deal and the high comic ironies of entrepreneurial capitalism." Lahr has outlined Mamet's family and career background, briefly discussed *Sexual Perversity in Chicago* and *American Buffalo*, and praised *Glengarry*—the "hilarious brutal sludge" of Mamet's characters' speech (476), the "pitch and roll of Mamet's stunning dialogue," (477)—as a major work.

Three short essays published as *1986–87 Humanities Booklet* 5 (Rhode Island Committee for the Humanities) accompanied the Trinity Repertory Company production of *Glengarry*. Coale discusses the myth of the self-made man in American society in the light of the figure of the confidence man. Klein explores the American myths in *Glengarry Glen Ross*—"rugged individualism, competition, and salesmanship" (3)—and suggests that the characters "sell illusions" (7). Mongeon chronicles the history of business in America and the emerging concern with business ethics as the backdrop for the "nightmare" of Mamet's play (10).

Allen offers an interesting perspective on Mamet's ideas about the play in an articles based on interviewing him just before the Broadway opening. Mamet told her that he "wanted to write a play . . . 'about those guys you see on planes' " who appear in *Glengarry* and use all the tricks, " 'not only to sell land. Everybody is always selling to everybody' " (40).

Adding to the growing critical commentary on Mamet's work and the playwright's indebtedness to Veblen, Roudané suggests that the "delicate balance between the public and the private which so engaged Tocqueville [particularly in *Democracy in America*] exerts an equally strong influence on Mamet's aesthetic" ("Public Issues," 35). Roudané further observes that throughout Mamet's theatre, he "tackles a Tocquevillian dialectic which, on the one hand, recognizes the individual's right to pursue vigorously entrepreneurial interest, but which, on the other, acknowledges that in an ideal world such private interests should, but do not, exist in equipoise with a sense of civic and moral duty" (35). He perceives the characters of *Glengarry Glen Ross* as "living the myth" of the American dream seen in other Mamet works, especially *American Buffalo*, their problem being that they "sell not only land but themselves as well" (39). Mamet explores a "business-as-sacrament world . . . public and private experiences become one . . . the most remarkable feature of *Glengarry Glen Ross* lies in its compelling presentation of a series of particular real-estate events which suddenly broaden to encompass universal experiences" (39). Kolin examines the thematic importance of Mamet's unseen bosses (Mitch and Murray) who are responsible for the fatal contest fueling and ultimately destroying the salesman; he discusses the onomastic irony behind their names and the false friendships they promote and typify in Mamet's capitalistic jungle ("Mitch and Murray").

Sexual Perversity in Chicago, which played in New York with *Duck Variations*, "first made Mamet's name in Chicago and New York, and was his first popular 'success' " (Carroll, 52). Discussing *Sexual Perversity* in relation to *The Woods*, which shares a similar theme of "heterosexual love" (52), Carroll points out that the two plays differ in "focus and milieu" and tone. In addition, *Sexual Perversity* "deals almost as much with male bonding as with heterosexual love" (52). Bigsby calls the play "one of Mamet's funniest" (*Mamet*, 52). "The sheer exuberance is compelling. But the . . . vitality is illusory, the energy largely neurotic" (52). Here, as in Mamet's other plays, his "characters deal with people as though they were commodities . . . they are sexual consumers, and relationships become no more than transactions" (50–51).

Sullivan describes *Sexual Perversity* as a "comic strip, a strain of bits and blackouts on Making Out in the Big Town" ("Young Playwright," 1). Cardullo, who suggests that it is a "modern American comedy that comments on the sexual attitudes and coupling rites of its time," considers the last scene generally misunderstood by both audiences and critics and that male and female bonding is the "true focus of this play" ("Comedy," 6).

Gale summarizes criticism and traces early productions of *The Duck Variations*, which was praised for "the accuracy of Mamet's language and the reality of the play's situation" (9). Storey examines Mamet's "dramatic strategies" as they emerge in the play, writing that this "very simple," "wonderfully funny play" is built of humor that depends on "the balance of power between the two characters shifting with their shifts in verbal perspective, each of those perspectives entertained with the solemnity of a naively incompetent rhetorician" (3–4). Carroll discusses *Duck Variations* as one of the "largest group of Mamet's plays," in which "the relationship is an educative one between two males" (70). In *Duck Variations*, the relationship is "one of teacher-pupil in two old men who are much the same age" (71). Sitting on their park bench, they conduct "a social ritual" (72) in which each "has a social role that shores him up against silence and too much self-questioning" (73). Gale has remarked that "the importance of their conversations lies...in the fact that they are conversing" (208). Carroll adds that more than conversing, the characters "are carrying out action...each exercising will to contact, then away, then back again, in a dynamic bond of friendship" (76). For Bigsby also, in Mamet, "character is action, and the evasive strategies of Emil and George a primary concern." The process by which the aging figures "contain their fears through narrative" is one "that fascinates Mamet" (27). George and Emil "maintain a constant and apparently meaningless chatter in order to avoid the silence they fear.... Sense is subordinate to the rhythms of relationship and the reassurance to be found in the simple sound of the human voice" (28). Bigsby discusses *Duck Variations* in relation to Albee's *The Zoo Story* and Beckett's *Waiting for Godot*, as well as the influence of Pinter. He concludes that while these influences are clear in this early play, "the voice is already Mamet's, as is the ironic tone and the concern for rhythm...that indicated clearly enough Mamet's emerging talent" (*Mamet*, 33).

Bigsby and Carroll both offer discussion of *The Water Engine*, while other criticism appears in articles on Mamet's plays in general by, for example, Storey and Gale. Bigsby calls the play "a neat parody of thirties social drama" (*Mamet*, 87) on one level, but the "apparent realism is presented ironically.... The story of Charles Lang is only part of the play; the radio drama is contained within another fiction...punctuated by the voice of a chain letter...this becomes in part a drama about fictionality" (87). According to Carroll, "the fable walks a fine line between optimism and ironic disillusionment" (132). He discusses *Water Engine* as "Mamet's most quintessential play as far as content is concerned. It weaves together 'business,' with its pressure to abrogate trust; the potential for communion in the mentor-protégé relationship; the tensions caused by sexual pressures" (131). In a chapter on "The Plays in the Theatre" (118–39), Carroll discusses *Water Engine* at some length as an example of how Mamet's work "comes alive only when it's on stage," in the words of set designer John Lee Beatty (quoted in Carroll, 118). Storey, who prefers *Water Engine* as a radio play, writes that here Mamet presents "Forces for Evil" that "are, in short, real." The source of their strength lies in their rhetoric, Storey continues: "rhetoric that shamelessly legitimizes chicanery...corruption at the heart of things, both verbal and political; it spawns a system in which business is mere thievery methodized" (8). Gale considers *Water Engine* Mamet's "weakest full-length published work" (214), one in which Mamet has drawn on clichés to dramatize distrust of business and the business ethic. He compares *Water Engine* to Mamet's other works in terms of theme, action, tone, language, style, and significance.

Carroll includes *A Life in the Theatre* in the group of Mamet's plays about learning, one "which reads and plays in a deceptively effortless manner" (78). The two characters—Robert, the aging actor and mentor, and John, the newcomer to the stage and protégé—are "well-observed individuals who at the same time carry representative weight" (78). Carroll discusses the play's "movement to a climax of a transfer of power from mentor to protégé" and the differing way the characters view the nature of the theatre: Robert, "as mostly an analogue of life" (80); John, as part of life. Robert comes to concede "that theatre and life are all one" (81). Carroll concludes that the play's significance lies in the precise structuring and development of the central relationship between Robert and John" (83). In an essay in *Writing in Restaurants*, Mamet confirms that "a life in the theatre need not be an analogue to 'life.' It *is* life" (106). "My play," he adds, "is...a comedy about this life" (106). Bigsby points out that the play's "title itself parodies Stanislavsky's autobiography, *My Life in Art*" (*Mamet*, 93). *Life* "consists of a string of episodes (twenty-six scenes in all) through which Mamet slowly creates a kind of pointillist portrait of the two men...a closer relationship between the two men than between most of Mamet's characters" (96). Bigsby comments that through Robert, Mamet contests "his own mode of representation...his own procedures as a playwright.... For the fact is that performance can be an evasive strategy, and the logic of the theatrical metaphor is no less implacable than that of the life for which it stands or with which it is contiguous" (98). In summary, *Life* "emphasizes the evanescence both of theatre and of life.... As to the audience—ourselves—Mamet seems to imply that we too are manoeuvred into playing parts not of our own devising" (99).

Gale effectively summarizes *Life*, pointing out the theatre as life theme and the related teacher-student subtheme. "Through a variety of circumstances and over a long period of time [the play] shows how two men overcome obstacles to form a solid relationship ... through it all there is an underlying sense of good humor and, ultimately, proportion" (219–20). Jacobs, examining Mamet's "working worlds," points out, "The actor as craftsman is one of the primary topics" of *Life* (51). In his brief commentary on the play, Weales discusses its scenes that show the actors in performance; these are "parody turns" ("1977–1978," 518), while "the backstage sequences trace the changing relationship" between Robert and John (519). Gussow's review includes comment on the play as a comedy and about the effects of the differences in the Chicago and New York productions ("Illusion"). Ditsky discusses the "interesting ... curious rituals of power" (31) going on between the two characters as "their professional standing as well as the locus of power between them, is ... reversed" (31). He sees Robert at the play's end as still "trapped in his role of actor" (32).

Christiansen describes the middle-aged New Yorker hero of *Edmond* as "the latest of Mamet's characters to learn the essential loneliness and isolation of the soul. Like most persons in Mamet's plays, ... Edmond struggles against but succumbs at last to a fate he has helped fashion through his own insensitivity toward his fellow man" (" 'Edmond' Savage," 14). Weales called the play a "skeletal descent-into-hell drama" in which Mamet's concern "is with the ways in which we become part of our destructive surroundings" ("1982–1983," 604). Weales discusses the play as uncharacteristic of Mamet in its darker view of contemporary society and its presentation of Edmond as a representative character rather than a completely conceived character like Mamet's others.

Bigsby writes that *Edmond* embodies the American "culture of narcissism" (*Mamet*, 101) of the 1970s, intent on self-realization with no interest in the wider community, and plunges into corruption that is "a wilful product of his own self-obsession" (108–9). Bigsby, who perceives the same narcissistic concern with the self in *American Buffalo, Sexual Perversity in Chicago, The Water Engine*, and *Glengarry Glen Ross*, comments that Edmond's "failure to relate his fragmented experiences to some central meaning is equally the failure of his culture ... a world in which alienation is a fundamental experience ... reflected in the linguistic and theatrical structure" of Mamet's plays (109). The "rhythmic, often staccato exchanges and veristic colloquialism" (Beaufort, "Edmond," 163), the "crisp, anecdotal style" (Barnes, "Stark Telling," 162), and the "series of many short, swift scenes" (Watt, "Edmond," 160), result in a play that is, like Mamet's others, "episodic for more than structural reasons"

(Bigsby 109). The short scenes invite comparison with *Sexual Perversity* specifically.

In an interview with Carroll, Mamet described *Edmond* as being "about a man trying to come to grips with his life in a society which he cannot understand and cannot support" (97). According to Carroll, "Mamet presents Edmond's journey as a fable-like allegory . . . qualified by ironies," a fable that "encompasses the disintegration and reintegration of a personality" (97) and culminates in the final scene that "reinforces Edmond's new-found vulnerability and indicates further growth in him . . . imprisoned—but at peace, learning about himself, and involved in a communing relationship with another human being" (103–5). Weales perceives "nothing but irony" in the final scene, which ends in "an image of isolation" rather than connection ("1982–1983," 605).

In his review of *Edmond*, Barnes discusses the play's comparison to Buchner's *Woyzech*, pointing to Dreiser's *An American Tragedy* as an influence "far nearer the mark" (162). Barnes connects Mamet's work with Pinter and also comments on the historical suggestions implied in the hero's being called Edmond Burke. Kissel explores the allusion to the eighteenth-century English political theorist further, suggesting that "the plot illustrates [Edmund] Burke's notions about the need for limits on liberty" ("Edmond," 159).

Mamet's other plays have received less critical attention than they deserve. While reviews, many of which can be found in the *New York Theater Critics' Reviews*, contain some criticism, there are few articles available. Among the few is Kolin's on *The Shawl*, in which he insightfully explores levels of illusion and the audience's need for illusions. General studies such as Bigsby's include brief comment on the lesser-known works, and Carroll's concluding chapter (140–55) focuses on the short plays and sketches (and Mamet's essays, adaptations of plays by others, children's plays and works in progress).

FUTURE RESEARCH OPPORTUNITIES

Judging by the amount of recent work done on him, Mamet is beginning to attract the scholarly attention he merits. The two central books by Bigsby and Carroll are only a start. As Mamet continues to write for stage and screen, longer, more comprehensive studies will be necessary. Such studies need to devote more time to Mamet's indebtedness to classical and Renaissance plays, his own views of theatre (as expressed most characteristically in *Writing in Restaurants*), the connections between his stage and Hollywood work, and Mamet's relationship to other Chicago writers (e.g. Bellow, Emily Mann, etc.). A rigorously formal linguistic analysis of Mamet's style is in order, as is a study of Mamet in the light of deconstruction theory. A continuation of and supplement to the Davis-Coleman bibliography would also be useful. It would be helpful to scholars to have Mamet's plays collected into a few volumes, as Atheneum has done for Albee or Random House for Neil Simon.

SECONDARY SOURCES

Allen, Jennifer. "David Mamet's Hard Sell." *New York* (9 April 1984): 38–41.
Almansi, Guido. "David Mamet, a Virtuoso of Invective." In *Critical Angles: European Views of Contemporary American Literature*, pp. 191–207. Edited by Marc Chénetier. Carbondale: Southern Illinois University Press, 1986.
Asahina, Roberts. Review of *American Buffalo. Hudson Review* 37 (Spring 1984): 101–2.
Barbera, Jack V. "Ethical Perversity in America: Some Observations on David Mamet's *American Buffalo.*" *Modern Drama* 24 (September 1981): 270–75.
Barnes, Clive. "Mamet's 'Glengarry': A Play to See and Cherish." *New York Post* (26 March 1984). Reprinted in *NYTCR*, 336–37.
———. "Stark Telling of Mamet's 'Edmond.' " *New York Post* (28 October 1982). Reprinted in *NYTCR*, 162–63.
———. " 'Woods' Lumbers Along." *New York Post* (26 April 1979). Reprinted in *NYTCR*, 252.
Beaufort, John. "Also: A New Mamet Play, Off-Broadway Drama, 'The Water Engine.' " *Christian Science Monitor* (12 January 1978). Reprinted in *NYTCR*, 336–37.
———. " 'Buffalo' Is Back—Tragicomedy Starring Al Pacino." *Christian Science Monitor* (8 November 1983): 23.
———. " 'Life' Tops List of New York Openings." *Christian Science Monitor* (29 October 1977). Reprinted in *NYTCR*, 143–44.
———. "On Stage: 'Edmond.' " *Christian Science Monitor* (8 November 1982): 18. Reprinted in *NYTCR*, 163.
———. "The Woods." *Christian Science Monitor* (9 May 1979). Reprinted in *NYTCR*, 251.
Bertin, Michael. "*American Buffalo.*" *Theatre Journal* (October 1981): 402–4.
Bigsby, C. W. E. *A Critical Introduction to Twentieth-Century American Drama: Beyond Broadway*, 3: 251–90. New York: Cambridge University Press, 1985.
———. *David Mamet*. Contemporary Writers Series. New York: Methuen, 1985.
Billington, Michael. "Theater in London: Mamet Turns to the World of Salesmen." *New York Times* (9 October 1983): B6.
Cardullo, Bert. "Comedy and *Sexual Perversity in Chicago.*" *Notes on Contemporary Literature* 12 (January 1982): 6.
Carroll, Dennis. *David Mamet*. Macmillan Modern Dramatists Series. London: Macmillan, 1987.
Chaillet, Ned. "*Sexual Perversity in Chicago/Duck Variations.*" *The Times* (London, 2 December 1977): 9.
Christiansen, Richard. "Chicago Playwright Wins Pulitzer Prize." *Chicago Tribune* (17 April 1984): A1.

———. "David Mamet." *Contemporary Dramatists*. 4th ed., pp. 338–40. Edited by D. L. Kirkpatrick. Chicago: St. James, 1988.

———. "David Mamet." *Performing Arts Journal* 15, no. 3 (1981): 36–40.

———. "Mamet's 'Edmond' Savage But Compassionate." *Chicago Tribune* (7 June 1982): C14.

———. " 'Glengarry' Gets Rave, Coolly Favorable N.Y. Reviews." *Chicago Tribune* (27 March 1984): E1, E3.

———. "The Young Lion of Chicago Theater." *Chicago Tribune Magazine* (11 July 1982): 9–14, 18–19.

Clurman, Harold. Introduction to *Nine Plays of the Modern Theater*, pp. xiii-xiv. New York: Grove, 1981.

———. "Theater." *Nation* (1 December 1979): 571–72.

Coale, Sam. "Have I Got a Deal for You: Self-Made and Selling It." *1986–87 Humanities Booklet #5*, pp 1–3. Providence: Rhode Island Committee for the Humanities, Trinity Repertory Company, 1986.

Cohn, Ruby. "Narrower Straits." In *New American Dramatists: 1960–1980*, pp. 41–46. New York: Grove, 1982.

Davis, J. Madison, and John Coleman. "David Mamet: A Classified Bibliography." *Studies in American Drama, 1945–Present* 1 (1986): 83–101.

Ditsky, John. " 'He Lets You See the Thought There': The Theatre of David Mamet." *Kansas Quarterly* 12, no. 4 (1980): 25–34.

Duberman, Martin. "The Great Gray Way." *Harper's* (May 1978): 79–87.

Eder, Richard. "David Mamet's New Realism." *New York Times Magazine* (12 March 1978): 40.

———. "Mamet's 'Perversity' Mosaic on Modern Mores, Moves." *New York Times* (17 June 1976): 29.

———. "Stage: 'Water Engine' Is Uptown." *New York Times* (7 March 1978): 42.

———. "Mamet's 'The Woods' Redone at Public." *New York Times* (26 April 1979). Reprinted in *NYTCR*, 250–51.

Ellis, Roger. "Theatre in Review: *Lone Canoe*." *Theatre Journal* 32 (May 1980): 256–57.

Freedman, Samuel G. "The Gritty Eloquence of David Mamet." *New York Times* (21 April 1985): F32, F40–41, F46, F50–51, F64.

Gale, Steven H. "David Mamet: The Plays, 1972–1980." In *Essays on Contemporary American Drama*, pp. 207–23. Edited by Hedwig Bock and Albert Wertheim. Munich: Max Hueber, 1981.

Gill, Brendan. "No News from Lake Michigan." *New Yorker* (28 February 1977): 54.

———. "The Theater: Valorous Failures." *New Yorker* (7 November 1983): 149–50.

Gottfried, Martin. "Cult of the Second-rate." *Saturday Review* 4 (March 1978): 41.

———. " 'Life in the Theater' Surges with Love." *New York Post* (21 October 1977). Reprinted in *NYTCR*, 143.

Gottlieb, Richard. "The Engine That Drives Playwright David Mamet." *New York Times* (15 January 1978): B1.

Gussow, Mel. "The Daring Visions of Four New, Young Playwrights." *New York Times* (13 February 1977): B1, B9, B13.

———. "Mamet's Hollywood is a School for Scoundrels." *New York Times* (15 May 1988): B5, B51.

———. "Stage: Illusion within an Illusion." *New York Times* (21 October 1977): C3.

———. "Stage: Mamet Explores the Fall of 'Edmond.' " *New York Times* (17 June 1982): C17.

———. "Stage: 'Reunion,' 3 Mamet Plays." *New York Times* (19 October 1979): C4.

———. "Two Pungent Comedies by New Playwright." *New York Times* (1 November 1975): 15.

Henry, William A., III. "Madonna Comes to Broadway." *Time* (16 May 1988): 98–99.

Herman, William. "Theatrical Diversity from Chicago: David Mamet." In *Understanding Contemporary American Drama*, pp. 125–60. Columbia: University of South Carolina Press, 1987.

Hughes, Catharine. "New American Playwrights." *America* (16 April 1977): 363–64.

Jacobs, Dorothy H. "Working Worlds in David Mamet's Dramas." In *Midwest Miscellany XIV, Being Essays on Chicago Writers*, pp. 47–57. Edited by David D. Anderson. East Lansing: Michigan State University Press, 1986.

Kalem, T. E. "Curtain Call: 'A Life in the Theater.' " *Time* (31 October 1977). Reprinted in *NYTCR*, 144.

———. "Trickle: The Water Engine." *Time* (20 March 1978). Reprinted in *NYTCR*, 335.

Kastor, Elizabeth. "The Brilliance of 'Buffalo': Playwright David Mamet, the Ups and Downs of His Bristling Life in the Theater." *Washington Post* (25 August 1983): E1, 17.

Kauffmann, Stanley. "American Past and Present." *Saturday Review* (November-December 1984): 59.

Kerr, Walter. "Language Alone Isn't Drama." *New York Times* (6 March 1977), B3.

———. "Theater: 'Water Engine.' " *New York Times* (15 January 1978): B3, B25.

King, Kimball. *Ten Modern American Playwrights*. New York: Garland, 1982.

Kissel, Howard. "Edmond." *Women's Wear Daily* (28 October 1982). Reprinted in *NYTCR*, 159.

———. " 'A Life in the Theatre.' " *Women's Wear Daily* (24 October 1977). Reprinted in *NYTCR*, 144.

———. "Mr. Happiness." *Women's Wear Daily* (8 March 1978). Reprinted in *NYTCR*, 336.

———. "The Water Engine." *Women's Wear Daily* (6 January 1978). Reprinted in *NYTCR*, 336.

———. "The Woods." *Women's Wear Daily* (26 April 1979). Reprinted in *NYTCR*, 251.

Klein, Maury. "Omnis Gall Est Divisa in Partes Tres." *1986–87 Humanities Booklet #5: The Dramatic Work as a Historical/Cultural Document*, pp. 3–7. Providence: Rhode Island Committee for the Humanities, Trinity Repertory Company 1986.

Kolin, Philip C. "Mitch and Murray in David Mamet's *Glengarry Glen Ross.*" *Notes on Contemporary Literature* 18 (March 1988): 3–5.

―――. "Revealing Illusions in David Mamet's *The Shawl.*" *Notes on Contemporary Literature* 16 (March 1986): 9–10.

Kroll, Jack. "Golden Age of Radio." *Newsweek* (10 January 1978). Reprinted in *NYTCR,* 337.

―――. "Hearts of Darkness." *Newsweek* (8 November 1982). Reprinted in *NYTCR,* 161–62.

―――. "Mamet's Jackals in Jackets." *Newsweek* (9 April 1984): 109.

―――. "The Muzak Man." *Newsweek* (28 February 1977): 79.

―――. "The Profane Poetry of David Mamet." *Newsweek* (19 October 1987): 85.

―――. "The Terrors of Tinseltown." *Newsweek* (16 May 1988): 82–83.

Lahr, John. "Winners and Losers." *New Society* (29 September 1983): 467–77.

Lape, Bob. Review of *The Water Engine.* WABC-TV, New York. 5 January 1978. Reprinted in *NYTCR,* 338.

Lewis, Patricia, and Terry Browne. "Mamet, David." In *Dictionary of Literary Biography,* 7, pt. 2: 63–70. Edited by John MacNicholas. Detroit: Gale, 1981.

A Life in the Theatre. By David Mamet. Videocassette. Stage version dir. Gerald Gutierrez. WNET Great Performances Series, 1979.

"Madonna Lands Role in Play." *Hattiesburg* (Mississippi) *American* (20 January 1988): 2A.

Maslin, Janet. "Paul Newman Stars in 'The Verdict.'" *New York Times* (8 December 1982): C24.

Mongeon, Joanne. "Something Unholy." *1986–87 Humanities Booklet #5: The Dramatic Work as a Historical/Cultural Document,* pp. 7–10. Providence: Rhode Island Committee for the Humanities, Trinity Repertory Company, 1986.

Mordden, Ethan. "The Me Decade." In *The American Theatre,* pp. 316–18. New York: Oxford University Press, 1981.

Nightingale, Benedict. "Is Mamet the Bard of Modern Immorality?" *New York Times* (1 April 1984): B5.

―――. "Shaping a Distinctive Dramatic Style." *New York Times* (23 February 1984): C21.

Oliver, Edith. "Mamet at the Movies." *New Yorker* (16 May 1988): 95.

―――. "Off Broadway." *New Yorker* (29 October 1979): 81.

―――. "Watered Down." *New Yorker* (16 January 1978): 69–70.

Nuwer, Hank. "A Life in the Theatre: David Mamet." *Rendezvous* 21, no. 1 (Fall 1985): 1–7.

―――. "Two Gentlemen of Chicago: David Mamet and Stuart Gordon." *South Carolina Review* 17 (Spring 1985): 9–20.

Porterfield, Christopher. "David Mamet's Bond of Futility." *Time* (28 February 1977): 54–55.

"Profile of a Writer, Vol. 6: David Mamet." Videocassette. Home Vision, 1987.

Rich, Frank. "Mamet's 'Edmond' at the Provincetown." *New York Times* (28 October 1982). Reprinted in *NYTCR,* 161.

―――. "Theater: A Mamet Play, 'Glengarry Glen Ross.'" *New York Times* (26 March 1984). Reprinted in *NYTCR,* 334.

Rogoff, Gordon. "Albee and Mamet: The War of Words." *Saturday Review* (2 April 1977): 37.

Roudané, Matthew C. "An Interview with David Mamet." *Studies in American Drama, 1945–Present* 1 (1986): 73–81.

———. "Public Issues, Private Tensions: David Mamet's *Glengarry Glen Ross.*" *South Carolina Review* 19 (Fall 1986): 35–47.

Savran, David. "Trading in the American Dream." *American Theatre* (September 1987): 12–18.

Schlueter, June, and Elizabeth Forsyth. "America as Junkshop: The Business Ethic in David Mamet's *American Buffalo.*" *Modern Drama* 26 (December 1983): 492–500.

Sharp, Christopher. "The Water Engine." *Women's Wear Daily* (6 January 1978): Reprinted in *NYTCR*, 336.

Siegel, Joel. Review of *Glengarry Glen Ross.* WABC-TV, New York. 25 March 1984. Reprinted in *NYTCR*, 339.

Simon, John. "Word Power." *New York* (16 May 1988): 106.

Solomon, Alisa. "Production Notes." *Performing Arts Journal* 7, no. 1 (1983): 78–83.

Sterritt, David. "Playwright David Mamet's Impressive Jump to Screen: Strong Script Is Backbone of Paul Newman Film." *Christian Science Monitor* (21 October 1982): 19.

Storey, Robert. "The Making of David Mamet." *Hollins Critic* 16 (October 1979): 1–11.

Stothard, Peter. "*Sexual Perversity in Chicago* and *Duck Variations.*" *Plays and Players* 25 (February 1978): 30–31.

Sullivan, Dan. "Waiting for Mamet." *Los Angeles Times* (27 November 1977): Calendar: 72.

———. "Stage Review: A Young Playwright Who Listens." *Los Angeles Times* (19 January 1977): D1, D10.

TOFT (Theatre on Film and Tape) Collection. Billy Rose Theatre Collection. New York Public Library at Lincoln Center.

Ventimiglia, Peter James. "Recent Trends in American Drama: Michael Cristofer, David Mamet, Albert Innaurato." *Journal of American Culture* 1 (1978): 195–204.

Watt, Douglas. "A Comic Masterpiece by Mamet." *New York Daily News* (21 October 1977). Reprinted in *NYTCR*, 141–42.

———. "'Edmond' Goes Round the Bend." *New York Daily News* (28 October 1982). Reprinted in *NYTCR*, 160.

———. "The Engine' Works Uptown." *New York Daily News* (7 March 1978). Reprinted in *NYTCR*, 333.

Weales, Gerald. "American Theater Watch: 1977–1978." *Georgia Review* 32 (1978): 515–21.

———. "American Theater Watch: 1982–1983." *Georgia Review* 37 (1983): 604–5.

———. "American Theater Watch: 1983–1984." *Georgia Review* 38 (1984): 594–96.

———. "Birthday Mutterings." *Modern Drama* 19 (1976): 417–21.

———. "Decay Is Our Destiny." *American Theatre* (January 1987): 33.

——. "Rewarding Salesmen." *Commonweal* (4 May 1984): 278–79.

——. "Stronger Than Water." *Commonweal* (14 April 1978): 244, 246.

Wetzsteon, Ross. "David Mamet: Remember That Name." *Village Voice* (5 July 1976): 101.

Wilson, Edwin. "Chicago: New Plays, Tradition, Fresh Laughs." *Wall Street Journal* (1 June 1979): 21.

——. "Mamet's 'Engine' Rolls But Where Is It Going?" *Wall Street Journal* (10 March 1978). Reprinted in *NYTCR*, 334.

Winer, Linda. "David Stages a Victory over a Village Goliath." *Chicago Tribune* (15 August 1976): F2.

Witt, Linda. "David Mamet." *People* (12 November 1979): 58–63.

Yakir, Dan. "The Postman's Words." *Film Comment* (March-April 1981): 21–24.

Carson McCullers

(19 FEBRUARY 1917–29 SEPTEMBER 1967)

MARY ANN WILSON

ASSESSMENT OF McCULLERS'S REPUTATION

Carson McCullers wrote two plays: *The Member of the Wedding* and *The Square Root of Wonderful*. The first, based on her 1946 novel of the same name, was a popular, if not a critical, success; it was voted the best play of the 1949–1950 season by the New York Drama Critics Circle. Reviewers praised *Member* for its haunting evocation of adolescence and of the South in 1945. The play solidified a growing trend in the theatre toward the mood play as opposed to the drama of action. Weales calls the meandering plotlessness of the first two acts of *Member* "the most obvious structural innovation in the recent American theatre" (177). In *The Square Root of Wonderful* McCullers attempted playwriting rather than adapting a previous prose work to the stage; it echoes her obsessive themes of loneliness and desire for love and community but was not so successful as *Member* in conveying these feelings to the audience. Critics panned *Square Root* for its stilted dialogue, its confusing shifts from tragic to comic, and its too obvious indebtedness to McCullers's dramatic mentor, Tennessee Williams. Weales called the play "disastrous" (198), and *Member*'s director, Clurman, saw it as a "total dud" (394).

PRIMARY BIBLIOGRAPHY OF McCULLERS'S WORKS

Plays

The Member of the Wedding. New York: New Directions, 1951.
The Square Root of Wonderful. Boston: Houghton-Mifflin, 1958. London: Cresset, 1958.

Interviews

Pollock, Arthur. "Theatre Time—Carson McCullers Talks about Self and First Play." *New York Daily Compass* (7 October 1949): 18.

Breit, Harvey. "Behind the Wedding—Carson McCullers Discusses the Novel She Converted into a Stage Play." *New York Times* (1 January 1950): 2: 3.

Rice, Vernon. "A Little Southern Girl Speaks from a Well of Despair." *New York Post* (29 January 1950): 8.

Morehouse, Ward. "Broadway after Dark—Carson McCullers Cuts Her Own Hair." *New York World-Telegram and the Sun* (31 March 1950): 36.

" 'Quarrels and Cussing'—Playwright Tells of Pangs." *Philadelphia Inquirer* (13 October 1957): I:5.

"The *Marquis* Interviews Carson McCullers." *Marquis* (Lafayette College) (1964): 5–6, 20–23.

White, Terence de Vere. "With Carson McCullers: Terence de Vere White Interviews the American Novelist at the Home of Her Host, John Huston." *Irish Times* (Dublin) (10 April 1967): 12.

Reed, Rex. "Frankie Addams at 50." *New York Times* (16 April 1967): 11: 15.

Critical Essays and Prefaces

"The Russian Realists and Southern Literature." *Decision* (July 1941): 15–19. Collected in *The Mortgaged Heart*.

"How I Began to Write." *Mademoiselle* 27 (September 1948): 256–57. Collected in *The Mortgaged Heart*.

"Loneliness... An American Malady." *This Week* Magazine, *New York Herald Tribune* (19 December 1949): 18–19.

"The Vision Shared." *Theatre Arts* 34 (April 1950): 23–30. Collected in *The Mortgaged Heart*.

"A Personal Preface." Preface to *The Square Root of Wonderful*. Boston: Houghton Mifflin, 1958.

"The Flowering Dream: Notes on Writing." *Esquire* 52 (December 1959): 162–64. Collected in *The Mortgaged Heart*.

"The Dark Brilliance of Edward Albee." *Harper's Bazaar* 97 (January 1963): 98–99. Collected in *The Mortgaged Heart*.

PRODUCTION HISTORY

McCullers's two plays have been produced on Broadway, off-Broadway, at regional theatres across the country, and abroad. A 1950 box office hit, *The Member of the Wedding* had its pre-Broadway opening at the Walnut Theatre in Philadelphia, 22 December 1949, and opened on Broadway 5 January 1950 at the Empire Theatre for 501 performances. Critics praised the production for its evocation of mood, its sensitivity, its depth of characterization, and its excellent cast and direction. *Member* struck critics and American theatregoers as something new, not quite a play but art. Atkinson's comment was typical: "If the drama were nothing but character sketches and action then 'The Member of the Wedding' ... would be a masterpiece" (26).

Shortly after its Broadway success, *Member* appeared as a Columbia Pictures film (1952), closely copying the stage version with the original Broadway cast, directed by Fred Zinnemann and produced by Stanley Kramer. It did not translate well to the screen because of its lack of action, and the unfamiliarity of two of its actors (Brandon de Wilde and Julie Harris) with the conventions of film acting. Tyler declared: "Miss McCullers's story has deteriorated progressively from book to stage to screen" (86).

Member of the Wedding opened in London with an English cast at the Royal Court Theatre on 5 February 1957 and ran for thirty-six performances, closing 9 March. On the whole it was well received. While London newspapers mentioned the play's style and beautiful moments, Shulman called it "a very tender bloom that has failed to stand up to the rigours of transplanting" ("Salute," 10).

The following year, 1958, André Bay and William Hope presented their French adaptation of *Member*, called *Frankie Addams*, in Paris at the Théâtre d'aujourdhui. What American critics had seen as exciting and innovative—its plotlessness, focus on character delineation, and creation of mood—the more classical French critics saw as faults. Falb explains that before the Theatre of the Absurd, the American freedom "from rules, restrictions, and traditions" disturbed French audiences (126). The play closed after three weeks (31 December 1958).

Member saw an extremely successful 1963 revival at the Pasadena Playhouse with Ethel Waters in her original role as Berenice. It ran from 7 February to 8 March 1963, and Evans's biography records that it broke all previous records there. The year 1971 saw a musical version of *Member*, *F. Jasmine Addams*, off-Broadway at the Circle in the Square Theatre in New York. This event marked the first time that the Circle in the Square had produced a musical. Barnes wrote that the play had lost some of its freshness and that its musical adaptation added nothing to the original. In 1975, twenty-five years after its Broadway premiere, the Phoenix Repertory Co. presented *Member* at the Helen Hayes Theatre in New York to lukewarm reviews citing the play's bookishness. Since 1975, there have been no major revivals, though *Member* continues to be produced at regional theatres throughout the country and seems destined to be a favorite with high school, college, and professional acting companies.

McCullers's second play, *The Square Root of Wonderful*, had its pre-Broadway opening at the Walnut Theatre in Philadelphia on 14 October 1957. It opened on Broadway on 30 October at the National and closed after only forty-five performances. Critics invariably compared *Square Root* to its more successful predecessor: it lacked "the tenderness and understanding of *Member*" (Wyatt, 306); and its southern characters seemed "transplanted from other and far better plays about the South," notably McCullers's own (Gibbs, 104). Plagued by last-minute changes in director and by McCullers's own uncertainty about writing for the theatre, *Square Root* began a progressive decline in her critical reputation. On 9 March 1970, *Square Root* opened in London at the Hampstead Theatre Club but closed after twenty-three performances. Almost all the reviews were negative: critics such as Barber and Shulman stressed the "sensitivity" and "delicacy" of her novels, which they thought she sacrificed to the constraints of the stage. *Square Root* confirmed the fact that McCullers was a far better novelist than playwright.

SURVEY OF SECONDARY SOURCES

Bibliographies

The most complete and helpful bibliography to date is by Shapiro, Bryer, and Field. Part I contains a chronological listing and description of all of McCullers's books, plays, and other publications, including all first printings, adaptations of McCullers's works, recordings, and English-language foreign editions. Part II is an annotated listing of books and articles, sections of books, dissertations about McCullers, and reviews of her books and plays. This second section supplements and updates Stewart, Robert S. Phillips, and a more recent (1976) annotated checklist prepared by Kiernan.

The most comprehensive bibliographical essay on McCullers to date is by Carr and Millichap (1983). Their five-part essay annotates the bibliographical materials and supplements the printing history of McCullers's books found in the Shapiro, Bryer, and Field bibliography. It also discusses collections of McCullers materials and discusses in detail the writing of the two major biographies of McCullers (Evans and Carr). A useful addition to the Carr and Millichap essay is Carr's entry in *Contemporary Authors Bibliographical Series: American Novelists*.

Biographies

There are two biographies of Carson McCullers. Evans's is a critical biography written during the author's lifetime and perhaps is less helpful in its factual reliability than in its analyses of the works. Evans devotes an entire chapter to *Member* and also offers a perceptive analysis of *Square Root*, echoing critical response to the play. Carr's more recent and exhaustively researched *The Lonely Hunter* was written without the cooperation of McCullers's literary executors. *The Lonely Hunter* nevertheless contains a staggering amount of useful biographical material, including information concerning how and why the plays came to be written and produced. Carr's book offers little critical examination of McCullers's works but does contain a primary bibliography of her published works.

Of further interest are books written by Graver, Edmonds, and Cook; all contain introductory biographical chapters.

Influences

Perhaps the two most fruitful sources discussing influences on McCullers are Carr's definitive biography and McCullers's own comments in selected essays from *The Mortgaged Heart*. Early in her biography Carr mentions a host of writers whom the young McCullers read and imitated, notably the nineteenth-century Russian realists and her southern contemporaries such as William Faulkner. McCullers herself linked the nineteenth-century Russians and twentieth-century Southern realists (as she called them) in her "The Russian Realists and Southern Literature," citing their preoccupation with death, "the cheapness of human life" (252) and their ironic juxtaposition of the tragic and the comic. Gassner similarly links McCullers's dramas to the Chekhovian tradition of the plotless semi-comic, semi-tragic play (79). Carr's biography stresses a later influence on McCullers's playwriting in her friendship with Tennessee Williams and his encouraging her to adapt *Member* for the stage.

Certainly the most obvious influence McCullers's works have had is on Albee, who adapted her novella *Ballad of the Sad Café* for the stage. Bigsby offers a perceptive discussion of the reasons why Albee was drawn to McCullers's novella, and Missey offers further demonstration of McCullers's lingering influence in Albee's *The Zoo Story*.

General Studies

Most studies of American drama since 1945 devote only a few sentences to McCullers who, after all, is known and considered principally as a writer of fiction. Overviews of American drama that do cite her focus on *Member* and lament *Square Root* as an unfortunate attempt. Weales, who offers useful commentary on how *Member* differs from its prose fiction prototype and why he considers it a successful adaptation, places McCullers in the context of other novelists whose works have been adapted for the stage, a group that includes Truman Capote, Eudora Welty, and Henry James. Another piece dealing with the transition from novelist to playwright is by L. Phillips, whose interest is in why these successful novelists felt the need to turn to drama to express their artistic concerns.

Some thematic and generic studies of American drama since 1945 have also included consideration of Carson McCullers. A thematic study by Dusenbury amplifies McCullers's obsession with family and belonging in its discussion of *Member of the Wedding* and Frankie's isolation from family and society. Kiernan's *American Writing since 1945* provides brief but incisive commentary on postwar fiction, drama, and poetry, positing that *Member of the Wedding* is a "successful play that should have been a failure" (77).

Most feminist studies in the 1970s deal with McCullers as novelist, but a notable exception is Olauson, who attempts to show the range of women characters in American drama over the forty-year period 1930–1970. She discusses Frankie in *Member* as a type of awkward child on the threshold of womanhood and discovery of the world.

Analyses of Individual Plays

Although most secondary sources on McCullers's dramas treat them in the context of her other works, two articles deal with *Member of the Wedding* exclusively. Dedmond discusses the circumstances surrounding the writing of *Member*, points to the loose structure of the dramatic version, and claims, along with most other critics, that the third act is inferior to the rest. Dedmond concludes that whatever structural defects the play had were more than compensated for by McCullers's "ability to dramatize the abstract values of the play" (52).

Giannetti, who provides insights into the movie version and contrasts it to both the novel and the play, calls *Member* "one of the neglected minor masterpieces of the American cinema" (28). He reiterates McCullers's obsession with the themes of loneliness, entrapment, and isolation and ascribes the film's success to its closely following the stage version. Giannetti's in-depth analysis of cinematic techniques throws new light on the dramatic qualities in McCullers's story.

FUTURE RESEARCH OPPORTUNITIES

The distressing uniformity of McCullers criticism points to several areas of research that have been neglected. Her association with Tennessee Williams deserves fuller investigation than it has yet received, especially the extent to which she borrowed or adapted materials from such dramas as *The Glass Menagerie*. Another area for further investigation is McCullers's treatment of the family in her two plays. Relationships shift, dissolve, and sometimes blossom in McCullers's protean definition of family, linking her to contemporary women writers such as Alice Walker,

Toni Morrison, or Gail Godwin. Finally, a detailed feminist interpretation of the complex female characters in McCullers's dramas and their relationships with each other would shed light on McCullers's own ambivalent sexuality and her essentially androgynous vision.

SECONDARY SOURCES

Atkinson, Brooks. "At the Theatre." *New York Times* (6 January 1950): 26.

Barber, John. "Lost Chances of Play by Delicate Writer." *Daily Telegraph* (London, 10 March 1970): 14.

Barnes, Clive. "Stage: Musical Based on McCullers." *New York Times* (28 October 1971): 49.

Bigsby, C. W. E. "Edward Albee's Georgia Ballad." *Twentieth Century Literature* 13 (January 1968): 229–36.

Carr, Virginia Spencer. "Carson McCullers." In *Contemporary Authors Bibliographical Series: American Novelists*, vol. 1. Edited by Matthew Bruccoli and C. E. Frazer Clark, Jr. Detroit: Gale Research, 1986.

———. *The Lonely Heart: A Biography of Carson McCullers*. Garden City, N.Y.: Doubleday, 1975.

———, and Joseph Millichap. "Carson McCullers." In *American Women Writers: Bibliographical Essays*. Edited by Maurice Duke, Jackson R. Bryer, and M. Thomas Inge. Westport, Conn.: Greenwood, 1983.

Clurman, Harold. "Theatre." *Nation* (23 November 1957): 394.

Cook, Richard. *Carson McCullers*. New York: Ungar, 1975.

Dedmond, Francis. "Doing Her Own Thing: Carson McCullers's Dramatization of 'The Member of the Wedding.' " *South Atlantic Bulletin* 40 (May 1975): 47–52.

Dusenbury, Winifred. "An Unhappy Family." In her *The Theme of Loneliness in Modern American Drama*, pp. 57–85. Gainesville: University of Florida Press, 1960.

Edmonds, Dale. *Carson McCullers*. Austin, Tex.: Steck-Vaughn, 1969.

Evans, Oliver. *The Ballad of Carson McCullers*. New York: Coward-McCann, 1966.

Falb, Lewis. *American Drama in Paris 1945–1970: A Study of Its Critical Reception*. Chapel Hill: University of North Carolina Press, 1973.

Gassner, John. *The Theatre in Our Times: A Survey of the Men, Materials and Movements in the Modern Theatre*. New York: Crown, 1954.

Giannetti, Louis D. *"The Member of the Wedding." Literature/Film Quarterly* 4 (Winter 1976): 28–38.

Gibbs, Wolcott. "The Theatre: Music and Words." *New Yorker* (9 November 1957): 103–5.

Graver, Lawrence. *Carson McCullers*. St. Paul: University of Minnesota Press, 1969.

Kiernan, Robert. *American Writers Since 1945: A Critical Survey*. New York: Ungar, 1983.

———. *Katharine Anne Porter and Carson McCullers: A Reference Guide*. Boston: G. K. Hall, 1976.

Missey, James. "A McCullers Influence on Albee's *The Zoo Story.*" *American Notes and Queries* 13 (April 1975): 121–23.

Olauson, Judith. *The American Woman Playwright: A View of Criticism and Characterization.* New York: Whitson, 1981.

Phillips, Louis. "The Novelist as Playwright: Baldwin, McCullers, and Bellow." In *Modern American Drama: Essays in Criticism.* Edited by William E. Taylor. Deland, Fla.: Everett/Edwards, 1968.

Phillips, Robert S. "Carson McCullers 1956–1964: A Selected Checklist." *Bulletin of Bibliography* 24 (September-December 1964): 113–16.

Shapiro, Adrian, Jackson R. Bryer, and Kathleen Field. *Carson McCullers: A Descriptive Listing and Annotated Bibliography of Criticism.* New York: Garland, 1980.

Shulman, Milton. "Darn Agonizing 'Way down South." *London Evening Standard* (10 March 1970): 17.

———. "Salute for a Valiant Failure." *London Evening Standard* (6 February 1957): 10.

Smith, Margarita G., ed. *The Mortgaged Heart.* Boston: Houghton Mifflin, 1971.

Stewart, Stanley. "Carson McCullers 1940–1956: A Selected Checklist." *Bulletin of Bibliography* 22 (January-April 1959): 182–85.

Tyler, Parker. "Toulouse-Ferrer." *Theatre Arts* 37 (March 1953): 84–89.

Weales, Gerald. *American Drama since World War II.* New York: Harcourt Brace, 1962.

Wyatt, Euphemia Van Rensselaer. "Theatre." *Catholic World* 185 (January 1958): 304–8.

Terrence McNally

(3 NOVEMBER 1939–   )

GERALDO U. DE SOUSA

ASSESSMENT OF McNALLY'S REPUTATION

Terrence McNally established his reputation as a major American comic writer in the 1968–1969 season when he had seven plays produced on Broadway and off-Broadway. He is America's Ben Jonson, a talented satiric writer who examines the faults, delusions, and shibboleths of society. With a bleak outlook on life and a sharp sense of humor, which is not always appreciated by his critics, McNally has been described as "an angry and sometimes vicious observer of personality types" (Kanfer, 373). His subjects include self-delusion, violence and cruelty, the Vietnam War, and popular culture. His early characters exhibit much anger and frustration at what seems to be a schizophrenic society, but his more recent work reveals exuberance and lyricism—what one critic has referred to as "a wondrous joy" (Ballet, 537). As a social satirist, McNally is undoubtedly "one of the most original and brilliant of contemporary playwrights" (Sanders, 376).

PRIMARY BIBLIOGRAPHY OF McNALLY'S WORKS

Plays

The Roller Coaster. Columbia Review 40 (Spring 1960): 42–60.
The Lady of the Camellias (adaptation of Giles Cooper play based on play by Dumas fils. New York, 1963).
And Things That Go Bump in the Night. In *Playwrights for Tomorrow: A Collection of Plays*, 1: 159–274. Edited by Arthur H. Ballet. Minneapolis: University of Minnesota Press, 1966. New York: Dramatists Play Service, 1966.

Here's Where I Belong, based on John Steinbeck's *East of Eden*. Book by Terrence
     McNally. Music by Robert Waldman. First produced on Broadway at Billy
     Rose Theatre, 20 February 1968.
Tour. In *Collision Course*, pp. 85–97. Edited by Edward Parone. New York: Ran-
     dom House, 1968.
Bringing It All Back Home (produced New Haven, 1969; New York, 1972).
Apple Pie. New York: Dramatists Play Service, 1969. Includes three one-act plays:
     Apple Pie, Next, Botticelli, and *Tour*.
Sweet Eros, Next, and Other Plays. New York: Random House: 1969. Includes
     Botticelli, Next, ¡ Cuba Si! Sweet Eros, and *Witness*.
Sweet Eros. In *Off-Broadway Plays 2*. London: Penguin, 1972.
Let It Bleed (produced New York, 1972).
Noon. In *Morning, Noon and Night*. With Israel Horovitz and Leonard Melfi. New
     York: Random House, 1969.
Three Plays: ¡ Cuba Si! Bringing It All Back Home, Last Gasps. New York: Dramatists
     Play Service, 1970.
Let It Bleed. (produced New York, 1972).
Botticelli. In *Off-Broadway Plays 2*. London: Penguin, 1972.
Where Has Tommy Flowers Gone? New York: Dramatists Play Service, 1972.
Whiskey. New York: Dramatists Play Service, 1973.
Bad Habits: Ravenswood and Dunelawn. New York: Dramatists Play Service, 1974.
     Garden City, N.Y.: Nelson Doubleday, 1974.
Tubs (produced New York, 1974).
The Ritz and Other Plays. New York: Dodd, Mead, 1976. Includes *Bad Habits,
     Where Has Tommy Flowers Gone?* "...*And Things That Go Bump in the Night*,"
     Whiskey, and *Bringing It All Back Home*.
Broadway, Broadway (produced Philadelphia, 1978).
It's Only a Play (produced New York, 1982–83).
The Lisbon Traviata (produced New York, 1985).
Frankie and Johnny in the Claire de Lune (produced New York, 1987).

Screenplays

Noon. 1970.
The Ritz. Warner Bros., 1976.

Television Plays

Apple Pie. 1966.
Botticelli. 1968.
Last Gasps. 1969.
Adaptation of John Cheever's *The Five Forty-Eight*. PBS, 1979.
Mama Malone. CBS, 1984.

Radio Plays

The Lisbon Traviata. 1979.

Essays

"Theatre Isn't All on Broadway." *New York Times* (28 April 1974): 2:1.
"*The Ritz* on Stage and Screen." *Dramatists Guild Quarterly* 14, No. 1 (Spring 1977), 26: 32–36.

Interviews

"Three Young Playwrights Talk Shop." *New York Times* (10 December 1968): 54.
"Humor: A Cool Discussion." *Dramatists Guild Quarterly*, 14, No. 4 (Winter 1978): 8–25. (Discussion with Russell Baker, Jules Feiffer, Bruce Jay Friedman, etc.)
"Sex and the Theater: Doing What Comes Naturally." *Dramatists Guild Quarterly* 17, no. 3 (1980): 22–33. (Symposium with Robert Anderson, Terrence McNally, etc.)
"Landmark Symposium: *Tea and Sympathy*." *Dramatists Guild Quarterly* 19, no. 4 (1983): 11–27. (Discussion between McNally, Elia Kazan, etc.)
"Edward Albee in Conversation With Terrence McNally," *Dramatists Guild Quarterly* 22 (Summer 1985): 12–23.
"Frank Rich in Conversation With Terrence McNally." *Dramatists Guild Quarterly* 24 (Autumn 1987): 11–29.

PRODUCTION HISTORY

McNally's plays have been produced on Broadway and off-Broadway and at a number of regional theatres. His first Broadway credit, *The Lady of the Camellias*, adapted from Giles Cooper's play based on Alexandre Dumas, opened on 20 March 1963 at the Winter Garden, New York, running for thirteen performances (Robins and Downing, 74). Although short-lived, this production, staged and designed by Franco Zeffirelli, introduced McNally to Broadway. Nadel praised the dialogue, which "seems spontaneous, Gallic, passionate and hearty" (Review of *The Lady*, 306). While commending this production for the acting, settings, and costumes, Watts, Jr., thought that "the narrative sometimes creaks, and the creakiness threatens to get dangerously in the way" ("Two on the Aisle," 307). Taubman called this production "inept and the writing needlessly explicit and coarse" ("Zeffirelli's," 306).

McNally's next play, *And Things That Go Bump in the Night*, was produced 4–7 February 1964 at the Tyrone Guthrie Theatre, Minneapolis; and on 26 April 1965 it opened at the Royale Theatre, New York, for sixteen performances staged by Michael Cacoyannis. The Minneapolis show caused a scandal when the University of Minnesota censored the play "on grounds that it was offensive to public taste" (Robins and Downing, 75), but McNally decided to go ahead with the production. The producer Theodore Mann, who was in the audience on opening night, decided to take the play to New York (75). The production at the Royale Theatre was essentially a failure (Taubman, "Theater," 342; Nadel, "Dead End at the Royale," 343; Chapman, " 'Things that Go Bump' Weirdest," 343). It was condemned "for its violence, dismal vision of mankind, and its bizarre action" (Robins and Downing, 75). Hewes, however, praised McNally's talent for "imagery and ambitiousness of purpose" (" 'Ello, Tommy," 24).

McNally's next play, *Tour*, was much better received than *Things That Go Bump*. It was produced as part of *The Scene*, an ensemble of eleven plays by various playwrights, in November 1967 at the Mark Taper Forum, Los Angeles. *Tour* was again staged as part of *Collision Course*, an ensemble of several one-act plays, on 8 May 1968 at the Cafe Au Go Go, New York, running for eighty performances, and at the Berkshire Theatre Festival on 7 August 1968 (Robins and Downing, 74).

Next, the most successful McNally play, was first presented at the White Barn Theatre, Westport, Connecticut, on 13 August 1967; it was also seen on Channel 13, New York City. A revised version of this play was staged at the Berkshire Theatre Festival, Stockbridge, Massachusetts, in 1968. Later this version was produced at the Greenwich Mews Theatre, New York, on 10 February 1969, running for 707 performances (Robins and Downing, 74). Subsequently the play was also staged on a double bill with *Sweet Eros* at the Open Space Theatre, London, 13 July 1971 (Herbert, 450–51) and at the Drama Ensemble Co. in April 1976 (Salem, 342). Barnes considered the two plays "funny, provocative and, in their own way, touching" ("Theater: Off Broadway," 269–70). Gottfried saw a welcome shift in McNally's career away from *Things that Go Bump* to a more universally appealing comedy (" 'Adaptation'—'Next,' " 270).

Botticelli, first produced by Channel 13 in New York City on 14–15 March 1968, was staged at the Berkshire Theatre Festival on 7 August 1968 and at the Mark Taper Forum, Los Angeles on 7 October 1969 (Robins and Downing, 74), and at the Old Post Office, Easthampton, New York, in 1971.

Sweet Eros and *Witness* were presented as a double bill on 21 November 1968 at the Gramercy Arts Theatre, New York, running for seventy-eight performances (Robins and Downing, 74). *Sweet Eros* was also presented by the Theatre-in-Progress Workshop, Berkshire Theatre Festival, 22 July 1968, and by the Act IV Theatre on 30 July 1968, at the Gifford House, Provincetown, Massachusetts. This last production was invited to the First International Experimental Theatre Festival at Brandeis University, Waltham, Massachusetts, on 20 August 1968. *Witness* was presented by Albee-Barr-Wilder on 4 June 1968 at the Playwrights Unit, New York City. *Sweet Eros* created a sensation off-Broadway because it was one of the first modern plays to feature total nudity, but most critics considered the double bill almost a failure. Many thought that what redeemed the production was James Coco's superior performance as a window washer in *Witness* (Watts, "Disappointing News," 135; Gottfried, "Sweet Eros—Witness," 136; O'Conner, 136; Barnes, "Common Threads," 137; Oliver, "Support Mental Health," 140–42; Funke, 34).

Noon was staged as part of an ensemble, entitled *Morning, Noon and Night*, on 28 November 1968 on Broadway at Henry Miller's Theatre, New York, running for fifty-two performances (Robins and Downing, 74), and off-off-Broadway (Direct Theater) on 14 April 1976 (Salem, 342).

¡Cuba Si! was produced by the Act IV Theatre on 16 July 1968 at the Gifford House, Provincetown, Massachusetts; on 9–10 December 1968, it was presented off-Broadway by Lucille Lortel at Theatre de Lys, New York City.

Bringing It All Back Home was produced in New Haven, Connecticut, in 1969 and at the off-Broadway La Mama Experimental Theatre Club, New York (Robins and Downing, 74).

Bad Habits: Ravenswood and Dunelawn, a thematically unified double bill, was first presented at the John Drew Theatre, East Hampton, New York, in 1971; subsequently it was produced on 4 February 1974 off-Broadway at Astor Place Theatre and then transferred 5 May 1974 to Broadway's Booth Theatre, running for 126 performances (Robins and Downing, 74). In his review of the Astor Place Theatre production, Watts praised McNally's "gift for laughter" ("Doctors and Their Patients," 373). Kanfer noted that this double bill was one of McNally's masterpieces (373). Watt wrote that though funny, the plays also had macabre aspects ("Eight with 'Bad Habits,' " 374). Wilson noted McNally's "unmistakable gift for caricature" ("Doctor Pepper," 374). Gottfried remarked that the two plays are "extended skits" and present "cardboard characters and mechanical construction" ("Bad Habits," 375). In his review of the Booth Theatre production, Gussow praised the "tonic" quality of the plays' satire and their "spontaneity and modesty" ("McNally's 'Bad Habits,' " 226). Oliver noted that McNally "continues to be a source of joy" ("Bad Habits," 52).

McNally's very successful *Where Has Tommy Flowers Gone?* was first produced in New Haven at the Yale Repertory Theatre on 7 January 1971 and was subsequently staged on 11 August 1971 at the Berkshire Theatre Festival. This same production opened on 7 October 1971 at the Eastside Playhouse, New York, running for seventy-eight performances (Robins and Downing, 74). Writing of the Yale performance, Kerr praised Robert Drivas as Tommy Flowers, especially Drivas's impersonation of Marilyn Monroe in heaven, but on the whole Kerr thought that McNally was "unwilling to distinguish between random vaudeville and apt parody" ("Tommy's Bag," 12). Writing about the

Eastside Playhouse production, which used three large television screens, Kerr deemed the play "singularly empty, empty above all of a character named Tommy Flowers" and strongly condemned the playwright for his inability "to put a finger on a time, a place, a person or a quality" and for indulging in "grossly easy vaudeville routines" ("Go On, Relax," 136). Watt compared the play to a "screenplay": the Eastside Playhouse production "can't quite make up its mind whether it's a movie or a play" (" 'Tommy Flowers,' " 213). Watts wrote that this production had "some amusing scenes and a disarming air of geniality. But it also has several episodes of excessive tastelessness and toward the end it becomes almost unbearably flat and tiresome" ("Adventures," 214). Heldman observed that this play was "sardonic, funny, exuberantly theatrical," adding that "it is not so much a play as a vaudeville, a series of loosely connected vignettes, a multimedia show-and-tell of what makes Tommy Flowers run" (214). Oliver, on the other hand, noted that the play has a "hollow center" (*"Tommy Flowers,"* 101).

Let It Bleed was produced as part of *City Stops* at the Bronx Community College, New York, on 8 May 1972 (Robins and Downing, 74).

Whiskey was presented on 29 April 1973 at the Theatre at St. Clement's, New York, running for seven performances (Robins and Downing, 74). In his review, Gussow wrote: "Actually *Whiskey* is not so much a play as an extended skein of caricatured sketches, loosely stitched together and infiltrated with Western ballads" ("Stage," 24). Oliver considered *Whiskey* one of McNally's strongest plays and "a very inventive and touching one, although it runs, I'd say, about a third too long" ("Whiskey," 69).

The Tubs, later revised as *The Ritz*, was originally staged at the Yale University Theatre, New Haven, in January 1974. Under the title of *The Ritz*, it was presented on 20 January 1975 on Broadway at the Longacre Theatre, running for nearly 400 performances (Robins and Downing, 74). Gussow called the play "a spirited Feydeauvian farce about a combination health and nightclub—a cousin of the Continental Baths," but occasionally "the play falters . . . whenever the author begins to take his comedy seriously" (" 'The Tubs,' " 28). The Longacre Theatre production with Rita Moreno as the *chanteuse* Googie Gomez received mixed reviews. Barnes thought that though amusing, the play did not have much of a plot, and he also suspected that "lurking beneath Mr. McNally's sunnyside-up raunchiness, there is, one suspects, something darker, deeper and more serious" ("The Ritz," 40). Kerr called it a comedy of errors that makes "merriment out of little more than the multiplication tables," and he said that the play relied too much on four-letter words ("Albee's Unwritten Part," 5). Watt thought that McNally made a "desperate attempt to stretch out one joke, the spectacle of a straight in gay company, for a couple of hours"; moreover, he concluded that though genuinely funny, *The Ritz* was "both trying and a bit nasty"

("Being Gay," 377). Kissel, however, thought it was "a first-rate farce" (" 'The Ritz.' " 378). Kalem noted a change in McNally's career: "In *The Ritz*, McNally abandons the idiosyncratic comic vision he brought to *Bad Habits* in favor of old vaudeville and burlesque routines" ("Imps of the Perverse," 378). The movie (Warner Bros, 1976) received negative reviews (see Eder, C12; Canby, 2:13).

Broadway, Broadway opened 4 September 1978 at the Forrest Theatre in Philadelphia and closed during its pre-Broadway tryout there on 16 September 1978 (Willis, 35:159; Buckley, 13; Delatiner, 14). This play was later revised and presented under the title *It's Only a Play* at the Actors and Directors Theater on 26 November 1982. Rich thought that it was "an uncompromising in-joke about current personalities and fashions in the Broadway theater," and that may be the reason why the earlier version was not successful ("Funny Valentine," 3).

The musical *The Rink*, the book written by McNally and music by Fred Ebb, starring Chita Rivera and Liza Minelli, opened at the Martin Beck Theater on 9 February 1984 and closed on 4 August 1984 after 204 performances and 29 previews (Willis, 40:19). Rich considered the production "static": "Mr. McNally is a smart and witty playwright, but you'd never know it from this synthetic effort. His dialogue is banal, and his characters are ciphers" ("Theater: 'The Rink,' " 374). Watt thought it was a "mishmash" (" 'Rink' Glides and Tumbles," 375). Kissel commented on McNally's "nasty book"—"an unusually sordid chapter in the history of the Broadway musical" (" 'The Rink,' " 375–76). Barnes decided that the show was neither well envisioned nor well produced, but he found much to enjoy in it ("Chita and Liza," 376–77). And Wilson found the clichés annoying and the subject of the show as a whole a bit outdated ("A Turkey on Skates," 377).

SURVEY OF SECONDARY SOURCES

Bibliographies

No full-length bibliography on McNally has been compiled. There are partial bibliographies on McNally's works (and/or reviews of his plays) in Bradish (359–60); Ballet (536–37); Robins and Downing (74–82), Falco (1226–33), Straub (457–58), O'Donnell (363); Harris (332–33), Salem (341–43), and Eddleman (*American Drama Criticism*, 233–34; and *Supplement I*, 110).

Biographies

Short biographical sketches are available in Freedman (229–331), O'Donnell (363), Anderson et al. (198–99), Miller (301), Ballet (536–37),

Robins and Downing (74–82), Falco (1226–1233), Straub (457–58), and
Bradish (359). A very helpful and recent article, which includes many
comments from McNally's interviews, appears in *Current Biography*
(March 1988).

Influences

Although many reviewers and critics have noted several sources of
influence on McNally's work, no full-length study of influence exists.
Falco notes, for example, that McNally "draws on experimental techniques pioneered by Samuel Beckett and Bertolt Brecht" (1227). Other
critics have noted McNally's use of burlesque techniques (Straub, 457),
vaudeville routines and picaresque novel elements (Kalem, "Holden
Caulfield's Return," 215), and television, movie, and operatic techniques
(Heldman, 214). Emphasizing this last "special dimension" of McNally's
work, Bradish points to "the influence of his well known and erudite
appreciation of opera, with its duets, trios, ensembles, its disguises, its
mistaken identities, and its frequent preoccupations with the possibilities
of *la maledizione*" (360).

General Studies

The best and most detailed general studies of McNally are Robins and
Downing, Falco, Straub, and Ballet. These sources also provide brief
analyses of individual plays.

Analyses of Individual Plays

Robins and Downing discuss *And Things That Go Bump, Tour, Next,
Botticelli, Witness, Noon, ¡Cuba Si! Bringing It All Back Home, Where Has
Tommy Flowers Gone? Bad Habits, Whiskey*, and *The Ritz* (2: 74–82). Falco's
discussion is limited to *Tommy Flowers, Next, ¡Cuba Si!* and *The Ritz* (1229–
33). Straub briefly summarizes the reviews of several plays (457–58). For
more detailed discussions of each play, the reader would have to turn
to reviews of individual productions.

FUTURE RESEARCH OPPORTUNITIES

Many research opportunities remain open for scholars and students of
McNally's drama, which needs to be assessed for its place in the context
of developments in contemporary drama and in the satiric tradition. His
Bad Habits, for example, shows clear affinity to Ben Jonson's *The Alchemist*,
and some of the other comedies reveal a kinship to the comedies of
Terence and Plautus. Other possible topics of research are McNally's

indebtedness to the Theatre of the Absurd, vaudeville, and opera, the structure of the plays, and their allegorical nature. Another area of research is McNally's portrayal of the effects of the Vietnam War on American life. Finally it would be helpful to know more of McNally's importance as a officer-member of the Dramatists Guild, an organization he has served well for many years.

SECONDARY SOURCES

Anderson, Michael et al., eds. *Crowell's Handbook of Contemporary Drama*. New York: Thomas Y. Crowell Company, 1971.

Andrews, Nigel. "*Sweet Eros/Next*." *Plays and Players* 18, no. 12 (September 1971): 47–48.

Ballet, Arthur H. "McNally." In *Contemporary Dramatists*, 2d ed., pp. 536–38. Edited by James Vinson. London: St. James Press; New York: St. Martin's Press, 1977.

Barnes, Clive. "Chita and Liza Set the Wheels in Motion in 'Rink.' " *New York Post* (10 February 1984). Reprinted in *New York Theatre Critics' Reviews* (1984): 376–77.

———. "Common Threads Run through the Plays." *New York Times* (22 November 1968). Reprinted in *New York Theatre Critics' Reviews* (1968): 137.

———. "Making the Most of 'Ritz' Steam Bath." *New York Times* (21 January 1975): 40. Reprinted in *New York Theatre Critics' Reviews* (1975): 377.

———. Review of *Adaptation—Next*. *New York Times* (12 March 1970): 46.

———. Review of *The Ritz*. *New York Times* (21 January 1975): 40.

———. "Theater: McNally's 'Tommy Flowers.' " *New York Times* (8 October 1971): 32.

———. "Theater: Off Broadway Brings a Happy Double Bill." *New York Times* (11 February 1969). Reprinted in *New York Theatre Critics' Reviews* (1969): 269.

———. "Theater: A Reappraisal." *New York Times* (12 March 1970): 46.

———. "Theater: 'Sweet Eros' and 'Witness.' " *New York Times* (22 November 1968): 38.

Buckley, Tom. " 'Broadway, Broadway' Gets Under Way on East 73d Street." *New York Times* (6 July 1978): C13.

Bradish, Gaynor. "Terrence McNally." In *Contemporary Dramatists*. 4th ed., pp. 359–60. Edited by D. L. Kirkpatrick. Chicago: St. James Press, 1988.

Canby, Vincent. "The Daze and Nights of a Movie Critic." *New York Times* (7 November 1976): 2:13. Reprinted in *New York Times Film Reviews* (1975–1976): 281–82.

Chapman, John. Review of *The Lady of the Camellias*. *New York Daily News*. Reprinted in *New York Theatre Critics' Reviews* (1963): 305.

———. " 'Things That Go Bump' Weirdest." *Daily News* (27 April 1965). Reprinted in *New York Theatre Critics' Reviews* (1965): 343.

Clurman, Harold. "Theatre." *Nation* (16 December 1968): 665.

———. "Theatre." *Nation* (3 March 1969): 281–82.

Coleman, John. "Camille Struggles But Doesn't Live." *New York Mirror* (1 April 1963). Reprinted in *New York Theatre Critics' Reviews* (1963): 307.

Delatiner, Barbara. "McNally: 'If a Play Goes Well...'" *New York Times* (30 July 1978): 21:14.

Eddleman, Floyd Eugene, ed. *American Drama Criticism: Interpretations 1890–1977.* 2d ed. Hamden, Conn.: Shoe String Press, 1979.

———. *American Drama Criticism: Supplement I to the Second Edition.* Hamden, Conn.: Shoe String Press, 1984.

Eder, Richard. Review of *The Ritz* (movie). *New York Times* (13 August 1976): C12. Reprinted in *New York Times Film Reviews* (1975–1976): 241.

Falco, Jane. "Terrence McNally." In *Critical Survey of Drama: English Language Series*, pp. 1226–33. Edited by Frank N. Magill. Englewood Cliffs, N.J.: Salem Press, 1985.

Flatley, Guy. "He Won't Kick His 'Bad Habits.'" *New York Times* (10 March 1974): 2:1.

Freedman, Samuel G. "For McNally, a New Show and an Old Struggle." In *New York Times Biographical Service* 15, no. 1 (January 1984): 229–31.

Funke, Lewis. "Candy Store Goes Public." *New York Times* (24 November 1968): 2:34.

Gottfried, Martin. "'Adaptation'—'Next.'" *Women's Wear Daily* (11 February 1969). Reprinted in *New York Theatre Critics' Reviews* (1969): 270.

———. "'Bad Habits.'" *Women's Wear Daily* (6 February 1974). Reprinted in *New York Theatre Critics' Reviews* (1974): 375.

———. "'Sweet Eros'—'Witness.'" *Women's Wear Daily* (22 November 1968). Reprinted in *New York Theatre Critics' Reviews* (1968): 136.

———. "Throwing in the Towel." *New York Post* (21 January 1975). Reprinted in *New York Theatre Critics' Reviews* (1975): 376.

———. "'Where Has Tommy Flowers Gone.'" *Women's Wear Daily* (12 October 1971). Reprinted in *New York Theatre Critics' Reviews* (1971): 215.

Gussow, Mel. "McNally's 'Bad Habits' Moves to the Booth." *New York Times* (6 May 1974): 45. Reprinted in *New York Times Theater Reviews* (1973–1974): 226.

———. "Stage: 'Whiskey' Opens: Comedy by McNally Is at St. Clements." *New York Times* (30 April 1973): 24. Reprinted in *New York Times Theater Reviews* (1973–1974): 65.

———. "'The Tubs.'" *New York Times* (7 January 1974): 28. Reprinted in *New York Times Theater Reviews* (1973–1974): 167–68.

Harris, Richard H. *Modern Drama in America and England, 1950–1970: A Guide to Information Sources.* Detroit: Gale Research Company, 1982, 332–33.

Heldman, Irma Pascal. "'Tommy Flowers' as a Comic Find." *Wall Street Journal* (11 October 1971). Reprinted in *New York Theatre Critics' Reviews* (1971): 214.

Herbert, Ian, et al. "McNally, Terrence." In *Who's Who in the Theatre*, 7th ed. pp. 450–51. Detroit: Gale Research Company, 1981.

Hewes, Henry. "'Ello, Tommy." *Saturday Review* (15 May 1965): 24.

———. "Present Mirth." *Saturday Review* (1 March 1969): 45.

Kalem, T. E. "Holden Caulfield's Return." Review of *Tommy Flowers. Time* (18 October 1971). Reprinted in *New York Theatre Critics' Reviews* (1971): 215.

———. "Imps of the Perverse: *The Ritz.*" *Time* (3 February 1975). Reprinted in *New York Theatre Critics' Reviews* (1975): 378.

Kanfer, Stefan. "Funny Farm." Review of *Bad Habits. Time* (18 February 1974). Reprinted in *New York Theatre Critics' Reviews* (1974): 373.

Kerr, Walter, "Albee's Unwritten Part; McNally's Missing Joke." Review of *The Ritz. New York Times* (2 February 1975): II:5. Reprinted in *New York Times Theater Reviews* (1975–1976): 17–18.

———. "Elaine May Just Kill You." Review of *Next. Sunday Times* (23 February 1969): 2:5. Reprinted in *New York Theatre Critics' Reviews* (1969): 271.

———. "Go On, Relax, You May Get Kissed." *New York Times* (17 October 1971): 2:1. Reprinted in *New York Times Theater Reviews* (1971–1972): 135–36.

———. Review of *Noon. New York Times* (8 December 1968): 2:5.

———. "Tommy's Bag Is Full of Bombs (and Clichés)." *New York Times* (24 January 1971): II:3. Reprinted in *New York Times Theater Reviews* (1971–1972): 12.

Kissel, Howard. " 'The Rink.' " *Women's Wear Daily* (10 February 1984). Reprinted in *New York Theatre Critics' Reviews* (1984): 375–76.

———. " 'The Ritz.' " *Women's Wear Daily* (21 January 1975). Reprinted in *New York Theatre Critics' Reviews* (1975): 378.

Kroll, Jack. "Please Omit Flowers." *Newsweek* (18 October 1971). Reprinted in *New York Theatre Critics' Reviews* (1971): 215.

McLain, John. "A Bumpy Road to Bafflement." *Journal American* (27 April 1965). Reprinted in *New York Theatre Critics' Reviews* (1965): 341.

Miller, Terry. "McNally." In *McGraw-Hill Encyclopedia of World Drama*, 2d ed., p. 301. Edited by Stanley Hochman. New York: McGraw-Hill, 1984.

Nadel, Norman. Review of *The Lady of the Camellias. New York World-Telegram* and *The Sun.* Reprinted in *New York Theatre Critics' Reviews* (1963): 306–7.

———. " 'Things That Go Bump' Hits Dead End at the Royale." *New York World-Telegram and the Sun,* (27 April 1965). Reprinted in *New York Theatre Critics' Reviews* (1965): 343.

O'Conner, John J. "McNally Time." *Wall Street Journal* (4 December 1968). Reprinted in *New York Theatre Critics' Reviews* (1968): 136.

O'Donnell, Monica M., ed. *Contemporary Theatre, Film, and Television,* 1: 363. Detroit: Gale Research Company, 1984.

Oliver, Edith. Review of *Bad Habits. New Yorker* 49 (18 February 1974): 52.

———. Review of *Tommy Flowers. New Yorker* 47 (16 October 1971): 101.

———. Review of *Whiskey. New Yorker* 49 (12 May 1973): 69.

———. "Support Mental Health." *New Yorker* 44 (7 December 1968): 140–42.

Pasolli, Robert. "Theatre." *Nation* 206 (10 June 1968): 772–74.

Rich, Frank. "Funny Valentine." *New York Times* (26 November 1982). Reprinted in *New York Times Theater Reviews* (1982): 426–27.

———. "Theater: 'The Rink.' " *New York Times* (10 February 1984). Reprinted in *New York Theatre Critics' Reviews* (1984): 374.

Robins, William Mattathias, and Craig L. Downing. "Terrence McNally." In *Twentieth-Century American Dramatists*, pp. 74–82. Edited by John Mac-Nicholas. Detroit: Bruccoli Clark, 1981.

Salem, James M. *A Guide to Critical Reviews: Part I: American Drama, 1909–1982.* 3d ed. Metuchen, N.J.: London: Scarecrow Press, 1984.

Sanders, Kevin. Review of *Bad Habits.* WABC-TV, New York. Reprinted in *New York Theatre Critics' Reviews* (1974): 376.

Straub, Deborah A. "McNally." In *Contemporary Authors*, 2: 457–58. Edited by Ann Evory. Detroit: Gale Research Company, 1981.

Taubman, Howard. "Theater: *Things That Go Bump in Night*." *New York Times* (27 April 1965): 27. Reprinted in *New York Theatre Critics' Reviews* (1965): 342.

———. "Zeffirelli's 'Lady of the Camellias.' " *New York Times* (22 March 1963): 7. Reprinted in *New York Theatre Critics' Reviews* (1963): 306, and *New York Times Theater Reviews* 7 (1960–1966).

"Terrence McNally." *Current Biography* 49 (March 1988): 23–27.

Watt, Douglas. "Being Gay Is Hard Work in 'The Ritz.' " *Daily News* (21 January 1975). Reprinted in *New York Theatre Critics' Reviews* (1975): 377.

———. "Eight with 'Bad Habits' Make Dandy Company." *Daily News* (5 February 1974). Reprinted in *New York Theatre Critics' Reviews* (1974): 374.

———. " 'Rink' Glides and Tumbles." *Daily News* (10 February 1984). Reprinted in *New York Theatre Critics' Reviews* (1984): 375.

———. " 'Tommy Flowers' Youth Portrait." *Daily News* (8 October 1971). Reprinted in *New York Theatre Critics' Reviews* (1971): 213.

Watts, Richard. "Adventures of Tommy Flowers." *New York Post* (8 October 1971). Reprinted in *New York Theatre Critics' Reviews* (1971): 214.

———. "Doctors and Their Patients." *New York Post* (5 February 1974). Reprinted in *New York Theatre Critics' Reviews* (1974): 373.

———. "Disappointing News for Voyeurs." *New York Post* (22 November 1968). Reprinted in *New York Theatre Critics' Reviews* (1968): 135.

———. "Enigmas of a Basement Shelter." *New York Post* (27 April 1965). Reprinted in *New York Theatre Critics' Reviews* (1965): 342.

———. "Two on the Aisle: New Life in a Romantic Classic." *New York Post* (21 March 1963). Reprinted in *New York Theatre Critics' Reviews* (1963): 307.

Willis, John. *Theatre World, 1978–1979 Season*, 35: 53. New York: Crown Publishers, 1984.

———. *Theatre World, 1983–1984 Season*, 40: 29. New York: Crown Publishers, 1985.

Wilson, Edwin. "Doctor Pepper and His Clinic." *Wall Street Journal* (12 February 1974). Reprinted in *New York Theatre Critics' Reviews* (1974): 374.

———. "A Turkey on Skates." *Wall Street Journal* (14 February 1984). Reprinted in *New York Theatre Critics' Reviews* (1984): 377.

Arthur Miller

(17 OCTOBER 1915–)

ALVIN GOLDFARB

ASSESSMENT OF MILLER'S REPUTATION

Arthur Miller's critical reputation has taken a rollercoaster ride in the almost four decades since the premiere of his classic *Death of a Salesman*. While most critics would agree with Bigsby's statement that "it [*Salesman*] is undoubtedly one of the finest plays ever written by an American" (*Twentieth Century American Drama*, 2:186), the thematic, structural, and linguistic qualities of the rest of his dramaturgy have been called into question by many contemporary analysts.

Miller is best known as a social dramatist of ideas, in the tradition of Henrik Ibsen. In *All My Sons, Salesman, Incident at Vichy*, and *The Price*, as well as in his adaptation of Ibsen's *An Enemy of the People*, Miller has questioned the values and integrity of contemporary society. Most often, he has focused on attacking the hypocrisy of the American dream. His protagonists are isolated from mainstream society, fighting to protect their individual dignity. Clurman noted, in discussing *All My Sons*, that Miller is a "moral talent with a passionate persistence that resembles that of the New England preacher who fashioned our first American rhetoric" (*Lies Like*, 68).

Miller's traditional realistic techniques have been questioned. Although his "old-fashioned" realism has been taken to task by contemporary analysts, the playwright himself has not shied away from his conventional dramatic style: "I have stood squarely in conventional realism" (*Collected Plays*, 52). While Miller has experimented successfully with symbolism and expressionism, particularly in *Death of a Salesman* and *After the Fall*, he has often been criticized for not being able to match his thematic concerns with his stylistic approaches. Moss notes: "Miller's construction, if rarely flawless, is never formless. His metaphors, if some-times obvious, are sometimes subtle" (*Miller*, 103).

If Miller's linguistic shortcomings have been compared to the weak-nesses found in the dialogue of Eugene O'Neill, with Moss, for example, pointing to his "self-conscious oratory" (*Miller*, 105), the playwright has been quite articulate about his dramatic work and his characters. Miller forced critics to reevaluate their definition of tragedy, tragic heroes, and the purpose of drama by creating protagonists like Willy Loman and Eddie Carbone and by publishing theoretical works like "Tragedy and the Common Man" and "On Social Plays."

Critical respect for Miller's work is reflected in the many awards he has won. As a student at the University of Michigan, he won the Avery Hopwood Drama Award for *Honors at Dawn* and *They Too Arise*, the latter also receiving the Theatre Guild Bureau of New Plays Award. *All My Sons* won the New York Drama Critics Circle Award. *Death of a Salesman* won all of the major awards for the 1949 season, including the Tony, the Pulitzer Prize, and the New York Drama Critics Circle Award. *The Crucible* won the 1953 Tony and Donaldson awards. In 1959 Miller received the Gold Medal for Drama by the National Arts and Letters Institute and in 1965 Brandeis University's Creative Arts award. The recent success of revivals of Miller's classic plays, including *Death of a Salesman, After the Fall* and *All My Sons*, as well as the success of his two newest one-acts, produced at Lincoln Center under the title *Danger: Memory!* may signal a reevaluation of Arthur Miller's career and place in contemporary American drama.

PRIMARY BIBLIOGRAPHY OF MILLER'S WORKS

The following is a selected primary bibliography of Arthur Miller's works and plays (dates of premiere productions noted; unproduced plays have dates of completion noted).

No Villain. 1936.
They Too Arise. Revision of *No Villain*. 1936.
Honors at Dawn. 1937.
The Great Disobedience. 1938.
The Grass Still Grows. Revision of *They Too Arise*. 1939.
Listen My Children. With Norman Rosten. 1939.
The Golden Years. 1939–1940.
The Half-Bridge. 1941–43.
That They May Win. 1943. In *The Best One Act Plays of 1944*, pp. 45–60. Edited by Margaret Mayorga. New York: Dodd, Mead, 1945.
The Man Who Had All the Luck. 1944. In *Cross-Section 1944*. Edited by Edwin Seaver. New York: L. B. Fischer, 1944.
All My Sons. 1947. New York: Reynal and Hitchcock, 1947.

Death of a Salesman. 1949. New York: Viking, 1949; London: Cresset, 1949.
An Enemy of the People. Adaptation of Henrik Ibsen play. 1950. New York: Viking, 1951.
The Crucible. 1953. New York: Viking, 1953. London: Cresset, 1956.
A Memory of Two Mondays and *A View from the Bridge*. 1955. New York: Viking, 1955.
A View from the Bridge. 1956. Revised two-act version. New York: Dramatists Play Service, 1957. London: Cresset, 1957.
After the Fall. 1964. New York: Viking, 1964. London: Secker and Warburg, 1965.
Incident at Vichy. 1964. New York: Viking, 1965. London: Secker and Warburg, 1966.
The Price. 1968. New York: Viking, 1968. London: Secker and Warburg, 1968.
Fame. 1970.
The Reason Why. 1970. In *Yale Literary Magazine* 140 (March 1970): 34–40.
The Creation of the World and Other Business. 1972. New York: Viking, 1973.
Up from Paradise. 1974. New York: Samuel French, 1984.
The Archbishop's Ceiling. 1977. London: Methuen, 1984. New York: Dramatists Play Service, 1985.
The American Clock. 1980. New York: Viking, 1980; London: Methuen, 1983.
Some Kind of Love Story and *Elegy for a Lady*. Produced as *2 by* A.M.. 1982. Published as *Two-Way Mirror*. London: Methuen, 1984.
I Can't Remember Anything and *Clara*. 1987. In *Danger: Memory!* New York: Grove Press, 1986.

Screenplays and Teleplays

The Misfits. 1961. New York: Viking, 1961.
Fame. 1978.
Playing for Time. 1980. New York: Bantam, 1981.

Radio Plays

The Pussycat and the Expert Plumber Who Was a Man. In *One Hundred Non-Royalty Radio Plays*, pp. 20–30. Edited by William Kozlenko. New York: Greenberg, 1941.
William Ireland's Confession. In *One Hundred Non-Royalty Radio Plays*, pp. 512–21. Edited by William Kozlenko. New York: Greenberg, 1941.
Grandpa and the Statue. In *Radio Drama in Action*, pp. 267–81. Edited by Erik Barnouw. New York: Farrar and Rinehart, 1947.
The Guardsman. By Ferenc Molnar. Adapted by Miller. In *Theatre Guild on the Air*, pp. 65–98. Edited by H. William Fitelson. New York: Rinehart, 1947.
The Story of Gus. In *Radio's Best Plays*, pp. 303–19. Edited by Joseph Liss. New York: Greenberg, 1947.
Three Men on a Horse. Adaptation. In Fitelson, *Theatre Guild on the Air*.

Fiction and Non-Fiction

Situation Normal. New York: Reynal and Hitchcock, 1944.
Focus. New York: Reynal and Hitchcock, 1945.
"The Plastic Masks." *Encore: A Continuing Anthology* 9 (April 1946): 424–32.
"It Takes a Thief." *Collier's* (8 February 1947): 23, 75–76.
"Monte Saint Angelo." *Harper's* (March 1951): 39–47.
"The Misfits." *Esquire* (October 1957): 158–66.
"I Don't Need You Anymore." *Esquire* (December 1959): 270–309.
"Please Don't Kill Anything." *Noble Savage* 1 (March 1960): 126–31.
"The Prophecy." *Esquire* (December 1961): 140, 268–87.
"Glimpse at a Jockey." *Noble Savage* 5 (October 1963): 138–40.
Jane's Blanket. New York: Crowell-Collier, 1963.
"The Recognitions." *Esquire* (July 1966): 76, 118.
"Search for a Future." *Saturday Evening Post* (13 August 1966): 64–68, 70.
I Don't Need You Anymore: Stories. New York: Viking, 1967; London: Secker and
      Warburg, 1967.
"Lines From California" (poem). *Harper* (May 1969): 97.
In Russia, photographs by Inge Morath. New York: Viking, 1969.
In the Country. New York: Viking, 1977.
Chinese Encounters, photographs by Inge Morath. New York: Farrar, Straus, and
      Giroux, 1979.
Salesman in Beijing. New York: Viking, 1984; London: Methuen, 1984.
Timebends: A Life. New York; Grove Press,1987.

Critical Essays

"Subsidized Theatre." *New York Times* (22 June 1947): 2:1.
"Tragedy and the Common Man." *New York Times* (27 February 1949): 2:1, 3.
"Arthur Miller on 'The Nature of Tragedy.' " *New York Herald-Tribune* (27 March
      1949): 5:1, 2.
"The 'Salesman' Has a Birthday." *New York Times* (5 February 1950): 2: 1, 3.
"Ibsen's Message for Today's World." *New York Times* (24 December 1950): 2:
      3, 4.
"Many Writers: Few Plays." *New York Times* (10 August 1952): 2: 1.
"Journey to 'The Crucible.' " *New York Times* (8 February 1953): 2: 3.
"The American Theatre." *Holiday* 17 (January 1955): 90–104.
"On Social Plays." Preface to the original edition of *A View from the Bridge.* New
      York: Viking, 1955.
"The Family in Modern Drama." *Atlantic Monthly* (April 1956): 35–41.
"The Playwright and the Atomic World." *Colorado Quarterly* 5 (1956): 117–37.
Introduction to *Arthur Miller's Collected Plays.* New York: Viking, 1957.
"Brewed in 'The Crucible.' " *New York Times* (9 March 1958): 2: 3.
"The Shadows of the Gods" (essay). *Harper's* (August 1958): 35–43.
"Art and Commitment." *Anvil and Student Partisan* 11 (Winter 1960): 5.
Preface to *A View from the Bridge* (two-act version). New York: Compass, 1960.
"A New Era in American Theatre?" *Drama Survey* 3 (1963): 70–71.

"On Recognition." *Michigan Quarterly Review* 2 (1963): 213–20.

"Foreword, *After the Fall.*" *Saturday Evening Post* (1 February 1964): 32.

"With Respect for Her Agony—But with Love." *Life* (7 February 1964): 66.

"Our Guilt for the World's Evil." *New York Times* (3 January 1965): 6: 10–11, 48.

"What Makes Plays Endure?" *New York Times* (15 August 1965): 2: 1, 3.

"It Could Happen Here—and Did." *New York Times* (30 April 1967): 2: 17.

"Arthur Miller Talks." *Michigan Quarterly Review* 6 (1967): 153–84.

"Broadway, from O'Neill to Now." *New York Times* (21 December 1969): 2:3, 7.

"When Life Had at Least a Form." *New York Times* (24 January 1971): 2: 17.

"Arthur Miller vs. Lincoln Center." *New York Times* (16 April 1972): 2: 1, 5.

"Politics as Theatre." *New York Times* (4 November 1972): 33.

"The Measure of Things Is Man." *Theatre* 4 96–97.

"Symposium: Playwriting in America." *Yale/Theatre* 4 (Winter 1973): 19–21.

The Theatre Essays of Arthur Miller. Edited by Robert A. Martin. New York: Viking, 1978.

"Every Play Has a Purpose." *Dramatists Guild Quarterly* 15 (Winter 1979): 13–20.

"The American Writer: The American Theatre." In *The Writer's Craft: Hopwood Lectures. 1965–81*, pp. 254–70. Edited by Robert A. Martin. Ann Arbor: Michigan University Press, 1982.

Miller, Arthur. "Arthur Miller on McCarthy's Legacy." *Harper's* 269 (July 1984): 11.

Interviews

Roudané, Matthew. *Conversations with Arthur Miller* (Jackson: University Press of Mississippi, 1988). Contains, thirty-seven Miller interviews from the 1940's through 1986.

PRODUCTION HISTORY

Arthur Miller's early works were produced in the commercial Broadway theatre; however, in the 1960s, 1970s, and 1980s, after some commercial failures, Miller produced outside Broadway, with some of his plays receiving productions at Lincoln Center (*After the Fall, Incident at Vichy, Danger: Memory!*), at the Kennedy Center in Washington, D.C. (*The Archbishop's Ceiling*), and off-Broadway (*Fame* and *The Reason Why* and *The American Clock*). The playwright has occasionally directed his own plays in revivals. Miller's recent works have been more successfully produced and received in England.

The first professional production of a Miller play was *The Man Who Had All the Luck*, which premiered on 23 November 1944 and had a run of only four performances. The production was not critically well received, with Miller's play being characterized as too pedantic.

In 1947, *All My Sons*, which won the Drama Critics Circle Award, was staged by Elia Kazan with settings by Mordechai Gorelick. Ed Begley played Joe Keller and Arthur Kennedy, Chris. Atkinson spoke for the New York critics when he remarked that *All My Sons* is the "most talented work by a new author in some time" (2:1). Nathan, however, touched on critical problems that would be echoed later by analysts when questioning Miller's theatrical significance: "*[All My Sons]* says what we already know too well in a manner . . . and language that are undistinguished" (293). *All My Sons* has been revived frequently, with the Long Wharf (New Haven, Connecticut) production in 1987 again bringing the play to the public's attention. This presentation, directed by Arvin Brown and starring Richard Kiley, was well received, but many critics shared Rich's assessment that "*All My Sons* may be too topical for its own theatrical good" (23 April 1987).

Death of a Salesman, which premiered on 10 February 1949 in a production directed by Elia Kazan and designed by Jo Mielziner, is Miller's classic. Its original presentation, which starred Lee J. Cobb as Willy Loman, is the one against which all revivals are measured. The skeletal set, which received a Tony Award, is a landmark in theatre history, perfectly underscoring the deterioration of Willy's existence. Cobb's internal intensity and his ability to make the audience see him as an Everyman won him unanimous praise. Paul Muni, in the London production, received less positive notices, and Frederic March, in the 1952 film directed by Laszlo Benedek and with a screenplay by Handley Roberts, was characterized as too melodramatic and emphasizing Loman's negative traits. George C. Scott, who starred in and directed a Circle in the Square production in 1975, was generally criticized for diminishing the universal qualities of Willy Loman. Kerr suggested that Scott's Loman was not destroyed by the emptiness of the American dream but was someone who "always had to compensate, to inflate his indeterminate place in the scheme of things, to substitute for his sickened hollowness an equally hollow image in which . . . only his adoring sons could possibly believe. . . . [Scott's production is] a play of persons not of social prophecy or some archetypal proclamation of an already failed American myth" ("This Salesman," B5).

Possibly the most controversial revival was a 1984 production directed by Michael Rudman and starring Dustin Hoffman as Willy and John Malkovich as Biff. (Virtually the same cast was employed in a later television adaptation.) Critics questioned Hoffman's physical size and therefore also his stature, as well as his youthfulness; most reviewers agreed with Rich that "Mr. Hoffman is not playing a larger-than-life protagonist but the small man described in the script—the little boat looking for a harbor, the extremely adolescent American male who goes to the grave without ever learning who he is" (30 March 1984). John Malkovich's Biff, for which he later won a television Emmy Award, redefined the significance of the character: "John Malkovich, who plays the lost Biff gives a performance of such spellbinding effect that he becomes the evening's anchor. When Biff finally forgives Willy and nestles his head lovingly on his father's chest . . . we know we're watching the salesman arrive at the only safe harbor he'll ever know" (Rich, 30 March 1984). A unique revival of *Salesman* was the production Miller staged at the Beijing People's Art Theatre in 1983.

Miller's adaptation of Henrik Ibsen's *An Enemy of the People* opened on 28 December 1950 in a production directed by Robert Lewis and starring Frederic March as Dr. Stockmann and Morris Carnovsky as his brother. The play has been revived frequently, most notably off-Broadway in 1959, at Lincoln Center in 1971, and at the Arena Stage in Washington, D.C.

The Crucible, supposedly Arthur Miller's response to McCarthyism, opened on 22 January 1953 in a production directed by Jed Harris, designed by Boris Aronson, and starring Arthur Kennedy as John Proctor, Beatrice Straight (later replaced by Maureen Stapleton) as Elizabeth, and E. G. Marshall as Hale. The play, while winning a number of critical awards, was attacked for being too rhetorical by reviewers such as Walter Kerr, who complained that *"The Crucible* lives not in the warmth of humbly observed human souls, but in the ideologic heat of polemicism" ("The Crucible," 12). In 1955, Jean-Paul Sartre wrote the screenplay for a French film adaptation, *Les Sorcières de Salem*, starring Yves Montand and Simone Signoret, which critics pointed out totally changed *The Crucible* into a rhetorical vehicle and a proletarian allegory. Miller strongly argued with Sartre's adaptation: "I thought it was Marxist in the worst sense. . . . He was . . . imposing a simplistic class analysis on the play" (Bigsby, *Twentieth-Century American Drama*, 2:193).

The Crucible has been revived frequently since its premiere, including many international productions such as the one directed by George Devine in 1956 at the Royal Court Theatre and the presentation staged by Laurence Olivier in 1965 at the Old Vic. A television version of the play was adapted by the playwright in 1967 and starred George C. Scott and Colleen Dewhurst who, according to Nelson, "turned in the finest portrayals of John and Elizabeth Proctor I have seen" (175). Other well-received revivals included an off-Broadway presentation in 1958, a Lincoln Center production in 1972, and the Stratford, Connecticut, staging in 1976.

Miller's two one-acts *A View from the Bridge* and *A Memory of Two Mondays* premiered in New York on 29 September 1955 on a single bill, directed by Martin Ritt and designed by Boris Aronson. The plays received the weakest reviews of any Miller play since *The Man Who Had All the Luck*. Few praised Miller's experimentation with verse, the shortened dramatic form, or the use of narrator in *A View from the Bridge*.

Few agreed with Miller's perception of Eddie Carbone as a modern tragic hero. Miller transformed *A View from the Bridge* into a two-act play with the verse turned into prose and a greater focus on psychological realism for its 11 October 1956 London premiere, directed by Peter Brook and starring Anthony Quayle as Eddie. The production was well received, but again Miller's higher dramatic intentions were questioned. Most reviewers agreed with Trewin, who categorized the presentation as an "honest theatrical melodrama" (720). Brook also staged the French premiere of the play.

Two revivals have enhanced the reputation of *A View from the Bridge:* Ulu Grosbard's off-Broadway staging in 1965 with Robert Duvall and Jon Voight and Arvin Brown's 1983 production, which premiered at the Long Wharf Theatre and then moved to Broadway. Both productions shifted critics' focus away from the question of tragedy and pointed up the script's theatrical strengths. Oliver explained in her *New Yorker* review of the 1965 revival: "If the play never attains the status of classical tragedy, it is still an effective and exciting melodrama" (94). Rich praised Arvin Brown for having "emphasized psychosexual drama over the playwright's unrealistic aspirations to Greek tragedy" ("Theatre: Richard Kiley"). The National Theatre in London produced the play in 1987; it was directed by Alan Ayckbourn and starred Michael Gambon. A film version, directed by Sidney Lumet and starring Raf Vallone, Maureen Stapleton, Morris Carnovsky, and Carol Lawrence, was poorly received in 1962.

While *A Memory of Two Mondays* has not been revived as often, it too has been reevaluated because of recent productions. A television adaptation in 1971 led Julius Novick to describe it as a "gentle lyrical Chekhovian evocation of the past" (17).

Miller did not present another new work until nine years later when, on 23 January 1964, *After the Fall* premiered for the new Lincoln Center Repertory Theatre at the remodeled ANTA Washington Square Theatre, directed by Elia Kazan, designed by Jo Mielziner, and starring Jason Robards and Barbara Loden. The debate among reviewers over the autobiographical versus universal qualities of the play continues into the current critical commentary. Nadel, in the *World Telegram and Sun* defended the play: "It will be a long time before another playwright will reveal more about the form and content of man's self examination" (26). Brustein led the attack by those critics who believed that Miller was simply exorcising the demons of his marriage to Marilyn Monroe: "*After the Fall* is a three-and-one-half hour breach of taste, a confessional autobiography of embarrassing explicitness" ("Miller's Mea Culpa," 26).

Significant international productions include Luchino Visconti's Parisian staging and Franco Zeffirelli's Italian presentation. An off-Broadway revival at Playhouse 91 in 1984 with Frank Langella fared little better than the original, as did a television adaptation written by Miller and televised in 1974. Welland's view that "its text can reveal to the student a carefully-patterned structure and an intensity of approach to which, in the future, when the rawness of feeling about Marilyn Monroe has tempered more with the passing of time, a revival may be able to do more justice on the stage" *(Miller: The Playwright,* 104) has yet to be upheld by a new production.

Later in the same year, on 3 December, *Incident at Vichy* was produced by Lincoln Center Repertory Theatre at the ANTA Washington Square Theatre; Harold Clurman directed and Boris Aronson designed. The London production premiered on 26 January 1966 and was directed by Peter Wood and starred Alec Guiness as Von Berg and Anthony Quayle as Leduc. Critics who praised the play applauded its focus on the moral question of individual responsibility during the Holocaust. Taubman in the *New York Times* labeled it "a moral inquest that has the most searching pertinence for man today or any time" (2:3). Brustein, however, spoke for those critics who castigated Miller's old-fashioned dramatic techniques and philosophical ideas, which, according to the *New Republic* reviewer, reflected "noisy virtue and moral flatulence" ("Muddy Track," 26).

Miller's *The Price*, which premiered in New York on 7 February 1968 in a production directed by Ulu Grosbard (although Miller took over after a dispute in the final week of previews) and designed by Boris Aronson, was directed by the author in its London production a year later and marked a return to commercial and critical success. The New York production ran for 425 performances, while the English production ran for 51 weeks, a record for the Duke of York's Theatre at which it was performed. While some critics, such as Brustein and Bermel, suggested that the play did not deal with current concerns and was rooted in old-fashioned 1930s ideology, others, best represented by Clurman, pointed to Miller's continued concern with the American dream. The defense is possibly best summed up by Nelson: "*The Price* is an intriguing play. In form and structure it hearkens back to *All My Sons;* in its themes it is similar to *After the Fall.* Consequently, while it seems somewhat dated (one reviewer wrote it off as 'vintage 1930s') it also appears to herald new directions in Miller's thought (another critic saw it exhibiting not one but 'two new faces' of its author)" (295). The play was adapted for television in 1971 with a cast that included George C. Scott, Colleen Dewhurst, and David Burns.

As Welland points out: "Miller's plays since *The Price* have been his least successful, but they are not for that reason his least interesting and it would be premature to imply an end to his career" *(Miller: The Playwright,* 125). In 1970, two one-acts, *Fame* and *The Reason Why,* were staged at the off-off-Broadway New Theatre Workshop with Eli Wallach and

Anne Jackson. The shows at this theatre were not publicly advertised or reviewed.

The Creation of the World and Other Business, a retelling of Genesis, opened on Broadway on 30 November 1972 after a tumultuous rehearsal and out-of-town tryout period during which Harold Clurman was replaced as the director by Gerald Freedman. The production was almost universally attacked. While many saw recurring family drama themes in the play and noted Miller's continued experimentation with comedy— *The Price* had been praised for its use of the comic character Solomon— most agreed with Weales's conclusion that *Creation* was "the dullest, the least dramatic, the most pretentious and the most vulgar reworking of the Biblical material this critic can recall" ("Cliches in the Garden," 276). Miller reworked *Creation* into *Up From Paradise*, a musical version on which he collaborated with Stanley Silverman. Miller simplified the original, added a narrator, a part he performed, and directed the musical adaptation at the University of Michigan with a professional cast in April 1974.

On 30 April 1977 Miller's *The Archbishop's Ceiling*, directed by Arvin Brown, premiered at the Kennedy Center in Washington, D.C. Set in a room in a former archbishop's palace in Eastern Europe, which is probably bugged by the secret police, the play focuses on an author who has the opportunity to defect to the West, two of his friends, an ex–political prisoner writer who is now in favor with the regime and a visiting American, as well as the woman who has been a mistress to all three. The reviewers in the Washington and Baltimore press attacked the play for, as Coe suggested, "belabor[ing] his [Miller's] moral concerns" (B7). However, Bigsby defended "the play which moves closer to Beckett and Pinter than ever before. . . . That it failed in performance had less to do with its intensive merit than with a resolutely realistic production. Played for its realism, it was in fact a work which set out to deconstruct that realism and dramatise anxieties which go far beyond a concern for psychological veracity or social analysis" (*Twentieth-Century American Drama*, 2:237–38). England's Royal Shakespeare Company revived *Ceiling* in 1986.

The American Clock, an epic presentation of the effects of the Great Depression, was first performed at the Harold Clurman Theatre in New York prior to its official premiere at the Spoleto Festival's Dockside Theatre in Charleston, South Carolina, on 24 May 1980. This presentation was directed by Daniel Sullivan. A revised version of the script was staged by Vivian Matalon on Broadway on 20 November 1980. While not well received, many critics noted Miller's return to an earlier subject matter, the effects of the depression, and the dramatic style of the 1930s. Rich led the attack on the Broadway revision: "Mr. Miller has tinkered with his play to the point of dismantling it. . . . He has also interjected too much sentimentality, thematic signposting and slapdash comedy" (21

November 1980). More successful revivals were staged at the Mark Taper Forum in Los Angeles and at the National Theatre in London.

In November 1982 two one-acts, *Elegy for a Lady* and *Some Kind of Love Story*, were staged at the Long Wharf Theatre by Arthur Miller. (This regional theatre produced the critically acclaimed revivals of *A View from the Bridge* and *All My Sons.*) Again dismissed by the reviewers, the one-acts are defended by Bigsby for experimenting with techniques reminiscent of Harold Pinter's drama and for breaking with Miller's traditional well-made realism.

On 8 February 1987 two new one-acts, *I Can't Remember Anything* and *Clara*, directed by Gregory Mosher, were presented at the Mitzi E. Newhouse at Lincoln Center as *Danger: Memory!* In *I Can't Remember Anything*, a wealthy widow disillusioned with the brutality and hypocrisy of society debates with her husband's best friend, a depression-age Communist who holds a more optimistic view. In *Clara*, the liberal father of a murdered social worker is questioned by an investigating detective, who has given up his own liberal ideals and who believes the killer is one of the murdered woman's "reformed" clients. Rich's review summarizes critical reaction to *Danger: Memory!* and possibly to all of Miller's plays since *Death of a Salesman:* "While Arthur Miller's admirable voice of conscience remains firm as always, 'Danger: Memory!' is an evening in which the pontificator wins over the playwright" ("Miller's 'Danger: Memory!' " 9 February 1987).

Significant critical attention has been paid to Miller's two full-length film and television plays: *The Misfits* and *Playing for Time. The Misfits*, a modern western focusing on the triangle of the younger Perce, the cowboy Gay, and the beautiful Roslyn, starred Marilyn Monroe, Clark Gable, and Montgomery Glift and was directed by John Huston. The film was not a critical or box office success. Many analysts focused on Miller's use of Monroe and his own relationship with her (foreshadowing the later attacks on *After the Fall*). Many, including Kauffmann, attacked the film for being too talky and traditionally melodramatic. However, Kauffmann also noted that *The Misfits* is, "in idea and in much of its execution, several universes above most American films" (26). Various critics have pointed out that many of the themes are developed from Miller's earlier dramatic works.

Miller's teleplay *Playing for Time*, an adaptation of Auschwitz survivor Fania Fenelon's memoirs, was well received. (The 1980 presentation also generated controversy due to the casting of Vanessa Redgrave as Fenelon, who survived as a member of the concentration camp orchestra.) Of the three works by Miller that touch on the Holocaust—the other two are *After the Fall* and *Incident at Vichy—Playing for Time* was critically acclaimed as the most successful. Bigsby explains: "More than either of the other two plays with which Miller attempted to tackle the experiences of the camps, *Playing for Time* dramatizes not merely the horror which has quite clearly haunted his imagination for more than forty years but also the problem of justifying to himself his survival as a Jew and as a writer condemned to continue after the death of his own early optimism and after the extinction of a certain kind of hope" (*Twentieth-Century American Drama*, 2: 231). Welland sees "in these last two plays [*The American Clock* and *Playing for Time*] more parallels with and echoes of the earlier plays.... The big themes of personal responsibility, guilt, the relation between the microcosm of the family and the macrocosm of modern society, the effect of the passing of time and memory and on perspective, the moral stance and value of protest, public and private integrity, all these recur" (*Miller: The Playwright*, 156).

SURVEY OF SECONDARY SOURCES

Bibliographies

The major bibliographies on Arthur Miller are Ungar's, Jensen's, Hayashi's, and Carpenter's. Ferres's is the most comprehensive bibliography covering writing by and about Miller through 1977, including reviews of productions, and doctoral dissertations. The annotations are helpful and concise. Hayashi's bibliography, which catalogs criticism, as well as works by the playwright and noncritical articles, is not annotated, nor is it as comprehensive or as well organized as Ferres's. Carpenter's bibliography fills in gaps in Ferres's work, including ninety entries not found in the full-length bibliography, half of them in foreign languages. Jensen's is a descriptive bibliography of the publications of Miller's works and provides some useful publication information. Ungar's bibliography is no longer useful and much less complete than either Ferres's or Hayashi's. One additional bibliography is Tetsumaro Hayashi's *Arthur Miller and Tennessee Williams: Research Opportunities and Dissertation Abstracts*, which contains abstracts of all dissertations on Arthur Miller through 1980 and reveals gaps in doctoral research on the playwright. Dwain E. Manske's dissertation has a catalog of the Arthur Miller Collection at the University of Texas at Austin appended to it. An excellent bibliographical essay is Martine's Introduction to *Critical Essays on Arthur Miller*.

Biographies

Most of the critical works that survey Miller's plays contain biographical chapters and chronologies of his career, including: Hayman's *Arthur Miller*, Hogan's *Arthur Miller*, Huftel's *Arthur Miller: The Burning Glass*, Moss's *Arthur Miller*, and Welland's *Miller: The Playwright*. Nelson's *Arthur Miller: Portrait of a Playwright* is a critical study that heavily emphasizes biographical information. Walden provides biographical context for Miller's early work and concludes: "In the first phase of his creative life, up to and including *Death of a Salesman*, [Miller] was a playwright intensely concerned with and close to his Jewish heritage" (194).

Influences

Many critics have cited specific influences on Miller, as well as his influence on other contemporary dramatists. Tynan compares and contrasts Williams and Miller; Willett points out thematic similarities (1965). Nolan discusses the means of dramatizing and employing memory in *The Glass Menagerie* and *After the Fall*. The influence of *The Glass Menagerie* on *Death of a Salesman* is outlined by Hays.

Groff contrasts Miller's employment of flashbacks with O'Neill's in *The Emperor Jones* and how both use the technique to create an expressionist point of view. A comparison between Eddie Carbone in *A View from the Bridge* and Katherine in O'Neill's *A Long Day's Journey into Night* can be found in Rothenberg and Shapiro.

Hurrell's introduction points up the influences of Greek tragic playwrights and Ibsen on Miller. Johnson's doctoral dissertation reviews the ways in which Miller has been influenced by Ibsen, Chekhov, and expressionism, while Flaxman focuses on how indebted the playwright is to Ibsen and Strindberg. Steene compares *After the Fall* to Strindberg's *To Damascus*. Bronson reviews the relationship of Ibsen's original *An Enemy of the People* to Miller's adaptation, as does Haugen. Williams reviews Miller's indebtedness to Ibsen, Marxism, and German expressionism; he also points up the similarities in *After the Fall* to Tennessee Williams's dramaturgy (1968).

Sheldon's doctoral dissertation compares Odets and Miller, as does Jeanne-Marie Miller's article, which focuses on *The Crucible* and *Till the Day I Die*.

Koppenhaver compares and contrasts *After the Fall* and *The Fall*, as does Cismaru, while Moss's "Biographical and Literary Allusion in *After the Fall*" notes the personal and literary sources, including Camus. Long's dissertation points up the themes of Jean-Paul Sartre in Miller's *Death of a Salesman*, while Lowenthal does the same for *Incident at Vichy*. Hayman, in his full-length study, points up Miller's debt to traditional realistic playwrights and to Sartre's philosophical views, an idea he also presents in "Arthur Miller: Between Sartre and Society." Centola deals with alienation in the works of Miller and Sartre (1984).

Bergeron points up the relationship between *The Crucible* and *The Scarlet Letter*, as does Bergman. Heilman identifies similarities between *Death of a Salesman* and Eudora Welty's short story "The Death of a Traveling Salesman" (1969). Vogel compares Willy Loman to Oedipus.

Gianakaris compares Miller's expressionistic technique in *After the Fall* with similar techniques in the drama of Osborne and Shaffer.

General Studies

Numerous full-length studies critically treat Arthur Miller's oeuvre. Welland's *Miller: The Playwright* is the most recent revision of his *Arthur Miller*, published in 1961, the first full-length study of the playwright. Welland's 1961 book was also revised in 1979 under the title *Miller: A Study of His Plays*. Welland analyzes Miller in the context of American literature, particularly Emerson, tracing his development from *The Man Who Had All the Luck* through *Playing for Time*.

Moss's *Arthur Miller*, first published in 1967 and then in a revised edition in 1980, traces his dramatic development from his unpublished college plays through *The Creation of the World*. Moss focuses on the question of tragedy in the author's works, as well as recurrent dramatic techniques, including "dialogue styles, narrative conventions, symbolic devices, and structural principles" (Preface). The most recent edition also contains an interview with Miller.

Hayman's *Arthur Miller* discusses the dramas through *The Price*, reviewing his work as social commentator and his Sartrean concerns. English critic Huftel analyzes the playwright's work and theoretical writings through *Incident at Vichy*. Huftel notes Miller's synthesis of social and psychological in all of his plays, his respectful dramatization of the individual in spite of his limitations, and the representation of characters "who cannot settle for half" (63). Huftel's work also contains analyses of Miller's novel *Focus* and his screenplay for *The Misfits*. Nelson defends Miller's social didacticism and his seemingly old-fashioned craftsmanship. The study also provides a good deal of biographical context for Miller's development.

Among the many other full-length studies that treat Arthur Miller's dramaturgy are Hogan's long pamphlet, *Arthur Miller*, Murray's *Arthur Miller, Dramatist*, which analyzes Miller's major dramas through *Incident at Vichy*, and White's short *Guide to Arthur Miller*, which treats Miller's work up to *The Price*, with the primary focus on *Death of a Salesman*. Neil Carson, in his 1982 *Arthur Miller*, surveys the dramatist's life and career and analyzes his major plays, concluding, "His characters are a peculiar combination of insight and blindness, doubt and assertiveness, which makes them alternately confront and avoid their innermost selves.... [Miller] has come to realize that the greatest enemy to life is not doubt but despair" (155–56). Panikkar's *Individual Morality and Social Happiness in Arthur Miller* treats Miller's plays through *Creation of the World*, focusing on the theme of the individual's search for happiness in a changing social structure. June Schlueter's and James K. Flanagan's *Arthur Miller* provides analyses of all of Miller's dramas through *Danger: Memory!* as well as a biographical essay.

A significant number of articles and sections of books analyze Miller's common dramatic techniques or thematic concerns. A number of essays treat Miller's attempts to create modern tragedies. Wiegand suggests that the tragedy of Miller's protagonists is that they have knowledge of society's ills but cannot communicate them and are martyred. Adler points up the failure of Miller's drama because it "springs from rationalist, sociological fallacy which argues ... everything human is dramatic and therefore art should focus upon the feeblest man" (61). Trowbridge argues that Miller's early characters evoke pathos but are not tragic, though with *After the Fall*, "he hovers between pathos and tragedy" (232). Steinberg reviews Miller's theoretical statements and dramas in order to see how he attempts to define modern tragedy. McAnany contrasts the playwright's statements on modern tragedy in his essay "Tragedy and the Common Man" with those found in the introduction to his *Collected Plays* and "reading Willy in his role as father, McAnany clearly points to the tension between two goals which drive Willy to tragic proportions" (Martine, xiv). Hynes points up how the limitations of naturalism keep Miller from being able to create a traditional tragedy (1963). Prudhoe reviews Miller's struggle to reconcile his realism with his quest for tragedy. Aylen's chapter on Miller in his *Greek Tragedy and the Modern World* compares and contrasts *Salesman*, *The Crucible*, and *A View from the Bridge* with Greek tragedy. Heilman, in *The Iceman, the Arsonist and the Troubled Agent*, suggests that Miller's plays from *Salesman* through *After the Fall* were becoming less melodramatic and more tragic but that *The Price* returned to the earlier style. Stambusky compares and contrasts Miller's theories and works to Aristotle's concepts of tragedy.

Many critical studies characterize Miller's plays as social problem plays and provide analyses of his social and political consciousness. Among these are works by Cassell, Dillingham, Driver, Popkin ("Arthur Miller: The Strange Encounter"), Weales ("Arthur Miller: Man and His Image" and "Theatre Without Walls"), Ganz, Mottram, Corrigan ("The Achievement of Arthur Miller"), Blumberg, Porter ("The Mills of the Gods"), and Brater ("Ethics and Ethnicity in the Plays of Arthur Miller").

Other critics have attempted to review the structural, thematic, and linguistic qualities inherent in Miller's dramas. These include: Moss's "Arthur Miller and the Common Man's Language," Bigsby in *Confrontation and Commitment*, Reno, Cohn, Freedman, McMahon, Overland, Scanlan, and Schroeder.

Analyses of Individual Plays

There is a significant body of critical essays dealing with each of Arthur Miller's plays. An excellent essay that places the plays Miller wrote as a student at the University of Michigan in the context of his later work is Rowe's "Shadows Cast Before." *The Man Who Had All The Luck* has received little attention. Scholarly articles treating *All My Sons* focus on the social issues posed in the play, the Ibsen-like dramatic techniques, the family dilemma, or the relationship of the play to traditional tragedy. Schneider points up the Oedipal struggles in both *All My Sons* and *Death of a Salesman*, while Whitley argues that neither of these early plays contains characters of tragic stature. Loughlin reviews the similarities between *All My Sons* and the Cain and Abel tale, ancient Greek epics, and medieval morality dramas. Boggs, in *"Oedipus* and *All My Sons,"* shows that the Miller play is not a tragedy because of its focus on the responsibility of the individual to the collective rather than focusing on the tragic hero's individual downfall. Samuel A. Yorks, in "Joe Keller and His Sons," points up that the family drama implies that personal responsibilities should not be discarded for general social loyalties. Wells concludes that Miller "leaves a dual impression: the action affirms the theme of the individual's responsibility to humanity but, at the same time, it suggests that the standpoint of even so fine an ideal is not an altogether adequate one from which to evaluate human beings, and that a rigid idealism operating in the actual world of men entails suffering and waste" (8). Gross suggests that *All My Sons* fails because the focus of the play is on the naive Chris and because the verbal and dramatic contrivances violate our belief in the reality of the play. Vos notes how both *All My Sons* and *Death of a Salesman* focus on the destructiveness of the American dream.

Many of the seminal articles dealing with *Death of a Salesman* focus on the question of whether Miller had created a contemporary tragedy. Eric Bentley, in the reprint of his original 1949 review in *In Search of Theatre*, argues that the play is a social drama rather than a tragedy in the Aristotelian sense. In "Willy Loman and King Lear," Siegel draws parallels between Shakespeare's tragic protagonist and Miller's. Gassner argues that *Salesman* is a modern tragedy that focuses on a common person rather than the traditional aristocratic protagonist. In the *Tulane Drama Review*'s *"Death of a Salesman:* A Symposium," Gelb, along with Gore Vidal, J. Y. Miller, and Watts, review the tragic and non-tragic characteristics found in the play. Schweinitz argues that the play has the traditional epic and tragic structures. Saisselin suggests that Miller has not created a modern tragedy because Willy, unlike the characters in absurdist drama, never realizes that his values are absurd and therefore does not have the insight of the traditional tragic hero. Foster posits that *Salesman* is not a tragedy because the play is too filled with social and moral clichés, as well as stock emotional responses. Hagopian counters those who argue against *Salesman* as a tragedy by answering that Biff is the focal character and that his struggle is one of man trying to discover his own identity. Jackson delineates how Miller uses classical and romantic characteristics of tragedy to create an industrial age tragic hero. Otten compares Willy Loman to Oedipus, arguing that both tragic protagonists search to discover who they are. Field summarizes the debate over *Salesman* as tragedy and concludes: "Willy committed a crime for which he is justly punished" (19). Susan Cole, in *The Absent One: Mourning Ritual, Tragedy, and the Performance of Ambivalence*, theorizes that "this profound communal experience [the enactment of mourning] resides at the heart of tragedy" (5) and that *Death of a Salesman* clearly illustrates her thesis.

A significant body of criticism addresses the stylistic and structural techniques inherent in *Death of a Salesman*. Hunter analyzes the unique manner in which Miller treats time in the play, while Groff compares the flashback technique in *Salesman* and in O'Neill's *The Emperor Jones*. Sister M. Bettina shows how Ben is employed as another expressionistic device. Hynes, in "Attention Must Be Paid . . . ," points up contradictions in structure, theme, and character within *Salesman*. Parker argues that the dramatic success of *Salesman* comes from the blurring of the real and expressionistic in the play. Oberg shows how Miller uses language expressionistically to "reveal the disparities between Willy's pipe dreams" and reality (311). Brater, in "Miller's Realism and *Death of a Salesman*," shows how the symbolic devices in the play help to give expressionistic insights into Willy Loman. Gordon reviews Miller's dramatic techniques and devices in order to prove that "*Death of a Salesman*, the major American drama of the 1940s, remains unequalled in its brilliant and original fusion of realistic and poetic techniques, its richness of visual and verbal texture, and its wide range of emotional impact" (274).

Other significant analyses focus on the social criticism found in the play or attempt to show how Miller employs the family and/or secondary characters in *Salesman*. Couchman draws parallels between *Death of a Salesman* and Sinclair Lewis's *Babbitt*. Williams, in "The Realism of Arthur Miller," argues that the American dramatist experimented with and developed beyond the tradition of realistic social drama in his first five plays, including *Death of a Salesman*, while Mander rejects as simplistic Freudian and Marxist explanations of the difficulties Willy encountered. Barksdale shows how the protagonists in *Salesman* and *A View from the Bridge* are victimized by the socioeconomic system in which they exist. Lawrence explains that society, having forsaken traditional human values, shares responsibility with Willy for the salesman's death. Jordan Y. Miller suggests that Miller does not really show the American dream as responsible for Willy's downfall, especially in the light of Bernard's success, while Siegel in "The Drama and the Thwarted American Dream," argues that the symbolism in *Salesman* reflects how Willy succumbs to his thwarted dreams. Bates argues that Willy is an embodiment of past

American personae and values that do not fit in his contemporary world. Eisinger, Gross in "Peddler and Pioneer in *Death of a Salesman*," and Weales in "Arthur Miller: Man and His Image" focus on the conflict in *Salesman* between a romanticized rural world and the contemporary capitalist society. Spindler characterizes Willy as a "consumer man in crisis." Bliquez suggests that Linda shares responsibility for Willy's downfall since she supports his mistaken dreams of success. Cook shows how Willy's admiration of his brother and the archetypal salesman reflects his own incompatible ideals and dreams. Shaw, analyzing the ironic characterization of Bernard, notes that the successful lawyer clearly represents Miller's revulsion for an inhuman technological society. Porter's *Salesman* essay concludes that the "play is an anti-myth, the rags-to-riches formula in reverse so that it becomes the story of a failure in terms of success, or better, the story of the failure of the success myth" (131). Irving Jacobson argues that "[Willy's] death changes nothing; it implies instead that a man's frenetic attempt to make the world a home can defeat the viability of his private home, even cost him his life" (1975, 258). Brucher compares *Salesman* with Tracy Kidder's *The Soul of a New Machine* in order to illustrate how both works "invoke the spirit of Whitman, Thoreau, and Emerson, who before them sought peace with technology while defining a new individualism and freedom" (336).

A seminal full-length study of Miller's *Death of a Salesman* is by Harshbarger who tackles most of these issues in a detailed and carefully developed analysis.

Much of the criticism dealing with *The Crucible* focuses on the relationship of the play to actual historical fact, to other pieces of literature that deal with the Puritan witch-hunt, and to McCarthyism. Warshow attacks Miller for not dealing honestly with the Salem witch trials and using the material to support present-day dissent. Walker criticizes the playwright for not deciding whether his play is a traditional tragedy or a political allegory. Blau argues that *The Crucible* is not a strong political play that forces us to call into question or transform our beliefs. Henry Popkin's "Arthur Miller's *The Crucible*" shows the weakness in the analogies drawn between the Salem trials and the McCarthy hearings, as well as Miller's failure to turn Proctor into a tragic hero. Both Bergeron and Bergman point up parallels between Miller's *The Crucible* and Nathaniel Hawthorne's *The Scarlet Letter*. Willis argues that the thematic emphasis on the individual's responsibility to stand up for truth makes the play relevant to all political times, as does John H. Ferres in his essay "Still in the Present Tense: *The Crucible* Today." In his introduction to *Arthur Miller, "The Crucible": Text and Criticism*, Weales suggests that critics have spent too much time focusing on the politics of the play while ignoring many of its dramaturgical strengths.

Studies that focus on the historicity of *The Crucible* include McGill's, O'Neal's, Strout's, and Budick's. Martin's "Arthur Miller's *The Crucible:*

Background and Sources" is an excellent summary of the historical context and dramatic transformations made by Miller. Martin concludes that "*The Crucible* has attained a life of its own; one that both interprets and defines the cultural and historical background of American society" (290).

A few critics focus on the linguistic and structural techniques employed by Miller in *The Crucible*. Fender shows how Miller uses language to point up the hypocrisy of the Puritans in Salem. Hill defends the play against Nathan's arguments that the play is "all 'internal,' that it is not communicated to an audience," that its characters are poorly developed, that it is relevant only to the McCarthy era, and that it is structurally deficient because the courtroom scene is the climax (312). Porter's "The Long Shadow of the Law" shows how the "play not only uses the formula [of the trial ritual] as a framing device, but also raises the question about the value of the trial itself as an instrument of justice" (181). Meserve focuses on Miller's characterization of his protagonist (1982). Liston's analysis of Proctor concludes that what separates the protagonist from the others "is the ability to think and speak in metaphor: i.e., the ability to think and speak poetically, playfully, imaginatively, non-literally" (395). Bonnet points up that the "fundamental duality" in the play is that it is both a tragic drama of an individual and a "drama involving a whole group of people" (32). A full-length study that reviews many of these critical issues is Welland's *Arthur Miller, The Crucible: Notes.*

Criticism of *A View from the Bridge* focuses primarily on Eddie Carbone as tragic protagonist, the unique dramatic conventions found in the play, and the changes made when the one-act was revised into a full-length work. Arthur Epstein analyzes Miller's intent to make Eddie Carbone a tragic hero and suggests that his revision was weaker than the original because of changes in the dramatic conventions. Rothenberg and Shapiro provide psychoanalytic portraits of Eddie and Katherine. Orr discusses primarily *The Crucible* and *A View from the Bridge* as attempts at reviving traditional tragedy. Hurd concludes that "the reference to angels and other sexual symbols...indicate that his [Eddie Carbone's] repressed homosexuality is a major source of his conflict" (6). An excellent study of the revision of *A View from the Bridge* can be found in Styan. There have been few critical essays touching on *A Memory of Two Mondays*, in most cases, it is only referred to in surveys of Miller's oeuvre.

The most recent of Miller's plays to receive extensive critical attention is *After the Fall*. Criticism usually focuses on the autobiographical content of the play, the expressionistic technique of the play, or its relationship to other major literary works.

Steene compares Miller's play to Strindberg's *To Damascus* and labels *Fall* "a Strindbergian failure." Koppenhaver compares and contrasts *After the Fall* with Camus's *The Fall*, as does Cismaru. Nolan shows how Tennessee Williams in *Glass Menagerie* and Miller in *After the Fall* create

memory plays that focus on action contained in the minds of the protagonists. Buitenhuis categorizes *After the Fall* as Arthur Miller's *King
Lear*. Terry Otten analyzes Miller's portrayal of the fall. Moss's "Biographical and Literary Allusion in *After the Fall*" catalogs various literary
allusions, including Miller's first works, the Bible, and *The Fall*, as well
as personal sources for the play.

Many critics try to focus discussion on *After the Fall*'s structural techniques and thematic concerns rather than on its autobiographical plot
line. Ganz suggests that there are structural problems in the play but
argues it is Miller's first successful treatment of the theme of guilt. Price
argues that in *After the Fall* Miller is finally successful in merging the
psychological, sociological, and political concerns of his previous works.
Leslie Epstein's "The Unhappiness of Arthur Miller" suggests that *After
the Fall*, as well as *Incident at Vichy*, are not successful because the playwright has not confronted his own guilt and that their "weakness...is
...in Miller's understanding" (Martine, xx). Epstein draws parallels between Quentin and Hamlet, as well as between Miller and Ibsen. Brashear argues that *After the Fall* again proves Miller to be a dramatist who
deals with social concerns rather than tragic ones. Murray argues, in
"Point of View in *After the Fall*," that the representation of Quentin's
subjective view results in a flawed dramatic structure and *Fall* is basically
an "old-fashioned thesis play" (140). Bigsby, in "The Fall and After:
Arthur Miller's Confession," notes that the play attempts to revolt against
the simple responses to social problems of the dramatists of the 1930s
and 1940s but is not totally successful because his protagonist's credibility
is not fully established. Stinton defends the play against critics who argue
that it is structurally weak and points out the clear thematic and symbolic
ties between the first and second acts. Jacobson's "Christ, Pygmalion,
and Hitler in *After the Fall*" delineates the various facets of Quentin's
personality and how these help shape the action and theme of the play.
Centola's "Unblessed Rage for Order" concludes that "Quentin's journey
through the labyrinth of his mind ends with a revelation that is life-
renewing and life-sustaining, but that also explains why man's search
for meaning must ultimately remain an unblessed rage for order" (70).

Incident at Vichy is most often analyzed in terms of Miller's approach
to the theme of guilt and the Holocaust. Clurman's "Director's Notes:
Incident at Vichy" are interesting for their insights into characters and
themes within the play. Rahv criticizes the play's sententiousness and
melodramatic contrivances. Lowenthal proves "that *Vichy* is an explicit
rendition of Sartre's treatise on Jews, as well as a clear structural example
of Sartre's definition of the existential 'theatre of situation' " (143).

Miller's plays from *The Price* through *Danger: Memory!* have not received much critical attention. Bigsby, in "What Price Arthur Miller?"

argues that Miller successfully balances his recurrent thematic conflict between freedom and determinism and has "emerged from the personal and artistic difficulties he has experienced since the mid-fifties" (25). Willett describes the similarities in *The Price* to Miller's earliest works (1971), while Weales, in "All About Talk: Arthur Miller's *The Price*," notes how "Miller is using and questioning the dramatic, social, and therapeutic uses of talk" (189). Chaikin deals with the enigmatic denouement and "suggests it affirms the power of life" (44). Higgins's article focuses on the comic character of Solomon and his central function in the dramatic action. Centola, in "What Price Freedom?" argues that *The Creation of the World* "deserves our attention not only because it represents Miller's first experiment with comedy, but also because it contributes to our understanding of his enduring vision of the human condition and gives us valuable insight into his interpretation of the process of the fall into that condition" (3). Centola goes on to compare Miller's depiction of humanity's fall with Sartre's and concludes with a brief analytical allusion to *Up From Paradise*.

Detailed analyses of many of Miller's plays since *The Price* are found in Welland's full-length work, *Miller: The Playwright*, and Bigsby's chapter on Miller in his *Twentieth-Century American Drama*. Albert Wertheim's essay "Arthur Miller: *After the Fall* and After" is an excellent reevaluation of Miller's later works, from *After the Fall* through *The American Clock*. Wertheim points out similarities to Miller's earlier dramas as well as new thematic and structural approaches. He concludes that "what is clear, however, in viewing the dramatic output of Arthur Miller from *After the Fall* to the present is that he is a playwright who has not stood still. He continues to develop new ideas as well as new dramaturgy to convey them" (31).

Many of the seminal articles dealing with Arthur Miller's dramaturgy are found in collections of essays; the major anthologies are Corrigan, Ferres, Koon, Martin, Martine, Meserve, and Weales's two volumes on *The Crucible* and *Salesman*.

FUTURE RESEARCH OPPORTUNITIES

A number of scholarly and critical questions need to be explored in future research on Arthur Miller. Studies dealing with his dramatic works since *The Price* are most needed. These plays, including *The Creation of the World and Other Business, The Archbishop's Ceiling, The American Clock, Playing for Time, Elegy for a Lady, Some Kind of Love Story, I Can't Remember Anything*, and *Clara*, need to be placed within the context of Miller's work. Furthermore many of Miller's earlier works, particularly in the light of recent successful revivals, need reevaluation; this may be most important for *All My Sons, Death of a Salesman*, and *After the Fall*.

Given Miller's position as the senior statesman among contemporary American dramatists, an updated analysis of his complete dramatic output and of his place in the contemporary American theatre is necessary.

SECONDARY SOURCES

Adler, Henry. "To Hell with Society." *Tulane Drama Review* 4 (May 1960): 53–76.

Atkinson, Brooks. "Welcome Stranger." *New York Times* (9 February 1947): 2: 1.

Aylen, Leo. "Miller." In *Greek Tragedy and the Modern World*, pp. 248–57. London: Methuen, 1964.

Barksdale, Richard K. "Social Background in the Plays of Miller and Williams." *CLA Journal* 6 (March 1963): 161–69.

Bates, Barclay W. "The Lost Past in *Death of a Salesman*." *Modern Drama* 11 (September 1968): 164–72.

Bentley, Eric. *In Search of Theatre*. New York: Knopf, 1953.

Bergeron, David M. "Arthur Miller's *The Crucible* and Nathaniel Hawthorne: Some Parallels." *English Journal* 58 (January 1969): 47–55.

Bergman, Herbert. "The Interior of a Heart: *The Crucible* and *The Scarlet Letter*." *University College Quarterly* 15 (May 1970): 27–32.

Bettina, Sister M. "Willy Loman's Brother Ben: Tragic Insight in *Death of a Salesman*." *Modern Drama* 4 (February 1962): 409–12.

Bigsby, C. W. E. "Arthur Miller." In *Confrontation and Commitment*, pp. 26–49. Columbia: University of Missouri Press, 1968.

———. "The Fall and After: Arthur Miller's Confession." *Modern Drama* 10 (September 1967): 124–36.

———. *Twentieth-Century American Drama*. Vol. 2: *Tennessee Williams, Arthur Miller, Edward Albee*. Cambridge: Cambridge University Press, 1984.

———. "What Price Arthur Miller?: An Analysis of *The Price*." *Twentieth-Century Literature* 16 (January 1970): 16–25.

Blau, Herbert. "Counterforce I: The Social Drama." In *The Impossible Theatre*, pp. 186–92. New York: Macmillan, 1964.

Bliquez, Guerin. "Linda's Role in *Death of a Salesman*." *Modern Drama* 10 (February 1968): 383–86.

Blumberg, Paul. "Work as Alienation in the Plays of Arthur Miller." In *Arthur Miller: New Perspectives*, pp. 48–64. Edited by Robert A. Martin. Englewood Cliffs, N.J.: Prentice-Hall, 1982.

Boggs, W. Arthur. "*Oedipus* and *All My Sons*." *Personalist* 42 (Autumn 1961): 555–60.

Bonnet, Jean M. "Society versus the Individual in Arthur Miller's *The Crucible*." *English Studies* 63 (1982): 32–36.

Brashear, William R. "The Empty Bench: Morality, Tragedy, and Arthur Miller." *Michigan Quarterly Review* 5 (Fall 1966): 270–78.

Brater, Enoch. "Ethics and Ethnicity in the Plays of Arthur Miller." In *From Hester Street to Hollywood: The Jewish-American Stage and Screen*, pp. 123–

36. Edited by Sarah Blacher Cohen. Bloomington: Indiana University Press, 1983.

———. "Miller's Realism and *Death of a Salesman*." In *Arthur Miller: New Perspectives*, pp. 115–26. Edited by Robert A. Martin. Englewood Cliffs, N.J.: Prentice-Hall, 1982.

Bronson, David. "*An Enemy of the People:* A Key to Arthur Miller's Art and Ethics." *Comparative Drama* 2 (Winter 1968): 229–47.

Brucher, Richard T. "Willy Loman and *The Soul of a New Machine:* Technology and the Common Man." *Journal of American Studies* 17 (1983): 325–36.

Brustein, Robert. "Arthur Miller's Mea Culpa." *New Republic* (8 February 1964): 26–28, 30.

———. "Muddy Track at Lincoln Center." *New Republic* (26 December 1964): 26–27.

Budick, E. Miller. "History and Other Spectres in Arthur Miller's *The Crucible*." *Modern Drama* 28 (December 1985): 535–52.

Buitenhuis, Peter. "Arthur Miller: The Fall from the Bridge." *Canadian Association for American Studies Bulletin* 3 (Spring-Summer 1967): 55–71.

Carpenter, Charles A. "Studies of Arthur Miller's Drama: A Selective International Bibliography, 1966–1979." In *Arthur Miller: New Perspectives*, pp. 205–19. Edited by Robert A. Martin. Englewood Cliffs, N.J.: Prentice-Hall, 1982.

Carson, Neil. *Arthur Miller*. London: Macmillan, 1982.

Cassell, Richard A. "Arthur Miller's 'Rage of Conscience.' " *Ball State University Forum* 1 (Winter 1960): 31–36.

Centola, Steven R. "Confrontation with the Other: Alienation in the Works of Arthur Miller and Jean-Paul Sartre." *Journal of Evolutionary Psychology* 5, nos 1–2 (1984): 1–11.

———. "Unblessed Rage for Order: Arthur Miller's *After the Fall*." *Arizona Quarterly* 39 (Spring 1983): 62–70.

———. "What Price Freedom? The Fall Revisited: Arthur Miller's *The Creation of the World and Other Business*." *Studies in the Humanities* 12, no. 1 (June 1985): 3–10.

Chaikin, Milton. "The Ending of Arthur Miller's *The Price*." *Studies in the Humanities* 8, no. 2 (1981): 40–44.

Cismaru, Alfred. "Before and *After the Fall*." *Forum* 11 (Winter 1974): 67–71.

Clurman, Harold. "Arthur Miller." In *Lies Like Truth*, pp. 64–72. New York: Macmillan, 1958.

———. "Director's Notes: *Incident at Vichy*." *Tulane Drama Review* 9 (Summer 1965): 77–90.

Coe, Richard. "Arthur Miller's 'Ceiling.' " *Washington Post* (2 May 1977): B1, B7.

Cohn, Ruby. "The Articulate Victims of Arthur Miller." In *Arthur Miller: New Perspectives*, pp. 65–74. Edited by Robert A. Martin. Englewood Cliffs, N.J.: Prentice-Hall, 1982.

Cole, Susan L. *The Absent One: Mourning Ritual, Tragedy, and the Performance of Ambivalence*. University Park: Pennsylvania State University Press, 1985.

Cook, Larry W. "The Function of Ben and Dave Singleman in *Death of Salesman*." *Notes on Contemporary Literature* 5 (January 1975): 7–9.

Corrigan, Robert W. "The Achievement of Arthur Miller." *Comparative Drama* 2 (Fall 1968): 141–60.

———, ed. *Arthur Miller: A Collection of Critical Essays.* Englewood Cliffs, N.J.: Prentice-Hall, 1969.

Couchman, Gordon W. "Arthur Miller's Tragedy of Babbitt." *Educational Theatre Journal* 7 (October 1955): 206–11.

Dillingham, William B. "Arthur Miller and the Loss of Conscience." *Emory University Quarterly* 16 (Spring 1960): 40–50.

Driver, Tom F. "Strength and Weakness in Arthur Miller." *Tulane Drama Review* 4 (May 1960): 45–52.

Eisinger, Chester E. "Focus on Arthur Miller's *Death of a Salesman:* The Wrong Dreams." In *American Dreams, American Nightmares,* pp. 165–74. Edited by David Madden. Carbondale: Southern Illinois University Press, 1970.

Epstein, Arthur. "A Look at *A View from the Bridge.*" *Texas Studies in Literature and Language* 7 (Spring 1965): 109–22.

Epstein, Leslie. "The Unhappiness of Arthur Miller." *Tri-Quarterly* 1 (Spring 1965): 165–73.

Fender, Stephen. "Precision and Pseudo Precision in *The Crucible.*" *Journal of American Studies* 1 (April 1967): 87–98.

Ferres, John H. *Arthur Miller: A Reference Guide.* Boston: G. K. Hall, 1979.

———. "Still in the Present Tense: *The Crucible* Today." *University College Quarterly* 17 (May 1972): 8–18.

———, ed. *Twentieth Century Interpretations of The Crucible.* Englewood Cliffs, N.J.: Prentice-Hall, 1972.

Field, B. S. "Death of a Salesman." *Twentieth Century Literature* 18 (January 1972): 19–24.

Flaxman, Seymour L. "The Debt of Williams and Miller to Ibsen and Strindberg." *Comparative Literature Studies* (1963): 51–59.

Foster, Richard J. "Confusion and Tragedy: The Failure of Miller's *Salesman.*" In *Two Modern American Tragedies,* pp. 82–88. Edited by John D. Hurrell. New York: Scribner's, 1961.

Freedman, Morris. "The Jewishness of Arthur Miller." In *American Drama in Social Context,* pp. 43–58. Carbondale: Southern Illinois University Press, 1971.

Ganz, Arthur. "The Silence of Arthur Miller." *Drama Survey* 3 (Fall 1963): 224–37.

Gassner, John. "Tragic Perspectives: A Sequence of Queries." *Tulane Drama Review* 2 (May 1958): 20–21.

Gelb, Phillip. "*Death of a Salesman:* A Symposium." *Tulane Drama Review* 2 (May 1958): 63–9.

Gianakaris, C. J. "Theater of the Mind in Miller, Osborne, and Shaffer." *Renascence* 30 (Autumn 1977): 33–42.

Gordon, Lois. "*Death of a Salesman:* An Appreciation." In *The Forties: Fiction, Poetry, Drama,* pp. 273–83. Edited by Warren French. Deland, Fla.: Everett/Edwards, 1969.

Groff, Edward. "Point of View in Modern Drama." *Modern Drama* 2 (December 1959): 268–82.

Gross, Barry. "*All My Sons* and the Larger Context." *Modern Drama* 18 (March 1975): 15–27.

———. "Peddler and Pioneer in *Death of a Salesman*." *Modern Drama* 7 (February 1965): 405–10.

Hagopian, John V. "Arthur Miller: The Salesman's Two Cases." *Modern Drama* 6 (September 1963): 117–25.

Harshbarger, Karl. *The Burning Jungle: An Analysis of Arthur Miller's Death of a Salesman*. Washington, D.C.: University Press of America, 1978.

Haugen, Einar. "Ibsen as Fellow Traveler: Arthur Miller's Adaptation of *An Enemy of the People*." *Scandinavian Studies* 51 (1979): 343–53.

Hayashi, Tetsumaro. *Arthur Miller and Tennessee Williams: Research Opportunities and Dissertation Abstracts*. Jefferson, N.C.: McFarland, 1983.

———. *An Index to Arthur Miller Criticism*. 2d ed. Metuchen, N.J.: Scarecrow Press, 1976.

Hayman, Ronald. *Arthur Miller*. New York: Ungar, 1972.

———. "Arthur Miller: Between Sartre and Society." *Encounter* 37 (November 1971): 73–9.

Hays, Peter L. "Arthur Miller and Tennessee Williams." *Essays in Literature* 4 (1977): 239–49.

Heilman, Robert B. *The Iceman, the Arsonist, and the Troubled Agent*. Seattle: University of Washington Press, 1973.

———. "Salesmen's Deaths: Documentary and Myth." *Shenandoah* 20 (Spring 1969): 20–28.

Higgins, David. "Arthur Miller's *The Price:* The Wisdom of Solomon." In *Itinerary 3: Criticism*, pp. 85–94. Edited by Frank Baldanza. Bowling Green, Ohio: Bowling Green State University Press, 1977.

Hill, Philip G. "*The Crucible:* A Structural View." *Modern Drama* 10 (December 1967): 312–17.

Hogan, Robert. *Arthur Miller*. Minneapolis: University of Minnesota Press, 1964.

Huftel, Sheila. *Arthur Miller: The Burning Glass*. New York: Citadel, 1965.

Hunter, Frederick J. "The Value of Time in Modern Drama." *Journal of Aesthetics and Art Criticism* 16 (December 1957): 199–200.

Hurd, Myles R. "Angels and Anxieties in Miller's *A View from the Bridge*." *Notes on Contemporary Literature* 14, no. 4 (1983): 4–6.

Hurrell, John D., ed. *Two Modern American Tragedies: Reviews and Criticism of Death of a Salesman and Streetcar Named Desire*. New York: Scribner's, 1961.

Hynes, Joseph A. "Arthur Miller and the Impasse of Naturalism." *South Atlantic Quarterly* 62 (Summer 1963): 327–34.

———. "Attention Must Be Paid . . . " *College English* 23 (April 1962): 574–78.

Jackson, Esther M. "*Death of a Salesman:* Tragic Myth in the Modern Theatre." *CLA Journal* 7 (September 1963): 63–76.

Jacobson, Irving F. "Christ, Pygmalion, and Hitler in *After the Fall*." *Essays in Literature* 2 (August 1974): 12–27.

———. "Family Dreams in *Death of a Salesman*." *American Literature* 47 (1975): 247–58.

Jensen, George. *Arthur Miller: A Bibliographical Checklist*. Columbia, S.C.: Faust, 1976.

Johnson, Vernon E. "Dramatic Influences in the Development of Arthur Miller's

Concept of Social Tragedy." Ph.D. dissertation, George Peabody College for Teachers, 1962.

Kauffmann, Stanley. "Across the Divide." *New Republic* (20 February 1961): 26, 28.

Kerr, Walter. "The Crucible." *New York Herald Tribune* (23 January 1953): 12.

———. "This Salesman Is More Man Than Myth." *New York Times* (29 June 1975): B1, B5.

Koon, Helene Wickham, ed. *Twentieth Century Interpretations of Death of a Salesman.* Englewood Cliffs, N.J.: Prentice-Hall, 1983.

Koppenhaver, Allen J. "*The Fall* and After: Albert Camus and Arthur Miller." *Modern Drama* 9 (September 1966): 206–09.

Lawrence, S. A. "The Right Dreams in Miller's *Death of a Salesman.*" *CollegeEnglish* 25 (April 1964): 547–49.

Liston, William T. "John Proctor's Playing in *The Crucible.*" *Midwest Quarterly* 20 (1979): 394–403.

Long, Madeline J. "Sartrean Themes in Contemporary American Literature." Ph.D. dissertation, Columbia University, 1967.

Loughlin, Richard L. "Tradition and Tragedy in *All My Sons.*" *English Record* 14 (February 1964): 23–7.

Lowenthal, Lawrence D. "Arthur Miller's *Incident at Vichy:* A Sartrean Interpretation." In *Critical Essays on Arthur Miller*, pp. 143–54. Edited by James J. Martine. Boston: G. K. Hall, 1979.

McAnany, Emile G. "The Tragic Commitment: Some Notes on Arthur Miller." *Modern Drama* 5 (May 1962): 11–20.

McGill, William J. "The Crucible of History: Arthur Miller's John Proctor." *New England Quarterly* 54 (1981): 258–64.

McMahon, Helen. "Arthur Miller's Common Man: The Problem of the Realistic and the Mythic." *Drama and Theatre* 10 (Spring 1972): 128–33.

Mander, John. "Arthur Miller's *Death of a Salesman.*" In *The Writer and Commitment*, pp. 138–52. London: Secker and Warburg, 1961.

Manske, Dwain E. "A Study of the Changing Family Role in the Early Published and Unpublished Works of Arthur Miller, to Which Is Appended a Catalogue of the Arthur Miller Collection at the University of Texas at Austin." Ph.D. dissertation, University of Texas at Austin, 1970.

Martin, Robert A., ed. *Arthur Miller: New Perspectives.* Englewood Cliffs, N.J.: Prentice-Hall, 1982.

———. "Arthur Miller's *The Crucible:* Background and Sources." *Modern Drama* 20 (1977): 279–92.

Martine, James J., ed. *Critical Essays on Arthur Miller.* Boston: G. K. Hall, 1979.

Meserve, Walter J. "*The Crucible:* The Fool and I." In *Arthur Miller: New Perspectives*, pp. 127–38. Edited by Robert A. Martin. Englewood Cliffs, N.J.: Prentice-Hall, 1982.

———. *The Merrill Studies in Death of a Salesman.* Columbus, Ohio: Merrill, 1972.

Miller, Jeanne-Marie A. "Odets, Miller, and Communism." *College Language Association Journal* 19 (June 1976): 484–93.

Miller, Jordan Y. "Myth and the American Dream: O'Neill to Albee." *Modern Drama* 7 (September 1964): 190–98.

Moss, Leonard. *Arthur Miller.* Rev. ed. Boston: Twayne, 1980.

————. "Arthur Miller and the Common Man's Language." *Modern Drama* 7 (May 1964): 52–59.

————. "Biographical and Literary Allusion in *After the Fall.*" *Educational Theatre Journal* 18 (March 1966): 34–40.

Mottram, Eric. "Arthur Miller: The Development of a Political Dramatist in America." In *American Theatre*, pp. 127–61. Edited by J. R. Brown and Bernard Harris. London: Edward Arnold, 1967.

Murray, Edward J. *Arthur Miller, Dramatist.* New York: Ungar, 1967.

————. "Point of View in *After the Fall.*" *CLA Journal* 10 (December 1966): 135–42.

Nadel, Norman. "After the Fall." *New York World Telegram and Sun* (3 February 1964): 26.

Nathan, George Jean. "All My Sons." In *Theatre Book of the Year, 1946–1947*, pp. 290–93. New York: Alfred A. Knopf, 1947.

Nelson, Benjamin. *Arthur Miller: Portrait of a Playwright.* London: Peter Owen, 1970.

Nolan, Paul T. "Two Memory Plays: *The Glass Menagerie* and *After the Fall.*" *McNeese Review* 17 (1966): 27–38.

Novick, Julius. "Arthur Miller: Does He Speak to the Present?" *New York Times* (7 February 1971): 17.

Oberg, Arthur K. "*Death of a Salesman* and Arthur Miller's Search for Style." *Criticism* 9 (Fall 1967): 303–11.

Oliver, Edith. "The Theatre: Off-Broadway." *New Yorker* (6 February 1965): 94.

O'Neal, Michael J. "History, Myth, and Name Magic in Arthur Miller's *The Crucible.*" *Clio* 12 (1983): 111–22.

Orr, John. "Williams and Miller: The Cold War and the Renewal of Tragedy." In *Tragic Drama and Modern Society: Studies in Social and Literary Theory of Drama from 1870 to the Present*, pp. 206–40. Totowa, N.J.: Barnes and Noble, 1981.

Otten, Charlotte F. "Who Am I? A Re-investigation of Arthur Miller's *Death of a Salesman.*" *Cresset* 26 (February 1963): 11–13.

Otten, Terry. *After Innocence: Visions of the Fall in Modern Literature.* Pittsburgh: Pittsburgh University Press, 1982.

Overland, Orm. "The Action and Its Significance: Arthur Miller's Struggle with Dramatic Form." *Modern Drama* 18 (March 1975): 1–14.

Panikkar, N. Bhaskara. *Individual Morality and Social Happiness in Arthur Miller.* Atlantic Highlands, N.J.: Humanities, 1982.

Parker, Brian. "Point of View in Arthur Miller's *Death of a Salesman.*" *University of Toronto Quarterly* 35 (January 1966): 144–57.

Popkin, Henry. "Arthur Miller's *The Crucible.*" *College English* 26 (November 1964): 139–46.

————. "Arthur Miller: The Strange Encounter." *Sewanee Review* 68 (Winter 1960): 34–60.

Porter, Thomas E. "Acres of Diamonds: *Death of a Salesman.*" In *Myth and Modern American Drama*, pp. 127–52. Detroit: Wayne State University, 1969.

————. "The Long Shadow of the Law: *The Crucible.*" In *Myth and Modern American Drama*, pp. 177–99. Detroit: Wayne State University, 1969.

————. "The Mills of the Gods: Economics and Law in the Plays of Arthur

Miller." In *Arthur Miller: New Perspectives*, pp. 75–96. Edited by Robert A. Martin. Englewood Cliffs, N.J.: Prentice-Hall, 1982.

Price, Jonathan. "Arthur Miller: Fall or Rise?" *Drama* 73 (Summer 1964): 39–40.

Prudhoe, John. "Arthur Miller and the Tradition of Tragedy." *English Studies* 43 (October 1962): 430–39.

Rahv, Philip. "Arthur Miller and the Fallacy of Profundity." In *The Myth and the Powerhouse*, pp. 225–33. New York: Farrar, Straus, and Giroux, 1965.

Reno, Raymond H. "Arthur Miller and the Death of God." *Texas Studies in Language and Literature* 11 (Summer 1969): 1069–87.

Rich, Frank. "Play: Miller's 'American Clock.' " *New York Times* (21 November 1980). Reprinted in *New York Theatre Critics' Reviews* (1980): 80–81.

———. "The Stage: Arthur Miller's 'Danger: Memory!' " *New York Times* (9 February 1987). Reprinted in *New York Theatre Critics' Reviews* (1987): 343.

———. "Theatre: Hoffman, 'Death of a Salesman.' " *New York Times* (30 March 1984). Reprinted in *New York Theatre Critics' Reviews* (1984): 324.

———. "Theatre: Richard Kiley in Miller's 'All My Sons.' " *New York Times* (23 April 1987). Reprinted in *New York Theatre Critics' Reviews* (1987): 272.

Rothenberg, Albert and Eugene D. Shapiro. "The Defense of Psychoanalysis in Literature: *Long Day's Journey into Night* and *A View from the Bridge*." *Comparative Drama* 7 (Spring 1973): 65–7.

Rowe, Kenneth. "Shadows Cast Before." In *Arthur Miller: New Perspectives*, pp. 13–32. Edited by Robert A. Martin. Englewood Cliffs, N.J.: Prentice-Hall, 1982.

Saisselin, Remy G. "Is Tragic Drama Possible in the Twentieth Century?" *Theatre Annual* 17 (1960): 20–1.

Scanlan, Tom. "Family and Society in Arthur Miller." In *Family, Drama, and American Dreams*, pp. 126–55. Westport, Conn.: Greenwood, 1978.

Schlueter, June and James K. Flanagan. *Arthur Miller*. New York: Ungar, 1987.

Schneider, Daniel E. "Play of Dreams." *Theatre Arts* 33 (October 1949): 18–21.

Schroeder, Patricia R. "Arthur Miller: Illuminating Process." *REAL: Yearbook of Research in English and American Literature* 3 (1985): 265–93.

Schweinitz, George de. "*Death of a Salesman:* A Note on Epic and Tragedy." *Western Humanities Review* (Winter 1960): 91–6.

Shaw, Patrick W. "The Ironic Characterization of Bernard in *Death of a Salesman*." *Notes on Contemporary Literature* 11, no. 3 (1981): 12.

Sheldon, Neil. "Social Commentary in the Plays of Clifford Odets and Arthur Miller." Ph.D. dissertation, New York University, 1963.

Siegel, Paul N. "The Drama and the Thwarted American Dream." *Lock Haven Review* 7 (1965): 52–62.

———. "Willy Loman and King Lear." *College English* 17 (March 1956): 341–45.

Spindler, Michael. *American Literature and Social Change: William Dean Howells to Arthur Miller*. London: Macmillan, 1983.

Stambusky, Alan S. "Arthur Miller: Aristotelian Canons in Twentieth Century Drama." In *Modern American Drama: Essays in Criticism*, pp. 91–115. Edited by William E. Taylor. Deland, Fla.: Everett/Edwards, 1968.

Steene, Birgitta. "Arthur Miller's *After the Fall*." *Moderna Sprak* 58 (1964): 446–52.

Steinberg, M. W. "Arthur Miller and the Ideas of Modern Tragedy." *Dalhousie Review* 40 (Autumn 1960): 329–40.

Stinton, John J. "Structure in *After the Fall:* The Relevance of the Maggie Episode to the Main Themes and the Christian Symbolism." *Modern Drama* 10 (December 1967): 233–40.

Strout, Cushing. "Analogical History: *The Crucible*." In *The Veracious Imagination: Essays on American History, Literature, and Biography*, pp. 139–56. Middletown, Conn.: Wesleyan University Press, 1981.

Styan, J. L. "Why *A View from the Bridge* Went Down Well in London: The Story of a Revision." In *Arthur Miller: New Perspectives*, pp. 139–48. Edited by Robert A. Martin. Englewood Cliffs, N.J.: Prentice-Hall, 1982.

Taubman, Howard. "Inquiry into Roots of Evil." *New York Times* (20 December 1964): 2:3.

Trewin, J. C. "Quick Change." *Illustrated London News* (27 October 1956): 720.

Trowbridge, Clinton W. "Arthur Miller: Between Pathos and Tragedy." *Modern Drama* 10 (December 1967): 221–22.

Tynan, Kenneth. "American Blues: The Plays of Arthur Miller and Tennessee Williams." *Encounter* 2 (May 1954): 13–19.

Ungar, Harriet. "The Writings of and about Arthur Miller: A Checklist 1936–1967." *Bulletin of New York Public Library* 74 (February 1970): 107–34.

Vogel, Dan. "Willy Tyrannos." In *Three Masks of American Tragedy*, pp. 91–102. Baton Rouge: Louisiana State University, 1974.

Vos, Nelvin. "The American Dream Turned to Nightmare: Recent American Drama." *Christian Scholar's Review* 1 (Spring 1971): 200–201.

Walden, Daniel. "Miller's Roots and His Moral Dilemma: or, Continuity from Brooklyn to *Salesman*." In *Critical Essays on Arthur Miller*, pp. 189–96. Edited by James J. Martine. Boston: G. K. Hall, 1979.

Walker, Philip. "Arthur Miller's *The Crucible*: Tragedy or Allegory?" *Western Speech* 20 (Fall 1957): 222–24.

Warshow, Robert. "The Liberal Conscience in *The Crucible*." *Commentary* 15 (March 1953): 265–71.

Weales, Gerald. "All about Talk: Arthur Miller's *The Price*." In *Arthur Miller: New Perspectives*, pp. 188–99. Edited by Robert A. Martin. Englewood Cliffs, N.J.: Prentice-Hall, 1982.

———. "Arthur Miller: Man and His Image." *Tulane Drama Review* 7 (Fall 1962): 165–80.

———. "Cliches in the Garden." *Commonweal* (22 December 1972): 276.

———. Introduction to *Arthur Miller, The Crucible: Text and Criticism*, pp. ix-xvii. Edited by Gerald Weales. New York: Viking, 1971.

———, ed. *Arthur Miller: The Crucible: Text and Criticism*. New York: Viking, 1971.

———, ed. *Arthur Miller: Death of a Salesman: Text and Criticism*. New York: Viking, 1967.

———. "Theatre Without Walls." In *A Time of Harvest*. Edited by Robert E. Spiller. New York: Hill and Wong, 1962. p. 142–43.

Welland, Dennis. *Arthur Miller*. New York: Grove, 1961.

———. *Arthur Miller: The Crucible: Notes*. London: Longman, 1980.

———. *Arthur Miller: The Playwright*. London: Methuen, 1983.

———. *Arthur Miller: A Study of His Plays*. London: Methuen, 1979.

Wells, Arvin R. "The Living and the Dead in *All My Sons*." In *Critical Essays on Arthur Miller*, pp. 5–9. Edited by James J. Martine. Boston: G. K. Hall, 1979.

Wertheim, Albert. "Arthur Miller: *After the Fall* and After." In *Essays on Contemporary American Drama*, pp. 19–32. Edited by Hedwig Bock and Albert Wertheim. Munich: Max Hueber, 1981.

White, Sidney Howard. *Guide to Arthur Miller*. Columbus, Ohio: Charles E. Merrill, 1970.

Whitley, Alvin. "Arthur Miller: An Attempt at Modern Tragedy." *Transactions of the Wisconsin Academy of Science, Arts and Letters* 42 (1953): 257–62.

Wiegand, William. "Arthur Miller and the Man Who Knows." *Western Review* 21 (Winter 1957): 85–103.

Willett, Ralph. "The Ideas of Miller and Williams." *Theatre Annual* 22 (1965): 31–40.

———. "A Note on Arthur Miller's *The Price*." *Journal of American Studies* 5 (December 1971): 307–10.

Williams, Raymond. *Drama from Ibsen to Brecht*. London: Chatto and Windus, 1968.

———. "The Realism of Arthur Miller." *Critical Quarterly* 1 (Summer 1959): 140–49.

Willis, Robert J. "Arthur Miller's *The Crucible:* Relevant for All Times." *Faculty Journal (East Stroudsberg State College)* 1 (1970): 5–14.

Yorks, Samuel A. "Joe Keller and His Sons." *Western Humanities Review* 13 (Autumn 1959):401–7.

Marsha Norman

(21 SEPTEMBER 1947–   )

IRMGARD H. WOLFE

ASSESSMENT OF NORMAN'S REPUTATION

Marsha Norman belongs to the group of female playwrights who have recently made successful inroads on a still very much male-dominated preserve. Her best-known plays, *Getting Out* and *'night, Mother*, have won the John Gassner New Playwrights Medallion (1979) and the Pulitzer Prize (1983), respectively. Her plays center on female protagonists and discuss questions of female identity, the mother-daughter relationship, and the severing of ties. These concerns, however, owe less to feminist polemics than to Norman's desire to depict the human condition from the vantage point of active female characters.

Her strongest points are her recreation of meticulously observed everyday life, her ear for the nuances of dialogue, her dry, often sardonic humor, and her emotional honesty. Like Beth Henley and Maria Irene Fornes, Norman possesses a regional orientation, although she does not tie herself to a specific locale.

PRIMARY BIBLIOGRAPHY OF NORMAN'S WORKS

Plays

Getting Out. In *The Best Plays of 1978–1979*. Edited by Otis L. Guernsey. New York: Dodd, Mead, 1979. (Abridged.) New York: Dramatists Play Service, 1979; Garden City, N.Y.: Doubleday, 1979; New York: Avon Books, 1980.
Third and Oak—The Laundromat. New York: Dramatists Play Service, 1980.
'night, Mother. New York: Dramatists Play Service, 1983; New York: Hill and Wang, 1983; London: Faber, 1984; in *The Best Plays of 1982–1983*. Edited by Otis L. Guernsey. New York: Dodd, Mead, 1983. (Abridged.)

Third and Oak—the Pool Hall. New York: Dramatists Play Service, 1985.
The Holdup. New York: Dramatists Play Service, 1987.

Interviews

Beard, Sherilyn. "An Interview With Marsha Norman." *Southern California Anthology* 3 (1985): 11–17.
Guernsey, Otis R. "Five Dramatists Discuss the Value of Criticism." *Dramatist's Guild Quarterly* 21 (March 84): 11–25.
Brustein, Robert. "Conversations with...Marsha Norman." *Dramatists Guild Quarterly* 21 (September 84): 9–21.
The Guernsey and Brustein interviews are reprinted in:
Guernsey, Otis L., ed. *Broadway Song and Story*. New York: Dodd, Mead, 1985.
Betsko, Kathleen, and Koenig, Rachel. *Interviews with Contemporary Women Playwrights*. Beech Tree Books: New York, 1987.

Selected Articles and Novel

"How Can One Man Do So Much? And Look So Good? A Meditation on a Mystery." *Vogue* (February 1984): 356–58.
"Articles of Faith: A Conversation with Lillian Hellman." *American Theatre* 1 (May 1984): 10–15.
"Ten Golden Rules for Playwrights." *Writer* (September 1985): 13, 45.
"Why Do We Need New Plays? And Other Difficult Questions." *Dramatists Guild Quarterly* 24 (Winter 1987): 18, 31–33.
The Fortune Teller. New York: Random House, 1987; London: Collins, 1988.

PRODUCTION HISTORY

Norman's plays have followed a familiar pattern. First produced at regional theaters, they then moved to off-Broadway or Broadway. Her first play, *Getting Out*, was produced by Jon Jory at the Actors Theatre of Louisville, Kentucky, in 1977 for the Festival of New Plays. *Getting Out* concentrates on one main character, a woman just released from prison, who is split into two persons appearing onstage simultaneously to show the protagonist before and after her imprisonment and thus present her interactions with the people around her and her choices for remaking her life. The play won the festival prize and was also judged the best new play produced in a regional theater by the American Theater Critics Association.

Subsequently *Getting Out* was staged at the Mark Taper Forum in Los Angeles in February 1978 by Gordon Davidson. Metzger reviewed that production for *Ms. Magazine* and highlighted the feminist aspects of the drama (27).

In October 1978 the play opened at the Phoenix Theatre's off-Broadway season at the Marymount Manhattan Theatre in New York. Critics were impressed with Norman's first effort. Simon called it "a spiny, realistic play ... written with such a brisk, fresh, penetrating touch that sordid, brooding things take on the glow of honesty, humanity, very nearly poetry" ("Free, Bright," 152). On the other hand, Clurman found the play "not altogether convincing" (557); he objected particularly to the dramatic handling of the transformation from Arlie into Arlene.

The Marymount production of *Getting Out* was so successful that the company revived it at the Theatre de Lys for an eight-month run. Weales was impressed with director Jory and Susan Kingsley as Arlene and Pamela Reed as Arlie, but he had some reservations: "*Getting Out* is an effective theater piece which has a genuine concern for the traps of both heredity and environment and a wicked way of suggesting the ambiguities of its title" ("Getting Out"). Other reviewers also praised the acting (Kalem, 80) and judged the play a persuasive first effort (Raidy, 36–37). Kauffmann, who saw the play at both New York theatres, liked it at neither ("All New," 25). Weales and Simon both refined their critical responses to *Getting Out* in their expanded review essays, "American Theater Watch, 1979–1980" (Weales, 506–7) and "Kopit, Norman and Shepard" (Simon, 81–85). *Getting Out* received in addition to the Gassner New Medallion the first annual George Oppenheimer Newsday Playwriting Award.

Norman wrote her next works when she was playwright in residence at the Actors Theatre in Louisville. *Third and Oak* (two one-act plays) was produced in 1978, and *Circus Valentine* premiered in 1979 but received poor reviews. Aided by a Rockefeller playwrights in residence award, she worked on another play, *Holdup*, which was staged by the Actors Theatre as a workshop production. After undergoing some revisions, it was staged in 1983 in San Francisco by the American Conservatory Theatre under the direction of Edward Hastings. *Holdup*, in which Norman dramatized tales from the West told by her grandfather, did not win the critics over. Weiner's comment was typical: "However, as cute and lively as the dialogue is, it can't conceal a certain thinness in the material."

Norman's most important play to date, *'night, Mother*, was written in 1981 and produced by Brustein at the American Repertory Theatre in Cambridge, Massachusetts, in January 1983. Directed by Tom Moore, with Anne Pitoniak as Thelma Cates and Kathy Bates as her daughter, Jessie, the play garnered favorable reviews, particularly for its emotional honesty—"If there is such a thing as a benign explosion, this play is it: it detonates with startling quietness, showering us with truth, compassion and uncompromising honesty" (Kroll, "End Game," 41)—and for its dialogue—"a spare, suspenseful and entirely realistic dialogue between a mother and a daughter" (Henry, "Reinventing the Classics," 85). The critics were unanimous in their praise of the cast. Brustein (25–26) stressed the realism in '*night, Mother*, especially in the details of commonplace life, as well as the unity of elapsed time measured by the functioning clocks on stage. An indication of the play's importance to and for women can be gauged by Norman's winning (in January 1983) the first Susan Smith Blackburn prize to be given annually to a woman playwright from an English-speaking country.

On 31 March 1983 '*night, Mother*, with the original cast, moved to the John Golden Theatre on Broadway, where it ran for ten months. On the whole, the critical reception was favorable. The realistic, nonsentimental depiction of everyday lives without aim or purpose was again noted. Said Rich: "As she perfectly captures the intimate details of two individual, ordinary women, this playwright locates the emptiness that fills too many ordinary homes on too many faceless streets in the vast country we live in now" (333). Simon ("Journeys," 58) concurred with this view, as did Wilson, who also stressed Norman's psychological perceptiveness: "The surface life of the two women is depicted with astonishing accuracy, but beyond that, the play is filled with remarkable insights" (335). Despite the central mother-daughter relationship, the drama was not labeled feminist (Bosworth, 203).

Not all reviewers liked the play, though. What some critics saw as inexorable dramatic structure (Wilson, Gill, Rich), Kauffmann described as "a device, a stunt" ("More Trick," 48) and Barnes as "a two-character, one-idea play" (335) and as "a worthy try, just not true enough." Kissel objected to the "drabness" (336) of the characters and the play. Gilman took issue with his colleagues' enthusiasm: "Upon a modest two-character play with nothing flagrantly wrong with it—but not much to get excited about either—the reviewers have lavished nearly their whole stock of ecstatic adjectives" (586). He agreed with Barnes that the play was well intentioned but fell short. Hughes thought the play did not deserve the Pulitzer Prize (361), and so did Asahina, who believed *Getting Out* should have won instead of '*night, Mother*, which he castigated as "yet another deadening display of Idiot Realism" (100). The reviewers did, however, agree on the performances by Pitoniak and Bates, calling them "superb" (Rich, 333), "flawless" (Gill, 110), and "expressive" (Hughes, 36).

On 18 April 1984 '*night, Mother* moved with the original cast off-Broadway to the Westside Arts Theatre. For two weeks (last week of March through first week of May 1986) Bates and Pitoniak, directed by Tom Moore, reprised their roles at the Mark Taper Forum. The play was also performed by a touring company with actresses Mercedes McCambridge and Phyllis Somerville and the original set by Heidi Landesman. It has been performed by regional companies throughout the United States, such as the Guthrie, the Arena Stage, and the Geary Theatre.

In Canada numerous productions followed the premiere at the Belfry Theatre in Victoria in October 1984. Canadian critical opinion was favorable. O'Hara wrote: "And the play itself emerges as a near masterpiece of pathos, punctuated with the humor of desperation" (52). Smith pointed out that males are characterized as inadequate and peripheral to the main drama: "This is a story of women, full of valour, irony and liberating laughter" (38).

Norman wrote the screenplay for the movie adaptation of *'night, Mother* (1986), and Tom Moore directed actresses Anne Bancroft and Sissy Spacek. Critical response was mixed: Kroll repeated his glowing review of the play ("Ultimate Family Quarrel," 81), Kauffmann still considered the drama a stunt ("Stanley Kauffmann," 26) and Denby agreed with Kauffmann's verdict ("Fighting Back," 159). O'Brien felt that the play did not translate well to the screen. Feminist critic Stone was not impressed with "this two-character talkathon," which she faulted as "artificial from word one" (20).

This movie probably would not have been as successful without the prestige value of its stars. Critics were divided in their assessment of the performances. Denby described the movie as "reasonably well acted"; O'Toole (79) and Kroll liked both actresses very much, especially Spacek's portrayal of Jessie. On the other hand, Kauffmann called Bancroft "a vulgar actress" and found Spacek "insufficiently interesting" (Stanley Kauffmann on Films, 26); O'Brien shared these sentiments and also accused Bancroft of mugging (472).

In February 1984 Marsha Norman's sixth play, *Traveler in the Dark*, was produced by the American Repertory Theatre and again directed by Tom Moore. Reviewers credited Norman with a valiant attempt to come to grips with moral and philosophical issues but also thought the play unconvincing, didactic, and overwritten. DeVries (19) called her writing "forced and self-conscious, as if the playwright knows she is addressing 'Big Themes' and 'Real Psychic Pain.' " Similarly Kroll concluded, "Norman is one of those writers who are natural lightning rods for the shattering assaults on faith and hope that come to all of us. The danger is that her moral urgency will drive her into the too-conscious role of crisis laureate" ("Modern Crisis," 76). Henry called the play "altogether too clever" but commended the playwright for extending her range: "The play seeks to debate science and faith, love and self-knowledge, the rage to grow and the resistance to change. Norman writes candidly and capably about God, reason and honor" (Blasted Garden, 101).

From late January through 10 March 1985, a revised version of *Traveler in the Dark* played at the Taper Forum directed by Gordon Davidson. It had a lukewarm reception, ranging from " 'Traveler in the Dark' leaves us confused; it makes large, dark gestures, but its tone is oddly cozy"

(Sullivan) to "meanders hopelessly, exploring one area of anguish or another, usually with too many words, going nowhere" (Viertel). All reviewers were, however, unanimous in praising the set by Ming Cho Lee. Later that year the play was staged by Jon Jory at the Actors' Theatre in Louisville.

SURVEY OF SECONDARY SOURCES

Bibliographies

The most complete bibliography of primary and secondary material available is Wolfe. Partial listings can be found in Miller, Guerrini and O'Donnell.

Biographies

No biography of Marsha Norman is available, although biographical sketches are found in *Current Biography Yearbook 1984* and *The New York Times Biographical Service* and in interviews (Stout, Stone, Gross).

Influences

Marsha Norman pointed out to Betsko that as a child growing up in Kentucky, she knew of only one female playwright, Lillian Hellman. Hellman's example eventually inspired Norman's goal of writing for the theatre. In an interview with Brustein, Norman listed *Oedipus, Medea*, and *King Lear* as plays whose tragic dimensions have had a bearing on her work. As an undergraduate in college, she majored in philosophy and mentioned Aristotle, Kierkegaard, and Jaspers as thinkers for whom she felt a particular affinity. Norman also stressed the influences of her professional experiences with emotionally disturbed children on the subject matter of her plays.

General Studies

Gussow's contribution in the *New York Times Magazine* investigated the impact of female dramatists and found them to be a diverse group, with Beth Henley and Marsha Norman sharing the fewest similarities. Stout has described Norman's compulsion to portray in her plays people for whom no one speaks. Stone dwelt on the meaning of the mother-daughter relationship for the plays, Norman's interest in overheard chance snippets of dialogue, and her emphasis on "speaking the unspoken" (57).

General scholarly studies of Norman's works have been confined to a few articles and to brief mentions in works on the American theatre and on women playwrights. Bigsby cites *'night, Mother* in his chapter on women's theatre as an example of a commercially successful play by a female author, and he outlined some of the criticism of the play by the women's movement (438–439). In a concise entry, Hoffmann interprets both Arlene's survival in "Getting Out" and Jessie's suicide in *'night, Mother* as "a victory for individual choice" (403). Keyssar discusses Norman in a chapter entitled "Success and Its Limits," putting Norman's work in context with other female dramatists who share the same themes: "Mother-daughter relationship, sisterhood, sexuality and female autonomy" (150). Keyssar found the success of *'night, Mother* problematical from a feminist perspective, since "off-stage suicide does not transform society. It denies it" (166).

In her perceptive comparison McDonnell characterizes Henley and Norman as writers who recognizably share certain southern literary traits: "their remarkable gift for story telling, their use of family drama as framework, their sensitive delineation of character and relationships, their employment of a bizarre Gothic humor and their use of the southern vernacular to demonstrate the poetic lyricism of the commonplace" (95). She also enumerates the differences between the two, calling Henley more "theatrical" and Norman more "literary."

Hart analyzes Marsha Norman's work from a feminist and psychological perspective in a well-documented, thoughtful essay. Concentrating on *Getting Out* and *'night, Mother*, she uses the twin symbols of food and hunger to interpret these plays: "Norman's hunger imagery captures the elemental struggle for autonomy that her characters undergo" (73). Hart also emphasizes the struggle for liberation from confinement, which is embodied with different emphases in the main characters' desire to escape. The mother-daughter relationship in its psychological ramifications is for Hart another major theme. Morrow covers similar ground in her intriguing and detailed investigation of the overriding importance of food and eating in Henley's *Crimes of the Heart* and Norman's *'night, Mother*. Wertheim discusses Norman's use of a divided main character in *Getting Out* within the context of modern American drama and compares her technique with Eugene O'Neill's early attempt to integrate that device in a play.

Analyses of Individual Plays

Almost all scholarly attention has focused on Norman's two major plays. Readers should also consult Hart, McDonnell, and Morrow for specific readings. Murray brings a valid sociological and socioeconomic perspective to *Getting Out* by stressing the importance of institutions of authority, of patriarchal control as the overriding forces in Arlie/Arlene's life, which she can only subvert with humor and bad jokes but cannot overcome, either in or out of prison. Miner's essay also emphasizes the absence of truly free choices for either Arlie or Arlene; Miner goes beyond the absence of concrete options for unskilled lower-class women to state " 'Getting Out' suggests that ghosts can be neither expelled nor conquered, that acts of excision merely doom the presumed 'self' to incompletion and alienation" (143). Spencer's investigation of *'night, Mother* examines the play's effect on the female audience. She probes the psychological dilemmas posed by the mother-daughter relationship and the play's symbolic presentation of the female experience of limited options. But the drama with its naturalistic portrayal of the traditional domestic setting does not offer women the option of either understanding or changing "the broader social dynamics of their specific situation" (374).

FUTURE RESEARCH OPPORTUNITIES

Although it is too early in Norman's promising career for a definitive biography or critical study, the need exists nonetheless for initial work. An analysis of Norman's southern roots and their influence on her work would be welcome. Another promising avenue for research would be the relationship of Norman's nondramatic writings, such as her work in children's literature and for educational television, with her dramatic themes and techniques. The adaptation of *'night, Mother* to film would seem worthy of a separate study, as well as a comparison with the film version of Henley's *Crimes of the Heart*. An investigation of Norman's screenplays for films and television programs might offer new insights. Norman's latest published work, the novel *The Fortune Teller*, may represent a new departure for the playwright.

SECONDARY SOURCES

Asahina, Robert. "The Real Stuff." *Hudson Review* 37 (Spring 1984): 100–101.

Barnes, Clive. " 'night, Mother Is a Long Days Night." *New York Post* (1 April 1983: 37). Reprinted in *New York Theatre Critics' Reviews* 1983): 335.

Bigsby, C. W. E. *Beyond Broadway*. Vol. 3 of *A Critical Introduction to Twentieth Century American Drama*. Cambridge: Cambridge University Press, 1985.

Bosworth, Patricia. "Some Secret Worlds Revealed." *Working Woman* 8 (October 1983): 204.

Brustein, Robert. "Don't Read This Review!" *New Republic* (2 May 1983): 25–27.

Clurman, Harold. "Theatre." *Nation* (18 November 1978): 557–58.

Denby, David. "Fighting Back." *New York* (22 September 1986): 158–59.

———. "Stranger in a Strange Land." *Atlantic Monthly* (January 1985): 44–45.

DeVries, Hilary. "Marsha Norman's 'Traveler' Stumbles into a Pedantic Wilderness." *Christian Science Monitor* (22 February 1984): 19.

Gill, Brendan. "Portrait of the Artist as a Young Saint." *New Yorker* (11 April 1983): 109–12.

Gilman, Richard. " 'Night, Mother." *Nation* (7 May 1983): 585–86.

Gross, Amy. "Marsha Norman." *Vogue* (July 1983): 200–201, 256–58.

Guerrini, Anne M. "Norman, Marsha, 1947– ." *Contemporary Authors* 102 (1982): 105.

Gussow, Mel. "Marsha Norman Savors Pulitzer Prize for Drama." *New York Times Biographical Service* (April 1983): 455–56.

———. "Women Playwrights: New Voices in the Theater." *New York Times Magazine* (1 May 1983): 22–40.

Hart, Lynda. "Doing Time: Hunger for Power in Marsha Norman's Plays." *Southern Quarterly* 25 (Spring 1987): 67–79.

Henry, William A. "Blasted Garden." *Time* (27 February 1984): 101.

———. "Reinventing the Classics." *Time* (7 February 1983): 85.

Hoffmann, Tess. "Marsha Norman." In *Contemporary Dramatists*, 4th ed., pp. 403–4. Edited by D. L. Kirkpatrick. Chicago: St. James Press, 1988. 403–4.

Huges, Catherine. "The Pulitzer Puzzle." *America* (7 May 1983): 361.

Kalem, T. E. "Seared Soul." *Time* (28 May 1979): 80.

Kauffmann, Stanley. "All New, All American." *New Republic* (7 July 1979): 24–25.

———. "More Trick Than Tragedy." *Saturday Review* (September 1983): 47–48.

———. "Stanley Kauffmann on Films: High Pressure and Low." *New Republic* (13 October 1986): 26.

Kerr, Walter. "Variety Never Hurts." *New York Times* (3 June 1979): 112–13.

Keyssar, Helene. *Feminist Theatre: An Introduction to Plays of Contemporary British and American Women.* New York: Grove Press, 1985.

Kissel, Howard. " 'night, Mother." *Women's Wear Daily* (1 April 1983). Reprinted in *New York Theatre Critics' Reviews* (1983): 336.

Klemesrud, Judy. "Playwright Marsha Norman." *New York Times Biographical Service* 12 (May 1979): 673–75.

Kroll, Jack. "A Modern Crisis of Faith." *Newsweek* (27 February 1984): 76.

———. "End Game." *Newsweek* (3 January 1983): 41–42.

———. "The Ultimate Family Quarrel." *Newsweek* (22 September 1986): 81.

McDonnell, Lisa J. "Diverse Similitude: Beth Henley and Marsha Norman." *Southern Quarterly* 25 (Spring 1987): 95–104.

Metzger, Deena. "Getting Out." *Ms.* (June 1978): 26–28.

Miller, Mary Ellen: "Marsha Norman." *Dictionary of Literary Biography Yearbook* (1984): 308–12.

Miner, Madonne. " 'What's These Bars Doin' Here?'—The Impossibility of *Getting Out*." *Theatre Annual* 40 (1985): 115–34.

Morrow, Laura. "Orality and Identity in *'night, Mother* and *Crimes of the Heart*." *Studies in American Drama, 1945–Present* 3 (1988).

Murray, Timothy. "Patriarchal Panopticism, or the Seduction of a Bad Joke: *Getting Out* in Theory." *Theatre Journal* 35 (October 1983): 376–88.

O'Brien, Tom: " 'night, Mother." *Commonweal* (12 September 1986): 471–72.

O'Donnell, Monica M., ed. "Norman, Marsha, Playwright, Producer." *Contemporary Theatre, Film, and Television* 1 (1984): 400–401.

O'Hara, Jane. "Saturday Night, Alive or Dead" *Maclean's* (5 November 1984): p. 52.

O'Toole, L. " 'night, Mother." *Maclean's* (6 October 1986): 79.

Raidy, William A. "Getting Out after Time." *Plays and Players* 26, no. 10 (1979): 36–37.

Rich, Frank. "Suicide Talk in *'night, Mother.*" *New York Times* (1 April 1983). Reprinted in *New York Theatre Critics' Reviews* (1983): 333.

Simon, John. "Free, Bright, and 31." *New York Magazine* (13 November 1978): 152, 155.

——. "Journeys into Night." *New York Magazine* (11 April 1983): 55–58.

——. "Theater Chronicle: Kopit, Norman and Shepard." *Hudson Review* 32 (Spring 1979): 78–88.

Smith, Patricia Keeney. "Theatre of Extremity." *Canadian Forum* (April 1985): 37–40.

Spencer, Jenny S. "Norman's *'night, Mother:* Psycho-drama of Female Identity." *Modern Drama* 30, no. 3 (1987): 364–75.

Stone, Elizabeth. "Playwright Marsha Norman: An Optimist Writes about Suicide, Confinement and Despair." *Ms.* (July 1983): 56–59.

Stout, Kate. "Marsha Norman: Writing for the "Least of Our Brethren.' " *Saturday Review* (September–October 1983): 28–33.

Sullivan, Dan. "*Traveler in the Dark* at Taper." *Los Angeles Times* (25 January 1985): 7:1, 7.

Viertel, Jack. " 'Traveler' Remains in the Dark." *Los Angeles Herald Examiner* (25 January 1985). NewsBank, Performing Arts 1985, fiche 77, grid F13.

Weales, Gerald. "American Theater Watch, 1979–1980." *Georgia Review* 34, no. 3 (1980): 497–519.

——. " 'Getting Out': A New American Playwright." *Commonweal* (12 October 1979): 559–60.

Weiner, Bernard. "Comic Look at an Era Gone Sour." *San Francisco Chronicle* (14 April 1983). Newsbank, Performing Arts, 1983, fiche 90, grid f13.

Weiner, Bernard. "Norman's 'Traveler' in L.A." *San Francisco Chronicle* (4 February 1985). NewsBank, Performing Arts, 1985, fiche 77, grid G3.

Wertheim, Albert. "Eugene O'Neill's *Days Without End* and the Tradition of the Split Character In Modern American and British Drama." *Eugene O'Neill Newsletter* 6. 3 (Winter 1982): 5–9.

Wilson, Edwin. " 'night, Mother." *Wall Street Journal* (6 April 1983): 334–335. Reprinted in *New York Theatre Critics' Reviews* (1983): 334–35.

Wolfe, Irmgard H. "Marsha Norman: A Bibliography." *Studies in American Drama, 1945–Present* 3 (1988).

David Rabe

(10 MARCH 1940–   )

PHILIP C. KOLIN

ASSESSMENT OF RABE'S REPUTATION

David Rabe is best known for his highly controversial Vietnam trilogy. As Berkowitz maintains, Rabe "dramatized the damage done to the American spirit by the Vietnam War more eloquently, perhaps, than any writer in any genre" (137). *Basic Training of Pavlo Hummel* (1971) received an Obie and New York Drama Critics' Circle Award; *Sticks and Bones* (1971) won a Tony; and *Streamers* (1976) was voted the Best Play of the Year. The televised version of *Sticks* in 1973 hurled Rabe into confrontation with CBS when it refused to air the play for fear of offending the families of returning prisoners of war; and the 1983 film of *Streamers*, directed by Robert Altman with screenplay by Rabe, shocked audiences worldwide. Rabe's early successes also form an important chapter in the history of the New York Shakespeare Festival/Public Theater. Five of his plays *(Pavlo, Sticks, Orphan, Boom Boom Room,* and, after its New Haven run, *Streamers*) were produced by Joe Papp who described Rabe as "the most important writer we've ever had" (quoted in Gussow, "Second Pavlo," 43).

Although rightly acclaimed as the most important dramatist of the Vietnam War, Rabe himself vigorously denied (Berkvist, "If You Kill Somebody," 3) that he wrote antiwar plays. In listing some of Rabe's wide-ranging themes, Marranca points out that his plays "expose the turmoil of American life, and his characters represent attitudes toward heroism, maleness, alienation, violence, racism, and interpersonal communication" (86). Schier has isolated what might be the most telling concern of his work: "There may be no other playwright in America writing against violence with as much passion and commitment" as Rabe ("Villanova's David Rabe," 21). The hallmarks of Rabe's style complement his recurrent interest in violence—grotesque lyricism, haunting symbolism, and an eerie admixture of realism and surrealism.

The themes and style of Rabe's soldier plays spill over into what Kolin *(Stage History*, 98) has called "Rabe's second trilogy"—*I'm Dancing* (1982 screenplay), *Hurlyburly*, and *Goose and Tomtom*—which deal with the war at home with drugs, betrayals, and the burden of male bonding. Rabe's most recent success, *Hurlyburly*, "offers some of Mr. Rabe's most inventive and disturbing writing" (Rich, C3). And although it has never received a performance sanctioned by Rabe, *Goose and Tomtom* (1982, 1986) has been described as "an existential comedy exploring the fictions and the fantasies out of which a postmodern reality is constructed and ultimately deconstructed" (Kolin, "*Goose*," 128).

PRIMARY BIBLIOGRAPHY OF RABE'S WORKS

Plays

The Chameleon. Unpublished. Performed 12 April 1959 at Holy Trinity Auditorium, Dubuque, Iowa.
The Basic Training of Pavlo Hummel. New York: Samuel French, 1972.
Sticks and Bones. New York: Samuel French, 1972.
The Basic Training of Pavlo Hummel; Sticks and Bones. New York: Viking, 1973. Introduction by Rabe.
In the Boom Boom Room: A Drama in Three Acts. New York: Samuel French, 1975.
The Orphan. A Play in Two Acts. New York: Samuel French, 1975.
Streamers. New York: Knopf; distributed by Random House, 1976.
Streamers. In *Coming to Terms: American Plays and The Vietnam War.* Introduction by James Reston. New York: Theatre Communication Group, 1985.
Hurlyburly: A Play. New York: Samuel French; Grove, 1985.
In the Boom Boom Room: A Play by David Rabe. Revised to the original two acts. New York: Grove, 1986.
Goose and Tomtom. New York: Grove, 1987.
Oddo's Response to the Queen. Scene from an unpublished play. *Studies in American Drama, 1945–Present* 3 (1988): 3–7.

Screenplays

Sticks and Bones. Unpublished screenplay written by Rabe, Joseph Papp, and Robert Downey. 1972.
First Blood. Unpublished screenplay. 1974–1975.
In the Boom Boom Room. Unpublished screenplay. 1975.
It Gave Everybody Something To Do. Unpublished screenplay. 1976.
Prince of the City. Unpublished screenplay based on work by Robert Daley. 1978.
I'm Dancing as Fast as I Can. Unpublished screenplay based on Barbara Gordon's autobiography. 1981.
Just Married. Unpublished screenplay. 1983.

Streamers. Unpublished screenplay. 1983. Videocassette available from Streamers International Distributors, Media Home Entertainment, 1984.

Casualties of War. Unpublished screenplay. 1988.

Articles and Letters

Twenty-six stories written between June 1969 and April 1971 for the *New Haven Register*, specific bibliographic information can be found in Kolin's *Stage History and A Primary and Secondary Bibliography.*

"So We Got Papp in to See a Runthrough." *New York Times* (4 June 1972): 2: 1.

"Each Night You Spit in My Face." *New York Times* (18 March 1973): 23, 20.

"Admiring the Unpredictable Mr. Kubrick." *New York Times* (21 June 1987): H34, H36.

Interviews

"Lorasman's Play Produced." *Witness* [archdiocese of Dubuque] (26 March 1959): 12.

Fields, Sidney. "Viet Vet, Teacher, Author." *New York Daily News* (15 November 1971): 50.

Michener, Charles. "The Experience Thing." *Newsweek* (20 December 1971): 59, 61.

Tallmer, Jerry. "The Basic Training of David Rabe." *New York Post* (11 March 1972): 2: 15.

Kaye, Ellen. "The Private War of David Rabe." *Philadelphia Inquirer Magazine* (19 March 1972): 18–20, 22, 26, 27, 31.

Brockway, Jody. "Defining the Event for Myself." *After Dark* 5 (August 1972): 56–57.

Berkvist, Robert. "How Nichols and Rabe Shaped *Streamers.*" *New York Times* (25 April 1976): B1, B12.

Gussow, Mel. "Rabe Is Compelled 'To Keep Trying.' " *New York Times* (12 May 1976): 34.

Simmons, Ira. "Oh, No . . . Another Success." *Courier Journal/Louisville Times* (10 July 1976): 7, 21.

Prochaska, Bob. "David Rabe: 'There's No Audience That Ever Experiences Everything I Haven't Experienced When I Wrote It.' " *Dramatics* 48 (May-June 1977): 18–20.

Newquist, Jay. "*Streamers* Author Ponders Play as Film." *New Haven Register* (6 November 1983): D1.

Bennetts, Leslie. "Interview with Rabe." *New York Times* (11 May 1984): C2.

Dudar, Helen. " . . . And as Rabe Sees Hollywood." *New York Times* (17 June 1984): B1, B5.

[Freedman, Samuel G., and Michaela Williams]. "A Conversation between Neil Simon and David Rabe: The Craft of the Playwright." *New York Times Magazine* (26 May 1985): 37–38, 52, 56, 57, 60, 61, 62.

Gale, William K. "This Hurlyburly Is the Real One." *Providence Sunday Journal* (14 December 1986): A1, A4.

Savran, David. "Interview with David Rabe." In *In Their Own Words: Contemporary American Playwrights*. New York: Theatre Communication Group, 1988. 193–206.

PRODUCTION HISTORY

For a full, nearly exhaustive account of productions and revivals, consult Kolin's *Stage History*.

Although Rabe saw a few of his early works *(Pavlo, Sticks* then called *Bones*, and *Orphan*, then entitled *Bones of Birds)* performed at Villanova in 1968–1970, his career on the New York stage was launched on 20 May 1971 when the *Basic Training of Pavlo Hummel* premiered at the Newman Theater of the Public Theatre and continued its run for 363 performances. Rabe was hailed as the bright new star—"a new authentic voice" (Barnes, "Theater: *Training of Pavlo Hummel*," 25) and "possibly the most promising new talent" of the 1971 New York season (Hewes, "Taps for Lenny Bruce," 36). Speaking for many critics, Kroll applauded *Pavlo* as "the first play to deal successfully with the Vietnam War and the contemporary army" ("This Is the Army," 70). Oliver went even further: "It makes everything else I've seen on the subject seem skimpy and slightly false" (55). The reason for *Pavlo*'s popularity was, again in Kroll's words, that Rabe's army (with its deadening rituals) is a "microcosm of the ironies and personalities at large in society itself" (70). A few critics faulted Rabe for a "fragmentary" plot (Oppenheimer, A1) and "tiresome and depressing" characters (Lahr, 57). Rabe's dogface Pavlo, however, was praised as a comic and grotesque creation: "an eternal patsy in a phony world" (Watts, 31). Generally the critics thought William Atherton played the addled yet gung-ho Pavlo to perfection. Of Atherton, Rabe pointed out: "He had a Huck Finn mix of innocence, toughness, and mischievousness" (Introduction, xviii). These were the disparate qualities Rabe sewed into the role. As he would with other Rabe roles, Joe Fields won hearty commendation for his Sergeant Tower, the "apotheosis of all first sergeants" (Kroll, "This Is the Army," 70). Rabe and director Jeff Bleckner each won an Obie.

Two landmark revivals of *Pavlo* deserve notice. On 24 April 1977 the Theatre Company of Boston, directed by David Wheeler, brought *Pavlo* back to New York, this time to Broadway's Longacre Theatre, with Al Pacino in the lead role. Pacino's jumpy mannerisms won the critics' approval; he generated a great deal of sympathy—regardless of Rabe's original intention—for the character. In the spring of 1979 the Gladsaxe Theatre in Copenhagen staged a poignantly antimilitaristic *Pavlo*.

Under the title of *Bones*, Rabe's *Sticks and Bones* made its world premiere on 7 February 1969 at Villanova's Vasey Theater. The local reviewers applauded Rabe as a new talent. Schier called him a "poet playwright with a future" ("Villanova Has Fine Play," 33). On 7 November 1971, after revisions, *Sticks and Bones* opened at the Anspacher at the Public Theater joining *Pavlo*, which had been playing to appreciative audiences at the Public's Newman stage since May. *Sticks* ran for 121 performances and, like *Pavlo*, was directed by Jeff Bleckner. *Sticks* earned bountiful praise from the New York critics, who naturally compared it with *Pavlo* as a companion piece. While *Pavlo* presented battlefield conditions, *Sticks* depicted a painful homecoming. Barnes proclaimed that *Sticks* was a "play that takes a decently satirical glance at chaos, and a play that has moral force that neither flinches nor sermonizes" ("Theater: A Most Gifted Playwright," 60). Rabe's story of the fate awaiting one veteran led Hewes to conclude that *Sticks* represents the "painful ambiguities that affect" ("Only Winter in White," 70) all American society. The symbolic mode of *Sticks* helped to establish Rabe's reputation as a highly moral and gifted playwright. Watt perceptively observed: "It is a play written out of rage . . . but it has not been written in rage. It is, instead, a beautifully controlled and even poetic work of the imagination that becomes almost unbearably moving" ("*Sticks* Brings the Vietnam War Home," 64). The New York Public Theater cast basked in the critics' praise—David Selby (David), Tom Aldredge (Ozzie), Elizabeth Wilson (Harriet), Cliff De Young (Ricky), and Asa Gim (the silent Zung).

On 1 March 1972, *Sticks* moved to the Golden Theater, marking Rabe's first appearance on Broadway. As they had at its Public Theater opening, the New York critics profusely acknowledged Rabe's talent and rejoiced over his deeply troubling play, which more than one reviewer saw as salutary for Broadway. Wallach, for example, claimed that *Sticks* "brings a fresh sense of seriousness and urgency to Broadway" (A7). *Sticks* brought Rabe a host of awards, honors, and national fame. He won a Tony, a New York Drama Critics' Circle award, and (with *Pavlo*) a coveted Hull-Warriner award for dramatizing contemporary social issues.

If *Sticks* brought Rabe fame, it also embroiled him in controversy at home and abroad. Rabe's troubles with CBS are well chronicled by Little. CBS had agreed with Papp to air a televised version of *Sticks* (which Rabe had worked on with Robert Downey) in March 1972 but thought such a program would be offensive to returning prisoners of war and so cancelled *Sticks* and refused to air it until August. The editorials and stories (especially Krebs) provide interesting reading. Rabe's trouble with the Russians over *Sticks* stemmed from their unauthorized and distorted production of the play in March 1972. Rabe's letter to the Soviets protesting their piracy ("Each Night") is important reading.

Sticks remains one of Rabe's most popular works. It has been staged overseas a number of times: in Zurich (1973), Hungary (1974), Poland (1974), London (1978), and Tokyo (1981).

Rabe's most ambitious work, *The Orphan*, was also his least popular.

Commenting on violence and family disruption, Rabe combined modified versions of the myths in the *Oresteia* with contemporary references
to the Manson murders and Einstein's theory of relativity. Growing out
of his early script *The Bones of Birds, The Orphan, or Orestes and the $E = MC^2$*
premiered on 14 October 1970 at Villanova's Vasey Theater where Rabe
was playwright in residence. The play was greeted by positive reviews
from Childs (a work of "much intellectual and emotional pleasure," D7)
and Schier (Rabe could "handle many complex deeply interwoven characters and situations," "A Lively Production," 49). These sentiments were
not echoed by the critics when a revised *Orphan* (directed by Bleckner)
opened at the Public Theatre on 18 April 1973. Closing after only one
month, Rabe's play was branded a failure, although many critics still saw
much promise in the young Rabe. Kroll ("Greek Salad," 87) claimed that
The Orphan offered "callow excuse for thought"; Watt judged it "confusing and static" ("Rabe Orphan Ambitious Failure," 104); and Africano
complained it had "no real characters," (7). But not all reviews were
bleak. In a highly positive review, Bermel held that the play was "crowded
with exciting scenes and some of the most interesting soliloquies" (24).

A new and greatly revised *Orphan* was directed by Kellman at the
North Carolina School of the Arts on 12 November 1973. Through
Kellman's urging—and his cooperation—Rabe reworked the play. This
new North Carolina *Orphan* opened on 15 March 1974 at Philadelphia's
Manning Street Theater, a production in part supported by Papp.
Judged a bold attempt, the play still failed to win support, for, in Collins's
words, it "succeeds as statement but fails as drama" (B4).

Rabe's next play, *Boom Boom Room*, departed from his previous work
on the war by dramatizing the victimization of a Philadelphia go-go
dancer (Chrissy) by a series of sexually aberrant individuals—her incestuous father, a bisexual dance captain, a homosexual neighbor, and a
wife-pounding husband. Premiering on 8 November 1973 at Lincoln
Center and directed by Papp, *Boom Boom Room* launched Papp's controversial "new play policy," which gave preference to the work of living
writers. With some reservations, the critics applauded Rabe's new work,
which Clurman (and others) linked with the Vietnam plays. A consistently strong Rabe supporter, Gottfried proclaimed that the play was "a
near masterpiece, theatrically thrilling . . . technically and poetically pro-
ficient beyond ordinary expectations" ("*Boom*," 30). Schier pronounced
it Rabe's "finest play" ("*Boom*," B19). A few critics strenuously objected,
however, to Rabe's symbolism and plot, which was attacked as "structurally chaotic" (Stasio, 7).

Madeline Kahn's interpretation of Chrissy contributed both to the
critics' respect and their reservations. Kroll approved Kahn's "fighting
vulnerability" ("Go-Go in Hell," 96) while Novick thought that such feisty
behavior lessened the audience's pity. Barnes, too, was disappointed by

Kahn's spunky comedy, which he feared bordered on caricature ("Rabe Revised," 55). Voicing a representative complaint, Barnes feared that "we really know no more about her [Chrissy] at the end than we did at the beginning" ("Stage: New Papp Home," L31).

Chrissy's dancing partners—the glittery go-gos—also drew mixed reviews. Albrecht astutely saw their gilded cages as symbols of the audience's own "captivity" ("We Too May Be Trapped," 36) At the most cerebral, Kroll philosophized that the go-gos represented "the eternal feminine lobotomized to an apoplectic travesty of femininity" ("Go Go in Hell," 96), and at the most psychoanalytic, Harris speculated that the girls were "a brassy counterpart to the Freudian agonies of Chrissy" (199). Charles Durning as Chrissy's father and Mary Woronov as Susan (the bisexual leader of the go-gos) received highly strong reviews.

A revised, much tighter *In the Boom Boom Room* (directed by Robert Hedley) opened a year later at Papp's Public Theater. The critics who liked the 1973 play approved of it in 1974, and vice-versa. Although he complimented Rabe for getting "into the feminine mind," Barnes nonetheless protested that Chrissy "never develops" ("Theatre: Rabe Revisited," 55). "Though some things about her ring toughingly true, she is inconsistent," wrote Simon (92). Clurman liked the new, smaller stage but feared that the Public Theater made "the faults of the script and staging . . . more glaring" (28 December 1974, 701). Ellen Greene, a well-known jazz singer who replaced Kahn, portrayed Chrissy as less earthy and street smart but "so vulnerable and emotionally virginal" that the audience would be as "shattered" as Chrissy was at her "sleazy end" (Ogden). Albrecht claimed that Greene's performance placed the production "in constant jeopardy of becoming camp" ("Go-Go Dancer's Other Dimensions Ugly," 34).

Chrissy continues to dance for audiences. In December 1976 *In the Boom Boom Room* became the first Rabe play to be performed in England when it opened at the Square One in London. In 1979 Jill Clayburgh (Rabe's wife) starred in a highly successful production at a Long Beach revival. In 1986, the Orange Theatre Company brought the play to off-Broadway.

Streamers, the last play in the Vietnam trilogy, premiered on 30 January 1976 at New Haven's Long Wharf Theatre where it ran until 27 February. Rabe's play about violence and homosexuality in a stateside barracks where recruits await transfer to Vietnam was masterfully directed by Mike Nichols, whose influence is chronicled by Berkvist. The New York critics gave the New Haven *Streamers* high marks, favorably comparing it to Rabe's earlier work. Watt proclaimed that *Streamers* "was the most powerful piece of theatre we've had all season" ("*Streamers* Is Worth a Trip," 25). Like *Pavlo* and *Sticks*, *Streamers* was, in Kroll's words, a "tough" and "explosive play" ("Three Cuts to the Quick," 89). For Barnes

("David Rabe's *Streamers* in New Haven," L+: 45) and others, *Streamers* was a " straightforward play" whose economy of action intensified the violence, making it a better play than the more diffuse *Pavlo* or the symbolically strained *Sticks*. The New Haven cast, which was universally praised, included Joe Fields as the menacing Carlyle, John Heard as the all-American boy Billy, and Dolph Sweet and Kenneth McMillan as the liquor-swilling sergeants.

On 21 April *Streamers* moved to the Newhouse Theater at Lincoln Center, then run by Joe Papp, who produced Rabe's new play, which ran for over 400 performances. Reed was effusively laudatory, professing that *Streamers* redeemed the New York season from "lethargy" because it was "quite the most accomplished new American play in years." Barnes, Gottfried, and Watt repeated their endorsements from New Haven. Sharp called *Streamers* "hard hitting" and "solid and intelligent" (36). For Weales, Rabe was to be praised for "telling a plain tale plainly," (45). The violence shocked almost every reviewer of the play. Gottfried pointed out, "Tension fills the place as tight as a pressure cooker" ("Rabe's *Streamers*," 21). The streamers metaphor was interpreted as symbolic of death, lunacy, meaninglessness. Wilson identified its importance when he observed that "many people today are hurtling toward destruction, cut off from those things which might sustain or save them" ("The Bomb," 22). Dorian Harewood's portrayal of Carlyle was chillingly accurate (Chase). A stream of honors flowed to Rabe, including having *Streamers* voted as the Best New Play of 1976 and a Drama Desk Award.

Streamers may be the most frequently performed Rabe play. Among the most memorable productions are those at the Goodman Theatre in 1977, in Tokyo by the Seihai Company in 1979, and the Steppenwolf Theatre Company's savage triumph at the Lincoln Center in 1985. Speaking of this last production, Payne observed that Steppenwolf played Rabe's "vision for all the horror and pathos that it's worth" (109). The same might be said of the film version of *Streamers* (1983), directed by Robert Altman. The highly favorable review by Crist needs to be balanced against the low opinion of the film by Canby.

Rabe's next stage success, *Hurlyburly*, grew out of his experience looking for work as a screenwriter in Hollywood in 1975, although as Rabe has pointed out (Freedman), the play could have been set anywhere. *Hurlyburly* explores the lives of two casting directors and their sordid antics to find meaningful relationships in the cocaine culture. Premiering in March 1984 at the Goodman Theatre, *Hurlyburly* was directed by Mike Nichols, who had also worked on *Streamers* in 1976. Rabe revealed two years after this premiere (Gale, "This *Hurlyburly* is the Real One, 11"), however, that he was unhappy with Nichols's interpretation (emphasizing the satiric) and the cuts he made in the script. The Chicago critics voiced mixed reactions. Pointing to vices and virtues (*Hurlyburly* was "beautifully lyrical, grossly misshapen and precisely formed"), Christiansen pronounced that with *Hurlyburly*, "David Rabe [is] at his most brilliant and excessive" (E1). Syse, however, refused to see the brilliance and condemned Rabe's effort as "garrulous to the extreme" (47), a criticism later reviewers forcefully echoed. The stellar cast included William Hurt (Eddie), Christopher Walken (Mickey), Sigourney Weaver (Darlene), and Jerry Stiller (Artie). With one exception—Candace Bergen replacing Weaver—this cast opened the play in New York. In both Chicago and New York, their performances were heartily applauded.

When *Hurlyburly* came to New York's Promenade Theatre on 21 June, it "made theatre history of a sort," according to Kroll ("Hollywood Wasteland," 65). Rabe's dazzling, provocative play quickly moved in early August to Broadway's Ethel Barrymore Theatre where it ran for 343 performances. Once again, as he had with *Streamers*, Rabe received numerous accolades. But not every critic shared Kroll's rave opinion ("a powerful and permanent contribution to American drama," 65). Barnes liked the play, which he said "entertained, horrified, and intrigued" him but found the length worrisome ("Rabe's *Hurlyburly*," 43). Wilson quipped that *Hurlyburly* was "not a play but a series of incidents and vignettes that could go on forever" ("On Theater: Rambling Rabe," 32). Most cruel, Beaufort argued that *Hurlyburly* was "disappointing" because it lacked "some clarity" (27).

Many reviewers inevitably focused on Rabe's Hollywood (a central image, in Barnes's words, of a "wasteland of lost meanings"), and a few offered comparisons with the Vietnam in Rabe's earlier plays. Stitt interestingly observed that *Hurlyburly* issued "war zone reports from the battlefield of the sexes" (17). Rich discerned parallels between the psychotic Phil and Carlyle ("Theatre: *Hurlyburly*"). Most instructive was Freedman's comment that while the "subjects" of Rabe's plays "may appear wildly different, they share one of his common concerns: the difficulty of manhood" (C3).

Hurlyburly was exported to Australia in August 1986 where it was produced by Melbourne's Russell Street Theatre. Perhaps the most significant post-1984 production was by Trinity Rep (Providence, Rhode Island) in December 1986. Directed by David Wheeler, this *Hurlyburly* restored Rabe's script and was faithful to his original intention. As far as Rabe was concerned, this was the "definitive" production.

SURVEY OF SECONDARY SOURCES

Bibliographies

Kolin's bibliography of 1,200 entries (primary and secondary items) is the most complete to date, far surpassing the listings in King. The primary bibliography includes Rabe's early poetry, fiction, and his work for the *New Haven Register* in addition to plays and screenplays. The secondary bibliography annotates critical studies and lists theatre reviews.

Biographies

The official, full-scale Rabe biography has yet to be written. Assisted by the playwright's sister Marsha and by Rabe himself, Kolin (*Stage History*) supplies relevant information about Rabe's early years in Dubuque, at Villanova, and in New Haven. Supplementing his coverage (in *Stage History*) of Rabe's early years in Dubuque, Kolin assesses the biographical significance of Rabe's *The Chameleon* ("Notices of David Rabe's First Play"). Reprinting four local reviews of *The Chameleon*, Kolin documents Rabe's early interests in playwrighting as a career, filmmaking, and James Dean's acting style. Kolin also points out how *The Chameleon* foreshadows Rabe's later works, especially the Vietnam Trilogy. A useful biographical sketch by Tigges and McMahon also discusses Rabe in light of his Dubuque roots.

Briefer biographical sketches are in Hartnoll and Hart; a fuller discussion is found in Wakeman and in *Current Biography* (July 1973). Rabe's relationship with Papp is an important part of Little's book. Important biographical details can be gleaned from Rabe's interviews with Simmons, Brockway, Michener, Prochaska, Bennetts, and Savran.

Influences

The greatest influence on Rabe's work has been the Vietnam War. Beidler briefly discusses Rabe's plays up to *Streamers* within the context of the war. Wakeman interestingly alludes to comparisons between *Sticks* and the Heimkehier plays of World War II Germany. Classical myths—and Rabe's alteration of them—lie behind *The Orphan*, especially the Orestes myth. Adler claims that *Sticks* is indebted to *King Lear* "for certain symbols, character configurations, and thematic motifs" (203). Another unquestionably strong influence on Rabe's *Sticks* is Arthur Miller's *All My Sons*, as Brustein, Weales, and Mordden point out. In a number of interviews (Savran), Rabe has acknowledged Miller's influence on him. Bernstein compares Rabe with a host of authors, including Sophocles, Conrad, Ibsen (especially *Ghosts*), Eliot, Ionesco, and van Itallie. In passing, Simard compares and contrasts Rabe's themes and techniques with those of Albee, Shepard, Beckett, and Pinter. Rosen contrasts and compares Rabe's dramas with those of Arnold Wesker as "plays of impasse" where the individual is claustrophobically caught in a no-exist situation. Christopher Durang savagely parodied *Sticks* in *Vietnamization of New*

Jersey (1976), demonstrating a perverse type of influence Rabe's play had.

General Studies

Except for Kolin's stage history and bibliography, there is no book-length study on Rabe. Herman devotes a chapter to Rabe but explores only four plays (*Pavlo, Sticks, Streamers, Hurlyburly*), asserting that *Orphan, Boom Boom Room,* and *Goose* "constitute a small body of less assured and less coherent drama." (119). Especially good at identifying some major Rabe themes (e.g., violence, racism, sex, language drained of emotion, drugs, a longing for something grand), Herman concludes that Rabe "has searched for the right forms of ritual theatre to embody his high sense of overriding purpose" (86). A number of worthwhile general assessments, however, are found in a few articles (assessments by Marranca, Hertzbach ["The Plays of David Rabe: A World of Streamers"]), and Phillips are among the most rewarding) and as part of larger theatre histories and critical studies. Estrin provides a brief but insightful overview of Rabe's themes and techniques. Although he admits that the war is at the center of Rabe's work, Bigsby contends that Rabe uses it as "a dramatic device" to expose America's "profound uncertainties" (331). Arriving at a similar conclusion, Marranca believes that Rabe is most concerned with "the *effect* of the Viet Nam experience on ordinary individuals" (86). In her two essays (1981, 1984), Hertzbach identifies Rabe's metaphors, topical references, and themes: violence, racism, alienation, and family disruption. Especially convincing in her treatment of Rabe's use of rituals, Hertzbach concludes that *Hurlyburly* is "both a continuation and a break with" Rabe's earlier work ("David Rabe," 1553). For Phillips (as for Simard) "the core of all existence" for Rabe is a bleak "existential nothingness" (108). The overview of the canon (up to *Streamers*) by Patterson offers a useful summary of key ideas.

Rabe's language is the subject of three studies. Cohn believes that his plays have a "stylistic rather than thematic consistency," (31) whereas Homan argues that Rabe's style changes from the nonrepresentational mode of the 1960s to the new realism of the 1980s in order "to challenge our everyday sense of reality" (74). The most extensive assessment of Rabe's language is by Werner, who holds that "the problem of language lies at the center" (518) of Rabe's Vietnam plays and classifies them according to "the language of brutality" (*Pavlo*), "the language of evasion" (*Sticks*), and "the collapse of metaphor" (*Streamers*).

Many general discussions praise Rabe's talent but fault his art. Hughes, for example, proclaims Rabe "as the most significant playwright to appear since Albee" (*American Playwrights 1945–75*, 81) yet disapproves of the "diffused" focus in *Palvo*, the bizarre combination of "menace and melodrama" in *Sticks*, and the "intellectual clutter" (85) in *Orphan*. Asahina honors Rabe for avoiding autobiography and polemics but disapproves of Rabe's "overblown symbolism" and mysterious characters and concludes, as most other critics do, that *Streamers* is his best work, exhibiting "real dramatic movement" and offering the "perfect metaphor" (37).

Analyses of Individual Plays

Rabe's antihero Pavlo stands at the center of critical attention. Identifying many facets of his character, Weales notes that Pavlo "is a mixture of two pacifist stereotypes—the clown, the foul up, the yardbird, the victim-hero and also the sacrificial innocent of the sentimental anti-war play" (14). However, in her balanced chapter on the play, Hughes argues that *Pavlo* is not "polemical" and that it would be misleading to talk of the character's "dehumanization" since this "gung-ho" and "mixed up ... oddball" is mechanized by the army to tap his "capacity for the inhumane" (*American Playwrights*, 78). Seeing Pavlo as a "misplaced Everyman" whose ancestors are among "vaudeville types," Rosen explores the "dreamlike" world of loss and fragmentation; her bleakly existential Pavlo demands comparison with assessments of Rabe's recruit by Phillips and Simard. More traditionally, Bigsby accuses the entire American culture of betrayal in making Pavlo a pawn of the system (326). The army rituals in *Pavlo* are discussed insightfully by Brockett and Berkowitz, who believe that Pavlo's major mistake is in confusing manhood with soldiering. Loser, victim, buffoon, Pavlo ultimately is, in Jacobus's words, a "weird" character who is "not a figure who can be taken symbolically or allegorically" (617).

Ardell, Pavlo's mysterious sidekick, has also been variously interpreted. Expressing a frequent criticism, Hughes (*American Playwrights*) complains that he is "the weakest element" in the play since he "is never fully integrated or defined" (82). Other, more salutary views of Ardell have been advanced: he is Pavlo's "inner voice" (Marranca, 88), Tiresias in sunglasses (Asahina, 36), or "a kind of chorus" (Bigsby, 325). Herman believes that Ardell is "at once Pavlo's wish and his destiny" (100).

The most convenient starting point to enter the world of *Sticks* is Bernstein's chapter, which first surveys criticism and reviews (up to 1979) and then analyzes possible sources (Rabe's skillful "intertwining" of realism and absurdism) and the structure and symbols, which are like those of a "traditional tragedy." Two recent articles, by Cooper and McDonald, build upon previous criticism. The more formalistic of the two, Cooper identifies Rabe's targets ("consumer society," television, sick American manhood, violence) as part of the "stylistic strategy" in *Sticks* where David's lyrical expression contrasts with the family's savage clichés but then is adopted by a perplexed Ozzie (621). Regarding *Sticks* as representing the mystery of Vietnam, McDonald assesses the levels of knowing, not knowing, and not wanting to know in the play. He is especially convincing in discussing the "significant absences" (212) and "displaced" signals (219), which create such a mystery.

Whether as returning veteran, stranger, invader, ghost, or martyr, Rabe's protagonist (David) has not been universally accepted as the honorable truth-teller. Cooper stresses the ambiguity (victim and intruder) in the character, while Adler concludes that David is "arrogant in moral superiority" (206). Relating character to audience dynamics, Colette Brooks observes that David frees the audience from painful self-identification with the Nelsons (102–03). However we view David, his blindness, a major symbolic dimension in the play, is carefully explicated by Phillips (111–12).

Almost all criticism of Rabe's Tony Award–winning play touches on what Beidler has called "the whole American mythology of a happy life" (113). At the center of that life is the Nelson family and the ethos of American values. Cooper, Hurrell, and Marranca provide consistent and instructive assessments of Rabe's cliché-speaking, plastic, cartoon family. Among others, Hertzbach points out that "the domestic violence is as terrible" in *Sticks* as the battlefield or barracks variety in the other Rabe plays ("Plays," 176). That violence—the immediate product of family life—is studied in psychoanalytic detail by Metcalf. Hurrell offers a worthwhile reading of the existential struggle with "self" and "other" (99).

No one would quibble that *The Orphan* is Rabe's least appreciated, most maligned work. The scathing reviews by Kauffmann and Simon ("Stinkweed" 98) exhaust the negatives expended on Rabe's pastiche of classical and modern worlds. Although Patterson praises the writing, he too faults the play for its lack of "narrative energy." The essential article is Kellman's "casebook study," which tells "the story of the writing of *The Orphan*, its development through no fewer than five productions, and [Kellman's] participation during the process" (72).

In the Boom Boom Room has persistently evoked comparisons with Rabe's Vietnam plays. Bode, for example, claims that *Boom Boom Room* lacks the "precision" of the Vietnam work (661), and going even further Brown charges that Rabe is unable to write anything "not directly associated with the war" (38). On the other hand, Simard claims that the play is "the touchstone of Rabe's canon to date" (125). For many critics, Chrissy is unable to sustain either interest or sympathy; she is, according to Hughes, "yet another in a long line of Marilyn Monroe-like figures" (*American Playwrights*, 86). Concurring, Patterson labels the play "static," for Chrissy has little sense of her "self worth." To Cohn, however, Chrissy is the "obverse" of Pavlo since she has a deeper understanding of her fate as a victim (34). Expanding her role as victim to embrace larger existential issues, Phillips sees Chrissy's "mental disintegration" as the result of being "surrounded by people who offer her definitions of existence that reinforce her own incapacity to discover meaning" (113). The most detailed reading of the play (and sympathetic view of Chrissy) is Brown's feminist interpretation, which emphasizes Chrissy's struggle to obtain "autonomy" in a "socio-sexual" and dangerously patriarchal "hierarchy."

Critics have generally regarded *Streamers* as the most successful play in Rabe's Vietnam trilogy. Departing from the nonrealistic techniques (flashbacks, nonlinear staging) of *Sticks* and *Pavlo*, *Streamers* was praised for its straightforward, realistic plot moving with terrifying logic toward its inevitable doom. Cohn judges it "the least pretentious and most coherent" (35) of Rabe's plays; Marranca labels it "a modern well-made play"; Kiernan finds that Rabe's "forte is realism" (89); and Patterson concludes that *Streamers* shows "promise of becoming an American classic." Berkowitz convincingly labels *Streamers* "the darkest of the three" Vietnam plays (138). An indispensable introduction to the ideas in *Streamers* is Kerr, who argues that Rabe's metaphoric use of the word *house* is central to his "view of . . . a troubled universe." Kerr expresses the message of the play in these oft-quoted words: "We are all—black, white, straight, queer, parents, children, foes, stable, unstable—living together in the same 'house.' And we cannot do it" (B5). Also examining the implications of Rabe's house, Kolin ("Rabe's *Streamers*") discusses "an archetypical theme—the rite of passage into manhood"—and concludes that the young recruits are abused by "destructive father figures" in both army and civilian life (64). The loss of logic and the inability of the characters to establish human contact mark *Streamers* as a play of impasse for Rosen, who believes its cruel jokes lay bare a "system which promises nothing" (258). Joining a group has dangerous implications in *Streamers*. Studying one key group in the play, Brockett finds that *Streamers* undercuts the myth that "army life is the essence of masculinity" (477).

Among the most vital elements of the play are Rabe's two recurring metaphors: the Viet Cong trapped in a bunker with an exploding grenade and the streamer (or falling parachute, which fails to open). The implosive image of the Viet Cong applies to everyone in the *Streamers* barracks trapped in the oppressively claustrophobic world of the barracks. Interestingly, however, Hertzbach observes that Carlyle is the "Rabean grenade ready to explode" ("Plays"), an opinion shared by Herman, who claims that Carlyle "functions as a magnetic emotional field" (105). Critics found that the streamer perfectly summarized the action of the play. Among representative interpretations of this central image are Bigsby's that it refers to the men "having lost whatever values, whatever structures, that support their lives" (330); Phillips's that it is the instrument and sign of "impending death," which underscores the "meaninglessness of all life" (116); or Asahina's that like "parachutists at the mercy of their packers," the men in *Streamers* are divided between those "who will float" and those "who will plunge" to their fate (37).

The only article devoted exclusively to *Hurlyburly* is Kolin's study of its "provocative dramaturgy" ("Staging *Hurlyburly*," 77). Examining the "acoustical, visual, and physical elements," Kolin shows that the staging, costumes, "Hollywood props," and delivery of lines, turning words into "combative weapons," convey Rabe's twin themes of "dehumanization and despair" (65–66). Regarding *Hurlyburly* as "what is so far his masterpiece," Herman says that "Rabe has gone deeply into the male psyche, a kind of heroic journey into a damnable underground place . . . " (119). Also singling out *Hurlyburly* for high praise, Estrin believes that it is "Rabe's most intricate, verbally dazzling theatrical statement to date" (442). A valuable short guide (containing three brief notes) to the play was produced as part of the Trinity Repertory production: Coale examines the characters as victims of the information age whose "language can lie . . . distort and spiral inward"; Klein sees the "deal making" in the play as a reflection of the market economy, each character seeking to make the "Big Score." Most valuable of all, Brooks points out how the characters confuse the semantic and phatic levels of language. Bruckner also considers the language as an essential ingredient in the characters' malaise: "As they diminish, their language builds up a vision of the repulsive world they live in, work in and believe in even as they are destroyed by it" (12).

FUTURE RESEARCH OPPORTUNITIES

Unlike many other dramatists of the period, Rabe has a relatively complete stage history and bibliography, although a study of the textual changes over the many revisions of his plays would be a welcome addition. Most needed in a book-length assessment of Rabe's plays exploring his artistic development, his use and modification of sources, and his themes and techniques. Such assessment needs to include a chapter on Rabe's *Goose and Tomtom*, one of the most dynamic works in the Rabe canon. Also necessary is a chapter on Rabe's Vietnam plays in a history of the Vietnam War on the American stage. By comparing and contrasting Rabe's works with other plays on the war, we can better validate the claims made for his trilogy. Worth far more attention, too, are Rabe's screenplays, especially in the light of his own comments on the film, and an appreciative assessment of the cinematic qualities in his plays.

SECONDARY SOURCES

Adler, Thomas P. "Blind Leading the Blind: Rabe's *Sticks and Bones* and Shakespeare's *King Lear*." *Papers on Language and Literature* 15 (1979): 203–206.

Africano, Lillian. "Rabe's *The Orphan*." *Villager* (26 April 1973): 7.

Albrecht, Ernest. "*Boom Boom Room:* We, Too, May Be Trapped in Go-Go Cage of Life." *New Brunswick Home News* (9 November 1973): 36.

———. "Go-Go Dancer's Other Dimensions Ugly." *New Brunswick Home News* (5 December 1974): 34.

Asahina, Robert. "The Basic Training of American Playwrights: Theatre and the Vietnam War." *Yale/Theatre* 9 (Spring 1978): 30–37.

Barnes, Clive. "Rabe's *Hurlyburly* Pins Hollywood to the Wall." *New York Post* (22 June 1984): 43.

———. "Stage: A Most Gifted Playwright at the Anspacher." *New York Times* (9 November 1971): 60.

———. "Stage: New Papp Home." *New York Times* (9 November 1973) L + 31.

———. "Stage: Rabe's *The Orphan* Arrives." *New York Times* (19 April 1973): L + 51.

———. "Theatre: David Rabe's *Streamers* in New Haven." *New York Times* (8 February 1976): L + 45.

———. "Theatre: Rabe Revised." *New York Times* (5 December 1974): 55.

———. "Theatre: *Training of Pavlo Hummel*." *New York Times* (21 May 1971): 25.

Beaufort, John. "*Hurlyburly* Is Confused Comedy." *Christian Science Monitor* (3 July 1984): 27.

Beidler, Philip D. *American Literature and the Experience of Vietnam*. Athens, Ga.: University Press of Georgia, 1982.

Berkowitz, Gerald M. *New Broadways: Theatre Across America 1950–1980*. Totowa, New Jersey: Rowman and Littlefield, 1982. 83, 126, 136–38, 157.

Berkvist, Robert. "How Nichols and Rabe Shaped 'Streamers.' " *New York Times* (25 April 1976): B1, B12.

———. "If You Kill Somebody . . ." *New York Times* (12 December 1971): 2: 3.

Bermel, Albert. "From Greece to America." *New Leader* (11 June 1973): 24–25.

Bernstein, Samuel J. *The Strands Entwined: A New Direction in American Drama*. Boston: Northeastern University Press, 1980. 17–34, 139–40, et passim.

Bigsby, C.W.E. *A Critical Introduction to Twentieth-Century American Drama*. Vol. 3. Cambridge: Cambridge University Press, 1984.

Bode, Walt, "David Rabe." In *Contemporary Authors*, 660–62. New York: St. Martin's, 1983.

Brockett, Oscar. "Streamers." In *Historical Edition. The Theatre: An Introduction*, pp. 400–404. New York: Holt, 1979.

Brooks, Colette. "In Pursuit of the Self: Actor and Society." *Yale/Theatre* 8 (Spring 1978): 94–103.

Brooks, Tom. "Blah-blah-blah." In *1986–87 Humanities Booklet #3*, pp. 6–9. Providence, R.I.: Rhode Island Committee for the Humanities for Trinity Rep.

Brown, Janet. *Feminist Drama: Definitions and Critical Analyses*. Metuchen, N.J.: Scarecrow, 1979.

Bruckner, D. J. R. "Strong Language." *San Jose Mercury News* (14 July 1985): 12.

Brustein, Robert. "The Crack in the Chimney: Reflections on Contemporary American Playwrighting." *Yale/Theatre* 9 (Spring 1978): 21–29.

Canby, Vincent. "Film Festial: Play *Streamers* Adapted by Altman." *New York Times* (9 October 1983): A73.

Chase, Chris. "The Audience Can Almost Hear Him Ticking." *New York Times* (13 June 1976): B5.

Childs, James. "Today's Reality Turned in on Mythology." *New Haven Register* (25 October 1970): D1, D7.

Christiansen, Richard. "Rabe's *Hurlyburly* Probes the Depths But Hits the Heights." *Chicago Tribune* (4 April 1984): E1, E3.

Clurman, Harold. "Theatre." *Nation* (26 November 1973): 572–73.

———. "Theatre." *Nation* 219 (28 December 1974): 701.

Coale, Sam. "Phone Booths in the Shopping Mall in Your Head." *1986–87 Humanities Booklet #3*, pp. 1–3. Providence, R.I.: Rhode Island Committee for the Humanities for Trinity Rep.

Cohn, Ruby. *New American Dramatists: 1960–1980*. New York: Grove, 1982.

Collins, William B. "Manning's *Orphan* Makes a Statement But Is a failure." *Philadelphia Inquirer* (18 March 1974): B4.

Cooper, Pamela. "David Rabe's *Sticks and Bones:* The Adventures of Ozzie and Harriet." *Modern Drama* 29 (December 1986): 613–25.

Crist, Judith. "A Fallen Star." *Saturday Review* (November 1983): 43.

Donohue, John. "*Sticks and Bones* on TV." *America* (1 September 1973): 120.

Estrin, Mark W. "David Rabe." *Contemporary Dramatists*, Fourth Edition, Ed. D. L. Kirkpatrick. Chicago: St. James Press, 1988. 440–42.

Freedman, Samuel G. "Rabe and the War at Home." *New York Times* (28 June 1984): C13.

Gale, William, K. "This *Hurlyburly* is the Real One." *Providence Sunday Journal*, December 14, 1986, "Arts," I 1, 4.

Glover, William. "Rabe Misses Epic Drama But Effort Not Timid." *New Haven Register* (19 April 1973): 38.

Gottfried, Martin. "*Boom Boom Room*." *Women's Wear Daily* (12 November 1973): 30.

———. "Rabe's *Streamers*—Theater at Its Peak." *New York Post* (22 April 1976): 21.

Gussow, Mel. "2nd David Rabe to Join *Pavlo Hummel* at Public Theater." *New York Times* (3 November 1971): 43.

Harris, Leonard. "Boom Boom Room." WCBS-TV (8 November 1973). Reprinted in *New York Theater Critics' Reviews* (1973): 199.

Hart, James D. "David Rabe." *The Oxford Companion to American Literature*. 5th Edition. New York: Oxford University Press, 1983. 623.

Hartnoll, Phyllis. "David Rabe." *The Oxford Companion to the Theatre*. New York: Oxford University Press, 1983. 677.

Henry, William A. "Playwright Rabe in Profile." *Boston Globe* (19 April 1972): 28.

Herman, William. "David Rabe." *Understanding Contemporary American Drama*. Columbia: University of South Carolina Press, 1987.

Hertzbach, Janet. "David Rabe." In *Critical Survey of Drama*, 4:1545–54. English Language Series. Edited by Frank Magill. Englewood Cliffs, N.J.: Salem, 1984.

———. "The Plays of David Rabe: A World of Streamers." In *Essays on Contem-*

porary American Drama, pp. 173–86. Edited by Hedwig Bock and Albert Wertheim. Munich: Hueber, 1981.

Hewes, Henry. "Only Winter Is White." *Saturday Review* (27 November 1971): 70–71.

———. "Taps for Lenny Bruce." *Saturday Review* (10 July 1971): 36.

Hoffman, Ted. Introduction to *Famous American Plays of the 1970s*, pp. 20–21. New York: Dell, 1981.

Homan, Richard L. "American Playwrights in the 1970s: Rabe and Shepard." *Critical Quarterly* 24 (Spring 1982): 73–82.

Hughes, Catharine. *American Playwrights 1945–75*. New York: Pitman, 1976.

———. *Plays, Politics, and Polemics*. New York: Drama Book Specialists, 1973.

Hurrell, Barbara. "American Self-Image in David Rabe's Vietnam Trilogy." *Journal of American Culture* 4 (1981): 95–107.

Jacobus, Lee A. "David Rabe's *The Basic Training of Pavlo Hummel*." In *The Longman Anthology of American Drama*, pp. 615–77. New York: Longman, 1982.

Kauffmann, Stanley. "Sunshine Boys." *New Republic* (26 May 1973): 22.

Kellman, Barnet. "David Rabe's *The Orphan:* A Peripatetic Work in Progress." *Theatre Quarterly* 7 (1977): 72–93.

Kerr, Walter. "David Rabe's 'House' Is Not a Home." *New York Times* (2 May 1976): B5.

Kiernan, Robert F. *American Writing Since 1945: A Critical Survey*. New York: Frederick Ungar, 1983.

King, Kimball. "David Rabe." In *Ten American Playwrights: An Annotated Bibliography*. New York: Garland, 1982.

Klein, Maury. "Misdeals." *1986–87 Humanities Booklet #3*, pp. 3–6. Providence, R.I.: Rhode Island Committee for the Humanities for Trinity Rep.

Kolin, Philip C. "Notices of David Rabe's First Play, *The Chameleon* (1959)." *Resources for American Literary Study* (forthcoming).

———. *David Rabe: A Stage History and A Primary and Secondary Bibliography*. New York: Garland, 1988.

———. "David Rabe's *Streamers*." *Explicator* 45 (Fall 1986): 63–64.

———. "*Goose and Tomtom*." *World Literature Today* 62 (Winter 1988): 128–29.

———. "Staging *Hurlyburly:* David Rabe's Parable for the 1980s." *Theatre Annual* 41 (1986): 63–78.

Krebs, Albin. "Paley, C.B.S. Chairman, Personally Vetoed Showing of *Sticks and Bones*." *New York Times* (20 March 1973): 78.

Kroll, Jack. "Go-Go in Hell." *Newsweek* (19 November 1973): 96.

———. "Greek Salad." *Newsweek* (30 April 1973): 87.

———. "Hollywood Wasteland: Off-Broadway, and All-Star Cast Makes Theater History." *Newsweek* (2 July 1984): 65, 67.

———. "This Is the Army." *Newsweek* (14 June 1971): 70.

———. "Three Cuts to the Quick." *Newsweek* (23 February 1976): 89, 91.

Lahr, John. "On-Stage." *Village Voice* (27 May 1971): 57.

Little, Stuart W. *Enter Joseph Papp: In Search of a New American Theater*. New York: Coward, McCann & Geoghegan, 1974.

Marranaca, Bonnie. "David Rabe's Viet Nam Trilogy." *Canadian Theatre Review* 14 (Spring 1977): 86–92.

McDonald, David. "The Mystification of Vietnam: David Rabe's *Sticks and Bones*." *Cultural Critique* 3 (Spring 1986): 211–34.

Metcalf, William A. *A Search for the Causes of Violence in the selected plays of David*

Rabe and Sam Shepard compared to the Patterns of Violence Found in Rollo May's "Power and Innocence; A Search for the Sources of Violence." Diss., University of Minnesota, 1982. Ann Arbor: UMI, 1986. PUV 83–01971.

Mordden, Ethan. *American Theatre.* New York: Oxford University Press, 1981.

Novick, Julius. "Papp Goes Boom at Beaumont." *Village Voice* (15 November 1973): 74.

Ogden, Jean. "On Stage." WBRW Radio. Somerville, New Jersey. 4 December 1974.

Oliver, Edith. "The Theatre: Off-Broadway." *New Yorker* (29 May 1971): 55.

Oppenheimer, George. "Stage: Salute to Pavlo." *Newsday,* (21 May 1971): A1, 9.

Patterson, James A. "David Rabe." In *Dictionary of Literary Biography,* 7, pt. 2: 172–78. *Twentieth-Century American Dramatists.* Edited by John Mac-Nicholas. Detroit: Gale, 1982.

Payne, Deborah C. *"Streamers." Studies in American Drama, 1945–Present* 1 (1986): 107–9.

Phillips, Jerrold A. "Descent into the Abyss: The Plays of David Rabe." *West Virginia University Philological Papers* 25 (February 1979): 108–17.

Reed, Rex. "*Streamers* Shatters Broadway's Doldrums." *New York Daily News* (23 April 1976): 70.

Rich, Frank. "Theater: *Hurlyburly.*" *New York Times* (22 June 1984): C:3.

Rosen, Carol. *Plays of Impasse: Contemporary Drama Set in Confining Institutions.* Princeton: Princeton University Press, 1983.

Schier, Ernest. "A Lively Production of *Orphan.*" *Philadephia Evening Bulletin* (15 March 1974): 49.

———. *"Boom Boom Room* Is Rabe's Finest." *Philadelphia Evening Bulletin* (9 November 1973): B19.

———. "Villanova's David Rabe: Impressive." *Philadelphia Evening Bulletin* (27 October 1970): 21.

———. "Villanova Has Fine Play, Playwright." *Philadelphia Evening Bulletin,* 11 February 1969: 33.

Sharp, Christopher. "Streamers." *Women's Wear Daily* (22 April 1976): 36.

Simard, Rodney. *Postmodern Drama: Contemporary Playwrights in America and Britain.* Lanham, Md.: University Press of America, 1984.

Simon, John. "Bad and Good Evenings." *New York* (26 November 1973): 92.

———. "Stinkweed Among the Asphodel." *New York* (30 April 1973): 98.

Stasio, Marilyn. *"Boom Boom Room." Cue* (19 November 1973): 7.

Stitt, Milan. "Gratitude Must Be Paid." *Horizon* (December 1984): 17.

Syse, Glenna. "*Hurlyburly:* Talent without Heart or Pain." *Chicago Sun-Times* (4 April 1984): 47.

Tigges, John, and Kay McMahon. "David Rabe." In John Tigges, compiler. *They Came From Dubuque.* Dubuque: Kendall/Hunt, 1983.

Wakeman, John, ed. "David Rabe." In *World Authors 1970–1975,* pp. 666–69. New York: H. W. Wilson, 1980.

Wallach, Allan. "Recasting a Success." *Newsday* (28 December 1971), A7, A9.

Watt, Douglas. "Rabe *Orphan* Ambitious Failure." *New York Daily News* (19 April 1973): 104.

———. "*Sticks and Bones* Brings the Vietnam War Home." *New York Daily News* (8 November 1971): 64.

————. "*Streamers* Exerts Its Power Anew." *New York Daily News* (22 April 1976): 91.

————. "*Streamers* Is Worth a Trip to New Haven." *New York Daily News* (9 February 1976): 25.

Watts, Richard. "An Innocent in Vietnam." *New York Post* (21 May 1971): 31.

Weales, Gerald. "Rampant Rabe." *Commonweal* (10 March 1972): 14–15.

Werner, Craig. "Primal Screams and Nonsense Rhymes: David Rabe's Revolt." *Educational Theatre Journal* 30 (December 1978): 517–29.

Wilson, Edwin. "On Theater: Rambling Rabe." *Wall Street Journal* (26 June 1984): 32.

————. "Time Bomb in an Army Barracks." *Wall Street Journal* (27 April 1976): 22.

Ronald Ribman

(28 MAY 1932–   )

PHILIP J. EGAN

ASSESSMENT OF RIBMAN'S REPUTATION

Although Ronald Ribman lacks a spectacular commercial success, his plays have been an important presence in American drama since the appearance of *Harry, Noon and Night* in 1965. He has won a number of impressive awards, including an Obie for the 1966 production of *Journey of the Fifth Horse;* a Straw Hat Award for *The Poison Tree;* an Emmy nomination for *The Final War of Olly Winter*, written for CBS Playhouse in 1967; and a Dramatists Guild Award for *Cold Storage* in 1977. He has won many grants over the years, including Rockefeller and Guggenheim fellowships.

Ribman, who came to the theater through an apprenticeship in poetry, is noted among his admirers for his unusual sensitivity to language, his bold experimentation with form, and his consistent treatment of the ambiguous relationship between victims and oppressors. As Weales correctly points out, Ribman offers a vision of man "limited by the situation . . . which, as likely as not, he helped to create" ("Ronald Ribman: The Artist of the Failure Clowns," 78).

PRIMARY BIBLIOGRAPHY OF RIBMAN'S WORKS

Plays and Screenplays

Day of the Games. Ideas and Figures (University of Pittsburgh) 1 (Spring 1959): 34–53. Never produced.
Harry, Noon and Night. In *The Journey of the Fifth Horse and Harry, Noon and Night.* Boston: Little, Brown, 1967. In *Five Plays by Ronald Ribman.* New York: Avon, 1978.

The Journey of the Fifth Horse. Based on Ivan Turgenev's short story "The Diary of a Superfluous Man." In *The Journey of the Fifth Horse and Harry, Noon and Night*. Boston: Little, Brown, 1967; in *Five Plays by Ronald Ribman*. New York: Avon, 1978.

The Journey of the Fifth Horse and Harry, Noon and Night: Two Plays. Boston: Little, Brown, 1967.

The Final War of Olly Winter. Television drama. In *Great Television Plays*, pp. 259–301. Edited by William I. Kaufman. New York: Dell, 1969; in *One Act Plays for Our Time*, pp. 271–328. Edited by Dr. Francis Griffith, Joseph Mersand, and Joseph B. Maggio. New York: Popular Library, 1973.

The Ceremony of Innocence. New York: Dramatists Play Service, 1968; in *Five Plays by Ronald Ribman*. New York: Avon, 1978.

The Most Beautiful Fish. Television drama. In " 'How Beautiful the Air Is!' " *New York Times* (23 November 1969): 2:21.

Passing Through from Exotic Places. Includes *The Son Who Hunted Tigers in Jakarta*, *Sunstroke*, and *The Burial of Esposito*. New York: Dramatists Play Service, 1970.

The Angel Levine. With Bill Gunn. Screenplay. Adapted from Bernard Malamud's short story "Angel Levine." United Artists, 1970.

Fingernails Blue as Flowers. In *The American Place Theatre: Plays*, pp. 1–30. Edited by Richard Shotter. New York: Dell, 1973.

A Break in the Skin. Produced in New Haven, Connecticut, 1972; New York, 1973. Never published.

The Poison Tree. New York: French, 1978; in *Five Plays by Ronald Ribman*. New York: Avon, 1978.

Cold Storage. New York: French, 1978; New York: Doubleday, 1978; in *Five Plays by Ronald Ribman*. New York: Avon, 1978.

Five Plays by Ronald Ribman. Includes *Harry, Noon and Night, The Journey of the Fifth Horse, The Ceremony of Innocence, The Poison Tree*, and *Cold Storage*. New York: Avon, 1978.

Buck. In *New Plays USA 2*, pp. 155–217. Edited by Elizabeth Osborn and Gillian Richards. New York: Theatre Communications Group, 1984.

Sweet Table at the Richelieu. American Theatre (July-August 1987): twelve-page insert between pages 28 and 29 in this issue.

A Serpent's Egg. Produced Cambridge, Massachusetts, April 1987.

The Cannibal Masque. Produced Cambridge, Massachusetts, April 1987.

Seize the Day. Screenplay. Adapted from Saul Bellow's novel *Seize the Day*. Learning in Focus, 1985. Televised on PBS, May 1987.

Fiction and Poetry

"Death of a Unicorn Hunter." *Ideas and Figures* 1 (Winter 1959): 42–47.

"Appendix: The Poems." In Susan H. Dietz, "The Work of Ronald Ribman: The Poet as Playwright". Ph.D. dissertation, University of Pennsylvania, 1974. Ann Arbor: UMI, 1975. 75–2720.

Nonfiction

"John Keats: The Woman and the Vision." Ph. D. dissertation, University of Pittsburgh, 1962. Ann Arbor: UMI, 1962. 63–7528.

"The Poor Man in the Scales." With Samuel Ribman. *Harper's Magazine* (April 1964): 150–58.

Interviews

Gruen, John. "He Refuses to Be 'With It.' " *New York Times* (7 June 1970): B15–16.

Wilson, Barbara. " Censorship Lives in Philadelphia: *The Poison Tree* Edited for Our Childish People." *Philadelphia Inquirer* (22 July 1973): G6.

O'Haire, Patricia. "Play That Will Not Die." *New York Daily News* (7 May 1977): 9.

Roiphe, Anne. " 'I Write about the Human Game.' " *New York Times* (25 December 1977): D2, 26.

Cunningham, Barry. "Ribman Defrosts Own Happy Ending." *New York Post* (13 January 1978): 41.

Wahls, Robert. "Healthy Revelations." *New York Daily News* (22 January 1978): 2:4.

Leahey, Mimi. "Ron Ribman: A Play about Cable TV." *Other Stages* (New York) (24 February 1983): 8.

Bennetts, Leslie. "Ronald Ribman Writes of a Violent World." *New York Times* (6 March 1983): B4–5.

DiNovelli, Donna. "Ronald Ribman's Journey to the Sweet Table." *A.R.T. News* (Cambridge, Massachusetts) (February 1987): 1, 8.

PRODUCTION HISTORY

Most of Ribman's plays have first appeared in off-Broadway productions, especially at the American Place Theatre, a noncommercial operation supported by subscribers. Several, however, have premiered at theatres associated with Robert Brustein at Harvard or Yale Universities.

Harry, Noon and Night (1965) played off-Broadway first at the American Place Theatre and later at the Pocket Theatre. The American Place production is noteworthy for providing Dustin Hoffman with his first important character role as Immanuel, a role Ribman has claimed partially inspired Hoffman's later performance as Ratso Rizzo in *Midnight Cowboy* (Wahls). The Pocket Theatre production, which aroused the entire range of reactions from enthusiastic praise to extreme loathing, was either credited with energy or accused of hysteria. Smith called the production "baroque and generally impressive."

The Journey of the Fifth Horse opened at the American Place on 21 April 1966 and again involved Dustin Hoffman, who won an Obie for his performance as Zoditch. Hoffman's difficulties in rehearsal, differences with the director, and inspired improvisations on opening night have been detailed in many accounts, the best of which is Kempton's (80). Brustein eloquently praised the intricate parallels between Zoditch and Chulkaturin in the *New Republic*, while acknowledging that the play is sometimes tedious and clumsy.

Ribman's television play, *The Final War of Olly Winter*, aired on CBS Playhouse 29 January 1967 with Ivan Dixon playing the lead as a black American soldier in Vietnam. Critics generally praised Dixon for the delicacy and gentleness in his portrayal of Olly Winter (Gould, "TV: 'The Final War' "), but some accused the play of sentimentality (Dietz, 140). Still, the drama was seen as important beyond its specific impact because, as the first show in the CBS Playhouse series, it struck many critics as heralding CBS's return to "serious" drama (Laurent).

The Ceremony of Innocence, opening at the American Place Theatre in December 1967, was directed by Arthur S. Seidleman and starred Donald Madden as Ethelred. Reviewers commonly praised Madden's Ethelred; Clive Barnes said his performance was "full of nervous energy" and "a strange yet believable mixture of strength and weakness" ("Ribman's *The Ceremony of Innocence*," 33). Yet many saw the play as lacking the vitality of Ribman's earlier efforts (Weales, *The Jumping-Off Place*, 233–34). The play was subsequently produced for National Educational Television, where it was more favorably received than on stage. Gould, the reviewer for the *New York Times*, claimed that the television version had found the "right medium" for the material because it could handle flashbacks smoothly, and he was impressed as well with Richard Kiley's performance as Ethelred ("TV: Play Finds Right Medium," 79).

Passing Through from Exotic Places, consisting of the three one-act plays—*Sunstroke*, *The Son Who Hunted Tigers in Jakarta*, and *The Burial of Esposito*—opened off-Broadway at the Sheridan Square Theatre in December 1969. While the production was generally praised, especially the acting of Vincent Gardenia and Tresa Hughes (Barnes, "Theater: 3 One-Acts"), the plays themselves were often seen as light and gimmicky (Weales, "Sour Notes").

Ribman was the second author of the feature film *The Angel Levine*, adapted from Bernard Malamud's short story "Angel Levine" and released in 1970. Given the fact of collaboration, Ribman's influence is difficult to identify; reviews focused principally on the acting of Harry Belafonte and Zero Mostel and the direction of Jan Kadar.

Ribman's one-act play *Fingernails Blue as Flowers* opened on 22 December 1971, the first play staged at the splendid new home of the American Place Theatre, and in general reviews celebrated the new theatre while expressing mocking puzzlement at the play's meaning. In a typical review, Simon dismissed the play as "bargain-basement absurdism" (58).

Others, such as *Newsweek's* Jack Kroll praised Albert Paulsen's performance as the millionaire tycoon without penetrating the play's meaning ("Broadway Breakthrough"). Gottfried, calling the piece "an authentic dramatic puzzle," was one of the few critics who explained and defended the play's intricate time scheme ("One New Theatre," 14).

A Break in the Skin, Ribman's only science fantasy, opened at the Yale Repertory Theatre on 13 October 1972 and then ran in a revised version off-Broadway in May 1973. Critics, like Gussow of the *New York Times* and the anonymous reviewer of *Variety* ("Bone"), praised the acting, directing, and the set but faulted the loose structure and use of science-fiction clichés.

The Poison Tree opened in Philadelphia at the Playhouse in the Park on 23 July 1973 and won the Straw Hat Award as the best play of the 1973 stock season. A revised version was mounted, first in Philadelphia in November 1975 and later at the Ambassador Theatre on Broadway in January 1976. According to Kerr and Kroll ("Locking the Door"), this production fielded some of the finest black actors in the country: Dick Anthony Williams (as pimp Bobby Foster), Cleavon Little (as revolutionary Willie Strepp), and Moses Gunn (as Hurspool). Both critics singled out Gunn's performance as outstanding. Others alleged that the play relied too much on the tradition of the 1930s prison movies (Gottfried, "Ribman"). Although the production was widely seen as powerful, it closed after only four Broadway performances, partly because the grim theme did not suit audiences.

Cold Storage opened in April 1977 at the American Place Theatre to an enthusiastic reception, and in January 1978 this production moved to the Lyceum Theatre on Broadway where, in a somewhat revised version, it ran for 180 performances. As virtually a two-character piece, this play made extraordinary demands on actors Martin Balsam and Len Cariou, who received great praise from critics in the national press, including *Newsweek's* Kroll ("Where Is Thy Sting?") and *Time's* Kalem. Ribman's only real commercial and popular success, *Cold Storage* has been widely produced in foreign countries. Because of its direct discussion of cancer, it sometimes is produced in conjunction with seminars on death and dying, as it was at the University of Wyoming ("Theatre Department").

Ribman's next play, *Buck*, opened as a combined effort of the American Place Theatre and Playwrights Horizons on 10 March 1983. It was hostilely received and widely charged with shapelessness and inconsistency, for which both the play itself and the production bore the blame. Rich claimed, for example, that Elinor Renfield's production "never finds a style that might help fit Mr. Ribman's pieces together" (C5).

Ribman's most recent major play to date, *Sweet Table at the Richelieu*, opened at the American Repertory Theatre on 11 February 1987. Reviewed only by the local press, *Sweet Table*'s reception was mixed, but the production generally fared well in critics' opinions (Kelly, "Remarkable 'Richelieu' Premieres"). Two one-act plays, *A Serpent's Egg* and *The Cannibal Masque*, were mounted by the American Repertory Theatre in April 1987. Designed as part of a trilogy with *Sweet Table*, these plays also received mixed reviews. *The Cannibal Masque*, however, won some praise for its relentless vision of human predation and what Kelly called its "creepy originality" ("Ribman Double Bill," 46).

SURVEY OF SECONDARY SOURCES

Bibliographies

Egan's classified bibliography in *Studies in American Drama, 1945–Present* is the most substantial bibliography to date and supersedes the "Selected Bibliography" of Ribman in Dietz's 1974 dissertation. Egan's bibliography divides the items into Ribman's work, interviews, criticism, reviews, and biographical/informational articles; the primary bibliography is essential for any Ribman research; the secondary bibliography lists almost four hundred items.

Biographies

Ribman has led a varied life and came to playwrighting relatively late. Although many interviews briefly document his early life and its connection with his plays (Cunningham, DiNovelli, Wilson), Roiphe's is the most useful. Weales's "Ronald Ribman" in *Contemporary Dramatists* also gives valuable and concise information. In addition, Dietz supplies a reasonably full account of Ribman's early professional career, including his association with the American Place Theatre (3–8).

Influences

No extended study of influences on Ribman has been done, and the playwright himself evades the question of contemporary dramatic mentors, admitting to influence only from such figures as Shakespeare, Keats, and Wallace Stevens (Roiphe, 26D). Nevertheless, so many reviewers and critics have seen "absurdist" or "Beckettian" elements in his plays that such dramatic influence seems eminently likely, even if it is undocumented. As for influence from the poets, Weales suggests that Wallace Stevens inspires Ribman's fascination with "the artist's way of seeing" and his preference for "antirealistic devices" ("Ronald Ribman: The Artist of the Failure Clowns," 85).

General Studies

For any thorough study of Ribman's work, Dietz's 1974 dissertation is indispensable for two reasons. First, although Dietz conceives her work as a critical commentary, she received Ribman's permission to print the text of many primary items—including more than thirty poems, an introduction to *Day of the Games*, and generous quotations from letters and interviews—that appear nowhere else. Second, Dietz is an intelligent and sensitive critic, whose comments are all the more powerful because she had access to early drafts and unproduced scripts. She devotes a chapter each to *Harry, Noon and Night*, *The Journey of the Fifth Horse*, *The Ceremony of Innocence* (including both stage and television versions), the one-act plays (including *Passing Through from Exotic Places* and *Fingernails Blue as Flowers*), the television plays (including both *The Final War of Olly Winter* and the unproduced *If My Father's House Be Evil*), *A Break in the Skin* (including unproduced early versions *Marginal Man* and *Skew*), and *The Poison Tree*. Her treatments are particularly useful because for each play (except *A Break in the Skin* and *The Poison Tree*), she begins with a summary of reviewers' reactions and uses the issues raised as the starting point of her analysis. The dissertation's subtitle ("The Poet as Playwright") reveals its principal bias; Dietz, who frequently cites connections between Ribman's poetry and plays, consistently concerns herself with language and with the dramatic presentations of imagery and metaphor. She notes as well the ambiguous relationship between oppressor and oppressed in many of the plays.

Weales has written important assessments of Ribman's work. In *The Jumping-Off Place: American Drama in the 1960's*, Weales gives much of value on Ribman's early plays (228–34). Most impressive is his treatment of *Harry, Noon and Night*, which he sees as revealing a deeply felt sibling rivalry between Harry and his conventional brother. In his other treatment of Ribman's works, "Ronald Ribman: The Artist of the Failure Clowns," Weales develops the thesis that images of the "failure clown" from *Harry, Noon and Night* and the title image of *The Journey of the Fifth Horse* represent a recurrent theme in Ribman's work: "man is limited by the situation, mundane or metaphysical, in which he finds himself and which, as likely as not, he helped to create" (78). Weales shows that this theme is central to *The Final War of Olly Winter*, *The Ceremony of Innocence*, *The Poison Tree*, and *Cold Storage*. He emphasizes, however, that Ribman is an artist of the failure clown because he is concerned in all plays with ways of seeing. Noting Ribman's use of Wallace Stevens's poetry in *Harry, Noon and Night*, Weales rejects the label of realism often applied to Ribman's plays. Even when Ribman is realistic, he often chooses dramatic methods that emphasize imagination, memory, or interpretation (rather than simple transcription) of reality. In documenting this ingenuity,

Weales corrects the idea, perpetrated in part by the playwright himself, that Ribman is a "verbal" playwright; he writes with an excellent visual sense as well. Weales does honor Ribman's verbal brilliance with two examples from *Cold Storage*, but he is careful to show that Ribman subordinates language to character. Weales supplies a brief, useful overview of Ribman's themes and techniques in *Contemporary Dramatists*, 4th ed.

In addition to these general studies, Lamont compares *Buck* to *Cinders*, a play by Polish author Janusz Glowacki. For Lamont, both authors explore how users of the camera, driven by the power structure of their particular society, corrupt themselves and those whose lives they scrutinize. Both authors use the play-within-a-play technique that shows how filmmakers change the reality they attempt to reenact. In *Buck* this technique combines with metaphors of eating and images of cannibalism to reveal the predatory nature of our society at large.

FUTURE RESEARCH OPPORTUNITIES

Some of the current critical responses to Ribman's canon should be deepened with a historical perspective or extended to cover his new plays. First, many critics claim that Ribman uses (or even joins) the absurdist tradition in his plays. Although the claim appears most frequently in reviews of *Fingernails Blue as Flowers*, many other plays, including even *The Ceremony of Innocence*, are also alleged to have absurdist elements (Dietz, 93–94). Most of these suggestions, however, are casual and lack depth. Clearly Ribman occasionally uses absurdist dialogue, but does the influence penetrate more deeply? We can well use a study, thoroughly grounded in both absurdist texts and Ribman's canon, that pins down the way Ribman appropriates absurdist tradition and how he changes it when he does so. Second, Ribman's use of language can use more attention. There is, for example, a remarkable disagreement among critics about whether Ribman uses archaic or modern idiom in *The Ceremony of Innocence* (Dietz 100–102). Both this play and *The Poison Tree* suggest that Ribman can invent an idiom for special circumstances without rendering it unintelligible to contemporary audiences. It would be instructive to know the concessions Ribman makes—and those he refuses to make—in the direction of archaism or dialect. Finally, although both Dietz and Weales have probed the oppressor-oppressed relationship in Ribman's early work, this theme can be further analyzed in the light of the recent plays (*Buck, Sweet Table, A Serpent's Egg*, and *The Cannibal Masque*), where it appears with even more frightening intensity. It is time to take stock of how this theme has evolved since its appearance in *Harry, Noon and Night* more than twenty years ago and to note as well the imagery that expresses it. The images of eating and cannibalism Lamont finds in *Buck* continue in *Sweet Table* and rise to suggestions of actual cannibalism in *The Cannibal Masque*. While these image patterns imply a predatory world, it is worth establishing what values can remain in such a world.

SECONDARY SOURCES

Barnes, Clive. "Theater: 3 One-Act Plays Stretch Out at the Sheridan Square." *New York Times* (8 December 1969): 60.

———. "Theater: Ribman's *The Ceremony of Innocence* Opens." *New York Times* (2 January 1968): 33.

Bone. Review of *A Break in the Skin*. *Variety* (15 November 1972): 74.

Brustein, Robert. "Journey and Arrival of a Playwright." *New Republic* (7 May 1966): 31, 33–34.

Cunningham, Barry. "Ribman Defrosts Own Happy Ending." *New York Post* (13 January 1978): 41.

Dietz, Susan H. "The Work of Ronald Ribman: The Poet as Playwright." Ph.D. dissertation, University of Pennsylvania, 1974. Ann Arbor: UMI, 1975. 75–2720.

DiNovelli, Donna. "Ronald Ribman's Journey to the Sweet Table." *A.R.T.* [American Repertory Theatre] *News* (February 1987): 1, 8.

Egan, Philip J. "Ronald Ribman: A Classified Bibliography." *Studies in American Drama, 1945–Present* 2 (1987): 97–117.

Gottfried, Martin. "One New Theatre, One Superb Play." *Women's Wear Daily* (23 December 1971): 14.

———. "Ribman Out on a Limb." *New York Post* (9 January 1976): 15.

Gould, Jack. "TV: 'The Final War of Olly Winter.' " *New York Times* (30 January 1967): 59.

———. "TV: Play Finds Right Medium on N.E.T. Tonight." *New York Times* (12 June 1970):79.

Gussow, Mel. "Theater: Yale Repertory Stages 'Break in the Skin.' " *New York Times* (20 October 1972): 32.

Kalem, T. E. "Ferrying on the Styx." *Time* (18 April 1977): 31.

Kelly, Kevin. "Remarkable 'Richelieu' Premieres at ART [American Repertory Theatre]." *Boston Globe* (12 February 1987): 94.

———. "Ribman Double Bill is Compelling Theatre." *Boston Globe* (8 April 1987): 46.

Kempton, Sally. "Little Big Man Clings to Life." *Esquire* (July 1970): 78–81.

Kerr, Walter. "Did I See the Same Show You Did?" *New York Times* (21 March 1976): D7.

Kroll, Jack. "Locking the Door." *Newsweek* (19 January 1976): 81.

———. "Broadway Breakthrough." *Newsweek* (3 January 1972): 49.

———. "Where Is Thy Sting?" *Newsweek* (25 April 1977): 90.

Lamont, Rosette C. "Murderous Enactments: The Media's Presence in the Drama." *Modern Drama* 28 (1985): 148–61.

Laurent, Lawrence. "Quality Back in TV Drama." *Washington Post* (30 January 1967): D6.

Rich, Frank. "*Buck*, Sleaze, and Cable TV." *New York Times* (11 March 1983): C5.

Simon, John. "Absurdism and Absurdity." *New York* (3 January 1972): 58.

Smith, Michael. Review of *Harry, Noon and Night*. *Village Voice* (15 May 1965): 18.

"Theatre Department, College of Medicine Join in Unique Project." *Laramie* (Wyoming) *Sunday Boomerang* (19 August 1979): 3.

Wahls, Robert. "Healthy Revelations." *New York Daily News* (22 January 1978): Leisure sec.:4.

Weales, Gerald. "Ronald Ribman." In *Contemporary Dramatists*, 4th edition, pp. 449–51. Edited by D. L. Kirkpatrick. Chicago: St. James Press, 1988.

———. "Ronald Ribman: The Artist of the Failure Clowns." In *Essays on Contemporary American Drama*, pp. 75–90. Edited by Hedwig Bock and Albert Wertheim. Munich: Hueber, 1981.

———. "Sour Notes." *Commonweal* (30 January 1970): 482–83.

———. *The Jumping-Off Place: American Drama in the 1960's*. New York: Macmillan, 1969.

Wilson, Barbara. "Censorship Lives in Philadelphia: *The Poison Tree* Edited for Our Childish People." *Philadelphia Inquirer* (22 July 1973): G6.

Ntozake Shange
(18 OCTOBER 1948–   )

KENNETH WATSON

ASSESSMENT OF SHANGE'S REPUTATION

Shange's work in the theatre is an important contribution to a still-emerging black feminist dramatic aesthetic. She combines poetry with dance and jazz as integral parts of her plays. She draws her materials almost exclusively from the experience of contemporary urban black women, and her technical innovations are designed to give this group a theatrical voice and presence. Such an effort has not been unattended by controversy, especially regarding Shange's treatments of black men. Nonetheless, her first play, *for colored girls who have considered suicide/when the rainbow is enuf*, enjoyed considerable popular and critical success, and her subsequent work in the theatre and a variety of other media has made her a crucial artist in the development of black feminist perspectives. Official recognition of her work has included two Obies, the Outer Circle Critics Award, the Andelco Award, and the Mademoiselle Award, as well as fellowships from the Guggenheim Foundation and the National Endowment for the Arts.

PRIMARY BIBLIOGRAPHY OF SHANGE'S WORKS

Plays

for colored girls who have considered suicide/when the rainbow is enuf. New York: Macmillan, 1977.
Negress. Unpublished. 1977.
where the mississippi meets the amazon. Unpublished. 1977.
Black and White Two-Dimensional Planes. Unpublished, 1979.
Mother Courage. Unpublished. 1980.
A Photograph: Lovers-in-Motion. New York: French, 1981.

three pieces: Spell #7, A Photograph: Lovers-in-Motion, Boogie Woogie Landscapes.
    New York: St. Martin's Press, 1981.
Three for a Full Moon, and Bocas. Unpublished, 1982.
from okra to greens: a different kinda love story. New York: French, 1983.
Educating Rita. Unpublished, 1983.
Spell #7. London: Methuen, 1985.
mouths. Unpublished. 1981.
carrie. Unpublished operetta 1981.

Novels

Sassafrass. San Lorenzo, Calif.: Shameless Hussy Press, 1977.
Sassafrass, Cypress, Indigo: A Novel. New York: St. Martin's Press, 1982.
Betsey Brown: A Novel. New York: St. Martin's Press, 1985.

Poetry

Melissa and Smith. St. Paul: Bookslinger, 1976.
Natural Disasters and Other Festive Occasions. San Francisco: Heirs, 1977.
Nappy Edges. New York: St. Martin's Press, 1978.
a daughter's geography. New York: St. Martin's Press, 1983.
Ridin' the Moon in Texas: Word Paintings. New York: St. Martin's Press, 1987.

Essays and Interviews

"Women and the Creative Process: A Discussion (with Susan Griffin, Norma
    Leistiko, Ntozake Shange, and Miriam Schapiro)." *Mosaic* 8 (1974–1975):
    91–117.
"Ntozake Shange." *New Yorker* (2 August 1976): 17–19.
"Ntozake Shange Interviews Herself." *Ms.* 6 (December 1977): 35, 70, 72.
"An Interview with Ntozake Shange" (with Henry Blackwell). *Black American
    Literature Forum* 13 (Winter 1979): 134–38.
"Interview with Ntozake Shange" (with James Early). In *In Memory and Spirit of
    Frances, Zora, and Lorraine: Essays And Interviews on Black Women and Writ-
    ing,* pp. 23–26. Edited by Juliette Bowles. Washington, D.C.: Institute for
    the Arts and the Humanities, Howard University, 1979.
"N. S." In *Black Women Writers at Work*, pp. 149–74. Edited by Claudia Tate. New
    York: Continuum Publishing Company, 1983.
"Ntozake Shange." In *Interviews with Contemporary Women Playwrights*, pp. 365–
    78. Edited by Kathleen Betsko and Rachel Koenig. New York: Beech Tree
    Books, 1987.
See No Evil: Prefaces, Essays, and Accounts, 1976–1983. San Francisco: Momo's
    Press, 1983.

PRODUCTION HISTORY

For several months in 1977–1978, Shange had three pieces playing simultaneously in New York City. One of them, in collaboration with poet-performers Thulani Nkabinde and Jessica Hagedorn (who, together with Shange, were collectively billed as "The Satin Sisters"), brought Shange herself to the stage. This was in a Public Theatre Cabaret presentation of *where the mississippi meets the amazon*, a dance-poetry-jazz evening in the form that Shange calls a choreopoem. The music was provided by a quintet led by avant-garde saxophonist David Murray. Another, just then beginning its own brief run under the aegis of the Public Theatre, *a photograph: a study in cruelty*, remains Shange's only excursion to date into somewhat more traditional playwriting. It was not a critical or popular success (however, see Murray for an account of its highly interesting elements). Meanwhile, uptown on Broadway, the original choreopoem *for colored girls who have considered suicide/when the rainbow is enuf* was going strong at the Booth.

Shange began performances of versions of *for colored girls* in bookstores and women's bars in San Francisco in 1974. Its gradual local success encouraged Shange and her collaborators to take the show to New York in July 1975, where they established themselves in a series of jazz lofts and bars in the East Village. Woodie King moved them to the stage at the Henry Street Settlement in November 1975, and Joseph Papp took the show to the Public Theater in June 1976. There, having successfully run a difficult gauntlet to a major off-Broadway stage, *for colored girls* received its first significant reviews. Shange was proclaimed "an incisive new playwright" by Frazer, and Barnes joined in the general adulation (27). Not long after, in September 1976, *for colored girls* moved to Broadway. Shange continued to perform in the piece but only briefly. Nonetheless, it proved durable enough to succeed without her presence, by all accounts formidable.

Gussow praised the Broadway opening as "a joyful celebration" and asserted that "the coda is discovery: The 'colored girl' learns to trust herself, to believe in her own elemental value" ("Stage: 'Colored Girls' Evolves," 53). An extremely simple set by Ming Cho Lee and brilliant performances by Shange herself and by Trazana Beverly received high compliments. Among the few less than celebratory reviewers, Sanders thought it "a long and shrill harangue . . . over-wrought and over-acted" (202). Meanwhile muted reservations appeared in the black press. Rogers, in an otherwise favorable review, attacked what he called Shange's "unrelenting stereotyping of Black men" (38). This, rather than any formal or technical criticism, has proved to be the central controversy over Shange's work. *for colored girls* played on Broadway from September

1976 to July 1978, and regional companies continued to tour the United States and Canada well after that.

a photograph: a study in cruelty was much less successful. In a typical notice, Eder complained that Shange's attempt at more conventional theatre suffered from flabby dramatic structure ("New Production at the Public Theater"). In the context of his notice of Shange's next major offering, *Spell #7*, Eder referred to *a photograph* as "an awkward experiment" ("Stage: 'Spell #7' by Ntozake Shange," 12). *a photograph* played only briefly at the Public Theater, never moved on to Broadway, and has not been widely performed since.

Spell #7 was more favorably received than *a photograph*, although it never achieved the popularity of *for colored girls*. In it, Shange reverted to the choreopoem form she had evolved for her Broadway hit. It opened in July 1979 at the Public Theatre, and Eder's initial notice termed it "a most lovely and powerful work" ("Stage: 'Spell #7' by Ntozake Shange," 12). Of its substance, Eder noted an available comparison to *A Chorus Line*, of which he found *Spell #7* to be a sort of black version. Oliver found the piece "a kind of miracle" and joined with Eder in singling out the play's director Oz Scott (who also directed *for colored girls*) and actor Mary Alice for special praise ("The Theater: Off-Broadway," 73). Although *Spell #7* stayed at the Public Theater and lasted only a season, regional companies toured with it, to general acclaim.

Shange's most recent major production on the New York stage represented a considerable departure from her other works in the form of a radically revisionist adaption of Brecht's classic *Mother Courage and Her Children*. This opened at the Public Theater in May 1980 to generally respectful but somewhat chagrined mixed notices. The respectful tone of the reviews apparently resulted from the seriousness of the effort. *Mother Courage* was transposed to the post–Civil War American Indian wars. The main character became a freed black woman, wandering the war-torn western plains, surviving by selling her wares to anyone who will buy them and speaking Shange's inimitable black stage idiom. Gussow, one of Shange's most loyal champions, found this adaption "a venturesome feat of re-interpretation" and "a considerable dramatic achievement," but even he was forced to admit certain "shortcomings" ("Stage: 'Mother Courage,'" 20). Still, Wilford Leach's direction and economical stage setting and Gloria Foster's performance in the lead role won Gussow's praise. Oliver was much less forgiving, questioning the wisdom of the transposition and finding the production "slack" even as she admired the "strength" and "control" (26 May 1980, 77). In the black press, Allen found the adaption "pointless" and wished that Shange had created a play that did not equivocate between "half-Brecht, half-Black" (20). *Mother Courage* had a brief run and has not been widely performed elsewhere or since.

SURVEY OF SECONDARY SOURCES

Bibliographies

There is no adequate bibliography of Shange's work. Listings of varying completeness and accuracy can be located in Richards (1988), Woll, *Current Biography*, and *Who's Who*. Blackwell's, Betsko and Koenig's, and Tate's interviews are each prefaced with brief bibliographic paragraphs.

Biographies

Sketchy biographical information is available in Woll, *Current Biography*, and *Who's Who*. The eight interviews with Shange that are available help to flesh out and complete these rather skeletal accounts.

Influences

In interviews, Shange frequently credits her artistically minded upper-middle-class family for interesting her and encouraging her participation in black poetry, dance, and music. She also mentions the names of the many writers and musicians she admires. Rushing summarizes Shange's evaluations of specific influences on her work as conveyed in interview. Subsequent interviews, especially Tate's, extend the list of possible influences to be explored. Richards (1983) argues that Brecht's dramatic theories and those that Amiri Baraka derived from Antonin Artaud are of prime importance to Shange's mode of theatre.

General Studies

There is no full-length study devoted to Shange's work. Almost all of the few critical considerations available have been largely devoted to *for colored girls*. Chinoy and Jenkins situate Shange's work in the context of feminist theatre. Among the few exceptions is Richards, who undertakes a concurrent reading of Shange's published dramatic works, concentrating on *for colored girls* and *Spell #7*. Richards argues that Shange's drama can be viewed as an open-ended dialectic "between the felt constrictions of the social order and the perceived limitlessness of the natural order" (73). Besides this attempt to develop a structure within which all of Shange's theatre may be seen to operate, Richard's essay has two other important features: its serious attention to dramatic influences on Shange and the best defense mounted to date against the attacks on Shange's supposedly stereotypifying portrayals of black men.

Analyses of Individual Plays

for colored girls has elicited most of the critical attention that Shange has thus far received. The mild demurrals in the notices of this play in the black press expanded into an extended controversy over the role of men in Shange's plays and the role of feminism in black American culture. Peters stated the negative case first, and his essay remains the most lucid and balanced statement of it. Staples stated the negative case much more harshly, from a sociological perspective. He combined his attack on Shange's version of black feminism with one on that of Michele Wallace's *Black Macho and the Myth of the Superwoman* (1979). Staples's essay provoked a massive response, printed as "The Black Scholar Reader's Forum on Black Male-Female Relations." This is essential reading for anyone interested in the issues of black feminism as they bear on Shange's plays. Rushing offers an important critique of *for colored girls* from the perspective of a different version of black feminism, and her essay too is required reading for the same interest. Christ's positive and systematic close reading undertakes to integrate Shange's black feminism with feminism in general, laying special stress on women's spirituality as a means to counter oppression. Flowers mounts a defense of *for colored girls* against the sort of attack represented by Peters. Flowers's project is to integrate Shange's black feminism with the black liberation struggle in general. Mitchell's essay departs from the history of the criticism on *for colored girls* by focusing on the city and the means of transcending it as metaphor in the play. Murray is the only critic to write on Ntozake Shange without mentioning *for colored girls*. His essay puts Shange's *a photograph* in the context of Jackson's *Toe Jam*, Amiri Baraka's *The Motion of History*, and Adrienne Kennedy's *An Evening with Dead Essex*. His focus is an ideological critique of theatrical convention implicit in these plays, and he brings to the discussion of Shange's work a theoretical sophistication lacking heretofore.

FUTURE RESEARCH OPPORTUNITIES

While this essay has made a first attempt at primary bibliography on Shange, more work will undoubtedly need to be done in this area. It is too early in Shange's career to consider a critical biography. The fact remains that most of her work, in the theatre and in other media, has gone undiscussed. This is a serious gap in the criticism of contemporary letters. Of special interest is her combination of jazz, dance, and poetry in the mode she calls a choreopoem; this kind of purely formal and technical innovation stands in need of careful investigation. The issue of the influences Shange has assimilated and extended also needs much more exploration.

SECONDARY SOURCES

Allen, Bonnie. "A Home Instinct." *Essence* 11, no. 4 (August 1980): 17, 20.

Chinoy, Helen Krich and Linda Walsh Jenkins. *Women in American Theatre*. Revised And Expanded Edition. New York: Theatre Communications Group, 1987.

Christ, Carol P. " 'i found god in myself . . . & i loved her fiercely': Ntozake Shange." In her *Diving Deep and Surfacing: Women Writers on Spiritual Quest*, pp. 97–118. Boston: Beacon Press, 1980.

"The Black Scholar Reader's Forum on Black Male-Female Relations." *Black Scholar* 10, nos. 8/9 (May-June, 1979): 15–67.

Barnes, Clive. "Off Broadway." *New York Times* (2 June 1976): 18.

Eder, Richard. "New Production at the Public Theater." *New York Times* (4 October 1977): 24.

———. "Stage: 'Spell #7' by Ntozake Shange." *New York Times* (16 July 1979): 12.

Flowers, Sandra Hollin. "*Colored Girls:* Textbook for the Eighties." *Black American Literature Forum* 15, no. 2 (Summer 1981): 51–54.

Frazer, C. Gerald. "Theatre Finds an Incisive New Playwright." *New York Times* (16 June 1976): 27.

Gussow, Mel. "Stage: 'Colored Girl' Evolves." *New York Times* (16 September 1976): 53.

———. "Stage: 'Mother Courage.' " *New York Times* (14 May 1980): 20.

Mitchell, Carolyn. " 'A Laying On of Hands': Transcending the City in Ntozake Shange's *for colored girls who have considered suicide/when the rainbow is enuf*." In *Women Writers and the City: Essays in Feminist Literary Criticism*, pp. 230–48. Edited by Susan Merrill Squier. Knoxville: University of Tennessee Press, 1984.

Murray, Timothy. "Screening the Camera's Eye: Black and White Confrontations of Technological Reproduction." *Modern Drama* 28, no. 1 (March 1985): 110–24.

Oliver, Edith. "The Theatre: Off-Broadway." *New Yorker* (16 July 1979): 73.

———. "The Theatre: Off Broadway." *New Yorker* (26 May 1980): 77.

Peters, Erskine. "Some Tragic Propensities of Ourselves: The Occasion of Ntozake Shange's 'for colored girls who have considered suicide/when the rainbow is enuf.' " *Journal of Ethnic Studies* 6, no. 1 (1978): 79–85.

Richards, Sandra L. "Shange, Ntozake." In D. L. Kirkpatrick, ed., *Contemporary Dramatists*. Fourth Edition. Chicago: St. James Press, 1988. 477–78.

———. "Conflicting Impulses in the Plays of Ntozake Shange." *Black American Literature Forum* 17, no. 2 (Summer 1983): 73–78.

Rogers, Curtis E. "Good Theatre But Poor Sociological Statement." *New York Amsterdam News* (9 October 1976): 38.

Rushing, Andrea Benton. "*For Colored Girls:* Suicide or Struggle." *Massachusetts Review* 22 (Autumn 1981): 539–50.

Sanders, Kevin. "Commentary." WABC-TV, New York, 19 September 1976. Reprinted in *New York Theatre Critics' Reviews* (1976): 202.

Staples, Robert. "The Myth of Black Macho: A Response to Angry Black Feminists." *Black Scholar* 10, nos. 6–7 (March-April 1979): 24–33.

Woll, Allen. "Shange, Ntozake." In his *Dictionary of the Black Theatre*, pp. 248–50. Westport, Conn.: Greenwood Press, 1983.

Sam Shepard

(5 NOVEMBER 1943–   )

WILLIAM KLEB

ASSESSMENT OF SHEPARD'S REPUTATION

Sam Shepard arrived in New York in 1963 at age 19 determined to become an actor. Two years later, Lester in the *New York Times* had named him "the acknowledged 'genius' of the OOB circuit"—not as an actor but as a playwright (100). In a sense, however, Shepard has always been both. His plays, as he has said, are not only written with the act of performing in mind—"In my experience the character is visualized, he appears out of nowhere in three dimensions and speaks" ("Visualization," 50)—they are often about the act of performance itself, the process of self-identification through self-projection. In this, as in so much else, Shepard reflects an age fascinated with, and often confounded by, its own theatricality. How to come to terms with or improvise a way out of this "gestalt" (as many Shepard critics have put it) has been the constant theme of his work.

Shepard's plays have always evoked a divided response from audiences and reviewers, if not from academic critics. Only since he won the Pulitzer Prize (1979) has a real awareness of his work entered the theatrical mainstream—and then only via off-Broadway, regional, and university theatre. His writing has won dozens of awards, including Obies for eleven plays (more than anyone else), the New York Drama Critics Circle Award, and the Golden Palm at Cannes. Many consider him to be, in Mazzocco's words, "the dominant American playwright of his generation" (27). Having produced forty-two plays in just over half that number of years, he is surely among the most prolific. According to Esslin, "He *is* contemporary American theatre" (Coe, "Saga," 58).

PRIMARY BIBLIOGRAPHY OF SHEPARD'S WORKS

Most of Shepard's plays are in print in three major anthologies: *Seven Plays* (New York: Bantam, 1981); *Fool for Love and Other Plays* (New York: Bantam, 1984); and *The Unseen Hand and Other Plays* (New York: Bantam, 1986). Abbreviations of these titles (*Seven, Fool, Unseen*) are included, along with place and date of publication, after each play title listed below. Earlier publications in anthologies—most now out of print or going out of print—are then indicated by shortened title and year of publication only. The few publications in separate books or periodicals are given full citations.

Plays

Cowboys. Unpublished play. 1964.

The Rock Garden. Unseen, New York: Bantam, 1986; *Angel City,* 1976; *Scripts* 3 1, no. 3 (January 1972): 24–30; *Mad Dog,* 1972; final scene included in *Oh! Calcutta,* 1969, and in *Evergreen Review* 13, no. 69 (August 1969): 49, 51.

Up to Thursday. Unpublished play. 1965.

Dog. Unpublished play. 1965.

Rocking Chair. Unpublished play. 1965.

Chicago. Unseen, New York: Bantam, 1986; *Chicago,* 1981; *Five Plays,* 1967; *Eight Plays from Off-Off-Broadway,* 1966.

4–H Club. Unseen, New York: Bantam, 1986.

Untitled. Unpublished play. 1965. (Produced as part of *BbAaNnGg!*)

Icarus's Mother. Unseen, New York: Bantam, 1986; *Chicago,* 1981; *New Underground Theatre,* 1968; *Five Plays,* 1967.

Red Cross. Unseen, New York: Bantam, 1986; *New Underground Theatre,* 1968; *Five Plays,* 1967.

Fourteen Hundred Thousand. Unseen, New York: Bantam, 1986; *Chicago,* 1981; *Five Plays,* 1967.

La Turista. Seven, New York: Bantam, 1981; *Four Two-Act,* 1980; *La Turista,* Indianapolis: Bobbs-Merrill, 1968.

Melodrama Play. Fool, New York: Bantam, 1984; *Chicago,* 1981; *Five Plays,* 1967.

Cowboys #2. Unseen, New York: Bantam, 1986; *Angel City,* 1976; *Mad Dog,* 1972; *Collision Course,* 1969.

Forensic and the Navigators. Unseen, New York: Bantam, 1986; *Unseen,* 1981; 1972. *Best of Off-Off Broadway,* 1969.

The Holy Ghostly. Unseen, New York: Bantam, 1986; *Unseen,* 1981; 1972.

The Unseen Hand. Unseen, New York: Bantam, 1986; *Unseen,* 1981; 1972. *Plays and Players* May 1973: II-XI; *Off-Off Broadway Book,* 1972.

Operation Sidewinder. Unseen, New York: Bantam, 1986; *Four Two-Act,* 1980; *Angel City,* 1976; *Operation Sidewinder,* Indianapolis: Bobbs-Merrill, 1970. *Esquire* (May 1969): 152 ff. (Variant text).

Shaved Splits. Out of print. *Unseen,* 1981; 1972.

Mad Dog Blues. Unseen, New York: Bantam, 1986; *Mad Dog,* 1972.

Cowboy Mouth. Fool, New York: Bantam, 1984. *Mad Dog,* 1972.

Back Bog Beast Bait. Unseen, New York: Bantam, 1986. *Unseen,* 1981; 1972.

The Tooth of Crime. Seven, New York: Bantam, 1981; *Four Two-Act,* 1980; *Tooth/ Geography,* 1974; *Performance* (March-April 1973): 67–91 (variant text).

Nightwalk ("The House and the Fish"). In *Three Works by the Open Theatre.* Edited by Karen Malpede. New York: Drama Book Specialists, 1974.

Geography of a Horse Dreamer. Fool, New York: Bantam Books, 1984. *Four Two-Act,* 1980; *Tooth/ Geography,* 1974.

Little Ocean. Unpublished play. 1974.

Action. Fool, New York: Bantam, 1984; *Angel City,* 1976.

Killer's Head. Unseen, New York: Bantam, 1986; *Angel City,* 1976.

Angel City. Fool, New York: Bantam, 1984; *Angel City,* 1976.

Flat Suicide in B Flat. Fool, New York: Bantam, 1984; *Buried,* 1979.

The Sad Lament of Pecos Bill on the Eve of Killing His Wife. Fool, San Francisco: City Lights Books, 1983. *Theatre* 12, no. 3 (Summer-Fall 1981): 32–38 (libretto only).

Inacoma. Unpublished play. 1977.

Curse of the Starving Class. Seven, New York: Bantam, 1981; *Angel City,* 1976.

Seduced. Fool, New York; Bantam, 1984; *Buried,* 1979.

Tongues. Seven, New York: Bantam, 1981.

Buried Child. Seven, New York: Bantam, 1981; *Famous American Plays of the 1970s,* 1981; *Buried,* 1979.

Jacaranda. Unpublished monologue. 1979.

Savage/Love. Seven, New York: Bantam, 1981.

True West. Seven, New York: Bantam, 1981.

Superstitions. Unpublished play. 1981.

Fool for Love. Fool, New York: Bantam, 1984; *Fool for Love,* San Francisco: City Lights, 1983.

The War in Heaven: Angel's Monologue. A Lie of the Mind, New York: New American Library, 1987.

A Lie of the Mind. New York: New American Library, 1987.

True Dylan. Esquire (July 1987): 59–62, 64, 66, 68.

Screenplays

Me and My Brother. Unpublished filmscript with Robert Frank. 1965–1969.

Zabriskie Point. New York: Simon and Schuster, 1972. With Michelangelo Antonioni, Fred Gardner, Tonino Guerra, and Clare Peploe.

Renaldo and Clara. Unpublished filmscript with Bob Dylan. 1978.

Paris, Texas. Berlin: Road Movies, 1984; Nordlingen (Bavaria): Greno, 1984. Adaptation by L. M. Kit Carson.

Fool for Love. Unpublished filmscript based on Shepard's play *Fool for Love,* 1985.

Short Stories, Poems, Monologues, and Memoirs

Hawk Moon. New York: Performing Arts Journal, 1981. Reprint of *Hawk Moon: A Book of Short Stories, Poems, and Monologues.* Los Angeles: Blacksparrow Press, 1973.

Rolling Thunder Logbook. New York: Viking, 1977 Rpt. Limelight, 1987.
Motel Chronicles. San Francisco: City Lights, 1982; London, Faber, 1985.

Essays and Autobiographical Notes

"Author's Notes to *Melodrama Play*." In *Five Plays by Sam Shepard*, p. 126. Indianapolis: Bobbs-Merrill, 1967. Reprinted in *Chicago and Other Plays*. New York: Urizen, 1981.

"Sam Shepard." In *The New Underground Theatre*, pp. 79–80. Edited by Robert J. Schroeder. New York: Bantam, 1968.

"OOB and the Playwright (Two Commentaries)." *Works* 1, no. 2 (Winter 1968): 70–73.

Untitled autobiographical statement. In *News of the American Place Theatre* 3, no. 3 (April 1971): 1–2.

Untitled comment. In *Contemporary Dramatists*, pp. 720–23. Edited by James Vinson. London: St James, 1973.

Untitled comment. In "Symposium: Playwriting in America." *yale/theatre* 4, no. 1 (Winter 1973): 24–25.

"News Blues." *Time Out* (31 May–6 June 1974): 17.

"Emotional Tyranny." *Theatre Quarterly* 4, no. 15 (August-October 1974): 22.

"Time." In *News of the American Place Theatre* 7, no. 3 (March 1975): n.p. Reprinted in *American Dreams: The Imagination of Sam Shepard*, pp. 210–11. Edited by Bonnie Marranca. New York: Performing Arts Journal, 1981.

"Note on the Music; Note to the Actors." In *Angel City and Other Plays*, p. 6. New York: Urizen, [1976].

Letter. *Village Voice* (13 June 1977): 44.

Untitled comment. In "American Experimental Theatre: Then and Now." *Performing Arts Journal* 2, no. 2 (Fall 1977): 13–14. Reprinted in *American Dreams: The Imagination of Sam Shepard*, pp. 212–13. Edited by Bonnie Marranca. New York: Performing Arts Journal, 1981.

"Visualization, Language and the Inner Library." *Drama Review* 21, no. 4 (December 1977): 49–58. Reprinted in *American Dreams: The Imagination of Sam Shepard*, pp. 214–19. Edited by Bonnie Marranca. New York: Performing Arts Journal, 1981.

"AZUSA is a real place." *Plays and Players* (May 1978): 1.

"Note to *Tongues*." In *Sam Shepard: Seven Plays*, p. 302. New York: Bantam, 1981.

"Peter Handke's Inner Self." *Vanity Fair* (September 1984): 106–7.

Introduction to *The Unseen Hand and Other Plays*. New York: Bantam, 1986.

Interviews and Feature Articles Based on Interviews

Gussow, Mel. "Sam Shepard: Writer on the Way Up." *New York Times* (12 November 1969): 42.

Khan, Naseem. "Free Form Playwright." *Time Out* (13–17 July 1972): 30–31.

White, Michael. "Underground Landscapes." *Manchester Guardian* (20 February 1974): 8.

"Metaphors, Mad Dogs and Old Time Cowboys." *Theatre Quarterly* 4, no. 15

(August-October 1974): 3–16. Reprinted in *American Dreams: The Imagination of Sam Shepard*, pp. 187–209. Edited by Bonnie Marranca. New York: Performing Arts Journal, 1981.

"The Most Promising Playwright in America Today Is Sam Shepard" (with Irene Oppenheim and Victor Fascio). *Village Voice* (27 October 1975): 81–82.

"Sam Shepard—Off Broadway's Street Cowboy" (with Robert Goldberg). *Rolling Stone College Papers* (Winter 1980): 43–45.

Wren, Scott Christopher. "Camp Shepard: Exploring the Geography of Character." *West Coast Plays* 7 (Fall 1980): 75–106.

"The 'True West' Interviews" (with John Dark). *West Coast Plays* 9 (Summer 1981): 51–71.

"A Conversation with Sam Shepard about a Very Corny Subject" (with Johnny Dark). *San Francisco* (September 1983): 68–72.

"Joe Chaikin Going On" [Conversation between Sam Shepard and Joe Chaikin] Film, 1983. Performing Arts Research Center, New York Public Library at Lincoln Center.

Hamill, Pete. "The New American Hero." *New York* (5 December 1983): 75–76 ff.

"A Conversation with Sam Shepard" (with Amy Lippman). *Gamut* 5 (1984): 11–27. Reprinted as "Rhythm and Truths: An Interview with Sam Shepard." *American Theatre* 1, no. 1 (April 1984): 9–13, 40–41.

Fay, Stephen. "Renaissance Man Rides Out of the West." *Times Sunday Magazine* (London) (26 August 1984): 11–19.

"The Rolling Stone Interview: Sam Shepard" (with Jonathon Cott). *Rolling Stone* (18 December 1986–1 January 1987): 166–72, 198, 200.

PRODUCTION HISTORY

A detailed production history of Sam Shepard's prolific output would be impossible in an essay of this length. Although virtually all of his plays have been seen (and reviewed) in New York, many premiered elsewhere, and most have received a number of important (often radically different) revivals. None has been done on Broadway. The most detailed, sympathetic, and influential critical response to Shepard's early one-acts may be found in a series of articles (called "theatre journal") by Michael Smith, published in the 1960s in the *Village Voice*. His strongly positive review of *Cowboys* and *The Rock Garden* (Theatre Genesis, 16 October 1964) not only launched Shepard's career in New York, it outlined an anti-interpretative, antinaturalistic approach to Shepard's theatre that became central to its subsequent critical reception and acceptance: "His is a gestalt theatre which evokes the existence behind behavior" ("Cowboys," 13). In the years that followed, Smith was unwavering in his support, favorably noticing off-off-Broadway productions that other critics ignored—*Dog* and *Rocking Chair, BbAaNnGg!*—and explicating the major one-acts at length. In his reviews of *Chicago* and *Red Cross*, Smith was the first to compare Shepard's imagistic method and structure to happenings and collage. He even directed the world premiere of *Icarus's Mother* (Caffe Cino, 16 November 1965) and then, responding to Albee's negative review, blamed himself for its failure: "Any logical or psychological approach makes many of [Shepard's] choices seem arbitrary" ("Journal," 19, 24). The other off-Broadway reviewers apparently agreed; *Icarus's Mother*, along with *Chicago* and *Red Cross*, won Shepard his first Obie (1966).

Away from this milieu, Shepard found less support. Douglas Davis called *The Rock Garden* obscene; Tallmer thought *Cowboys* derivative; six of the twelve negative reviews of *Up to Thursday* reported a too obvious debt to the Theatre of the Absurd. Despite a generally hostile or indifferent response to Shepard's early plays, however, there was occasional, even strategic, praise from a few major reviewers. Kauffmann, for instance, pronounced *Chicago* the "best play" on the *6 from La Mama* program (*Chicago*, 36), while Barnes saved the double bill of *Red Cross* and Guare's *Muzeeka* by calling it "the most interesting theatrical evening New York can offer" ("Where," 41). Hardwick, ignoring Shepard's decision not to have his first full-length play, *La Turista*, reviewed, published an especially influential account in the *New York Review of Books:* with its "electrifying set," its transformational characters, and its "truly meaningful central image," *La Turista* fulfilled the promise of the "lofts of off-off-Broadway" ("Word," 6, 8). She also reported that Shepard's next one-act, *Melodrama Play*, was "the most beautiful and intriguing event of the New York season" ("Notes," 5). Both plays won Obies.

By 1970, Shepard was widely regarded (at least in New York), as the leading *avant-garde* playwright of his generation; his plays, however, remained controversial, and critical reaction was often sharply divided. Shepard canceled the premiere of *Operation Sidewinder* at Yale when a group of Drama School students protested his portrayal of black revolutionaries (Brustein, *Making Scenes*, 73–79), and the subsequent opening that spring at Lincoln Center (12 March 1970) became a media event. Many of the reviews were quite analytical (perhaps because a version of the text was printed prior to production in *Esquire*), and several included appraisals of Shepard's career and reputation. Nevertheless, Lahr's was the only unqualified rave; most were mixed, and a number were strongly negative, agreeing that the production had failed but assigning a variety of reasons: the director, the theatre, and the music were all singled out. Clurman, making a point he has returned to over the years, blamed the writing, and he urged Shepard "to discipline himself to sharper thought or cultivate more incisive powers of lyrical expression" (*Operation*, 380). Two weeks later, Poland's elaborate pop-style revival of *The Unseen Hand* and *Forensic and the Navigators* drew a slightly more favorable response. For Kraft, "it was an evening of total immersion in camp," a new critical term in those days (40). Barnes ended up "mildly loving" the whole thing, coming up with his famous *aperçu* about early Shepard: "the first person to write good disposable plays ("Theatre," 43). The run was disappointing (twenty-one performances). The initial London production of *The Unseen Hand* (Royal Court Theatre Upstairs, 12 March 1973) also had a mixed critical reception, but according to Chubb, it "really got London excited about Sam Shepard" ("London," 119). Brustein praised it highly there—"[the characters] mingle past, present and future into a pastiche of legend and actuality which describes prole America more effectively than the most fastidious documentary"—but he finally questioned the play's political-moral ambivalence ("Shepard's," 34).

From a critical point of view, the most successful of Shepard's one acts during the early 1970s was *Mad Dog Blues* (Theatre Genesis, 4 March 1971). By this time, the experiential approach to Shepard's work had become a journalistic commonplace, and Gussow advised audiences to "relax and let yourself be carried away" by this "Shepard and family vaudeville" ("Mad," 25). Recurrent themes were also becoming apparent. Sainer, who described the staging in vivid detail, noted in Shepard's work "that yearning for an Arcadia, a Lost America, for a time when needs were simpler, action more direct" ("Shepard's" 53). Other reviews were favorable to mixed, but the run was brief.

The first New York showings of Shepard's next two one-acts, *Cowboy Mouth* and *Back Bog Beast Bait* (American Place, 29 June 1971), were not reviewed but only because Shepard (who played Slim in the first performance of the former) exercised his option and excluded the critics. At the first public New York production of *Back Bog* (Unit 453, 6 December 1973), several critics pointed out the radically disjunctive (and to some, self-defeating) mix of styles, but Michael Smith blamed his reservations on the production: "The terror of the beast didn't come alive" ("*Back Bog*," 83). The play is rarely revived, but George Ferencz's 1984 production (La Mama, 16 December) was greeted as an "authentic discovery" by Gussow ("Prophetic," 24). Unit 453 also presented the first public performance of *Cowboy Mouth* in New York (11 July 1974). Feingold called it "a statement of a condition" and expressed the current favorable consensus toward this, the most realistic of Shepard's one-act plays ("Games," 56).

In the fall of 1971, Shepard and his family moved to London. There he wrote the play that many consider his masterpiece, *The Tooth of Crime*. Under Charles Marowitz's direction, it was first produced at the Open Space in London (17 July 1972). Marowitz analyzed the play at length in the *Village Voice* ("Sam," 59); later Shepard publicly attacked Marowitz's directing style ("emotional tyranny") in *Theatre Quarterly* (72). When *The Tooth of Crime* finally opened (after being postponed), it was widely and seriously reviewed. Although *Time Out* (Shepard's chief journalistic ally in London) championed the play, general critical reaction was negative or reserved. In particular, there was dissatisfaction with Marowitz's direction and confusion over Shepard's extraordinary use of language. The first American production took place at Princeton's McCarter Theatre (9 November 1972), and it drew a number of New York critics. While some had reservations about the staging, they generally had high praise for Shepard's play. Feingold saw Crow as a new character type: "the post-emotional protean man" ("Biting," 75). When *The Tooth of Crime* opened in New York, however (7 March 1973), the radical production by the Performance Group aroused a heated debate about the relationship between text and performance. Again most reviewers agreed that *The Tooth of Crime* was a major work but not in this version. Michael Smith called the production "damaging and extraneous" to the play and launched a theoretical attack on the "environmental" theories of director Richard Schechner ("*Tooth*," 57). Clurman wished that he could see a production "in which Shepard's written stage directions were scrupulously followed on the highest level of competence" ("Tooth," 410). Lahr, on the other hand, liked the "added visual power and much-needed emotional detail" (*Tooth*, 55), while Sainer praised the "marvel" of Spaulding Gray's Hoss and thought the production better than the play ("Playing," 117). Schechner later published an account of his disagreement with Shepard during the group's collaborative work on the script, a classic statement of the conflict between the playwright's vision and creative directorial prerogative ("Writer"). *The Tooth of Crime* won Shepard another Obie, and the Performance Group's version has been filmed.

Shepard's uneasy relationship with directors is a major subtextual theme throughout the performance history of his work, and clearly the issue came to a head with the Marowitz and Schechner versions of *The Tooth of Crime*. When the Royal Court decided to produce *Geography of a Horse Dreamer* (21 February 1974), Shepard took a major step and directed the play himself. Critical reaction was mixed on both counts. Lahr's poetic review was among the most positive, describing the play as a meditation on America's preoccupation with dreams and dreaming (*Geography*, 46). (A studio version of this production was broadcast on Granada Television, 31 March 1974.) The directorial issue came up again when Shepard's play crossed the Atlantic. The American premiere at Yale University (8 March 1974) had an expressionistic tilt to it, while the first New York production, under Levy's direction, was more naturalistic. Gussow, who described the play as "a passionate, almost patriotic longing for a sensibility that has disappeared," discussed the two productions in detail (*Horse*, 21), while Harris compared Levy's New York version to Shepard's London original (*Geography*, 28). Most critics agreed, as Clurman put it, that *Geography* was "not [Shepard's] best work" ("*Georgraphy*,"

27). In fact, Wetzsteon, usually one of Shepard's strongest advocates, in a major dissent, again raised the issue of creative self-consciousness: "[Its] meaning doesn't emerge from its being but exists prior to its being" ("Looking, " 71).

London saw two more Shepard premieres in 1974, both radically different. The first, "a 45 minute fantasia on childbirth" called *Little Ocean* (developed collaboratively with his wife, O-Lan, Dinah Stabb, and Caroline Hutchison), played a series of late-night performances at the Hampstead Theatre Club (25 March 1974) and received a number of favorable reviews (Wardle, *"Little,"* 11). The second was a grimly comic dramatization of anomie, *Action*, at the Royal Court Theatre Upstairs (17 September 1974). After the "relative clarity and logic" of Shepard's more recent work, *Action* struck several reviewers as obscure and undefined (Nightingale, *"Action,"* 440). Lahr, reporting back to the *Village Voice*, called it "a dead end" (*Action*, 90). Coveney, on the other hand, thought it "delicately hypnotic" (29), and Hobson, in an impressionistic response, urged audiences "to be utterly relaxed, with the mind surrendered to the images [the play] summons up from the depths of one's being" (10). Perhaps because of the metatheatrical nature of Shepard's play, many London reviewers compared *Action* to other dramatic (and nondramatic) works, but interestingly the names Beckett and Pinter were rarely evoked.

When the play opened in New York, however, at the American Place (15 April 1975), the apparent debt to both writers, as well as the European flavor of the play, became a major issue. On the negative side, Simon dismissed it as "flagrant and mindless borrowing" (*Action*, 74), but Feingold pointed approvingly to Peter Handke as an influence and in a lucid analysis found the play to be "rich and perfect" ("Everything's," 87). During the summer of 1974, Shepard and his family had ended their three-year residency in England and moved to Marin County north of San Francisco. He chose Nancy Meckler to direct *Action* both in London and New York, the first time a woman had directed a Shepard premiere. When *Action* opened at the Magic Theatre (2 May 1975) in San Francisco, however, Shepard himself directed; play and production were both highly praised. In New York and San Francisco, *Action* was preceded by a short monologue, *Killer's Head*. Feingold stressed the thematic relationship between the two plays, but most reviewers on both coasts agreed with Weiner that it was "a slight work" ("Powerful," 40).

Shepard returned to the Magic Theatre to direct the premiere of *Angel City* (2 July 1976). New York critics did not get a chance to see it until Michael Kahn's version opened at the McCarter Theatre in Princeton (3 March 1977). Although acknowledged by some as a major work, Shepard's play met resistance on both coasts. Fennell, among others, complained of the length, while Marranca criticized the "fundamental incoherence" ("Sam," 31). Only Feingold completely approved: "It's his most playful work and one of his most accessible" ("Sam," 72).

With Michael Smith gone from the *Village Voice*, Feingold had now become chief Shepard advocate and explicator. When *Suicide in B Flat* opened at the Yale Repertory (15 October 1976), Feingold outlined the "plot" and criticized director Walt Jones for obscuring the clarity ("almost comically non-mysterious") of Shepard's design ("Kleist," 113). Other critics, while praising the play, were less dogmatic. For Gussow, the "never fully deciphered story" made a social point about cultural disorientation ("Yale," 42); Kroll emphasized the stylistic mix—"like a free-form jazz opus by Ornette Coleman to a text by Wittgenstein translated by Abbott and Costello" ("High," 109). Wholly opposed, Kerr attacked Shepard's "cavalier discontinuity" and "slippery non sequiturs" ("Play," D3). The London premiere (1977) evoked a similarly mixed reaction, while the first New York production (1979) was not widely reviewed. Gussow compared it to the Yale production and found it wanting ("*Suicide*"). Shepard collaborated with director Robert Woodruff on the Magic Theatre version (3 August 1979), which featured a jazz score improvised every night by pianist Harry Mann.

The Sad Lament of Pecos Bill on the Eve of Killing His Wife, a one-act opera, opened first at the Legion of Honor Theatre in San Francisco (23 October 1976) and then was done by the Overtone Theatre in New York in 1983. The critical consensus was expressed by Nightingale who found the piece agreeable but "minimal" ("Even," 45). *Inacoma*, inspired by the plight of comatose Karen Ann Quinlan, has been produced only once, at the Magic Theatre (18 March 1977). Kleb described the collaborative process by which Shepard and a group of actors created the piece and concluded that what was missing was Shepard's language and his "personal vision" ("*Inacoma*," 64).

Shepard received an Obie in 1977 for a work that had been published in New York but not yet staged, *The Curse of the Starving Class*. The award was controversial but much less so than the first two productions of the play. In London, where Meckler directed the world premiere at the Royal Court (21 April 1977), the play drew many strongly negative reviews. Nightingale identified three levels of meaning, each a cliche ("Only," 577); Wardle objected to the "lack of psychological details" in the characters ("*Curse*," 11g); Marowitz asked the rhetorical question, "Is this Shepard or Saroyan?" and drew a parallel to *The Hungerers* ("Is," D3). Others compared the play (unfavorably) to *The Cherry Orchard* and to a string of domestic melodramas from *Desire Under the Elms* to *Tobacco Road*. Lahr, in a thoughtful and provocative analysis, again accused Shepard of poor craftsmanship ("Curse"). If Meckler's staging tended toward a kind of lyric realism—see Adler's description of Sue Plummer's wall-less set with its "vistas of telephone poles and tufts of grass, of the hard earth and blue white sky of America's furtherest frontiers" ("Curse," 410)—Woodruff's at the New York Shakespeare Festival (14 February 1978) was much more stylized, even surreal. Barnes described Santo Loquasto's "stripped-down setting, a white box on a high, raked stage" ("Shepard's," 29), and Fox reported that the "soliloquies are spoken against saxophone solos" ("Family," 77). Again there were a number of negative reviews. Kerr called it "intellectual driftwood" ("From," D3); Duberman, "high-flown allegorical allusion in tandem with unacknowledged sentimentality" (83); Kauffmann, in a long assessment of Shepard's artistic development, concluded that this was another of his "heartbreakers—it contains so much but it finally comes to not enough" ("What," 24). The play, however, had its defenders, and finally reception was sharply divided. On the issue of faulty structure, for instance, Rabkin insisted that the "radical visual and verbal juxtapositions" are part of what makes the play "work" ("Like," 4), while Clurman approved of the rough-hewn improvisational style: "Its faults are part of its virtues" ("*Curse*," 349).

Shepard's "mythic" preoccupations had by this time become an obvious trait in his work, and *The Curse of the Starving Class* was quickly recognized (and analyzed) as an exploration of the "myth of the family." *Rolling Thunder Logbook* (1977), as Palmer pointed out, explored mythology of another sort, with Bob Dylan ("an invention of his own mind") and his Rolling Thunder concert tour ("an unusually self-conscious brand of mythmaking") as its subject (21). *Logbook* clearly related to the growing Shepard "myth" as well. This had always been an issue in criticism of his work (as Patti Smith's "biographical" poem attests), but now, with Shepard's triumphant appearance as the laconic, brooding Texan in the film *Days of Heaven* (1978), it often became a premise from which his work was viewed and evaluated. Gussow, for instance, called Shepard "more definably an American playwright than most of his contemporaries" ("*Seduced*," 23), while Kroll found it appropriate that this "most American" of playwrights should be attracted to the "myth" of American billionaire Howard Hughes ("Crazy," 94). Both were reporting, in strongly positive terms, on the world premiere of *Seduced*, which Shepard had assigned to the Trinity Square Repertory in Providence (25 April 1978). Local reviews, however, were negative, and when the play, with Rip Torn as Hackamore, opened at the American Place in New York (18 January 1979), it was not well received. Mythic themes were discussed at length (Feingold compared Hackamore to the "old cowboys" of early Shepard), but the play and production were both strongly criticized (Feingold, "Seductive," 93). For Rabkin, "*Seduced* focuses inappropriately on what should be a minor theme: the power (or loss of it) of sexuality" ("Sam's," 62). Clurman again found the writing undisciplined, and Jack

Gelber's direction was "too overt, too plain, too raucous and crude, entirely without mystery or legendary dimension" ("*Seduced*," 221).

In a change of pace, Shepard next collaborated with Joseph Chaikin on *Tongues*, a piece for voice and percussion, which they performed together at the Magic Theatre (7 June 1978) to strongly positive reviews. A month later, Shepard returned to family matters with the premiere, again at the Magic Theatre (7 July 1978), of *Buried Child*. Woodruff directed this production, as well as the New York premiere, which opened, first as a showcase and then officially (19 October 1978) at the Theatre de Lys. Reviews in San Francisco were sharply divided, and the New York response was similar. Many detected a strong family resemblance between *Buried Child* and a long list of predecessors, including *Ghosts, Tobacco Road, Who's Afraid of Virginia Woolf?* and, especially, *The Homecoming*. Fox called it "son of *Curse*" and criticized Woodruff's direction as too pictorial and too static ("Many," 119). Kerr made his strongest and most lucid statement yet about why he felt "shut out" from Shepard's work ("Sam," D3). Rabkin, on the other hand, gave a detailed and positive explication of style and theme, relating the piece to "classic Absurdism" ("Bones," 74). Clurman seemed to have resolved, for the moment at least, his problems with Shepard's lack of discipline. *Buried Child*, he argued, was the work of "an improviser, a tramp-like bard who doesn't concern himself with total coherence or immediate lucidity"; the play was a "tattered song" (*Buried*, 621). Three months later, East Coast critics had a chance to compare the New York production to Adrian Hall's intentionally more "optimistic" version at the Yale Repertory Theatre (Brantley, C11). Here Feingold made a point of explaining Shepard's relationship to Pinter as one of "kinship" and not "imitation"; he called the Fraserian corn god motif "a *jeu*" ("Seductive," 93). The day after the Theatre de Lys production closed, *Buried Child* won the Pulitzer Prize—17 April 1979. Later that year, it also won an Obie.

In San Francisco, Shepard and Chaikin created their second major piece together, *Savage/Love*. It opened at the Eureka Theatre (5 September 1979) with Chaikin again performing the text but this time with music by Harry Mann and Skip LaPlante. Chaikin, Mann, and LaPlante also performed a new version of *Tongues* (without Shepard's participation on stage), and the two pieces then had their premieres together in New York at the Public Theatre Other Stage (6 November 1979). Reviews of both were favorable, but most critics thought that *Tongues* was the stronger of the two. Gussow called it "a collage of echoes from the dead . . . that pulsates with the heartbeat of life" ("Intimate," B36). Finally, Shepard took part in another collaboration resonant with the past, a "performance event," called *Drum War*, which he conceived and performed with five other drummers (28 March 1980).

The performance history of Shepard's next major play, *True West*, has as much to do with theatrical politics as it does with critical response. Both Weiner ("True," 25) and Shewey ("True," 115) give detailed accounts of this fascinating bicoastal custody battle. In brief, Woodruff staged the original, highly praised production at the Magic Theatre in San Francisco with well-known local actors (10 July 1980), but when he attempted to direct the New York premiere at the New York Shakespeare Festival, with a different, more famous New York cast, a squabble broke out with producer Joseph Papp that eventually led to Woodruff's resignation and Shepard's long-distance repudiation of the entire production. Papp opened it anyway (23 December 1980), to a barrage of negative notices—although several reviewers defended the play while attacking the production. Feingold, for one, preferred it to *The Tooth of Crime* and *Buried Child* ("Truthful"), while Rich called it a "very good play" which "looked as if it hadn't been directed at all" ("Stage," C9). Most, however, dismissed the play as well: "a feeble imitation of Pinter" (Simon, *True West*, 45); "tedious wrangling" (Watt, " 'True West,' " 37). Kerr again attacked the "too obvious" mythic element as lacking "a necessary connection to the narrative" ("Of," 3).

That spring, Shepard, Woodruff, and the Magic Theatre restaged *True West* with most of the original San Francisco cast. This time, however, the San Francisco reviews were disappointing, and *True West* did not, as promised, travel to New York. Thus the critical reputation of the play was very much in doubt when the Steppenwolf Company opened its production in New York in 1982. Directed by Gary Sinise, with Sinise as Austin and John Malkovitch as Lee, it was greeted by Gussow and others as "an act of theatrical restitution and restoration" (Gussow, "West," C18). The Steppenwolf *True West* ran for 762 performances, a Shepard record in New York at that time, and it was shown on PBS American Playhouse (31 January 1984).

In 1981, Shepard contributed material to only one new theatrical production, *Superstitions*, and then, initially, under the pseudonym Walker Hayes. Developed collaboratively by the Overtone Theatre, which included O-Lan Shepard, it opened at the Intersection Theatre, San Francisco (1 July 1981). Essentially a mood piece, with music by Catherine Stone, Winn found it "unusual and satisfying" (48). *Superstitions* played New York in 1983, and a videotape with the Overtone cast was shown on National Educational Television (18 Dec. 1984).

Shepard did not produce another new play until *Fool for Love* opened at the Magic Theatre (9 February 1983), with Ed Harris as Eddie, Kathy Baker as May, and Will Patton as the Old Man. Shepard directed the explosive production in Andy Stacklin's tight, boxlike set. The play was instantly hailed as a "major Shepard work" (Weiner, "Passion," 64), and there was high praise for the "physical staging" (DeRose, *Fool*, 100). The entire Magic Theatre production was then sent to New York (26 May

1983), but there the reception was mixed. The main issue had to do with substance: what, if anything, was all the sound and fury on stage about? Feingold argued that "the Punch and Judy knockabout is only the surface of something rich and dense" ("Fool's," 81), while Barnes noted "the planes of meaning" ("Fool," 29). For Simon, however, it was "inconclusive" and "opaque," as well as "overdirected" ("Soft," 110). Denby called it "even more an acting exercise" than *True West* (45). *Fool for Love* set another long-run New York record for a Shepard play (1,000 performances); each member of the cast won an Obie, as did Shepard— for playwriting and directing. *Fool for Love* had another unpredictable result: After nearly a decade as one of Shepard's staunchest opponents in the popular New York press, Watt reported that this was Shepard's "purest and most beautiful play" ("Fool," 16).

Shepard wrote a series of unproduced filmscripts in the 1970s and tried unsuccessfully to have several of his plays made into films. His efforts finally paid off, first when he and German director Wim Wenders collaborated on *Paris, Texas* (1984) and then when he and Robert Altman made a film version of *Fool for Love* (1985), with Shepard himself in the lead. Shepard's contribution to *Paris, Texas* has yet to be established, but apparently Wenders's vision predominated, an aspect that bothered many American reviewers. According to Canby, for example, when it stuck to the "almost surreal world of Sam Shepard," *Paris, Texas* was "funny, mysterious and moving"; otherwise it seemed inauthentic, the work of "informed tourists" ("Paris," 64). Outside the United States, however, *Paris, Texas* won many major awards, including the Golden Palm at the Cannes Film Festival. The film adaptation of *Fool for Love* had less success. Comparisons to the play were inevitable. For Canby, as for others, the problem was that by moving the play out of its one-room set, the emotional tension had been "dissipated" ("Small," B23).

In January 1985, a third Shepard-Chaikin collaboration, *The War in Heaven: Angel's Monologue*, called "a radio play with music," was first broadcast over WBAI (New York) with Chaikin as the voice and Shepard on percussion. There were no reviews. Nearly a year later, Shepard's most recently produced play, *A Lie of the Mind*, opened at the Promenade Theatre, New York (5 December 1985). Shepard came east to direct an all-star cast including Harvey Keitel, Aidan Quinn, Amanda Plummer, and Geraldine Page. It was Shepard's first world premiere in that city since *Back Bog Beast Bait* in 1971. Much had changed. Then the press had been disinvited by the playwright; now the media coverage, with Shepard's full cooperation, was massive. The many reviews and satellite features provide a fascinating overview of the current state of Shepard's theatrical reputation, at least in New York City. In place of the *Village Voice*, Shepard's chief journalistic advocate had now become the *New York Times*. First it introduced *A Lie of the Mind* with Freedman's long feature in which Shepard discussed, among other family matters, the death of his father—an important biographical connection to the play. Then there were two lengthy reviews. Rich was rhapsodic: "the unmistakable expression of a major writer reaching the height of his powers" ("Lie," 19). Gussow was triumphant. A Shepard supporter since the 1960s, when the two had promoted off-off-Broadway together in *Newsweek*, he concluded that this was a "synthesis and advancement" over themes and motifs that had preoccupied the playwright throughout his career ("Revisits," 3). According to Honan, in another *Times* feature, *A Lie of the Mind* exemplified the reawakening of optimism on the American stage—"a message radiant with hope and the prospect of redemption" (2:156). Finally, summing up the season, Rich called it "the most exhilarating new American play of 1985–86" ("At," B36). The *Times* was not alone. Henry thought it the "best" of Shepard's plays (83); Kroll, the work of a "great poet of our theatre" ("Savage," 58); and even Watt, now apparently firmly in the Shepard camp, thought it "hilarious and pathetic," if a little too long ("On").

But as usual with Shepard, there was dissent, some of it mixed with praise and some not. Rogoff, in the *Village Voice*, appreciated the "epic" aspirations but concluded that the play had failed: the imagery retreats into "seductive technicolor simplicities masquerading as ideas"; "the words seem branded onto the characters"; the action "keeps running into detours and dead ends"; the themes are too ambiguous; and there is a lack of discipline and a sense of reality—"does he know America or does he only know its myths and movies?" (117). Brustein found the love story "somewhat banal," the symbolism "crude," and the text "bloated" ("Enigma," 25). Berman used it to attack Shepard's artistic reputation broadside: "He's not a major playwright and the effort to become more than what he is has led to fiascos like *A Lie of the Mind*" (215). Perhaps as a final indication of the complex "politics of reception" (Marranca, "Controversial," 25) surrounding the premiere of Shepard's latest play, it should be noted that *A Lie of the Mind* won the 1986 Drama Critics Circle Award for best play but was not even mentioned in the Obies. In short, if the critical ground seemed to be shifting as Shepard's work (and his professional interests) evolved and changed, many of the old attitudes and issues still persisted, and clearly Shepard remained as controversial and provocative a writer as he had been forty-two world premieres ago.

SURVEY OF SECONDARY SOURCES

Bibliographies

No major, formal bibliographical work on Shepard exists. The most complete to this point, though necessarily limited, has been King's chapter on Shepard, which includes a list of the various early editions of plays (all now out of print), as well as a brief, annotated list of other primary and secondary materials—essays (by Shepard), criticism, and reviews. The Salem and Eddleman bibliographies of reviews and critical articles usefully supplement King. Salem also includes dates for key New York productions. (These lists must be used with care; they are far from complete and contain inaccuracies.) Carpenter gives a partial account of recent volumes containing Shepard criticism and a limited number of critical articles. Of the books about Shepard, Hart's contains the most complete bibliography, as well as a detailed, if not entirely reliable, account of Shepard premieres and publications.

Biographies

Two popular biographies have appeared. Oumano's is notable chiefly for details from several key people who worked with Shepard off-off-Broadway in the 1960s and early 1970s. Shewey's, written in a lively, journalistic style, is more meticulously researched and better balanced; its informality (no bibliography, no index) belies the author's critical acuity. The Shepard article in *Current Biography Yearbook* emphasizes the critical response to the first productions of Shepard's plays, while Engle describes and comments on the plays themselves. Biographical notes may be found in the usual books: *Notable Names in American Theatre, Who's Who in the Theatre*, and *Contemporary Dramatists*. Both Auerbach and Mottram organize their studies chronologically and include numerous biographical references. Much of this material comes from the interviews listed above and from the dozens of news items and features that have appeared in diverse publications.

Influences

Very little detailed critical work has been done with what Gilman calls "the far flung network of influences, interests and obsessions" operating on Shepard and on his plays (*Seven*, xiii). Many of these seem to be extratheatrical or extraliterary, and Gilman provides a useful summary—including popular music (rock, modern jazz, blues, country-western, and folk), happenings and mixed media events, science fiction, Hollywood westerns, television ("in its pop or junk aspects"), mystery novels, and all facets of the southern California road culture of the 1950s. (Shepard identifies many of these roots in interviews and dedications.)

The clearest theatrical influence seems to have been Joseph Chaikin and the Open Theatre, a debt that promises to be fully exposed in Daniels's forthcoming book. Gilman also suggests that Shepard was influenced by the experimental dramaturgy going on around him in New

York in the 1960s, but Shepard has acknowledged this only in general terms. The two playwrights who have had the most obvious impact on his work are Beckett ("surpasses everyone") and Handke (McBride, B3). The influence of Handke, as Marranca points out, seems apparent in Shepard's emphasis on phenomenological detail and in his development of a verbal linguistics "built upon the techniques of rock music" (*Playwrights*, 98, 102). The debt to Beckett, much more general (and pervasive), has yet to be clearly charted. Brecht's influence was also apparent in the late 1960s and early 1970s; Auerbach in particular discusses the relationship between *The Tooth of Crime* and *In the Jungle of Cities*. During his London years, Shepard began to read the classics, and he mentions "the Greek guys" (especially Sophocles), Marlowe, Shakespeare, and Strindberg with appreciation (Cott, 170). Shepard also met Peter Brook, who impressed him with his knowledge of theatre history and who taught him that "a playwright has to understand what an actor goes through" (McBride, B3). Both shared an interest in the philosopher-mystic Gurdjieff. The relationship to Pinter, so apparent to so many reviewers, remains unexamined and unacknowledged by Shepard.

Shepard's debt to the American dramatic tradition is probably even more tenuous. In 1987, he told Cott (172) that he had "always thought" O'Neill's *Long Day's Journey Into Night* was "the truly great American play," but although there may be echoes of late O'Neill in recent Shepard, the debt to popular American melodrama and farce, probably by way of the movies, seems much more obvious. Indeed, if Shepard belongs to the "transcendental and romantic traditions" of American literature, as Earley convincingly argues (126), it is because the spirits of Emerson, Melville, Hawthorne, and Whitman (whom Shepard has clearly read and admired) spoke to him not directly but through the lenses of John Huston and John Ford and from the pages and mouths of Jack Kerouac, Allen Ginsburg, Gregory Corso, and Bob Dylan.

The nature and extent of Shepard's influence on others remains to be defined. According to Bruckner, he "has had a greater effect on theatre than anyone now writing, including Beckett," (C3) and Brustein says that Shepard has encouraged writers in their twenties and thirties "to release themselves from realistic conventions" (Hall, 27), but neither names names. For a glimpse of Shepard at work as a teacher, see Wren's extraordinary record of the playwriting workshop Shepard conducted at the Bay Area Playwrights Festival during the summer of 1980.

General Studies

Two book-length monographs have been published. Both adhere to a chronological scheme, and both ground their readings on pertinent biographical information. Hart looks at ten key plays that demonstrate the "organic development" of Shepard's style and content; she traces the roots of his technique to the "great European innovators" and to two American groups, the Living Theatre and the Open Theatre (2–3). Mottram divides Shepard's career into three major periods, summarizes the plot of each of the plays, extracts recurrent themes (such as the father-son relationship), and notes typical stylistic devices (the verbal arias, the use of striking visual imagery).

A pamphlet-sized monograph by Patraka and Siegel attempts (in much too little space) to relate Shepard's plays to thematic concerns typical of western American writers. Auerbach also identifies Shepard's subject as "America"; his method is the use of "American myths to explain the world about him and to explore the causes of the current American malaise" (1, 4). Her book, which includes a study (though not, as she promises, a comparative one) of Arthur Kopit, emphasizes Shepard's incantatory use of language and contains valuable materials from Shepard letters in which he discusses his compositional methods.

Five book-length surveys of American playwrights contain chapters on Shepard (each from a different point of view) and thus place him, at least by proximate publication, in a contemporary context. Marranca's valuable critical essay looks at Shepard's work through *Buried Child* and praises his "ear," his "musicality," the imagistic (verbal and visual) quality, and the sensuality of his writing; "his predominant weakness is his carelessness in the plotting of the plays." The most important aspect of the Shepard style, for Marranca, is his "transformation of realism from its psychological weightiness to a lean, poetic exploration of individual consciousness" (*Playwrights*, 81–111). Bigsby's critical introduction to the plays makes an interesting and valid connection between Shepard and the Beat Generation writers and suggests further comparisons to Nathanael West, Robert Coover, John Barth, and Albert Camus, as well as the obvious ones to Beckett and Pinter. Despite his appreciation for this "neoromantic," experiential element in Shepard's writing, Bigsby finds him "at his best when there is a dominating idea, as in *Operation Sidewinder*"—a controversial notion to say the least (*Critical*, 219–50). Cohn divides Shepard's work into three periods: "collage, fantasy and the recent, larger-than-life tragic realism." She compares Shepard's stylistic development to O'Neill's but resists hyperbole, clearly preferring Shepard's earlier work to his later, more realistic family plays. For Cohn, "It is not theme . . . but image and rhythm that render Shepard's plays memorable—some of them" (*New*, 171–86). Hughes's brief account of Shepard's work (ending in the mid-1970s) has been largely superseded by the studies already listed, but it contains some valid insights about the early plays nonetheless.

Simard places Shepard in an Anglo-American context ("the American counterpoint to the British Stoppard") and calls him "the first totally postmodern voice in American drama." Defining the postmodern style as "a new form of existential realism, wherein reality is displayed as subjective," Simard analyzes several Shepard plays from this point of view but focuses on *Buried Child*—Shepard's "first sustained work of conscious dramatic allusion . . . a postmodern dramatization of *The Waste Land*" (75–97). Finally, Herman offers a brief biographical sketch before explaining how Shepard's "expressive theatre" works (29). Identifying major Shepard themes, including "the quarrel with paternal authority, the loss of the land and the fall from an Edenic possibility into an iron city, the transgressions and impingements on the artists by the interests of commercial greed, and the recesses of the psyche and the personifi-cations of the beasts in its crevices, the old West and the new" (29), Herman discusses *Tooth, Curse, Child, True West*, and *Fool for Love*.

Since most Shepard plays were initially published and are now in print as parts of anthologies, a number of introductions contain commentary on the plays included and occasionally on Shepard's work as a whole. Early examples reflect the anti-interpretative critical strategies of the 1960s, encouraging the reader, as Gelber puts it, to "receive" Shepard's plays on their own terms, as "trips" created between audience and actor by a playwright-shaman (2). The style is tempered, but the attitude re-mains the same in Wetzsteon's later, longer introduction. He divides the Shepard canon (to *Fool for Love*) into three periods and identifies four ways in which his theatre has "transformed the rigid categories of nat-uralism in order to achieve a kind of hyperrealism." Still, he insists that Shepard's plays are actually about "their highly charged atmospheres" and argues against an attempt to reduce his plays to their "meanings" (*Fool*, 1–15). Gilman agrees that these plays should not be probed for "single 'meanings' or ruling ideas"; they are "dispositions, pressures, points of inquiry." Nevertheless, despite the formal difficulties (and im-perfections), a "strategy of discourse to deal usefully" with the work is needed, Gilman says, and he attempts to move in this direction, first by placing Shepard clearly in a cultural context and then by examining the "surfaces" of his plays. There he finds evidence of Shepard's central theme, "the quest for identity" (ix–xxv).

To date, two anthologies include Shepard criticism. Parker's contains four essays reprinted from *Modern Drama;* Marranca's, a series of articles (some are reprinted from journals) covering the Shepard canon through *True West*. Marranca's introduction offers a concise, thoughtful, and provocative overview of critical issues amplified in the articles that follow and dealt with (occasionally contradicted) by other critics. Mazzocco's lengthy essay-review of Shepard's work also provides a summary of crit-ical attitudes (from a thematic point of view), while Rabillard's essay, based on Ubersfeld, suggests a meta-theatrical approach to Shepard's work as a whole.

Analyses of Individual Plays

Critical analysis of individual Shepard plays began slowly in the late 1960s following the production (and Hardwick's review) of *La Turista*. Nevertheless, certain dominant themes were sounded forcefully at the beginning. Madden focused on the divided audience response to the "antiliterary" *La Turista*, concluding that both playwright and director had achieved "their highest aspiration: to violate their audience" (713). Valgemae agreed that Shepard's "underlying ideas" were "not always easy to find" but praised the "expressionistic" surface of the play, its use of "brilliant colors, elaborate patterning and constant objectification" (232). Frutkin sought meaning in a structural device (also apparent in *Cowboys #2* and *Red Cross*), "paired existence" characterized not by "union" but "displacement"; Shepard's "dramatic subject," he concluded, was "the character as performer" (24). Later critics of *La Turista* have looked at style, structure, and sexual politics. Cohn calls it "a metaphysical farce" and relates it to the camp sensibility of the 1960s ("Camp," 301); Erben finds Salem allied with the doctors ("other men") against Kent (33). Whiting explains the effect (to "jolt the audience") and meaning of the "inverted chronology" of acts 1 and 2 (417).

The one-acts that preceded and immediately followed *La Turista* have not received much individual attention. Donohue traces key themes through the early plays, including Shepard's fascination with cowboys, Indians, and rock 'n' roll, while Bloom (following Michael Smith) calls them "gestalt theatre" and attempts to define the type of "consciousness" evoked (72–73). Richard A. Davis reads these plays symbolically (emphasizing *Icarus's Mother*), identifying the central themes as "self-destructive energy" and a "desire to escape [from] the fragmentation of the material world" to a "kind of ideal manhood" (14, 18). He also emphasizes Shepard's language, as does Rabillard, who uses *Icarus's Mother* to exemplify the "conative" and "phatic" element in Shepard's dialogue (60–61). The early one-acts also provide Falk with evidence of Shepard's "vision of an America overrun by a horde of renegade cowboys, and their women trailing at heel" ("Men," 102)—a position shared by Marranca and Londré. For Erben, on the other hand, Joy, in *Chicago*, is the typical Shepard woman, "modern, independent and socially active" (31). Leverett detects a melodramatic "atmosphere" at work in *Melodrama Play* but few of the traditional conventions (110), while Wilson uses *Cowboys #2* to demonstrate "the complexity of Shepard's interest in performance" (47).

Shepard's next two full-length plays have attracted one major critical reading each, though both plays are mentioned frequently in other (often developmental) contexts. Stambolian, in the earliest major analysis of a single Shepard text, identifies *Mad Dog Blues* as both a "pop-like display and a psychodrama" dealing with the "desperate search for identity" (780), while Carroll contends that the use in *Mad Dog Blues* of disjunctive structural devices borrowed from film (the cut and the switch-back) depicts "a profound schism of both identity and vision in the playwright's artist-surrogate" (136). The only major piece on *Operation Sidewinder* is Lahr's energetic defense (*Astonish*), although Bigsby ampli-fies his earlier favorable opinion in a more recent assessment of Shepard's work as a whole ("Word," 216–17). *Operation Sidewinder* is briefly analyzed by Davis and Bloom in their discussions of early Shepard, and Cohn uses the plays in her piece on Shepard's comedy.

The Tooth of Crime stands as a critical point of reference for much Shepard criticism, yet little detailed work has been done on it. Herbert Blau connects "the obsession with language in Shepard's play" to a post-structural theory of the comic ("Comedy," 558), while Kennedy sees the verbal battle between Hoss and Crow as a "new mode of interactive dramatic dialogue" (with roots in Brecht) that "refuses to suggest, or enter, inner states of being" (250). See also Auerbach on the relation to Brecht. Powe analyzes the musical component, as does Coe in a major piece on Shepard's rock plays (including *Melodrama Play, Mad Dog Blues*, and *Cowboy Mouth*). For Coe, "the search for authentic values to sustain the performing self" is a crucial concept in *The Tooth of Crime;* Shepard's characters are either "paranoid or nostalgic" or "escape artists . . . leaping into the void to find themselves on stage" ("Image," 58). Weales also finds "a series of escape images" in these early plays and relates Shepard's "transformational" approach to character to the author's protean per-sonal "image" (38). Finally, in *The Tooth of Crime* (as well as in *Cowboy Mouth* and *Geography of a Horse Dreamer*), Bachman isolates a recurrent and evolving pattern of action related to the potential for (and ultimate avoidance of) violence.

The performing self is also a key structural and thematic principle in Falk's important article focusing on Shepard's next three major plays, *Action, Angel City*, and *Suicide in B Flat*. Each, she argues, contains a "series of performance rituals" in which "the self" searches "ghostlike" for "im-ages ('pictures') to complete itself" ("Role," 184). In the same vein, McCarthy finds moments of "perfect stasis" for the actor in *Action* that build up "a strong metaphor for a disintegrating society" (3). The met-aphor for Savran is theatrical; *Action* is the play that "most clearly reveals the theatre to be a prison for all those concerned in its operation" (58). Cima contradicts Savran's ingenious deconstructive analysis on one ma-jor point: "The actions of Lupe and Liza suggest that they refuse to acknowledge their supposed marginality" (75). Her comparison of *Action, Angel City*, and *Buried Child* to the combines of Robert Rauschenberg remains the most complete and convincing explication of Shepard's tech-nique as theatrical collage. Rosen's earlier piece on the filmic structure of *Angel City* makes a related point, as does Carroll's in reference to *Suicide in B Flat*. Putzel uses both of these plays as the central examples of the way in which Shepard manipulates audience response, confuting expectations ("naive interpretation proves ineffective") and compelling a "complicit reading" (150).

Curse of the Starving Class, like *The Tooth of Crime*, is discussed briefly in a variety of contexts. Rabillard, for example, uses it as a metatheatrical "paradigm": "It disturbs the audience with a peculiarly unresolved clash of disparate elements" (65); Herbert Blau, to demonstrate "the persistence of desire in language to overcome the failed promise" of the American dream ("American Dream," 521); Falk, Londré, and Erben to demonstrate their different perspectives on sexual politics. Glore sees *Curse* as a "watershed play"; from this point on "all Shepard's plays will share an 'indraught' of classical interpretability that one doesn't find in his earlier work" (57). Glore's concomitant reading of *Buried Child* makes an interesting companion piece to both Simon's attempt to explain the play's "seeming contradictions" ("Chronicles," 87) and to Wilson's analysis of the way in which *Buried Child* (through Shelly) "constitutes its spectators; "we want the play to be meaningful because it sates our desire for theatrical action which signifies" (50). All three should be read with Cima's provocative, if too brief, deconstruction of the play in which she finds "two (or more) conflicting main actions, which enter the realm of the surreal as they attempt, unsuccessfully, to cancel each other out" ("Shifting," 73). In an earlier essay-review, Cima also compares the visual style of *Buried Child* to the superrealist painters, a point amplified by Zinman ("Super Realism)." Nash applies Lévi-Strauss's theory of "the overrating and underrating of blood relations" to the incest of Halie and Tilden and to the infanticide of Dodge (487); Adler says the play "deflates the myth of America as the new Eden" and (unlike Nash) sees the ending as ironic (*Mirror*, 107); Callens links the water symbolism to a "holistic (feminine) longing" rooted in the precolonial American dream (413).

Daniels's forthcoming book will document fully the Chaikin-Shepard collaborations; a selection of critical essays will include a reprint of Kleb's detailed analysis of the text of *Tongues* as performed by the authors in San Francisco. Blumenthal's description of the piece (amplified from an earlier article) appears in her book on Chaikin. Kleb also examines the San Francisco productions of *True West* and *Fool for Love* in two extended essay-reviews. In the former, he connects the stylistic ambiguity of both text and performance to the dialectical treatment of three major themes: artistic creation, the American West, and the "psychic state of modern (western) man" (71). Orbison outlines several "mythic" levels apparent in the text of *True West* (506). Kleb's piece on *Fool for Love* questions the meaning (and function) of the incest element, as well as the sexual politics. Wilson makes a similar point about May's ambiguous position in the play by showing that "the perspective of the spectator is that of the

Old Man" (55). Londré, on the other hand, contends that Shepard succeeded in giving May "equal dramatic weight in the battle of the sexes that constitutes the through-line of action" (19). For Rabillard, the booming walls, and the other metatheatrical effects, emphasize that the text is "troué"—a technique intended to make the spectator "aware of his place in the auditorium, of his efforts to interpret" (64).

Both Rabillard and Londré also examine the role of women in *A Lie of the Mind*. Agreeing that women are no longer marginalized in this play, Rabillard nevertheless detects "sexually differentiated performance styles" and argues that the "logic" of the plot exposes the dangers of female "theatricality" (69). Putzel sees *Lie* as evidence "that the nature of audience complicity in Shepard's productions may be degenerating" (158), while DeRose notes the many parallels to earlier Shepard plays but misses "the mythic density" and "wild theatricality" of his best work ("Slouching," 74).

Little critical work has been done on Shepard's screenplays, although Londré uses *Paris, Texas* to bolster her postfeminist reading of the recent plays, and Thomson, in a lively analysis of Shepard's personal film image ("paranoia searching for its grievance"), suggests parallels between the parts Shepard has created on and for the screen and the parts he has written for the stage (49).

A central problem with Shepard's theatre from the beginning has been practical—how to achieve the Shepard style in performance—and thus a body of critical comment has developed that addresses itself specifically to this issue. Predictably much material comes from directors, starting with the fascinating (and still valid) introductory notes to *Five Plays* and ending with interviews of Wenders and Altman. In between, Chubb outlines his "difficulties" directing early Shepard ("lack of traditional structure"; "the flow of the imagery seems to overpower and negate character and structure"), and urges actors "to forget much of what they have learned about building a character and sustaining a performance" ("Fruitful," 17–18; 20). Sharman also offers a useful account of his work on *The Unseen Hand*. The director most closely associated with Shepard personally, Robert Woodruff, discusses his method in two major interviews, with Harris and then with Coe. In the latter, he talks about the "enormous freedom" he and Shepard give actors to discover the "rules" within the text (156). This is confirmed by several eyewitness accounts of rehearsals directed by Shepard alone—Coe ("Saga"), VerMeulen, Wetzsteon ("Unknown")—as well by interviews with actors who have worked under Shepard's direction (see Funke, Robertson, and E. Blau). Aaron says that "Sam himself—his presence and instinct—was usually the most illuminating element whenever I worked on his plays" (173). Another director who has successfully staged a number of Shepard plays is George Ferencz. In an interview with Zinman, he and Max Roach discuss the musical structure in the jazz plays (*Suicide in B Flat, Back Bog, Angel City*), as well as the improvisational ensemble style they tried to achieve with their actors ("Suite"). A decidedly different directorial approach is expressed by Schechner, whose account of the Performance Group's work on *The Tooth of Crime* ("Drama") should be read along with Gray's more personal, and considerably less programatic, memories of playing Hoss in the same production (Dasgupta).

FUTURE RESEARCH OPPORTUNITIES

Shepard scholarship has just begun. Clearly a critical biography is needed. Many research opportunites exist in the Shepard Collection at the Mugar Library (Boston University) and in the Toby Cole Collection (University of California at Davis). Though restricted, both contain unpublished manuscripts and early (often multiple) versions of published plays. A full-scale bibliography is needed. More critical pressure needs to be put on the texts themselves. Several recent poststructural readings have yielded promising results, but perhaps more traditional approaches might prove equally useful. Linguistic and psychoanalytic (especially neo-Freudian) strategies are applicable. The political dimension has been explored almost exclusively from a feminist perspective; ideological issues raised by metatheatrical and sociological studies might be brought into the foreground. Shepard's work needs to be placed more firmly in context, both artistic and social. Influences, especially from the visual arts, music, and film, require more rigorous and knowledgeable explications. The literary connections remain largely unexplored. No attempt has been made to evaluate Shepard's impact on his contemporaries. Finally, despite the sharply divided public reception of his plays, there has been little serious critical dissent. Surely, as Shepard's plays continually demonstrate, there are at least two sides to every story.

SECONDARY SOURCES

Aaron, Joyce. "Clues in a Memory." In *American Dreams: The Imagination of Sam Shepard*, pp. 171–74. Edited by Bonnie Marranca. New York: Performing Arts Journal, 1981.

Adler, Thomas P. "Curse of the Starving Class." *Educational Theatre Journal* 29 (October 1977): 409–10.

———. *Mirror on the Stage: The Pulitzer Prize Plays as an Approach to American Drama*. West Lafayette: Purdue University Press, 1987.

Albee, Edward. "Theatre: *Icarus's Mother*." *Village Voice* (25 November 1965): 19.

Ansen, David. "The Reluctant Star." *Newsweek* (24 November 1980): 117–18.

Auerbach, Doris. *Sam Shepard, Arthur Kopit, and the Off-Broadway Theatre*. Twayne's United States Authors Series 432. Boston: Twayne, 1982.

Bachman, Charles R. "Defusion of Menace in the Plays of Sam Shepard." *Modern Drama* 19 (December 1976): 405–15. Reprinted in *Essays on Modern American Drama: Williams, Miller, Albee and Shepard*, pp. 167–73. Edited by Dorothy Parker. Toronto: University of Toronto Press, 1987.

Barnes, Clive. " 'Fool for Love'—Powerful Play about a Divided U.S." *New York Post* (27 May 1983).

———. "Shepard's 'Starving Class' Offers Much Food for Thought." *New York Post* (3 March 1978): 29.

———. "Theatre: A Sam Shepard Double Bill." *New York Times* (2 April 1970): 43.

———. "Where Is U.S. Theatre? It's Alive Off Broadway." *New York Times* (28 May 1968): 41.

Berman, Paul. Review of *A Lie of the Mind*. *Nation* (22 February 1986): 215.

Bigsby, C. W. E. *A Critical Introduction to Twentieth-Century American Drama*. 3 vols. Cambridge: Cambridge University Press, 1985.

———. "Sam Shepard: Word and Image." In *Critical Angles: European Views of Contemporary American Literature*, pp. 208–19. Edited by Marc Chénetier. Carbondale: Southern Illinois University Press, 1986.

———. Kenneth Chubb, and Malcolm Page. "Theatre Checklist No. 3, Sam Shepard." *Theatrefacts* 3 (August-October 1974): 3–11.

Blau, Eleanor. "Stars of 'Fool for Love' Find Success Can Hurt." *New York Times* (10 June 1983): C3.

Blau, Herbert. "The American Dream in American Gothic: The Plays of Sam Shepard and Adrienne Kennedy." *Modern Drama* 27 (December 1984): 520–39.

———. "Comedy since the Absurd." *Modern Drama* 25 (December 1982): 545–68.

Bloom, Michael. "Visions of the End: The Early Plays." In *American Dreams: The Imagination of Sam Shepard*, pp.72–78. Edited by Bonnie Marranca. New York: Performing Arts Journal, 1981.

Blumenthal, Eileen. *Joseph Chaikin: Exploring at the Boundaries of Theatre*. Cambridge: Cambridge University Press, 1984.

Brantley, Robin. "Yale Gives Its Own Version of 'Buried Child.' " *New York Times* (19 January 1979): C11.

Bruckner, D. J. R. "Forging a New Dramatic Language." *New York Times* (7 July 1985): C3.

Brustein, Robert. *Making Scenes: A Personal History of the Turbulent Years at Yale 1966–1979*. New York: Random House, 1981.

———. "The Shepard Enigma." *New Republic* (27 January 1986): 25, 28.

———. "Shepard's America." London *Observer*, (18 March 1973): 34.

Callens, Johan. "Memories of the Sea in Shepard's Illinois." *Modern Drama* 29 (September 1986): 403–15.

Canby, Vincent. " 'Paris, Texas' from Wim Wenders." *New York Times* (14 October 1984): 64.

———. "Small Screens Breed Small Movies." *New York Times* (15 December 1985): B23.

Carpenter, Charles A. *Modern Drama Scholarship and Criticism 1966–80: An International Bibliography*. Toronto: University of Toronto Press, 1986.

Carroll, Dennis. "The Filmic Cut and 'Switchback' in the Plays of Sam Shepard." *Modern Drama* 28 (March 1985): 125–38.

Chubb, Kenneth. "Fruitful Difficulties of Directing Shepard." *Theatre Quarterly* 4, no. 15 (August-October 1974): 17–25.

———. "Sam Shepard's London." *Canadian Theatre Review* 10 (Spring 1976): 119–22.

Cima, Gay Gibson. "Buried Child." *Theatre Journal* 35 (December 1983): 559–60.

———. "Shifting Perspectives: Combining Shepard and Rauschenberg." *Theatre Journal* 38 (March 1986): 67–81.

Clurman, Harold. Review of *Buried Child. Nation* (2 December 1978): 620–22.

———. Review of *Curse of the Starving Class. Nation* (25 March 1978): 348–49.

———. Review of *Geography of a Horse Dreamer. Nation.* (10 January 1976): 27–29.

———. Review of *Operation Sidewinder. Nation* (30 March 1970): 380–81.

———. Review of *Seduced. Nation* (24 February 1979): 221.

———. Review of *The Tooth of Crime. Nation* (26 March 1973): 410–12.

Coe, Robert. "Image Shots Are Blown: The Rock Plays." In *American Dreams: The Imagination of Sam Shepard*, pp. 57–66. Edited by Bonnie Marranca. New York: Performing Arts Journal, 1981.

——— "Interview with Robert Woodruff." In *American Dreams: The Imagination of Sam Shepard*, pp. 151–58. Edited by Marranca. New York: Performing Arts Journal, 1981.

———. "Saga of Sam Shepard." *New York Times Magazine* (23 November 1980): 56–58, 118, 120, 122, 124.

Cohn, Ruby. "Camp, Cruelty, Colloquialism." In *Comic Relief: Humor in Contemporary American Literature*, pp. 281–303. Edited by Sarah B. Cohen. Urbana: Illinois University Press, 1978.

———. *New American Dramatists, 1960–1980*. New York: Grove, 1982.

———. "Sam Shepard: Today's Passionate Shepard and His Loves." In *Essays on Contemporary American Drama*, pp. 161–72. Edited by Hedwig Bock and Albert Wertheim. Munich: Max Hueber Verlag, 1981.

Cott, Jonathan. "The Rolling Stone Interview: Sam Shepard." *Rolling Stone* (18 December 1986–1 January 1987): 166–72, 198, 200.

Coveney, Michael. "*Action.*" *Plays and Players* (November 1974): 29.

Current Biography Yearbook. Edited by Charles Moritz. New York: H. W. Wilson, 1979.

Daniels, Barry, ed. *In Front of You Is the Moon: Correspondence and Texts by Joseph Chaikin and Sam Shepard*. New York: Sun and Moon, 1988.

Dasgupta, Gautam. "Interview with Spalding Gray." In *American Dreams: The Imagination of Sam Shepard*, pp. 175–83. Edited by Bonnie Marranca. New York: Performing Arts Journal, 1981.

Davis, Douglas. Review of *Cowboys* and *The Rock Garden. New York Herald Tribune* (6 February 1966).

Davis, Richard A. " 'Get Up Out A' Your Homemade Beds': The Plays of Sam Shepard." *Players* 47 (October-November 1971): 12–19.

Denby, David. "A Stranger in a Strange Land: A Moviegoer at the Theatre." *Atlantic Monthly* (January 1985): 45.

DeRose, David. Review of *Fool for Love*. *Theatre Journal* 36 (March 1984): 100–101.

———. "Slouching Towards Broadway: Shepard's *A Lie of the Mind*." *Theatre* 17 (Spring 1986): 69–74.

Donohue, Walter. "American Graffiti: Walter Donohue on the Pulsating World of Sam Shepard." *Plays and Players* (April 1974): 14–18.

Duberman, Martin. "The Great Gray Way." *Harper's* (May 1978): 83.

Earley, Michael. "Of Life Immense in Passion, Pulse and Power: Sam Shepard and the American Literary Tradition." In *American Dreams: The Imagination of Sam Shepard*, pp. 126–32. Edited by Bonnie Marranca. New York: Performing Arts Journal, 1981.

Eddleman, Floyd E. *American Drama Criticism: Interpretations, 1890–1977*. Hamden, CT: Shoe String, 1979.

Engel, David W. "Sam Shepard." In *Dictionary of Literary Biography*, Vol. 7: *Twentieth-Century American Dramatists*, Pt. 2: 231–38. Edited by John MacNicholas. Detroit: Gale Research, 1981.

Erben, Rudolf. "Women and Other Men in Sam Shepard's Plays." *Studies in American Drama, 1945–Present* 2 (1987): 29–41.

Falk, Florence. "Men without Women: The Shepard Landscape." In *American Dreams: The Imagination of Sam Shepard*, pp. 90–103. Edited by Bonnie Marranca. New York: Performing Arts Journal, 1981.

———. "The Role of Performance in Sam Shepard's Plays." *Theatre Journal* 33 (May 1981): 182–98.

Feingold, Michael. "Biting Shepard." *Village Voice* (16 November 1972): 75.

———. "Everything's So Shocking Inside." *Village Voice* (21 April 1975): 87.

———. " 'Fool's Gold." *Village Voice* (7 June 1983): 81.

———. "Games and Saviors." *Village Voice* (1 August 1974): 56.

———. "Kleist and Shepard Flirt with Death." *Village Voice* (15 November 1976): 113.

———. "Sam Shepard, Part-Time Shaman." *Village Voice* (4 April 1977): 72.

———. "Seductive." *Village Voice* (12 February 1979): 93–94.

———. "Truthful and Consequential." *Village Voice* (24–30 December 1980): 83.

Fennell, Patrick J. Review of *Angel City*. *Educational Theatre Journal* 20 (March 1977): 112–13.

Fox, Terry Curtis. "Family Plot." *Village Voice* (13 March 1978): 77.

———. "Many Deaths in the Family." *Village Voice* (30 October 1978): 119.

Freedman, Samuel G. "Sam Shepard's Mythic Vision of the Family." *New York Times* (1 December 1985): B1.

Frutkin, Ren. "Paired Existence Meets the Monster." *Yale/Theatre* 2, no. 2 (Summer 1969): 22–30. Reprinted in *American Dreams: The Imagination of Sam Shepard*, pp. 108–16. Edited by Bonnie Marranca. New York: Performing Arts Journal, 1981.

Funke, Phyllis Ellen. "Wizard of the Way-Out." *Showbill* (September 1983): 3–10.

Gelber, Jack. "Sam Shepard: The Playwright as Shaman." In Sam Shepard, *Angel City and Other Plays*, pp. 1–41. New York: Urizen, 1973. Reprinted in *American Dreams: The Imagination of Sam Shepard*, pp. 45–48. Edited by Bonnie Marranca. New York: Performing Arts Journal, 1981.

Gilman, Richard. Introduction to *Sam Shepard: Seven Plays*, pp. ix–xiv. New York: Bantam, 1981.

Glore, John. "The Canonization of Mojo Rootforce: Sam Shepard Live at the Pantheon." *Theatre* 12 no. 3 (Summer-Fall 1981): 53–65.

Goldberg, Robert. "Sam Shepard—Off Broadway's Street Cowboy." *Rolling Stone College Papers* (Winter 1980): 43–45.

Gussow, Mel. "Intimate Monologues That Speak to the Heart." *New York Times* (9 December 1979): B36.

———. "Sam Shepard Revisits the American Heartland." *New York Times* (15 December 1985): B3, B7.

———. "Sam Shepard's Prophetic 'Beast' Retains Its Comedic Bite." *New York Times* (16 December 1984): B3, B34.

———. "Sam Shepard's *Seduced.*" *New York Times* (28 April 1978): C3.

———. "Shepard's 'Suicide in B Flat' Presented by Yale Repertory." *New York Times* (25 October 1976): 42.

———. "Stage: *Horse Dreamer.*" *New York Times* (13 December 1975): 21.

———. "Stage: 'Mad Dog Blues.' " *New York Times* (9 March 1971): 25.

———. "Stage: Shepard and 'Suicide.' " *New York Times* (14 March 1979): C19.

———. "Stage: Shepard's 'West' Revived and Restored." *New York Times*, (18 October 1982): C18.

Hall, Trish. "Sam Shepard: Theatre's Reluctant Star." *Wall Street Journal*, (8 April 1983): 27.

Hardwick, Elizabeth. "Notes on the New Theatre." *New York Review of Books*, (20 June 1968): 5.

———. "Word of Mouth." *New York Review of Books* (6 April 1967): 6, 8. Reprinted as "An Introduction: *La Turista.*" In *American Dreams: The Imagination of Sam Shepard*, pp. 67–71. Edited by Bonnie Marranca. New York: Performing Arts Journal, 1981.

Harris, William. Review of *Geography of a Horse Dreamer*. *Soho Weekly News* (18 December 1975): 28.

———. "Woodruff on Shepard." *Soho Weekly News* (26 October 1978): 74, 79.

Hart, Lynda. *Sam Shepard's Metaphorical Stages.* Contributions in Drama and Theatre Studies 22. Westport, Conn.: Greenwood Press, 1987.

Henry, William A., III. "Achieving a Vision of Order." *Time* (16 December 1985): 83.

Herman, William. "Geography of a Play Dreamer: Sam Shepard." In his *Understanding Contemporary American Drama.* pp. 23–80. Columbia: University of South Carolina Press, 1987.

Hobson, Harold. "An Act of Defiance." *Sunday Times* (London, 22 September 1974): 10.

Honan, William M. "The American Dream Moves to Center Stage." *New York Times*, (13 April 1986): B1, B6.

Hughes, Catherine. *American Playwrights, 1945–1975.* London: Pitman, 1976.

Kakutani, Michiko. "Myths, Dreams, Realities—Sam Shepard's America." *New York Times*, (29 January 1984): B1, B26–28.

Kauffmann, Stanley. Review of *Chicago* (as part of *6 from La Mama*). *New York Times*, (13 April 1966): 36.

———. "What Price Freedom?" *New Republic* (8 April 1978): 24–25. Reprinted in *American Dreams: The Imagination of Sam Shepard*, pp. 104–7. Edited by Bonnie Marranca. New York: Performing Arts Journal, 1981.

Kennedy, Andrew K. *Dramatic Dialogue: The Dialogue of Personal Encounter*. Cambridge: Cambridge University Press, 1983.

Kerr, Walter. "A Play That Binds Us Knot by Knot." *New York Times*, (7 November 1976): D3.

———. "From Tasseled Parasols to Intellectual Driftwood." *New York Times*, (12 March 1978): D3.

———. "Of Shepard's Myths and Ibsen's Men." *New York Times* (11 January 1981): B3, B17.

———. "Sam Shepard—What's the Message?" *New York Times* (10 December 1978): D3.

Kihss, Peter. "Shepard Takes the Pulitzer for Drama, Baker of *Times* Wins for Comment." *New York Times* (17 April 1979): 1, B8.

King, Kimball. *Ten Modern American Playwrights: An Annotated Bibliography*. New York: Garland, 1982.

Kleb, William. "Sam Shepard's Free-for-All: *Fool for Love* at the Magic Theatre." *Theatre* 14, no. 3 (Summer-Fall 1983): 77–82.

———. "Sam Shepard's *Inacoma* at the Magic Theatre." *Theatre* 9, no. 1 (Fall 1977): 59–64.

———. "Shepard and Chaikin Speaking in *Tongues*." *Theatre* 10, no. 1 (February 1977): 66–69.

———. "Theatre in San Francisco: Sam Shepard's *True West*." *Theatre* 12, no. 1 (Fall-Winter 1980): 65–71. Reprinted as "Worse Than Being Homeless: *True West* and the Divided Self." In *American Dreams: The Imagination of Sam Shepard*, pp. 117–25. Edited by Bonnie Marranca. New York: Performing Arts Journal, 1981.

Kraft, Daphne. "Shepard Double Bill." *Newark Evening News* 2 April 1970): 40.

Kroll, Jack. "Crazy Henry." *Newsweek*, (8 May 1978): 94.

———. "High Pressure Jazz." *Newsweek*, (8 November 1976): 109.

———. "Savage Games People Play." *Newsweek*, (16 December 1985): 85.

Lahr, John. "Spectacles of Disintegration." In *American Dreams: The Imagination of Sam Shepard*. Ed. Bonnie Marranca. New York: Performing Arts Journal, 1981. pp. 49–56.

———. *Automatic Vaudeville: Essays in Star Turns*. New York: Knopf, 1984.

———. "Curse of the Starving Class." *Plays and Players* (June 1977): 24–25.

———. "On-stage." *Village Voice* (19 March 1970): 43–44.

———. Review of *Action*. *Village Voice* (31 October 1974): 90.

———. Review of *Geography of a Horse Dreamer*. *Plays and Players* (April 1974): 46–47.

———. "*The Tooth of Crime*." *Village Voice* (8 March 1973): 55.

Lester, Elenore. "The Pass-the-Hat Theatre Circuit." *New York Times Magazine* (5 December 1965): 90, 95, 98, 100, 102, 106, 108.

Leverett, James. "Old Forms Enter the New American Theatre: Shepard Foreman, Kirby and Ludlam." In *Melodrama*, pp. 107–12. Edited by Daniel Gerould. New York: New York Literary Forum, 1980.

Londré, Felicia. "Sam Shepard Works Out: The Masculinization of America." *Studies in American Drama, 1945–Present* 2 (1987): 19–26.

Madden, David. "The Theatre of Assault: Four Off-Off-Broadway Plays." *Massachusetts Review* 8 (Autumn 1967): 713–25.

Marowitz, Charles. "Is This Shepard or Saroyan?" *New York Times* (15 May 1977): D3.

———. "Sam Shepard: Sophisticate Abroad." *Village Voice* (7 September 1972): 59.

Marranca, Bonnie. "Sam Shepard in Hollywood." *Soho Weekly News* (17 March 1977): 31–39.

———, ed. *American Dreams: The Imagination of Sam Shepard*. New York: Performing Arts Journal, 1981.

———, and Gautam Dasgupta. *American Playwrights: A Critical Survey*. New York: Drama Book Specialists, 1981.

———. Gerald Rabkin, and Johannes Birringer. "The Controversial 1985–86 Theatre Season: A Politics of Reception." *Performing Arts Journal 28* 10, no. 1 (1986): 7–33.

Mazzocco, Robert. "Heading for the Last Roundup." *New York Review of Books* (9 May 1985): 21–27.

McBride, Stewart. "Sam Shepard: Listener and Playwright." *Christian Science Monitor*, (23 December 1980): B2–3.

McCarthy, Gerry. " 'Acting It Out': Sam Shepard's *Action*." *Modern Drama* 24 (March 1981): 1–12.

Mottram, Ron. *Inner Landscapes: The Theatre of Sam Shepard*. Columbia: University of Missouri Press, 1984.

Nash, Thomas. "Sam Shepard's *Buried Child:* The Ironic Use of Folklore." *Modern Drama* 26 (December 1983): 486–91. Reprinted in *Essays on Modern American Drama: Williams, Miller, Albee and Shepard*, pp. 203–9. Edited by Dorothy Parker. Toronto: University of Toronto Press, 1987.

Nightingale, Benedict. "Even Minimal Shepard Is Food for Thought." *New York Times* (25 September 1983): H5.

———. "Only When We Laugh." *New Statesman* (London, 29 April 1977): 577.

———. Review of *Action*. *New Statesman* (London, 27 September 1974): 440.

Orbison, Tucker. "Mythic Levels in Shepard's *True West*." *Modern Drama* 27 (December 1984): 506–19. Reprinted in *Essays on Modern American Drama: Williams, Miller, Albee and Shepard*, pp. 188–202. Edited by Dorothy Parker. Toronto: University of Toronto Press, 1987.

Oumano, Ellen. *Sam Shepard: The Life and Work of an American Dreamer*. New York: St. Martin's, 1986.

Palmer, Robert. "A Rock Tour Recalled." *New York Times* (17 September 1977): 21.

Parker, Dorothy, ed. *Essays on Modern American Drama: Williams, Miller, Albee and Shepard*. Toronto: University of Toronto Press, 1987.

Patraka, Vivian M., and Mark Siegel. *Sam Shepard*. Western Writers Series 69. Boise: Boise State University, 1985.

Peachment, Chris. "American Hero." *Time Out* (23–29 August 1984): 14–17.

Powe, Bruce W. "*The Tooth of Crime:* Sam Shepard's Way with Music." *Modern Drama* 24 (1981): 13–25. Reprinted in *Essays on Modern American Drama:*

Williams, Miller, Albee and Shepard, pp. 174–87. Edited by Dorothy Parker. Toronto: University of Toronto Press, 1987.

Putzel, Steven. "Expectation, Confutation, Revelation: Audience Complicity in the Plays of Sam Shepard." *Modern Drama* 30 (June 1987): 147–60.

Rabillard, Sheila. "Sam Shepard: Theatrical Power and American Dreams." *Modern Drama* 30 (March 1987): 58–71.

Rabkin, Gerald. "The Bones Underneath." *Soho Weekly News* (26 October 1978): 74, 78, 81.

———. "Like One Whole Thing." *Soho Weekly News* (16 March 1978): 4.

———. "Sam's Endgame." *Soho Weekly News* (8 February 1979): 62, 66.

Rich, Frank. " 'A Lie of the Mind' by Sam Shepard." *New York Times* (6 December 1985): 19–20.

———. "At Its Best, It Was a Season That Illuminated Our World." *New York Times* (1 June 1986): B1, B36.

———. "Stage: Shepard's 'True West.' " *New York Times* (24 December 1980): C9.

Robertson, Nan. "The Multidimensional Sam Shepard." *New York Times* (21 January 1986): C15.

Rogoff, Gordon. "America Screened." *Village Voice* (17 December 1985): 117–18.

Rosen, Carol. "Sam Shepard's *Angel City:* A Movie for the Stage." *Modern Drama* 22 (March 1979): 39–46.

Sainer, Arthur. "Playing Top Dog in a Turd Paradise." *Village Voice* (17 November 1975): 117.

———. "Shepard's Collision Course: Stung in the Land of Honey." *Village Voice* (11 March 1971): 53.

Salem, James. *A Guide to Critical Reviews: Part I: American Drama. 1909–1982.* 3d. ed. Metuchen, N.J.: Scarecrow, 1984.

Savran, David. "Sam Shepard's Conceptual Prison: *Action* and the Unseen Hand." *Theatre Journal* 38 (March 1984): 57–73.

Schechner, Richard. "Drama, Script, Theatre, and Performance." *Drama Review* 17, no. 3 (September 1973): 5–36.

———. "The Writer and the Performance Group: Rehearsing *The Tooth of Crime.*" *Performance* 5 (March-April 1973): 60–65. Also rpt. in *American Dreams: The Imagination of Sam Shepard.* Ed. Bonnie Marranca. New York: Performing Arts Journal, 1981. 162–68.

Sharman, Jim. "It'll Get You In the End." *Plays and Players* (May 1973): xiii–xv.

Shewey, Don. *Sam Shepard.* New York: Dell, 1985.

———. "The True Story of 'True West.' " *Village Voice* (30 November 1982): 115.

Simard, Rodney. *Postmodern Drama: Contemporary Playwrights in America and Britain.* Lanham, Md.: University Press of America, 1984.

Simon, John. Review of *Action. New York* (5 May 1975): 94.

———. Review of *True West. New York* (12 January 1981): 45–46.

———. "Soft Centers." *New York* (6 June 1983): 110.

———. "Theatre Chronicle: Kopit, Norman and Shepard." *Hudson Review* 32 (Spring 1979): 77–88.

Smith, Michael. Review of *Back Bog Beast Bait*. *Village Voice* (13 December 1973): 82–83.

———. Review of *BbAaNnGg! Village Voice* (11 November 1965): 19.

———. Review of *Chicago*. *Village Voice* (13 May 1965): 17.

———. Review of *Cowboys* and *The Rock Garden*. *Village Voice* (22 October 1964): 13.

———. Review of *Red Cross*. *Village Voice* (27 January 1966): 19.

———. Review of *The Tooth of Crime*. *Village Voice* (26 July 1973): 57.

———. "Theatre: New Playwrights I." *Village Voice* (18 February 1965): 12.

———. "Theatre Journal." *Village Voice* (2 December 1965): 19, 24.

Smith, Patti. "Sam Shepard: 9 Random Years [7 + 2]." In *Sam Shepard: Mad Dog Blues and Other Plays*, pp. 153–58. New York: Winter House, 1972.

Stambolian, George. "Shepard's *Mad Dog Blues:* A Trip through Popular Culture." *Journal of Popular Culture* 7, no. 4 (Spring 1974): 776–86. Reprinted in *American Dreams: The Imagination of Sam Shepard*, pp. 79–89. Edited by Bonnie Marranca. New York: Performing Arts Journal, 1981.

Stasio, Marilyn. "Sam Shepard: An Outlaw Comes Home." *After Dark* (January 1980): 58–63.

Tallmer, Jerry. "Tell Me about the Morons George." *New York Post* (12 October 1964): 16.

Thomson, David. "Shepard." *Film Comment* 19, no. 6 (November-December 1983): 49–56.

Valgamae, Mardi. "Expressionism and the New American Drama." *Twentieth Century Literature* 17 (January-October 1971): 227–34.

VerMeulen, Michael. "Sam Shepard: Yes, Yes, Yes." *Esquire* (February 1980): 79–86.

Wardle, Irving. "*Curse of the Starving Class*." *Times* (London, 22 April 1977): 11g.

———. "*Little Ocean*." *London Times* (27 March 1974): 11.

Watt, Douglas. " 'Fool for Love' Shows Shepard at His Starkest, Bleakest Best." *New York Daily News* (27 May 1983): 16.

———. "On Stage: 'A Lie of the Mind.' " *New York Daily News* (6 December 1985).

———. " 'True West' Moves Shepard in Right Direction." *New York Daily News* (24 December 1980): 37.

Weales, Gerald. "The Transformations of Sam Shepard." In *American Dreams: The Imagination of Sam Shepard*, pp. 37–43. Edited by Bonnie Marranca. New York: Performing Arts Journal, 1981.

Weiner, Bernard. "Passion Fuels 'Fool for Love.' " *San Francisco Chronicle* (11 February 1983): 64.

———. "Sam Shepard's Powerful Drama on Confusion." *San Francisco Chronicle* (6 May 1975): 40.

———. "The True Story of Shepard's 'True West.' " *San Francisco Chronicle and Examiner Datebook* (12 April 1981): 25–26.

"Wender's á la recherche d'un lieu (entretien sur *Paris, Texas*)." *Cahiers du cinema*, 360/361 (Summer 1984): 6–17.

Wetzsteon, Ross. Introduction to Sam Shepard, *Fool for Love and Other Plays*, pp. 1–15. New York: Bantam, 1984.

————. "Looking a Gift Horse Dreamer in the Mouth." *Village Voice* (5 January 1976): 71.

————. "Unknown Territory." *Village Voice* (10 December 1985): 55–56.

Whiting, Charles G. "Inverted Chronology in Sam Shepard's *La Turista*." *Modern Drama* 29 (September 1986): 416–21.

Wilson, Ann. "Fool of Desire: The Spectator to the Plays of Sam Shepard." *Modern Drama* 30 (March 1987): 46–57.

Winn, Stephen. " 'Superstitions': A Sparkling But Slight Show." *San Francisco Chronicle* (9 July 1981): 48.

Wren, Scott Christopher. "Camp Shepard: Exploring the Geography of Character." *West Coast Plays* 7 (Fall 1980): 43–45.

Zinman, Toby Silverman. "Sam Shepard and Super Realism." *Modern Drama* 29 (September 1986): 423–29.

————. "Shepard Suite." *American Theatre* 1, no. 8 (December 1984): 15–17.

Neil Simon

(4 JULY 1927–   )

LAURA MORROW

ASSESSMENT OF SIMON'S REPUTATION

Neil Simon is famous for commercially successful humorous plays that celebrate marriage and the family through exploring serious themes such as sibling rivalry, sexual awakening, love, marriage, parenting, infidelity, and divorce. Although he exposes human folly and criticizes the shallowness of modern life, Simon's drama is neither didactic nor harshly satirical. His characters are variations of types, their speech and concerns reflecting his Brooklyn Jewish heritage. Loney suggests that "the farther removed from New York a Simon production is, the less easily do audiences respond and empathize" (485); nevertheless, Simon's comedies are staples of the repertoires of local theatres throughout the country and have enjoyed considerable success as films.

Simon's plays are not structurally complex. Typically, they present a single plot line and draw some of their humor from farce. The main source of the comedy, however, is the violation of expectation in situation and language (McGovern, 188–89). As Martin Gottfried observes, "Simon doesn't write situation comedy—he writes verbal comedy—he was really born for radio" ("Lovers," 125). Though characters may lapse into one-liners, their words always sound as if voiced by real people.

One weakness in Simon's plays is an overreliance on running jokes and one-liners reminiscent of television sitcoms. Clive Barnes found the humor in Simon's earlier plays often contrived and heartless: "You always felt that his characters would die with a jaunty wisecrack stuck in their mouths like a Groucho cigar" ("Theatre: Neil Simon Play," 120). A more serious problem for Simon is structure. "He just isn't a man with a plot" ("Lovers," 125), Gottfried complains. Simon's least successful comedies have been described as "hairline plots upon which are strung rows of gags in wide assortment, ranging from the bright and dry to the wisecrack-funny to the obvious and old-time comedian" (Gottfried, "Star-Spangled Girl," 194). When he finds his characters in difficult situations, he sometimes substitutes the microstructure of the joke for the macro-structure of the drama.

The morality reflected in Simon's plays is conventional, but tolerant of human fallibility. A recurring theme in the plays is, as Johnson suggested, manhood: "For Simon, a man is someone who asserts his independence and experiments with a variety of life's offerings, but who ultimately does not ignore the traditionally richest human experiences founded on love, marriage, and the family" (4). Simon believes that a prime source of hope, dignity, and fulfillment lies in family and friendship, despite the conflicts and frustrations that arise in such relationships. His traditional values make him distinct from many other contemporary playwrights, especially male playwrights.

For his work in television, he received the Emmy in 1957 and again in 1959. In 1963, 1965, 1970, and 1985 he received the Tony; in 1967, the London *Evening Standard* award; and in 1968, the Shubert award. In 1969, 1971, 1972, and 1976 he was the recipient of the Writer's Guild of America West Award for his screenplays and in 1982 of the PEN Los Angeles Center Award. In 1983, he received both the New York Drama Critics Circle Award and the Outer Circle Award, and received the latter again in 1985. Simon also received the New York State Governor's Award in 1986.

PRIMARY BIBLIOGRAPHY OF SIMON'S WORKS

Plays

Sketches (produced Tamiment, Pennsylvania, 1952, 1953).

Sketches, with Danny Simon, in *Catch a Star!* (produced New York, 1953).

Sketches, with Danny Simon, in *New Faces of 1956* (produced New York, 1956).

Come Blow Your Horn (produced New York, 1961; London, 1962). New York and London: French, 1961.

Barefoot in the Park (produced New York, 1963; London, 1965). New York: Random House, 1964; London: French, 1966.

The Odd Couple (produced New York, 1965; London, 1966; revised, with female leads, New York, 1985). New York: Random House, 1966.

The Star-Spangled Girl (produced New York, 1966). New York: Random House, 1967.

Plaza Suite (produced New York, 1968; London 1969). New York: Random House, 1969.

Last of the Red-Hot Lovers (produced New York, 1969; Manchester and London, 1979). New York: Random House, 1970.

The Gingerbread Lady (produced New York, 1970; Windsor and London, 1974). New York: Random House, 1971.

The Prisoner of Second Avenue (produced New York, 1971). New York: Random House, 1972; London: French, 1972.

The Sunshine Boys (produced New York, 1972; London, 1975). New York: Random House, 1973.

The Good Doctor (produced New York, 1973; Coventry, 1981). Based on stories by Chekhov. Music by Peter Link, lyrics by Neil Simon. New York: Random House, 1974; London: French, 1974.

God's Favorite (produced New York, 1974). New York: Random House, 1975.

California Suite (produced Los Angeles, New York and London, 1976). New York: Random House, 1977.

Chapter Two (produced Los Angeles and New York, 1977). New York: Random House, 1979; London: French, 1979.

I Ought to Be in Pictures (produced Los Angeles and New York, 1980; Perth, 1983; London, 1986). New York: Random House, 1981.

Fools (produced New York, 1981). New York, Random House, 1982.

Actors and Actresses (produced Stamford, Connecticut, 1983).

Brighton Beach Memoirs (produced Los Angeles and New York, 1983; London, 1986). New York: Random House, 1984; London: French, 1984.

Biloxi Blues (produced New York, 1985). New York: Random House, 1986.

Broadway Bound (produced New York, 1986). New York: Random House, 1987.

Musicals

Adventures of Marco Polo: A Musical Fantasy, with William Friedberg. Music by Clay Warnick and Mel Pahl. New York: French, 1959.

Heidi, with William Friedberg. Adaptation of the novel by Johanna Spyri. Music by Clay Warnick. New York: French, 1959.

Little Me (produced New York, 1962; London, 1964; revised version New York, 1982; London, 1983). Based on the novel by Patrick Dennis. Music by Cy Coleman, lyrics by Carolyn Leigh. In *Collected Plays*, Vol. II.

Sweet Charity (produced New York, 1966; London, 1967). Based on the screenplay of Federico Fellini's *Nights of Cabiria*. Book by Neil Simon, music by Cy Coleman, lyrics by Dorothy Fields. New York: Random House, 1966.

Promises, Promises (produced New York, 1968; London, 1969). Based on the screenplay *The Apartment* by Billy Wilder and I. A. L. Diamond. Music and lyrics by Burt Bacharach and Hal David. New York: Random House, 1969.

They're Playing Our Song (produced Los Angeles, 1978; New York, 1979; London, 1980). Book by Neil Simon, music by Marvin Hamlisch, lyrics by Carole Bayer Sager. New York: Random House, 1980.

Screenplays

After the Fox (1966)
Barefoot in the Park (1967)
The Odd Couple (1968)
The Out-of-Towners (1970)

Plaza Suite (1971)
The Heartbreak Kid (1972)
Last of the Red-Hot Lovers (1972)
The Sunshine Boys (1974)
The Prisoner of Second Avenue (1975)
Murder by Death (1976)
The Goodbye Girl (1977)
The Cheap Detective (1978)
California Suite (1979)
Chapter Two (1979)
Seems Like Old Times (1980)
Only When I Laugh (1981)
I Ought to Be in Pictures (1982)
Max Dugan Returns (1983)
The Slugger's Wife (1985)
Brighton Beach Memoirs (1986)
Biloxi Blues (1987)

Collections

The Collected Plays of Neil Simon, Vol. II. New York: Random House, 1979. (Includes *The Sunshine Boys, Little Me, The Gingerbread Lady, The Prisoner of Second Avenue, The Good Doctor, God's Favorite, California Suite, Chapter Two*).
The Comedy of Neil Simon. New York: Random House, 1971. (Includes *Come Blow Your Horn; Barefoot in the Park; The Odd Couple; The Star-Spangled Girl; Plaza Suite; Promises, Promises; Last of the Red-Hot Lovers*).

Essay

"Notes from the Playwright." In *Neil Simon: A Critical Study.* By Edythe M. McGovern. New York: Ungar, 1977. 3–5.

Interviews

Barthel, Joan. "Life for Simon—Not That Simple." *New York Times* (25 February 1968): 2: 9.
Zimmerman, Paul D. "Neil Simon: Up From Success." *Newsweek* (2 February 1970): 52–56.
Kerr, Walter. "What Simon Says." *New York Times Magazine* (22 March 1970): 6, 12, 14, 16.
Meryman, Richard. "When the Funniest Writer in America Tried to Be Serious." *Life* (7 May 1971): 60B-60D, 64, 66–69, 71, 73, 75, 77, 79–80, 83.
Hirschhorn, Clive. "Make 'em Laugh." *Plays and Players* 24 (September 1977): 12–15.
Linderman, Lawrence. "Playboy Interview: Neil Simon." *Playboy* 26 (February 1979): 58+.

Corry, John. "Why Broadway's Fastest Writer Cannot Slow Down." *New York Times* (5 April 1981): 2: 1.

[Freedman, Samuel G. and Michaela Williams.] "A Conversation Between Neil Simon and David Rabe: The Craft of the Playwright." *New York Times Magazine* (26 May 1985): 37–38, 52, 56, 57, 60, 61, 62.

PRODUCTION HISTORY

From the Broadway opening of his first play, *Come Blow Your Horn*, Neil Simon has been honored as one of the foremost writers of American comedy. *Come Blow Your Horn* was directed by Stanley Prager and opened on 22 February 1961. This play, like Simon's Brighton Beach trilogy, has autobiographical origins: it concerns how he and his brother Danny left their parents' home to have their own apartment (Linderman 68). The play received largely favorable reviews, despite the thinness of its plot and its overreliance on type characters (Taubman, "Horn," 356). Although the characterization of Harry Baker was uniformly praised for originality, Simon was criticized for elsewhere sacrificing depth of characterization to humor—for being "more interested in keeping the customers howling than in fashioning characters with depth and warmth" (Coleman, 358)—and for that humor's being corny and forced (Kerr, "Horn," 357). The structure was also considered weak; the play seemed "a thing of shreds and patches at the start, come to life in [individual scenes]" (Watts, "Comedy," 356).

An indisputable critical and popular success was Simon's next play, *Barefoot in the Park*, which was directed by Mike Nichols and opened 23 October 1963. *Barefoot* focusses on the problems of a newlywed couple of opposite temperaments. Whereas Paul is an upwardly mobile representative of traditional values, Corie is a free spirit whose values anticipate those that would dominate the latter part of the decade. The emphasis in this play—as in most of Simon's plays—is on the need to compromise, to respect and appreciate those whose values are not wholly congruent with one's own.

Although Simon has often been criticized for overreliance on the running gag, here the running gag of the steps was singled out for praise by the critics (Nadel, "Barefoot," 222; Taubman, "Bubbling," 223). As Johnson demonstrates, this gag not only elicits laughter but also helps to "define individual characters by inviting the audience to compare these characters' reactions to climbing all those steps" (10). The funny lines also "are not often simply wisecracks here [as they were in *Come Blow Your Horn*] but natural to character and situation" (Taubman, "Bubbling," 223). Kerr also praised the clever use of the empty, sky-blue set to foreground the exposition ("Horn," 357).

Simon's success continued with his next play, *The Odd Couple*, which opened 10 March 1965 and was also directed by Mike Nichols. The play centers around the complications that arise when a man, cast out by his wife, is taken in by a divorced friend of opposite habits. Taubman lauded Simon's "gift for the deliciously surprising line and attitude" and deemed his "instinct for incongruity . . . faultless" ("Odd Couple," 363). Whereas Simon's earlier plays had been considered frothy, though very funny, entertainment, for the first time Simon showed real depth and insight into the human condition—what Kerr called "interior truth" (untitled review 362). "This new seriousness behind the comedy, a technique he will develop further in later plays, heightened the humor and increased the breadth of audience appeal of the play" (Taubman, "Odd Couple," 364).

Simon himself was never altogether happy with the third act of *The Odd Couple* (McGovern, 3–4), which he revised several times during the tryout period (Johnson, 16). Though he conceived of the play as a black comedy (Linderman, 74), he wanted his characters to end happily. Johnson maintains that, short of violating verisimilitude by having Felix and Oscar undergo sudden reformation, a fully happy ending is really impossible, for Felix and Oscar are static characters—they have not changed those qualities in themselves that brought their troubles upon them (Johnson, 21). But close examination of the conclusion of the play reveals that each character has come to recognize and regret his role in his marital difficulties, particularly the sloppy Oscar, who can now speak politely to Blanche and who now insists his poker-playing friends use coasters.

In 1985, under the direction of Gene Saks, a female version of *The Odd Couple* was staged. Brendan Gill's negative response was similar to that voiced by most critics: he argued that poker games and sloppiness bear different weights of meaning for men and women and that attempts to "feminize" the details (e.g., substituting Trivial Pursuit for poker) were unsuccessful (78).

Simon's next Broadway offering was *The Star-Spangled Girl*, which opened 21 December 1966. In an interview with Kerr, Simon called this "the least successful play I've written" ("What Simon Says," 14). The central problem with the play was most memorably identified in Kerr's review, which opened thus: "Neil Simon . . . hasn't had an idea for a play this season, but he's gone and written one anyway" ("Star," 196). *The Star-Spangled Girl* is unsatisfying in virtually every respect—it has weak and predictable plotting, poor characterization, and forced, repetitious jokes. Only the first act was considered at all funny (Nadel, 222). Part of the problem, according to Kerr, was George Axelrod's direction, "particularly in the overwrought, undernourished second act. Mr. Axelrod is driving the whole droshky as though the wolves were after him and gaining steadily" ("Theatre . . . Star," 196).

With his next play, *Plaza Suite*, Simon resumed his customary success. Watts deemed him "currently our most brilliant writer of comedy" ("Hilarity," 346). This play, which opened 14 February 1968 under the direction of Mike Nichols, consists of three one-act plays with a common setting, a suite in the Plaza Hotel. The three playlets are united by their concern with the difficulty of obtaining or sustaining love. The first playlet, "Visitor from Mamaroneck," presents Karen and Sam, a middle-aged couple with marital problems who are celebrating their twenty-third anniversary; Karen unsuccessfully tries to rekindle their love. The couple in the next playlet, "Visitor from Hollywood," are Jesse, a Hollywood producer, and Muriel, his former high-school girlfriend, who is now an unhappily married housewife. Some of the credit for the success of "Hollywood" is due those who acted these roles, George C. Scott and Maureen Stapleton. The last play, "Visitors from Forest Hills," concerns the mother and father of a bride who has locked herself in her hotel bathroom, terrified lest her marriage turn out like her parents'.

In reviewing *Plaza Suite*, Kerr observed again that Simon was able to present a play with genuine insight and depth as well as humor. Kerr noted that, unfortunately, people tend to dismiss the work of a skilled comedy writer as fluff: "No man who can turn a laugh so readily, so unfailingly, so *compulsively* really, could possibly be mistaken for a serious craftsman" ("Simon's Funny," 347). Kerr was responding to a view of Simon advanced by critics such as Barnes. Regarding "Mamaroneck," which Kerr singled out for praise, Barnes expressed contempt: "[Simon] is at his worst when at his most serious," Barnes accused; his humor does "nothing to show any genuine insight" in any of the three "farces" that constitute this trilogy ("Theatre: Plaza Suite" 384). Barnes's reservations about form and characterization were shared by Gottfried: "I wouldn't call them one-act plays—they're barely sketches and are more nearly vaudeville routines" ("Plaza Suite" 349).

Simon's next play, *The Last of the Red Hot Lovers*, was directed by Robert Moore and opened 28 December 1969. *Lovers*—which consists again of a triad of one-acts—centers around the unsuccessful seduction attempts of Barney Cashman. Once again, Simon presents a male character in the throes of a midlife crisis. The play received strongly conflicting reviews. Barnes, who was impressed by the character of Barney, deemed it Simon's "most considerable achievement to date," remarking that Simon "is now controlling that special verbal razzle-dazzle that has at times seemed mechanically chill" ("Stage: Red Hot," 124). Watts found it "delightfully hilarious and witty," "genuinely brilliant," and praised this play, as Kerr had earlier work, for being "filled with the wisdom about human nature characteristic of all his work" (Watts, "Neil Simon," 125).

Not everyone responded to *Lovers* so favorably, however. Gottfried, for example, said the play was "a very inconsistent business, sometimes hysterically funny and sometimes shaky on its feet"; he attributed some of the weakness to a tendency to preach after the first act ("Last" 125). In a review titled "Why Do the Laughs Grow Fewer?" Kerr expressed disappointment with the repetitiousness of the scenes and the lack of a specific, sustained comic tone; "at the very best," he concluded, "it's so-so Simon" (126).

The darkest comedy Simon has produced to date comes next—*The Gingerbread Lady*, which presents an alcoholic woman reminiscent of Judy Garland. Directed by Robert Moore, the play opened 13 December 1970. Though some of the dialogue is humorous, the serious elements of the drama often overwhelm the comic. The play's central weakness, according to Kerr, "is the plainness of its outline. . . . We see not only what's being done, we see how" ("She is a Woman," 119). The characters lack depth and the plot lacks variation, he also maintains (119). Gottfried found it "weak in almost every way—trivial, plotless, characterless" ("Gingerbread," 121). Even the talents of Maureen Stapleton, who acted the lead role of Evy Meara, could not offset the play's many flaws.

Though *The Gingerbread Lady* was not in itself a success, it is evidence of a shift in Simon's comic orientation: from this point on, Simon strives for greater poignancy than he did in the earlier portion of his career. This movement toward seriousness is evident in his next comedy, *The Prisoner of Second Avenue*, which was directed by Mike Nichols and opened 11 November 1971. The pressures of contemporary life drive the protagonist, Mel, into depression and paranoia and, finally, into a nervous breakdown. In this play, the scope of Simon's concerns broadens beyond problems between family members and friends to those of urban life, such as the psychological consequences of unemployment, crime and the anonymity of city living. Simon's overreliance on one-liners persists, as do his failure to develop character fully and his tendency to set up jokes rather than construct plot. Once again, then, we are presented with a male protagonist caught in a midlife crisis; again Simon emphasizes the importance of marriage and family to emotional stability. The problems faced by Mel and his wife inhere in human nature rather than in living in New York; as McGovern suggests, "moving to another place won't necessarily alter or ameliorate the situation" (105).

Simon's next play, *The Sunshine Boys*, opened on 20 December 1972 with Alan Arkin as director. It was a substantial critical and popular success. Whereas Simon had, in earlier plays, presented the theme of aging (through middle-aged characters who resisted it), here, for the first time, he chose elderly protagonists. Al Lewis and Willie Clark are a once famous vaudeville team who have not been on speaking terms for years; Willie's nephew, Ben, persuades them to reunite for a television special. The central theme is the importance and difficulty of retaining human dignity in old age (McGovern, 109). The one-liners that flaw others of Simon's plays here function successfully as an aspect of characterization, for they echo vaudevillian speech patterns (Johnson, 64). The play is also unusually well structured (Johnson, 69). Gottfried suggested that *The Sunshine Boys* "demonstrates Simon's first discovery of a real reason to write a play—an appreciation of old-time comics— and his first creation of a real character—one of these comics" ("Sunshine," 135). Jack Kroll considered the play not merely a veneration of the past but "an apologia for Simon's own work: see, he is saying, my plays are vaudeville for our time" ("Exploring," 136).

Simon's concern with expanding his dramatic horizons is also evident in *The Good Doctor*, "his first straight play that did not have a New York setting or any New York characters" (Johnson 80). Directed by A. J. Antoon, *The Good Doctor* opened 11 December 1973. With this piece, Simon returns once more to the playlet format, here basing each of the sketches on one of Chekhov's short stories; by employing a metatheatrical structure, Simon circumvents the difficulty of structuring a single-focus full-length play: "two women and three men play all the roles, with one of the men doing both Narrator (and Writer) and, at times, various characters within the sketches" (McGovern 123). Moreover, the structure anticipates the self-reflexivity of Simon's later plays, the writing about writing evident in his most recent autobiographical trilogy.

The title of *The Good Doctor* refers simultaneously to Chekhov and to Simon himself, whose nickname is "Doc" (Johnson 80). Surprising as this collaboration might initially seem, Simon and Chekov are not incongruous playwrights—they share a comic world-view, employ a wide range of comic forms (from the very serious to the very farcical), and are tolerant of human folly despite their criticism of it (McGovern 123). Unfortunately, however, their talents are not combined well here. Simon, Gottfried said, "seems to have noticed only the superficial, sentimental elements of the stories. . . . He has not only drained Chekhov's (minor at that) stories of their subtlety and charm, but made the mistake of assuming that to gain seriousness he must lose his sense of humor" ("Neil Simon's," 157).

Simon's commitment to experimentation and growth is also apparent in his next play—*God's Favorite*, which was first presented on 11 December 1974. Michael Bennett directed this adaptation of the story of Job, one of Simon's least successful efforts. The main problems are Simon's choice and lack of development of characters, especially the protagonist's family; such weaknesses had also detracted from the effectiveness of *Prisoner, The Star-Spangled Girl,* and *Gingerbread Lady.* Unlike the Biblical Job, as McGovern points out, Joe Benjamin is discontented even before he undergoes his test of faith (139). Barnes felt Simon could have done a better job of defining this character, whom we see in embryo in his other plays (in *Prisoner*, especially): "When you think back, Job—with a slow burn of pain extinguishing the natural optimism of success—is an archetypal Simon character" ("Theatre: God's Favorite," 146). Simon included as characters neither God nor the inherently interesting and complex figure of Satan. Joe's greedy wife, another potentially interesting character, serves as little more than the locus for a running gag involving her rather unsavory interest in rapists. The most successful character is Sidney Lipton, the the messenger of God; with his poor eyesight, unhappy home life, and dissatisfaction with his job, he is complex and amusing. The play is further weakened by an excess of one-liners, and even these are not up to Simon's usual standard: characters repeat too often their own and each others' lines (Johnson, 87).

With *California Suite*, Simon resumes his position as a master of comedy. Appropriately this play, which is set in a Beverly Hills hotel, opened not in New York but at the Ahmanson Theatre in Los Angeles on 23 April 1976; two months later, it opened at the O'Neill in New York. Gene Saks directed both productions. Like *Plaza Suite, California Suite* consists of a series of comic one-acts; it, too, received mixed reviews despite its popular success. Although the four plays concern marriage and the family, they are not as tightly linked thematically as are those in *Plaza Suite*. And though all are funny, Simon alternates a farcical with a more serious playlet; the first and third comedies are the stronger and more sophisticated offerings (Barnes, "Stage: California Suite," 224).

The first, "Visitor from New York," presents Hannah and Bill Warren, a divorced couple who are meeting to debate who will obtain custody of their teenaged daughter. As McGovern suggests, the humor "depends almost entirely on the traditional rivalry which exists between New Yorkers and Angelenos, particularly the transplanted variety" (153). The one-liners do work here, as they fit Hannah's character; but though her lines are often very funny, there is real poignancy behind them. Hannah rather unkindly twits Bill for the affected casualness of his stereotypical "Southern California" lifestyle; he (more gently and more justly) accuses her of overintellectualized competitiveness and insincerity in the guise of sarcasm. When Bill recognizes the degree of her vulnerability and leaves the decision to her, Hannah relinquishes custody to him, then immediately resumes her abrasive mask as the playlet closes.

The second piece, "Visitors from Philadelphia," is a light farce in the manner of Feydeau (McGovern, 158). Awakening from a drunken sleep, Marvin Michaels finds the still-unconscious body of a hooker in his bed, a "gift" from his brother. A heretofore faithful husband, Marvin tries to remove, then conceal, the girl but is nevertheless discovered and, ultimately, forgiven by his wife, who plans to solace herself by buying expensive clothes in Beverly Hills.

With "Visitors from London," Simon returns to a more serious mood. The first half of the playlet presents Diana Nichols and her husband, Sidney, dressing for the Academy Awards; in the last half, Diana and Sidney have gotten drunk because she did not win Best Actress. Venting her spleen on Sidney, the insecure Diana targets her hostility on his homosexuality. Their exchanges are as clever as they are mutually painful. "Their normal mode of communication," as McGovern says, "[is] sharp, witty, high-comedy repartee—the kind of verbal exchange usually connected with characters created by Noel Coward" (163). Despite this verbal skirmish, Diana and Sidney will remain married, partly because each has a pragmatic interest in maintaining the union and partly because of their genuine mutual affection, their desire to help each other cope with their vulnerabilities.

Simon concludes *California Suite* with "Visitors From Chicago," a slapstick about two couples who have been on vacation together for three weeks and whose friendship is consequently endangered.

Chapter Two, Simon's next play, also opened first in Los Angeles (on 7 October 1977) and then, two months later, in New York. Simon calls this "the most autobiographical and the most painful play he has ever written" (McGovern, 171). In it are reflected his sorrow over the death of his beloved first wife, Joan Simon, and his guilt-filled courtship of and marriage to actress Marsha Mason. The play received mixed reviews: Barnes, for example, praised it ("Touching," 110), while Richard Eder objected to the subplot and found the character of Jennie unrealistic (108). The Leo and Faye subplot—a device Simon does not usually employ (McGovern 172)—is not integrated well into the main plot and contributes to the play's excessive length.

Simon's next effort, *I Ought to Be in Pictures*, which opened 3 April 1980, was even less successful. Libby Tucker visits Herb, the father who abandoned her sixteen years before. In the course of the play, Libby solves virtually all Herb's personal and professional problems; she is, as one may gather, a highly idealized character. Kerr finds her naivete about life in general, especially about sex, utterly unconvincing; he found the play "pallid" and compared it, with its simplistic sentimentality, to an Andy Hardy movie ("New Neil Simon," 292). One of the weakest scenes is that in which Libby asks her father questions about sex appropriate to a much younger girl; one of the few critics to praise this scene was Barnes, who found not only this but the entire play "terrific" ("Simon Turns," 295). Even those critics who find merit in the characterization do not think Herb sufficiently well drawn. As Johnson argued, Herb is insufficiently introspective—though he recognizes that his inability to write is related to his fear of emotional commitment, he never examines this conflict in detail, and his recovery thus seems facile and contrived (125).

Simon's next play, *Fools*, was one of his least successful; it opened 7 April 1981 under the direction of Mike Nichols. *Fools* focusses on a mythological Ukrainian village, all of whose inhabitants are cursed by stupidity; an outsider, the intelligent, educated protagonist, Leon, falls in love with Sophia, one of the stupid village girls. Leon decides to stay and risk the curse, which warns that anyone who remains in the village more than twenty-four hours will himself become stupid. Johnson suggests that here, as in *Chapter Two* and *Pictures*, Simon "attacks the negative, hobbling effect of guilt" and reprises the theme of the importance of self-respect (130); though Johnson saw some merit in the play, he thought it flawed by a sluggish plot and by unconvincing, repetitious characterization (131). *Fools* is clearly derivative of two successful musicals, *Fiddler on the Roof* and *Brigadoon*; in his review, T. E. Kalem renames the village "Anatevka-cum-Brigadoon" (294). There is plenty of visual and verbal humor, but *Fools* is essentially a one-joke play, "stupidity at its most obvious and least amusing," and the joke wears thin rather quickly (Barnes, "Fools," 295).

With *Brighton Beach Memoirs*, which opened to mixed reviews 27 March 1983, Simon comes full circle: as in *Come Blow Your Horn*, he employs memories of his family as an autobiographical basis for the action. The play is set in Brooklyn during the 1940s. The hero, Eugene, is a fifteen-year-old aspiring writer modeled closely, if self-indulgently, on Simon himself. We again encounter themes familiar in Simon's play—sibling rivalry, parent-child relationships, the importance of human dignity—and they are presented with warmth and humor. For the first time, Simon's characters are explicitly Jewish, and he reveals once more his gift for blending poignancy and humor. Barnes praised the especially well wrought scene in which Eugene's cousin describes the meaning her deceased father's coat pockets held for her ("Memoirs," 345). But, as Barnes also suggested, this play "showed Simon's limitations almost as clearly as his virtues": "He never pushes beyond pain. He always shrugs deprecatingly, makes a slight Jewish joke and hides his heart behind his well-tailored sleeve" ("Memoirs," 345). Eugene is also not a wholly successful character; Frank Rich found him "so saintly and resilient [that] he becomes elusive and opaque—a vacuum where the play's sensitive center should be" ("Stage: Neil Simon's," 344). After comparing this play unfavorably with Marsha Norman's *'night, Mother*, Kroll identified *Brighton's* central weakness—that the playwright omitted or sugar-coated the dark truth of his life ("Simon Says Laugh," 348). Rich also accused Simon of "papering over the rough edges of the lives in view" ("Stage: Neil Simon's" 344). In both plot and characterization, Simon withdraws, using facile resolutions.

Biloxi Blues, which opened 28 March 1985, was essentially a continuation of *Brighton Beach Memoirs*. We now meet Eugene as a member of the 1943 wartime army who must contend with such serious issues as antisemitism and homophobia. The reviewers split in their judgements of this play: Rich thought this a much more honest play than its predecessor ("Biloxi," 322), but Kroll refused to accept the "phantom virtues" other critics saw in either play, finding Simon's more recent effort "thin stuff," a formulaic army comedy that waxed sentimental over serious isssues ("Simon Says Laugh . . . Cry," 327). Barnes would later deem this the weakest in the trilogy ("Simon Says," 117).

The third and most successful play in this series is *Broadway Bound*, which opened in December of 1986. Barnes suggested that this play's form resembles that of a Williams memory play more than that of a traditional comedy ("Simon Says," 118). Simon's most significant achievement here is the creation of Kate, the mother; unlike his past heroines, who were "either sentimentalized or caricatured" (Rich, "Broadway," 112), she is real and moving, especially in the scene in which she recalls the high point of her life—having once danced with George Raft.

SURVEY OF SECONDARY SOURCES

Bibliography

Listings of primary and secondary works concerning the plays of Neil Simon are available in *Contemporary Authors, Contemporary Dramatists, Critical Survey of Drama, Crowell's Handbook of Contemporary Drama, Twentieth-Century Dramatists, Part Two* (Vol. 7 of *The Dictionary of Literary Biography*), *Notable Names in the American Theatre*, and *Who's Who in the Theatre: A Biographical Record of the Contemporary Stage*.

Biography

Although no full-length biography of Neil Simon is available, details of Simon's biography are offered by McGovern and Johnson and may be gleaned from the interviews and reference works listed above.

Influence

As is evident in *The Sunshine Boys*, Simon owes much of the style and form of his comedy to the vaudeville, movie and radio comics of the first half of this century and to his experience in television writing. Johnson, for example, finds echoes of the work of Charlie Chaplin, Buster Keaton, Laurel and Hardy, Jackie Gleason, Phil Silvers, and Sid Caeser (139). In her "Overview" (6–12), McGovern also finds in his work the influence of the work and tradition of Jonson, Moliere, Shaw, Yeats, and Feydeau. Beaufort sees in *Fools* traces of Lewis Carroll, Sholom Aleichem, the

Marx Brothers, and W. S. Gilbert (293). Simon's own influence may be seen in television comedy such as Norman Lear's *All in the Family*, which treats serious issues with a blend of comedy and poignancy. On Broadway, he is to be credited with keeping alive the tradition of the well crafted realistic play, for helping preserve the genre playwrights such as Marsha Norman and Beth Henley would employ in a more overtly literary style.

Analyses of Individual Plays

Simon's own plays have received very little scholarly attention: at present, virtually nothing has been done except for the book-length studies by McGovern and Johnson. Given the proliferation of scholarly activity in recent years, one wonders why this is so, for Simon's work merits closer examination. His experimentation with form and characterization in plays such as *God's Favorite, The Good Doctor,* and *Fools* attests to the seriousness with which Simon approaches his art, to his desire to be considered more than the creator of formulaic popular comedies.

Why, then, have scholars turned elsewhere? Perhaps because of Simon's persistent difficulties with plot and his habit of lapsing into one-liners; perhaps because each of Simon's experiments has thus far failed; or perhaps because of prejudice on the part of scholars against Simon for having written comedies that were popular with the public and financially successful. (*Real* artists, many scholars implicitly believe, are never appreciated by the masses, nor do they ever profit by their labors: we shall know them by their anonymity and poverty.) Thus, the very real shortcomings of Simon's plays and the unconscious but equally real prejudice of the academy render him vulnerable to easy dismissal by scholars in search of more "serious" drama.

An excellent starting point for those interested in studying Simon's work is Loney's overview in *Contemporary Dramatists*. One might then turn to the pioneering study done by Edythe McGovern, which offers detailed summaries of the plays through *Chapter Two;* each summary is accompanied by information about performance history and brief but insightful commentary. Preceding her own text is "Notes from the Playwright," the only essay Simon has thus far published. In it he gives his own impression of his plays in specific terms. Certainly required reading for any Simon scholar is Robert Johnson's more recent book, which examines the plays through *Fools*. Johnson offers careful, perceptive analyses of each play, drawing appropriate and often subtle links between them. His annotated bibliography (149–50), though brief, is well worth consulting.

FUTURE RESEARCH OPPORTUNITIES

Given the paucity of scholarship on Simon, a substantial number of research opporunities exist. Foremost among these are a scholarly biography of Simon and studies comparing the realities of that biography with his dramatic presentation of it. An examination of his transformation of his dramas into screenplays is also long overdue, as are source studies supplementing McGovern's work. An annotated bibliography supplementing Johnson's is absolutely necessary. At least a few critical articles need to discuss ethnicity in Simon's more recent plays, comparing his drama with that of other playwrights concerned with their Jewish heritage—Israel Horovitz, David Mamet, or Clifford Odets, for example. Or one might consider language games in the plays, or themes such as male (or female) mid-life crises, or Simon's use of time and memory. Also needed is a study of the plays as performances, the various effects of specific directorial and casting choices. A fashionable topic one might pursue is self-reflexivity, that is, a writer's writing about being a writer: *The Good Doctor, I Ought to Be in Pictures*, and Simon's autobiographical trilogy obviously lend themselves to such treatment.

SECONDARY SOURCES

Barnes, Clive. " 'Fools' Die—Or Should." *New York Post* (7 April 1981). In *New York Theatre Critics' Reviews* (1981): 295.

———. " 'Memoirs' is Simon's Best Play." *New York Post* (28 March. 1983). In *New York Theatre Critics' Reviews* (1983): 345.

———. *"Simon Says: This is Life."* *New York Post* (5 December 1986). In *New York Theatre Critics' Reviews* (1986): 117–18.

———. "Simon Turns Out Terrific 'Picture.' " *New York Post* (4 April 1980). In *New York Theatre Critics' Reviews* (1980): 295.

———. "Stage: 'California Suite Opens.' " *New York Times* (22 June 1976). In *New York Theatre Critics' Reviews* (1976): 224–25.

———. "Stage: 'Red Hot Lovers.' " *New York Times* (12 December 1969). In *New York Theatre Critics' Reviews* (1969): 124.

———. "Theatre: 'God's Favorite,' New Simon." *New York Times* (12 December 1974). In *New York Theatre Critics' Reviews* (1974): 146.

———. "Theatre: Neil Simon Play." *New York Times.* (14 December 1970). In *New York Theatre Critics' Reviews* (1970): 120.

———. "Theatre: 'Plaza Suite,' Neil Simon's Laugh Machine." *New York Times* (15 February 1968). In *New York Theatre Critics' Reviews* (1968): 348.

———. "A Touching Play Tiptoes on the Heart." *New York Post* (5 December 1977). In *New York Theatre Critics' Reviews* (1977): 110.

Beaufort, John. "From Neil Simon, a Fairy-Tale Farce?" *Christian Science Monitor* (8 April 1981). In *New York Theatre Critics' Reviews* (1981): 293.

Coleman, Robert. " 'Blow Your Horn' a Funny Show." *New York Mirror* (23 February 1961). In *New York Theatre Critics' Reviews* (1961): 358.

Eder, Richard. "For Neil Simon, 'It's Chapter Two.' " *New York Times* (5 December 1977). In *New York Theatre Critics' Reviews* 1977: 108.

Gill, Brendan. "Self-Sabotage." *New Yorker* (24 June 1985): 78.

Gottfried, Martin. " 'The Gingerbread Lady' . . . Trivial, plotless, characterless." *Women's Wear Daily* (15 December 1970). In *New York Theatre Critics' Reviews* 1970: 121.

———. "Last of the Red Hot Lovers." *Women's Wear Daily* (29 December 1969). In *New York Theatre Critics' Reviews* (1969): 125.

———. "Neil Simon's 'The Good Doctor.' " *Women's Wear Daily (29 November 1973). In New York Theatre Critics' Reviews* (1973): 157

———. "Plaza Suite." *Women's Wear Daily* (15 February 1968). In *New York Theatre Critics' Reviews* (1968): 349

———. "The Star Spangled Girl." *Women's Wear Daily* (22 December 1966). In *New York Theatre Critics' Reviews* (1966): 194.

———. "The Sunshine Boys." (22 December 1972). In *New York Theatre Critics' Reviews* (1972): 135.

———. Untitled Review of *Prisoner. Women's Wear Daily* (15 November 1971). In *New York Theatre Critics' Reviews* (1971): 192.

Johnson, Robert K. *Neil Simon*. Boston: Twayne, 1983

Kalem T. E. "Nudniks." *Time* (20 April 1981). In *New York Theatre Crritics' Reviews* (1981): 294.

Kerr, Walter. " 'Come Blow your Horn.' " *New York Herald Tribune* (23 February 1961). In *New York Theatre Critics' Reviews* (1961): 357.

———. "The New Neil Simon Comedy." *New York Times* (4 April 1980). In *New York Theatre Critics' Reviews* (1980): 292.

———. "She is a Woman Who Drinks, and That is That." *New York Times* (20 December 1970). In *New York Theatre Critics' Reviews* (1970): 119–20.

———. "Simon's Funny—Don't Laugh." *New York Times* (18 February 1968). In *New York Theatre Crittics' Reviews* (1968): 347.

———. "The Theatre: Neil Simon's 'Star Spangled Girl.' " *New York Times* (22 December 1966). In *New York Theatre Critics' Reviews* (1966): 196.

———. Untitled Review of *The Odd Couple. New York Herald Tribune* (11 March 1965). In *New York Theatre Critics' Reviews* (1965): 363.

———. "Walter Kerr Reviews 'Barefoot in the Park.' " *New York Herald Tribune* (24 October 1963). In *New York Theatre Critics' Reviews* (1963): 222.

———. "What Simon Says." *New York Times Magazine* (22 March 1970): 6, 12, 14, 16.

———. "Why Do The Laughs Grow Fewer?" *New York Times* (4 July 1970): In *New York Theatre Critics' Reviews* (1970): 126.

Kroll, Jack. "Exploring Lewis and Clark." *Newsweek* (1 January 1973): In *New York Theatre Critics' Reviews* (1973): 136.

———. "Simon Says Laugh." *Newsweek* (11 April 1983). In *New York Theatre Critics' Reviews* (1983): 348.

———. "Simon Says Laugh, Simon Says Cry." *Newsweek* (29 March 1985). In *New York Theatre Critics' Reviews* (1985): 327.

Linderman, Lawrence. "Playboy Interview: Neil Simon." *Playboy* (26 February 1979): 58 + .

Loney, Glenn. "Neil Simon." In *Contemporary Dramatists*. Fourth Edition, pp. 484–86. Edited by D. L Kirkpatrick. Chicago: St. James Press, 1988.

McGovern, Edythe M. *Neil Simon: A Critical Study*. New York: Ungar, 1979.

Nadel, Norman. " 'Barefoot in the Park' Due for a Long, Long Run." *New York World-Telegram and The Sun* (24 October 1963). In *New York Theatre Critics' Reviews* (1963): 222.

———. " 'Star-Spangled Girl' Funny—For One Act." *World Journal Tribune* (22 December 1966). In *New York Theatre Critics' Reviews* (1966): 196.

Rich Frank. "Simons 'Broadway Bound.' " *New York Times* (5 December 1986). In *New York Theatre Critics' Reviews* (1986): 112–13

———. "Stage: 'Biloxi Blues,' Neil Simon's New Comedy." *New York Times* (29 March. 1985). In *New York Theatre Critics' Reviews* (1985): 322.

———. "Stage: Neil Simon's 'Brighton Beach.' " *New York Times* (28 March 1983). In *New York Theatre Critics' Reviews* (1983): 344.

Taubman Howard. "Bubbling Comedy." *New York Times* (24 October 1963). In *New York Theatre Critics' Reviews* (1963): 223.

———. " 'Come Blow Your Horn' by Neil Simon Opens." *New York Times* (23 February 1961). In *New York Theatre Critics' Reviews* (1961): 356

———. "Theatre: Neil Simon's 'Odd Couple.' " *New York Times* (11 March 1965). In *New York Theatre Critics' Reviews* (1965): 363–64.

Watts, Richard, Jr. "A Comedy of Two Rebellious Brothers." *New York Post* (23 February 1961). In *New York Theatre Critics' Reviews* (1961): 356.

———. "Hilarity in a Hotel Suite." *New York Post* (15 February 1968). In *New York Theatre Critics' Reviews* (1968): 346.

———. "Neil Simon Comes Through Again." *New York Post* (29 December 1969). In *New York Theatre Critics' Reviews* (1969): 292.

Stephen Sondheim

(22 MARCH 1930–)

KATHLEEN SULLIVAN

ASSESSMENT OF SONDHEIM'S REPUTATION

Stephen Sondheim's lyrics and scores have revolutionized the musical. His probing lyrics have moved the musical away from escapist art. Sondheim's works explore the difficulty of commitment, the disillusionment of lost dreams, the obsession of vengeance, the collapse of values, and the artist's struggle for integrity. Sondheim frequently abandons the linear plot and unifies the musical through theme. His creation of intricate word play, wit, and parody distinguishes his lyrics. Commenting on Sondheim's lyrics, Shevelove asserted that Sondheim is "the first and perhaps the only true theatre lyricist we have" (quoted in Locher, 482). His break with traditional melodic and rhythmic structures has also heightened the dramatic power of the musical. While his songs often develop character, they also comment on the action of the scene. The winner of four Tony Awards, three New York Drama Critics Circle Awards, and the recipient of the Pulitzer Prize for Drama, Sondheim has enlarged the possibilities of the musical.

PRIMARY BIBLIOGRAPHY OF SONDHEIM'S WORKS

Musicals

West Side Story. Lyrics by Stephen Sondheim. Music by Leonard Bernstein. Book by Arthur Laurents. New York: Random House, 1958. Original cast recording, Columbia Records. OS 2001.

Gypsy. Lyrics by Stephen Sondheim. Music by Jule Styne. Book by Arthur Laurents. New York: Random House, 1960. Original Broadway cast recording, Columbia Records OS 2017.

A Funny Thing Happened on the Way to the Forum. Music and lyrics by Stephen Sondheim. Book by Burt Shevelove and Larry Gelbart. New York: Burthen Music Co., 1964.

Do I Hear a Waltz? Lyrics by Stephen Sondheim. Music by Richard Rodgers. Libretto by Arthur Laurents, 1965. Original Broadway cast recording, Columbia Records AKOS 2770.

Company. Music and lyrics by Stephen Sondheim. Book by George Furth. New York: Random House, 1970. Original Broadway cast recording, Columbia Records OS 3550.

Follies. Music and lyrics by Stephen Sondheim. Book by James Goldman. New York: Random House, 1971. Original Broadway cast recording Capitol Records SO 761.

Candide. Lyrics by Stephen Sondheim and John Latouchi. Music by Leonard Bernstein. Libretto adapted from Voltaire by Hugh Wheeler, 1973.

A Little Night Music. Music and lyrics by Stephen Sondheim. Book by Hugh Wheeler. New York: Dodd, Mead, 1974. Original Broadway cast recording, RCA Victor Records KS 32265.

Anyone Can Whistle. Music and lyrics by Stephen Sondheim. Book by Arthur Laurents. New York: L. Amiel, 1976. Original Broadway cast recording, Columbia Records KOS 2480.

Pacific Overtures. Music and Lyrics by Stephen Sondheim. Book by John Weidman. New York: Dodd, Mead, 1977. Original Broadway cast recording, RCA Victor Records ARL 1 1367.

Sweeney Todd. Music and lyrics by Stephen Sondheim. Book by Hugh Wheeler. New York: Dodd, Mead, 1979. Original Broadway cast recording, RCA Victor Records CBL 2 3379.

Merrily We Roll Along Music and lyrics by Stephen Sondheim. Libretto by George Furth, 1981. Original Broadway Cast recording, RCA Victor Records CBLI 4197.

Frogs. Music and lyrics by Stephen Sondheim. Book by Burt Shevelove. New York: Dodd, Mead, 1985.

Sunday in the Park with George. Music and Lyrics by Stephen Sondheim. Book by James Lapine. New York: Dodd, Mead, 1986. Original Broadway cast recording, RCA Victor Records HBCI 5042.

Films

Topper. Written by Stephen Sondheim. NBC, 1953.

The Last Word. Written by Stephen Sondheim. CBS, 1956.

Evening Primrose. Music and Lyrics by Stephen Sondheim. ABC, 1966.

The Last of Sheila. Written by Stephen Sondheim and Anthony Perkins. A Warner Bros. Presentation of a Herbert Ross film, 1973.

Stavisky. Music and lyrics by Stephen Sondheim. Cerito Films, 1974.

The Seven Percent Solution. Music and lyrics by Stephen Sondheim. Universal Pictures, 1977.

Reds. Music and lyrics by Stephen Sondheim. Paramount, 1981.

Interviews

Kresh, Paul. "Stephen Sondheim Talks to Paul Kresh about the Future of American Musical Comedy." *Stereo Review* (July 1971): 73–74.

Savran, David. "Stephen Sondheim." *In Their Own Words: Contemporary American Playwrights*, pp. 223–39. New York: Theatre Communications Group, 1988.

Essays

"Theatre Lyrics." *Dramatists Guild Quarterly* 8, no. 3 (1971): 6–36.
"The Musical Theatre." *Dramatists Guild Quarterly* 15, no. 3 (1978): 6–27.
"Larger Than Life: Reflections on Melodrama and Sweeney Todd." In *Melodrama*, pp. 3–14. Edited by Daniel Gerould. New York: New York Literary Forum, 1980.

PRODUCTION HISTORY

Sondheim's musicals have been produced twenty-two times, with most of the shows originating on Broadway. The eleven revivals have included Broadway and off-Broadway theatres and London's West End. On 26 September 1957, *West Side Story* opened at the Winter Garden. The reviewers applauded the collaboration of composer Leonard Bernstein, director and choreographer Jerome Robbins, librettist Arthur Laurents, and lyricist Stephen Sondheim. McClain summarized the critics' responses: "There has never been a happier integration, a more sensitive blending of story, song and movement" (254). Although the 1968 revival at Lincoln Center disappointed the critics, the 1961 film, starring Natalie Wood, won eleven Academy Awards, including Best Picture of the year.

Gypsy, starring Ethel Merman, opened at the Broadway Theatre on 21 May 1959. Critics enthusiastically supported the musical as they celebrated the performance of the leading lady. Atkinson proclaimed: "Since Ethel Merman is the lead woman in *Gypsy* . . . nothing can go wrong. She would not permit *Gypsy* to be anything less than the most satisfying musical of the season" (31). The 1963 motion picture, starring Natalie Wood, however, proved disastrous. Angela Lansbury's performance in the London and Broadway revivals renewed the public's support of the musical.

After *Gypsy*, Sondheim received his first opportunity to write both the lyrics and the music. *A Funny Thing Happened on the Way to the Forum* received excellent reviews despite a disastrous preshow run. The 1972 Broadway revival, starring Phil Silvers, received even better reviews than the original show. The motion picture version of *Forum*, cast with the original leading man, Zero Mostel, failed at the box office. Changes in script and internal conflict doomed the film.

The major critics detested Sondheim's next show, *Anyone Can Whistle*. Opening on 4 April 1964 at the Majestic Theatre, the show closed eight performances later. The *New York Times's* hostile criticism jeopardized the musical's survival. "There is no law against saying something in a musical," wrote Taubman, "but it's unconstitutional to omit imagination and wit" (36).

Collaborating with composer Richard Rodgers, Sondheim wrote the lyrics for the 1965 musical *Do I Hear a Waltz?* Reviewers deplored the show's music. Sondheim was spared assault and even received a Tony nomination for best lyrics.

Sondheim established his reputation as an outstanding lyricist and composer with his 1970 musical, *Company*. This show marked the beginning of his long and fruitful collaboration with Harold Prince. Critics recognized the originality of the musical, though several disliked the show. Kerr admitted that "Sondheim has never written a more sophisticated, more pertinent or—...more melodious scores" but conceded, "I didn't like the show" ("Company," B:1). Watt however, argued that the show balanced innovation and sensitivity: "It is Broadway's first musical treatment of nerve ends.... But Sondheim's songs, while equally scintillating, shine through time and again with a welcome and essential warmth" (p. 260). The show received the New York Drama Critics Circle Award for Best Musical and the Tony Awards for Best Musical and Best Lyrics. Closing after twenty months, *Company* went to London, receiving some of the best reviews ever written by the British critics.

A diversity of opinion greeted Sondheim's next work, *Follies*, which opened at the Winter Garden on 4 April 1971. *Follies* impressed some with its poignant theme and tragic characters and dazzled others with its theatricalities. Several critics, however, were bored with the show: "Follies is intermissionless and exhausting, an extravaganza that becomes tedious," reported Kerr ("Yes, Yes, Alexis!"). Kalem disagreed with the derogatory comments: "Rarely have such searching unsentimental questions and answers been put to a Broadway audience with such elegance and expertise" (78). Although *Follies* earned the Drama Critics Circle Award as Best Musical of the Year and Tony Awards for Best Music and Best Lyrics, the show closed after a year's run at a loss of its entire investment.

On 25 February 1973, *A Little Night Music* opened at the Shubert Theatre. Barnes proclaimed Sondheim's achievement: "Yet perhaps the real triumph belongs to Stephen Sondheim who wrote the music and lyrics. People have long been talking about Mr. Prince's conceptual musicals; now I feel I have actually seen one of the actual concepts.... Good God!—an adult musical!" (26). On 8 March 1978, a movie starring Elizabeth Taylor as Desiree received a bombardment of fatal reviews. Sondheim admitted, "I never wanted the movie made because I didn't think it would translate well onto the screen" (Zadan, 199).

Pacific Overtures' Broadway opening on 11 January 1976 elicited divergent responses. Gottfried championed Sondheim's score since it "places him at the very pinnacle of American stage composers and entirely apart from conventional theater songwriters" (389). Others complained that the hybrid musical was atonal and the story uninteresting. The 1984 off-Broadway revival fared significantly better with the critics since the Japanese influence was diluted and the acting was more personal. Prior to the 1976 Broadway closing, the show was videotaped for a Japanese television network, making it the first telecast of an American stage musical in that country.

Sweeney Todd, Sondheim's most acclaimed work, appeared on Broadway 1 March 1979. Beaufort heralded the score: "A dazzling achievement of variety and invention" (16). Certain critics debated the genre of the work—musical or opera; others discussed the morality of the play, but nearly all agreed that the score was Sondheim's greatest success and the production a triumph of Prince's directing skills. Angela Lansbury and Len Cariou also reaped lavish praise. The musical won eight out of nine of its nominated Tony Awards, including Best Musical, Best Score, Best Book, and Best Director. Lansbury and George Hearn starred in an outstanding videotaped performance of the musical, and the New City Opera repertoire performed *Sweeney Todd* in 1984.

After the success of *Sweeney Todd*, Sondheim's 1981 debut of *Merrily We Roll Along* failed dismally. Critics complained of the backward plot, the mundane theme, and the stale music. After only sixteen performances, the play closed.

Sunday in the Park with George introduced Sondheim to a new team of collaborators, most importantly to director James Lapine. The show's Broadway opening on 2 May 1984 received mixed reviews. The support by the *New York Times* enabled the musical to have a successful run. "What I do know is that Mr. Sondheim and Mr. Lapine have created an audacious, haunting and, in its own intensely personal way, touching work," wrote Rich ("Sunday in the Park," 21). Brustein praised the musical for its experimentation but complained that if "*Sunday in the Park with George* had been a musical piece exclusively concerned with the execution of painting on stage, it would have been a masterpiece. In its present inflated form, it is merely a handsome, pleasing, if occasionally meretricious entertainment" (25–26). Although the musical received the 1985 Pulitzer Price for Drama, it lost 25 percent of its $24 million investment.

SURVEY OF SECONDARY SOURCES

Bibliographies

No bibliography of Sondheim exists.

Biographies

Zadan offers the most comprehensive biographical material. Its composite of interviews illuminates the history and accomplishment of Stephen Sondheim. Locher provides a brief but in-depth overview of Sondheim's musicals, lists of awards, songs, recordings, and an insightful analysis of each play by referencing comments to the critics and Sondheim's interviews (479–85). Hitchcock and Sadie sketch Sondheim's adolescence and highlight the composer-lyricist's accomplishments through his most recent musicals (258–60). The biographical material of Sondheim's early musical training originates from "Stephen "Sondheim: Theatre Lyrics." Sondheim's talk on lyrics includes his anecdotal account of Hammerstein's impact on the young musician (6–8). The *New York Times Biographical Service* provides a few pieces of information not mentioned in other sources. "The Words and Music of Stephen Sondheim" incorporates original interview material and a chronological development of Sondheim's lyrics and music (548–56).

Influences

Critics have not identified the influences on Sondheim's work, nor have they investigated Sondheim's influence on contemporary composers or lyricists. Sondheim, however, does speak of those musicians and writers who have shaped his art: Oscar Hammerstein, Shevelove, and Laurents ("Stephen Sondheim: Theatre Lyrics"). He also acknowledges his debt to Harold Arlen, Jerome Kern, Cole Porter, Yip Harburg, Dorothy Fields, and Frank Loesser ("Words and Music of Stephen Sondheim"). Both Adler and Hirst point to a thematic similarity between Stephen Sondheim and Edward Albee.

General Studies

Zadan explores Sondheim's musical achievements by effectively linking the interview material of Sondheim and the producers, directors, librettists, and actors of the shows. Zadan discusses Sondheim in the context of the musical performance, with each of the primary chapters chronologically exploring a major work and the transitional chapters explaining a particular element of the overall production. The primary chapters successfully discuss the origins and development of a Sondheim musical and the problems unique to a production and include an edited reprint of significant reviews. Zadan's appendixes provide all pertinent information about Sondheim's productions and his recordings.

Adams's useful dissertation explores how Sondheim's lyrics function as structural devices, reveal characters, and enhance thematic development. Adams also identifies Sondheim's accomplishments by tracing the development of the American musical and provides a comprehensive overview of the critics' reaction to the work, a lengthy plot summary and an in-depth analysis of the lyrics.

Sheren and Sutcliffe also explore the lyrics of Stephen Sondheim. Unlike Adams, these critics classify Sondheim as poet: "Sondheim's poems, although they are merely more specific in their dramatic intention than lyric poetry was historically, are among the most interesting and cleverest products of the modern tradition" (194). Sheren and Sutcliffe effectively cite examples from an array of Sondheim musicals to demonstrate his cleverness with images, his verbal wit, intriguing characters, and the tension and uncertainty characteristic of his music. These critics highlight the achievements of *West Side Story, Gypsy, Anyone Can Whistle, Company, Follies*, and *A Little Night Music*.

Exploring Sondheim's work through generic, formalistic, and thematic approaches, Adler argues that while critics recognize the influence of the musical's heritage on Sondheim, they ignore the impact of the non-musical on the artist. Adler also compares Sondheim's dramatic technique to that of Brecht and relates Sondheim's thematic concerns to O'Neill's and Albee's to show "the qualitative difference between him and nearly every other writer for the American musical stage" (521). In his analysis of *A Little Night Music, Company, Follies, Pacific Overtures, Anyone Can Whistle*, and *Do I Hear a Waltz?* Adler argues that Sondheim has revolutionized the musical by creating songs that move beyond plot and character development.

Focusing on theme, Hirst effectively traces the history of the musical by analyzing its treatment of the American dream. *Gypsy, Anyone Can Whistle, Company, Follies* reflect Sondheim's refusal to "enhance the optimism and belief in American values which characterized the United States in the immediate Post War period through the early 1960's" (26).

Mordden concludes *Broadway Babies* with an overview of Sondheim's musicals. Mordden's pointed language captures Sondheim's accomplishments and failures. His assessment includes Sondheim's more recent works—*Pacific Overtures, Side by Side, Sweeney Todd*, and *Merrily We Roll Along*. Characterizing a Sondheim show as the blending of tradition and innovation, Mordden identifies Sondheim's later works as the "most influential shows in the American musical at present" (185).

While contemporary critics recognize Sondheim's contributions to the musical, Lahr attacks Sondheim's works, labeling him the "laureate of disillusion." Lahr complains that Sondheim's characters lack depth since they exist as numbed survivors (10). After reviewing Sondheim's musicals through *Merrily We Roll Along*, Lahr concludes that Sondheim's music suffers from "a lack of heart . . . his real nemesis" (18). This imbalanced assessment of Sondheim concludes with Lahr's outrageous reading of *Sweeney Todd:* "The show justifies Sondheim's flexing his misanthropic muscle" (20).

Two collections that discuss popular songwriters acknowledge Sondheim's talent. White provides a short history of Sondheim's musicals through *Sweeney Todd*, and Suskin lists data on the individual songs.

Analyses of Individual Plays

While critics have investigated Sondheim's collective works, few scholars have extensively explored the individual musicals. Zadan analyzes Sondheim's individual musicals through a performance approach. Zadan along with others has analyzed *Company*, Sondheim's first award-winning musical. While Zadan highlights the reflections of director Hal Prince, choreographer Michael Bennett, and Stephen Sondheim on issues of production, staging, casting, and choice of music, other critics explore lyrics, style, and theme. Berkowitz argues that the paradox inherent in the lyrics and music of *Company* characterizes the protagonist's struggle to comprehend the inevitable paradox of fulfillment and loneliness in marriage (94–100). Frankel scrutinizes the lyrics of *Company* according to principles of effective lyric writing (123–38). By analyzing the lyrics in *Company*, Adams identifies the thematic concerns of the work, the correlation between theme and lyric, the function of song in *Company*, and Sondheim's effective use of ambiguity, contradiction, and ironic juxtaposition (126–34). Wilson provides a highly technical study of the musical unity in *Company*.

Sweeney Todd has also attracted a handful of studies. Sondheim's own discussion provides insights into genre, character portrayal, staging, theme, and musical composition ("Reflections of Melodrama and *Sweeney Todd*," 3–11). Blyton details the musical accomplishments of the work. Lahr's analysis asserts that Sondheim sanctions vengeance and damns human goodness (5–21). Zadan's study highlights the challenges of creating a sympathetic Sweeney Todd and Mrs. Lovett and explains Sondheim's musical innovations.

FUTURE RESEARCH OPPORTUNITIES

While critics analyze Sondheim's singular accomplishments as lyricist and composer, they ignore his influence on contemporary musicals and plays. Research needs to explore the impact of his nonescapist musicals on the American musical and theatre. In particular, how has Sondheim's nonlinear plot influenced the structure of contemporary plays? In what ways has Sondheim's break with traditional lyrics affected the language of modern playwrights? Though critics have nodded at the similarity in theme between Sondheim's and Albee's work, further study should explore the relationship of Sondheim's music and Albee's dramatic structure. Since Albee insists that his drama is structured according to musical composition, Sondheim's disturbing musicals, akin in theme to the playwright's works, may have influenced the dramatic structure of an Albee play.

SECONDARY SOURCES

Adams, M. C. "The Lyrics of Stephen Sondheim: Form and Function." Ph.D. dissertation, Northwestern University, 1980.

Adler, Thomas P. "The Musical Dramas of Stephen Sondheim: Some Critical Approaches." *Journal of Popular Culture* 12 (1978–1979): 513–25.

Atkinson, Brooks. "Theatre: Good Show!" *New York Times* (22 May 1959): 31.

Barnes, Clive. "*A Little Night Music.*" *New York Times* (26 February 1973): 26.

Beaufort, John. "Grand Guignol to Music." *Christian Science Monitor* (7 March 1979): 16.

Berkowitz, Gerald. "The Metaphor of Paradox in Sondheim's *Company.*" *West Virginia Philological Papers* 25 (February 1979): 94–100.

Blyton, Carey. "Sondheim's 'Sweeney Todd'—The Case for the Defence." *Tempo* 149 (1984): 19–26.

Brustein, Robert. "Monday on the Stage with the Steve." *New Republic* (18 June 1984): 25–26.

Frankel, Aaron. *Writing the Broadway Musical.* New York: Drama Book Specialists, 1977.

Freedman, Samuel G. "The Words and Music of Stephen Sondheim." *New York Times Biographical Service* (April 1984): 548–56.

Gottfried, Martin. "Overtures—A Remarkable Work of Theater Art." *New York Post* (12 January 1976). Reprinted in *New York Theatre Critics' Reviews* (1976): 389–90.

Hirst, D. "The American-Musical and the American Dream, from 'Show Boat' to Sondheim." *New Theater Quarterly,* no. 1 (1985): 24–38.

Hitchcock, H. Wiley, and Stanley Sadie, eds. *New Grove Dictionary of American Music* 4 (1986): 258–60.

Kalem, T. E. "Seascape with Frieze of Girls." *Time* (12 April 1971): 78.

Kerr, Walter, " 'Company': Original and Uncompromising." *New York Times* (3 May 1970): B1.

———. "Yes, Yes, Alexis! No, No, *Follies.*" *New York Times* (11 April 1971): B1.

Lahr, John. *Automatic Vaudeville: Essays on Star Turns.* New York: Knopf, 1984.

Locher, Francis C., ed. *Contemporary Authors* 103 (1982): 479–85.

McClain, John. "Music Magnificent in Overwhelming Hit." *Journal American* (27 September 1957). Reprinted in *New York Theatre Critics' Reviews* (1957): 254.

Mordden, Ethan. *Broadway Babies: The People Who Made the American Musical.* New York: Oxford University Press, 1973.

Rich, Frank. "A Musical Theater Breakthrough." *New York Times Magazine* (21 October 1984): 52–54.

———— " 'Sunday in the Park with George': New Musical by Sondheim and Lapine." *New York Times* (3 May 1984): 21.

Sheren, P., and T. Sutcliffe. "Steven Sondheim and the American Musical." In *Theatre '74*, pp. 187–215. Edited by S. Morley. London: Hutchinson, 1974.

Stein, J. C., and Daniel G. Marowski, eds. *Contemporary Literary Criticism* 3 (1984): 375–403.

Suskin, Steven. *Show Tunes, 1905–1985*. New York: Dodd, Mead, 1986, 466.

Taubman, Howard. "The Theater: 'Anyone Can Whistle.' " *New York Times* (6 April 1964): 36.

Watt, Douglas. " 'Company' Has Brilliant Time with Couples in Manhattan." *New York Daily News* (27 April 1970). Reprinted in *New York Theatre Critics' Reviews* (1970): 260.

White, Mark. *You Must Remember This*. New York: Scribner's, 1985.

Wilson, S. B. "Motivic, Rhythmic and Harmonic Procedures of Unification in Stephen Sondheim's 'Company' and 'A Little Night Music.' " Ph.D. dissertation, Ball State University, 1983.

Zadan, Craig. *Sondheim and Co.* 2d ed. New York: Harper & Row, 1986.

Megan Terry

(22 JULY 1932–)

LYNDA HART

ASSESSMENT OF TERRY'S REPUTATION

Megan Terry's early interest in the political possibilities of the theatre has been sustained and expanded since she joined Jo Ann Schmidman to become playwright in residence of the Omaha Magic Theatre in 1974. Together Terry and Schmidman have produced and directed a body of women-centered theatre pieces that "consistently reveal a precise criticism of stereotyped gender roles, an affirmation of women's strength, and a challenge to women to better use their own power" (Keyssar, 54). Helene Keyssar has rightfully acknowledged Terry as the Mother of American Feminist Drama.

Terry was a founding member of the Open Theatre (with Joseph Chaikin), the New York Theatre Strategy, and the Women's Theatre Council. She revolutionized the American theatre by creating the first rock musical, *Viet Rock* (1966), which premiered at La Mama Experimental Theatre Club and was chosen by Robert Brustein to inaugurate his first season as artistic director of the Yale Repertory Theatre. Since 1965, Terry has created and published over sixty plays that have altered the course of American drama through their innovative use of transformational characters and constructions, a concept derived from the Open Theatre's workshop strategies.

In 1970, Terry's *Approaching Simone*, based on the life of the French philosopher Simone Weil, was awarded an Obie for Best New Play. In 1977, she was awarded the Silver Medal for Distinguished Contribution to and Service in the American Theatre by the American Theatre Association. Terry's work represents a sustained project to offer alternatives to realism as a form that perpetuates male-centered power structures. Her feminist vision focuses on process and change in contradiction to mainstream American drama's reinforcement of the status quo. In 1983, she was awarded the Dramatists Guild Annual Award in "recognition of [her] work as a writer of conscience and controversy and [her] many lasting contributions to the theatre." As David Savran correctly points out, Megan Terry "remains a key figure in the development of American alternative theatre" (242).

PRIMARY BIBLIOGRAPHY OF TERRY'S WORKS

The Dirt Boat. King-TV, Seattle. 1955.
Beach Grass. Produced in Seattle. 1955.
Seascape. Produced in Seattle. 1955.
Go Out and Move the Car. Seattle. 1955.
Avril and Helen. Never produced. 1958.
Attempted Rescue on Avenue B. Written in 1960. Produced in 1979 at Chicago's
    Theater Strategy at Hull House.
New York Comedy: Two. Saratoga, New York. 1961.
When My Girlhood Was Still All Flowers. Produced at the Open Theatre at the
    Sheridan Square Playhouse, New York. 1963.
Eat at Joe's. New York. 1964.
Ex-Miss Copper Queen on a Set of Pills. In *Playwrights for Tomorrow*, Vol. 1. Edited
    by Arthur H. Ballet. Minneapolis: University of Minnesota Press, 1966;
    also in *A Century of Plays by American Women*. Edited by R. France. New
    York: Rosen Press, 1979. Also published with *The People vs. Ranchman*.
    Samuel French, 1970.
Calm Down Mother. In *Plays by and about Women*. Edited by Victoria Sullivan. New
    York: Random House, 1973; in *Eight Plays from Off-Off Broadway*. Edited
    by Michael Smith and Nick Orzel. New York: Bobbs Merrill, 1966.
The Gloaming, Oh My Darling. In *Four Plays*. New York: Simon and Schuster,
    1967; in *The Norton Introduction to Literature*. Edited by Carl E. Bain. New
    York: W. W. Norton and Co., 1973. Also New York: Samuel French,
    1980.
Viet Rock: A Folk War Movie. In *Four Plays*. New York: Simon and Schuster, 1967;
    Tulane Drama Review (Summer 1966): T33.
The Key Is on the Bottom .Los Angeles: Mark Taper Forum, 1967.
The People vs. Ranchman. New York: Dramatists Play Service, 1968.
Jack-Jack. Produced in Minneapolis. 1968.
Keep Tightly Closed in a Cool Dry Place. In *Four Plays*. New York: Simon and
    Schuster, 1967; *Tulane Drama Review* 10 (Summer 1966): 177–200.
The Tommy Allen Show. In *Scripts 2*. New York, 1971.
Home; or, Future Soap. New York: Samuel French, 1972.
Sanibel and Captiva. In *Three One-Act Plays*, 1972; in *Spontaneous Combustion*. Edited
    by Rochelle Owens. New York: Winterhouse, 1972.
Massachusetts Trust. In *The Off-Off-Broadway Book*. Edited by Albert Poland and
    Bruce Mailman. Indianapolis: Bobbs Merrill, 1972.
One More Little Drinkie. In *Three One-Act Plays*. New York: Samuel French, 1972.
Couplings and Groupings. New York: Pantheon, 1972.

Grooving. Produced at Brooklyn Academy of Music, New York. 1972.
The Magic Realists. In *Three One-Act Plays.* New York: Samuel French, 1972. Also
 in *The Best One-Act Plays of 1968.* Edited by Stanley Richards. Philadelphia:
 Chilton Press, 1969.
Choose a Spot on the Floor. With Jo Ann Schmidman. Produced in Omaha. 1972.
Thoughts. Lyrics only; book by Lamar Alford. Produced in New York. 1973.
Approaching Simone. Old Westbury, N.Y.: Feminist Press, 1973; Also in *Women
 in Drama.* Edited by M. Kriegel. New York: New American Library, 1975.
 Also Samuel French, 1980.
Susan Peretz at the Manhattan Theatre Club. Produced in New York. 1973.
American Wedding Ritual, Monitored/Transmitted by the Planet Jupiter. In *Places: A
 Journal of the Theatre* 1 (1973).
St. Hydro Clemency; or A Funhouse of the Lord: An Energizing Event. Produced in
 New York, 1973.
Hothouse. Produced 1974. New York: Samuel French, 1975.
All Them Women. With others. Produced in New York. 1974.
We Can Feed Everybody Here. Produced in New York. 1974.
Hospital Play. Omaha. 1974.
Special Material. For Anne Meara on PBS television. 1974.
Henna for Endurance. Omaha. 1974.
Nightwalk. With Sam Shepard and Jean-Claude van Itallie. In *Three Works by the
 Open Theatre.* New York: Bobbs-Merrill, 1975.
The Pioneer and Pro-Game. Holly Springs, Miss.: Ragnarok Press, 1975.
100,001 Horror Stories of the Plains. With others. Omaha. 1976.
Women and the Law. Four half-hour television shows, PBS (Nebraska). 1976.
Sleazing towards Athens. Omaha, 1977.
Willie-Willa-Bill's Dope Garden. Birminghams Ala.: Ragnarok Press. 1977.
Brazil Fado. Omaha. 1977.
Lady Rose's Brazil Hide Out. Omaha. 1977.
American King's English for Queens. Omaha. 1978.
Babes in the Bighouse. Omaha. 1979.
Goona Goona. Omaha. 1979. Omaha Magic Theatre, 1985.
Attempted Rescue on Avenue B: A Beat Fifties Comic Opera. Omaha. 1979.
Fireworks. In *Independence Day.* Louisville, 1979.
Running Gag. Lyrics. Book by Jo Ann Schmidman. Omaha. 1979. Omaha Magic
 Theatre, 1981.
Objective Love I. Omaha. 1980.
Scenes from Maps. Omaha. 1980.
Objective Love II. Omaha Magic Theatre, 1981.
The Trees Blew Down. Los Angeles. 1981.
Winners (Santa Barbara) 1981.
Flat in Afghanistan. Omaha Magic Theatre. 1981.
Kegger. Omaha Magic Theatre. 1982.
Fifteen Million Fifteen Year Olds. Omaha Magic Theatre. 1983.
Molly Bailey's Traveling Family Circus; Featuring Scenes from the Life of Mother Jones.
 New York: Broadway Play Publishing, 1983.
X-rayed-Late. Omaha Magic Theatre. 1984.
Katmandu. Omaha Magic Theatre. 1985.
Astro-Bride. Omaha Magic Theatre. 1985.

Sea of Forms (with Jo Ann Schmidman.) Omaha Magic Theatre. 1986.
Family Talk. Omaha Magic Theatre. 1986.
Walking Through Walls (with Jo Ann Schmidman). Omaha Magic Theatre. 1987.
Dinner's in the Blender. Gordon, Nebraska, and Omaha Magic Theatre. 1987.
Retro. Omaha Magic Theatre. 1988.
Amtrak. Omaha Magic Theatre. 1988.
Head Light. Arkansas Art Center. Little Rock. 1988.

Articles

"Cool Is Out! Uptight Is Out!" *New York Times* (14 January 1968): 2: 17.
"Who Says Only Words Make Great Drama?" *New York Times* (10 November 1968): 2: 1, 3.
"American Experimental Theatre: Then and Now." *Performing Arts Journal* 2, no. 2 (1977): 13–24.
"Two Pages a Day." *Drama Review* 21, no. 4 (1977): 59–64.
"Janis Joplin." In *Notable American Women*. Edited by Barbara Sicherman and Carol Hurd Green. Cambridge: Harvard University Press, 1980.

Interviews

Betsko, Kathleen, and Rachel Koenig. "Megan Terry." *Interviews with Contemporary Women Playwrights*, pp. 377–401. New York: Beech Tree Books, 1987.
Savran, David. "Megan Terry." *In Their Own Words: Contemporary American Playwrights*. pp. 240–56. New York: Theatre Communications Group, 1988.

PRODUCTION HISTORY

Megan Terry's first three plays, *Beach Grass, Seascape,* and *Go Out and Move the Car,* were produced in Seattle, Washington, by the Cornish Theatre. She also wrote a television play, *The Dirt Boat,* produced by Seattle's King-TV. From 1965 to 1974 her primary identification was with the New York–based Open Theatre, and her plays were produced by such off-off Broadway playhouses as La Mama Experimental Theatre Club, the Cherry Lane Theatre, and Theatre Genesis. From 1974 to the present, she has been playwright in residence at the Omaha Magic Theatre.

Her first play to premiere in New York City was *Ex–Miss Copper Queen on a Set of Pills,* which opened 24 January 1963, produced by the Playwright's Unit at the Cherry Lane Theatre, and then in 1968 at the New York Players Workshop. Most recently the play was produced at the Edinburgh Theatre Festival (August 1987). Marranca and Dasgupta describe this play as "highly sentimental in the realistic mode offering characters whose lives of fantasy energize the mundane reality of their existence, a frequent theme in Terry's work" (184–85). In 1960 Terry's *The Magic Realists* was produced in New York by La Mama and later included in *The Best Short Plays of 1968*, described as an example of the

off-off-Broadway movement's "withering satirical attacks on establishment orthodoxy, bourgeois social graces, and middle-class vegetation"
(Richards, 329).

On 10 November 1966, *Viet Rock: A Folk War Movie*, the first antiwar
play and the first rock musical, opened at New York's Martinique Theatre. Some reviewers had difficulty appreciating *Viet Rock's* style and
content. Clurman was "embarrassed" (587) by the play, describing it as
"an irregular chain of improvisations, in feeble rock'n'roll style, intended
to protest and mock the indignity and stupidity of our action in Vietnam"
(586). Richardson was offended by the presentation of "our military . . .
made up of infants in arms" (87). Hughes found its writing "amateurish"
and its message "sophomoric" (759). Mordden suggests a probable cause
for *Viet Rock's* unfavorable reception by the mainstream critics: "It ran
counter to the gathering sixties vogue for anti-American expression. A
synthesis of images relating to war, *Viet Rock* failed to take sides in any
specific war; it asserted that war is wrong, therefore all sides are wrong"
(262). Schechner thought the "theme and scope, the variety and density,
of *Viet Rock* would have excited Brecht" (17). The play became a "popular
favorite" in the Samuel French catalog, remains her best-known work,
and has been widely translated.

During her association with the Open Theatre, Terry saw six additional plays produced, including *When My Girlhood Was Still All Flowers*
(1963), *Eat at Joe's* (1964), *Calm Down Mother* (1965), and *The Gloaming,
Oh My Darling* (1967), and she was a contributing writer with Sam Shepard and Jean-Claude van Itallie to *Nightwalk*, the Open Theatre's final
production.

In 1970, *Approaching Simone* earned Terry an Obie Award for Best
Play. Inspired by the life of the French philosopher and mystic Simone
Weil, who died at the age of thirty-four following a hunger strike, *Approaching Simone* is considered by many critics to be Terry's best play. In
his review following the play's opening at La Mama, Barnes proclaimed:
"Terry's treatment of her story is masterly. . . . There is nothing unnec-
essary. It is as sparse, as vital and as undemonstrative as Simone's own
life" ("Simone" 43). Hughes found that the play "records the journey
of a soul—into one of the most powerful and engrossing pieces of theatre
to be seen" ("Avant Garde," 612). *Calm Down Mother*, first performed by
the Open Theatre at the Sheridan Square Playhouse in New York in
1965, was later included in Victoria Sullivan's *Plays by and about Women*,
one of the first anthologies of women's plays. Sullivan and Hatch describe
this transformation play for three women as an exploration of "the
fearful limitations of biological essentialism" (xii). Examining mother-
daughter relationships, Keyssar identifies this play as "the first truly
feminist American drama" (62). *Keep Tightly Closed in a Cool Dry Place*,
also produced by the Open Theatre in 1965, casts three men who have

all been convicted of the murder of one of their wives. Peter Feldman, who directed the first production, believed the play is "about those who are tormented and those who torment; about imprisonment—literal, psychological and metaphysical—[it is] about dependency and father-hood" (quoted. in Schechner, 204).

In January 1974 Terry moved to the Midwest and joined the Omaha Magic Theatre as literary manager and playwright in residence. Through her work with the Magic Theatre, Terry has written and directed dozens of plays, consistently demonstrating her artistic courage in addressing vital issues of topical and lasting interest to American social practices. *Babes in the Bighouse*, the first full-length script Terry developed after joining the Omaha Magic Theatre, characteristically uses comedic trans-formations to expose profound social problems. Set in a women's prison and making connections between incarceration and the dehumanization of people and sexual stereotyping, in *Babes*, "the most distressing and aggressive actions of the production are not predictable prison behaviors but are the stories the women tell us of their past and present anguish" (Keyssar, 73).

From this point on, Terry's plays became increasingly feminist. In *American King's English for Queens*, she was concerned with "how language is used to control people, define them, and keep them in boxes. For instance, the English language was invented by men and the whole pro-noun thing—god is a 'he,' the generic term is 'he' and 'man'.... Our female gods have been taken away from us" (Leavitt, 289). *Goona Goona*, which premiered in November 1979, took domestic violence as its sub-ject. In this play, Terry, according to Catlin, confronts her audience: "We are the next door neighbors and we aren't supposed to say that whatever happens in a man's home (his proverbial castle) is his business. We are supposed to call the police, or the Flying Nuns of Mercy, depicted here as the Visiting Nurses Association" (15). Critics like Barnes who could appreciate Terry's play about the dead martyr Simone Weil balked at plays like *Hothouse:* "What is a nice playwright like that doing with a comic melodrama like this, all about how three alcoholic nymphoman-iacs—an old woman with her daughter and granddaughter—find love and comfort with one another?" (24 October 1974, 49). Barnes failed to appreciate Terry's subject: the "positive side of matriarchal love, and how women have been able to maintain themselves, even though they've had no power, through the love that is passed from grandmother to mother to daughter" (Leavitt, 289).

Again in Terry's words, *Attempted Rescue on Avenue B* "shows a woman coming to terms with her power which women have been afraid of, showing and experiencing her creative power, aside from procreative power, and being able to create new products to send out into the world" (quoted in Leavitt, 289), an apt description of Megan Terry's own progress as an artist. In recent years Terry has continued to write plays that address serious social problems. *Kegger* (1985) confronts adolescent alcohol abuse. *Family Talk* (1986), about failed communication, offers professional solutions based on research with family counselors. *Sleazing Toward Athens* (1986) "takes a worried look at what she considers the excessively materialistic orientation of today's college students" (Millburg, 16).

Terry continues to experiment with new themes and styles of dramatic presentation. *Sea of Forms* (1986) combines sculpture, music, dance, and chanting in a performance piece inspired by the work of Omaha sculptor Bill Farmer, whose work fills the set. Illustrating such themes as "violence, body building, consumerism, lawyers, and the role of the artist in society," *Sea of Forms* incorporates transformational strategies as "each scene feeds into the next without slowing down or stopping the work, so the audience is laughing one minute and considering a serious idea the next" (Nelson, 2).

One of her latest theatre pieces, *Walking Through Walls* (November 1987), is a giant-scale interdisciplinary project that combines the efforts of composers, visual artists and textile artists to explore autonomy and the unity of self and planet.

SURVEY OF SECONDARY SOURCES

Bibliographies

No individual bibliography, primary or secondary, of Megan Terry's work exists. A useful publication list of her plays is available upon request from the Omaha Magic Theatre, 1417 Farnam Street, Omaha, Nebraska 68102. The most complete listing of secondary sources on Terry through 1980 is in Rose. For limited bibliographies, see volume 4 of Mainiero, which includes a listing of plays through 1980. Eddleman 2 lists early secondary criticism, Gunton contains excerpts from reviews of the earlier plays, and Rose contains a comprehensive listing of Terry's plays through 1980. See also Coven.

Biographies

The best biography in a reference work is by Rose. Also see Betsko's, Savran's, and Leavitt's interviews with Terry. Terry's biography is published in *The World Who's Who of Women, American Women Writers, National Playwright's Directory*, and *Contemporary Authors*.

Influences

The women's movement of the past three decades is probably the most important influence on her work. Initially it freed her to leave New York and give up "the man's world of career stuff" and also allowed her "to see really clearly that there's a necessity to write about very strong women so women can know that there have been strong women in the past" (Leavitt, p. 287). Megan Terry's work with Joseph Chaikin and the Open Theatre and her participation in and contributions to the development of the off-off-Broadway movement in the 1960s were extremely influential in the development of her performance style and methods. Terry was trained as a designer, and this background is clearly present in her interest in set design and innovative use of theatrical spaces and shapes. Terry says that the sources of inspiration for the transformational techniques that have become her signature were her "grandmother and a lot of children, Bugs Bunny and stand-up comics. I was crazy about radio when I was growing up. Impersonators or impressionists would come on who could do Jimmy Cagney or James Stewart and would change these characters quickly. I loved it!" (Leavitt, 291–92).

General Studies

No one has written an individual study of Megan Terry's work. Keyssar's chapter offers a good overview and a feminist perspective on selected plays by Terry. Marranca and Dasgupta devote a chapter to Terry. Natalle's *Feminist Theatre* includes brief discussion of *Babes in the Bighouse* and *American King's English for Queens*. Klein discusses the social function of language and its relationship to meaning in *American King's English for Queens, Babes in the Bighouse, Brazil Fado*, and *The Tommy Allen Show*. Asahina discusses Terry and David Rabe. Schlueter effectively links transformational techniques with feminist purpose; she persuasively argues that Terry's early work paved the way for the burgeoning of feminist theatre in the 1980s. The most distinguished piece of writing on Terry to date is Diamond, who reads Terry in the company of Roland Barthes, Bertolt Brecht, Julia Kristeva, and others.

FUTURE RESEARCH OPPORTUNITIES

Terry's contributions to the American theatre are vast. Her career has been and continues to be innovative, exciting, and artistically vital. Critical coverage of her work has been grossly neglected. No significant biography or comprehensive bibliography of her work has been written or compiled, and scholarly journals publish little about her work. Most of the traditional histories of the theatre and collections of critical essays on American dramatists fail to give Terry's work the recognition that she is surely due. As feminist scholars continue to restore, recover, and revise the canon of American drama, they will find in Megan Terry's career fruitful material for analysis. Keyssar's *Feminist Theatre* has recognized Terry's crucial role in the development of a woman-centered drama, but a critical introduction to Terry's work, a full-length study of her plays, is long overdue.

SECONDARY SOURCES

Asahina, Robert. "The Basic Training of American Playwrights" Theater and the Vietnam War." *Theater* 9 (Spring 1978): 30–37.

Barnes, Clive. "Stage: Terry's 'Simone.' " *New York Times* (9 March 1970): 43.

———. "Stage: Flaccid 'Hothouse.' " *New York Times* (24 October 1974): 49.

Catlin, Roger. "Nuclear Family Melts Down in 'Goona Goona.' " *Omaha World-Herald* (17 November 1979): 15.

Clurman, Harold. "Theatre: 'Viet Rock.' " *Nation* (28 November 1966): 586–87.

Coven, Brenda. *American Women Dramatists of the Twentieth Century: A Bibliography.* Metuchen, N.J.: Scarecrow Press, 1982.

Diamond, Elin. "(Theoretically) Approaching Megan Terry." *Art and Cinema* 3 (Fall 1987): 3, 5–6.

Eddleman, Floyd Eugene, compiler. *American Drama Criticism,* supplement 2. Hamden, Conn.: Shoe String Press, 1976.

Gunton, Sharon R. *Contemporary Literary Criticism,* 19: 438–41. Detroit: Gale Research Co., 1981.

Hughes, Catherine. "The Theatre Goes to War." *America* (20 May 1967): 759–61.

———. "An Avant-Garde Simone Weil." *America* (6 June 1970): 612.

Kay, Ernest, ed. *The World Who's Who of Women.* 7th ed. Cambridge, England: International Biographical Centre, 1984.

Kaye, Phyllis Johnson, ed. *The National Playwrights Directory.* 2d ed. Waterford, Conn.: Eugene O'Neill Theater Center, 1981.

Keyssar, Helene. *Feminist Theatre.* London: Macmillan, 1984; New York: Grove Press, 1985.

Klein, Kathleen Gregory. "Language and Meaning in Megan Terry's 1970s 'Musicals.' " *Modern Drama* 27 (December 1984): 574–83.

Leavitt, Dinah L. "Interview with Megan Terry." In *Women in American Theatre.* Edited by Helen Krich Chinoy and Linda Walsh Jenkins. New York: Crown Publishers, 1981.

Locher, Frances Carol, ed. *Contemporary Authors,* 77–80: 543–45. Detroit: Gale Research Co., 1979.

Mainiero, Lina, ed. *American Women Writers.* New York: Frederick Ungar, 1982.

Marranca, Bonnie, and Gautam Dasgupta. *American Playwrights: A Critical Survey.* New York: Drama Book Specialists Publishers, 1981.

Millburg, Steve. "Sleazing toward Athens' Satirizes Careerism of '80s." *Omaha World-Herald* (9 June 1986): 16.

Mordden, Ethan. *The American Theatre*. New York: Oxford University Press, 1981.

Natalle, Elizabeth J. *Feminist Theatre: A Study in Persuasion*. Metuchen, NJ: Scarecrow Press, 1985.

Nelson, Karen. "Styrofoam Sculpture Is the Real Star of 'Sea of Forms.' " *Gateway* (10 September 1986): 2.

Richards, Stanley. *The Best Short Plays of 1968*. New York: Chilton Book Company, 1968.

Richardson, Jack. "Satires." *Commentary* 43 (March 1967): 86–87.

Rose, Phyllis Jane. *Dictionary of Literary Biography*, 7: 277–90. Edited by John MacNichols. Detroit: Gale Research Co., 1981.

Schechner, Richard. Introduction to *Viet Rock and Other Plays* by Megan Terry. New York: Simon and Schuster, 1966.

Sullivan, Victoria, and James Hatch. *Plays by and about Women*. New York: Vintage, 1974.

Jean-Claude van Itallie
(25 MAY 1936–   )

ALEXIS GREENE

ASSESSMENT OF VAN ITALLIE'S REPUTATION

Jean-Claude van Itallie's main contribution to the American theatre occurred from 1963 to 1973, when he was principal writer for the Open Theatre in New York City. Under the direction of Joseph Chaikin, van Itallie drew inspiration from the Open Theatre's acting exercises, notably its transformation exercise, and was able to structure his texts around the Open Theatre's improvisational work and create rich examples of the melding of the spoken word and the visual image, as physicalized by the Open Theatre's actors. van Itallie brought to his plays a political sensibility that decried what he perceived as the mechanization of American life. His use of the transformation technique expressed the individual's loss of identity, and his use of film and television imagery served his vision of America as a dehumanizing and potentially annihilating society. As Dasgupta observed: "Van Itallie has given us theatrical experiences that are vibrantly imaginative and some of the best of their time. . . . His work reflects a strong awareness of social and political issues while many of his contemporaries are content to explore personal problems in an isolationist fashion (p. 79).

PRIMARY BIBLIOGRAPHY OF VAN ITALLIE'S WORKS

The majority of van Itallie's papers are at Special Collections, Kent State University Library, Kent, Ohio, including unpublished notes and typescripts (designated KSU).

Plays and Workshop Material

War. New York, 1963. In *War and Four Other Plays*. New York: Dramatists Play
    Service, 1967.

Variations on a Clifford Odets Theme. Odets dialogue by van Itallie. New York, 1963. KSU.

An Airplane, Its Passengers, and Its Portent. New York, 1963. KSU.

Picnic in Spring. New York, 1964. KSU.

The Murdered Woman. New York, 1964. KSU.

The Hunter and the Bird. New York, 1964. In *War and Four Other Plays.* New York: Dramatists Play Service, 1967.

From an Odets Kitchen. New York, 1964. KSU.

I'm Really Here. New York, 1964. In *War and Four Other Plays.* New York: Dramatists Play Service, 1967.

It's Almost Like Being. New York, 1965. In *War and Four Other Plays.* New York: Dramatists Play Service, 1967.

The Airplane. New York, 1965. An improvisation with scripted dialogue by van Itallie. KSU.

The First Fool. New York, 1965. *Theatre Quarterly* (London) 4 (November 1964–January 1975): 49.

The Girl and the Soldier. New York, 1965. In *Seven Short and Very Short Plays.* New York: Dramatists Play Service, 1967.

Pavane: A Fugue for Eight Actors. New York, 1965. Retitled and performed as *Interview,* 1966. Under this title, in *American Hurrah and Other Plays.* New York: Grove Press, 1978.

America Hurrah, A Masque for Three Dolls. New York, 1965. Retitled and performed as *Motel,* 1966. As *Motel,* in *America Hurrah and Other Plays.* New York: Grove Press, 1978.

Dream. New York, 1965. Revised and retitled as *Where Is De Queen?* Minneapolis, 1965. As *Where Is De Queen?* in *War and Four Other Plays.* New York: Dramatists Play Service, 1967.

TV. New York, 1966. In *America Hurrah and Other Plays.* New York: Grove Press, 1978.

Thoughts on the Instant of Greeting a Friend on the Street. With Sharon Thie. New York, 1967. In *Seven Short and Very Short Plays.* New York: Dramatists Play Service, 1973.

The Serpent. Rome, Italy, 1968. In *America Hurrah and Other Plays.* New York: Grove Press, 1978.

Take a Deep Breath. New York, 1968. In *Seven Short and Very Short Plays.* New York: Dramatists Play Service, 1973.

Photographs: Mary and Howard. Los Angeles, 1969. In *Seven Short and Very Short Plays.* New York: Dramatists Play Service, 1973.

Eat Cake. Denver, Colorado, 1971. In *Seven Short and Very Short Plays.* New York: Dramatists Play Service, 1973.

Harold. New York, 1972. In *Seven Short and Very Short Plays.* New York: Dramatists Play Service, 1973.

The King of the United States. New York, 1972. New York: Dramatists Play Service, 1975.

Mystery Play. New York, 1973. New York: Dramatists Play Service, 1973.

Nightwalk, with Megan Terry and Sam Shepard (produced New York and London, 1973). Published in *Open Theatre,* New York: Drama Book Specialists, 1975.

The Sea Gull. Adapted from the play by Anton Chekhov. Princeton, New Jersey, 1973. New York: Dramatists Play Service, 1974.

A Fable. Lenox, Massachusetts, 1975. In *American Hurrah and Other Plays*. New York: Grove Press, 1978.

Rosary. In *Seven Short and Very Short Plays*. New York: Dramatists Play Service, 1975.

The Cherry Orchard. Adapted from the play by Anton Chekhov. New York, 1977. New York: Dramatists Play Service, 1977.

Three Sisters. Adapted from the play by Anton Chekhov. Rhinebeck, New York, 1979. New York: Dramatists Play Service, 1979.

Medea. Adapted from the play by Euripides. Kent, Ohio, 1979. KSU.

Bag Lady. New York, 1979. New York: Dramatists Play Service, 1980.

Naropa, music by Steve Gorn (produced New York, 1982). In *Wordplays 1*. New York: Performing Arts Journal Publications, 1980.

Early Warnings (includes *Bag Lady, Sunset Freeway, Final Orders*.) Produced New York, 1983. New York: Dramatists Play Service, 1983.

The Tibetan Book of the Dead. New York, 1983. New York: Dramatists Play Service, 1983.

The Master and Margarita. Adapted from the novel by Mikhail Bulgakov, 1980. KSU.

Uncle Vanya. Adapted from the play by Anton Chekhov. New York, 1983. New York: Dramatists Play Service, 1980.

Pride, in Nagel Jackson's *Faustus in Hell* (produced Princeton, New Jersey, 1985).

The Balcony. Translated from the play by Jean Genet. Cambridge, Massachusetts, 1986. KSU.

The Traveler. Los Angeles, 1987. KSU.

Paradise Ghetto. Los Angeles, 1987. KSU.

Television Scripts

Between June 1963 and July 1967, van Itallie wrote a number of adaptations for the Look Up and Live Series, produced by CBS News. These adaptations include *Blues for Mister Charlie; The Brig; Camino Real;* and *Hamlet*. He wrote two scripts for New York Illustrated, produced by WNBC-TV: *Kind Deeds and Cornets*, December 1964; and *Asia in Manhattan*, February 1965. He wrote the television script for *Hobbies, or, Things Are All Right with the Forbushers* (1967), for *Take a Deep Breath* (1969), and for *Picasso—A Painter's Diary*, which was produced by PBS and broadcast in 1980.

Screenplays

Three Lives for Mississippi. Based on a novel by William Bradford Huie. 1970. Unproduced.

The Box is Empty. Privately produced. 1975.
Motel. Adapted from the play of the same title. Equinox Films, 1976.

Nondramatic Writing

"Francois Yattend." *Transatlantic Review* 7 (Fall 1961): 114–18.
Karma to India: A Journal. 1972. KSU.
"Discovering the Real Fountain of Youth... in South America" (with Wendy Gimbel). *Vogue* (February 1981): 196, 201–4.

Interviews

"About the One That Succeeds: Interview with van Itallie." Julius Novick, *New York Times* (27 November 1966): 2:1.
" 'America Hurrah': Search for Adaptability and Seductiveness." Paine Knickerbocker. *San Francisco Examiner and Chronicle* (14 May 1967): 3.
" 'America Hurrah' Author Firm on 'Involved' Plays." Dan Sullivan, *The New York Times* (7 November 1967): 46.
"Van Itallie Hurrah." Anne Youens, *Pittsurgh Point* (20 March 1969): 1.
"A Reinvention of Form." Bill Simmer, *Drama Review* 21 (December 1977): 65–74.
"Rogues' Gallery." Terry Helbing, *Chiristopher Street* (June 1978): 16–23.
"Morning Edition." Connie Goldman, National Public Radio, 1980. KSU.
"Van Itallie's 'Traveler' Springs from Personal, Artistic Journeys." Kathleen O'Steen, *Variety* (27 February 1987): 82.
"An Interview with Jean-Claude van Itallie." Alexis Greene, *Studies In American Drama, 1945–Present* 3 (Fall 1988): 135–46.

Articles

"Playwright at Work: Off-Off Broadway." *TDR* 10 (Summer 1966). 154–58.
"The Adaptation of Theatre Plays to the Media of Television and Films." Unpublished report prepared at the request of UNESCO for presentation to the Budapest Round-Table Meeting (19–24 September 1966) on "The Sound-track in the Cinema and Television." August 1966. KSU.
"Should the Artist Be Political in His Art?" *New York Times* (17 September 1967): 2:3.
"Polish Lab Director Plays for Total Stakes." *Village Voice* (7 March 1968): 38, 44.
"The Integrity of the Dramatic Text; An Open Letter to the Odyssey Theatre." *New England Theatre* 1 (Spring 1970): 109–13.
"Chekhov's Characters Seem to Be Ourselves." *New York Times* (13 February 1977): B1, B7.

PRODUCTION HISTORY

van Itallie joined the Open Theatre in 1963, and his first one-act plays were performed by the company in 1964. Ironically the production that brought van Itallie extensive critical recognition was the presentation of his *America Hurrah* trilogy at the Pocket Theatre on 6 November 1966. Although Chaikin directed *Interview* (second play in the trilogy), and van Itallie's work with the Open Theatre informed this play in particular, *America Hurrah* was neither produced by nor for the Open Theatre.

Critics viewed the three plays as radically different from the content and form of traditional American playwriting. Brustein noted that "the triumph of this occasion is to have found provocative theatrical images for the national malaise we have been suffering in Johnsonland these last three years" ("Three Views"). Kerr urged that "you'll be neglecting a whisper in the wind if you don't look in on 'America Hurrah' " ("A Whisper,"). *Motel*, which was directed by Jacques Levy, was praised by Lahr for the "gigantic *papier-maché* people" who eventually tear the equally giant Motel Keeper apart and "march off the stage carrying her arm like a baton and down the aisle." Wrote Lahr: "*Motel* is van Itallie's apocalypse. A vision of surfaces and masks, violence, vulgar irresponsibility, hilarious and terrible destruction. Like Swift, van Itallie has an 'excremental vision' and *Motel* is it.... To say, as Walter Kerr did, that these plays were a 'whisper in the wind' is to be out of touch with the life blood of American life and to be too old to be scared" (*Manhattan East*, p.7).

van Itallie's next significant production was *The Serpent*, which opened at Rome's Teatro delle Arti on 2 May 1968 under the direction of Chaikin and presented by the Open Theatre. Italian critics were generally favorable, enthralled, as many other critics in Europe would be, by what they perceived as an unusually lyrical physicalization of both modern and ancient myths. Tian, theatre critic for Rome's *Il Messagero*, described in particular the physicalization of the serpent itself: "A group of a dozen actors twined around each other, but in such a way that this twisting of arms legs hands torsos faces formed a self-propelled monster that slinked sinuously, breathed, darted restless tongues" (p. 12). When Chaikin toured the United States with a revised production, American critics were divided in their responses. Hardwick called the work "soft, sentimental...sadly trivial and banal.....When the beauty of the Biblical language intrudes, your first thought is relief and the second is that the physical representation of the Biblical text, by the actors, is quite unbearable in its inadequacy. In the begetting scenes, actors straddle each other, ramming front and back: and no matter, it is all appallingly mushy and weak" ("Scalp!" 40). Writing in the *Boston Globe*, Kelly called the play a "poignant, provocative parable" (p. 24). Reviewing the Open Theatre's performances at New York's Washington Square Methodist Church, Gussow called *The Serpent* "an eloquent reexamination of Genesis" (2 June 1970, 35).

The Serpent was van Itallie's last major collaborative effort with the

Open Theatre, which disbanded in 1973. Subsequent plays produced in New York City from 1973 until 1979 often drew the general response from critics that van Itallie was unsuccessful at finding new forms for his social satire. *The Fable*, produced at the Exchange Theater at Westbeth in October 1975, directed by Chaikin and employing a number of Open Theatre actors, elicited positive assessments from Sainer (in the *Village Voice*) and from Gussow, who wrote that "it is verbal as well as gestural, with the actors as performing instruments, improvising upon themes and acting as natural objects. 'A Fable' strips the stage bare (the main prop is a long shower-like curtain), and then populates it with the artists' imaginations (28 October 1975, 26). However, Kerr used the occasion of this production to call on van Itallie to write more words in his plays: "Mr. Van Itallie has more and more surrendered himself to the ritualistic investigations, the compilings of evocative stage pictures with nonrational sound, that Mr. Chaikin has been conducting. . . . Always, always Mr. Van Itallie was writing less. . . . Is he limited, creatively, to the fleeting hint?" (30 November 1975, p. 5).

Not until the production of *Bag Lady* on 21 November 1979 at Theatre for the New City did van Itallie receive the acclaim that he had won for *America Hurrah* thirteen years earlier. Mainstream reviewers in particular were effusive about both the play and the production. "As directed by Elinor Renfield," wrote Gussow, "the play is an enviroment as well as a monologue. The stage is a triangular cul de sac, a dead-end zone. The designer, Barbara Sonneborn, has covered one wall with a wire grating, which serves for prison bars as well as playground fence, and another wall with jagged pieces of hanging plastic, like shards from a broken mirror" (27 November 1979, 24).

Between 1973 and 1983, van Itallie's four adaptations of plays by Chekhov were produced in the United States and generally earned praise from critics for their idiomatic fluency. Munk, writing about van Itallie's adaptation of *The Cherry Orchard* for the controversial production directed by Andrei Serban at the New York Shakespeare Festival, noted that "Jean-Claude van Itallie's adaptation is splendid, colloquial without being cute, simple, moving, funny" (7 March 1977, 65). However, a suit brought by translator Ann Dunnigan regarding this particular adaptation cast doubt for a time on van Itallie's work in this vein, resulting in 1983 in a near accusation of plagiarism by *New York Magazine's* Simon (26 September 1983, 102). This in turn prompted a defense of van Itallie from Brustein (24 October 1983).

van Itallie continues to wrestle with the creative problem of finding an appropriate dramatic form for his ideas, which by 1987 seem to have departed from the acute social satire that infused his writing during the 1960s and early 1970s. His play *The Traveler*, which is based on Chaikin's experience of recovering from a stroke that affected memory and speech, received its world premiere on 4 March 1987 at the Mark Taper

Forum in Los Angeles. The overall critical response was that the play possessed considerable potential but required further work. Sullivan summed up the thoughts of many of his colleagues: "'The Traveler' (*sic*) is really two plays. The first is a monodrama.... The other... is a hospital drama that we seem to have seen on TV.... These scenes may be based on fact, but they play like fiction, and not particularly well-worked-out fiction at that" (6 March 1987, F16). A revised version of the play was produced from 30 September to 24 October 1987 at the Haymarket Theatre in Leicester, England, under the direction of Keith Boak.

SURVEY OF SECONDARY SOURCES

Bibliographies

The most accurate bibliography covering the years of van Itallie's association with the Open Theatre was assembled by Daniels. A good supplement to this bibliography is in Brittain, which, in addition to a solid listing of interviews and primary articles from this period, contains the only bibliography to date of published translations of van Itallie's plays. Also consult Vinson and Kaye. A more accurate and up-to-date bibliography exists in the 1988 edition of Contemporary Dramatists, with a brief critical essay by van Itallie's dramaturg William Coco.

The most up-to-date bibliography of secondary sources is in Carpenter, who also provides international sources of criticism not listed in any other reference works. Gildzen lists some entries not included elsewhere. The bibliography in *Twentieth-Century American Dramatists* is incomplete in comparison to the others mentioned, as is the bibliography of plays at the end of van Itallie's essay in *Contemporary Authors*.

Biographies

The most detailed and up-to-date biography is the personal essay that van Itallie himself wrote for *Contemporary Authors* surveying the origins of his family, his close relationship with his mother, the challenge of being influenced by two cultures (the American one of his peers and the European one of his parents), the decisions that led him to become a practicing Buddhist, and his homosexuality.

Also worth consulting is an issue of *Serif*, the quarterly of Kent State University, devoted to van Itallie, which includes "A Chronology" that encapsulates details of van Itallie's life from 1936 to 1972, and three brief essays by friends and colleagues who offer insightful memories of van Itallie as a young man and emerging artist. The essay on van Itallie in *Twentieth-Century American Dramatists* contains pertinent biographical information. An encapsulated biography in *Contemporary Dramatists* contains reliable information about awards, fellowships, and teaching appointments that van Itallie received through 1977.

Influences

Wagner succinctly notes the relationship between the theories of Antonin Artaud as expressed in *The Theatre and Its Double* and van Itallie's *Motel*, written prior to his joining the Open Theatre. Bigsby also draws connections between Artaud's theories and van Itallie's "theatre of dissonance," as exemplified by *Motel's* cacophony of sound, intense lighting, and enormous doll-like figures (3:113). The greatest influence on van Itallie's work during the 1960s, however, were the acting exercises and the philosophies of the Open Theatre. Wagner quotes van Itallie extensively on his creative responses to the improvisational and nonverbal nature of the Open Theatre. Pasolli helps fill in connections between specific Open Theatre exercises and their reappearance as concrete visual metaphors in a number of van Itallie's plays and provides links to the Open Theatre's "investigation of social roles" (62). Pasolli's commentary on *The Serpent*, however, is superseded by Jacquot's detailed examination of the relationship between rehearsal explorations and final text (these analyses themselves draw on Glickfield's log and notes by Open Theatre actor Peter Maloney). Lahr's essay on *The Serpent* adds to our understanding of van Itallie's creative process here, as does Mohan's dissertation; Blumenthal's volume on Chaikin lends further insights.

General Studies

General studies can be located in Cohn's *New American Dramatists: 1960–1980*, where she discusses van Itallie's work through the New York premiere of *Bag Lady* in 1979, in Dasgupta, which provides a more discursive exploration of van Itallie's styles and themes during the course of his career, and in Coco. Bigsby's segment on van Itallie and Richter's thesis provide the only other general studies of any substance, although in both cases the focus is solely on van Itallie's work from the 1960s.

Analyses of Individual Plays

Unquestionably van Itallie's *America Hurrah* trilogy and *The Serpent* have elicited most of the critical commentary. Cohn, in "Camp, Cruelty, Colloquialism," analyzes *Motel* as comic grotesquerie: "Literally dehumanized, van Itallie's giant dolls are at once funny and horrifying. . . . Representatives of the triviality and artifice of a motel civilization, the dolls invite us, through uneasy laughter, to indict such triviality and artifice" (292). Much of the significant criticism of *America Hurrah* analyzes this trio of one-acts from the viewpoint of their social satire. Grabes finds that van Itallie uses expressionist techniques to demonstrate social criticism and the inevitable destruction of civilization, a conclusion that is also found in Wagner, who writes that "the destruction of a culture is a political problem.... With these causes as their subjects, *Interview, TV*, and *Motel* are political plays" (58). These ideas are echoed in milder form by Madden and Jackson.

Critical analyses of *The Serpent* also consider van Itallie as a political playwright, notably in Taylor. However, other criticism of *The Serpent* addresses the play's humanistic values and religious viewpoints, a theme underlying the arguments in Kerr (*God on the Gymnasium Floor*) and Adler. "God in van Itallie's play," writes Adler, "springs from within human history as a necessary creator to fulfill man's need for some curb to stave off the anarchy of freedom without responsibility" (13). Lahr approaches *The Serpent* as ceremony and analyzes it in terms of the myths that both van Itallie and Chaikin were trying to interpret. *The Serpent*, writes Lahr, is "a dialectic exploration of mythology, playing off conventional theological attitudes and discovering new input in old myths" ("Open Theatre's Serpent," 169).

FUTURE RESEARCH OPPORTUNITIES

A significant bibliography of primary and secondary sources is needed, including international reviews and criticism. We need to determine which of the television scripts van Itallie wrote for CBS News were actually produced and, if produced, broadcast. It is necessary to determine whether any of these videotapes still exist, since several, particularly van Itallie's adaptation of Kenneth Brown's *The Brig*, might have value for students of this period.

A critical reassessment of van Itallie's work is also in order, both to reevaluate his work from the 1960s and to place his canon in perspective, with special attention going to the stylistic and thematic relationships between his work of the 1960s and subsequent writing; the relationship between van Itallie's stylistic and thematic development and changing trends in American culture and theatre; and his adaptations of Chekhov to determine in what ways they may reinterpret Chekhov for a contemporary audience.

SECONDARY SOURCES

Adler, Thomas P. "Van Itallie's *The Serpent:* History after the Fall." *Drama and Theatre* 11 (Fall 1972): 12–14.
Berk, Philip R. "Memories of John." *Serif* 9 (Winter 1972): 9–11.
Blumenthal, Eileen. *Joseph Chaikin: Exploring at the Boundaries of Theater.* Cambridge, England: Cambridge University Press, 1984.

Bigsby, C. W. E. *A Critical Introduction to Twentieth-Century American Drama.* Vol. 3: *Beyond Broadway.* Cambridge, England: Cambridge University Press, 1985.

Breed, Paul F., and Florence M. Sniderman, eds. *Dramatic Criticism Index.* Detroit: Gale Research Co., 1972.

Brittain, Michael J. "A Checklist of Jean-Claude van Itallie 1961–1972." *Serif* 9 (Winter 1972): 75–77.

Brustein, Robert. "Three Views of America." *New Republic* (3 December 1966): 31–33. Reprinted in *The Third Theatre*, pp. 50–54. New York: Knopf, 1969.

———. "Serban under Seige." *New Republic.* (24 October 1983): 33–34.

Carpenter, Charles, A., ed. *Modern Scholarship and Criticism 1966–1980.* Toronto: University of Toronto Press, 1986.

Coco, William. "Jean-Claude van Itallie." In *Contemporary Dramatists.* Fourth Edition, pp. 535–37. Edited by D. L. Kirkpatrick. Chicago: St. James Press, 1988.

Cohn, Ruby. "Camp, Cruelty, Colloquialism." In *Comic Relief: Humor in Contemporary American Literature*, pp. 281–313. Edited by Sara B. Cohen. Urbana: Illinois University Press, 1978.

———. *New American Dramatists: 1960–1980.* New York: Grove Press, 1982.

Daniels, Barry V. "The Open Theatre: A Chronology, 1963–73." Program of the Open Theatre Conference at Kent State University. Special Collections, Kent State University Library.

Dasgupta, Gautam. "Jean-Claude van Itallie." In *American Playwrights: A Critical Survey*, pp. 65–80. New York: Drama Book Specialists, 1981.

Freedman, Samuel G. "Translations of Plays Spark Debate." *New York Times* (4 January 1984): C17.

Gassner, Rhea. "Jean-Claude van Itallie: Playwright of the Ensemble: Open Theater." *Serif* 9 (Winter 1972): 14–17.

Gildzen, Alex. "The Open Theatre: A Beginning Bibliography." In *Three Works by the Open Theatre*, pp. 188–91. Edited by Karen Malpede. New York: Drama Book Specialists, 1974.

Glickfeld, Kenneth. "Serpent Log." Special Collections, Kent State University Library. Sections of the log are included in Roberta N. Mohan. "The Open Theater Production of *The Serpent: A Ceremony:* An Examination of Aesthetic Purpose and Creative Process." Master's thesis, Kent State University, 1973.

Grabes, Herbert. "Moglichkeiten der Gesellschaftskritik im Drama: Jean-Claude van Itallie's *America Hurrah.*" In *Amerikanishes Drama und Theater im 20. Jahrhundert*, pp. 328–46. Edited by Alfred Weber and Siegfried Neuweiler. Gottingen: Vandenhoeck & Ruprecht, 1975.

Gussow, Mel. "Stage: A Bite into an Apple Long Ago." *New York Times* (2 June 1970): 35.

———. "Stage: 'Fable' Is Lighthearted Fancy." *New York Times* (28 October 1975): 26.

———. "Stage: Van Itallie's 'Bag Lady' a Soul of Imagination." *New York Times* (27 November 1979): C24.

Hardwick, Elizabeth. "Scalp!" *New York Review of Books* (6 November 1969): 39–40.

Harris, Richard. H., ed. *Modern Drama in America and England 1950–1970*. Detroit: Gale Research Co., 1982.

Jackson, Esther M. "American Theatre in the Sixties." *Players Magazine* 48 (1973): 236–49.

Jacquot, Jean. "The Open Theatre: *The Serpent* création par l'open Théâtre Ensemble en collaboration avec Jean-Claude van Itallie, sous la direction de Joseph Chaikin." In *Les Voies de la création théâtrale*, pp. 278–308. Edited by Jean Jacquot and Denis Bablet. Paris: Centre nationale de la recherche scientifique, 1970.

Kaye, Phyllis Johnson, ed. "Jean-Claude van Itallie." In *The National Playwrights Directory*. Waterford, Conn: O'Neill Theater Center, 1981.

Kelly, Kevin. "Open Theater Disciplined, Gifted." *Boston Sunday Globe* (19 January 1969): A24.

Kerr, Walter. "The Theater: A Whisper in the Wind." *New York Times* (7 November 1966): 66.

———. "God on the Gymnasium Floor." In *God on the Gymnasium Floor*, pp. 21–27, 41–44. New York: Simon and Schuster, 1971.

———. "Playwrights Who Evade Writing." *New York Times* (30 November 1975): D5.

Lahr, John. "Theater." *Manhattan East* (17 November 1966): 4, 7.

———. "The Open Theater's Serpent." In *Up against the Fourth Wall*, pp. 158–74. New York: Grove Press, 1970.

LaMont, Rosette. " 'The Book of the Dead': A Meditation on Mortality." *Other Stages* (13 January 1983): 4.

MacNicholas, John, ed. *Twentieth-Century American Dramatists*. Detroit: Gale Research Co., 1981.

Madden, David. "The Theatre of Assault: Four Off-Off-Broadway Plays." *Massachusetts Review* 8 (1967): 712–25.

Maloney, Peter. "The Making of *The Serpent*." In *The Open Theater-Europe 1968* (souvenir program), pp. 9–25. Edited by Richard Snyder and Peter Maloney.

———. "An Actor's View, Part I: Lee." *Changes* 2 (15 May 1971): 28–29.

———. "An Actor's View, Part II: *The Serpent*." *Changes* 3 (1 June 1971): 26–27.

Munk, Erika. *Village Voice* (7 March 1977): 65.

Ortolani, Benito, ed. *International Bibliography of Theatre: 1983*. Brooklyn: Theatre Research Data Center, 1983.

Pasolli, Robert. *A Book on the Open Theatre*. New York: Avon, 1970.

Richter, George R., Jr. "Jean-Claude van Itallie, Improvisational Playwright: A Study of His Plays." Master's thesis, University of Colorado, 1969.

Simon, John. "Overdirected, Underachieved." *New York Magazine* (26 September 1983): 102.

Stasio, Marilyn. "City's 'Bag,' a Study in Acting." *New York Post* (12 January 1980).

Sullivan, Dan. " 'The Traveler' Almost Makes It." *Los Angeles Times* (6 March 1987): F16.

Taylor, Karen Malpede. *People's Theatre in Amerika*. New York: Drama Book Specialists, 1973.

Tian, Renzo. "Mimano anche la 'Bibbia' gli attori dell'Open Theatre." *Il Messagero* (4 May 1968): 12.

Tonma, Kesang. "A Short Autobiography of Kesang Tonma." *Serif* 9 (Winter 1972): 12–13.

Van Itallie, Jean-Claude. "Jean-Claude van Itallie." In *Contemporary Authors*. Edited by Adele Sarkissian. Detroit: Gale Research Co., 1985.

Vinson, James, ed. *Contemporary Dramatists*. 3d ed. New York: St. James Press, 1982.

Wagner, Phyllis Jane. "Jean-Claude van Itallie: Political Playwright." *Serif* 9 (Winter 1972): 19–69.

Wendy Wasserstein

(18 OCTOBER 1950–   )

PATTI P. GILLESPIE

ASSESSMENT OF WASSERSTEIN'S REPUTATION

Wendy Wasserstein, "the first woman playwright from the nascent 'Yale School' to truly make her mark" (Lamb, 14), is one of several female writers currently attracting attention in America's commercial theatre. Although *Uncommon Women and Others*, both on stage and in its televised version, is Wasserstein's most widely known work to date, *Isn't It Romantic*, the musical *Miami*, and "The Man in a Case" have also captured the interest of New York's reviewers. Neither the playwright nor her plays have attracted the sustained attention of scholars, however. Considered "a savvy voice for the urban '80s" (Wallace, 10), Wasserstein writes "nouvelle cuisine comedy" (Gussow, "Stage," C3) whose subject is the choices facing young women in today's world, a concern that causes her to walk an uncomfortable tightrope between commercialism and feminism. Reviewers' comments help suggest her strengths ("socko dialogue" [Sweeney, 27] and "a darting sense of the ridiculous" [Newton, 140]) and her weaknesses ("too external, revue-sketchy, flashy" [Simon, "Review," 106], "episodic and uneven" [Watt, 3]). Simon probably offers the most honest current assessment: with *Uncommon Women and Others*, "Wendy Wasserstein proved herself a playwright to watch and wait for.... [With her later works] the promise continues to be brighter than the delivery" ("Failing," 36).

PRIMARY BIBLIOGRAPHY OF WASSERSTEIN'S WORKS

The dates refer to the date of first production.

Plays

Any Woman Can't. 1973.
Happy Birthday, Montpelier Pa-zazz. 1976.
When Dinah Shore Ruled the Earth. With Christopher Durang. 1977–1978. Written as a filmscript; performed as a play.
Uncommon Women and Others. (Produced New Haven, 1975) New York: Dramatists Play Service, 1978.
Isn't It Romantic. New York: Avon Books, 1979; Nelson Doubleday: Garden City, © 1984; Dramatists Play Service, © 1985.
Tender Offer. 1983.
The Man in a Case in *Orchards* (adaptation of a short story by Chekhov). 1985–1986. New York: Alfred A. Knopf, 1986.
Miami. 1986.

Interviews

"Your 30s: The More Decade." *Harpers Bazaar* 117 (June 1984): 146–47, 180.
Betsko, Kathleen, and Rachel Koenig. *Interviews with Contemporary Women Playwrights.* New York: Beech Tree Books, 1987.
Sturgeon, J. M. "The Phoenix Focus Talks to Wendy Wasserstein." *Phoenix Focus* 4, no. 5 (May 1981), unpaginated.

Television Plays

Uncommon Women and Others. Television script, 1978.
The Sorrows of Gin. Television script, 1979.
Comedy Zone. Television script, 1984.

Other

"The Itch to Get Hitched." *Mademoiselle* (November 1981): 146–47.
"Phil and Molly the New Romantics." *New York Times* (4 November 1984): F36–37, F72, F74.
"Giving in to Gluttony." *Esquire* 106 (July 1986): 60–61.
"New York Theatre: Isn't It Romantic?" *New York Times* (11 January 1987): B1.
"The Girl from Fargo: A Play." *New York Times* (8 March 1987): B5, B18.

PRODUCTION HISTORY

Before her first hit, Wasserstein had three plays produced, the first two at Playwrights Horizons, a not-for-profit theatre in New York City with which Wasserstein's career remains closely tied. In *Any Woman Can't* (1973), Wasserstein's heroine decides to marry because she failed a tap-dancing audition—modern women's choices. *Montpelier Pa-zazz* (opened 29 June 1976, with Wasserstein's book and David Hollister's music) was praised for its "sharp and clever" dialogue but criticized for using "every college fraternity and sorority cliché" to explore its themes of self-discovery (Bicknell, 17). She next wrote *When Dinah Shore Ruled the Earth* with Christopher Durang, who taught playwriting at Yale while Wasserstein pursued her master of fine arts degree there. Yale's Cabaret Theatre produced this piece during its 1977–1978 season. These three productions would be of little interest, however, were it not for the success of Wasserstein's fourth play, *Uncommon Women and Others*.

Begun as a one-act play for her graduate thesis at Yale (where it was first produced in December 1975), *Uncommon Women and Others* was given a staged reading at Playwrights Horizons (19 March 1977). At the National Playwrights' conference of the Eugene O'Neill Memorial Theatre Center during the summer, the one-act version was expanded and developed, and performed (26 July 1977). In its full-length version, *Uncommon Women and Others* received its first New York production at Marymount Manhattan Theatre, on 21 November 1977, produced by the Phoenix Theatre, directed by Steven Robman, and featuring Jill Eikenberry as Kate, Alma Cuervo as Holly, Swoosie Kurtz as Rita, and Glenn Close as Leilah. Although this production played only about three weeks, the play was quickly revived for television production as a part of PBS's Theatre in America series (1978), for which Wasserstein provided the adaptation and Steven Robman shared directing credit with Merrily Mussman.

Critical response was mixed, but reviews were more favorable than otherwise. Although Clurman complained that there was "more description than development of a situation" (667) and Frank that the play "lacked conflict" (39), Eder praised Wasserstein's "gifts for characterization" (48), Newton the "genuine thigh smack[ing] laughs" (22), and Kalem, the "affectionately bantering humor and . . . gamy ration of powder-room candor" (111). On the strength of this largely autobiographical play, critics agreed that Wasserstein was a playwright of promise.

Within ten years, more than a thousand college and regional theatres had produced *Uncommon Women*, most notably San Francisco's Magic Theatre, St. Nicholas Theatre (Chicago, March 1978), the Los Angeles Stage Company (April 1981), the Huntington Theatre Company (Boston, 1984), and the Caldwell Playhouse (Boco Raton, Florida, 1984–1985). As it played around the country, the play and its casts earned several awards: an Obie, a Joseph Jefferson Award, a Dramalogue Award, and an Inner Boston Critics Award.

The success of *Uncommon Women and Others* was not quickly repeated. In 1979 Wasserstein adapted John Cheever's short story, "The Sorrows of Gin," for PBS's *Great Performances*. Among reviewers, Demp was least enthusiastic: "Wasserstein's adaptation never catches fire" (72). More positively, Unger found the adaption "thought-provoking, sensitive television—true to its own scale of ambition" (19), and Wolcott thought that despite some "embroidering" and "slang [ing] up," Wasserstein managed to do "justice to Cheever's exploration" (56). In 1980, she wrote additional material for Murray Horwitz's *Hard Sell* (January 1980).

For Marathon '83, a six-week festival of one-act plays sponsored by the Ensemble Studio Theatre (4 May–20 June 1983), Wasserstein contributed *Tender Offer*, the story of a young girl whose father missed her dance recital. Massa pronounced it "easily the sweetest play in the festival" (100); Sommers termed it "amiable" and "sitcomable" (83); and Gussow thought that "despite its occasional stretch of credibility, . . . the play achieves an engaging wistfulness" ("Two Evenings," 17).

Not until *Isn't It Romantic* was revised and revived in late 1983 did critics echo their earlier enthusiasm for Wasserstein's work. Although the Phoenix Theatre had commissioned the play in 1979, Wasserstein began writing in 1980 as an attempt to resolve her own responses to a friend's marriage. Critics viewed this play as a sequel to *Uncommon Women:* two of the characters from *Uncommon Women* "figuratively, if not literally, matured into the heroines of *Isn't It Romantic*" (Haun, "Is It or," 5). The Phoenix Theatre opened it officially for a three-week run on 13 June 1981 at Marymount Manhattan Theatre. Directed by Steven Robman, with a cast that included Alma Cuervo as Jamie and Laurie Kennedy as Harriet Cornwall, the play received decidedly mixed reviews.

The play was revived on 15 December 1983 at Playwrights Horizons, this time directed by Gerald Guttierez, who, with artistic director André Bishop, helped Wasserstein sharpen the play. As revised and shortened (from 103 to 81 pages, or about forty-five minutes), this, the seventh version of the play, was "a laugh-till-you-cry-hit. . . . one⁄ of the best 10 plays of the year," according to Corliss (80). Kerr, citing the improved characterization of the two mothers, termed the result "altogether delightful" (7). The most negative assessments came from Munk of the *Village Voice*, who likened the play to a television sitcom whose commercials sold "upper middle class reconciliation" (109–110), and Nightingale who thought that Wasserstein was making "too big a deal of what should, after all, be an everyday fact: Growing up" (2). Sirkin found in the play an "ugly reverse bigotry" (202).

But the generally favorable reception encouraged a number of regional productions, most notably those at the Caldwell Playhouse, Boco Raton, Florida (July 1984), Arena Stage, Washington, D.C. (April 1985), Los Angeles Stage Company (May 1985), Ivanhoe Theatre, Chicago (October 1985), and the Walnut Street Theatre, Philadelphia (November 1985).

Wasserstein's growing reputation led the Acting Company to select her as one of the seven contemporary playwrights to adapt selected short stories by Anton Chekhov for an evening of short plays to showcase the company's actors. Collected under the title *Orchards*, the resulting seven plays were deemed unsuccessful by almost all reviewers. Even the most negative reviewers, however, agreed with Beaufort that "the experiment comes off best in Wendy Wasserstein's 'The Man in a Case' " (140). Gussow thought she "successfully merged her voice with that of Chekhov" (" 'Orchards,' " C15), and Barnes pronounced her adaptation "the best, by an indecent margin" (45). The Acting Company opened its national tour of *Orchards* at the Krannert Center of the University of Illinois in September 1985, where it was reviewed by Sid Smith for the *Chicago Tribune* (14). The tour ended at the Lucille Lortel Theatre in New York City, playing there 22 April-4 May 1986.

Following a brief service as a core writer for CBS's *Comedy Zone*, Wasserstein returned to theatre with *Miami*, a musical for which she wrote the book, with lyrics and music by Bruce Sussman and Jack Felman, again on commission from Playwrights Horizons. Offered in a workshop production for subscribers only for one month in January 1986, the piece played to all-but-sold-out houses. Gerald Guttierrez directed a cast that included John Aller, John Cunningham, Joanna Glushak, and Catherine Wolf. In keeping with the goal of showing to its subscribers a musical in progress, Playwright's Horizon did not have the performances reviewed.

SURVEY OF SECONDARY SOURCES

Bibliographies

Only Coven's brief bibliography of Wasserstein has been published. Out of date and incomplete, it lists only three plays, one biographical article, and five reviews.

Biographies

The most complete biographical sketch appears in Bennetts, originally published in the *New York Times* and subsequently included in its May 1981 *Biographical Service*.

General Studies

Wasserstein has entries in works edited by Stine and Marowski, Eddleman, and Kirkpatrick, each of which offers a very modest bibliography. Most recent is the entry on her by Swain. No book or dissertation takes Wasserstein as a major subject, although occasional dissertations, like Pevitts's, treat her as part of the larger scene of female writers. Typical of Wasserstein's treatment in general surveys of American dramatists is that of Weales, who skates over her with a single note about her "charming if too cute version of 'The Man in a Case' " (525). Because scholarly attention has been extremely slight, students of Wasserstein must depend largely on interviews, reviews, and occasional articles published in newspapers and popular magazines.

Analyses of Individual Plays

Only four extended treatments of Wasserstein's work appear in books or journals, and all of these take as their subject *Uncommon Women and Others*.

Cattaneo, the literary manager at the Phoenix Theatre, joins with ten other dramaturgs to discuss the role of dramaturgy in today's American theatre, using her experience with *Uncommon Women and Others* as an example of an extended process of revision (Alper, 19–20).

In a chapter called "Success and its Limits," Keyssar deals with the influence of commerce upon the content and production patterns of plays by women. As part of her analysis, she briefly turns to the issues introduced in *Uncommon Women* (154–55). Following equally brief analyses of one play each by Beth Henley, Mary O'Malley, Nell Dunn, Catherine Hayes, and Marsha Norman, Keyssar concludes that "the most innovative and challenging plays by feminists are produced in obscure venues and are heralded by a relatively small group of supporters, [while] the dramas of women that have achieved commercial success . . . tend to take fewer theatrical risks and to be less threatening to middle-class audiences" (148). Among the strengths of commerical plays like Wasserstein's, according to Keyssar, are their focus on female characters, their exploration of themes like sisterhood, sexuality, and female autonomy, and their ability to make audiences laugh. Their major weakness is that "no matter how serious the topic, they are all comedies of manners. . . . they are not challenges to the deeper social structures that allow those manners to endure" (150).

Like Keyssar, Crane seems interested in the degree to which *Uncommon Women and Others* is a feminist play. Focusing on the relationships among the play's women, she concludes that "the play is worth doing on the basis of its exploration of the dilemma of contemporary women, uncommon or not" (13). She avoids answering the question she initially set for herself: "Is *Uncommon Women* a feminist play?" She seems to feel some discomfort with the answer she sensed was emerging.

The most sustained scholarly analysis of Wasserstein's work to date is Carlson's, who compared Boothe's *The Women* with *Uncommon Women*. After a careful treatment of each play, Carlson proposes that "Wasserstein, with her play's openness of form and retaliation against some of comedy's sexist assumptions, has avoided some of the limitations which cornered Boothe." Carlson finds in *Uncommon Women* "a comic world where women can work within a female community to challenge social roles," but she is unable to conclude (as she had hoped) that Wasserstein had discovered "a way to translate comedy from its inherent social conservatism without destroying comedy itself" (572).

And so, although scholars to date have paid scant attention to Wasserstein's work, their conclusions seem correctly captured by Swain's entry on Wasserstein for the fourth edition of *Contemporary Dramatists*, which proposes that "Wasserstein's notable contribution to comedic playwrighting is her challenge of that vision [of a male-dominated world of values] with her comic worlds of women who do strike out and make a difference" (549).

Influences

No study presently takes as its focus influences on Wasserstein. Scattered through interviews and reviews, however, are three recurring references from which influences can perhaps be inferred. Christopher Durang is the playwright with whom she is most often compared. Cattaneo in *Theatre Crafts* writes of the works of Wasserstein and Durang as instances of the commercial requirements of popular comedy. This extended comparison finds echo in Bennetts; Betsko and Koenig; Haun ("Is it or") and Sirkin. Televised situation comedies are the comparative reference in unfavorable reviews by Corliss and Munk. The women's movement, contemporary female playwrights, feminism, and her personal experiences as a woman Wasserstein herself credits with influencing her plays (Betsko and Koenig, Sturgeon), as do reviewers Bennetts, Gold, and Lamb. Wasserstein's influence, if any, on other playwrights has yet to be explored and may still be in the making.

FUTURE RESEARCH OPPORTUNITIES

Wasserstein's works, because of their frankly commercial nature, can be more profitably studied as expressions of popular culture than as examples of literary or theatrical art. Among the cultural implications, those offering insights into the worlds of contemporary women are the most provocative. Thus, in the near future at least, research on Wasserstein will want to pursue the directions pointed by Carlson and Crane.

SECONDARY SOURCES

Alper, J. et al. "Dramaturgies in America: 11 Statements and Discussion." *Theater 10* (1978–1979): 15–30.

Barnes, Clive. "Chekhov Ambushed by Writers." *New York Post* (23 April 1986): 45.

Beaufort, John. "A Wry Reunion and a Bitter Eulogy: Wasserstein and Pinero Dramas Open in New York." *Christian Science Monitor* (30 November 1977): 26. Reprinted in *New York Theatre Critics' Reviews 1977: Off-Broadway Supplement*, 4: 140.

Bennetts, Leslie. "An Uncommon Dramatist Prepares Her New York Work." *New York Times* (14 May 1981): B1.

Bicknell, Arthur. "Montpelier Pa-zazz." *Show Business* (8 July 1976): 17.

Carlson, Susan L. "Comic Textures and Female Communities 1937 and 1977 Clare Boothe and Wendy Wasserstein." *Modern Drama* 27 (December 1984): 564–73.

Cattaneo, Anne. "When Comedy Is Commercial: Wasserstein and Durang." *Theatre Crafts* (November-December 1984): 32, 85–87.

Clurman, Harold. "Theatre." *Nation* (17 December 1977): 667–68.

Corliss, Richard. "Broadway's Big Endearment." *Time* (26 December 1983): 80.

Corry, John. Review of *Comedy Zone*. *New York Times* (17 August 1984): C24.

Coven, Brenda. *American Women Dramatists of the Twentieth Century: A Bibliography*. Methuen, N.J.: Scarecrow Press, 1982.

Crane, Gladys. "Playwriting Images to Improve Women's Position." *Indiana Theatre Bulletin* (February 1983): 11–13.

Demp. "T.V. Review: 'The Sorrows of Gin.' " *Variety* (31 October 1979): 72, 78.

Eddleman, Floyd Eugene. *American Drama Criticism*. Hamden, Conn.: Shoestring Press, 1979.

Eder, Richard. "Dramatic Wit and Wisdom Unite in 'Uncommon Women and Others.' " *New York Times* (22 November 1977): 48.

Frank, Leah D. "Two Views: 'Uncommon Women and Others' at Marymount College." *New York Theatre Review* (January 1978): 39.

Gold, Sylvaine. "Wendy, the Wayward Wasserstein." *Wall Street Journal* (7 February 1984).

Gussow, Mel. "Theater: Two Evenings of One-Act Plays." *New York Times* (1 June 1983): C17.

———. "Stage: New 'Romantic' by Wendy Wasserstein." *New York Times* (16 December 1983): C3.

———. "Theater: 'Orchards' Seven One-Acts." *New York Times* (23 April 1986): C15.

Haun, Harry. "Theatre." *Daily News* (19 February 1984): 5.

———. "Is It or . . . 'Isn't It Romantic.' " *Showbill* (March 1984): 4–7.

Kalem, T. E. "Stereotopical." *Time* (5 December 1977): 111.

Kerr, Walter. "Are Parents Looking Better on Stage?" *New York Times* (26 February 1984): 7, 36.

Keyssar, Helene. *Feminist Theatre*. New York: Grove Press, 1985.

Lamb, Pat. "Theatre: Seventh Sister." *East Side Express* (22 December 1977): 14.

Massa, Robert. "I Like You, I Like You Not." *Village Voice* (14 June 1983): 100.

Munk, Erika. "Review." *Village Voice* (27 December 1983): 109–10.

Newton, Edmund. " 'Women' One Can't Forget." *New York Post* (22 November 1977). Reprinted in *New York Theatre Critics' Reviews 1977: Off-Broadway Supplement*, 4:140.

Nightingale, Benedict. "There Really Is a World beyond 'Diaper Drama.' " *New York Times* (1 January 1984): B2, B14.

Pevitts, Beverley Byers. "Feminist Thematic Trends in Plays Written by Women for the American Theatre: 1970–1977." Ph.D. dissertation, University of Southern Illinois, 1980.

Simon, John. "Failing the Wasserstein Test." *New York Magazine* (29 June 1981): 36.

———. "Review." *New York Magazine* (26 December 1983): 106.

Sirkin, Elliot. *Nation* (18 February 1984):202.

Smith, Sid. " 'Orchards' Salutes Chekhov Works." *Chicago Tribune* (21 September 1985): 14.

Sommers, Michael. "Ensemble Marathon, Series C." *Backstage* (10 June 1983): 83.

Stine, Jean C., and Daniel G. Marowski, eds. *Contemporary Literary Criticism*. Vol. 33. Detroit: Gale, 1987.

Swain, Elizabeth. "Wendy Wasserstein." In *Contemporary Dramatists*. 4th ed., pp. 547–49. Edited by D. L. Kirkpatrick. Chicago: St. James Press, 1988.

Sweeney, Louise. "Being a Single Woman in Manhattan Has Its Funny Side." *Christian Science Monitor* (20 May 1985): 27–28.

Unger, Arthur. "John Cheever Buffs Should Be Relieved." *Christian Science Monitor* (22 October 1979): 19.

Wallace, Carol. "A Kvetch for Our Time." *Sunday News Magazine* (19 August 1984): 10–11, 17.

Watt, Douglas. " 'Isn't It Romantic' Sometimes." *New York Daily News* (16 December 1983): 3, 8.

Weales, Gerald. "American Theatre Watch, 1985–1986." *Georgia Review* 40 (Summer 1986): 520–31.

Wolcott, James. "Medium Cool: Television and Its Discontents: A Little Culture Won't Hurt You." *Village Voice* (29 October 1979): 56.

Michael Weller

(26 SEPTEMBER 1942–   )

RICHARD M. LEESON

ASSESSMENT OF WELLER'S REPUTATION

The late director Alan Schneider wrote that Michael Weller "manages to sum up the attitude of a generation: social, political, sexual and comedic" (xii). Indeed, for almost two decades, Weller has been writing about his own generation. From *Moonchildren* (1971), *Fishing* (1975), *Split* (1977), to *Loose Ends* (1979), his sadly comic plays have conjured a dramatic atmosphere of loss, humor, and human coping not unlike that found in Chekhov.

A student at Brandeis University in the 1960s, Weller is acutely aware of the trials of his generation: the disillusionment of the Vietnam War; reactionary escapism into the counterculture of drugs and "nature"; and the growth into "yuppiehood," selfish sex, and impersonal relationships. His plays vividly portray the contemporary Me Generation with its reliance on things to counter an overriding sense of boredom and fear that comes with the realization of age and morality. Yet in a recent interview with Sid Smith, Weller said, "I don't think [merely] in terms of the '60's generation.... Each play involves a set of circumstances I'm trying to solve, a number of things that seem to be happening to a number of friends of mine, things with a common thread" (*Chicago Tribune*, 11 January 1987). Lately he has felt that his reputation as a spokesman for his age has hampered the chances of success for more recent works such as *Dwarfman* (1981), *The Ballad of Soapy Smith* (1983), and *Ghost on Fire* (1985).

PRIMARY BIBLIOGRAPHY OF WELLER'S WORKS

Productions of Adaptations and Musical Compositions

Fred. Adaptation of the novel *Malcolm* by James Purdy. Weller, adapter/composer. Waltham, Massachusetts, 1965.

How Ho-Ho Rose and Fell in Seven Short Scenes. Weller, adapter/composer. Exeter, England, 1968.

The Making of Theodore Thomas, Citizen. Adapter/composer. Adaptation of the play *Johnnie Johnson* by Paul Green. London, 1968.

More Than You Deserve. Lyricist with Jim Steinman. New York, 1973.

Adaptor of Chekhov story *The Skit* in *Orchards* (adaptations of seven Chekhov stories by seven playwrights). New York, 1986.

Unpublished Plays and Productions

Cello Days at Dixon's Place. Loeb Experimental Theatre, Cambridge, Massachusetts, 1965.

Happy Valley. Edinburgh, 1969.

Poison Come Poison. London, 1970.

Twenty-three Years Later. Los Angeles, 1973.

"Alice" in *After Calcutta*. London, 1976.

Dwarfman, Master of a Million Shapes. Chicago, 1981.

Spoils of War. New York, 1988.

Published Plays

Cancer. Produced in London. 1970. London: Faber, 1971. Produced as *Moonchildren* in Washington, D.C. 1971, and New York, 1972. New York: French, 1971; with Introduction by Jack Kroll. New York: Delacorte, 1971.

The Bodybuilders and *Now There's Just the Three of Us*. Produced in London, 1969. In *The Bodybuilders, and Tira Tells Everything There is to Know about Herself*. New York: Dramatists Play Service, 1972; *Off-Broadway Plays 2*, London: Penguin, 1971.

Grant's Movie. Produced in London, 1971. In *Grant's Movie and Tira*. London: Faber, 1972.

Fishing. New York and London: French, 1975.

Split. New York and London: French, 1979.

Loose Ends: A Play in Eight Scenes. New York: French, 1980.

At Home (Split, part I). New York: French, 1981.

Now There's Just the Three of Us. New York: French, 1982.

Five Plays by Michael Weller. Contains *Moonchildren, Fishing, At Home (Split, part I), Abroad (Split, part II)*, and *Loose Ends*. Introduction by Alan Schneider. New York: New American Library, 1982.

The Ballad of Soapy Smith. New York: French, 1985.

Ghost on Fire. New York: Grove Press, 1987.

Screenplays

Hair. New York: Script City Distributors, 1977.
Ragtime. New York: Citron Manuscripts, 1980.

Translation

Barbarians. Adaptation of Maxim Gorky's play by Kitty Hunter Blair, Jeremy
    Brooks, and Michael Weller. New York: French, 1982.

Interviews

Berkvist, Robert. "We're Different But We See Life the Same." *New York Times*
    (4 July 1979): 7–8.
Johnson, Wayne. " 'Odd Little Play' Gets Varied Reaction from Seattle Rep.
    Audience." *Seattle Times* (20 January 1981).
Christiansen, Richard. "Hit Dramatist Takes Screen, Stage in Stride," *Chicago
    Tribune* (24 May 1981): F8.
Christon, Lawrence. "Michael Weller Examines Values in 'Ghost on Fire.' " *Los
    Angeles Times* (6 August 1985): 6: 3.
Smith, Sid. "Boomer-ing Voice," *Chicago Tribune* (11 January 1987): 13:10, 12.
Savran, David. "Michael Weller." *In Their Own Words: Contemporary American
    Playwrights*, pp. 272–87. New York: Theatre Communications Group,
    1988.

PRODUCTION HISTORY

Since the first productions of his plays in the early 1960s, Michael Weller's
works have achieved their greatest success on off-Broadway and regional
stages.

Weller began writing plays while he was still a student at Brandeis
University and continued to do so while completing his education at the
University of Manchester in England. Many of his early efforts were
first produced in England with the help of Charles Marowitz and his
Open Space Theatre. They received little formal critical attention.

Hammond, one of the few critics to comment on these early plays,
has described them as having dominant figures who "burst in on a situation and radically alter, by their actions and attitudes, the preoccupations and life-styles of the people in that situation" (801). In *Now There's
Just the Three of Us*, for instance, two American boys share a flat, along
with mutual adolescent sexual and identity anxieties. They are confronted by the mature, athletic Deke whose assertive behavior and perceptive observations bring the boys to some degree of self-awareness.
Hammond identifies the same pattern in *How Ho-Ho Rose and Fell*, a play
about fascism in which a group of young people become dominated and

then brainwashed by a strongman dictator. The fascist leader, Ho-Ho, is eventually rejected by the group, yet he lives on in the values he has ingrained in the members. Says Hammond, while Weller's early plays represent "experiments in a fresh, uncluttered realism," the protagonists who alter the directions of other characters exist "on a psychological and spiritual level outside [their] surface realism" (802).

Other apprentice plays starkly portray the social and political climate of the 1960s with acute realism. *Grant's Movie*, Chaillet notes, focuses on the point when the relationship between police and antiwar demonstrators has "come to be serious violence" (824). Yet a work like *Tira Tells Everything There Is to Know about Herself* turns inward for what Hammond describes as "a subtle and sensitive character study" (802) of an anguished, middle-class girl searching for a sense of completion and belonging in a careless world of impersonal sex and brutal perversion.

Weller's first major (and, to this date, greatest) success came with the production of *Cancer* in London (1970). The play was renamed *Moonchildren* and produced successfully in Washington, D.C. (1971) but was not as well received on Broadway the following year. It finally achieved critical acclaim off-Broadway in 1974.

"*Moonchildren*," Eichelbaum said in a review of the 1976 San Francisco production, "is a harshly realistic examination of eight college students' flight into fantasy at a time when alienation became the means for young people to cushion themselves against a hostile world." The students share a dingy, off-campus apartment during the 1965–1966 academic year at a Harvard-like college. With a background of rock-and-roll music, an atmosphere of smoke from marijuana, and an endless barrage of flippant, witty chatter, these "moonchildren" anticipate their futures playfully but with anxiety and bitterness. Indeed, Barnes noted a Chekhov-like happy-sad quality to the tone. The play, he said, is "about growing up in a hostile country . . . about taking a journey without maps, about developing ethics without ethics, about surviving without much belief in survival" ("Moonchildren", 45). Novick also noted the Chekhovian qualities of the play, suggesting that, with its characterization of "a bunch of high-spirited kids who live unconventionally, sass their elders, and communicate largely in put-ons," it "belongs to a tradition that also includes *La Bohême, A Hard Day's Night*, and *Hair*" (2:9). Sullivan was less laudatory, however, remarking of the characters: "There is nothing much in these kids. . . . They feel guiltier about their inability to 'relate' than the Class of 1955 did, yet they can't 'relate' nearly as well as the Class of 1975 will." He goes on to suggest that this is why they rely upon the put-on, two of the boys taking it "to a nearly pathological degree." We "never find out what is inside these boys," Sullivan laments, "but we are tempted not to care" ("College Roomies," 4: 9). Yet Kerr, while admitting that in "sustaining manic improvisation for so long, [the play] begins to gasp once or twice," concludes that after all the "desperate foolery," the audience will find itself "unexpectedly touched." By the end of the play, "you didn't know you'd taken them [the characters] so seriously or liked them so much" (2:3). Commenting on the structure of *Moonchildren* in his introduction to *Five Plays by Michael Weller,* director Alan Schneider says this play, like most of Weller's other works, is "loosely woven and yet deceptively well-made," his style involving "the careful putting together of accident, the bittersweet and the brash intertwined, pranks and profundity, the sense that life is so impossible that the only solution is to laugh at it" (xiv-xv).

In 1973, *Twenty-three Years Later* was produced in Los Angeles to a perplexed but entertained audience. This "odd little play," as Weller called it during an interview prior to a 1981 Seattle revival (Johnson), is about a suburban couple in their forties and the sudden appearance in their lives of the man's ninety-two-year-old grandmother (whom he has not seen for twenty-three years) accompanied by her eighty-seven-year-old East Indian consort. Sullivan describes the play as a slick "three-legged shaggy dog story, featuring a three-legged dog—about a boring suburban couple suddenly awash in extramarital sex and possibly extraterrestrial visitors." The dialogue is "alive" and Weller's point of view close to that of John Updike's in *Couples:* "There are more complicated things going on under those shake roofs than you might think," Sullivan concludes ("A Whole Lot," 4:8).

It was, however, with the productions of *Fishing* (New York, 1975), *Split* (New York, 1978), and *Loose Ends* (New York, 1979) that Weller's reputation as a "chronicler of his generation" was set. As Sid Smith put it, where *Moonchildren* was a rendering of the playwright's vision of "the counterculture and communal dormitories of the '60s" and implied that "the penchant for carefree change was at least partly rooted in a deep-seated inability to connect," *Fishing* is "a blistering look at an effort to flee convention through drugs and a back-to-the-basics, live-off-the-land enterprise" (13:10). The play shows the moonchildren a few years down the road, spaced out on drugs and hopeless dreams. Barnes found the theme to be "survival"—to "keep on." And while admiring the neat construction and the interesting characters, he lamented the rather slow beginning and the joking "pseudo-melodramatic ending that doesn't quite come off" ("Fishing," 41). Nelson admitted that the characters "ring true." Yet "their predicaments, however sensitively viewed, seem too well worn," the audience feeling a "trifle cheated at being routed through [Weller's] familiar territory without a fresh orientation." And Watt was disappointed that "we never do learn just what the friends are fishing for (outside of Life—with a big L, that is)" ("Moonchildren").

In *Split* and *Loose Ends,* the generation of the 1960s has grown well into the 1970s as Weller dramatizes the full flowering of a selfish, sterile generation. His characters have fallen into the malaise of casual sex, couple swapping, and empty materialism. *Split,* with its two parts, *At Home* and *Abroad,* traces the marital difficulties of Carol and Paul as they fight, make up, and fight again into the death of their six-year marriage. And while Christiansen found the play "charming" and "less predictable" than Weller's handling of similar situations elsewhere ("Lifeline," 3:8), Stasio lamented that Weller's characters, here and in other plays, "wrap themselves up in [the playwright's] razzle-dazzle dialogue to avoid confronting and articulating the pain of their inner alienation." The trouble is that Weller "refuses to articulate for his characters the intellectual and emotional roots of the feelings they are too disconnected to discover for themselves."

Beginning with Paul, a disillusioned former Peace Corps volunteer, and Susan, a free spirit trying to find herself, *Loose Ends* traces their life together from a chance meeting on a tropical beach, through marriage, to divorce. The play and the marriage end with the fact of Susan's abortion, her pregnancy becoming, director Francis Cullinan said concerning a 1982 production of the play, "a threat to her personal values and her relationship to Paul; she fears the changes that will come with motherhood" (quoted in Butler). She, like so many others of Weller's lost generation, dreads the very commitment for which she longs. The *Baltimore Sun* reviewer found the play to be "the other side of the coin to Ibsen's *Hedda Gabler,*" showing not what could happen when society offers women few alternatives to the traditional role of wife and mother but "what can happen in a society that does" ("Loose Ends"). Koehler of the *Los Angeles Times,* however, chided Weller for writing a play "so methodical, so conscious of itself as a decade report, that we almost feel that it may have more anthropological than theatrical value in the end." The characters "rarely rise above types"; Weller's world often feels "like the GE Carousel of Progress, written by the staff of Rolling Stone" (6:8). And, while Friedman criticized Weller for "cutting his scenes short just when they're getting inside the characters" and introducing "pointless stereotypes" as minor characters, Eder found that the playwright drew his characters "with sympathy as well as wit and a good ear"; many of his minor ones are but "caricatures" yet others are "effective" (C:17).

With the production in Chicago of *Dwarfman* (1981), Weller seemed to be trying to break out of the mold of chronicler of the 60s generation. Christiansen found this play about a cartoonist in crisis (the protagonist begins to doubt the truth and beauty of his black-and-white comic strip hero) "confused, overwrought, and pretentious," full of "anguished, breast-beating gobbledygook" (30 May 1981, 1:12). Syse, however, thought the play multidimensional, "provocative," and "dazzling." For her the play was a reminder "that we are losing our sense of awe, that we have become mindless machines determined to win the baubles of materialism, compromising our youthful aspirations."

The Ballad of Soapy Smith premiered in Seattle, Washington, in 1983 where it was hailed as "superbly-performed," "entertaining," and "funny" (Johnson). Yet Barnes found the New York Shakespeare Festival's production about con man Smith less successful. Soapy, a rogue, seeks to convince the people of Skagway, Alaska, in the Gold Rush days of the 1890s that he and his cohorts should bring law and order to the town. According to Barnes, Weller falls short of creating in Soapy an archly devilish Adolf Hitler because Soapy is not an interesting character. The play "is a true picture of neither a monster nor a society; nor does it tell anything new about the West (how won or how lost) or the Gold Rush, with its bonanza, avarice, hardship" (" 'Soapy' Sags"). Watt was also disappointed in the play, finding it somewhat hackneyed. "What Michael Weller has written," he said, "is the bloated outline for a Robert Preston musical with a fresh set of zippy and romantic Meredith Willson songs," the play standing "as a good example of regional theatre in a merry mood." Yet, Watt continued, "There is little genuine excitement. We've seen it all so many times before—the gamblers, prospectors, whores, outlaws and lawmen—Soapy or no Soapy" (" 'Soapy' mines). Rich agreed, commenting that Weller's satire of the American capitalistic dream with its "gilded-age Babbitts who deny their own ruthlessness and greed by spouting self-righteous pieties," is too familiar "to sustain" an audience "for nearly three hours" (C15).

The newest Weller play to come to the stage is *Ghost on Fire*, premiering in 1985 at the La Jolla playhouse in California and produced most recently in Chicago (1987). It is complex, revolving around two filmmakers who set forth to produce the great American movie together. Characters and caricatures slam wisecracks and sermons at each other and the audience, says Christiansen. "They're all glib, but most of them have no inner life, no reason for existing other than as mouthpieces or showboats." "For all the energizing performances in a play striving to grapple with the Big Issues of man's purpose in life, these are still little people parceling out little truths" ("Beneath 'Ghosts,' " 2:8). Vlertel summed it up this way: Weller's "attempt to use the internal combustion of the film industry as a mirror for a generation's exploding dream life is an extraordinary one. But *Ghost on Fire* needs serious rethinking." The play seems to call for revision, a taming down of its mannered, self-conscious eccentricity if it is to emerge as a credible landscape of the 1980s.

SURVEY OF SECONDARY SOURCES

Chaillet and Hammond offer short biographies and useful bibliographical listings.

Only a handful of critical works on Weller have appeared. O'Toole discusses the tensions playwrights experience when they are compelled, usually for financial (but sometimes for other) reasons, to turn away from the the theatre and write for the screen. "The lure of the theater is a little pale at the moment," Weller is quoted as saying. "There's simply not much of a serious theater in America, just a flop-hit mentality. Nor is there any feeling of community within the theater itself, or being taken seriously." Yet he concludes, "[you] write plays because you want to. You never write a screenplay without first being paid" (23–24).

Rudnick's "Recording Our Times" is a fine overview of Weller's work. It reviews the plays and their themes and discusses Weller's career as a playwright from its beginnings. Weller is quoted as lamenting the current American theatre: "You see," he says, "there are two branches of theater in America right now. The sacred, which deals with symbols and big images and confusing mumbo-jumbo, real art stuff." "Then," he goes on, describing his own aesthetic preferences, "you have the secular bunch, which is the popular theatre, and can entertain and also take joy in presenting descriptions of real peoples' lives, of things an intelligent audience wants to know about" (38–40).

Witham explores American playwrights' fascination with the Fourth of July. He discusses *Loose Ends*, which, in part, takes place on Independence Day, independence becoming a dominant theme of the work. The critic describes the America in Weller's play as "a photo album with ample evidence of where we have been. The past has been carefully preserved, the successes balanced by the failures. The problem with photo albums is that they cannot show us what to do next" (299). This problem is a major concern to Weller as an artist, a major concern of the play.

Most recently, Alexis Greene has written a concise overview of Weller's work on the occasion of the New York Second Stage's "retrospective" of his plays. In addition to reviewing the major themes of the plays, Greene discusses Weller's latest work, *Spoils of War*, to be directed at Second Stage by Austin Pendleton. According to Weller, the title of this family drama refers both to "the silent war between the parents, felt through the child," and to the post-World War II disillusionment experienced by idealists who expected a better world to come of it all. Says Greene, "Weller intends to 'situate' its [the play's] story in terms of politics and the disruptions World War II caused in people's lives" (21).

FUTURE RESEARCH OPPORTUNITIES

Because there have been few critical studies of Michael Weller's plays, the field is ripe for a variety scholarly projects. Not only should Weller's work be examined as an artistic record of a generation of political and moral change, it should also be investigated as postmodern dramatic art. Critical analyses by such reviewers as Syse, Vlertel, Smith, and Christiansen suggest the many unconventional qualities in script, staging, and audience-actor relationships appearing in such recent plays as *Dwarfman* and *Ghost on Fire*. The thematic as well as technical aspects of the plays' productions also warrant careful consideration. In addition, standard biography, bibliography, and reputation studies will surely be forthcoming. Weller's achievements as a screenplay writer merit attention considering of the enormous success of *Hair* and *Ragtime*.

SECONDARY SOURCES

Barnes, Clive. " 'Moonchildren': Bitterly Funny, Funnily Bitter Play at Royale." *New York Times* (22 Febuary 1972): 45.

———. "Weller's 'Fishing' at the Public Theatre." *New York Times* (13 February 1975): 41.

———. " 'Soapy' Sags a Bit Skagway." *New York Post* (13 November 1984).

Butler, Robert W. "An Unabashed Look at the 70s." *Kansas City Star* (1 Febuary 1982).

Chaillet, Ned. "Michael Weller." In *Contemporary Dramatists*, 4th ed. pp. 552–53. New York: Edited by D. L. Kirkpatrick. Chicago: St. James Press, 1988.

Christiansen, Richard. "Despite the Effort, 'Dwarfman' Is Overwrought and Pretentious." *Chicago Tribune* (30 May 1981):1:12.

———. "Lifeline Pulls It All Together with Fine 'Split.' " *Chicago Tribune* (16 Febuary 1983): 3: 8

———. "Beneath 'Ghost's' Cosmic Issues, Only Little Truths Emerge." *Chicago Tribune* (20 January 1987): 2: 8.

Eichelbaum, Stanley. "Uproarious Comedy of Distressed Youth." *San Francisco Examiner* (12 March 1976).

Eder, Richard. "Kevin Kline Stars in Loose Ends." *New York Times* (7 June 1979): C17.

Friedman, Arthur. " 'Loose Ends' Skims the Surface of Drifting '60s Couple." *Boston Herald* (12 February 1985).

Greene, Alexis. "The Times of Michael Weller." *American Theatre* 5, no.1 (April 1988): 18–22. Rpt. News Bank, Performing Arts, 89:A8.

Hammond, Jonathan. "Michael Weller." In *Contemporary Dramatists*. 3rd ed, pp. 800–802. Edited by James Vinson. New York: St. Martin's, 1973.

Johnson, Wayne. " 'Soapy' a Great Opener for New Rep." *Seattle Times* (27 October 1983).

Kerr, Walter. "Funny, Moving, and Alive." *New York Times* (27 February 1972): 2: 1, 3.

Koehler, Robert. " 'Loose Ends' Chronicles the Changes of the 1970s." *Los Angeles Times* (2 May 1986): 6: 8.

" 'Loose Ends' Well Executed in Arena Premiere." Review. *Baltimore Sun* (14 February 1979).

Nelson, Don. " 'Fishing': Strong Cast Outshines Weak Script." *New York Daily News* (30 April 1981).

Novick, Julius. "The Best New American Play? And Never Seen in New York?" *New York Times* (21 November 1971): 2:9

O'Toole, Lawrence. "Broadway to Hollywood." *Film Comment* 17, No. 6 (November-December 1981): 22–25.

Rich, Frank. "Michael Weller's 'Ballad of Soapy Smith.' " *New York Times* (13 November 1984): C15.

Rudnick, Paul. "Recording Our Times." *Horizon* 22 (December 1979): 36–41.

Schneider, Alan. Introduction to *Five Plays By Michael Weller*, pp. xi–xix. New York: New American Library, 1982.

Stasio, Marilyn. " 'Split' Breaks Up in the End." *New York Post* (5 April 1980).

Sullivan, Dan. "College Roomies Revived." *Los Angeles Times* (25 February 1972): 4:8.

———. "A Whole Lot of Plot in Suburbia." *Los Angeles Times* (4 October 1973): 4:8.

Syse, Glenna. " 'Dwarfman' Prophetic and Provocative." *Chicago Sun-Times* (30 May 1981).

Vlertel, Jack. "Specter of a Forceful Play Is Hidden Inside 'Ghost on Fire.' " *Los Angeles Herald Examiner* (13 August 1985). Rpt. NewsBank, Performing Arts, 32: F6–7.

Witham, Barry B. "Images of America: Wilson, Weller, and Horovitz." *Theatre Journal* 34, No. 2 (May 1982): 223–32.

Watt, Douglas. "The Moonchildren Go 'Fishing.' " *New York Daily News* (14 February 1975).

———. " 'Soapy' Mines No Gold." *New York Daily News* (13 November 1984). Rpt. in *New York Theatre Critics' Reviews* (1984): 138–39.

Tennessee Williams

(26 MARCH 1911–24 FEBRUARY 1983)

FELICIA HARDISON LONDRÉ

ASSESSMENT OF WILLIAMS'S REPUTATION

"He was the greatest American playwright. Period." Walter Kerr's unequivocal assessment (quoted in J. Phillips, 62) will surely be that of posterity. At present there are still those whose wavering judgments produce qualifications like that of Jack Kroll, who called him our "greatest playwright (after Eugene O' Neill)" (53), or safe understatements like "one of the premier American playwrights of the 20th century" (Singleton, 3) and "among the foremost of modern American playwrights" (Gould, 246). Too many critics have fallen prey to the assumption that a playwright is only as good as his latest play and have failed to consider the totality of Williams's work. Whether we take as a standard of judgment the literary and theatrical merit of individual works or the number of plays that have become a part of the standard repertoire of professional and educational theatre, or the impact that certain plays have had upon the development of American drama and dramatists, Tennessee Williams emerges as our best.

Indeed by any of those criteria, Williams's only serious contender for supremacy in all of American drama is Eugene O'Neill. O'Neill does have an apparent edge in the amount of scholarly criticism generated by his work, as indicated by the listings in Charles Carpenter's bibliography of modern drama scholarship for 1966 to 1980: 384 entries on O'Neill and 237 on Williams. *The New York Times Directory of the Theater* for 1920–1970 contains twice as many listings of New York productions and revivals for O'Neill as for Williams, but O'Neill had a twenty-year head start. A better index to lasting stageworthiness and acceptance by a broad spectrum of theatregoers is the number of productions in the not-for-profit regional theatres, as listed in Theatre Communications Group's biannual *Theatre Profiles* series; a compilation of all entries from

1977 to 1985 (volumes 4–7) shows that for every two productions of plays by O'Neill (a total of 71), there were three by Williams (a total of 113). Scholarly interest in Williams is rivaled by attention to Arthur Miller (224 entries in Carpenter) and Edward Albee (239 entries), but Miller and Albee fall woefully short of Williams in both the *New York Times* and Theatre Communications Group listings.

The early impact of Tennessee Williams's plays on the American theatre is succinctly recollected by Gilman: "If you don't know what the American theater was like when he first came into it, you can't know what he meant to so many of us. From the beginning he was an original, not simply a more 'talented' writer than his contemporaries but a different breed, an artist where the others were craftsmen. . . . In the bloodless, 'liberal,' cautious atmosphere of American drama, the Southern wildness, the sexual perversities and ferocities, the dangerous quality of what he dreamed gave his plays heart; their mingling of corruption and emotional accuracy touched us far more deeply than did any 'reasonable' American drama" (347). When *The Glass Menagerie* opened on Broadway in 1945, says Kalem, "it galvanized a theater that had exhausted its creative momentum. Onto this becalmed stage, Williams brought a kind of drama that reflected an entire generation's failure of nerve, and touched the exposed nerve ends" (88).

Williams was a trailblazer in dramatic form and content. Although he was often criticized as a better "scenewright" than a craftsman of overall dramatic structure, he must be credited with having transferred a cinematic concept of dramatic action to the American stage. And he eventually proved, with *Cat on a Hot Tin Roof*, that he could, when it suited him, write a play of concentrated continuous action. Although Maxwell Anderson had tried valiantly to put poetic language into the American theatre, Williams went one better, employing what the French call a "poetry *of* the theatre"—a harmonious blending and mutual reinforcement of dialogue, character, symbols, scenic environment, music, sound effects, and lighting. "Poetic naturalism" is the term often used to describe his theatre. "A play that thinks in images is a truly poetic play," wrote Simon, "and no other American dramatist, not even O'Neill, quite managed that" (77). Williams's dialogue is poetry in prose, distinctive in its rhythms and evocative power. That new voice was heralded in the first line of *The Glass Menagerie:* "Yes, I have tricks in my pocket, I have things up my sleeve." Although Williams tried in his late plays to adapt his style to a theatre that had come under the influence of Samuel Beckett and Harold Pinter, his last plays still offer flashes of the original voice, as in *Clothes for a Summer Hotel:* "The wisdom, the sorrowful wisdom, of acceptance. Wouldn't accept it. Romantics won't, you know."

Williams's subject matter was unusual in its strong focus on the misfits of humanity—the outcast, the destitute, the lonely—all treated with compassion. The private torments of some of those "tortured souls"

(Hughes)—Blanche Dubois, Val Xavier, Kilroy, Reverend T. Lawrence Shannon—earned them legendary stature in American drama. Going beyond the psychological explorations of human weakness, Williams shocked many theatregoers with his explicit sexual references. Among the taboos he overturned as fit topics for the stage were homosexuality (in *Cat on a Hot Tin Roof*), nymphomania (in *A Streetcar Named Desire*), social disease (in *Sweet Bird of Youth*), cannibalism (in *Suddenly Last Summer*), and sexual promiscuity (in *The Night of the Iguana*).

Most critics cite *The Glass Menagerie, A Streetcar Named Desire*, and perhaps *Cat on a Hot Tin Roof* as Williams's masterpieces. Other full-length plays that continue to be revived frequently are *Summer and Smoke, The Rose Tattoo, Sweet Bird of Youth*, and *The Night of the Iguana*. Although its large cast, complex staging, and expressionistic treatment prevent its being revived as often as other plays, *Camino Real* is recognized by many as one of Williams's most remarkable achievements. It was far ahead of its time when it premiered in 1953, just as *The Two-Character Play* (a variant of *Out Cry*) was advanced for the 1970s. Williams himself apparently believed that the latter work, as yet underappreciated, "would one day be regarded as his crowning achievement" (Kuehl, 9A). He continued to write prolifically up to his death, but he was never able to regain the popular press's critical favor after *The Night of the Iguana* (1961). Serious critics, however, continue to find value in the experimentations of his later plays. Ruby Cohn, for example, referred to *The Two-Character Play* as "what may be his masterpiece" (339), and Loney felt that with *Something Cloudy, Something Clear*, Williams "seemed to have regained his perspective and his control as a dramatist" (85).

It is difficult to pinpoint exactly how many plays Williams wrote, since a number of them were published in two or three different versions. Among the published variants with different titles are *Summer and Smoke/ Eccentricities of a Nightingale, Battle of Angels/Orpheus Descending, Kingdom of Earth/Seven Descents of Myrtle, Small Craft Warnings/Confessional, The Two-Character Play/Out Cry*, and *Baby Doll/Tiger Tail*. Three different versions of *Cat on a Hot Tin Roof* have been published. Boxill's tabulation of the canon seems as authoritative as any: "He published two books of poetry, two novels, four books of short stories (one including a novella), a book of essays, and his *Memoirs*. During his lifetime, at least sixty-three of his plays and playlets (thirty-two are short, twenty-four full-length and seven mid-length) were published or given a major professional production or both. He wrote or collaborated upon seven of the fifteen film adaptations" (21).

Williams won four New York Drama Critics Circle Awards: for *The Glass Menagerie* (which also won the Sidney Howard Memorial Award and the Donaldson Award), *A Streetcar Named Desire* (which also won the

Pulitzer Prize and the Donaldson Award), *Cat on a Hot Tin Roof* (which also won the Pulitzer Prize), and *The Night of the Iguana*. In 1969 he was awarded the Gold Medal for Drama by the American Academy of Arts and Letters and the National Institute of Arts and Letters. Honorary degrees were conferred by the University of Missouri (1969), the University of Hartford (1972), and Harvard University (1982). Among his other awards were the Brandeis University Creative Arts Award (1965), the National Theatre Conference Annual Award (1972), the Centennial Medal of the Cathedral Church of St. John the Divine (1973), the Entertainment Hall of Fame Award (1974), and the Medal of Honor for Literature by the National Arts Club (1975).

Williams's prominent position among American playwrights has held steady on the international theatre scene since the 1950s. "In Britain he remains America's best-loved playwright," declares Styan (11). Dotson Rader (in *Tennessee Williams Review*) recalls the success of *Vieux Carré* in London after it had failed in New York: "It opened in London to solid reviews and had a long run at the Picadilly Theatre in the West End. . . . He was happy. It was the last opening night (1978) he would enjoy" (23).

Paris critics were slower to appreciate Williams's episodic plot construction and carnal obsessions. As Falb explains, "The milieu of a Williams play is then viewed through a Parisian haze of social and political preconceptions, prejudices, or patterns already established by other American authors" (28). He also claimed, however, that "there has been a steady and considerable increase in the appreciation of Tennessee Williams's plays among the French" (35).

In 1982 Serge Schmemann reported from Moscow on Williams's popularity in the Soviet Union, which he attributed to the "Dostoyevskian tradition" of "appreciation for themes of human passion, despair and confession" and to an interest in the "forbidden" subject of sexual problems, which can be safely explored only through "imported" plays. With seven plays by Tennessee Williams then in the repertoires of Moscow theatres, one Soviet critic was quoted referring to him as "the biggest success since Chekhov" (C13). The "Tennessee Williams boom" had apparently hit Moscow theatre in 1980; Tass news agency reported at that time that "there are few foreign playwrights who are in a position to vie with Williams in popularity with Soviet audiences" (*Kansas City Times*, 13 October 1980).

According to Leverich, Williams's authorized biographer, "It can safely be said that no American playwright has ever been so widely recognized or so universally admired. Tennessee Williams cut across the grain of societies in countries all over the world to reach people on every level of life" (30).

PRIMARY BIBLIOGRAPHY OF WILLIAMS'S WORKS

The following bibliography lists the most accessible sources for Williams's works. Many of the plays are published in a number of different anthologies, as well as in acting editions from Dramatists Play Service. Textual variants exist, especially between the acting editions and the presumably definitive texts published by New Directions. For a fairly complete listing of works published in anthologies, pamphlets, and periodicals, see *Tennessee Williams: A Bibliography* by Drewey Wayne Gunn (Scarecrow Press, 1980; new edition forthcoming in 1988). For a listing of many unpublished works, see Arnott. References to some interviews not listed elsewhere may be found in *Tennessee Williams Newsletter* (Fall 1980): 26–28.

Plays and Screenplays

At Liberty. In *American Scenes*. Edited by William Kozlenko. New York: John Day Co., 1941.

American Blues: Five Short Plays (Moony's Kid Don't Cry; The Dark Room; The Case of the Crushed Petunias; The Long Stay Cut Short; or, The Unsatisfactory Supper; Ten Blocks on the Camino Real). New York: Dramatists Play Service, 1948.

You Touched Me! with Donald Windham. New York: Samuel French, 1947.

Baby Doll (the script for the film, with the two one-act plays that suggested it, *27 Wagons Full of Cotton* and *The Long Stay Cut Short; or, The Unsatisfactory Supper*). New York: New Directions, 1956.

Out Cry. New York: New York Directions, 1966.

27 Wagons Full of Cotton and Other Plays (27 Wagons Full of Cotton; The Purification; The Lady of Larkspur Lotion; The Last of My Solid Gold Watches; Portrait of a Madonna; Auto-Da-Fé; Lord Byron's Love Letter; The Strangest Kind of Romance; The Long Goodbye; Hello from Bertha; This Property Is Condemned; Talk to Me Like the Rain...; Something Unspoken). New York: New Directions, 1966.

Dragon Country (In the Bar of a Tokyo Hotel; I Rise in Flame, Cried the Phoenix; The Mutilated; I Can't Imagine Tomorrow; Confessional; The Frosted Glass Coffin; The Gnädiges Fräulein; A Perfect Analysis Given By a Parrot). New York: New Directions, 1970.

The Theatre of Tennessee Williams. Vol. 1 (*Battle of Angels; The Glass Menagerie; A Streetcar Named Desire*). New York: New Directions, 1971.

The Theatre of Tennessee Williams. Vol. 2 (*The Eccentricities of a Nightingale; Summer and Smoke; The Rose Tattoo; Camino Real*). New York: New Directions, 1971.

The Theatre of Tennessee Williams. Vol. 3 (*Cat on a Hot Tin Roof; Orpheus Descending; Suddenly Last Summer.*) New York: New Directions, 1971.

The Theatre of Tennessee Williams. Vol. 4 (*Sweet Bird of Youth; Period of Adjustment; The Night of the Iguana.*) New York: New Directions, 1972.

The Theatre of Tennessee Williams. Vol. 5 (*The Milk Train Doesn't Stop Here Anymore;*

Kingdom of Earth; Small Craft Warnings; The Two-Character Play). New York: New Directions, 1976.

Vieux Carré. New York: New Directions, 1979.

A Lovely Sunday for Crève Coeur. New York: New Directions, 1980.

The Theatre of Tennessee Williams. Vol. 6 (*27 Wagons Full of Cotton: The Purification; The Lady of Larkspur Lotion; The Last of My Solid Gold Watches; Portrait of a Madonna; Auto-Da-Fé; Lord Byron's Love Letter; The Strangest Kind of Romance; The Long Goodbye; Hello from Bertha; This Property is Condemned; Talk to Me Like the Rain . . . ; Something Unspoken; The Unsatisfactory Supper; Steps Must be Gentle; The Demolition Downtown*). New York: New Directions, 1981.

The Theatre of Tennessee Williams. Vol. 7 (*In the Bar of a Tokyo Hotel; I Rise in Flame, Cried the Phoenix; The Mutilated; I Can't Imagine Tomorrow; Confessional; The Frosted Glass Coffin; The Gnädiges Fräulein; A Perfect Analysis Given by a Parrot; Lifeboat Drill; Now the Cats with Jewelled Claws; This is the Peaceable Kingdom*). New York: New Directions, 1981.

Clothes for a Summer Hotel; A Ghost Play. New Directions, 1983.

Stopped Rocking and Other Screenplays (*All Gaul Is Divided; The Loss of a Teardrop Diamond; One Arm; Stopped Rocking*). New York: New Directions, 1984.

The Red Devil Battery Sign. 1988. New Directions.

Fiction and Poetry

One Arm and Other Stories. New York: New Directions, 1950.

The Roman Spring of Mrs. Stone. New York: New Directions, 1950.

Hard Candy: A Book of Stories. New York: New Directions, 1954.

In the Winter of Cities. New York: New Directions, 1954.

The Knightly Quest: A Novella and Four Short Stories. New York: New Directions, 1966.

Eight Mortal Ladies Possessed: A Book of Stories. New York: New Directions, 1974.

Moise and the World of Reason. New York: Simon and Schuster, 1975.

Memoirs. Garden City: Doubleday, 1975.

Androgyne, Mon Amour: Selected Poems. New York: New Directions, 1977.

Collected Stories. Introduction by Gore Vidal. New York: New Directions, 1985.

Essays, Letters, and Interviews

Letters to Donald Windham, 1940–65. Edited by Donald Windham. New York: Holt, Rinehart, and Winston, 1977.

Where I Live: Selected Essays. Edited by Christine R. Day and Bob Woods, with an Introduction by Christine R. Day. New York: New Directions, 1948.

Dictionary of Literary Biography, Documentary Series, An Illustrated Chronicle. Vol. 4: *Tennessee Williams*. Edited by Margaret Van Antwerp and Sally Johns. Detroit: Gale Research Co., 1984.

Conversations with Tennessee Williams. Edited by Albert J. Devlin. Jackson: University Press of Mississippi, 1986.

PRODUCTION HISTORY

All of Williams's major full-length plays have had at least one New York revival, and they are a staple of professional regional theatre repertoires. Gunn lists the number of performances in the runs of the major American productions and includes entries on some foreign productions. London productions between 1950 and 1975 are listed, with a bibliography of reviews, in Stanley. Falb offers a substantial chronology of productions but only a token nine-entry bibliography. University Press of America has announced its forthcoming publication of *Tennessee Williams on the Soviet Stage*, which analyzes Soviet production approaches to the major plays.

Although Williams had seen two of his earlier full-length plays staged by the Mummers of St. Louis, *Battle of Angels* was his first major production. Produced by the Theatre Guild, its disastrous opening in Boston on 30 December 1940 became a theatrical legend. Not only did many audience members leave during the performance, but the ending was marred when "the smoke pots miscarried and spewed grey clouds over the auditorium" (Wood, 136). Reviews were uniformly devastating, largely attacking the play as torrid melodrama, and the Boston City Council requested that offensive lines be cut. *Battle of Angels* closed within two weeks. The revised version that opened in New York seventeen years later, on 22 March 1957, under the title *Orpheus Descending*, achieved a run of sixty-eight performances. Critics found much to admire in it even as they noted its flaws. John Chapman of the *Daily News* saw in this "sprawling play of mercurial moods . . . the beauty of writing and the beauty of compassion; but there is also a great deal of obvious trash" (310). Brooks Atkinson found that while it was "written in his best style of mood, lyricism, and tenderness," it was also "overwritten in some of the scenes, uncertain at times in its progression" (310). For Richard Watts, Jr., it had a "disturbing fascination," and Robert Coleman wrote of "its brief lightning flashes and its flares of intensity" (*NYTCR*, 311). The 1959 Paris production starring Arletty had ninety-six performances despite generally unappreciative reviews like Robert Kemp's comment that seeing the play was like drinking raw liquor, "bitter and incendiary." In London that same season, critics gave it a "kindly but unenthusiastic reception." The 1961 Moscow production, however, scored a big success in Soviet audiences' first exposure to Tennessee Williams. *Orpheus Descending* was revived at the Gramercy Arts Theatre in New York, directed by Adrian Hall, on 5 October 1959. *Battle of Angels* was revived at Circle Repertory Company, directed by Marshall W. Mason, on 3 November 1974, for a run of thirty-two performances. A film version entitled *The Fugitive Kind* (1960) starred Anna Magnani and Marlon Brando.

Like *Battle of Angels*, *The Glass Menagerie* had a legendary opening but with quite different results. Icy weather deterred theatregoers from the opening on 26 December 1944 at the Civic Center in Chicago, but a crusade by the warmly enthusiastic Chicago critics to keep the play open was led by Claudia Cassidy of the *Chicago Tribune*. In a follow-up review (7 January 1945, reprinted in Van Antwerp and Johns, 61), Cassidy wrote: "It is an honest, tender, tough, and, to me, brilliant play." Director Eddie Dowling, who also played Tom, took a risk in casting Laurette Taylor as Amanda; she had achieved stardom in the title role of *Peg o'My Heart* in 1912 but had left the stage after the death of her husband in 1928 and was rumored to have a drinking problem. Evoking Taylor's "incredibly luminous, electrifying performance," Cassidy wrote: "At the beginning, this raddled belle of the old south is sunk deep in frustration pricked only by the nagging urge not to admit defeat. She looks like the scuffed, rundown slipper that outlived the ball. Yet when for a brief moment she knows hope, she leans on the tenement stoop and gazes at the moon that might have been that very slipper, brand new. And over her face flit all the lovely ghosts of girlhood when 17 gentlemen callers came riding to pay her tribute. You won't see a more radiant sight than Laurette Taylor at that magic moment" (Van Antwerp and Johns, 62–63). New York critics were equally impressed when the play opened on 31 March 1945 at the Playhouse Theatre. Thus Taylor's performance set a standard by which all other interpretations of Amanda would be measured, and the interpretation of that character became the crucial point of interpretation in all other productions of the play.

Helen Hayes's feisty Amanda in the November 1956 revival at the New York City Center brought "reminders of the downcast Taylor mouth, the fiercely bright face haloed by a straggling grey bob" (*NYTCR*, Kerr, 190) but focused on "the humorous possibilities" while scarcely touching "the tragic implications" (*NYTCR*, Donnelly, 191). Of the May 1965 revival at the Brooks Atkinson Theatre, directed by George Keathley, it was said that "Maureen Stapleton does not cause one to forget Miss Taylor; she makes one remember her own conception" (*NYTCR*, Taubman, 335). Walter Kerr described her as "dowdy and toppling slightly forward in her passion to discover a straightaway ahead, . . . beggar and bulldog at once" (334). Stapleton recreated the role in December 1975 under the direction of Theodore Mann at the Circle in the Square Theatre; Martin Gottfried called this Amanda "almost vulgar and hardly believable as a onetime Southern belle" (126). A 1980 revival at the Lion Theatre in New York featured the original Laura, Julie Haydon, in the role of Amanda. John Dexter directed the December 1983 revival at the Eugene O'Neill Theatre, which featured seventy-four-year-old Jessica Tandy as Amanda. She brought to the character "a vigor and sometimes an asperity that add greatly to the robustness of the play" (Gill, 157). And still there were comparisons to Laurette Taylor, as in Jack Kroll's review (*NYTCR*): "Jessica Tandy makes Amanda a living rhapsody of failure. Laurette Taylor's legendary Amanda in the original 1944 production seems to have had an ecstatic intensity that was almost a kind of madness. Tandy lacks that transcendent desperation; her Amanda is as real as the faded cotillion dress she puts on to recapture her lost romantic girlhood. Alternately hostile and tender toward her blighted children, Tandy shows us an Amanda whose love has become lethal through her balked passion for life. Putting her own stamp on the strongest woman character in American drama, Tandy makes this an occasion not to be missed" (*NYCTR*, 107).

In London, Amanda was played by Helen Hayes at the Theatre Royal, Haymarket, in July 1948, directed by John Gielgud. There, critics have been less tied to the vision of Amanda as the dramatic soul of the play. The *London Times* review of the December 1965 revival, for example, focused on the balance of the four characters. The play was revived there again on 13 June 1977 at the Shaw Theatre. *The Glass Menagerie* emerges as Williams's most popular play in Paris, where it was staged in 1963 and in 1969 in addition to English-language productions there in 1953 and 1961.

A much-acclaimed television production, broadcast on 16 December 1973, featured Katharine Hepburn as Amanda in a performance that "almost makes you forget that anyone else ever tried" (Waters, 61). She was "a wonderfully effective blend of Southen gentility and fierce determination" (O'Connor, 94). The 1950 film version starring Gertrude Lawrence was not successful; Williams, in fact, referred to it as "the first and worst screen adaptation ever done of his work" (G. Phillips, 50).

A Streetcar Named Desire opened at the Ethel Barrymore Theatre on 3 December 1947, directed by Elia Kazan. Critics hailed the play as an advance over *The Glass Menagerie* and seemed to recognize that in Blanche DuBois Williams had created an archetypal figure. John Chapman's comment (*NYTCR*) is typical: *The Glass Menagerie* was "a fragment, a cameo. The new play is full-scale—throbbingly alive, compassionate, heartwrenchingly human. It has the tragic overtones of grand opera and is, indeed, the story of a New Orleans Camille—a wistful little trollop who shuns the reality of what she is and takes gallant and desperate refuge in a magical life she has invented for herself." Jessica Tandy as Blanche, Marlon Brando as Stanley, Kim Hunter as Stella, and Karl Malden as Mitch all won critical acclaim. The play ran for 855 performances, with Uta Hagen, Anthony Quinn, Jorja Cartwright, and George Matthews eventually replacing the original cast. Three of the original cast members recreated their Broadway roles in the 1951 film version also directed by Elia Kazan, but because the producers insisted on "at least one box-office name" (Yacowar, p. 15), the role of Blanche was taken over by Vivien Leigh, who had won unanimous critical praise as

Blanche in the 1949 London production under the direction of Laurence Olivier. The play and the film together brought stardom to Marlon Brando, who felt in looking back on his interpretation of Stanley that he had missed one important facet of the character's personality: his gaiety (G. Phillips, p. 67). *A Streetcar Named Desire* remains one of the best of the fifteen movies based upon Williams's works, despite the cuts and changes demanded by the Motion Picture Association of America's Production Code and the Legion of Decency. The major changes were the removal of overt reference to the homosexuality of Blanche's former husband, the softening of the rape sequence, and Stella's apparent rejection of Stanley at the end. In industry circles, according to Gene D. Phillips, *A Streetcar Named Desire* was viewed "as an interesting exception to the rule that Hollywood should cater to family patronage" (p. 87).

There were several foreign productions of *A Streetcar Named Desire* in 1949 besides that in London: Mexico City; Goteborg, Sweden; Rome (directed by Luchino Visconti, designed by Franco Zeffirelli, with Vittorio Gassman as Stanley and Marcello Mastroianni as Mitch); Zurich; Paris (adapted by Jean Cocteau, directed by Raymond Rouleau, with Arletty as Blanche); and Berlin (adapted and directed by Berthold Viertel). A 1965 production in Havana was cheered by a standing-room-only audience who appreciated the "lavishness, the excellent acting," and "the "genuine poetry," despite the program's description of the play as "an implacable document of society in the south of the United States, a sordid and brutal ambience that leads man from a human sphere (normality) to the nonhuman one of alienation" (Hofmann, 27). The 1975 Paris revival used a new adaptation, by Paule de Beaumont, and the cast included Claude Brosset as Mitch.

The first of the play's many New York revivals was at the Originals Only Playhouse on 3 March 1955. Although it failed to convey the complexities of the script, that renewed experience of "the wildness, the pity, the insight of a work of dramatic art" (Atkinson, 4 March 1955, 18) led to a major revival the following year by the New York City Theatre Company. The reviews of that production focused almost exclusively on Tallulah Bankhead's interpretation of Blanche, and it was generally deemed that although "she was doing her level best to sink that fabled reputation into the broken and self-pitying terrors of the character called Blanche du Bois" (*NYTCR*, Kerr, 364), she "turned Mr. Williams's play into a vehicle" (*NYTCR*, Watts, 363). The twenty-fifth anniversary revival at the Vivian Beaumont Theatre on 26 April 1973 was well received, although there was little excitement about Rosemary Harris's "whimsical" approach to Stella (*NYTCR*, Watts, 281) and James Farentino's "lowbrow" Stanley (*NYTCR*, Kalem, 283). Ellis Rabb's direction was universally faulted for its "distracting" (*NYTCR*, Wilson) "introduction of droves of neighbors who kept darting about in the background" (*NYTCR*, Watts,

281). Another anniversary-year production was directed by James Bridges at the Ahmanson Theatre in Los Angeles, with Faye Dunaway as Blanche and Jon Voight as Stanley. Stephen Farber thought that Voight "underplayed" the role: "He even throws the dishes politely." He appreciated the comedy and the strength in Dunaway's performance, although "the one thing that eludes her is Blanche's fragile poetry" (15). New York saw another revival in 1973, only six months after the Vivian Beaumont production; directed by Jules Irving at the St. James Theatre, it was "low keyed and almost stealthily effective" (Barnes, 5 October 1973, 19).

A 1974 London revival directed by Edwin Sherin ran for over ninety performances. Irving Wardle wrote that "Claire Bloom presents a totally convincing image of Blanche; hollow-cheeked, delicate, dispensing Southern coquetry over an undertow of hysterical panic. What she leaves out is the comedy" (15). Other important revivals of *A Streetcar Named Desire* include that of the Academy Festival Theatre in Lake Forest (Chicago) in 1976, with Geraldine Page as Blanche and Rip Torn as Stanley; and the McCarter Theatre's (Princeton, New Jersey) 1976 production, which featured Shirley Knight as Blanche and Glenn Close as Stella. A television production broadcast on 4 March 1984 starred Ann-Margaret as Blanche and Treat Williams as Stanley. The play has been adapted as a ballet by Valerie Bettis, with music by Alex North; it premiered at Her Majesty's Theatre in Montreal on 9 October 1952 and was revived by the Dance Theatre of Harlem on 14 January 1982.

Summer and Smoke premiered on 8 July 1947 at Margo Jones's 200–seat Theatre '47 in Dallas and played to enthusiastic, sell-out audiences. Atkinson found the simplicity of the unusual arena staging "constructive" because it emphasized "the genuine truths of the play" and lay "the main emphasis on character" (10 August 1947, 1). The Broadway premiere on 6 October 1948 was again directed by Margo Jones with a different cast, but New York critics were generally disappointed. Having apparently expected the searing passions of *A Streetcar Named Desire*, they found the new work insubstantial and monotonous. Brooks Atkinson (17 October 1948) regretted the loss of intimacy in the New York production but spoke out for the play's values: "the incandescence of its search into the private agonies of a human being and the unostentatious beauty of the dialogue. It is as intangible as a piece of music—with modest themes that are balanced and contrasted and once or twice almost blended. These qualities are a rare treasure in our workaday theatre. Nothing is much more humbling and in this instance terrifying than a clairvoyant glimpse into the heart of another person. As far as spiritual tumult is concerned, *Summer and Smoke* is the most eventful drama on the stage today" (2:1).

La Jolla Playhouse produced a touring production of *Summer and Smoke* in 1950, which starred Dorothy McGuire as Alma Winemiller, John Ireland as John Buchanan, and Una Merkel as Mrs. Winemiller. The London production opened 22 November 1951 at the Lyric Theatre, Hammersmith, and was received well enough to move to the larger Duchess Theatre in the West End. The play began a second life with the sensitive production directed by Jose Quintero at the Circle in the Square Theatre in New York on 24 April 1952. Quintero describes in his book, *If You Don't Dance, They Beat You,* how the role of Alma made a star of Geraldine Page. She recreated the role in the 1961 film version, costarring with Laurence Harvey as John. In 1971, *Summer and Smoke* was made into an opera composed by Lee Hoiby to a libretto by Lanford Wilson. Directed by Frank Corsaro, it premiered at the St. Paul Opera, and was produced by the New York City Opera in 1972.

Eccentricities of a Nightingale, a substantially revised version of *Summer and Smoke,* was first produced at the Tappan Zee Playhouse in Nyack, New York, on 25 June 1964, followed by productions in Washington, D.C., in 1966 and in Guildford, England, in 1967. Not until 1976 did it reach Broadway, following the broadcast of a PBS television production starring Blythe Danner and Frank Langella on 16 June 1976. Critical reactions to the new version were mixed. Among the favorable responses was that of Alan Rich: "Miss Alma may be the younger Blanche DuBois, but she is an extraordinary creation on her own, and what Williams has done in *Eccentricities* is to shape her character more compellingly, and to set it far more skillfully into its milieu. Some new moments exhale a poetry beyond description" (116).

When *The Rose Tattoo* opened in New York on 5 February 1951, the critics split into two camps: those who found the play "offensive" (*NYTCR*, McClain, 364) and "sacrilegious" (*NYTCR*, Coleman, 364) versus those who found it "warm" (*NYTCR*, Guernsey, Jr., 363) and "compassionate and...hilarious" (*NYTCR*, Atkinson, 365). They were unanimous, however, in their enthusiastic praise for Maureen Stapleton in the "physically and emotionally taxing role" of Serafina (*NYTCR*, Chapman, 365); Eli Wallach for his "humorous, naive, frustrated performance in a light, buoyant style" (*NYTCR*, Atkinson, 365) as Mangiacavallo; Phyllis Love as the "dewy and dynamic" Rosa (*NYTCR*, Hawkins, 366); and Don Murray as her "perfect counterpart"(*NYTCR*, Atkinson, 365) in the role of the sailor. Daniel Mann directed both the stage premiere and the 1955 film, which featured Anna Magnani and Burt Lancaster.

The Rose Tattoo has been produced in Brussels (1952), Hamburg (1952), Munich (1953), Paris (1953), Dublin (1957), and Liverpool and London (1958–1959). In the 1966 New York revival at the City Center, Maureen Stapleton recreated her role, competing "not so much with herself as with Anna Magnani," for whom Williams had originally written the play.

"The comparison can be made with no discredit to either actress. Miss Magnani was immense in the role—a lusty, loud combination of Earth Mother and Mt. Vesuvius. Miss Stapleton's Serafina can also blow her top; but, in general, she is daintier and subtler than Miss Magnani was— less awe-inspiring perhaps, but more sympathetic" (Sullivan, 36).

Camino Real proved baffling to most reviewers of its original production on 19 March 1953. Richard Watts, Jr. (*NYTCR*, 330) called it an "enigma...bogged down in a kind of dogged determination to be as heavily symbolic as possible." Atkinson (29 March 1953) could not call it obscure but was shocked "to realize that Mr. Williams' conception of the world is so steeped in corruption." Elia Kazan "staged it with all the color and movement and artifice at his command" (*NYTCR*, Watts, Jr., 330). Eli Wallach led the cast as "an appealing Kilroy" (*NYTCR*, Kerr, 331). It ran for only sixty performances.

The 1957 London production, in which Denholm Elliott played Kilroy, achieved sixty-three performances. The play was also produced in Darmstadt (1954), Bochum (1955), and Hanover (1959), Germany. José Quintero directed the first New York revival in 1960, at the Circle in the Square. Although Brooks Atkinson (29 May 1960) could not summon much enthusiasm for the production, it ran eighty-nine performancees. A more noteworthy revival was directed by Milton Katselas for the Mark Taper Forum in Los Angeles and brought to the Vivian Beaumont Theatre in Lincoln Center, where it opened 8 January 1970 for fifty-two performances. No one complained of obscurity this time, and there was considerable praise for the "most striking production" (*NYTCR*, Barnes, 396), as well as performances by Al Pacino as Kilroy, Jessica Tandy as Camille, Jean-Pierre Aumont as Casanova, Patrick McVey as Don Quixote, Clifford David as "a splendidly passionate and tortured Byron" (*NYTCR*, Barnes, 396), Sylvia Syms as the Gypsy, Susan Tyrrell as Esmeralda, and Philip Bosco as the Baron de Charlus. In 1977 the Acting Company toured a production of *Camino Real* produced by John Houseman and directed by Gerald Freedman; David Schramm played Gutman.

One of Williams's longest-running plays (694 performances) was *Cat on a Hot Tin Roof*. It opened at New York's Morosco Theatre on 24 March 1955, directed by Elia Kazan with a set by Jo Mielziner and costumes by Lucinda Ballard. The brilliant cast included Barbara Bel Geddes as Maggie, Ben Gazzara as Brick, Burl Ives as Big Daddy, and Mildred Dunnock as Big Mama. "The tremendous dramatic impact" of Williams's "tormented and tormenting new drama" (*NYTCR*, Watts, Jr., 343) elicited raves from critics "torn between fascination and revulsion, but...held" (*NYTCR*, McClain, 344). The power of Williams's mature craftsmanship was fully acknowledged, though Williams had compromised in revising the play, against his better judgment, to accede to

Kazan's wish to bring Big Daddy back on stage in act 3. The play was subsequently published with both versions of the last act, and many directors in regional theatres over the years chose to use the original version. Finally, in 1974, for a production at the American Shakespeare Theatre in Stratford, Connecticut, Williams wrote a new version that combined the best features of both earlier options. That production, which was taken to New York on 24 September 1974, was directed by Michael Kahn. As Maggie, Elizabeth Ashley was outstanding in a strong cast that featured Keir Dullea as Brick, Fred Gwynne as Big Daddy, and Kate Reid as Big Mama. Clive Barnes (*NYTCR*, 242) wrote that "Miss Ashley's Maggie vibrantly combines charm with grit. She can stand outside a conversation like a cobra, or flutter in like a bird. Splendid."

Other outstanding interpretations of Maggie the Cat were by Elizabeth Taylor in the 1958 film version; Kim Stanley in the 1958 London production; Jeanne Moreau in the 1956 Paris production adapted by André Obey and directed by Peter Brook; Natalie Wood (supported by Laurence Olivier as Big Daddy and Robert Wagner as Brick) in the 1976 NBC-TV production; and Jessica Lange in a 1984 television production. Although the question of Brick's latent or actual homosexuality no longer shocks as it once did, the human drama played out by some of Williams's most compelling characters has lost none of its fascination.

Suddenly Last Summer premiered in New York on a double bill with Williams's one-act *Something Unspoken* under the umbrella title *Garden District*. Directed by Herbert Machiz, it opened on 7 January 1958 at the York Theatre off-Broadway. Anne Meacham as Catherine and Hortense Alden as Mrs. Venable gave intense performances, but most praise was directed at the play itself. Brooks Atkinson wrote (8 January 1958): "As an exercise that is both literary and dramatic, this brief, withering play is a superb achievement." Although the London production that year was coolly received, the 1965 Paris production marked a turning point in French acceptance of Williams's "strange, bewitching" dramatic world. Lewis W. Falb quotes Marc Bernard of *Les Nouvelles littéraires:* "a singular story . . . in which realism, fable, and symbolism mingle inextricably and required great artistry, meticulous craftsmanship to make us accept it" (33). The 1959 film directed by Joseph L. Mankiewicz is one of the better ones made of Williams's plays. Elizabeth Taylor and Katharine Hepburn were both nominated for Academy Awards for their performances as Catherine and Mrs. Venable, respectively.

Sweet Bird of Youth was first produced as a work in progress at Studio M Playhouse in Miami on 16 April 1956 under the direction of George Keathley. In his program note, Williams called it "the first draft of my play, something that ordinarily I would only dare show to my literary agent" (Van Antwerp, 163). Enthusiasm for that version prompted Williams to revise and expand the play. The full version reached New York on 10 March 1959 and ran for 383 performances. The production was directed by Elia Kazan, with sets by Jo Mielziner. Although critics were "repelled" (*NYTCR*, McClain, 350) by "a play that ranges wide through the lower depths, touching on political violence, as well as diseases of the mind and body" (*NYTCR*, Atkinson, 350), they found that Williams's "terrible gift for supercharged theatrical writing" (*NYTCR*, Chapman, 349) was " hypnotic theatre" (*NYTCR*, Coleman, 349). Geraldine Page gave a "compelling, bravura performance" (Coleman, 349) as the Princess, and Paul Newman as Chance Wayne was "superb in a role that requires him to be almost constantly repugnant" (*NYTCR*, Aston, 348). They were given excellent support by Sidney Blackmer as Boss Finley, Rip Torn as Tom Junior, Diana Hyland as Heavenly Finley, and Madeleine Sherwood as Miss Lucy. The 1962 film also featured Page, Newman, Torn, and Sherwood, now supported by Shirley Knight as Heavenly Finley, Ed Begley as Boss Finley, and Mildred Dunnock as Aunt Nonnie. Director Richard Brooks, who also wrote the screenplay, had to adapt the material considerably to meet the requirements of the Motion Picture Code, but the film has its own integrity.

Although the Princess disappears from act 2 of the play, the role has attracted outstanding actresses: Vivien Merchant in the 1968 British production, the incomparable Edwige Feullère in the 1971 Paris production of Françoise Sagan's adaptation, and Irene Worth in the 1975 revival. The last, directed by Edwin Sherin, opened at the Kennedy Center in Washington, D.C., on 9 October 1975 and moved to New York on 3 December. Edwin Wilson (*NYTCR*) wrote that Irene Worth "can take us on the full roller coaster ride of the woman's emotions. But she can do more: She can show us conflicting qualities simultaneously— energy, decadence, terror, talent, desire," (114). Christopher Walken played Chance Wayne opposite her, and Clive Barnes (*NYTCR*) found them both "superb—in timing, in temperament, even in dramatic temperature" (114).

"This is in many respects the most fruitful and versatile exercise by our best living playwright," John McClain (*NYTCR*, 132) wrote of *The Night of the Iguana* when it premiered in New York on 28 December 1961. The sentiment was echoed by other reviewers like John Chapman (*NYTCR*), who declared that "it will haunt you; haunt you with things said and unsaid; haunt you with its beauty. Having put aside the shock-treatment tactics of his recent works, Williams has given us one of his finest dramas, and Frank Corsaro has directed it to its full and fascinating depth" (131). The four principal roles were convincingly portrayed by a "marvelously brash and beguiling" Bette Davis as Maxine, Margaret Leighton as Hannah Jelkes, Patrick O'Neal in a "powerful performance as the sick and desperately disturbed" Reverend Shannon, and Alan

Webb as Nonno (*NYTCR*, McClain, 132). In 1965 it won the London Critics' Poll for Best Foreign Play. A 1976 New York revival at Circle in the Square Theatre, directed by Joseph Hardy, ran seventy-seven performances. Brendan Gill's comment sums up the critical response in general: "The production is satisfactory, if not exhilarating" (52). "At the heart of the play," wrote T. E. Kalem (*NYTCR*, 65), "Chamberlain captures the self-lacerating torment of Shannon, and McGuire the innate goodness of Hannah, but both are somewhat out of their depth where the play itself becomes deeper in certain late scenes and speeches that border on mystical transcendance." Sylvia Miles played Maxine "with the right brassiness, so that she gets her laughs, but without any real grasp of character" (*NYTCR*, Douglas Watt, 62). Foreign productions include those in Berlin (1963), London (1965), and Paris (1977). The 1964 film version featured Richard Burton as Shannon, Ava Gardner as Maxine, and Deborah Kerr as Hannah. Maurice Yacowar suggests that the film occupies "a central position in [director John] Huston's film canon.... Huston may laugh more robustly than Williams does in his work, but there is the same spirit in both men" (111–12).

The Two-Character Play premiered in London at the Hampstead Theatre Club on 12 December 1967, directed by James Roose-Evans. Although reviewers wrote favorably of the performances by Peter Wyndarde and Mary Ure, they could not come to grips with the play. As reported in the *New York Times* (13 December 1967), it was described as a "defiantly non-commercial" exercise of which the reviewer "could make no sense," and a play "in need of a psychoanalyst...to offer a rational interpretation of the enigmas that litter the stage like pieces of an elaborate jigsaw" (54). Philip French called it "elegantly produced hot air" (886), but David Wade of *The Times* was kinder: "Whatever his lapses and excesses Mr. Williams succeeds quite brilliantly in sustaining the idea that nothing whatever is to be relied upon and that if we go through one veil there is another just beyond.... For them [Wyngarde and Ure], for the change of voice and for what it has to say this play is worth a visit, but go soon—it has not the look of a long run" (9). Williams rewrote the play, retitled it *Out Cry*, and saw it produced first at the Ivanhoe Theatre in Chicago in 1971, directed by George Keathley, and then at the Lyceum Theatre in New York in 1973, directed by Peter Glenville, with Michael York and Cara Duff-McCormick as Felice and Clare. Again, critics were disappointed by the "entirely elusive" (*NYTCR*, Watt, 343) "shapeless, aimless, self-indulgent script, with its embarrassing use of the theater as a confessional, autobiographical medium and therapy" (*NYTCR*, Gottfried, 344). Further revised and once again entitled *The Two-Character Play*, it was presented at New York's Quaigh Theatre in 1975, directed by Bill Lentsch. Lawrence Van Gelder wrote of it: "Demonic, ghost-ridden, elliptical, it endures—and it appeals" (16). In 1977 it was produced by the Callboard Theater in Los Angeles, where it ran for twenty-four performances.

Small Craft Warnings began as a long one-act, *Confessional*, that was produced at the Maine Theatre Arts Festival in 1970. The expanded version opened in New York at the Truck and Warehouse Theatre on 6 June 1972, directed by Richard Altman. Although it received mixed notices, it moved to the New Theatre and achieved a run of 200 performances because Williams himself took the role of Doc in the play. According to Van Antwerp and Johns, "*Small Craft Warnings* was William's first moneymaker since *The Night of the Iguana* eleven years earlier." Richard Watts (*NYTCR*) praised its "characteristically eloquent writing and compassionate portraits of lost and brooding souls" but thought that "it suffers from any central drive in its narrative" (272). The sentiment was echoed succinctly by Betty Rollin (*NYTCR*): "No one can make nothing happen as eloquently as Tennessee Williams" (273). A London production was directed by Vivian Matalon in 1973.

Vieux Carré opened on Broadway, at the St. James Theatre, on 11 May 1977. It suffered from "inept direction"(*NYTCR*, Kalem, 246) by Arthur Allan Seidelman, a "cumbersome movable set" (*NYTCR*, Beaufort, 247), and "downright amateurish" lighting (*NYTCR*, Kissel, 246) but was helped by Sylvia Sidney as the "looney harridan landlady" (*NYTCR*, Barnes, 244) in a performance that "outclasses her company" (*NYTCR*, Gottfried, 244). Although Douglas Watt (*NYTCR*) thought that the play "ranks with his finest, and surely his most candid, works," most critics agreed with Leonard Probst ((*NYTCR*) that Williams was "confessing more and more about himself and homosexuality, but he is less interesting—less dramatic than in the past." It closed after only five performances. The 1978 London production was directed by Keith Hack and featured Sylvia Miles as Mrs. Wire, but still Joan F. Dean saw "precious little promise" in the play (27).

Williams scored a big success with *Crève Coeur* when it opened at the 1978 Spoleto Festival in Charleston, South Carolina. The premiere of a new Williams play had been touted as a highlight of the festival, and it did not disappoint the sellout audiences at the 500–seat Dock Street Theatre. T. E. Kalem (84) took note of the compassion and humor in the play, as well as the lively performances of Shirley Knight as Dorothea and Jan Miner as Bodey: "Like a magnifying glass, Knight can turn a role into a pinpoint of fire. With glares, hand signals and gusto, Miner kneads her part like the earthy dough of life." The 1979 New York production under the title *A Lovely Sunday for Crève Coeur* was not well received, and the play has been relatively neglected since then. However, a September 1987 revival by the People's Light and Theatre Company in Malvern, Pennsylvania, elicited excitement akin to that of discovering a new play. Dramaturg Lee Devin wrote that their production revealed it to be "a clear, subtle, complex, heartfelt, and harrowing play" and "a significant development in Williams' technique" (Letter to author).

SURVEY OF SECONDARY SOURCES

Bibliographies

Two major book-length bibliographies have been published. Gunn's is the broader in scope but is plagued by inaccuracies and omissions. Presumably many of those will be corrected in the second edition announced by Scarecrow Press for 1988. Some of the problems are noted in a review by George Miller. Despite those limitations, however, the book is an invaluable tool for any serious research on Williams. Part 1 lists William's writings categorized by type of publication: books and pamphlets (with reviews), works in anthologies and in books by other authors, works in periodicals, recordings, and translations. The latter section (185 entries) includes play translations in twenty-six different languages. Part 2 of Gunn's bibliography groups Williams's publications by genre; these entries have notes on composition and textual variants. Part 3 is a listing of Williams's manuscripts at various institutions; the great bulk of manuscripts are located in the Humanities Research Center of the University of Texas at Austin. Gunn states: "I make no attempt to indicate how many drafts of any work exist nor what state they are in. Nor do I attempt to list letters, untitled works, or such" (109). A glaring omission from this section is the New York Public Library's Theatre Collection housed at Lincoln Center, which includes vast clippings files on Williams. Part 4 covers all important productions of Williams's plays, both American and foreign, with all the reviews Gunn was able to find. Two categories of biographical information, interviews and biographies, make up part 5. Part 6, criticism, is divided into bibliographies, critical articles and books, and dissertations. The section listing critical articles and books contains only 418 entries.

Gunn's scant attention to critical articles and books is compensated by the other major bibliography, by McCann. McCann states: "This compilation represents an attempt to reckon with the vast storehouse of material on Tennessee Williams and his work, up to and including 1981. My parameters are basic ones: all popular and scholarly press criticism, with an emphasis on that which has appeared in the United States; production notices limited to Broadway premieres and important revivals, as well as notices from other domestic cities when significant premieres occurred somewhere other than New York; British notices for plays given important productions in London; interviews with Tennessee Williams, biographical material, and book reviews of his nondramatic works wherever they could be found; foreign language material limited to book-length studies; and doctoral dissertations" (ix). McCann also strove for neutrality—an avoidance of imposing his own critical bias—in his annotations describing the content of each entry. The listings are arranged chronologically, grouped by year of publication; thus it is easy to observe at a glance the waxing and waning of William's critical reputation from 2 entries on him in 1939, to 137 entries in 1960, to some 50 or 60 entries a year in the 1970s (but only 37 in 1978). The bibliography is prefaced by an eighteen-page introduction that succinctly describes and explains that trajectory of critical views.

Charles A. Carpenter's "Studies of Tennessee Williams's Drama: A selective International Bibliography: 1966–1978," in the *Tennessee Williams Newsletter* (Spring 1980): 11–23 filled a gap at the time and was subsequently expanded to cover two more years in his major publication, *Modern Drama Scholarship and Criticism 1966–1980*. The spring 1980 issue of the *Tennessee Williams Newsletter* also includes "Tennessee Williams in the Seventies: A Checklist" by Adler, Clark, and Taylor (24–29). A supplement to that checklist as well as to the Gunn bibliography appears in the spring-fall 1982 issue of the *Tennessee Williams Review* (46–50).

Arnott includes an invaluable listing of all the plays, published or unpublished, "arranged chronologically in order of their composition: information on first performances, major revivals, and publication" (5). The obvious omission from that listing is Williams's late play *Kirke, Kuche, und Kinder*. The Selected Bibliography in Falk is useful for its annotations. Both Yacowar and Gene D. Phillips include substantial bibliographies and filmographies. A six-page bibliography of reviews of London productions of Williams's plays is included in Stanley. Fayard lists French translations of Williams's plays. Among the numerous earlier bibliographies that have been superseded by Gunn, McCann, and Carpenter are Dony's ten-page bibliography and others listed in Gunn's bibliography of bibliographies.

Biographies

The best way to begin a study of Tennessee Williams's life is with *The World of Tennessee Williams*, edited by Leavitt. This profusely illustrated large-format book is divided into four sections: "Southern Gothic," "In the Winter of Cities," "Dramatist of Lost Souls," and "I Rise in Flame, Cried the Phoenix." Each chapter begins with a narrative account of Williams's life during that period. Those texts are followed by a wealth of photographs, as well as reproductions of newspaper clippings, manuscript pages, play programs, and posters, all generously captioned. Thus the book conveys a strong visual impression of the milieux in which Williams moved during various periods of his life. Also lavishly illustrated, but much richer in its supporting text is the *Dictionary of Literary Biography, Documentary Series, An Illustrated Chronicle 4: Tennessee Williams*, edited by Van Antwerp and Johns. The text is an excellent compilation of documents: letters, reviews, articles, and many of the major interviews that Williams gave, even two poems Williams wrote when he was in ninth grade. In addition, there are pertinent short quotations from various sources set off in boxes throughout the work. Not surprisingly, several of the same interviews are included in *Conversations with Tennessee Williams*, edited by Devlin: the ones with Mike Wallace, Lewis Funke and John E. Booth, Joanne Stang, David Frost, and Dotson Rader, for example. However, the three dozen interviews dating from 1940 to 1981, which comprise the latter book, include such unusual selections as a 1960 three-way CBS television hookup allowing Edward R. Murrow to converse with Tennessee Williams in Key West, Dilys Powell in London, and Yukio Mishima in Tokyo.

Three biographies appeared fairly soon after Williams's death, none of them authorized. The most comprehensive of the three is Spoto. This meticulously researched work by one who did not know Williams personally offers a balanced assessment but has been criticized for not allowing the playwright's own voice—his warmth and humor—to shine through the narrative. Spoto's 432–page book includes 34 black-and-white photographs, notes, a bibliography, and index. Published almost simultaneously was Rader's gossipy *Tennessee: Cry of the Heart*. Rader's anecdotal, almost sensation-seeking account—supported by a few photographs but no scholarly apparatus—emphasizes the period of his own association with Williams. In an "Author's Note" he declares that "during the years Tennessee Williams and I were friends, I kept, with his knowledge, notes, letters, journals, and other papers about my life with him. Also, from time to time, we would have conversations that we taped." *Tennessee Williams: An Intimate Biography* by his brother Dakin Williams and Shepherd Mead was begun in the late 1970s and was published a few months after Williams's death. While not a full-fledged biography, another recently published book contains many of Williams's reminiscences about his childhood in the South. Rasky's *Tennessee Williams* grew out of the friendship that developed between Rasky and Williams during the course of Rasky's filming for the CBC television documentary *Tennessee Williams' South*. It covers the making of the film and incorporates recollections that came out during their many hours of transcribed conversation.

Tennessee Williams's own *Memoirs* (1975) is an honest and compelling autobiography that jumps back and forth between present and past. Williams later claimed that his original manuscript had been much longer but that Doubleday had trimmed it considerably, leaving disproportionate emphasis on the sexual references. That candid and often witty revelation of the self from the perspective of his sixty-third year is interestingly complemented by *Tennessee Williams's Letters to Donald Windham 1940–1965*, published not long after the *Memoirs*. The letters reveal much about Williams's personality and his struggles as a writer during those decades. The book is edited, with commentary setting the letters in context, by Windham. Footnotes and an index add to its usefulness. The collected essays by Williams written between 1944 and 1979 and collected under the title *Where I Live* (1978) are largely autobiographical. Williams's mother, Edwina Dakin Williams, also wrote a biography, with Lucy Freeman, entitled *Remember Me to Tom*. It covers his childhood and early years as a playwright, often quoting from his letters home.

Earlier biographical studies include Nelson and Donahue, both of which relate themes in his plays to events in his life. Maxwell uses an omniscient narrator's technique to cover Williams's early life, but the bulk of the work is based on personal recollections of encounters with friends and professional associates during the productive years up to the opening of *The Night of the Iguana* and the death of Frank Merlo. A more varied and readable collection of reminiscences about Williams comprises Steen's *A Look at Tennessee Williams* (1969). Steen's twenty interviews with people like Karl Malden, William Inge, Geraldine Page, Jessica Tandy, and Maureen Stapleton focus on various episodes in Williams's career. *Represented by Audrey Wood*, a memoir written by Williams's long-time agent and friend Audrey Wood, with Max Wilk (1981), includes three chapters devoted to Williams concerning that important relationship. The chapter on Williams in J. William Miller's *Modern Playwrights at Work* offers not only a succinct biography but also a detailed assessment of his working methods from the genesis of a play to rewriting. Many other books and published interviews provide additional biographical material. Gunn's bibliography, for example, contains eighty-one entries in the biographies section, as well as fifty-four interviews. The most detailed account of Williams's death may be Hoffman's.

In 1986 a one-man play, *Confessions of a Nightingale*, by Charlotte Chandler and Ray Stricklyn was performed off-Broadway. Stricklyn played Williams, delivering a relaxed, witty, and at moments painfully self-revealing ninety-minute monologue based on material from Williams's interviews. On the whole, the mood of the piece was affectionate and upbeat, and audiences were warmly responsive. According to Henry, "The flavor is authentic" in this "ingratiatingly salty impersonation of Williams the raconteur" (97). One could only think that Williams would have approved of this sympathetic interpretation of his personality and recollections from his life.

Influences

Asked by Dotson Rader (Devlin, 331) about his literary influences, Williams replied: "What writers influenced me as a young man? *Chekhov!*

As a dramatist? Chekhov! As a story writer? Chekhov! D. H. Lawrence, too, for his spirit, of course, for his understanding of sexuality, of life in general." The most focused study of Chekhov's influence is "Tennessee Williams: America's Chekhov" by Styan. Fedder examines the latter influence in a monograph that covers Williams's poetry, fiction, early one-act plays, and full-length plays up to *The Milk Train Doesn't Stop Here Anymore*.

Hart Crane was the strongest influence on Williams's poetry. Williams often mentioned his interest in Crane's life and work, but some of his most extended commentary on poets and the qualities he admires in their work is found in his 1974 interview with Cecil Brown (Devlin, 267–69). He was also asked about influences in a 1973 interview with C. Robert Jennings (Devlin, 245–46) and replied that Chekhov and D. H. Lawrence were "the only ones of which I am conscious" but went on to mention a number of other writers whom he greatly admired: Rimbaud, Rilke, Hemingway, Jane Bowles, Flannery O'Connor, and Carson McCullers. Spoto also mentions his awakened interest in Ibsen and Strindberg when he attended the University of Missouri (37–39). An affinity for Federico García Lorca is apparent at least in Williams's short play *The Purification*. In the 1970s Williams professed great interest in the plays of Samuel Beckett and Harold Pinter, and some critics have speculated that it was their influence that undermined his own characteristic style.

Williams's influence on other playwrights is vast and immeasurable. Most contemporary American playwrights acknowledge his importance in their literary development. Among his contemporaries, William Inge was most directly stimulated both by Williams's writing and his personal encouragement. In the next generation, Arthur Kopit demonstrated Williams's influence through the parody in *Oh Dad, Poor Dad, Mama's Hung You in the Closet and I'm Feeling So Sad*. Lanford Wilson is the outstanding dramatist of today whose work exhibits the acknowledged influence.

General Studies

The enormous body of literature in this category precludes mention of few works other than the books devoted solely to Williams. Any survey of American dramatic literature includes a substantial section on his plays, but—other than the excellent treatment in Heilman—these are generally superficial. One other general study that is deserving of special mention is Bigsby's *A Critical Introduction to Twentieth-Century American Drama;* volume 2 covers Tennessee Williams, along with Arthur Miller and Edward Albee. Bigsby devotes 120 pages and seven photographs of Williams, including an overview of his life and substantial analyses of the major plays. The plays after *The Night of the Iguana* are treated less fully; of them Bigsby declares: "The familiar elements of Williams's work remain but they now have a parodic relationship to their originals" (110).

Boxill's 1987 study is an excellent survey of Williams's plays with full chapters on *The Glass Menagerie, A Streetcar Named Desire, Summer and Smoke*, and *Cat on a Hot Tin Roof* and chapters on the other plays grouped under three headings: "Wanderer Plays (1957–59)," "Reversals of the Pattern (1943-1961)," and "Late Plays (1962–1981)." Boxill distinguishes two main recurring character types: the wanderer (best exemplified by Val Xavier in *Orpheus Descending*) and the faded belle like Blanche Dubois. Another introductory survey, this by Londré, offers a straightforward reading of all the plays up to *The Two-Character Play*, with special attention to production values and major stage interpretations. In Twayne's United States Authors Series, Falk's *Tennessee Williams*, now in its second edition, follows the standard life and works format, including Williams's prose and poetry. Other life-and-works surveys are by Nelson, Donahue, Tischler and Fayard. The text of the last is heavily interspersed with quotations from Williams in keeping with the standard format of that French series; it includes Fayard's 1971 interview with Williams, comments by French actresses and directors who worked on plays by Williams in Paris, and excepts from the French press concerning the Paris productions of *The Glass Menagerie, A Streetcar Named Desire, Summer and Smoke, The Rose Tattoo, Cat on a Hot Tin Roof, Orpheus Descending, Suddenly Last Summer, Sweet Bird of Youth*, and an evening of one-act plays.

Tennessee Williams: A Tribute (1977), edited by Tharpe, is an invaluable collection of fifty-three essays covering the entire Williams canon, including his poetry and short stories. Only one of the essays is a reprint of a previously published article; thus all were written from the perspective of the late 1970s and reflect a sincere attempt to come to grips with Williams's late and lesser-known works, as well as with his homosexuality, to which he had publicly admitted in 1970. The latter topic is examined in the essays by Sklepowich and Jones. The essays in this collection are grouped under headings that include "European Contexts," "Themes," "Prose and Poetry," and "Techniques." Although many critics have acknowledged Williams's debt to the movies, Kalson offers some of the most specific examples of it in his piece. The book's three concluding essays, by Free, Pease, and Chesler, are balanced assessments of Williams's work as a whole and the critical responses to it.

Another well-rounded collection is *Tennessee Williams: A Collection of Critical Essays* (1977), edited by Stanton. Stanton's introduction and Hughes's short piece "Tennessee Williams: 'What's Left?'" tackle reasons for the often-stated judgment that "after *The Night of the Iguana* (1961), his career seemed over" (2). The articles in this collection, mostly reprints, are grouped under three headings: "Plays," "Themes," and

"Work in Progress," the last section comprised of two short pieces, on *The Red Devil Battery Sign* and *This Is (An Entertainment)*.

Jackson's *The Broken World of Tennessee Williams* (1966) is a somewhat unfocused study of the plays. The first chapter, "Reality! What Is It?" surveys Western dramatic tradition as a context for examining Williams's characteristic form. Chapter 2, "Williams and the Lyric Moment," quotes Hart Crane's "broken world" verse as a basis for the thesis that "form in [Williams's] drama is the imitation of the individual search for a way of redeeming a shattered universe" (26–27). Chapter 3, "The Synthetic Myth," shows how Williams's work evolved as he drew upon literary and philosophical systems beyond his early romantic impulses. Subsequent chapters—"The Antihero," "The Plastic Theatre," "*Camino Real:* The World as Spectacle," and "Williams and the Moral Function"—further analyze the evolution of Williams's dramatic form.

In *A Portrait of the Artist*, Hirsch presents Williams as a moralist working out confusing human problems through his plays, with particular emphasis on sex. He sees the "failure" of many of the plays after *The Night of the Iguana* as a consequence of "writing more to explore his own problems than to entertain audiences" (72). *Tennessee Williams: A Moralist's Answer to the Perils of Life* (1976) by Rogers is a more substantial study of Williams's moral outlook as manifested in the plays. Part I, "The Perils of Life," has chapters on the Flight from Reality, the American Dream, Fear of the Passage of Time, Improper Sexual Attitudes, Violence, Egocentrism and Material Goals, and Mendacity. Part II, "Means of Overcoming the Perils of Life," is comprised of the Concept of God, the Concept of Love, Art and the Perils of Life, and the Philosophy of Acceptance. Part III, "Formal Dramatization of the Perils of Life," treats various aspects of performamce: speech patterns, vocal sound, music and sound effects, lighting, clothing and appearance, setting, and gestures. The bibliography includes many works in German on Williams. Asibong's *Tennessee Williams: The Tragic Tension* is a slender volume devoted to identifying elements of tragedy and of melodrama in the plays from *The Glass Menagerie* to *The Milk Train Dosen't Stop Here Anymore*.

Analyses of Individual Plays

The Glass Menagerie has been the subject of numerous articles, including two interesting essays on the play in Tharpe's anthology (192–213). Among a number of studies of the genesis and variants of *The Glass Menagerie* are by Beaurline, Watson, and Parker. Similar studies have been published for most of the other major plays.

A Streetcar Named Desire is perhaps the most widely interpreted Williams's play. Miller has collected twenty previously published essays on the play. Seven new essays on this play appear in Tharpe's anthology, including Vivienne Dickson's interesting study of "Its Development through the Manuscripts." Another important document on the play is Elia Kazan's "Notebook for *A Streetcar Named Desire*," reprinted in Cole and Chinoy, *Directors on Directing*.

There are so many insightful and provocative articles on Williams's plays from *The Glass Menagerie* to *The Night of the Iguana* that it would be difficult to single out only a few for mention here. However, much remains to be explored in his plays written since 1961. An outstanding article on Williams's late plays is by Cohn. Other essays on the late plays are in Tharpe's anthology: Rexford Stamper on *The Two-Character Play*, Sy Kahn on *The Red Devil Battery Sign*, and the essays by William J. Free and Norman J. Fedder. The 1982 spring-fall issue of the *Tennessee Williams Review* includes several pieces on *Out Cry*. Stephen S. Stanton wrote on *Steps Must Be Gentle* in the spring 1983 issue.

FUTURE RESEARCH OPPORTUNITIES

The Tennessee Williams Collection in the University of Texas Humanities Research Center offers endless opportunities for future research; few scholars have yet availed themselves of this treasure trove of unpublished manuscripts and letters.

While the authorized biography by Lyle Leverich is eagerly anticipated, a glut of unauthorized biographies is available.

Williams's foreign reputation has not been adequately assessed, and there have been few articles concerning his cross-cultural influence, even on British dramatists. Nor has Williams been a subject for many comparative literature studies; one intriguing possibility would be a study of parallels in the work of Williams and of Japanese novelist-playwright Yukio Mishima. Almost no critical attention has been given to Williams's paintings, which occupied a great deal of his time during his last decade. There have been a number of articles on visual elements in his major plays, but there is room for more work in this area.

Above all, the plays written after *The Night of the Iguana* cry out for sympathetic critical attention. This is the most pressing area for further research, both in terms of literary and theatrical values in the plays.

SECONDARY SOURCES

Adler, Thomas P., Judith Hersh Clark, and Lyle Taylor. "Tennessee Williams in the Seventies: A Checklist." *Tennessee Williams Newsletter* 2, no. 1 (Spring 1980): 24–29.

Arnott, Catherine M. *Tennessee Williams on File*. London: Methuen, 1985.

Asibong, Emmanuel B. *Tennessee Williams: The Tragic Tension*. Elms Court: Arthur H. Stockwell Ltd., 1978.

Associated Press. "Williams' Plays a Big Hit in Moscow." *Kansas City Times* (13 October 1960): A2.

Beaurline, Lester A. *"The Glass Menagerie:* From Story to Play." *Modern Drama* 8(1965): 143–49.

Bigsby, C. W. E. *A Critical Introduction to Twentieth-Century American Drama*. Vol. 2. Cambridge: Cambridge University Press, 1984.

Boxill, Roger. *Tennessee Williams*. New York: St Martin's Press, 1987.

Camino Real. New York Theatre Critics' Reviews (20 March 1953): 330–32. Brooks Atkinson, "Camino Real," *New York Times* (29 March 1953): 2: 1. " 'Camino Real' in London," *New York Times* (9 April 1957): 41. Brooks Atkinson, "The Theatre: Black Phantasmagoria," *New York Times* (17 May 1960): 42. Brooks Atkinson," 'Camino Real,' " *New York Times* (29 May 1960): 2: 1. *New York Theatre Critics' Reviews* (9 January 1970): 395–99.

Cat on a Hot Tin Roof. New York Theatre Critics' Reviews (25 March 1955): 342– 44. Brooks Atkinson; "Williams' 'Tin Roof,' " *New York Times* (3 April 1955): B1. "London Sees Cat; Opinion Is Divided," *New York Times* (31 January 1958): 24. *New York Theatre Critics' Reviews* (25 September 1974): 242–46. T. E. Kalem, "Fate Strikes the Delta," *Time* (6 December 1976): 97–98.

Carpenter, Charles A. *Modern Drama Scholarship and Criticism 1966–1980: An International Bibliography*. Toronto: University of Toronto Press, 1986.

———. "Recent Bibliographies: Studies of Tennessee Williams' Drama: A Selective International Bibliography: 1966–1978." *Tennessee Williams Newsletter* 2, no. 1 (Spring 1980): 11–23.

Cohn, Alan M. "More Tennessee Williams in the Seventies: Additions to the Checklist and the Gunn Bibliography." *Tennessee Williams Review* 3, no. 2 (Spring-Fall 1982): 46–50.

Cohn, Ruby. "Late Tennessee Williams." *Modern Drama* (September 1984): 336– 44.

Cole, Toby and Helen Krich Chinoy. *Directors on Directing*. New York: Bobbs. Merrill, 1963.

Devlin, Albert J., ed. *Conversations with Tennessee Williams*. Jackson: University Press of Mississippi, 1986.

Donahue, Francis. *The Dramatic World of Tennessee Williams*. New York: Frederick Ungar, 1964.

Dony, Nadine. "Tennessee Williams: A Selected Bibliography." *Modern Drama* (December 1958):181–91.

Falb, Lewis W. *American Drama in Paris, 1945–1970: A Study of Its Critical Reception*. Chapel Hill: University of North Carolina Press, 1973.

Falk, Signi. *Tennessee Williams*. 2d ed. Boston: G. K. Hall, 1978.

Fayard, Jeanne. *Tennessee Williams*. Paris: Seghers, 1972.

Fedder, Norman. *The Influence of D. H. Lawrence on Tennessee Williams*. The Hague: Mouton and Co., 1966.

Gilman, Richard."Theatre: Tennessee Williams." *Nation* (19 March 1983): 347– 48.

The Glass Menagerie. New York Theatre Critics' Reviews (2 April 1945): 234–37; (22 November 1956): 190–93; (5 May 1965): 332–35; (19 December 1975): 125–28; (2 December 1983): 102–8. " 'Menagerie' in London," *New York*

Times (29 July 1948): 17. "Some Masterly Performances," *The Times* (London, 2 December 1965): 15. Harry F. Waters, "Deb Party," *Newsweek* (17 December 1973): 61. John J. O'Connor, "TV: Williams's Haunting 'Menagerie.' " *New York Times* (14 December 1973): 94. Brendan Gill, "Medicine of Make-Believe," *New Yorker* (12 December 1983): 157–58.

Gould, Jean. *Modern American Playwrights*. New York: Dodd, Mead, 1966.

Gunn, Drewey Wayne. *Tennessee Williams: A Bibliography*. Metuchen, N.J.: Scarecrow Press, 1980.

Heilman, Robert Bechtold. *The Iceman, the Arsonist, and the Troubled Agent*. Seattle: University of Washington Press, 1973.

Henry, William A., III. "Eerie Dancing at the Abyss: *Confessions of a Nightingale*." *Time* (6 October 1986): 97.

Hirsch, Foster. *A Portrait of the Artist: The Plays of Tennessee Williams*. Port Washington, N.Y.: Kennikat Press, 1979.

Hoffman, Peter. "The Last Days of Tennessee Williams." *New York* (25 July 1983): 41–49.

Hughes, Catharine. "Tennessee Williams, Remembered." *America* (26 March 1983): 231–33.

Jackson, Esther Merle. *The Broken World of Tennessee Williams*. Madison: University of Wisconsin Press, 1966.

Kalem, T. E. "The Laureate of the Outcast." *Time* (7 March 1983): 88.

Kazan, Elia. "Notebook for *A Streetcar Named Desire*." *Directors on Directing*, pp. 364–79. Edited by Toby Cole and Helen Chinoy. Indianapolis: Bobbs-Merrill, 1963.

Kroll, Jack. "The Laureate of Loss." *Newsweek* (7 March 1983): 53.

Kuehl, Claudia. "Tennessee Williams Returns to the St. Louis He Shunned." *Kansas City Star* (6 March 1983): 1A, 9A.

Leavitt, Richard F. *The World of Tennessee Williams*. New York: G. P. Putnam's Sons, 1978.

Leverich, Lyle. "Tennessee Williams' Vieux Carré." *Tennessee Williams Review* 4, no. 1 (Spring 1983): 26–30.

Londré, Felicia Hardison, *Tennessee Williams*. New York: Frederick Ungar Publishing Co., Inc., 1979; Paperback, 1983.

Loney, Glenn. "You Can't Retire from Being an Artist." *Performing Arts Journal* 20 (1983): 74–87.

A Lovely Sunday for Crève Coeur. "Williams' Comedy Works Well in Its World Premiere," *Dallas Morning News* (7 June 1978): 20A. T. E. Kalem, "Women Alone," *Time* (12 June 1978): 84. "Photo Essay/Preview: Tennessee Williams' *Crève Coeur*," *New York Theatre Review* (August-September 1978): 28. Edith Oliver, "Theatre," *New Yorker* (5 February 1979): 99–101. Lee Devin to Felicia Londré, 10 September 1987.

Maxwell, Gilbert. *Tennessee Williams and Friends*. Cleveland: World Publishing Company, 1965.

McCann, John S. *The Critical Reputation of Tennessee Williams: A Reference Guide*. Boston: G. K. Hall, 1983.

Miller, George. "Reviews of Books: *Tennessee Williams: A Bibliography*." *Tennessee Williams Review* 3 (Spring-Fall 1982): 51–54.

Miller, J. William. *Modern Playwrights at Work*. Vol. 1. New York: Samuel French, 1968.

Miller, Jordan Y., ed. *Twentieth-Century Interpretations of A Streetcar Named Desire*. Englewood Cliffs: Prentice-Hall, 1971.

Nelson, Benjamin. *Tennessee Williams: The Man and His Work*. New York: Ivan Obolensky, 1961.

The New York Times Directory of the Theater. New York: Quadrangle/New York Times Book Co., 1973.

The Night of the Iguana. *New York Theatre Critics' Reviews* (29 December 1961): 131–34. Brendan Gill, "The Theatre," *New Yorker* (27 December 1976): 52. *New York Theatre Critics' Reviews* (17 December 1976): 62–65.

Orpheus Descending. *New York Theatre Critics' Reviews* (22 March 1957): 310–13. "Paris Sees Arletty in Play by Williams," *New York Times* (18 March 1959): 44. "Williams' 'Orpheus' in London," *New York Times* (15 May 1959): 23. "Orpheus in Moscow," *New York Times* (28 August 1961): 21. "Williams Play Revived at Gramercy Arts," *New York Times* (6 October 1959): 45.

Parker, Brian. "The Composition of *The Glass Menagerie:* An Argument for Complexity." *Modern Drama* 25 (1982): 409–22.

Phillips, Gene D. *The Films of Tennessee Williams*. London and Toronto: Associated University Presses, 1980.

Phillips, Jerrold A. "A Giant's Passing—Press Coverage of Williams' Death." *Tennessee Williams Review* 4, no. 1 (Spring 1983): 60–72.

Quintero, José. *If You Don't Dance, They Beat You*. Boston: Little, Brown, 1974.

Rader, Dotson. "He Walks with Me . . . " *Tennessee Williams Review* 4, no. 1 (Spring 1983): 22–25.

———. *Tennessee: Cry of the Heart*. New York: Doubleday, 1985.

Rasky, Harry. *Tennessee Williams: A Portrait in Laughter and Lamentation*. New York: Dodd, Mead, 1986.

Rogers, Ingrid. *Tennessee Williams: A Moralist's Answer to the Perils of Life*. Frankfurt: Peter Lang, 1976.

The Rose Tattoo. *New York Theatre Critics' Reviews* (5 February 1951): 363–66. Dan Sullivan, "Theater: 'Minor Artist' in a Major Key," *New York Times* (21 October 1966): 36.

Schmemann, Serge. "The Russian Theatregoers Take Tennessee Williams to Their Hearts." *New York Times* (21 June 1982): C13.

Simon, John. "Poet of the Theater." *New York* (14 March 1983): 76–77.

Singleton, Don. "Drama Great Tennessee Williams Dead." *New York Daily News* (26 February 1983): 3.

Small Craft Warnings. *New York Theatre Critics' Reviews* (3 April 1972): 271–74. Irving Wardle, "Miss Stritch Shines as the Bar Room Wit," *Times* (London, 30 January 1973): 9. Benedict Nightingale, "Down at Monk's Place," *New Statesman* (9 February 1973): 208–9.

Spoto, Donald. *The Kindness of Strangers: The Life of Tennessee Williams*. Boston: Little, Brown, 1985.

Stanley, William T. *Broadway in the West End: An Index of Reviews of American Theatre in London, 1950–1975*. Westport, Conn.: Greenwood Press, 1978.

Stanton, Stephen S., ed. *Tennessee Williams: A Collection of Critical Essays*. Englewood Cliffs: Prentice-Hall, 1977.

————. "Some Thoughts about *Steps Must Be Gentle.*" *Tennessee Williams Review* 4 (Spring 1983): 48–53.

Steen, Mike. *A Look at Tennessee Williams.* New York: Hawthorn Books, 1969.

A Streetcar Named Desire. New York Theatre Critics' Review (4 December 1947): 249–52. Brooks Atkinson, "Streetcar Passenger," *New York Times* (12 June 1949): 1. Brooks Atkinson, "Streetcar Tragedy," *New York Times* (14 December 1947): 3. Brooks Atkinson, "Overseas Tornado," *New York Times* (11 December 1949): 3. "Vivien Leigh Scores as 'Streetcar' Star," *New York Times* (29 September 1949): 38. "London Sees 'Streetcar,' " *New York Times* (13 October 1949): 33. "Paris Likes, Critics Dislike, 'Streetcar,' " *New York Times* (19 October 1949): 36. Brooks Atkinson, "At the Theatre," *New York Times* (24 May 1950): 36. Brooks Atkinson, "Theatre: 'Streetcar,' " *New York Times* (4 May 1955): 18. *New York Theatre Critics' Reviews* (16 February 1956): 362–65. Paul Hofmann, " 'A Streetcar Named Desire' Is Cheered in Havana," *New York Times* (19 February 1965): 27. *New York Theatre Critics' Reviews* (27 April 1973): 281–85. Clive Barnes, "Stage: A Rare 'Streetcar,' " *New York Times* (27 April 1973): 31. Walter Kerr, "Of Blanche the Victim—and Other 'Women,' " *New York Times* (6 May 1973): 1, 10. Stephen Farber, "Blanche Wins the Battle," *New York Times* (1 April 1973): 1, 15. Clive Barnes, "Stage: Subtle 'Streetcar,' " *New York Times* (5 October 1973): 19. Irving Wardle, "New Trip on Old Streetcar," *The Times* (London, 15 March 1974): 15.

Styan, J. L. "Tennessee Williams: America's Chekhov." *Tennessee Williams Review* 4, no. 1 (Spring 1983): 8–11.

Suddenly Last Summer. Brooks Atkinson, "Theatre: 2 by Tennessee," *New York Times* (8 January 1958): 23. "Garden District," *Theatre Arts* (March 1958): 13. Brooks Atkinson, " 'Garden District,' " *New York Times* (19 January 1958): B1. "British See U.S. Play," *New York Times* (17 September 1958): 44.

Summer and Smoke. Brooks Atkinson, "Theatre in Dallas," *New York Times* (10 August 1947): B1. *New York Theatre Critics' Reviews* (7 October 1948): 205–9. Brooks Atkinson, "Author of 'Summer and Smoke' Displays Again the Gifts of the Poet," *New York Times* (17 October 1948): 2:1. Jack Goodman, "Western Triumph," *New York Times* (29 October 1950): 2:3. " 'Summer and Smoke' in London," *New York Times* (23 November 1951): 32. "Williams' Play in London." *New York Times* (25 January 1952): 13. Brooks Atkinson, "At the Theatre," *New York Times* (25 April 1952): 19. Brooks Atkinson, "Second Chance," *New York Times* (4 May 1952): 2:1. *New York Theatre Critics' Review* (24 November 1976): 107–10. Alan Rich, " 'Nightingale,' Williams's Sweet Bird of Middle Age," *New York* (13 December 1976).

Sweet Bird of Youth. New York Theatre Critics' Reviews (11 March 1959): 347–50. *New York Theatre Critics' Reviews* (4 December 1975): 113–17.

Tharpe, Jac, ed. *Tennessee Williams: A Tribute.* Jackson: University Press of Mississippi, 1977.

Tischler, Nancy M. *Tennessee Williams: Rebellious Puritan.* New York: Citadel Press, 1961.

The Two-Character Play. David Wade, "Tennessee Williams' New Voice," *The Times*

(London, 12, December 1967): 9. "Williams Drama Baffles Critics: Most London Reviews Cool to 'Two-Character Play,' " *New York Times* (13 December 1967): 54. Philip French, "The Tennessee Vaults," *New Statesman* (22 December 1967): 886–87. *New York Theatre Critics' Reviews* (2 March 1973): 343–46. Lawrence Van Gelder, "Stage: William's '2 Character Play,' " *New York Times* (22 August 1975): 16.

Van Antwerp, Margaret A., and Sally Johns, eds. *Dictionary of Literary Biography, Documentary Series, An Illustrated Chronicle. Vol. 4: Tennessee Williams.* Detroit: Gale Research Company, 1984.

Vieux Carré. New York Theatre Critics' Reviews (12 May 1977): 244–47. Joan F. Dean, "Vieux Carré," *Tennessee Williams Newsletter* 1(Spring 1979): 26–27.

Watson, Charles S. "The Revision of *The Glass Menagerie:* The Passing of Good Manners." *Southern Literary Quarterly* 8 (Fall 1975–Spring 1976): 74–78.

Williams, Dakin, with Shepherd Mead. *Tennessee Williams: An Intimate Biography.* New York: Arbor House, 1983.

Williams, Edwina, and Lucy Freeman. *Remember Me to Tom.* New York: G.P. Putnam's Sons, 1973.

Windham, Donald, ed. *Tennessee Williams's Letters to Donald Windham 1940–1965.* New York: Holt, Rinehart and Winston, 1976.

Wood, Audrey, with Max Wilk. *Represented by Audrey Wood.* Garden City, N.Y.: Doubleday, 1981.

Yacowar, Maurice. *Tennessee Williams and Film.* New York: Frederick Ungar Publishing Co., 1977.

August Wilson
(27 APRIL 1945–   )

MICHAEL C. O'NEILL

ASSESSMENT OF WILSON'S REPUTATION

Due to the critical and popular success of his major plays, *Ma Rainey's Black Bottom* and *Fences,* August Wilson has become one of the leading American dramatists of the 1980s. His work articulates the black experience in the United States through a vision informed by history. Wilson has said, "I think the black Americans have the most dramatic story of all mankind to tell" (DeVries, "A New Voice," 29). The freshness of Wilson's language is lauded by actors and critics alike for a rhythmic, colloquial accuracy that touches the realm of poetry, but critics generally are less enthusiastic about the structure of his plays. In his introduction to *Fences,* however, Richards, who has directed all of Wilson's major work for the stage, calls the playwright "one of the most compelling story tellers to begin writing for the theatre in many years" (vii).

Nominated for the Tony Award, Wilson's first Broadway play, *Ma Rainey's Black Bottom,* was named Best Play of the 1984–1985 season by the New York Drama Critics Circle. The Yale Repertory Theatre production of *Fences* won the American Theatre Critics' Association's first annual outstanding regional play award in 1986. After *Fences* moved to Broadway in 1987, it won both the Tony and the Drama Critics Circle awards as Best Play. Wilson completed the American theatre world's equivalent of the triple crown by winning the 1987 Pulitzer Prize in drama for *Fences.* A recipient of a Jerome Foundation Grant and Bush, McKnight, and Rockefeller playwrighting fellowships, Wilson in 1986 was awarded both a Guggenheim Fellowship and the Whiting Foundation Writer's Award. The rapidity and scope of Wilson's achievements have led Freedman to characterize his emergence in the 1980s as "the most auspicious arrival of an American playwright since that of David Mamet, some fifteen years ago" ("A Voice from the Streets," 36).

PRIMARY BIBLIOGRAPHY OF WILSON'S WORKS

Unpublished Plays

Black Bart and the Sacred Hills. Performed 1981, St. Paul, Minnesota.
The Mill Hand's Lunch Bucket. Produced 1983, New York.
Jitney. Performed 1982, Pittsburgh, PA; St. Paul, Minnesota.
Fullerton Street. Reading. Minneapolis, Minnesota.
The Piano Lesson. Performed 1987, New Haven, Connecticut.

Published Plays

Ma Rainey's Black Bottom. New York: New American Library, 1985.
Fences. New York: New American Library, 1986.
Joe Turner's Come and Gone. *Theatre* 17 (Summer-Fall 1986): 63–88.
The Piano Lesson. *Theater* 18 (Summer-Fall 1988): 35–68.

Poetry

"Theme One: The Variations." In *The Poetry of Black America: Anthology of The
Twentieth Century*, pp. 491–93. Edited by Arnold Adoff. New York: Harper
Row, 1973.

Critical Introductions

Black Tones of Truth. By Rob Penny. Pittsburgh: Oduduwa Productions, 1970.

Interviews

Powers, Kim. "An Interview with August Wilson." *Theater* 16 (Fall-Winter 1984):
50–55.
Palmer, Don. "Interview with August Wilson: He Gives a Voice to the Nameless
Masses." *Newsday* (20 April 1987): 47.
Savran, David. "August Wilson," In *In Their Own Words: Contemporary American
Playwrights*, pp. 288–305. New York: Theatre Communications Group,
1988.

PRODUCTION HISTORY

Wilson may have remained unknown if Lloyd Richards, dean of the Yale
Drama School and artistic director of the National Playwright's Conference at the Eugene O'Neill Center, had not selected *Ma Rainey*, which
Wilson had begun to write in 1976, for a staged reading in the summer
of 1982. The partnership between Wilson and Richards has proved to
be rich and rewarding for both men. DeVries, Freedman, Kleiman, and
Mitgang all provide commentary on the Richards-Wilson collaboration

and its effect on contemporary American theatre. Richards, who directed
the original production of Lorraine Hansberry's *A Raisin in the Sun* in
1959, has directed four of Wilson's plays at the Yale Repertory Theatre.
With the exception of *The Piano Lesson*, which was given its initial staging
in November 1987, the plays have gone on to successful runs in Boston,
Chicago, Los Angeles, New York, Rochester, San Francisco, Seattle, and
Washington, D.C.

Wilson wrote his first stage pieces in Pittsburgh for Black Horizons
on the Hill, a theatre that he helped to found in 1968 and that faded
in 1972. From 1978 to 1980 he worked as a scriptwriter for the Science
Museum of Minnesota, adapting plays for a theatre troupe attached to
the museum. No insightful critical appraisal exists in response to his first
professionally produced play, *Black Bart and the Sacred Hills*, staged in
1981 by the Penumbra Theatre in St. Paul, Minnesota. Productions of
Jitney, staged in 1982 at Pittsburgh's Allegheny Repertory Theatre and
in 1984 at the Penumbra Theatre, seem to have been neglected by critics
as well. *Fullerton Street* received a reading, not a production, at the Playwrights' Center in Minneapolis, and thus critical reaction to the play
cannot be expected.

Ma Rainey's Black Bottom, directed by Richards, opened on 6 April 1984
at the Yale Repertory Theatre in New Haven, Connecticut. Its portraits
of black jazz musicians in the 1920s are carefully drawn through humor
and storytelling that reflect a frustrating struggle with racism among
blacks themselves. The split-stage device of the band room and the recording studio provide ample opportunity for verbal and visual irony,
as well as a plausible reason to incorporate genuine—albeit, pre-
recorded—music of the period into the play. The success of *Ma Rainey*
in New Haven was duplicated in New York, where the play opened at
the Cort Theatre on 11 October 1984 with a slightly different cast and
played 267 performances. The critical response to the play, though cautious at times, seemed to acknowledge a major new talent. *Variety* cal-
culated eighteen favorable, two mixed, and one unfavorable review. Gill
compared Wilson's first Broadway play to Tennessee Williams's *The Glass
Menagerie*. Claiming that he welcomed the task of making an acquaint-
ence with a new playwright's work and watching it develop over time,
Gill went on to say, "*The Glass Menagerie* startled us when it first came
to Broadway—startled us not least because of the ease with which it
proved capable of moving us in spite of certain awkward dramaturgic
mishaps on the part of its youthful author. *Ma Rainey's Black Bottom* is
also startling, and in something like the same fashion" (152).

In their evaluation of the play, critics began to illuminate facets of *Ma
Rainey* that have since become recognizable characteristics of Wilson's
playwrighting. Simon called attention to Wilson's "vigorous, racy dialogue" and his ability to create "idiosyncratic character" ("Black Bottom,

Black Sheep," 148). Rich noted that the play's dialogue is funny, salty, carnal, and lyrical and that Wilson gradually allows the audience to know his characters and their dreams. Rich illuminated one of Wilson's major themes as a revisionist look at black American history. Responding to the play as "a searing account of what white racism does to its victims," Rich wrote, "In *Ma Rainey's Black Bottom*, the writer August Wilson sends the entire history of black America crashing down upon our heads" ("Wilson's 'Ma Rainey' Opens," C1). Wilson's use of music in general and the blues in particular, both as a dramatic device and metaphor, is mentioned by several critics in Hall's excellent and comprehensive survey of critical reaction to the play. Excluded from her survey, however, is the British reaction to *Ma Rainey*, represented by Hill's assessment of the play as a tapestry of black American history in which Levee and Ma acquire through their music a mythic stature equivalent to that of the characters in Greek tragedy.

Fences was originally presented as a staged reading at the O'Neill Center in 1983. Under the direction of Richards, its world premiere performance, with James Earl Jones as Troy Maxson and Mary Alice as Rose, took place at the Yale Repertory Theatre on 30 April 1985. Rich compared this version of *Fences* unfavorably with *Ma Rainey*, noting that the production was dominated by Jones and that, despite passages of potency, the play "doesn't always rise to the stature of its subject" ("Wilson's 'Fences,' " C17). DeVries remarked that Wilson's domestic drama about the conflict between a Negro league ex–baseball player and his son demonstrated an ear for dialogue and presented narratives that were "satisfying in their lyricism as well as their colloquial accuracy" ("Drama Reveals Angry Underside," 26). Other productions of *Fences*, which featured different casts under directors other than Richards, opened at the GeVa Theatre in Rochester, New York, on 18 February 1986 and at the Seattle Repertory Theatre on 19 March 1986.

After a prior-to-Broadway run at San Francisco's Curran Theatre during February 1987, *Fences* opened on 26 March 1987 at the Forty-Sixth Street Theater in New York City. The original Yale cast, except for the minor roles of Gabriel and Raynell, again was directed by Richards, who was crowned for his efforts with the Tony Award for Best Director. Critical reaction was overwhelmingly positive. *Variety* reported six enthusiastic and twelve favorable notices, as opposed to three reviews that gave *Fences* qualified approval and only one a qualified pan. Central to reviews by Barnes, Henry, Kroll, Siebert, and Simon is a discussion of James Earl Jones as Troy Maxson, a portrayal that seems destined to leave its mark on *Fences* in the way that Marlon Brando's Stanley Kowalski has informed all subsequent productions of *A Streetcar Named Desire*. Barnes predicted that as a result of Jones's performance, Wilson's Troy Maxson "will be remembered as one of the great characters in American drama" (23). Through Jones, observed Siebert, "Actor and character merge in a giant, heroic performance" (508). Oliver's review of *Fences* goes so far as to give equal billing to playwright and star; it is titled "Mr. Wilson and Mr. Jones."

In addition to Jones's performance, the most distinguished feature of *Fences* according to the reviews, was Wilson's language. Barnes called *Fences* "the strongest, most passionate American writing since Tennessee Williams" (23), whereas Henry wrote of Wilson, "In the decade or so since the emergence of David Mamet, the American stage has not heard so impassioned and authentic a voice" (81). An interesting parallel development to these comments occurs in reviews of *Fences* that attempt an immediate appraisal of Wilson's place among American dramatists through comparing the play to other family dramas written in the United States. In reviews of *Fences* by Siebert and Weales, Wilson is compared favorably with Arthur Miller, Eugene O'Neill, Sam Shepard, and Thornton Wilder. Only two reviewers—Kroll and, again, Weales—point out that Wilson's *Fences* is similar to the kind of black family play that was parodied earlier in the season in George C. Wolfe's *The Colored Museum*.

An instructive example of a negative review of *Fences* is that by Disch, who discusses the issue of press hype surrounding both the play and Jones's performance that resulted in raising expectations to impossible heights. Other objections to *Fences* can be found in reviews by Siebert and Simon; they are fair representatives of critics who called attention to the unsuccessful dramatic structure of *Fences*, a playwrighting weakness of Wilson noted by Kauffmann, among others, in *Ma Rainey*. Perhaps the most articulate review of *Fences* is that written by Feingold, who describes Wilson as "a mythmaker who sees his basically naturalistic panorama plays as stages in an allegorical history of black America" ("The Fall of Troy," 85).

Joe Turner's Come and Gone had its initial reading at the O'Neill Center in 1984 as *Mill Hand's Lunch Bucket*, a recognition by Wilson of the influence Ramore Bearden's painting by that name had upon his writing of the play. Revised as *Joe Turner's Come and Gone*, this third Wilson play to be staged by Richards, premiered at the Yale Repertory Theatre in April 1986; it opened in a joint Yale–Boston University production at the Huntington Theatre in Boston on 27 September 1986. The play was subsequently produced at the Seattle Repertory Theatre on 10 January 1987 and at the Arena Stage in Washington, D.C. for a limited run from 2 October through 22 November 1987. In reviewing the Yale production, Rich described the play as alive with religious feeling, historical detail, and musical cadences, adding that it may be Wilson's finest achievement to date. *Joe Turner's Come and Gone* played Broadway in the spring of 1988. Meanwhile, *The Piano Lesson*, also directed by Richards, premiered 27 November 1987 at the Yale Repertory Theatre in New

Haven. Both plays are part of Wilson's projected ten-play cycle that will chronicle the changing black experience in twentieth-century America by setting each play in a different decade. *Joe Turner's Come and Gone* takes place in a Pittsburgh boarding house in 1911; *The Piano Lesson* is set in 1936. *Jitney, Fullerton Street, Ma Rainey's Black Bottom,* and *Fences* are included in this cycle as well. Wilson's sole recent departure from his commitment to this cycle was his agreement to write the book for *Mr. Jelly Lord,* a musical tracing the evolution of jazz through the life of Jelly Roll Morton; the production, scheduled for the spring of 1987, has yet to come to the stage.

SURVEY OF SECONDARY SOURCES

Bibliographies

No complete primary or secondary bibliography on Wilson exists. A brief bibliography of biographical and critical sources is printed in *Contemporary Authors. Black American Writers Past and Present: A Biographical and Bibliographical Dictionary* also includes an entry on Wilson, although information within that listing concerning poems he published in two campus publications at the University of Pittsburgh, *Black Lines* and *Black World,* and in another small magazine, *Connection,* provides neither titles nor precise publishing dates. *Current Biography* includes a brief and incomplete secondary bibliography in its August 1987 portrait of Wilson.

Biographies

The sudden ascendance of Wilson into theatrical prominence has resulted in numerous articles on his life and his development as a playwright. Among the most thoughtful and detailed is Freedman's "A Voice from the Streets," which includes extensive quotations from Wilson about his boyhood in Pittsburgh. Similar biographical information is contained in "Spotlight: August Wilson" by Staples. Both articles reveal crucial early encounters with racism by Wilson that culminated with his leaving school at the age of fifteen, and each offers unsentimental portraits of the Catholic family life of Wilson, one of six children born to a black mother, who worked as a cleaning woman to support them, and a white father, who made only fleeting appearances throughout Wilson's youth. Both articles present different examples of Wilson's exposure to the matter and manner of the African storytelling tradition in black neighborhoods, a major consideration in the development of his dramatic voice.

Wilson's involvement in the black nationalist movement of the 1960s, something both Freedman and Staples touch upon, is also discussed by

DeVries, to whom Wilson explained, "I think black theatre of the 60s was angry, didactic, and a pushing outward. What I try to do is an inward examination" ("A New Voice," 30). The biographical details of the development of his dramatic technique, especially as it relates to his work with Richards, are the subject of helpful, though brief, articles by Christiansen, Freedman, Kleiman, and Mitgang. Perhaps the most memorable sketch of the playwright and director at work occurs not in a piece about Wilson but in Freedman's article on Richards, "Leaving His Imprint on Broadway," which describes in one section a meeting in which the director guides Wilson in preparing further rewrites of *The Piano Lesson*. Other biographical details, especially about the development of *Joe Turner* and *The Piano Lesson*, emerge in both the Palmer and Powers interviews. A gracefully written, concise, and informative biographical sketch, which incorporates much of the above material, was published in *Current Biography*.

Influences

Discussion of influences on Wilson can be found primarily in newspaper and magazine articles in which either the author paraphrases Wilson or quotes Wilson explaining the forces that help shape his work. Chief among these influences is music, particularly the blues. Freedman, for instance, quotes Wilson as saying, "I see the blues as the book, if blacks have one book that is going to inform their sensibilities" ("A Playwright Talks," C3). Staples relates how Wilson's first listening of a recording of Bessie Smith's "Nobody in town can bake a sweet jelly roll like mine" alerted the playwright to an inner song all black Americans share, thus providing in the blues "Wilson's source-book, the wellspring from which he gathers the centers of his plays" ("Spotlight," 111).

The influence of art on Wilson and of Ramore Bearden's paintings, in particular, on Wilson's work since *Fences* is mentioned briefly in the interview with Powers and in Johnson's article. Both pieces also mention the effect of Wilson's knowledge of poetry on his plays.

Specific literary influences on Wilson, including Amiri Baraka, John Berryman, Jorge Luis Borges, Ralph Ellison, and Dylan Thomas, are discussed briefly by Freedman ("A Voice") and by Wilson in his interview with Palmer. Freedman also compares Wilson to Arthur Miller, as do many other critics, and to Lorraine Hansberry, a playwright, incidentally, whom Wilson claims never to have read (Freedman, "A Voice," 36).

General Studies

Aside from those studies already mentioned De Vries (*American Theatre*) provides an overall assessment of Wilson's work, including *Fences* and *The Piano Lesson*. Christiansen supplies a brief overview of Wilson's themes and their social significance ("August Wilson," *Contemporary Dramatists*). No longer general studies of Wilson have been published. He is not included in any comprehensive studies of black American drama although one essay on Wilson by Phillip Smith appears in a collection on drama edited by Hartigan. As his reputation grows, this situation will change drastically.

Analyses of Individual Plays

Although Smith's essay treats the tradition of the blues in *Ma Rainey's Black Bottom*, the most insightful analysis of the play occurs in Feingold's commentary on the Broadway production that includes both a discussion of Wilson's development as a playwright and passages from an interview with Wilson.

Two analyses of *Fences* from different perspectives have appeared. Henderson's interview with James Earl Jones and Mary Alice emphasizes the acting challenges in the play, whereas Staples discusses the powerful impact the play has on black audiences who grew up in the 1950s.

FUTURE RESEARCH OPPORTUNITIES

Almost all writing about Wilson to date has been done in the popular press. While such source material is often helpful, the more intricate matters of theme, style and general dramatic achievement are only beginning to be addressed by scholars and critics. The facts about Wilson's life, although certainly illuminating, often conflict from article to article, so a solid biographical study, however brief, seems immediately necessary. An assessment of his work in relationship to other black playwrights, and vice-versa, is appropiate, and editors of both black drama anthologies and contemporary American play collections will do well to include *Fences* in future editions. Rich opportunities exist for critics to explore Wilson's poetry and its connection to his drama, and the influence of music on Wilson seems to be a crucial and nearly limitless field of critical play. Wilson's revisionist view of black American history should provide challenging material for research and debate, especially as he continues work on his monumental ten-play cycle, a project akin in scope and vision to the historical nine-play search into the American soul and psyche that O'Neill never completed. For any researcher interested in an analysis of the changing nature of contemporary commercial theatre, Wilson, Richards, and the Yale-Broadway connection would be necessary to include.

SECONDARY SOURCES

Barnes, Clive. "Fiery *Fences.*" *New York Post* (22 March 1987): 23.

Christiansen, Richard. "August Wilson: A Powerful Playwright Probes the Meaning of Black Life." *Chicago Tribune* (9 February 1986): M12–13.

———. "August Wilson." *Contemporary Dramatists.* Fourth Edition, pp. 571–72. Edited by D. L. Kirkpatrick. Chicago: St. James Press, 1988.

DeVries, Hillary. "A Song in Search of Itself." *American Theatre* 3, no. 10 (January 1987): 22–25.

———. "August Wilson—A New Voice for Black American Theatre." *Christian Science Monitor* (16 October 1984): 29–30.

———. "Drama Reveals Angry Underside of the Peaceful 1950s." *Christian Science Monitor* (23 May 1985): 25–26.

Disch, Thomas M. "Theatre." *Nation* (18 April 1987): 516–18.

Feingold, Michael. "August Wilson's Bottomless Blackness." *Village Voice* (27 November 1984): 117–18.

———. "The Fall of Troy." *Village Voice* (7 April 1987): 85.

Freedman, Samuel G. "Leaving His Imprint on Broadway." *New York Times Magazine* (22 November 1987): 38–48.

———. "A Playwright Talks about the Blues." *New York Times* (13 April 1984): C3.

———. "A Voice from the Streets." *New York Times Magazine* (15 May 1987): 36, 40, 49, 70.

———. "Wilson's New *Fences* Nutures a Partnership." *New York Times* (5 May 1985): 80.

Gill, Brendan. "Hard Times." *New Yorker* (22 October 1984): 152.

Hall, Sharon K., ed. "August Wilson: *Ma Rainey's Black Bottom.*" In *Contemporary Literary Criticism: Yearbook 1985*, 39: 275–86. Detroit: Gale Research Company, 1986.

Henderson, Heather. "Building *Fences:* An Interview with Mary Alice and James Earl Jones." *Theatre* 16, no. 3 (Summer-Fall 1985): 67–70.

Henry, William A. "Righteous in His Own Backyard." *Time* (6 April 1987): 81.

Hill, Holly. "Brilliant Drama, Bitter Irony." *The Times* (London, 6 November 1984): 17.

Johnson, Malcolm L. "Wilson: Acclaim Doesn't Alter His Mission." *Hartford* (Conn.) *Courant* (28 April 1985): G1, G4.

Kauffmann, Stanley. "Bottoms Up." *Saturday Review* (January-February 1985): 83, 90.

Kleiman, Dena. "*Joe Turner:* The Spirit of Synergy." *New York Times* (19 May 1986): C11.

Kroll, Jack. "Theater: Nine Innings against the Devil." *Newsweek* (6 April 1987): 70.

May, Hal, ed. *Contemporary Authors.* Vol. 115. Detroit: Gale Research Company, 1985.

Mitgang, Herbert. "Wilson, From Poetry to Broadway Success." *New York Times* (22 October 1984): C15.

Oliver, Edith. "Mr. Wilson and Mr. Jones." *New Yorker* (6 April 1987): 81.

Rich, Frank. "Theater: Wilson's *Fences.*" *New York Times* (7 May 1985): C17.

————. "Theater: *Joe Turner* at Yale Rep." *New York Times* (6 May 1986): C17.

————. "Wilson's *Ma Rainey's* Opens." *New York Times* (12 October 1984): C1, C3.

Rush, Theresa Gunnels et al. *Black American Writers Past and Present: A Biographical and Bibliographical Dictionary.* Vol. 2. Metuchen, N.J.: Scarecrow Press, 1975.

Siebert, Gary. "Theater: Adams and Sons." *America* (20–27 June 1987): 507–8.

Simon, John. "Black Bottom, Black Sheep." *New York* (22 October 1984): 148.

————. "Wall in the Family." *New York* (6 April 1987): 92.

Smith, Philip E. "*Ma Rainey's Black Bottom:* Playing the Blues as Equipment for Living." In *Without the Dramatic Spectrum*, pp. 177–86. Edited by Karelisa V. Hartigan. Lanham, Md.: University Press of America, 1986.

Staples, Brent. "*Fences:* No Barrier to Emotion." *New York Times* (5 April 1987): B1, B39.

————. "Spotlight: August Wilson." *Essence* (August 1987): 50–51, 111, 116.

Weales, Gerald. "Bringing the Light: *Fences* and *The Coloured Museum*." *Commonweal* (22 May 1987): 320.

"Wilson, August." *Current Biography* (August 1987): 53–56.

Lanford Wilson

(13 APRIL 1937–   )

C. WARREN ROBERTSON

ASSESSMENT OF WILSON'S REPUTATION

Marranca and Dasgupta report that Lanford Wilson is one of the few playwrights fortunate enough to develop his art working with a permanent repertory company (27). According to Simon, he is also the only American playwright "who is steadily growing, improving, paring himself down to essentials" ("*Folie à Deux*," 76). In Shewey's view, Wilson has captured the voice of the American people and the spirit of the times (18). The esteem in which he is held is attested to by the respect of numerous critics and by the many awards he has received: a Vernon Rice Award, several Rockefeller and Guggenheim fellowships, the Brandeis University Creative Arts Award, Obies for *The Hot l Baltimore* and *The Mound Builders*, and a Pulitzer Prize and a New York Drama Critics Circle Award for *Talley's Folly* (Branam, 2098).

Wilson's unusual success has been closely associated with the Circle Repertory Company, which he helped found in 1969. Sibley has characterized Wilson's collaboration with company cofounder, director Marshall Mason, as "perhaps unmatched in the annals of American theatre" (79). Wilson's plays contain the "greatest menagerie of characters in contemporary American drama—drag queens, freaks, prostitutes, academics, priests"—likable characters for the most part since the playwright has a deep sympathy for society's lost (Branam, 2097). The language these characters speak is extraordinary. To O'Connor the constant in his plays is his "ability to compose not so much patches of interesting dialogue as sustained series of quiet lyricism, resembling vocal duets, trios or complex ensemble pieces" ("Wilson Touch," 208). Simon ("All in the Family") echoes a similar sentiment: "At a time when most playwrights can produce only chamber music, Wilson can write for a whole orchestra" (47). Rich indicates that "Mr. Wilson is one of the few artists of our theatre who can truly make America sing" ("*Angels Fall*," C15).

PRIMARY BIBLIOGRAPHY OF WILSON'S WORKS

So Long at the Fair. Unpublished. Produced 1963.
Home Free! Unpublished. Produced 1964.
No Trespassing. Unpublished. Produced 1964.
Balm in Gilead and Other Plays. New York: Hill and Wang, 1965.
Sex Is between Two People. Unpublished. Produced 1965.
The Rimers of Eldritch and Other Plays. New York: Hill and Wang, 1967.
Miss Williams: A Turn. Unpublished. Produced 1967.
Untitled Play. Music by Al Carmines. Unpublished. Produced 1967.
The Sand Castle and Three Other Plays. New York: Dramatists Play Service, 1967.
The Gingham Dog. New York: Hill and Wang, 1969.
One Arm. Unproduced screenplay, written in 1969. Adapted from Tennessee
        Williams's short story.
Lemon Sky. New York: Dramatists Play Service, 1970.
Serenading Louie. New York: Dramatists Play Service, 1970; New York: Hill and
        Wang, 1985.
The Great Nebula in Orion and Three Other Plays. New York: Dramatists Play Service,
        1973.
The Hot l Baltimore. New York: Dramatists Play Service, 1973; ABC-TV-weekly
        series, 1975.
The Migrants. CBS Playhouse 90, 1974.
Summer and Smoke. Music by Lee Hoiby. Adaptation of the play by Tennessee
        Williams. Produced in St. Paul, 1971. New York: Belwin-Mills, c.1972.
The Mound Builders. New York: Hill and Wang, 1976.
Brontosaurus. New York: Dramatists Play Service, 1978.
"Observations of a Resident Playwright." *New York Times* (23 August 1978): D5.
Taxi! Aired on "Hallmark Hall of Fame," 2 February 1978.
5th of July. New York: Hill and Wang, 1979.
"Meet Tom Eyen, Tom Eyen." *Horizon* (July 1979):43.
Talley's Folly. New York: Hill and Wang, 1980.
A Tale Told. Unpublished. Produced 1981.
Thymus Vulgaris. New York: Dramatists Play Service, 1982.
Angels Fall. New York: Hill and Wang, 1983.
Three Sisters. Unpublished translation of Anton Chekhov. Produced in 1984.
Talley & Son. New York: Hill and Wang, 1986.
Burn This. New York: Hill and Wang, 1988.

Interviews

Sibley, William J. "Lanford Wilson." *Interview* (August 1983):79–80.
Feitlowitz, Marguerite. "An Interview with Lanford Wilson." *At the Rep* 1, no. 5
        (1984).

Barnett, Gene A. "Recreating the Magic: An Interview with Lanford Wilson."
    Ball State University Forum 25 (Spring 1984): 57–43.
Savran, David. "Lanford Wilson."*In Their Own Words: Contemporary American
    Playwrights*, pp. 306–20. New York: Theatre Communications Group,
    1988.

PRODUCTION HISTORY

Wilson's earliest plays were performed as a part of the off-off-Broadway movement at the Caffe Cino and the La Mama Experimental Theatre Club. Following the suicide of Joe Cino in 1967, Wilson turned to regional theatres such as the Washington Theatre Club and the Buffalo Studio Arena to produce his plays. However, unlike other playwrights of the 1960s who remained in isolation (Loney, 114), Wilson had the vision in 1969 to help establish the Circle Repertory Company, where he has continued as resident playwright. He has enjoyed Broadway and off-Broadway success, and he has been increasingly produced by college, community, and regional theatres in America. According to Marowski, Lanford Wilson's "plays are performed more often than those of almost any other dramatist currently working in the United States" (458).

The first one-acts to have a significant impact were *The Madness of Lady Bright* and *Home Free* which were produced in May and August 1964 at the Caffe Cino. *Lady Bright* depicts the psychological disintegration of an aging male homosexual who contemplates his lonely future with growing terror. *Home Free* shows incestuous siblings living in an isolated, make-believe world. Flatley provides background material on these early works (D21).

Wilson's first full-length play, *Balm in Gilead*, was produced at Cafe La Mama in January 1965 and caused a sensation. The play is a naturalistic documentary of twenty-nine low lifers. During Chicago's 1981 Joseph Jefferson Awards, the Steppenwolf Theatre Company's poetic production walked away with seven of the prizes (Christiansen, 2:4).

The Rimers of Eldritch, Wilson's second full-length play, premiered at Cafe La Mama in July 1966 and seven months later opened off-Broadway at the Cherry Lane Theatre (Tomo, 64). Characterized by Henry Hewes as "the best Off-Broadway play so far this season," the play is a portrait of malevolence, intolerance, and scapegoating in a small midwestern town ("Birdlime and Bobby Socks," 30).

The Gingham Dog, which examines an interracial marriage, opened in September 1968 at the Washington Theatre Club and was praised by Hewes for its "total honesty" (26 October 1968, 67). In April 1969 an Alan Schneider revival at the John Golden Theatre in New York was less successful and closed after only five performances (Hobe, 40).

In March 1970 the Washington Theatre Club premiered *Serenading*

Louise, which Fletcher characterized as Wilson's "best play to date" (6). The play features four suburban friends and two troubled marriages with the couples living in identical homes. The play has enjoyed a number of revivals, including a 1976 Circle Repertory production, which, Winer reported, "went into the Burns Mantle yearbook as one of the New York season's ten best plays" (10). A 1984 revival at the Public Theater by the Second Stage received positive reviews by Beaufort, Simon, Nightingale, and Feingold.

Wilson's most autobiographical play, *Lemon Sky*, is set in sun-drenched San Diego and is a memory piece. According to Rich, the play dramatizes "the way in which an adult tries to find peace with his parents and past" (*"Lemon Sky*," C17). The play opened in March 1970 at the Buffalo Arena Stage and then moved to the Playhouse Theatre in midtown Manhattan. Gottfried referred to the play as "a stage poem, Wilson at his loveliest and most true . . . written in absolutely gorgeous verbal choreography" (14). In December 1985 it was successfully revived in New York (Feingold, "Father and Sun," 83).

The Hot l Baltimore marked Wilson's full recovery from a period of writer's slump. Set in a rundown hotel, the play, in Lahr's words, "makes us feel the texture of the faded optimism that such 19th century 'palaces' once exuded" (64). *The Hot l Baltimore* premiered in January 1973 at the off-off-Broadway Circle Theatre Company and was moved in March to the off-Broadway Circle in the Square, where it ran for 1,166 performances (Madd, 76). In 1975 Norman Lear offered a short-lived weekly television series of the play on ABC (O'Connor, "TV Review," 63).

The Mound Builders, Wilson's most ambitious play and his personal favorite, was presented at the Circle Repertory Company in February 1975. This epic drama about an archaeological team's race with time to uncover the secrets of an American Indian tribe is rooted in conflicts between past and present, commerce and art, and preservation and development. One of the play's major themes, in Koyana's view, is our irreverence for history, our urge to throw things away before considering their value (70). On 11 and 15 February 1976, a televised version was presented on Channel 13's Theatre in America series (Finkle, 101).

Set in 1977 during the period following the Vietnam War, *Fifth of July* was the first of a series of plays about a Missouri family, the Talleys (Asahina, 101). The play opened 27 April 1978 at the Circle Repertory Theatre (Eder, C3). Two and a half years later, on 5 November 1980, it opened on Broadway at the New Apollo Theatre, where it enjoyed a run of 511 performances and nine previews (Canby, C13). On 10 May 1983, the American Playhouse televised a production of this "smash-hit Broadway play" ("Television and Radio," 6).

Weiner notes that *Fifth of July* deals with people who were "burned" physically and psychologically by the 1960s (47). Nevertheless, a number of critics, including Jack Kroll and Barry Witham, have seen a deep current of optimism in the play. Rich describes Wilson's vision as his "morning-after-Independence Day dream of a democratic America—a community with room for everyone, an enlightened place where the best ideals can bloom" ("Stage," 419).

Talley's Folly opened at the Circle Repertory Company on 22 April 1979 (Weales, "American Theatre Watch," 497). Set in the ruin of an old boathouse near Lebanon, Missouri, in July 1944, it is an unabashed love story about two very different people: the Jewish outsider, Matt, and the misfit of the Protestant Talley family, Sally. The run at the Circle was brief. However, it was produced in repertory with *Fifth of July* at the Mark Taper Forum in Los Angeles and then in February had a gala opening on Broadway at the Brooks Atkinson Theatre with its original cast (Gussow, 34–35).

Talley's Folly was a Valentine hit on Broadway. Feingold ("Wilson's Waltz") described the play as "an elegantly turned light entertainment with a strikingly bitter substratum; a double satisfaction, because it gives us enjoyment as a sentimental contrivance without falsity" (79). Productions of *Talley's Folly* have been equally successful in other cities. Paul responded to the Chicago production of *Talley's Folly* and analyzed it as a drama of character, a uniquely American type of "melting pot play" (25–26).

The third play in the Talley family cycle, *Talley and Son*, was originally produced under the title *A Tale Told*. It is set in Lebanon, Missouri, on precisely the same evening as *Talley's Folly*—4 July 1944. It opened 11 June 1981 at the Circle Repertory and was the twenty-ninth production of Lanford Wilson's work to be directed by Marshall W. Mason. The play was scheduled for a second opening in October at the Mark Taper Forum in Los Angeles using the New York cast (Lawson, C3).

Talley and Son is about the financial and other machinations of three generations of Talleys who, together with the Campbells, have run two of the most profitable businesses in Lebanon—the clothing factory and the bank. Because of the liberal use of plot devices, this story of meanness and greed has often been compared with Lillian Hellman's *The Little Foxes*. Critics noting the comparison have included Beaufort and Rich. As Novick points out, both Hellman and Wilson "are keenly aware of the connection between economics and morality" ("Talley Awhile," 77).

The world premiere of *Angels Fall* was on 19 June 1982 at the Coconut Grove Playhouse in Miami and was offered as a part of the New World Festival of the Arts (Zink, 74). The play enjoyed a short engagement at the Saratoga Performing Arts Center, Saratoga Springs, New York beginning 18 August 1982 and then opened at the Circle Repertory Theatre in New York on 16 October 1982. *Angels Fall* opened at the Longacre on Broadway on 18 January 1983 (Myers, 258) and received rave reviews by Simon (7 February 1983, 58), Larson, and Gill.

Angels Fall is set in a mission in northwestern New Mexico where an Irish priest, Father Doherty, presides over a small congregation of impoverished Navahos. An accident in a nearby uranium mine causes all of the roads in the vicinity to be closed, and as a consequence two couples who are traveling separately are trapped at the mission. The play at first seems as though it will be a comment on an impending apocalypse. However, as Simon points out in "Ideals Lost and Found," the real questions are daily ones: "how to live and love in the here and now . . . how to teach and learn, how to pick and do one's job" (58).

Midway through the play, Father Doherty reads from the second epistle of Peter: "What manner of persons ought ye to be" (3:11). As Weales points out, the answer to the Biblical question is "that a person should follow his vocation" ("*Angels Fall*," 690). Larson observes that "each of the characters has come to a crisis of confidence about his or her chosen vocation" (278), and in "Affirmative Actions," Novick notes that Wilson's theme "is the importance of finding a vocation and laboring in it" (103).

Burn This was previewed by the Circle Repertory subscribers in New York and then premiered 22 January 1987 at the Mark Taper Forum in Los Angeles. Shocking, outrageous, and larger than life, the play presents Wilson's views on art, human sexuality, and love. It is a poetic and cataclysmic work in which art is seen as a sacrament, as an outward sign for inward, often chaotic but exhilarating truths. The play has the fiery stature of Ibsen's *The Master Builder* and, like that play, was written at the pinnacle of its author's career. Stayton noted, "*Burn This* is Lanford Wilson's masterpiece" (34).

Burn This had its Broadway opening on 14 October 1987 at the Plymouth. Kroll described John Malkovitch's entrance as "the most sensational since the young Brando's in *A Streetcar Named Desire*" and added that "Brando's Stanley Kowalski was decorum itself compared with the character Malkovitch plays, who is called Pale" (88). In "Lonely World of Displaced Persons," Gussow described Pale as Wilson's "most incendiary character . . . a beast in a jungle of his own devising," and "the author's most original character" (5). In a review of the published play, Olson remarked, "The whole comes off like a collaboration between Robert Patrick and Sam Shepard, unlikely as that sounds" (967).

SURVEY OF SECONDARY SOURCES

Bibliographies

Play Index, 1968–1972 provides a brief synopsis of each of Lanford Wilson's early works. Another early bibliography, *A Guide to Critical Reviews:*

Part I: American Drama, 1909–1969, includes off-Broadway opening production dates, as well as information on important reviews. The 1976 *Notable Names in the American Theatre* provides a valuable source of production information for the early plays.

Sainer's primary bibliography includes a short essay analyzing Wilson's plays. The 1986 edition of *Contemporary Literary Criticism*, edited by Marowski, contains eighteen separate articles on Wilson by a variety of reviewers.

The excellent bibliographical checklist in *American Drama Criticism*, includes general works on Wilson by Baker, Dasgupta, and Schvey, as well as a bibliography of specific plays. Branam includes a checklist of Wilson's principal works from 1963 through 1984. Barnett also contains a first-rate annotated bibliography.

Biographies

Lanford Wilson's life story has captured the imagination of numerous journalists, critics, and scholars. In chronological order, some of the more important of these not already mentioned include: Grover, Drake, Berkvist, Sullivan, Kakutani, Gussow ("When the Playwright's Life Is Visible in His Work"), Gerard, Freedman, and Koehler.

Influences

An exceptionally valuable essay by Dreher (350–68) traces literary influences and analyzes several recurring themes: Wilson's interest in and respect for the past; his belief in the importance yet near impossibility of there being a stable and loving family unit; and his seemingly universal, Shakespearean love for humanity (353). Barnett claims that an early influence consisted of the plays he saw at Southwest Missouri State College; Wilson was "mesmerized" by a 1954 production of *Brigadoon* and in 1955 was drawn to the "magic" of a production of *Death of a Salesman* (1). Baker believes Ionesco's *The Lesson* had been a pivotal experience for Wilson, who said that he "never knew theatre could be dangerous and funny in that way at the same time" (41). Haller also notes the importance of *The Lesson* and states that Wilson "almost immediately ensconced himself in the coffeehouse theatre scene" (28).

Wilson was certainly one of off-off-Broadway's pioneering playwrights of the early 1960s. Not only has he survived, but as Wetzsteon observes, "he's won more public acceptance than the others combined" (40). He is a modest and hard-working craftsman who, as Blau notes, "attributes much of his success to the Circle Repertory Theatre Company (C15). Buckley sees Wilson's theatre as a "national resource" (37), and a number of respected critics see Wilson as a major American playwright. Simon, in "Ideals Lost and Found," notes that "Wilson writes very likely the best dialogue in America today" (58).

A number of critics, including Beaufort, Feingold, Munk, Novick, and Simon, see a strong Chekhovian flavor in Wilson's work. Many of his plays, however, combine experimental tendencies with traditional techniques. Wetzsteon sees Wilson as having combined avant-garde and mainstream drama to "take his place not as the descendant of Antonin Artaud but as the heir to Thornton Wilder" (45). In another article, "Demirep," Simon states that if playwriting were a horse race, he would "bet on Wilson, the heir of Tennessee Williams, because, though less strikingly original than Shepard, he is more literate, more disciplined, more humane" (64). The continuity of Wilson's work, according to Loney, recalls the dedication of earlier playwrights, such as Robert E. Sherwood and Maxwell Anderson, "proving it is still possible to make a career of writing for the theatre, despite the lures of film and televison projects" (*Encyclopedia of World Drama*, 119).

MacDougall and Scherer have noted that once "freed of the need to write only commercial hits, playwrights have experimented with a broad range of themes" (75). Lanford Wilson and the entire Circle Repertory Company can be seen as a part of a significant revitalizing trend away from the strictly commercial approach of Broadway to the not-for-profit experimentation typical of burgeoning regional theatres across the country.

Lanford Wilson is a distinctly American playwright whose works reflect his roots in the Ozarks as well as the streets and habitations of his adopted home, New York City. In Gussow's view, he is a major American playwright whose unified work speaks with eloquence about the importance of each person's individual history. Wilson's characters "reach back to the past not for nostalgia but for anchors, for a lineage with those who have preceded them, for sustaining values" ("*Talley's Folly*," 32).

General Studies

A number of dissertations, such as Harriot's, focus on Wilson's early and middle work. Three dissertations devoted exclusively to Wilson are by Leland, Myers, and Pauwels. Myers in particular provides an analysis of each of the individual plays in terms of plot, theme, and characterization.

The most valuable general study, however, is Barnett's *Lanford Wilson*, which contains chapters on all of the major plays through *Talley and Son*, as well as a family genealogy and family chronology for the entire Talley clan (154–56). Herman devotes a single chapter to Wilson, pointing out that in "his more than thirty plays he has undertaken to put on stage a kind of epic encompassment of American experience and mythologies"

(198). Explicating Wilson's major plays, Herman applauds the "delicate poetic language at the heart of his style" (228).

FUTURE RESEARCH OPPORTUNITIES

A number of critics have focused on characterization in Wilson's plays, and there seems to be considerable agreement that he is extraordinarily perceptive in this area. He is equally strong as a dramatic poet, and future research should focus on his use of language. Dreher observes, Wilson's poetic language is "loaded with sensory appeal" (353). Schvey notes that Wilson presents the paradox of having written a large body of work while still being young enough to be thought of as a developing artist (225). Future research should focus on Wilson's emerging works as he continues his unique blending of traditional and experimental techniques.

In terms of Aristotle's concept that the plot is the first and most important element of drama, Wilson would have to be evaluated as a good writer who is better with some scripts than with others. As a dramatic poet and as one who writes perceptively about a wide variety of people, however, he is unsurpassed. "Pale," the central figure in *Burn This*, is one of the great creations of the twentieth-century theatre and has been compared with O'Neill's "Hairy Ape," Steinbeck's Lenny, Williams's Kowalski, and Mamet's "losers." But there is a difference: Pale "knows his wounds" and can "articulate his agonies" (Stayton, 34).

SECONDARY SOURCES

American Drama Criticism. Edited by Floyd Eugene Eddleman. Hamden, Conn.: Shoe String Press, 1979.

Asahina, Robert. "Theatre Chronicle." *Hudson Review* 34 (Spring 1981): 99–104.

Baker, Rob. "Bill Hurt and Lanford Wilson: Player and Playwright Meet at the Circle." *After Dark* (June 1978): 38–41.

Barnett, Gene A. *Lanford Wilson.* Twayne's United States Authors Series. Boston: Twayne, 1987.

Beaufort, John. "Comedy with Chekhovian Grip." *Christian Science Monitor* (3 May 1978): 22.

———. "The Hot l Baltimore." *Christian Science Monitor* (9 February 1973): 14.

———. "Moral Malaise in Middle Class America." *Christian Science Monitor* (21 February 1984) Arts and Leisure: 33.

Berkvist, Robert. "Lanford Wilson—Can He Score on Broadway?" *New York Times* (17 February 1980): A33.

Blau, Eleanor. "How Lanford Wilson Writes with Actors in Mind." *New York Times* (27 January 1983): C15.

Branam, Harold. "Lanford Wilson." In *Critical Survey of Drama*, pp. 2097–98. Edited by Frank N. Magill. 6 vols. Englewood Cliffs, N.J.: Salem Press, 1985.

Buckley, Peter. "Circle Repertory Theatre." *Horizon* (May 1980): 36–37.

Canby, Vincent. *"Fifth of July* Will Close after Long Run." *New York Times* (22 January 1982): C13.

Christiansen, Richard. "Top Jefferson Awards Given to *Folies, Balm in Gilead.*" *Chicago Tribune* (20 October 1981): 2:4.

DeVries, Hilary. "A Twice-Told Tale." *Christian Science Monitor* (20 August 1985) Arts and Leisure: 25.

Drake, Sylvie. "Playwright Who Didn't Want a Job." *Los Angeles Times* (12 August 1979): C61.

Dreher, Ann Crawford. "Lanford Wilson." *Dictionary of Literary Biography*, 7:350–68. Detroit: Gale Research Company, 1981.

Eder, Richard. "Theatre: *Fifth of July* Is Staged." *New York Times* (2 April 1978): C3.

Feingold, Michael. "Father and Sun." *Village Voice* (31 December 1985): 83.

———. "Serenading Lanford." *Village Voice* (17 February 1984): 96.

———. "Wilson's Waltz." *Village Voice* (3 March 1980): 77, 79.

———. "Vodka and Apple Pie." *Village Voice* (12 November 1980): 91, 95.

Finkle, David. "TV Slouches Toward Maturity: *The Mound Builders." Village Voice* (9 February 1976): 101.

Flatley, Guy. "Lanford Is One 'L' of a Playwright." *New York Times* (22 April 1973): 2:1, 21.

Fletcher, Richard D. *"Serenading Louis* in a Split Level." *Christian Science Monitor* (15 April 1970): 6.

Freedman, Samuel G. "Lanford Wilson Enjoys a Triumph over Time." *New York Times* (26 December 1985): C13.

Gerard, Jeremy. "Circle Repertory Seeks to Rekindle Past Glory." *New York Times* (20 October 1985): B1, B4.

Gill, Brendan. "The Theatre: Events Before Mass." *New York Times* (31 January 1983): 101.

Gottfried, Martin. "The Theatre: Lemon Sky." *Women's Wear Daily* (18 May 1970): 14.

Grover, Stephen. "Little White Way." *Wall Street Journal* (20 August 1979): 1, 33.

A Guide to Critical Reviews. Pt.1: American Drama 1909–1969, 2d ed., pp. 532–34. Edited by James M. Salem. Metuchen, N.J.: Scarecrow Press, 1973.

Gussow, Mel. "Lonely World of Displaced Persons." *New York Times* (25 October 1987): 2:5.

———. *"Talley's Folly:* A Valentine Hit: Lanford Wilson on Broadway." *Horizon* (May 1980): 30–37.

———. "When the Playwright's Life Is Visible in His Work." *New York Times* (26 August 1984): B5.

Haller, Scott. "The Dramatic Rise of Lanford Wilson." *Saturday Review* (August 1981): 26–29.

Harriott, Esther. "Images of America: Four Contemporary Playwrights." *DAI* 44, no. 10 (April 1984): 306A.

Herman, William. "Down and Out in Lebanon and New York: Lanford Wilson." In his *Understanding Contemporary American Drama*, pp. 196–229. Columbia, S.C.: University of South Carolina Press, 1987.

Hewes, Henry. "The Theatre: Have Theater, Will Travel." *Saturday Review* (26 October 1968): 32, 67.

———. "The Theatre: Birdlime and Bobby Socks." *Saturday Review* (11 March 1967): 30.

Hobe. "Show on Broadway: *The Gingham Dog*." *Variety* (30 April 1969): 40.

Kakutani, Michiko. "I Write the World As I See It around Me." *New York Times* (8 July 1984): 4, 6.

Koehler, Robert. "Playwright, Director: The Long-Running Duo." *Los Angeles Times* (18 January 1987): 44–46.

Koyana, Christine. "Two Down, Three to Go." *Chicago* (May 1980): 70–71.

Kroll, Jack. "The Return of Theatricality." *Newsweek* (26 October 1987): 88–89.

Lahr, John. "On-Stage." *Village Voice* (22 March 1973): 64.

Larsen, Janet Karsten. "Scripts for the Living and the Dead." *Christian Century* (23–30 March 1983): 278–79.

Lawson, Carol. "3rd Play in Talley Cycle Opens June 11." *New York Times* (15 April 1981): C3.

Leland, Nicholas Frederick. "*A Critical Analysis of the Major Plays of Lanford Wilson*." Ph.D. dissertation, University of California, 1984. Ann Arbor: UMI, 1986. 8500010.

Loney, Glenn. "American Drama." *McGraw-Hill Encyclopedia of World Drama*, 1:114–19. Edited by Stanley Hochman. New York: McGraw-Hill, 1984.

MacDougall, William, and Ron Scherer. "Staging a Revolution in American Theatre." *U.S. News and World Report* (11 June 1984): 74–75.

Madd. "Off-Broadway Reviews: *The Hot l Baltimore*." *Variety* (11 April 1973): 76.

Marowski, Daniel G., ed. "Lanford Wilson." In *Contemporary Literary Criticism*, 36:458–66. Detroit: Gale Research, 1986.

Marranca, Bonnie, and Gautam Dasgupta. *American Playwrights: A Critical Survey*. New York: Drama Book Specialist, 1981.

Munk, Erika. "Home Rule." *Village Voice* (15 May 1978): 99.

Myers, Laurence Douglas. "*Characterization in Lanford Wilson's Plays*." Ph. D. dissertation, Kent State University, 1984. Ann Arbor: UMI, 1986. 8429799.

Novick, Julius. "Affirmative Actions." *Village Voice* (26 October 1982): 103.

———. "Talley Awhile." *Village Voice* (17–23 March 1983): 77.

———. "Theater." *Nation* (29 November 1980): 588–89.

Notable Names in the American Theatre. Edited by Raymond D. McGill. Clifton, N.J.: James T. White & Company, 1976.

O'Connor, John J. "TV Review: Hot l Baltimore Signs ABC Register at 9." *New York Times* (24 January 1975): L63.

———. "The Wilson Touch." *New York Theatre Critics' Reviews* (October 1970): 208.

Olson, Ray. Review of *Burn This*. *Booklist* (15 February 1988): 967.

Paul, John Steven. "Who Are You? Who Are We?" *Cresset* (September 1980): 25–27.

Pauwels, Gerard W. "A Critical Analysis of the Plays of Lanford Wilson." Ph.D. dissertation, Indiana University, 1986. Ann Arbor: UMI, 1987. 8617762.

Play Index, 1968–1972. Edited by Estelle A. Fidell. New York: H. W. Wilson Co., 1973.

Rich, Frank. "Play: *Angels Fall*, Lanford Wilson's Apocalypse." *New York Times* (18 October 1982): C15.

————. "Stage: *Fifth of July*, Talleys 33 Years Later." *New York Times* (6 November 1980): C19.

————. "Theatre: *Lemon Sky* by Lanford Wilson." *New York Times* (12 December 1985): C17.

————. "Theater: Wilson's 'Talley & Son.' " *New York Times* (23 October 1985): C19.

Sainer, Arthur, "Lanford Wilson." In *Contemporary Dramatists*, pp. 871–73. Edited by James Vinson. London: St. James Press, 1977.

Schvey, Henry I. "Images of the Past in the Plays of Lanford Wilson." In *Essays on Contemporary American Drama*, pp. 225–40. Edited by Hedwig Bock and Albert Wertheim. N.p.: Max Hueber Verlag, 1981.

Shewey, Don. "I Hear America Talking." *Rolling Stone* (22 July 1982): 18.

Sibley, William J. "Lanford Wilson." *Interview* (August 1983): 79.

Simon, John. "All in the Family." *New York* (22 June 1981): 47.

————. "*Folie à Deux*." *New York* (21 May 1979): 76.

————. "Ideals Lost and Found." *New York* (7 February 1983): 58.

————. "Likable But Unlikely Transplant." *New York* (15 May 1978): 77–78.

————. "Theater: Demirep." *New York* (4 November 1985): 64, 66.

Stayton, Richard. "The Critic Is for *Burn This:* Here's Why." *Los Angeles Herald Examiner* (23 January 1987): 34.

Sullivan, Dan. "Retracing the 'Roots' of Wilson." *Los Angeles Times* (15 November 1981): C48.

"Television and Radio: Audio Visual Treats." *Horizon* 26, no. 6 (May 1983).

Tomo. "Off-Broadway Review: *The Rimers of Eldritch*." *Variety* (22 February 1967): 64.

Weales, Gerald. "American Theatre Watch, 1979–1980." *Georgia Review* (Fall 1980): 497–508.

————. "American Theatre Watch, 1985–1986." *Georgia Review* (Summer 1986): 520–31.

————. "*Angles Fall:* Epistle of Peter to New Mexico." *Commonweal* (17 December 1982): 690–91.

Weiner, Bernard. "A Playwright Looks Back on '60s 'Innocence.' " *San Francisco Chronicle* (2 February 1979): 47.

Wetzsteon, Ross. "The Most Populist Playwright." *New York* (8 November 1982): 40–45.

Winer, Linda. "Wilson, Mason: The Duet Is in Perfect Stage Harmony." *Chicago Tribune* (27 August 1976): 4, 10

Witham, Barry B. "Images of America: Wilson, Weller and Horovitz." *Theatre Journal* (May 1982): 223–29.

Zink. "Resident Legit Reviews: *Angels Fall*." *Variety* (7 July 1982): 74.

Paul Zindel

(15 MAY 1936–   )

SUZANNE BURGOYNE DIECKMAN

ASSESSMENT OF ZINDEL'S REPUTATION

Paul Zindel's critical reputation as a dramatist rests chiefly on his Pulitzer Prize–winning *The Effect of Gamma Rays on Man-in-the-Moon Marigolds*. In addition to the 1971 Pulitzer, *Gamma Rays* garnered the 1970 Obie Award (Best play) and New York Drama Critics Circle Award (Best American Play). *Gamma Rays* was also named a 1971 Notable Book and a Best Book for Young Adults by the American Library Association. Zindel received the 1970 Vernon Rice Drama Desk Award for most promising playwright. His sensitivity to adolescent trauma, so clearly demonstrated in *Gamma Rays*, has also contributed to his success as a writer of novels for young people, of which he has authored some dozen to date. According to Hipple, "Few other writers match his awareness of teenagers' problems and attitudes" (410). Zindel's penchant for grotesque humor, which critics admire in *Gamma Rays*, marks his juvenile fiction as well.

Martin Gottfried bestowed upon Zindel the title of "most sympathetic writer for women since Tennessee Williams" (1971, 342). Zindel's wounded but ferociously funny heroines, portrayed on Broadway by performers of the magnitude of Estelle Parsons, Julie Harris, Shelley Winters, and Maureen Stapleton, continue to appeal to actresses in regional and amateur theatres.

PRIMARY BIBLIOGRAPHY OF ZINDEL'S WORKS

Dimensions of Peacocks. Unpublished play. 1959.
Euthanasia and the Endless Heart. Unpublished play. 1960.
A Dream of Swallows. Unpublished play, 1962.
Let Me Hear You Whisper. Television play. NET, 1966.

The Effect of Gamma Rays on Man-in-the-Moon Marigolds. Television play. NET, 3
    October 1966.
"The Theater Is Born Within Us." *New York Times* (26 July 1970): 2.
The Effect of Gamma Rays on Man-in-the-Moon Marigolds. Preface by Paul Zindel.
    New York: Harper & Row, 1971.
And Miss Reardon Drinks a Little. New York: Dramatists Play Service, 1971; New
    York: Random House, 1972.
Let Me Hear You Whisper and *The Ladies Should Be in Bed.* New York: Dramatists
    Play Service, 1973.
The Secret Affairs of Mildred Wild. New York: Dramatist Plays Service, 1973.
Ladies at the Alamo. (New York 1975).
Let Me Hear You Whisper. New York: Harper & Row, 1974.
A Destiny with Half Moon Street. Unpublished play 1983.

Screenplays

Up the Sandbox. National, 1972. Adapted from Anne Roiphe's novel.
Mame. Warner Bros., 1974. Adapted from Patrick Dennis's novel.
Maria's Lovers (coauthor). Cannon, 1985.
Runaway Train. CBS, 1985.
Alice in Wonderland. CBS, 1985.

Novel

When a Darkness Falls. New York: Bantam, 1984.

PRODUCTION HISTORY

With something less than humility, Zindel thanks the educational and
amateur theatres "for seeing that my plays are sometimes performed
with more frequency than those of any other playwright with the exception of Shakespeare" (Eaglen, 1980). Without substantiating Zindel's
claim, Dramatists Play Service confirms that *Gamma Rays* continues to be
one of its best-selling plays for the amateur market.

Zindel condemns critics for their tendency to "overpraise and then
annihilate" (Eaglen, 180). This is an accurate assessment of the trajectory
of critical response to Zindel's work. As is the case of so many other
contemporary American dramatists, to call a new playwright promising
is often to sound his death knell.

Little critical information exists regarding Zindel's first two produced
plays. *Dimensions of Peacocks,* written under the direction of Edward Albee
and produced in New York in 1959, deals with the now-familiar Zindel
situation of a sensitive youth dominated by a demented mother. *Euthanasia and the Endless Hearts* was performed by Take 3, a New York
City coffee house, in 1960.

A Dream of Swallows opened 14 April 1964 at Jan Hus House in New

York and closed after one performance. By all accounts, including Zindel's, it was a flop. Taubman opened his review with the line, "Egad, how they suffer," and went on to call the play "pretentious" and "inept" (1964, 46).

Zindel thus did not receive the dangerous label "promising" until the success of *Gamma Rays*, which he had actually written in 1962. Prior to its off-Broadway opening, the play appeared in several regional theatres, beginning with the Alley Theatre in Houston in June 1965. Taubman found the play "puzzling" and "murky" but admitted that it "created a mood" (1965, 48). Hewes noted "compelling moments of psychological insight and poetic overtones" (1965, 45). Negative reviews for a 1966 condensed television version starring Eileen Heckart may have retarded the play's arrival on the New York stage.

The Effect of Gamma Rays on Man-in-the-Moon Marigolds opened off-Broadway at the Mercer-O'Casey Theatre on 7 April 1970. Produced by Orin Lehman and directed by Melvin Bernhardt, the production featured Sada Thompson as Beatrice. On 11 August 1970, the production moved, with a new cast, to the New Theatre on Broadway where it closed after a total run of 819 performances.

Critical response was almost unanimously enthusiastic. Kerr promptly hailed Zindel as "one of our most promising new writers" (1970, 244). Critics tended to agree with Oliver's favorable evaluation of *Gamma Rays* as "a rather old-fashioned domestic drama" (82). Comparisons between *Gamma Rays* and *The Glass Menagerie* were quickly drawn, but in the general atmosphere of critical euphoria, those comparisons were to Zindel's credit. Words like *touching, honest, compassionate*, and *funny* abound in these reviews.

The implications of Zindel's mutation theme—that while intense psychological "radiation" destroys some souls, it engenders evolution in others—pleased critics such as Kerr, Barnes, and Clurman. The optimism of the play's ending held a powerful appeal; Kroll admired Zindel's "sane view of life which sees the agony of waste and the difficult beauty of hope" (1970, 64). Hewes (1970) sounded a dissenting note by questioning the believability of the hopeful ending, while Gottfried (1970) complained that Zindel made his mutation imagery overly explicit.

Cast and director also received accolades. Bernhardt's staging was complimented for being realistic, sensitive, and unobtrusively effective. Reviewers credited all five actresses for doing justice to Zindel's psychologically perceptive characterizations, although the juicy role of Beatrice naturally attracted the most comment. Hewes's evaluation of Sada Thompson's "sometimes hilarious but always desperate portrayal of a bitterly cynical mother" as "probably the finest performance of the current theatre season" (1970, 12) was confirmed by the same 1969–1970 *Variety* Critics Poll that named Zindel the most promising playwright.

Subsequent productions of *Gamma Rays* have not fared so well. Brustein summed up the critical reaction to the 1972 London production directed by Bernhardt: Zindel's play "was coldly received here after an indifferent production at the Hampstead Theatre Club exposed all its clumsy plotting, old-fashioned naturalism, and unacknowledged debts to *The Glass Menagerie*" (65). Greer, in dissent, castigated the (male) critics for chauvinism and gave an idiosyncratic feminist interpretation of the play.

The 1972 Twentieth-Century Fox film, with screenplay by Alvin Sargent, won praise for Paul Newman's direction and Joanne Woodward's Beatrice. Some reviewers attacked the inadequacies of Zindel's original script, but Farber found the material intelligently reshaped for the medium and the film itself "powerful and affecting" (13).

A 1974 Paris production at the Théâtre La Bruyère, directed by Michel Fagadeau and starring Lila Kedrova, failed to enhance Zindel's overseas reputation. *Le Figaro*'s Gautier declared his distaste for Zindel's psychopathic characters and Kedrova's melodramatic performance.

By the time the Broadway revival at the Biltmore Theatre opened on 14 March 1978, New York critics too were having second thoughts. In 1978, according to Gill, *Gamma Rays* seemed "far too literary in its construction and too meagre in its emotions" (1978, 95). Eder found the play dated and reeking "with self-pity" (C25). Eder condemned director A. J. Antoon for the allowing performers, especially Shelley Winters as Beatrice, to overact. The revival ran only sixteen performances.

The most common word to appear in the reviews of *And Miss Reardon Drinks a Little* is *disappointing*. Originally written in 1966, *Miss Reardon* went through numerous revisions and a 1967 Mark Taper Forum (Los Angeles) production before opening 25 February 1971 at the Morosco Theatre, where it ran for 108 performances.

Miss Reardon boasted a stellar cast including Estelle Parsons, Nancy Marchand, and Julie Harris as the three Reardon sisters. As Watt observed, Zindel "has a gift for writing parts for women. . . . But he hasn't found the play he was looking for in them" (341).

The reviews were mixed. Kroll maintained his *Gamma Rays* enthusiasm for Zindel as a playwright who can write intelligently for a general audience. Most reviewers conceded that *Miss Reardon* is funny. However, the majority of critics, including Watt, Kerr, Barnes, and Kalem, concluded that the plot goes nowhere and the point of the play is unclear. Again, Zindel depicts characters whose lives have been warped by a dominating mother, but this time, said Hewes, "the sickness on which the play feeds is more exploited than explored" (1971, 10). Reviewers complained that Zindel's alternation of wacky humor and poignant pathos, which they had found so effective in *Gamma Rays*, in *Miss Reardon* was jarring.

Performance reviews were also mixed, especially for Julie Harris's mad Anna, although most critics appreciated Estelle Parsons's wise-cracking Catherine. Zindel received his share of the blame for failing to write fully developed characters.

Gill castigated the critics themselves for having first "overpraised" *Gamma Rays* and then "underdamned" *Miss Reardon*, the latter a play that in his opinion put Zindel's "professional life in jeopardy" (1971, 67).

None of the critics could be accused of underdamning *The Secret Affairs of Mildred Wild*, which opened 14 November 1972 at the Ambassador Theatre in New York and closed after twenty-three performances. Kroll literally consigned Zindel to hell for writing down to his audience in order to score a commercial success.

Again, the consensus of opinion declared that *Mildred Wild* is pointless—and not funny. Barnes and Watts blamed Maureen Stapleton's performance on Zindel for having given Stapleton jokes instead of a character. Gottfried pointed the finger at director Jeff Bleckner's attempt to disguise the thinness of the plot with a frenzied pace.

Whereas *honest* had been a term of critical endearment for *Gamma Rays, Mildred Wild* earned the epithet *phony*. Watts summed up the chorus of discontent with his plaintive, "I wonder what has happened to the promising Paul Zindel" (186).

Zindel reworked a 1970 script, *Nymphs and Satyrs*, into *Ladies at the Alamo* and directed a 1975 Actors Studio production himself. Opening at Broadway's Martin Beck Theatre on 7 April 1977 under the direction of Frank Perry, *Alamo* closed after twenty performances. Estelle Parsons starred as Dede.

One gossipy topic of critical debate was whether Zindel had based his portrait of a power struggle among five bitchy women for control of a Texas theatre on his experiences at the Alley with Nina Vance. Zindel denied any such intention.

Reviewers renewed their charges of pointlessness: Gill considered all the characters equally unpleasant, and Kerr complained that Zindel gave no indication of who was right and who was wrong. In general, critics condemned *Alamo* as unbelievable, overwritten, overacted, and, as Barnes put it, "slick to the point of slippery" (1977, C3).

Two Zindel one-acts, *Let Me Hear You Whisper* and *The Ladies Should Be in Bed*, were produced off-off-Broadway at the Nat Horne Musical Theater 29 April 1982. Zindel's musical based on the life of Dorothy Parker, *A Destiny with Half Moon Street*, premiered in Florida on 3 March 1983 at the Coconut Grove Playhouse; José Ferrer directed. No reviews of these productions are available.

Thus the production history of Zindel's drama reveals a declining reputation after *Gamma Rays*, reflected in both critical response and length of run.

SURVEY OF SECONDARY SOURCES

Bibliographies

The article on Zindel in Stine provides the most up-to-date bibliography of primary sources. No complete bibliography of secondary sources has been compiled for Zindel. Salem's *Guide* includes listings of *New York Times* reviews and the *New York Theatre Critics' Reviews* references; Eddleman includes a few periodical references not found in Salem. *Twentieth-Century American Dramatists* gives the most comprehensive bibliography of interviews. Carpenter's monumental *International Bibliography* has only two Zindel citations (the Henke and Miner articles). Eddleman's *Supplement* also lists the Miner article, plus two reviews. *Something About the Author*'s bibliography includes a couple of interviews not listed elsewhere, but the bibliography's usefulness is impaired by the failure to include page numbers. The Zindel entries in *Contemporary Literary Criticism* and *Children's Literature Review* contain extensive excerpts from reviews of Zindel's juvenile fiction, with complete citations.

Biographies

The most useful compact biography of Zindel, interspersed with compact criticism of his plays, is Strickland's article. Since Zindel makes no secret of the autobiographical element in his writing, a series of interviews provides additional insights, if one can sort them out from a morass of wacky anecdotic detail.

Something about the Author arranges in chronological order excerpts from interviews, including anecdotes from Zindel's traumatic childhood. In the Eaglan interview, Zindel confesses that youthful feelings of worthlessness influenced him to become a writer and that he writes to encourage young readers to face their own problems with courage and hope. Zindel adds that he views himself as a born playwright and has to struggle with form to write novels and screenplays.

Flatley's 1970 interview includes a brief production history of *Gamma Rays* and Zindel's acknowledgment that his mother served as the model for Beatrice. Zindel also comments on his admiration for the plays of Tennessee Williams, although he does not discuss any direct influence. Mercier's article is notable for Zindel's affirmation of faith in psychoanalysis in helping him recover from his own childhood traumas and as an influence on his writing. Zindel's essay, "The Theater Is Born within Us," affirms his faith in the theatre as a kind of religion, since theatre assists people in their attempts to create a better world; to get to the point, one wades through more stories of childhood humiliation. Prideaux's combined interview and *Gamma Rays* review is rather skimpy but includes Zindel's comment that he tries "to arrive at the sublime through mundane, common material" (9). Janeczko's interview provides a brief discussion of the role played by pathos in Zindel's writing.

Bosworth deals primarily with Zindel's work on the *Alamo* script in collaboration with five actresses, two of whom withdrew from the project because they felt Zindel was exploiting them. The playwright explains that the subject of *Alamo* is intended to be transitional women confused by finding themselves playing male roles in a power-oriented world. Zindel also reveals that after the failure of *Mildred Wild*, he considered renouncing the theatre and going back to teaching. Perhaps none of the interviews is recent enough to have asked if Zindel has permanently renounced the theatre in favor of screenwriting and juvenile fiction.

Influences

No systematic analysis has been made of influences on Paul Zindel's dramatic writing, much less Zindel's possible influence on other playwrights. Zindel has consistently been compared with Tennessee Williams. A sample of the depth of such analyses is Simon's comment that Zindel "has approached his mentors, Tennessee Williams and Arthur Miller, with slavish reverence" (57). Although Zindel studied playwriting under the direction of Edward Albee, no one has analyzed that relationship. Zindel's interviews reveal that he views psychoanalysis as an important influence on his work; nobody has done a study of that either. The closest thing to even a sustained critical comparison is Adler's brief discussion of the similarities between *Gamma Rays* and *The Glass Menagerie* in terms of character relationships, setting, and technical effects.

General Studies

There is a dearth of critical studies dealing with Zindel as a playwright. Symbolic of critical disregard is C. W. E. Bigsby's sole reference to Zindel in the third volume of his *Critical Introduction*, an offhand comment that *Gamma Rays* demonstrates that "Off-Broadway could successfully accommodate the conventional as well as the innovative" (26). Bigsby, usually a careful scholar, even misspells Zindel's name. Dace's brief overview identifies major Zindel themes.

The sole comprehensive study of Zindel's drama is Stickland's *Twentieth-Century American Dramatists* entry, which, although limited by space, gives a good basic summary of Zindel's recurring themes and strengths and weaknesses, concluding predictably that Zindel has failed to live up to his promise as a playwright.

Two articles focusing on Zindel's juvenile fiction merit mention. Haley and Donelson trace Zindel's critique of society and the family through three novels and *Gamma Rays*, praising Zindel's "affirmation of his faith in people . . . and the collective human spirit" (945). Examining Zindel's first three novels, Henke proposes that Zindel's young protagonists prematurely seek to take over the parental role since their own parents have so abysmally failed. Henke argues his thesis most convincingly in his analysis of *The Pigman*, but he does not extend the concept to consideration of the plays.

Analyses of Individual Plays

Gamma Rays is the only Zindel play to have attracted critical attention beyond the review stage, and even that is scanty. Leonard gives an outline of the production history and brief excerpts from the film and stage reviews. Adler discusses Zindel's optimism about the future evolution of humanity, arguing that "Zindel's optimism does not grow organically from the play" (132). Furthermore, Adler finds *Gamma Rays* derivative and heavy-handed in its symbolism. Particularly attentive to metatheatrical implications in Pulitzer plays, Adler points to the science fair sequence in which the theatre audience is cast as the high school assembly audience; he does not, however, attempt the improbable task of arguing that *Gamma Rays* is metatheatre. Miner's article analyzes *Gamma Rays* as one of several examples of the varying use of grotesque imagery in contemporary drama. Miner suggests the almost "New Age" interpretation that Tillie embraces a vision of unity with the universe, while Ruth and Beatrice, inflexible in their isolation, represent "those who fear change" (102).

For analysis of other Zindel plays, one must fall back on the Strickland entry and the reviews. A few potentially useful items will be cited here. Kerr's reviews of *Gamma Rays* and *Miss Reardon* are particularly rich in detailed descriptions of performances, and his analysis of structural problems in *Miss Reardon* is worthy of attention. Gottfried claims that *Gamma Rays* and *Miss Reardon* both critique the American educational system; unfortunately his reviews merely propose that questionable thesis without developing it. While conceding that *Alamo* is a flawed play, W.L.T.'s review of the 1978 Dallas production commends Zindel for raising issues relevant to the survival of arts organizations, including the conflicting demands of human loyalty and public accountability in management.

FUTURE RESEARCH OPPORTUNITIES

So little sustained analysis of Zindel's drama has been done that the field remains wide open. The most intriguing question is why, given Zindel's concern for working through trauma to a hopeful conclusion in *Gamma Rays* and in his juvenile fiction, his other plays seem so pessimistic (with the exception of *Mildred Wild*, where the reconciliation appears forced). The real question, though, is how much, in the absence of new evidence to refute the decline of Zindel's critical reputation as a dramatist, further study is warranted.

SECONDARY SOURCES

Adler, Thomas P. *Mirror on the Stage: The Pulitzer Plays as an Approach to American Drama*. West Lafayette, Id.: Purdue University Press, 1987.

Barnes, Clive. "Ambush, Massacre." *New York Times* (8 April 1977): C3.

———. "And Miss Reardon Drinks a Little." *New York Times* (26 February 1971): 29.

———. "Paul Zindel Melodrama at Mercer-O'Casey." *New York Times* (8 April 1970): 38.

———. "The Secret Affairs of Mildred Wild." *New York Times* (15 November 1972): 38.

Bigsby, C. W. E. *Beyond Broadway*. Vol. 3 of *A Critical Introduction to Twentieth-Century Drama*. Cambridge: Cambridge University Press, 1985.

Bosworth, Patricia. "The Effect of Five Actresses on a Play-in-Progress." *New York Times* (3 April 1977): B1, B8, B9.

Brustein, Robert. *The Culture Watch: Essays on Theatre and Society, 1969–1974*. New York: Alfred A. Knopf, 1975.

Carpenter, Charles A. *Modern Drama: Scholarship and Criticism 1966–1980; An International Bibliography*. Toronto: University of Toronto Press, 1986.

Clurman, Harold. "Theatre." *Nation* (20 April 1970): 476.

Dace, Tish. "Paul Zindel." *Contemporary Dramatists*. Fourth Edition, pp. 586–88. Edited by D. L. Kirkpatrick. Chicago: St. James Press, 1988.

Eaglen, Audrey. "Of Life, Love, Death, Kids, and Inhalation Therapy: An Interview with Paul Zindel." *Top of the News* (Winter 1978): 178–85.

Eddleman, Floyd Eugene. *American Drama Criticism: Interpretations 1890–1977*. 2d ed. Hamden, Conn.: Shoe String Press, 1979.

———. *American Drama Criticism; Supplement I to the Second Edition*. Hamden, Conn.: Shoe String Press, 1984.

Eder, Richard. "The Effect of Gamma Rays on Man-in-the-Moon Marigolds." *New York Times* (15 March 1978): C25.

Farber, Stephen. "A Bouquet for Marigolds." *New York Times* (28 January 1973): 2:13.

Flatley, Guy. "...And Gamma Rays Did It!" *New York Times* (19 April 1970): B1, B5.

Gautier, Jean-Jacques. "De l'influence des rayons gamma sur les marguerites." *Le Figaro* (10 March 1974).

Gill, Brendan. "And So to Bed." *New Yorker* (27 March 1978): 95–96.

———. "Caterwauling." *New Yorker* (18 April 1977): 102.

———. "Shopworn." *New Yorker* (6 March 1971): 67.

Gottfried, Martin. "And Miss Reardon Drinks a Little." *Women's Wear Daily* (26 February 1971). Reprinted in *New York Theatre Critics' Reviews* (1971): 342.

———. "The Effect of Gamma Rays on Man-in-the-Moon Marigolds." *Women's Wear Daily* (8 April 1970). Reprinted in *New York Theatre Critics' Reviews* (1970): 243.

———. "The Secret Affairs of Mildred Wild." *Women's Wear Daily* (16 November 1972). Reprinted in *New York Theatre Critics' Reviews* (1972): 187.

Greer, Germaine. "The Effect of Gamma Rays on Man-in-the-Moon Marigolds." *Plays and Players* 20 (January 1973): 44–47.

Haley, Beverly A., and Kenneth L. Donelson. "Pigs and Hamburgers, Cadavers and Gamma Rays: Paul Zindel's Adolescents." *Elementary English* 51, no. 7 (October 1974): 941–45.

Henke, James T. "Six Characters in Search of the Family." *Children's Literature* 5 (1976): 130–40.

Hewes, Henry. "Broadway Postscript." *Saturday Review* (26 June 1965): 45.

———. "The Half-Life." *Saturday Review* (2 May 1970): 12.

———. "Under the Rainbow." *Saturday Review* (20 March 1971): 10.

Hipple, Theodore W. "Paul Zindel." In *American Writers for Children since 1960: Fiction*, pp. 405–10. Edited by Glenn E. Estes. *Dictionary of Literary Biography* 52. Detroit: Gale, 1986.

Janeczko, Paul. "An Interview with Paul Zindel." *English Journal* (October 1977): 20–21.

Kalem, T. E. "Overdrawn Account." *Time* (8 March 1971): 47.

Kerr, Walter. "Everything's Coming Up Marigolds . . . " *New York Times* (19 April 1970): 2:1, 3.

———. "Peculiar People, All Right, But What about Them?" *New York Times* (7 March 1971): 2:1.

———. "The Ring of Truth." *New York Times* (17 April 1977): B3.

Kroll, Jack. "Dream Girl." *Newsweek* (27 November 1972): 77.

———. "Fighting for Life." *Newsweek* (27 April 1970): 64.

———. "Teachers on the Rocks." *Newsweek* (8 March 1971). Reprinted in *New York Theatre Critics' Reviews* (1971): 342.

Leonard, William Torbert. "The Effect of Gamma Rays on Man-in-the-Moon Marigolds." In *Theatre: Stage to Screen to Television*, 1:537–41. Metuchen, N.J.: Scarecrow, 1971.

Mercier, Jean F. "Paul Zindel." *Publishers Weekly* (5 December 1977): 6–7.

Miner, Michael D. "Grotesque Drama in the '70s." *Kansas Quarterly* 12, no. 5 (1980): 99–109.

Oliver, Edith. "Why the Lady Is a Tramp." *New Yorker* (18 April 1970): 82–83.

"Paul Zindel." In *Contemporary Literary Criticism*, 26: 470–81. Edited by Jean C. Stine. Detroit: Gale, 1983.

"Paul Zindel." In *Contemporary Theatre, Film, and Television*, Vol. 3. Edited by Monica M. O'Donnell. Detroit: Gale, 1986.

Prideaux, Tom. "Man with a Bag of Marigold Dust." *Life* (4 July 1970): 8–9.

Salem, James M. *A Guide to Critical Reviews. Pt. 1: American Drama, 1909–1982*, 3d ed., pp. 603–4. Metuchen, N.J.: Scarecrow, 1984.

Simon, John. "No Foundations, All the Way Down the Line." *New York* (15 March 1971): 57.

Strickland, Ruth L. "Paul Zindel." In *Twentieth-Century American Dramatists*. Edited by John MacNicholas. *Dictionary of Literary Biography* 7. Detroit: Gale, 1981.

Taubman, Howard. "Houston's Alley Group Gives Zindel Play." *New York Times* (7 June 1965): 48.

———. "Swallows Hard to Swallow." *New York Times* (15 April 1964): 46.

Watt, Douglas. "Miss Reardon Drinks a Little." *Daily News* (26 February 1971). Reprinted in *New York Theatre Critics' Reviews* (1971): 341.

Watts, Richard. "Woman with Film Fantasies." *New York Post* (15 November 1972). Reprinted in *New York Theatre Critics' Reviews* (1972): 186.

W. L. T. "The Feminine Mistake." *Texas Monthly* 6 (June 1978): 136–37.

"Zindel, Paul." In *Children's Literature Review*, 3: 244–54. Edited by Gerard J. Senick. Detroit: Gale, 1978.

"Zindel, Paul." In *Contemporary Literary Criticism*, 6: 586–87. Edited by Carolyn Riley and Phyllis Carmel Mendelson. Detroit: Gale, 1976.

"Zindel, Paul." In *Something about the Author*, 16: 283–90. Edited by Anne Commire. Detroit: Gale, 1979.

Name Index

Play and Screenplay Index

About the Editor and Contributors

THOMAS P. ADLER is professor of English and associate dean of the Graduate School at Purdue University, where he teaches dramatic literature and film. Among his books are *Robert Anderson* (1978) and *Mirror on the Stage: The Pulitzer Plays as an Approach to American Drama* (1987).

THOMAS BONNER, JR., professor of English at Xavier University of Louisiana, has written *William Faulkner: The William B. Wisdom Collection* and *The Kate Chopin Companion* (Greenwood Press, 1988), as well as articles on Frederick Douglass and Victor Sejour. He is editor of *Xavier Review* and a frequent reviewer for the *New Orleans Times-Picayune*.

SCOTT T. CUMMINGS, assistant professor of theatre at Carnegie-Mellon University, is an associate editor of *Theatre Three*. He has published on Fornes and other contemporary playwrights in *American Theatre*, *Theatre Magazine*, and elsewhere.

FRANCIS DEDMOND is professor of English emeritus at Catawba College, where for eighteen years he served as chair of the English Department. He has published widely on American literature and lists among his acting credits roles in plays done off-Broadway.

WILLIAM W. DEMASTES has published on modern American playwrights in *Comparative Drama* and *Studies in American Drama, 1945- Present* and is the author of *Beyond Naturalism: A New Realism in American Theatre* (1988), published by Greenwood Press. He teaches American literature and drama at the University of Tennessee-Knoxville.

GERALDO U. DE SOUSA is an assistant professor of English at the University of Kansas and the author of articles and reviews in *Shakespeare Quarterly, Essays in Theatre, Research Opportunities in Renaissance Drama,* and *Notes and Queries.* With David Bergeron he has written *Shakespeare: A Study and Research Guide* (2d ed.).

SUZANNE BURGOYNE DIECKMAN is associate professor of theatre and chair of the Department of Fine and Performing Arts, Creighton University. An actress, director, translator, and playwright, she holds a Ph.D. in theatre from the University of Michigan, where she was a Rackham Prize scholar. Other awards include a Kellogg National Fellowship (1981–1984) and a Fulbright Fellowship to the National Theatre Institute of Belgium (1968–1969), where she returned in 1986–1987 as a visiting professor of directing and American drama.

PHILIP J. EGAN, who teaches at Western Michigan University, has published articles in *American Literature* and the *Journal of Paralegal Studies.* He contributed a Ronald Ribman bibliography to *Studies in American Drama, 1945–Present* in 1987.

PATTI P. GILLESPIE, professor and chair of the Department of Communication Arts and Theatre at the University of Maryland, is coauthor, with Kenneth Cameron, of *Enjoyment of Theatre* and *Western Theatre: Revolution and Revival.* Her numerous scholarly articles focus on theatre history, dramatic theory, academic administration, and women's studies.

DAVID H. GOFF is chair of the Radio, Television, and Film Department at the University of Southern Mississippi. He teaches a variety of courses concerning film and electronic media. His research interests include media history and policy, and he has published on these and other topics.

ALVIN GOLDFARB is chairperson and professor of theatre at Illinois State University. He has published articles, notes, and reviews in *Theatre Journal, Performing Arts Journal, Theatre Survey, Journal of Popular Culture, Southern Theatre, Exchange,* and *Tennessee Williams: A Tribute.* He is coauthor of *Living Theatre: An Introduction to Theatre History* and has published an annotated bibliography of Holocaust plays in *Plays of the Holocaust.*

ALEXIS GREENE teaches contemporary drama at Vassar College. The literary manager for the George Street Playhouse (New Brunswick, New Jersey), she has written for *Theatre Journal, Theatre Design and Technology,* and the *New York Times.* Her recent interview with Jean-Claude van Itallie appears in *Studies in American Drama, 1945–Present* (1988).

LYNDA HART is assistant professor at the University of Pennsylvania, where she teaches modern and contemporary theatre and feminism in drama. She is the author of *Sam Shepard's Metaphorical Stages* (Greenwood Press, 1987) and editor of a collection of feminist essays on contemporary women's theatre, forthcoming from the University of Michigan Press.

MARTIN J. JACOBI, an assistant professor of English at Clemson University, is coauthor of a forthcoming book on the American rhetorician Richard M. Weaver. He has also published on advanced writing and American literature and is the managing editor of *South Carolina Review*.

WILLIAM KLEB, who holds a D.F.A. from Yale University, is an associate professor in the Department of Dramatic Art at the University of California, Davis. An expert in late nineteenth-century and contemporary theatre, he publishes regularly in such journals as *Theatre Survey*, *Performing Arts Journal*, and *Theatre* (for which he serves as a contributing editor).

PHILIP C. KOLIN, professor of English at the University of Southern Mississippi, is coeditor and publisher (with Colby H. Kullman) of *Studies in American Drama, 1945–Present* and coeditor of the *Mississippi Folklore Register*. He has written or edited ten books, including *David Rabe: A Stage History and A Primary and Secondary Bibliography*, *Conversations with Edward Albee*, *Shakespeare in the South: Essays on Performance*, and *Successful Writing at Work*. The author of more than seventy articles, his work has appeared in *Theatre Annual*, *Eugene O'Neill Newsletter*, *Tennessee Williams: A Tribute*, English Literary Renaissance, *CLIA Journal*, *Explicator*, *American Speech*, *Resources for American Literary Study*, and *Research Opportunities in Renaissance Drama*. He has also reviewed books for *Theatre Journal*, *Modern Drama*, *Shakespeare Quarterly*, *Shakespeare Studies*, and *Comparative Drama*.

COLBY H. KULLMAN, assistant professor of English at the University of Mississippi, is coeditor and publisher (with Philip C. Kolin) of *Studies in American Drama: 1945–Present* and coeditor of *Theatre Companies of the World* (with William C. Young), the latter winning an award from *Library Journal* as a major reference work of 1986. He is also the author of numerous articles on theatre history, folklore, and English literature.

RICHARD M. LEESON, an associate professor of English at Fort Hays State University, has published articles on Flannery O'Connor and English education. He is president of the Kansas Association of Teachers of English.

FELICIA HARDISON LONDRÉ is Curators' Professor of Theatre at the University of Missouri-Kansas City and dramaturge for Missouri Repertory Theatre. She earned her B.A. at the University of Montana, studied on a Fulbright grant in France, and earned an M.A. in Romance languages at the University of Washington and a Ph.D. in speech/theatre at the University of Wisconsin. Her books include studies of Tennessee Williams, Tom Stoppard, and Federico Garcia Lorca, all published by Ungar, for which she is writing a history of world theatre. She is a playwright who has also translated plays from the French, Spanish, and Russian.

CHARLOTTE S. McCLURE, associate professor of English at Georgia State University, has taught modern drama and has presented papers on western regional theater. She is the author of a book and articles on Gertrude Atherton and coedited *Feminist Visions: Toward a Transformation of the Liberal Arts Curriculum.*

LINDA E. McDANIEL, a visiting instructor at the University of Southern Mississippi, teaches and publishes articles on southern and American literature. She served as editorial assistant on the *Mississippi Quarterly* Faulkner issues while working toward her Ph.D. degree at the University of South Carolina. She is currently writing annotations to William Faulkner's *Flags in the Dust* for Garland Press.

LAURA MORROW is coeditor of *Contemporary Literary Theory* (1988) and has published essays and reviews in such journals as *Studies in American Drama, 1945–Present, Modern Drama, Restoration and Eighteenth-Century Theatre Research, The Scriblerian,* and *Milton Quarterly.* She teaches English at Louisiana State University-Shreveport.

MIRIAM NEURINGER, who earned her M.L.S. from Indiana University, has published "The Burden of Meaning in Hunt's *Lady of Shallot*" in *Ladies of Shallot: A Victorian Masterpiece and Its Context.*

MICHAEL C. O'NEILL is associate professor of English and the director of theater at Wilkes College. His articles and reviews have appeared in, among other publications, *Theatre Journal* and the *New York Times.* His plays have been performed in colleges and off-off- Broadway.

VINCENT F. PETRONELLA, professor of English at the University of Massachusetts in Boston, holds a Ph.D. from the University of Massachusetts and is the author of articles in *Approaches to Teaching Shakespeare's "King Lear"* (Modern Language Association), *Studies in English Literature, Shakespeare Studies, Modern Language Review, Hamlet Studies, Studies in Philology, Theatre Journal, American Transcendentalist Quarterly,* and *Journal of English and Germanic Philology*. His article on Percy Bysshe Shelley as poetic dramatist appears in the Modern Language Association volume devoted to Shelley's works.

MAARTEN REILINGH teaches in the theatre program at Middle Tennessee State University. A field bibliographer for the *International Bibliography of Theatre* and editorial associate of Applause Theatre Books, he has also contributed essays to *Shakespeare Around the Globe* (Greenwood Press, 1988) and the *Cambridge Guide to World Theatre*.

DAVID H. ROBERTS is professor of English and director of writing at Samford University. He formerly directed the South Mississippi Writing Project. Roberts served two terms as president of the Southeastern Writing Center Association and is a member of the executive committee of the National Writing Centers Association. He recently published *A Guide to Computer Aided Instruction*.

C. WARREN ROBERTSON, director of theatre at East Tennessee State University, holds an M.F.A. from Tulane University and a Ph.D. in theatre from Florida State University. His play, *After the Wedding*, has been published by Oracle Press. He has written a number of papers and articles on the theatre and has edited a special issue of *Southern Quarterly: A Journal of the Arts in the South* on "Contemporary Theatre in the South" (1987).

MATTHEW C. ROUDANÉ, associate professor of English, teaches modern drama and American literature at Georgia State University in Atlanta. His books include *Understanding Edward Albee* (1987) and *Toward the Marrow: Who's Afraid of Virginia Woolf?* (forthcoming), and he is editor of *Conversations with Arthur Miller* (1987) and *Public Issues, Private Tensions: Contemporary American Drama*, a collection of essays appearing in *Studies in the Literary Imagination* (1988). Roudané serves on the editorial and advisory boards of five scholarly journals.

LESLIE SANDERS is associate professor in the Humanities and English departments of Atkinson College, Ontario. She has recently published *The Development of Black Theater in America*.

DAVID SAVRAN teaches drama at Brown University. He has published a book on the Wooster Group and a collection of interviews entitled *In Their Own Words: Contemporary American Playwrights*.

SUSAN HARRIS SMITH, assistant professor of English at the University of Pittsburgh, is the author of *Masks in Modern Drama*. A theatre critic for the *Pittsburgh Press*, she is also the author of sixteen plays.

MICHAEL STUPRICH, assistant professor of English at Ithaca College, has published a bibliographic essay on Samuel Johnson as a biographer and an article on John Donne.

KATHLEEN SULLIVAN received her Ph.D. in English from the University of Notre Dame in 1987. She teaches courses in American literature at Notre Dame and has published on modern drama, including an interview with Edward Albee.

JOYCELYN TRIGG, who holds an M.A. in English from the University of Southern Mississippi, is managing editor of *Southern Quarterly: A Journal of the Arts in the South*.

KENNETH WATSON is an assistant professor of English at the University of Southern Mississippi.

LAURA H. WEAVER is associate professor of English at the University of Evansville (Indiana). She is the author of articles on playwright David Storey, Canadian novelist Rudy Wiebe, theatre history, and technical writing. Her ethnic autobiographical essays have appeared in *Journal of Ethnic Studies, Mississippi Folklore Register, Children's Literature, The Road Retaken: Women Reenter the Academy*, and *The Ethnic American Woman* (forthcoming).

DON B. WILMETH, professor of theatre and English at Brown University, chaired the Department of Theatre, Speech, and Dance there until 1987. The author, editor, or coeditor of nine books, including the award-winning *George Frederick Cooke* (1980), his most recent projects have included serving as a coeditor of contributor to *The Cambridge Guide to World Theatre* (1988) and supplying the text for *Mud Show: American Tent Circus Life* (1988). He is an advisory editor for four journals and was book review editor for *Theatre Journal*, and theatre editor/columnist for the magazine *USA Today*.

MARY ANN WILSON, instructor of English at the University of Southwestern Louisiana, teaches courses in women's studies. She has written widely on women writers, notably Joyce Carol Oates and Alice Walker, and is at work on a study of motherhood in contemporary black female writers.

IRMGARD H. WOLFE is a cataloger at the University of Southern Mississippi. She and William Boyd have published a translation of *German*

Library History by Ladislas Buzas; a translation of Schottenloher's *Bucher bewegten die Welt* appeared in fall of 1988. She has also compiled a classified bibliography of Marsha Norman for *Studies in American Drama, 1945–Present* (1988).